The COM and COM+ Programming Primer

ISBN 0-13-085032-2
90000
9 780130 850324

PRENTICE HALL PTR MICROSOFT® TECHNOLOGIES SERIES

NETWORKING

- Microsoft Technology: Networking, Concepts, Tools
  Woodard, Gattuccio, Brain
- NT Network Programming Toolkit
  Murphy
- Building COM Applications with Internet Explorer
  Loveman
- Understanding DCOM
  Rubin, Brain
- Web Database Development for Windows Platforms
  Gutierrez

PROGRAMMING

- The COM and COM+ Programming Primer
  Gordon
- Windows 2000 Web Applications Developer's Guide
  Yager
- The Visual Basic Object and Component Handbook
  Vogel
- Developing Solutions with Office 2000 Components and VBA
  Aitken
- Windows Shell Programming
  Seely
- The Visual Basic Style Guide
  Patrick
- Introduction to Windows 98 Programming
  Murray, Pappas
- Developing Professional Applications for Windows 98 and NT Using MFC, Third Edition
  Brain, Lovette
- Win 32 System Services: The Heart of Windows 98 and Windows NT, Third Edition
  Brain
- Multithreaded Programming with Win32
  Pham, Garg
- Visual Basic 6: Design, Specification, and Objects
  Hollis
- ADO Programming in Visual Basic 6
  Holzner
- Visual Basic 6: Error Coding and Layering
  Gill
- Visual C++ Templates
  Murray, Pappas
- Introduction to MFC Programming with Visual C++
  Jones
- MFC Programming in C++ with the Standard Template Libraries
  Murray, Pappas
- COM-CORBA Interoperability
  Geraghty, Joyce, Moriarty, Noone
- Distributed COM Application Development Using Visual Basic 6.0
  Maloney
- Distributed COM Application Development Using Visual C++ 6.0
  Maloney
- Understanding and Programming COM+: A Practical Guide to Windows 2000 DNA
  Oberg
- ASP/MTS/ADSI Web Security
  Harrison
- Microsoft Site Server 3.0 Commerce Edition
  Libertone, Scoppa
- Building Microsoft SQL Server 7 Web Sites
  Byrne

ADMINISTRATION

- Windows 2000 Hardware and Disk Management
  Simmons
- Creating Active Directory Infrastructures
  Simmons
- Windows 2000 Registry
  Sanna
- Configuring Windows 2000 Server
  Simmons
- Tuning and Sizing NT Server
  Aubley
- Windows NT Cluster Server Guidebook
  Libertone
- Windows NT 4.0 Server Security Guide
  Goncalves
- Windows NT Security
  McInerney
- Supporting Windows NT and 2000 Workstation and Server
  Mohr
- Zero Administration Kit for Windows
  McInerney
- Designing Enterprise Solutions with Microsoft Technologies
  Kemp, Kemp, Goncalves

PRENTICE HALL PTR MICROSOFT® TECHNOLOGIES SERIES

GORDON

The COM and COM+ Programming Primer

PH PTR

Prentice Hall PTR, Upper Saddle River, NJ 07458
www.phptr.com

Editorial/Production Supervision: MetroVoice Publishing Services
Acquisitions Editor: Tim Moore
Editorial Assistant: Julie Okulicz
Development Editor: Jim Markham
Cover Design Director: Jerry Votta
Cover Designer: Anthony Gemmellaro
Buyer: Maura Goldstaub
Series Design: Maureen Eide
Art Director: Gail Cocker-Bogusz
Project Coordinator: Anne Trowbridge

Prentice-Hall, Inc.
Upper Saddle River, New Jersey 07458

Prentice Hall books are widely used by corporations and government agencies for training, marketing, and resale. The publisher offers discounts on this book when ordered in bulk quantities. For more information, contact:

Corporate Sales Department,
Prentice Hall PTR
One Lake Street
Upper Saddle River, NJ 07458
Phone: 800-382-3419; FAX: 201-236-7141
E-mail (Internet): corpsales@prenhall.com

Printed in the United States of America

10 9 8 7 6 5 4 3 2

ISBN 0-13-085032-2

Prentice-Hall International (UK) Limited, *London*
Prentice-Hall of Australia Pty. Limited, *Sydney*
Prentice-Hall Canada Inc., *Toronto*
Prentice-Hall Hispanoamericana, S.A., *Mexico*
Prentice-Hall of India Private Limited, *New Delhi*
Prentice-Hall of Japan, Inc., *Tokyo*
Pearson Education Asia Pte. Ltd.
Editora Prentice-Hall do Brasil, Ltda., *Rio de Janeiro*

CONTENTS

FOUR Building Your First COM Object 77

FIVE Making It Simple with ATL and Visual C++ COM Native Support 119

PART TWO Digging Deeper

SIX Creating an Out-of-Process Server 163

SEVEN Automation 197

NINE COM Threading *285*

TEN Distributed COM *351*

INTRODUCTION

Teaching my class at UCLA, an *Introduction to COM/ActiveX Programming Using Visual C++,* has given me a good background from which to write a book on COM and COM+. The target audience for this book is the same people who took my class at UCLA: intermediate-to-advanced programmers who have little or no knowledge of COM or COM+. By the time you finish this book, you should have enough knowledge of COM to begin using COM and COM+ professionally.

My Approach

My objective is to teach you the 90 percent of COM that, as an application developer, you will use every day. Most of this is surprisingly simple. But there is another 10 percent of COM that is very difficult to understand and this is the part with which I have often seen otherwise excellent programmers become bogged down. It's not that these "10 percent" topics aren't important, it's just that you can get started and begin using COM without understanding all of these topics. Some "10 percent" topics that immediately come to mind are Apartments, custom marshaling, aggregation in general, manual marshaling of interface pointers, and aggregating the Free-Threaded Marshaler. I do cover all of these topics in this book, but be forewarned you probably won't understand these topics the first time you try to learn them; I certainly didn't. But don't get discouraged and don't let topics like this "bog you down" as you try to learn COM. This is not what COM and COM+ is all about. COM is about making it simple for you to build location transparent and programming-language independent software components. COM+ is all about facilitating the development of enterprise-class, distributed applications. The objective of neither of these technologies is to aggregate the Free-Threaded Marshaler. Don't allow yourself to become lost in the minutia of COM as many people do. When I cover topics that I know tend to bog down people (like Apartments), I caution you to just keep going if you don't understand it right away. Please follow this advice. You will understand the other concepts as you begin using COM professionally and start tackling more difficult problems.

Visual C++ and Visual Basic

The primary programming language used in this book is Visual C++. The world seems to be turning away from languages like Visual C++ and to languages like Visual Basic, Java, and Delphi. Unfortunately these languages hide so much of the under-lying details of COM that it is difficult to understand what's going on under the hood if you only use these languages. Only in Visual C++ can you implement the `IUnknown` interface, and create your own class factory, as you will do in Chapter 4. I strongly believe that the additional insight that you gain by doing this is well worth the additional complexity. In addition, there are certain things that you can do in COM+ that you simply cannot do from Visual Basic 6, such as building an object that will run in the thread-neutral apartment and using object pooling. Once you understand COM+ using Visual C++, transferring your knowledge to a more productive development environment, like Visual Basic, will be easy. Don't worry; you don't have to be a C++ Guru to read this book. I really think that a beginning C++ programmer will have little problem following along with the code in this book. I do use Visual Basic to build some of the client programs. I mainly did this to save time. It is much easier to build GUIs with Visual Basic than Visual C++. In addition, using Visual C++ for server-side development and Visual Basic for client-side development is a popular combination that I have seen on a number of projects recently.

Use of the Word Component

If you read any books about COM you quickly see that the word *component* has two popular uses:

- It refers to a binary file (a Dynamic Link Library or Executable) that implements one or more COM classes
- It refers to a single COM class

Personally, I prefer the first definition of the word mainly because I believe that a COM class adequately describes the individual pieces of functionality that may reside in a single binary. People who use *component* to refer to a COM class usually use *component server* or just *server* to refer to the binary in which several components may be hosted. When you start using COM+ you will see that Microsoft refers to COM+ classes as components (even though they are not completely consistent either). I'm hardly a zealot on these kinds of issues so I concede the argument for now. I think there still are a few places in this book where my old bias shows through. I believe that in all places it is obvious from the context whether I am referring to a single COM class or a binary file in which several classes reside.

The Book's Structure

Of the 15 chapters in this text, eight chapters (1–8) are essentially pure COM, two chapters (9 and 10) are primarily COM with some COM+, and five chapters (chapters 11–15) are pure COM+. The simple reality is that you cannot understand COM+ without first understanding COM. COM+ is really just a vastly improved and more tightly integrated version of Microsoft Transaction Server along with some key refinements to the underlying COM infrastructure such as Thread Neutral Apartments. A book that only covered COM+ features would only be usable by people who understand COM already. I covered both COM and COM+ because I wanted this book to be usable by people who are new to COM. Having said that, I teach you only enough COM so that you can understand COM+. COM+ was designed primarily to facilitate the development of enterprise-class, distributed applications, so there are many COM topics (ActiveX controls for instance) that are not covered in this book because they have little relevance to enterprise-class development and COM+.

Most of the chapters start by explaining a problem that can be resolved by using COM/COM+. That is followed by a discussion of how the COM-related technology works and how you will use it. This discussion includes a lot of analogies, diagrams, and screen shots. Finally, in most of the chapters you build a demonstration program. I don't think any of the demonstration programs are terribly sophisticated (they weren't meant to be). The example programs are designed to reinforce the topic that you are learning in that chapter. I show you how to build the example program in enough detail that a beginning Visual C++ programmer (if you can work through the Scribble tutorial in the Visual C++ documentation you're good to go) should have no problems following along. I think you will learn the most by building the example programs yourself, but if you don't want to go through the steps yourself you can download the demonstration programs from the FTP site for this book ftp://ftp.prenhall.com/pub/ptr/windows_technology.056/gordon.

Part 1: Laying the Foundation

In the first chapter, I define all the names in the COM namespace. Confused as to what COM, OLE, ActiveX, and the Windows DNA are? Chapter 1 defines these names and more. In Chapter 2 you learn a number of object-oriented concepts that are important pre-requisites to understanding COM. In particular, you learn what it means to be object-oriented and I define a class, an object, and an interface. The discussion of interfaces in this chapter is particularly important. In Chapter 3 I define the notion of a software bus and use it to explain some of the intricacies of COM: GUIDs, the `IUnknown` interface, Type libraries, Marshaling, and how COM uses the registry. In Chapter 4 you build your first COM class in an in-process server. You do this "from scratch" without the help of any wizards. You also build a COM client application. In Chapter 5 you learn how to build a COM server much more easily using the Active Template Library (ATL) and the ATL Object Wizard. All of the work that you do from Chapter 5 on uses ATL and/or Visual Basic.

Part 2: Digging Deeper

In Chapter 6 you learn how to build an out-of-process server. In Chapter 7 you learn about Automation. In Chapter 8 you learn about connection points. These 8 chapters are the pure COM material in this book. In Chapter 9 I discuss COM threading and Apartments. This chapter features some material (primarily Thread Neutral Apartments) that will be new to COM programmers who have not used COM+. In Chapter 10 I discuss DCOM and again in this chapter I discuss, briefly, some new topics like the Kerberos Security Support Provider.

Part 3: COM+

Chapter 11 begins our discussion of COM+. In Chapter 11 I discuss the COM+ architecture. You learn about *Context's* and *Interception*. You also learn how to configure a component using the Component Services Explorer. In Chapter 12 you learn about each of the Services that COM+ provides to components: fine-grained security, transactions, concurrency, store-and-forward method invocation (queued components), loosely-coupled events, load balancing, improved scalability thru Just In Time activation and pooling of objects, and database connections. Chapter 13 is a big chapter in both size and significance. In this chapter you put it all together and build a 3-tiered, thin-client application using all the technologies in the Windows Distributed interNet Applications (DNA) Architecture: COM+, Active Server Pages, ADO, SQL Server 7, Visual C++, and Visual Basic. In Chapter 14 you use Queued Components to enhance your application. In this chapter you also learn how to use the Microsoft XML parser. Finally, in Chapter 15 you learn how to use COM+ Events.

In terms of reading suggestions: If you already understand COM you can skip Chapters 3–8. If you are not interested in writing code you can skip the hands-on part in the chapters. If you just want COM+ and nothing but COM+, read Chapters 11–15.

The Intended Audience

You need to have at least a beginner's level knowledge of both Visual C++ and Windows Programming, in general, in order to understand this book. Also, the more you know about object oriented concepts, pointers, distributed processing, and multi-threading the easier time you will have learning COM. None of this knowledge is required to understand this book, as I do start from first principles. But trust me, the more you understand these concepts, the easier time you will have understanding COM, whether you learn from this book, another book, or a class.

Conventions Used in This Book

This book uses different features to help highlight key information. These features are discussed in the following sections.

Code Presentation

You will notice that there are three types of code listings. Some do not have a listing number, some have a listing number, and some have a listing number and numbered lines. Code that does not have a listing number is usually a short snippet that is included to illustrate a point. For instance:

```
try {
   VARIANT_BOOL result=mSpellChecker.CheckSpelling(word);
}
catch (_com_error err) {
   cout << err.Description()'
}
```

Code with a listing number but without numbered lines is code that is usually longer in length. Typically this is code that is important enough that I want to explain it, but short enough and simple enough that I can explain it without going into line-by-line detail.

LISTING 5.5 *WRITERSCOMPONENT.CPP*

```
CComModule _Module;

STDAPI DllCanUnloadNow(void)
{
   return (_Module.GetLockCount()==0) ? S_OK : S_FALSE;
}
```

```
STDAPI DllGetClassObject(REFCLSID rclsid, REFIID riid, LPVOID* ppv)
{
   return _Module.GetClassObject(rclsid, riid, ppv);
}

STDAPI DllRegisterServer(void)
{
   // registers object, typelib and all interfaces in typelib
   return _Module.RegisterServer(TRUE);
}

STDAPI DllUnregisterServer(void)
{
   return _Module.UnregisterServer(TRUE);
}
```

Code that is important enough that I want to explain it in line-by-line detail will have both a listing number and individually numbered lines as shown here:

LISTING 5.15 *THE MESSAGE HANDLER FOR THE CHECKGRAMMAR BUTTON*

```
1.  void CNativecomclientDlg::OnGrammarcheckerButton()
2.  {
3.  VARIANT_BOOL isCorrect;
4.  UpdateData(TRUE);
5.  bstr_t word=m_word;
6.  IGrammarCheckerPtr grammarChecker;
7.  try {
8.     grammarChecker=mSpellChecker;
9.     isCorrect=grammarChecker->CheckGrammar(word);
10.       if (isCorrect)
11.          AfxMessageBox("Grammar check complete");
12.       else
13.          AfxMessageBox("Incorrect grammar");
14.    }
15.    catch (_com_error err) {
16.       AfxMessageBox(err.Description());
17.    }
18. }
```

I have also yet to become a true believer in Hungarian notation so I don't use it.

Sidebars

Sidebars are used to present parenthetical information: information that is related to the topic at hand but does not flow directly with the main body of the chapter. In a few cases, I also use sidebars as a soapbox where I present information that is strictly my opinion, such as when I discuss my idea for a new COM naming scheme in Chapter 1. If you put a "by the way" or a "for your information" before each sidebar then you've got the idea.

Icons

Notes are used as small sidebars. Whenever I want to present parenthetical information that consists of only a sentence or two, I make it a note.

Tips are used to provide recommendations or to present information that can either save you time or prevent you from encountering minor problems.

Warnings are used to present information that is so important that I want it to stand out. I also use warnings to inform you of things that you must do to avoid serious problems. It is particularly important for you to pay heed to warnings that are associated with the example programs. In most cases, not following the warning will cause the example program not to work.

About the FTP Site

The FTP site for this book can be found at the following URL: ftp://ftp.prenhall.com/pub/ptr/windows_technology.w-056/gordon/. The FTP site contains the errata for the book. It also contains the source code for all the example programs in the book. If you do not wish to build the example programs yourself, or you encounter problems building the examples, you can download the finished programs from the FTP site.

ACKNOWLEDGMENTS

My name may be listed as the sole author of this book, but it took the work of a team of people to make this happen. Let me begin by thanking the people at Prentice Hall who were directly involved in the production of the book: my acquisitions editor, Tim Moore, my developmental editor, Jim Markham, and my technical reviewer, John Vacca. Special thanks to Jim for being so patient with me. Thanks also to Scott Suckling and the team at MetroVoice who did the final production work to turn my manuscript into the book you now hold in your hand. Next, I would like to thank all the people at UCLA Extension. It was through my work there that I was given the opportunity to write this book. Standout people I would like to mention are Terry Warner, Ben Stein, Carolyn Diliberto, Joseph Mueller, Donald Haushnect, and Robert Abnous. At Logicon's Advanced Technology Group I would like to thank everyone on the CAMPS project including Mark Flores, Rick Clough, Betty Hampikian, Curtis Enge, Marilyn Leatherwood, Theresa Millette, and Ward Keenan. I would like to especially thank everyone who worked for me when I was the technical lead on the Channels component including Bill Bulaich, Curt Miller, Sanjukta Chowdhurry, and Steve Caton. Others I would like to thank at Logicon include Roger Fuji, Vince Goshi, Steve Altstatt, Mike Twymann, and Steve Cooper. Many thanks to my lunch buddies at Logicon, Bill Bulaich and Paul Firnett. Since late August 1999 I have been working at a new company called FieldCentrix, http://www.fieldcentrix.com. This startup company is located in Irvine, California, and develops software for field service workers using the latest technology in wireless communications, rugged handheld PCs, and the Windows CE operating system. Those I would like to thank at FieldCentrix include Dave Key (the company founder), Dr. Albert Lin (who hired me), Paul Osterhoudt, Gaurav Jalota, Ashu Shende, Calvin Shen, Lap Tran, and Kevin Bates.

Many thanks to friends who have influenced me including: Dr. Quintus Jett, Dr. George Shaw, Dr. Shozo Koshigoe, Carlos Castellanos, and Ruel Nuqui. Next, I would like to thank my family. Kudos to my older brother Winston Gordon, Jr. When I was an Aerospace Engineering major at UCLA, he scoffed when I was learning FORTRAN—told me that C was the way to go. Eventually, I bought books on C and on C++. He started me on a journey that culminated in my writing this book. I would also like to thank my parents, Agatha and Winston Gordon, Sr. I can never repay you for all you've done for me so I say thank you. Other members of my family I would like to thank include Vera LittleJohn, Dr. Mary Marin, Alma Horper, Kaylah Marin, Mikalynn Todd, Amber Saucedo, and Sharine Dinwiddie. Finally, and most importantly, I would like to thank the two special women in my life: my wife Tamber Lynn and my daughter Bria Almarie. Thank you both for all the love and support you gave me and continue to give me, before, during, and after this book was written. You sacrificed so much to make this a reality. Thank you, Tamber, for encouraging me when I was ready to give up this project and I'm sorry for all the times I wasn't at my best while writing this book. Bria, forgive me for the times I couldn't play with you while I was writing this book. I hope one day you will understand that I did it to help build a better life for us. To anyone I forgot, my apologies and heartfelt thanks.

PART ONE

Laying the Foundation

In This Part

▶ **CHAPTER 1**
What's in a Name?

▶ **CHAPTER 2**
Classes, Objects, and Interfaces

▶ **CHAPTER 3**
Get on the Software Bus

▶ **CHAPTER 4**
Building Your First COM Object

▶ **CHAPTER 5**
Making it Simple with ATL and Visual C++ COM Native Support

In this section we will lay the foundation for your further study of COM and COM+. If you're confused as to what ActiveX, OLE, the Windows DNA, MTS, and COM+ mean, chapter 1 will provide the answer. In chapter 2 you will explore some object-oriented concepts especially classes, objects, and interfaces prior to diving into COM. In chapter 3 we use the metaphor of a software bus to explain some COM fundamentals such as GUIDs, the `IUnknown` interface, and IDL. In chapter 4 we build our first COM component from scratch and we also build a client for it. Finally in chapter 5 you will see how to create a COM component in a much easier manner using the Active Template Library (ATL) and the ATL Object Wizard. In chapter 5 you will also learn how to use the Visual C++ Native COM Support, which makes developing COM clients much easier.

By the time you are done with this section you should understand the basics of COM and know how to create both a simple COM component and a COM client.

ONE

What's in a Name?

The first thing that any good book on COM+ should do is define what COM+ is. But it's difficult to define what COM+ is without first defining some other words such as COM, DCOM, and MTS. Once you define these names you quickly wind up on a slippery slope where words like ActiveX, OLE, and Windows DNA rocket past as you descend toward confusion.

I start this book the same way I start my class at UCLA: by defining all the words in the COM namespace. You've most likely heard many of the terms that are defined in this chapter: COM, COM+, DCOM, MTS, OLE, ActiveX, and Windows DNA. If you are confused as to what they all mean, you are not alone and it's not your fault. Microsoft has changed the meaning of many of these names over the last few years. The definition of OLE, for instance, has changed three times. If you are familiar with the definitions of COM, MTS, and Windows DNA, you can skip to the definition of COM+ and by all means read my soapbox about Microsoft's COM technology naming mess at the end of this chapter.

COM

COM is the foundation for everything else that is discussed in this book. It is a specification and supporting system software that enables the creation of *software components* that are *programming-language independent* and *location-transparent.* These italicized terms are defined in the next three sections. For now, remember that COM is first and foremost a specification. The COM specification tells you what you must do to COM-enable your software. But, unless you're using a tool like Visual C++, you have to do a lot of coding yourself, to make COM work. Also, because COM is a well-documented specification, it can and has been implemented on multiple platforms. There are COM implementations available for almost every UNIX platform (including Linux) and there's even a COM implementation available for Digital Equipment Corporation's VMS platform. Let's talk more about the italicized words in our COM definition.

Software Component

A software component is a binary, self-contained, *reusable,* language-neutral piece of software that is used as a building block for applications. It's important to understand the distinction between an application and a software component. You can use Microsoft Word as an application to write letters or even a book (in fact I am doing that right now). But Microsoft Word is also a software component. It has an Application Programming Interface (API)—that is exposed through COM—and through this API you can use Microsoft Word as a report writer. When you are writing a letter or book with Word, you are using it as an application; when you use Word as a report writer, you are using it as a software component. The key distinction in the second case is that Word is being used as a building block for another application. I emphasized the word reusable in the definition of software component because it's the motivation for the other elements of the definition. In other words, software components are binary, language-neutral, and self-contained so they are easy to reuse. Let's face it, the easiest way to build software is to *not build it at all* and reuse software that someone else has built. If you've worked in this business for a significant length of time, you know this is often easier said than done. One of the biggest barriers to reuse is that software developers, in the past, have often tried to reuse software at the code level. On one project I worked on, we were having trouble linking our software together with code that was developed by two subcontractors. An examination of the code showed there were four different definitions of a Boolean in the software. These problems might have been avoided if we could have reused our subcontractor's software in binary form.

On the Windows platform, software components are distributed like those shown in Figure 1.1.

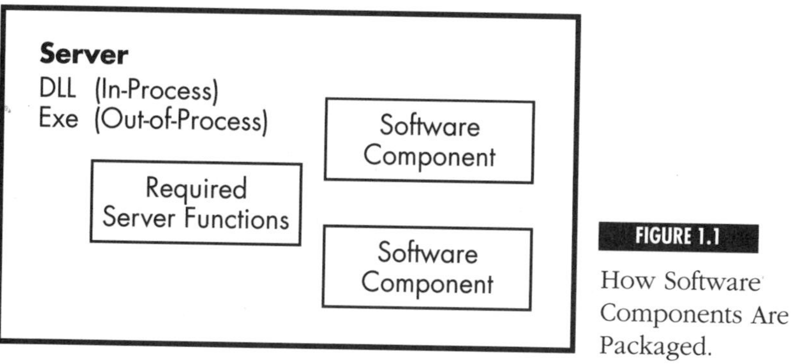

FIGURE 1.1

How Software Components Are Packaged.

Software components are distributed within a server. The server may be either a Dynamic Link Library (DLL) or an executable. A DLL based server is called an in-process server. This is because a DLL always runs within the same process as its client. An executable server is called an out-of-process server because it runs in a different process than its client.

Figure 1.1 shows that more than one software component can reside within a single server. There are also other functions within the server that must be present to tie the server into the COM system.

Programming-Language Independence

One of the primary goals of COM is to make it easy for you to write software that can be reused from any programming language. Ideally you should be able to use a COM object in exactly the same way regardless of what programming language you are using or what programming language the software component was implemented in. If you have been a programmer for any significant length of time, you've probably written software that spans multiple programming languages. Different programming languages have different ways of calling functions and handling exceptions and have different type systems. If you understand the calling conventions of both languages and how to map the types in one programming language into types in another language, you can write code that spans different programming languages. Of course, you will have to take a different approach depending on the two languages you are bridging and even the compiler you are using for each language, but it can be done.

However, if your code contains exception handling, you will probably have a more difficult time. The C++ programming standard specifies how exceptions should work; it does not specify how they should be implemented. For this reason, you'll probably have difficulty even reusing a software component that was built with a different C++ compiler, let alone a different programming language.

So how do you fix this problem? How do you make it easy for people to share software in binary form regardless of what programming language or compiler they are using? The solution is to create a software interface standard. This specification must define—at a binary level—how two pieces of software should interact.

Once this specification is in place, programming language vendors can map their programming languages to this specification. Developers can then write their software in the programming language and development environment they are most comfortable with. As you've probably guessed already, COM does define a binary-level software interface specification. COM components communicate using interfaces that are implemented as arrays of function pointers (more on this later). You can think of COM's binary interface standard as a common layer that everyone can write to as shown in Figure 1.2.

If the data-bound grid that was written in Delphi exposes its functionality through COM, then the Visual Basic code that interacts with the grid will look exactly the same as the code that interacts with the COM-based optimization component that was written with Visual C++ and the COM-based e-mail component that was written with Java (J++). As far as the Visual Basic application is concerned, all three components are COM objects. The programming language each software component was implemented in simply becomes an implementation detail.

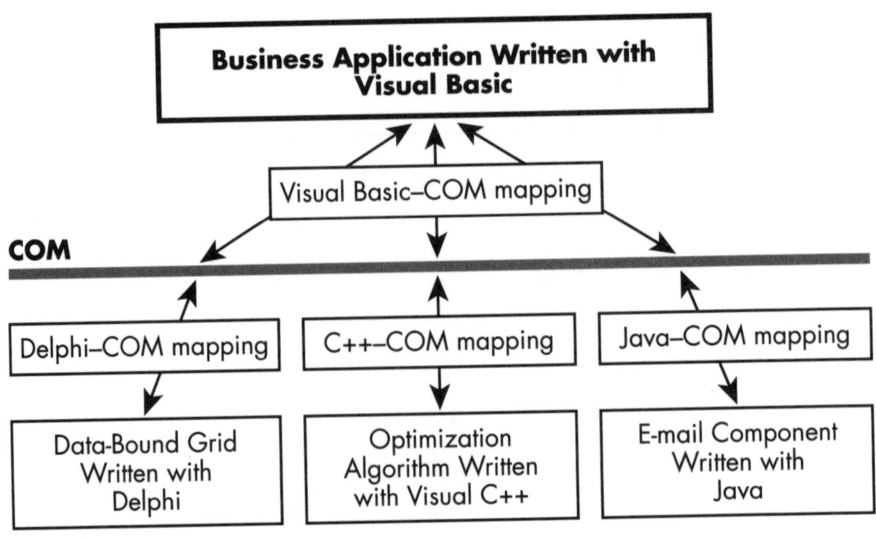

FIGURE 1.2 Programming-Language Independence.

Here's an example from my own experience of how effective COM is in this regard. If you design your applications in an object-oriented way using an object-oriented design methodology and process, one problem you immediately face is that most people are still using relational databases. At the company I work for, we found a COM-based product called the Data Access Add-In (DAA) that can be used to map Visual Basic classes to a relational database. The product worked great for us while we were building our software, but once we started running our software, we noticed that it was slower and used more memory than we would have liked. Upon further investigation we found that the DAA was implemented in Java. Had we known this, we might not have used it. But this shows that COM does an excellent job of hiding the programming language used to implement a software component.

Location Transparency

To understand location transparency, it's best to look at how you reuse software without the benefit of location transparency. As shown in Figure 1.3, a piece of software that you wish to reuse may be located in one of three places. It could be a dynamic or static link library, in which case reusing the software is fairly simple. You just have to link the library into your application. If the link library is implemented in a different programming language than the application using it, you will need to resolve some programming-language mapping issues.

If the software that you wish to reuse must run in its own process (in other words, it is a stand-alone executable), then things become more com-

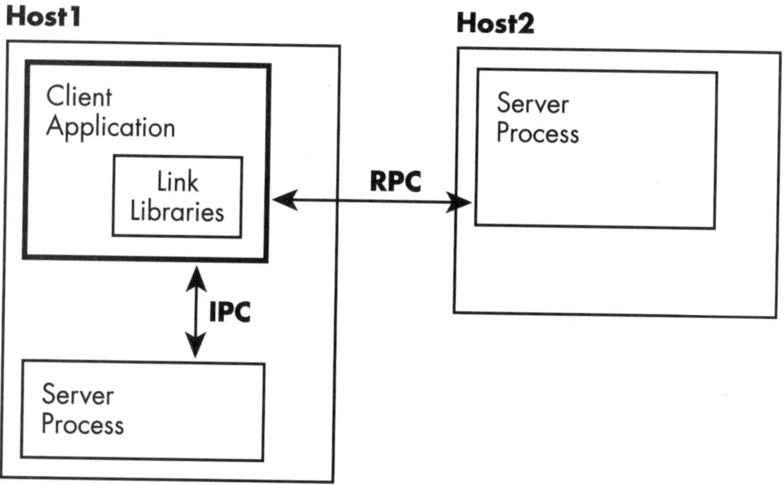

FIGURE 1.3 Reusing Software Without Location Transparency.

plicated. If the software that you wish to reuse (let's call it the server from now on) will run on the same host as the application that's using it (let's call this the client from now on), then you will need a mechanism for starting and communicating with the server. You cannot directly call functions that reside in a different process. You have to establish an Inter-Process Communication (IPC) link between the client and the server. Sockets or pipes are examples of IPC mechanisms that may be used to establish this link.

The situation gets even more complicated if the client and server must run on a different platform. For instance, if the server software is implemented on UNIX and the client software runs on Windows NT. In this situation, you will need to use some form of Remote Procedure Call (RPC). There are several cross-platform implementations of RPC. The most common one was created by the Open Software Foundation (OSF) and is called Distributed Computing Environment (DCE) RPC. This technology is not terribly difficult to use, but it does add an extra layer of complexity that makes reuse more difficult.

COM uses DCE RPC as its communication mechanism.

The main problem here is that without location transparency, the way in which you use a software component will vary according to how the component is implemented. If the software component is a link library, there is one mechanism for using it. If it is an executable that runs on the same host as the client, there is a different mechanism for using it. And if the software component cannot run on the same machine as its client, then there is yet another means for using the software component.

COM as a Software Bus

It would certainly make software development—and software reuse in particular—a lot easier if you could use a software component in exactly the same way, regardless of whether it is a Dynamic Link Library (DLL) or an executable, or whether it runs on the same machine as its client or on a remote machine. What you really need is the equivalent of a hardware bus but for software.

You probably know where the bus is on your computer. This is the part of your computer that you plug peripherals like sound cards and modems into. The interesting thing about the bus on most PCs is that you can plug a wide range of devices into it, even devices that were conceived and manufactured long after your computer was built. The key to making this work is that there are bus standards in place, such as Peripheral Component Interconnect (PCI) and Small Computer Systems Interface (SCSI). If you want to build peripheral devices for personal computers such as modems, sound cards, or disk drives, all you really have to do is make sure that your device adheres to one of these standards. Then, anybody who has a computer with a bus that is compliant with the bus standard of your device can plug your device into his or her computer.

Figure 1.4 shows, conceptually, what a software bus might look like. Notice the dotted line around the picture that indicates the software bus is not limited to a single machine; it encompasses all the machines on your network. You should be able to plug a software component into any machine on your network and then, subject to security constraints, use that software component from any machine on your network. Once this software bus is in place, there's no reason why system services such as graphics, the filesystem, even integrated speech support could not also be packaged as software components and plugged into the bus. Microsoft is doing precisely this. All new Microsoft APIs such as the DirectX and Speech APIs are being packaged as COM objects instead of C language APIs. This makes these functions easier to call from programming languages other than C.

As shown on Figure 1.4, COM is not the only software bus available. There is another technology called the Common Object Request Broker Architecture (CORBA). CORBA is conceptually similar to COM. Like COM, CORBA lets you create programming-language independent and location transparent software components.

The main difference with CORBA is that it was defined from the beginning to be a cross-platform technology. COM is still primarily a Windows-only technology, although implementations for other platforms are available now. See my sidebar about CORBA later in this chapter.

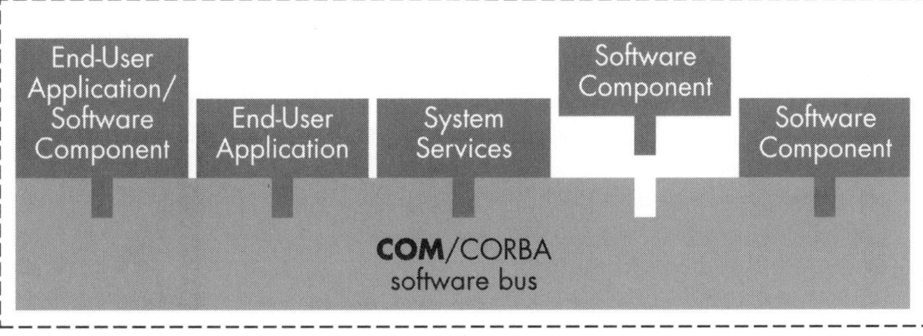

FIGURE 1.4 Reusing Location Transparent Software.

CORBA is an industry standard defined by a consortium of computer-involved companies (more than 600) called the Object Management Group (OMG). If you would like to learn more about it, visit www.omg.org or www.iona.com on the World Wide Web. These are fairly stable URLs, but if you search and do not find them, go to your favorite search engine and search on Object Management Group or Iona.

DCOM

DCOM is short for Distributed Component Object Model. DCOM is that part of COM that is concerned with enabling COM-based software components to be used over a network. Some people, myself included, feel that the name DCOM should not even exist. Location transparency is a key element of COM and location transparency implies that you should be able to use a software component, and use it in the same way, regardless of whether it resides on the same machine or on another machine on your network. By its very nature then, COM is a distributed technology and the use of the word DCOM is redundant.

I remember reading a review of a DCOM book on Amazon.com. One reader trashed the book and lamented the fact that 90% of this DCOM book simply covered COM. Well, the book was probably better than the user gave it credit for because 90% of DCOM is COM. The main new topic that DCOM adds to the COM world is security. If a COM object and its client are running on the same machine, security really is not a significant concern. If I want to let other machines use my software components from across my network, security becomes a major consideration. A significant amount of additional complexity that DCOM adds to COM is related to security.

DCOM was first implemented in NT 4.0. The introduction of DCOM represented a fundamental shift in the COM world. Before DCOM was introduced, COM was a desktop application integration technology. COM was being used to create and use ActiveX controls, to script office applications, and to paste Excel spreadsheets into Microsoft Word, and then double-click on the spreadsheet to see the Word menus and toolbars turn into those for Excel. Once DCOM was introduced, COM became an enterprise technology. People stopped talking about desktop application integration issues and started talking about using COM to create enterprise-class applications that would run their business. Technologies such as Microsoft Transaction Server and Microsoft Message Queue became the focal point of the literature written about COM. Maybe Microsoft COM introduced the name DCOM because it was important to mark the changeover in the focus of COM with the introduction of a new name.

MTS

Microsoft Transaction Server (MTS) is perhaps the most important COM-based technology that Microsoft has ever produced. DCOM made it *possible* to build distributed applications with COM; MTS made it *practical*. And unfortunately like most COM-based technologies, MTS is poorly named. A better name for MTS might be the COM Distributed Runtime Environment or the COM Application Server. In fact, most other companies that make products similar to MTS (Oracle and Powersoft, for example), call their products application servers. Transactions are only one of the things that MTS does.

Before MTS existed, you had to write a lot of infrastructure code to build enterprise-class, distributed applications. Enterprise-class, distributed applications usually require fine-grained security, scalability to thousands of clients, resource management, and distributed transactions. MTS frees you from having to write the code necessary to implement these requirements.

Version 2.0 of MTS is included with the NT Option Pack, which is a free add-on to Windows NT 4.0.

Fine-Grained Security

Enterprise-class distributed application usually needs a finer grain of security than DCOM provides. If you are developing a banking component, you may want a teller to be able to initiate a transaction involving less than $10,000. But only a bank manager can initiate a transaction involving more than $10,000. With MTS, implementing this kind of security is easy; with DCOM, you would have to write code directly to the Windows NT security API.

Scalability

Scalability is another big problem you'll encounter when building distributed applications. Let's say you deployed your component on a server and 1,000 clients tried to connect to the server at the same time. 1,000 clients may be holding a reference to COM objects on your server but at any given time only a few of those clients are actually executing a method on their COM object. It would improve the scalability of your application if you could create the illusion that each of these 1,000 clients has an object reference—even though they don't—and then quickly instantiate an actual object only when one of the clients actually makes a function call. This process is called Just-In-Time Activation. Imagine how difficult it would be to implement something like this yourself. With MTS, you get this functionality for free.

Resource Management

Another problem you will face when trying to implement distributed applications is managing a pool of scarce server-side resources such as database connections. Database connections are a scarce resource because not only are they expensive in terms of time to create, they can also be expensive in terms of money since most database server vendors require you to pay a per-connection licensing fee. MTS, OLEDB, and ODBC work together to implement database connection pooling. When a component tries to create a database connection, MTS first checks if there is an already established connection in the pool that can be reused. If there is an available connection, then this connection is used instead of a new one being created.

Distributed Transactions

Finally, MTS lets you create transactions that involve multiple databases on different servers and to do it in a way that does not require you to write code to explicitly start, commit, and rollback transactions.

Windows DNA

Windows DNA is an acronym that stands for the Windows Distributed interNet Applications Architecture. Basically, it is a distributed application development model that specifies how to build robust, scalable, distributed applications using the Windows platform. The central idea of the Windows DNA is that business applications developed for the Windows platform should be partitioned into three logical tiers: user interface, business logic, and data storage. These applications should use COM as their integration technology and use Internet Information Server (IIS), MTS, and Internet Explorer to provide integration with the World Wide Web.

IIS is Microsoft's Web server product. It is bundled with the server versions of Windows NT or Windows 2000. Internet Explorer is Microsoft's Web browser that, for now, is given away free with all of Microsoft's operating systems.

And of course the entire thing should be built with Visual Studio. The Windows DNA is a conceptual construct (it's not something you buy or install). It's the blue-print for how Microsoft's distributed technologies should be used to create business applications.

COM+

COM+ is the second generation of COM. It includes new features that make COM easier to use and simplifies the development of distributed, enterprise-class applications. COM+ builds on the distributed infrastructure provided by DCOM and it represents the final evolution of COM from a desktop, application integration technology to a distributed, application development infrastructure. With COM+, the features of MTS are tightly-integrated into the operating system. In addition, COM+ provides an all-new set of services that were designed to simplify the development of enterprise-class, distributed applications. Some of these exciting new features of COM+ are:

- Component load-balancing
- Publish and Subscribe events
- Asynchronous method invocation
- In-memory database
- Queued Components
- Improved administration services

In fact, the best description I have heard of COM+ is that it is MTS 3.0 plus additional services. Microsoft originally had more ambitious plans for COM+. It was to include a universal runtime and implementation inheritance. These other features are still planned but will not ship with the first release of COM+ in Windows 2000.

The In-Memory Database and Component Load Balancing will not appear in the first release of Windows 2000, but will likely follow in subsequent releases.

Now that you understand the underpinnings—COM, DCOM, MTS, and COM+—I define two more terms that have caused a great deal of confusion for people: ActiveX and OLE.

Whither CORBA?

In the 1996 book *Essential Distributed Objects Survival Guide* by Robert Orfali et. al., the authors state that if CORBA had not achieved significant market penetration by early 1997 then the battle to define the industry standard software bus would have been lost. More than 3 years have passed since this deadline. So is CORBA dead? Many of the technologies touted in *Essential Distributed Objects:* OpenDoc, Taligent CommonPoint, and NextStep are now faint memories. But that does not mean CORBA is dead. There is room in this market for one dominant standard and one minor standard. COM+, if it is stable, will most likely end any hope that CORBA has of being the dominant standard. So why did CORBA fail? My personal opinion is that nothing that is created by a standards group that involves more than 600 companies could possibly evolve fast enough to be competitive with a product that is controlled by a single company. Sun was right to maintain control of Java and not turn it over to a standards body as many people wanted them to do. It likely would have suffered the same fate as CORBA.

So where does CORBA fit in now? Despite what Microsoft says, COM/DCOM/COM+ is still not a cross-platform technology. There are COM implementations available on the UNIX and VMS platforms, but these products are still immature. CORBA was a cross-platform technology from the beginning and there are robust CORBA implementations available for almost every platform. So use COM if you are developing an all-Windows solution. But, if you have UNIX or mainframe servers and NT clients (as many people do these days), consider using CORBA to wrap the UNIX and mainframe servers, and then use a product such as Iona's COMet, to allow COM clients to invoke the CORBA servers. See the Prentice Hall book *COM-CORBA Interoperability* by Geraghty and colleagues if you would like to learn more.

ActiveX

ActiveX is the consumer brand name for all Microsoft COM-based technologies. None of the other names has caused even nearly as much confusion as this one. In fact, most publishers of computer books don't even like to publish books with ActiveX in the title. (How many books have you seen recently that included the word ActiveX in the title?) The main reason for this confusion is that the meaning of ActiveX has changed. Most everyone is familiar with the product Tylenol. Tylenol is an easy-to-remember, more consumer-friendly brand name for a drug called Acetaminophen. In the same way, ActiveX is an easy-to-remember, more consumer-friendly name for COM. ActiveX certainly sounds much cooler than COM. A company called Software AG has ported COM to several UNIX platforms. The consumer name for its product is EntireX. It is not using the name ActiveX—that's Microsoft's brand name—but it does advertise its product as an implementation of COM, just like other pharmaceutical companies sell Acetaminophen under different names than Tylenol.

The reason so many people are confused by the name ActiveX is because the definition changed. Originally ActiveX was a brand name for all COM-based Microsoft technologies that had utility on the World Wide Web. You probably remember back in 1995 when Bill Gates, after returning from his yearly sabbatical, decided that the Internet was a good thing. After Bill's revelation, Microsoft decided that COM could be used to deliver Active content on the Web.

Active content—in Internet terminology—is Web content that runs or executes as opposed to HTML pages that are static. Examples are a Java applet or ActiveX control.

All COM-based Microsoft technologies that had some Internet utility were then renamed as Active technologies. For instance, Ole Custom Controls (after some changes to the standard) were renamed as Active controls. Eventually the term ActiveX was coined, I guess because adding the X at the end of Active sounded cool. Finally, Microsoft—for reasons that escape me—decided to attach the name ActiveX to all COM-related technologies, even technologies that had nothing to do with the Internet. If you go into Visual Basic, for instance, you can see that two of the possible project types are an ActiveX DLL or Exe. These project types obviously have nothing to do with the Internet. So the end result of this naming saga is that you should think of ActiveX as being the consumer brand name for COM (at least until Microsoft changes its definition again). If you can remember that ActiveX is to COM as Tylenol is to Acetaminophen, then you've got the idea.

OLE

As if it wasn't bad enough that the definition of ActiveX has changed twice, the definition of OLE has actually changed three times. OLE is a collection of COM-based technologies that implement *compound documents*. What's a compound document? To create a compound document, open a Microsoft Word document. Type in a few words and then select Object from the Insert menu. Select Microsoft Excel Chart from the Object dialog that appears. Your screen should look like the one shown in Figure 1.5.

You probably noticed when you pasted the Excel Chart into Word that Word's menus and toolbars changed. If you looked closely, you probably realized they changed to look like Excel's menus and toolbars. Notice also that if you click back in the Word portion of the document, the menus and toolbars changed back into those for Word. Most computer-literate people I

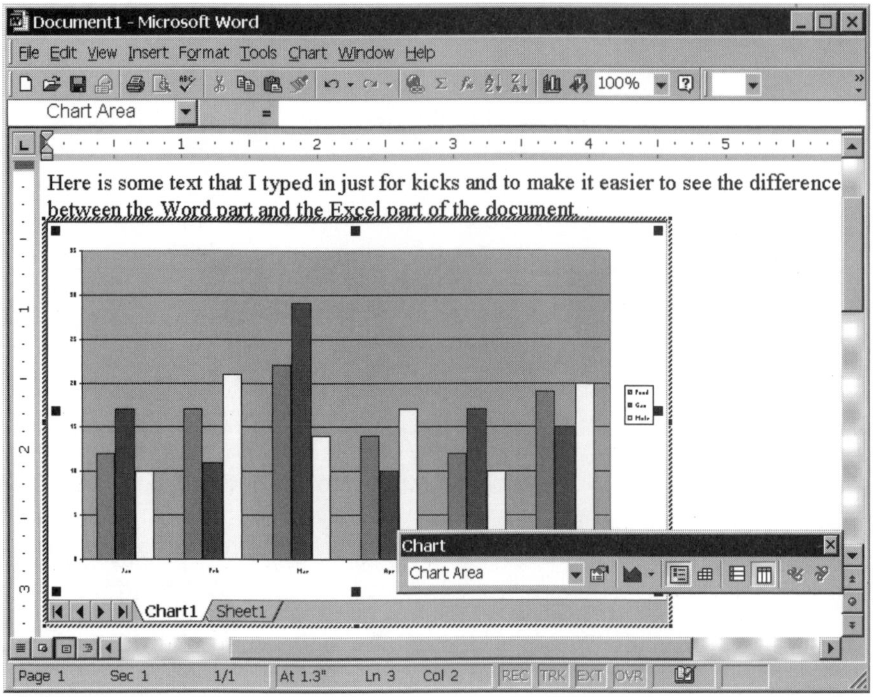

FIGURE 1.5 The Essence of OLE: A Compound Document.

know have used this feature, but I've found that many people believe this functionality is a Microsoft Office feature; it is not. The functionality you just used (in COM-speak, you just created a compound document) represents the very essence of OLE.

There are a set of COM interfaces that define what a piece of software must do to be a compound document server (Excel in this scenario). There is also a set of COM interfaces that define what a piece of software must do to be a compound document container (Word in this scenario). It's not terribly difficult to create your own compound document servers and containers. Visual C++ has wizard support for doing both.

So, why all the confusion about OLE? The name OLE actually predates COM. Before COM existed, there was OLE 1.0 that implemented a far less functional version of compound documents. OLE 1.0 used a technology called Dynamic Data Exchange (DDE) as its communication infrastructure. At that time, OLE was an acronym that stood for Object Linking and Embedding. In 1993, Microsoft came out with OLE 2.0, which was built on COM. In addition to providing the infrastructure for compound documents; OLE 2.0 saw the introduction of other COM-related technologies that had nothing to do with compound documents: OLE Custom Controls (OCXs) and OLE Automation. So, Microsoft decided to change the meaning of the name OLE. It was no longer thought of as Object Linking and Embedding, it was now simply OLE and was thought of as the consumer brand name for all COM-based technologies (sound familar).

This worked well for two years until ActiveX replaced OLE as the consumer brand name for COM. Rather than bury the name OLE, Microsoft decided to change the definition of OLE back to what it originally was: COM-based, compound document technologies. It's not clear to me whether OLE has gone back to being an acronym or if it's still OLE. And just to confuse you even more, Microsoft's new COM-based, Data Access technology is called OLEDB. This technology obviously has nothing to do with compound documents, but it still wears the OLE name.

A Modest Proposal: My New COM Naming Scheme

Successful brand names are ones where the company puts forth a consistent message. Microsoft has done the exact opposite with COM: constantly changing the definitions of names in the COM namespace and adding new ones. Oh, the humanity ... and confusion. I'm sure if someone in Microsoft's marketing department heard my complaint they would probably say that the software industry is a fast-paced, dynamic industry and they have to be allowed to make changes to their technology names as they see fit. But, when so many people are confused about what a product name means, then something may be amiss.

I'm a firm believer in the idea that you should not complain about a problem unless you have a solution to offer. So, here's my proposed solution for Microsoft's COM naming mess. The only COM-related name that has been around for a long period of time and has not changed is COM. It's not a coincidence that, of all the names in the COM namespace, this is the one that most people feel comfortable with. I think Microsoft should banish all the other COM-related names like ActiveX, OLE, DCOM, and even COM+ into a scrap heap. My proposed naming scheme would use the word COM and then a one- or two-word description of the technology. For instance, ActiveX controls would become COM Controls, OLE would become COM Compound Documents, DCOM would be COM Networking, OLEDB would become COM DB, and a good name for COM+ would be COM Enterprise. A naming scheme like this would clear up a lot of confusion and save me from having to explain the COM namespace to my students every semester.

■ Summary

In this chapter, you got an executive summary of all the names in the COM namespace. You also learned the history of some of the more confusing names, like OLE and ActiveX. With a firm grasp of the COM namespace, you can begin looking at COM in a more concrete way. In the next chapter, you can review some object-oriented concepts in preparation for a more technical introduction to COM.

TWO

Classes, Objects, and Interfaces

Before I get into the low-level details of implementing COM classes, objects, and interfaces, I want to wax philosophical about the meaning of object-orientation as applied to COM. It's important to do this because COM requires you to change the way you think about the idea of a class, an object, and an interface. So this chapter serves as both a review of object-orientation and an introduction to what Don Box (a noted expert on COM) calls the "second wave of object-orientation."

What is Object-Orientation?

To understand what object-orientation means, stop and think about how you solve complex problems. Unfortunately, the human brain has a limited ability to process information. There are limits as to how much information you can comprehend at any given time. How do we solve problems that are so complex they exceed our limited ability to comprehend either the problem or its solution? Well, instead of solving one, incomprehensible problem, you decompose the problem into smaller problems. You can then decompose each of these smaller problems into a set of even smaller problems. If you decompose a problem enough, it can be reduced to a form where each piece of the problem is easy to understand, communicate, and solve. Once you solve each of these smaller problems, you can combine these solutions to produce a solution to the overall problem. The question is: how do you perform your decomposition?

Algorithmic Decomposition

In the not-to-distant past, most software developers used an algorithmic decomposition to solve the kinds of complex problems you encounter every day when designing software. When using an algorithmic decomposition, you first determine the overall algorithm you are going to use to solve the problem at hand. An algorithm *breaks down* the overall task into a sequence of steps. You then break down each of these steps into even smaller steps until you finally reach a level where it is easy to understand each piece of the algorithm. Each of these small steps can then be implemented as a software module. In the software business, this approach is known as *structured design*. Figure 2.1 shows how you might decompose the problem of calculating the net pay of an employee using an algorithmic decomposition.

Your top-level task, calculate net pay, is broken into three major subtasks: calculate gross pay, calculate taxes, and calculate health care contribution. The calculate gross pay task is further broken down into two subtasks: get hourly rate and get hours worked. Get deductions is a subtask of calculate taxes and get number of dependents is a subtask of calculating health care contribution. Unfortunately, Figure 2.1 does not show all the information you need to completely specify your solution. The diagram only shows the dependencies between the different tasks. We also need some way to show how the tasks are ordered in time. In structured design, flow charts are usually used for this purpose. Figure 2.2 shows what a flow chart might look like for a problem like this.

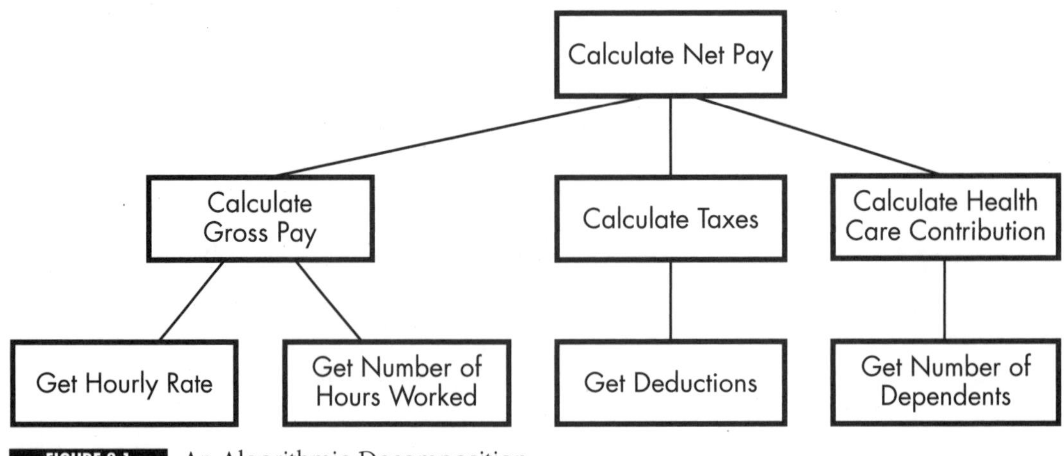

FIGURE 2.1 An Algorithmic Decomposition.

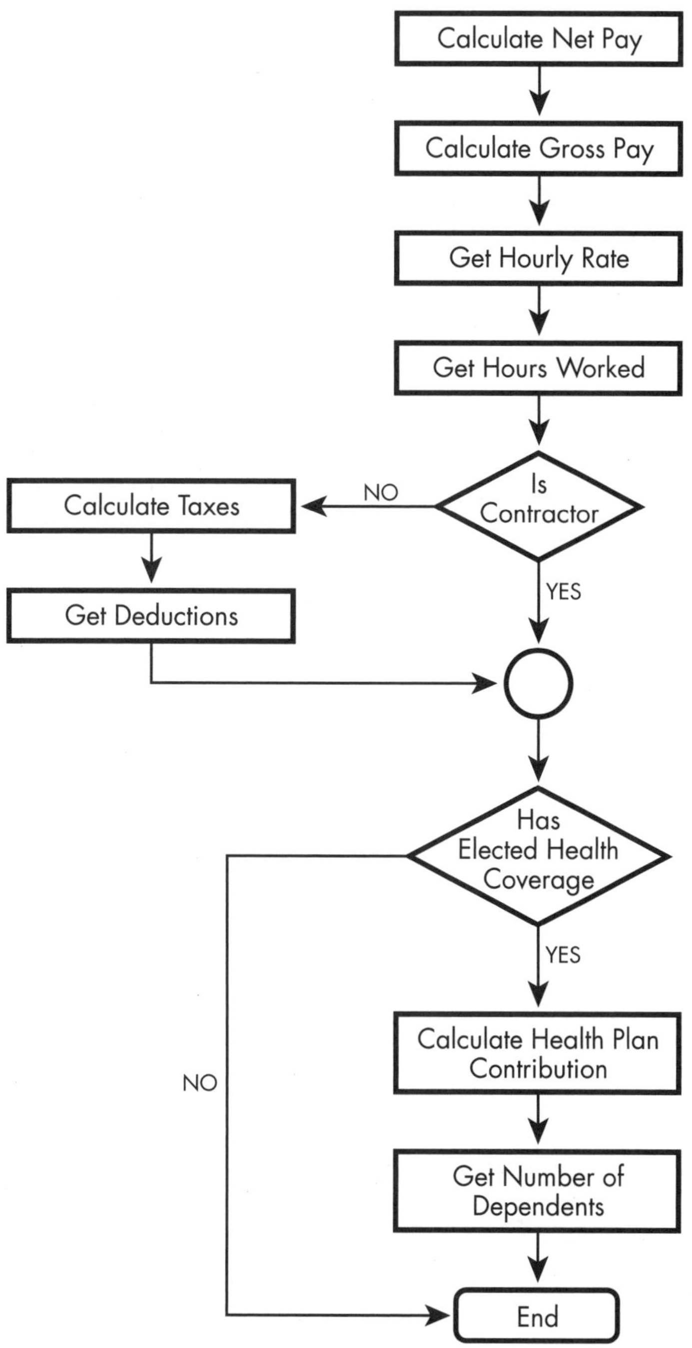

FIGURE 2.2 A Flow Chart.

Object-Oriented Decomposition

Another way to look at this problem is to use an object-oriented decomposition. In this approach, instead of concentrating on algorithms, you seek to identify the key abstractions in the problem domain. You can also try to discover the relationships that exist between both instances of these key abstractions (which are called objects) and between the abstractions themselves (which are called classes). Figure 2.3 shows how you might decompose the problem of calculating the net pay of an employee using an object-oriented approach. As the figure shows, four key abstractions (classes) have been identified: `Employee`, `Payroll`, `TaxCalculator`, and `HealthPlan`. This type of diagram is a Unified Modeling Language (UML) Collaboration Diagram. Diagrams like these are used to show how instances of classes (objects) interact to carry out a particular scenario.

Unified Modeling Language is an object-oriented design language. It is widely accepted as the standard notation for expressing object-oriented design.

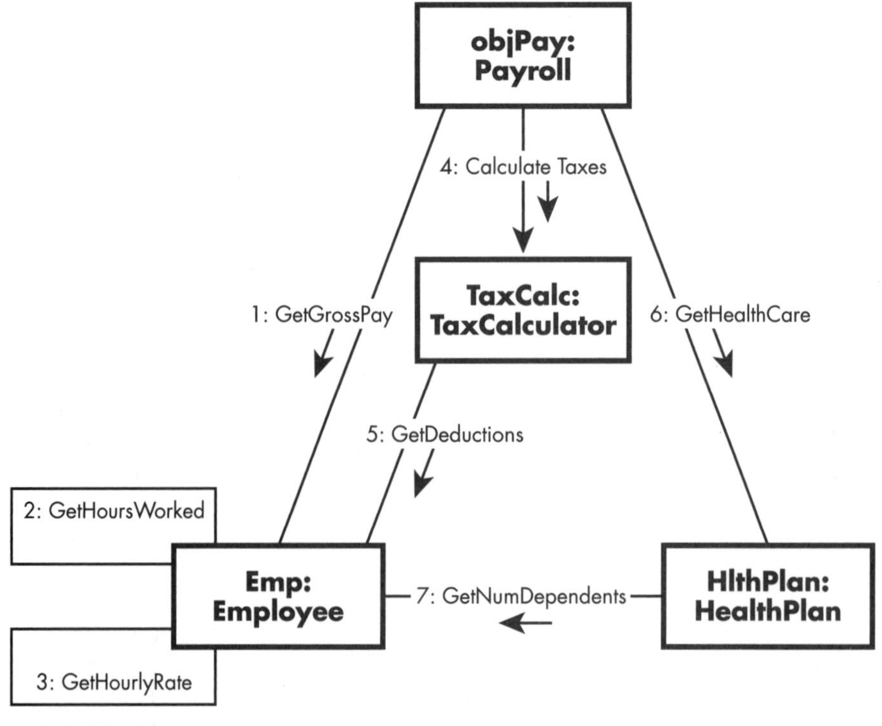

FIGURE 2.3 An Object-Oriented Decomposition.

The numbers on the lines connecting the objects shows the time ordering of the actions involved. The `Payroll` class is a controller class in this scenario. It initiates the sequence of events by calling the `GetGrossPay` method on the `Employee` object. The `Employee` object then calls the `GetHoursWorked` and `GetHourlyRate` methods on itself to calculate the gross pay of the employee. Next, the `Payroll` object calls the `CalculateTaxes` method on the `TaxCalculator` class that responds by calling the `GetDeductions` method on the `Employee` object. Finally, the `Payroll` object calls the `HealthPlan` object to get the employee's health plan contribution, the `HealthPlan` object responds by call the `GetNumDependents` method on the `Employee` object to calculate the contribution. Notice that what you have here is just a different way of looking at the same problem.

Just as in the case of structured design, it is difficult—and usually not desirable to display all the information needed to capture the design on a single diagram. In this example, there are some relationships that you really cannot capture on a collaboration diagram. For instance, a company may have many different types of employees and each of those types of employees may be paid differently: a manager may receive a salary plus a bonus that is calculated based on the amount of profit her department made. A salesperson's pay may be based solely on commission, a contractor might receive an hourly wage and no benefits. All of these types of employees share certain traits that all employees have—they work and are paid for instance, but they are paid differently. You need some way to capture the information that there are several types of Employees, each shares the essential characteristics of an employee, but each has certain important differences. Class diagrams are used to capture this kind of information, and Figure 2.4 shows what a class diagram would look like for the problem of calculating the net pay of an Employee.

Figure 2.4 shows several classes: `Manager`, `Contractor`, and `Salesperson` that inherit from the `Employee` class. In the object-oriented world, inheritance is your way of modeling an *is–a* relationship. In other words, you are showing here that a Manager *is–a* Employee as is a Contractor and a Salesperson. All of these classes share the essential characteristics of an Employee, but they each implement the `GetGrossPay` operation differently. It also shows that the `Payroll` class is dependent on the `Employee` class and maintains links to the `TaxCalculator` and `HealthPlan` classes because they are needed to calculate the net pay for Employees. Between Figures 2.3 and 2.4 you have captured the static structure and dynamic behavior of your problem.

So now that you have seen two ways to decompose a complex problem, the inevitable question is which type of decomposition is better? Some might argue that the best decomposition is the one you're most familiar with. Although it's hard to argue with that logic, I think the object-oriented decomposition is a superior approach in almost all situations. There are sev-

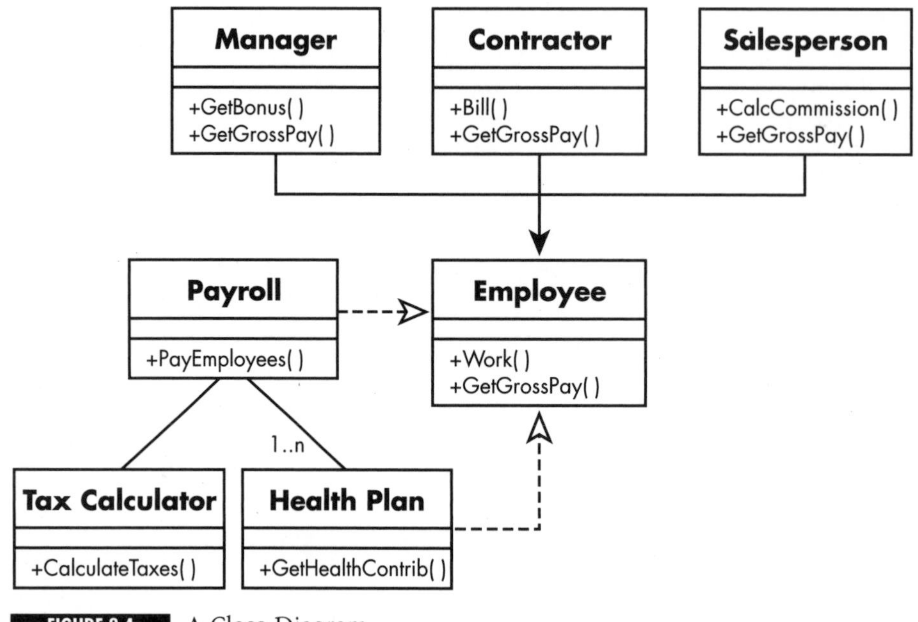

FIGURE 2.4 A Class Diagram.

eral advantages to the object-oriented approach: it yields smaller solutions because common mechanisms can more easily be reused. It also yields more stable solutions because the solution is built on stable, intermediate forms. Object-oriented solutions are also more resilient to change and because your solution is composed of entities from the problem domain, it is easier to communicate the design to end-users and this lowers the risk that you will build the *wrong* system. For these reasons Microsoft chose to base COM on object-oriented concepts.

But COM does not implement objects the same way that most object-oriented programming languages do. What works well when you are writing a few thousand lines of C++ that are going to be compiled into a single executable may not work well when you are trying to build a large, distributed system. So COM takes a different approach primarily in its use of interfaces and its lack of support of implementation inheritance. To understand why COM has to take a different approach in its implementation of object orientation, you must first understand the relationship between classes, objects, and interfaces.

Classes

You can think of classes as the templates from which objects are built. A class defines the state and behavior that all objects of that type will have. Listing 2.1 shows what an Employee class might look like when defined in C++.

LISTING 2.1 *EMPLOYEE.H*

```
#include<string>
using namespace std;
class Employee {
public:
   Employee(int id,const char *nm,float sal);
   virtual ~Employee();
   virtual float GetGrossPay() {
      return GetHoursWorked() * GetHourlyRate();
   }
   int GetHoursWorked() {
      return m_hoursWorked;
   }
   float GetHourlyRate() {
      return m_salary/40;
   }
   void BeginPayPeriod() {
      m_hoursWorked = 0;
   }
   void Work(short numHours) {
      m_hoursWorked += numHours;
   }
   short GetNumDependents() {
      return m_numDependents;
   }
   void SetNumDependents(short numDependents) {
      m_numDependents=numDependents;
   }
   string GetName() {
      return m_name;
   }
   float GetSalary() {
      return m_salary;
   }
private:
   int m_id;
   string m_name;
   float m_salary;
   short m_hoursWorked;
   short m_numDependents;
};
```

The state of the Employee class includes the identification (ID), name, salary, and number of hours worked in the current pay period. Notice that the member variables that hold the state of the Employee class are private. These variables can only be accessed by methods of the Employee class. The behavior of the Employee class is defined by the public methods of the class: GetGrossPay, Work, BeginPayPeriod, and so on. These methods define the interface that the Employee class exposes to the outside world. I mentioned that a Manager has all the behavior of an Employee but is paid differently. You captured this idea on our class diagram using inheritance. You can implement the Manager class in C++ using public inheritance from the Employee class. Because C++ supports implementation inheritance, it is easy for a subclass—Manager—to inherit the implementation of its superclass—Employee. Listings 2.2 and 2.3 show how little code is required to implement a Manager class using implementation inheritance.

LISTING 2.2 *MANAGER.H*

```
#include "employee.h"
class Manager : public Employee {
public:
   Manager(int id,const char *nm,float sal,short nDeps,float bonus);
   ~Manager();
   virtual float GetGrossPay() {
      return GetHoursWorked() * GetHourlyRate()+GetBonus();
   }
   float GetBonus() {
      return mBonus;
   }
   void SetBonus(float aBonus) {
      mBonus=aBonus;
   }
private:
   float mBonus;
};
```

LISTING 2.3 *MANAGER.CCP*

```
#include "manager.h"
Manager::Manager(int id,const char *nm,float sal,short deps,float bonus) :
   Employee(id,nm,sal,deps)
{
   SetBonus(bonus);
}

Manager::~Manager()
{
}
```

The Manager class declared above has inherited all the functionality and state of the Employee class. The manager has an ID, a name, and a base salary just like an employee. Notice that you only have to re-declare in the Manager class the private member variables that you are adding—in this case just mBonus—and the public methods that you are adding (GetBonus and SetBonus) or changing (GetGrossPay). All of the other methods and state in the Employee class automatically become part of the Manager class. To use your Employee and Manager classes, you have to write some code that creates instances of the classes—these are objects.

Objects

Listing 2.4 shows two functions (ShowEmployee and main) that create Employee and Manager objects.

LISTING 2.4 *MAIN.CCP*

```
#include <iostream>
#include "employee.h"
#include "manager.h"
void ShowPay(Employee *emp)
{
   cout << emp->GetGrossPay() << endl;
}
void main()
{
   Manager *mgr;
   Employee *emp1;
   Employee emp2(124,"John Smith",400.0,0);
   emp1=new Employee(123,"Alan Gordon",500.0,2);
   mgr=new Manager(25,"Mike Dunn",2000.0,3,500);
```

```
    Employee *empMgr=new Manager(2,"Carol Smith",2500.0,2,400);
    emp1->Work(50);
    emp2.Work(40);
    mgr->Work(40);
    cout << emp1->GetGrossPay() << endl;
    cout << emp2.GetGrossPay() << endl;
    ShowPay(mgr);
    delete emp1;
    delete mgr;
    delete empMgr;
}
```

Notice how you can declare an Employee pointer: empMgr and assign it to a Manager object as shown in the sixth line of the main routine.

```
Employee *empMgr=new Manager(2,"Carol Smith",2500.0,2,400);
```

It should make sense to you why you can do this. I said before that a Manager is an Employee, so it can do everything that an Employee can do. So all functions that can be called through an Employee pointer can be called on a Manager object. Of course the opposite would not work. You could not declare a Manager pointer and then assign it to an Employee object as follows:

```
Manager *mgr=new Employee(130,"John Smith",400.0,0);
```

There are certain functions that you should be able to call through a Manager pointer, such as SetBonus, that are not supported by an Employee object. Your C++ compiler will complain if you try to make an assignment like this. The ShowPay method illustrates a question that I like to ask when I'm interviewing a prospective C++ programmer. Notice that I'm passing a Manager object to the ShowPay method. The ShowPay method expects an Employee pointer. Can I do this? Certainly a Manager object can be used everywhere that an Employee object is expected. A manager is an employee. Now the ShowPay method calls the GetGrossPay method through the Employee pointer that is passed to it. The question is: if I pass a Manager object to GetGrossPay, which GetGrossPay method gets called? The one in the Employee class or the one in the Manager class? It does make a difference. For the case shown here, the manager whose name is Mike Dunn is defined to have a salary of $2,000 and a weekly bonus of $500 as shown on line 5 of the main routine.

```
mgr=new Manager(25,"Mike Dunn",2000.0,3,500);
```

If Mike Dunn works a 40-hour week, he will receive $2,000 if the Employee version of GetGrossPay is called, he will receive $2,500 if the Manager version of GetGrossPay gets called. In this case, the Manager method will be called. But only because I declared the `GetGrossPay` method using the virtual keyword as shown in the following code snippet from the definition of the `Employee` class:

```
virtual float GetGrossPay() {
   return GetHoursWorked() * GetHourlyRate();
}
```

Using the virtual keyword indicates to the compiler that I would like to use dynamic binding to find the correct function to call. So if I call a method on an object through a pointer that is typed to a base class of the object, I get the function that corresponds to the type of the object (in this case `Manager`) not the type of the pointer (in this case `Employee`). This is an example of an important object-oriented concept called polymorphism, which literally means many (poly) forms (morph). Essentially, it means that a class like `Manager` can assume many forms (types really). In this case, these many forms are all the types of its base classes. So if, for instance, I define an `Executive` class that inherited from `Manager` but also had stock options, I could use an `Executive` object anywhere that a Manager is required, I could also use an `Executive` object anywhere that an `Employee` is required. An `Executive` can assume the form of each of its base classes.

Polymorphism is wonderful, but there are a couple of problems with the way these classes are designed and with the use of implementation inheritance:

- The implementation inheritance exposes you to the fragile base class problem.
- The interface and implementation of these classes are too-tightly bound.

The Fragile Base Class Problem

If you've built Windows applications using Visual C++ and the Microsoft Foundation Classes (MFC), you have experienced the fragile base class problem. You experience the fragile base class problem every time you override a method in one of the MFC-based classes. Take a look at the following code, which is taken from an example that I use in my class:

LISTING 2.5 *ILLUSTRATING THE FRAGILE BASE CLASS PROBLEM*

```
void CDbpracticeView::OnInitialUpdate()
{
   m_pSet = &GetDocument()->m_dbpracticeSet;
   m_deptSet.Open();
   m_pSet->m_strFilter="DEPT_ID=?";
   m_pSet->m_deptIDParam=m_deptSet.m_ID;
   CRecordView::OnInitialUpdate();
   m_deptsCombo.ResetContent();
   int index=0;
   while (!m_deptSet.IsEOF())
   {
      m_deptsCombo.InsertString(index,m_deptSet.m_NAME);
      m_deptsCombo.SetItemData(index,m_deptSet.m_ID);
      m_deptSet.MoveNext();
      index++;
   }
   m_deptsCombo.SetCurSel(0);
}
```

In this example, I am developing a database application that uses a parameterized query. I have overridden the `OnInitialUpdate` in the `View` class (`CdbpracticeView`) of my project so I can setup the parameterized query. The question is: do I have to call the `OnInitialUpdate` method in my View's base class (`CRecordView`)? And if so, when do I need to make the call? It turns out that I do have to call the base class version of `OnInitialUpdate`. But, I have to setup the parameterized query before I make the call to `CRecordView::OnInitialUpdate` because the `CRecordView`'s implementation of `OnInitialUpdate` executes the query and performs other query-related initialization. However, if I want to load up any of my view's controls in my version of `OnInitialUpdate`, I have to do that after I make the call to `CRecordView`'s `OnInitialUpdate` because my application's window is created in `CRecordView::OnInitialUpdate`. How did I know all of this? I looked at the MFC source code. You've probably noticed that when you override a method in an MFC class using the ClassWizard, it usually inserts a call to the base classes version of the method if it is appropriate and puts comments guiding you as to where you should insert your code. Sometimes it will tell you to do your thing and then call the base class method. In other circumstances, you have to call the base class version of the method first before you work your magic. But I've encountered situations where to make something work the way I wanted it to, I had do something completely different than what the ClassWizard told me to do. If things aren't working the way I want, I usually figure out what to do by looking at the source code for the class. This always tells me what is done in the base class and what things I need to do if I choose not to call the base class version of the method that I just overrode.

So let's bring this back to the earlier employee example. Remember that you overrode the employee's `GetGrossPay` method in the `Manager` class. Imagine that the `GetGrossPay` method in the `Employee` base class inserted a record in a database every time somebody called the `GetGrossPay` method. Perhaps for privacy reasons a company wanted to keep a record of who and when someone accessed personal information about an Employee. If `GetGrossPay` was implemented this way, then you should call the `Employee` version of `GetGrossPay` method in the `Manager` as follows:

```
virtual float GetGrossPay() {
   return Employee::GetGrossPay()+GetBonus();
}
```

The problem is, how would you know that you needed to do this? Someone would have to tell you, or implementation details of the `GetGrossPay` method would have to be documented, or you would need the source code. Are you starting to see a recurring theme here? Implementation inheritance is what some people call a white-box form of reuse. In many situations, you cannot use implementation inheritance effectively without knowing some implementation details about the base class that you are using. You cannot treat the base class like a black box and be completely ignorant of its implementation. This is why Microsoft ships the source code for the MFC with Visual C++. The simple reality is that you cannot use MFC effectively without having it.

While it is okay to ship the source code for MFC, it's not okay to ship the source code for COM software components because, by definition, software components are always shipped in binary form. COM solves this problem by simply not letting you use implementation inheritance. If you have an `Employee` COM class, you cannot use implementation inheritance to create a `Manager` COM class. You can implement the `Employee` interface (I define interfaces further in the next section) in your `Manager` COM class. You can then reuse the implementation of the `Employee` methods by creating an `Employee` object within the `Manager` class. Then, when somebody calls one of the `Employee` methods in the `Manager` COM class, you can simply delegate these calls to the internal `Employee` instance (this is called containment). Or you could reuse the `Employee` class by exposing the Employee interface from the internal `Employee` object directly (this is called aggregation). But either way, you have to write a lot of duplicate and redundant code to delegate function calls. This extra code is not required if you use Implementation inheritance.

Before you start cursing COM as an abomination to all that is object-oriented, consider the following facts: (1) you *can* use implementation inheritance to *implement* a COM class, and (2) COM does support polymorphism. To understand the first point, remember that a COM class will likely be implemented by one or more C++, Visual Basic, or Java classes. There is no reason that these implementation classes cannot inherit their implementation from base classes that do most of the busy work. In fact, this is exactly how the Active Template Library (ATL) works. To understand the second point, recognize that different COM classes can implement an interface in different ways (just like the `Manager` and `Employee` classes implement the `GetGrossPay` method in different ways). If two different COM classes—let's say a `Manager` COM class and an `Employee` COM class—implement the same interface, you can use either of those classes in a situation where that interface is required. This is the equivalent of saying that you can pass either a `Manager` or an `Employee` to a method that expects an `Employee`. In other words, you have polymorphism.

The Active Template Library (ATL) is a C++ class library that ships with Visual C++. ATL simplifies the development of COM components by encapsulating most of the functionality required to implement COM components within a set of base classes that you can inherit from. I discuss ATL extensively later in this book.

COM's lack of support for implementation inheritance has been the subject of many debates within the software development community. My personal opinion is that everyone is overreacting. Microsoft's decision to not support implementation inheritance in COM is an overreaction on its part. If using implementation inheritance can cause problems, inform me what those problems are and how to avoid them. Don't prevent me from doing something just because there are potential problems with that thing. I think a lot of the detractors of COM are also overreacting because COM does support polymorphism and usually polymorphism is the real goal. Implementation inheritance is only one way of achieving that goal.

To Inherit or Not to Inherit

Microsoft initially announced in 1997 that COM+ would support implementation inheritance. Mary Kirtland, who is a COM program manager, wrote a pair of articles in the *Microsoft Systems Journal* (see the November 1997 and December 1997 issues) in which she outlined Microsoft's vision for COM+. At the time those articles were published, Microsoft's vision included implementation inheritance. Since then they have scaled back their plans and the first release of COM+ in Windows 2000 will *not* support implementation inheritance. However, Microsoft will likely include implementation inheritance in a later release of COM+.

If you would like a good—but not necessarily unbiased—view of this issue from the other side (the CORBA camp), see the book *Essential Distributed Objects Survival Guide* by

Orfali and colleagues. They, too, claim that Microsoft's lack of support for implementation inheritance is an overreaction to the fragile base-class problem. They also mention the problems that COM's lack of implementation inheritance causes: you have to write a lot of duplicate code to implement aggregation and delegation. But they don't mention that this is a relatively minor problem compared to the overall problem of developing software.

Separating Interface and Implementation

I mentioned that in addition to the fragile base class problem, there is another problem with the `Employee` and `Manager` classes as they are currently defined. The problem is that the interface and the implementation of the two classes are coupled too tightly together. You have already seen that the private member variables within the `Employee` class cannot be *accessed* by code outside the `Employee` class. Unfortunately, this does not mean that code that is outside of the `Employee` class does not have *knowledge* of the private member variables within the `Employee` class. In fact, the compiler generates code that is dependent on the size of the class every time an instance of the class is created. The C++ compiler also has to know how big the `Employee` class is so it can set up stack frames and function parameter lists properly. If you made a change to the `Employee` class that changed its size (changing the salary from a float to a double, for instance), you would have to recompile your client code. Remember I said that COM is all about creating software components and software components by definition are shipped in binary form. You certainly wouldn't want developers who use your software components to have to recompile their code whenever you changed the underlying implementation of your software component. So what you need is some way to further separate the interface and the implementation of your classes. C++ classes provide you with *Encapsulation*. In other words, they let you prevent clients from *accessing* the private part of your classes. You want to go one step further and prevent clients from even having *knowledge* of the private part of your classes. The key to this separation is to separate the interface of a class from its implementation. Let's talk about interfaces further and in the process you'll see why they are so important in the COM world.

Interfaces

Interfaces, as a programming language construct, are a concept that is unfamiliar to some C++ programmers. C++ does not support interfaces as a separate concept from a class. Java, being a more modern language, lets you define an interface as a separate construct from a class. In this section, I explore the concept of an interface and show how it can be used to construct classes that hide their implementation in such a way that clients have neither access to nor knowledge of the implementation of a class. To understand what interfaces are and how to use them, let's return to the definition of the `Employee` class provided in Listing 2.1.

You can separate this class into the following two pieces:

- Its interface, which is the set of public methods defined in the class minus the constructor and destructor.
- Its implementation, which includes the implementation of all of the methods in the interface, the constructor and destructor, and the private member variables of the class.

If you could separate these two pieces, you could hide the implementation and force clients to only use the interface. If these interfaces could be created in such a way that they were completely independent of the size (and even the programming language) of the class that implements them, then you could write client code that would not have to be recompiled, even if you radically changed the implementation of an interface.

Before I talk about how interfaces like these are constructed, let's define what an interface is, at least for this discussion. An interface is a set of related methods that define a behavior. An interface only has public methods and it contains no state (i.e., it has no private member variables). If you refer back to your `Employee` class, you could say that the public methods in the class define an `Employee` interface that the `Employee` class implements. The methods `GetGrossPay`, `Work`, `BeginPayPeriod`, and so on define your `Employee` interface. You can say that the Employee class implements this interface. Interfaces are independent of the size of their implementation because interfaces have no state.

Many object-oriented programming languages, such as Java, let you treat interfaces as separate concepts from classes. With Java, you can define an interface, and then define classes that implement the interface. A Java interface can be implemented by many Java classes, and a Java class can implement many Java interfaces. The following Java code shows how an interface can be defined using Java. The syntax should be familiar to a C++ programmer:

```
interface Employee
{
   float GetGrossPay();
   float GetHourlyRate();
   int GetHoursWorked();
   void BeginPayPeriod();
   void Work(short numHours);
   short GetNumDependents();
   void SetNumDependents(short numDeps);
   String GetName();
   float GetSalary();
}
```

Notice that your interface defines a set of methods that all relate to a particular type of behavior—the behavior of an Employee. But notice that no implementation is specified for any of the methods. Also notice there are no private member variables declared in this interface. The following code shows how you can define a class, in Java, that implements the `Employee` interface:

LISTING 2.6 *A JAVA CLASS THAT IMPLEMENTS THE EMPLOYEE INTERFACE*

```
class Person implements Employee
{
   private int m_id;
   private String m_name;
   private float m_salary;
   private short m_hoursWorked;
   private short m_numDeps;
   public Person(int id,String nm,float sal,short nDeps) {
      m_id=id;
      m_name=nm;
      m_salary=sal;
      m_numDeps=nDeps;
   }
   public float GetGrossPay() {
      return GetHourlyRate()*GetHoursWorked();
   }
   public float GetHourlyRate() {
      return m_salary/40;
   }
   public int GetHoursWorked() {
      return m_hoursWorked;
   }
   public void BeginPayPeriod() {
      m_hoursWorked = 0;
   }
   public void Work(short numHours) {
      m_hoursWorked += numHours;
   }
   public short GetNumDependents() {
      return m_numDeps;
   }
   public void SetNumDependents(short numDeps) {
      m_numDeps=numDeps;
   }
   public String GetName() {
      return m_name;
   }
   public float GetSalary() {
```

```
        return m_salary;
    }
}
```

Notice that your Person class uses the implements keyword to specify that it will implement the Employee interface. Once you specify that the Person class will implement the Employee interface, you must provide an implementation for each of the methods in the Employee interface. The Java compiler will complain if you do not implement all of the methods. Now you can pass an instance of the Person class to any method that expects an Employee interface as shown in the following code:

```
class Payroll
{
    public void PayEmployee(Employee emp) {
        float grossPay;
        grossPay=emp.GetGrossPay();
    }
}
```

Notice that the code in the Payroll class refers only to the Employee interface. It has no knowledge of the Person class that implements the interface. Interfaces allow you to create a better separation between the behavior and implementation of our classes, they also provide us with a richer set of tools that you can use to model certain kinds of problems. For instance, if you are modeling the real world, you know that a person is more than just an employee. A person might also be a parent. To model this idea, you can define a Parent interface that has the following functions:

```
interface Parent {
    public void Scold(String childName);
    public void Play(int game);
    public void ReadBedtimeStory(String bookTitle);
}
```

You can now implement the Parent interface in your Person class as shown here:

LISTING 2.7 *A JAVA CLASS THAT IMPLEMENTS TWO INTERFACES*

```
class Person implements Employee, Parent
{
    private int m_id;
    private String m_name;
    private float m_salary;
    private short m_hoursWorked;
    private short m_numDeps;
    private Vector m_children;
```

```
public Person(int id,String nm,float sal,short
                 nDeps,Vector children) {
   m_id=id;
   m_name=nm;
   m_salary=sal;
   m_numDeps=nDeps;
   m_children=children;
}
public void Scold(String childName) {
   ...
}
public void Play(int game) {
   ...
}
public void ReadBedtimeStory(String bookTitle) {
   ...
}
public float GetGrossPay() {
   return GetHourlyRate()*GetHoursWorked();
}
public float GetHourlyRate() {
   return m_salary/40;
}
public int GetHoursWorked() {
   return m_hoursWorked;
}
public void BeginPayPeriod() {
   m_hoursWorked = 0;
}
public void Work(short numHours) {
   m_hoursWorked += numHours;
}
public short GetNumDependents() {
   return m_numDeps;
}
public void SetNumDependents(short numDeps) {
   m_numDeps=numDeps;
}
public String GetName() {
   return m_name;
}
public float GetSalary() {
   return m_salary;
}
}
```

A `Person` object can now be used anywhere that the `Employee` interface is required. It can also be used anywhere that the `Parent` interface is required. You're probably thinking that this all sounds great, but what does it have to do with C++? Well, C++ does not support an interface keyword, but you can create C++ classes that function exactly like Java interfaces. These types of classes are called pure abstract classes and they are defined as follows:

```
#include <string>
using namespace std
class Employee
{
public:
   virtual float GetGrossPay()=0;
   virtual float GetHourlyRate()=0;
   virtual int GetHoursWorked()=0;
   virtual void BeginPayPeriod()=0;
   virtual void Work(short numHours)=0;
   virtual short GetNumDependents()=0;
   virtual void SetNumDependents(short numDeps)=0;
   virtual string GetName()=0;
   virtual float GetSalary()=0;
};
```

The Employee abstract class above shows how a COM interface is represented in C++, but I'm jumping ahead of myself.

The use of "=0" in a method declaration for a class indicates that the method is being declared, but not implemented, in the class. A method defined this way is called a pure virtual method. To implement the method, you must declare a class that inherits from `Employee` and then implement the pure virtual methods of the `Employee` class there as shown here:

LISTING 2.8 *A C++ CLASS THAT IMPLEMENTS AN EMPLOYEE INTERFACE*

```
class Person : public Employee
{
public:
   Person(int id,const char *nm,float sal,short nDeps);
   virtual ~Person();
   virtual float GetGrossPay();
   float GetHourlyRate();
   int GetHoursWorked() { return m_hoursWorked; }
   void BeginPayPeriod() { m_hoursWorked = 0; }
```

```
    void Work(short numHours) { m_hoursWorked += numHours;
}
    short GetNumDependents() { return m_numDeps; }
    void SetNumDependents(short numDeps) {
m_numDeps=numDeps; }
    string GetName() { return m_name; }
    float GetSalary() { return m_salary;}

private:
    int m_id;
    string m_name;
    float m_salary;
    short m_hoursWorked;
    short m_numDeps;

}
```

In this example, you have defined a class called `Person` that inherits from `Employee`. You have defined the state of the `Person` class, its private member variables, and have provided an implementation of all the methods declared in the `Employee` class. Do you see that this code is exactly equivalent to the Java code? The only difference is you do not have a separate keyword in C++ to represent the concept of an interface. Any class like `Employee` that contains pure virtual methods is called an abstract class. You cannot create an instance of abstract classes. The following code statement causes a compiler error:

```
Employee *emp=new Employee
```

It should make sense why this is so. Imagine if you could create an instance of the `Employee` class. What do you think would happen if after creating a new employee, you attempted to call the `GetGrossPay` method? Nothing could happen, because you have not defined an implementation of this method in the `Employee` class. So if you can't create an instance of the `Employee` class, what can you do with it? You can create an instance of the `Person` class and assign an `Employee` pointer to point to it as follows:

```
Employee *emp=new Person(130,"John Smith",400.0,0);
```

The key to implementation hiding is to always use the `Employee` pointer to communicate with the `Person` object. If you do this, then only the code that contains the instantiation of the `Person` object has any knowledge of how the `Employee` interface is implemented. Now, if you can just hide the instantiation of the `Person` class, then you would have totally hidden the implementation of the `Employee` interface. COM class factories are used for exactly this purpose as you will see in the next chapter.

COM Classes, Objects, and Interfaces

In most programming languages, the concept of an interface plays second fiddle to that of a class. In fact, in both C++ and Java you could write entire applications, and many people do, without ever using an interface or an abstract class. COM supports classes, objects, and interfaces just like C++. You define COM classes in a language called Interface Description Language (IDL) that COM provides. You can then create instances of these classes—COM objects—using a COM API function called `CoCreateInstance`. You can think of `CoCreateInstance` as COM's equivalent of the C++ new operator. That's where the similarities end between COM classes and C++ classes because in the COM world, interfaces are elevated in importance above that of a class. When you call `CoCreateInstance`, you do not receive a COM object. What you actually receive is a pointer to one of the interfaces that the COM class supports. In fact, a COM class is really just *an* implementation of a set of COM interfaces. COM classes also have something called a class factory that is used to hide the creation of the programming language class that implements the COM class.

Why did Microsoft choose this approach? As I said earlier, one of the goals of COM was to let people ship software in binary form. With COM, you should be able to change the implementation of a software component and distribute it without requiring clients of the component to recompile. The only way to achieve this goal is to completely hide the implementation class. Clients should only talk to COM objects through interfaces. These interfaces should only contain method signatures and no implementation details; COM was designed to solve a different set of problems then most C++ programming languages. As I mentioned in the previous chapter, COM was designed to be a distributed technology that uses binary coupling between software components and its clients.

■ Summary

So now you have the low down on classes, objects, and interfaces in the context of COM. You've seen that COM does not support implementation inheritance because it can cause problems if you wish to ship software in binary form only. You've also seen that COM uses interfaces extensively to completely hide the implementation of a COM class. Now it is time to begin a more technical discussion of COM and build your first COM object. Before you can build your first COM object, you must understand GUIDs, IDL, marshalling, and type libraries. In the next chapter, I discuss these concepts. Read on.

THREE

Get on the Software Bus

I first learned about COM in 1993, when I read an article in Byte magazine that hailed what was then called OLE as the most important new technology of the year. I figured if it was that important, I should find out more about it. So I went to a bookstore and bought the first edition of a book called Inside OLE. I got about 200 pages into the book and gave up. For the first time in my life I had found a computer book I could not understand. Part of the responsibility was mine. I was still a C++ programming novice and a Windows Programming novice at the time (I cannot emphasize enough that if you want to learn COM, learn C++ and Windows programming first). But even if I had known C++ and Windows programming better, I still would have had problems with this book or any other COM book. There are a lot of new concepts that you have to grasp as you learn COM. Globally unique identifiers, interfaces, reference counting, marshaling, and interface description language are all important concepts in COM, but they will likely be foreign concepts to someone who has not already had experience with distributed computing. At that time most of my programming experience was on my home PC and doing numerical analysis on VAX, Cray, and IBM mainframe computers. I was ill-prepared to digest all of this information at once.

What would have helped me is to have a unifying concept to aid my understanding. In this book, I attempt to provide this unifying concept. The concept that I use is the notion that COM implements a software bus—a software equivalent of a hardware bus. Globally unique identifiers, interfaces, reference counting, marshaling, and interface description language are a part of COM because they solve specific problems related to implementing a software bus.

As shown in Figure 3.1, the idea behind this software bus is that you can plug software components into any machine on your network and those components are available for use (subject to security constraints) by any client application on any machine on your network. The software bus should work as transparently as possible and you should be able to use a COM object in the exact same way regardless of what language the component is implemented in and regardless of whether the component is implemented as a Dynamic Link Library or an executable. If you've done any low-level, network or cross-language programming, you know that this is a fairly tall order. Your software bus has to do a lot of work and like most things in life, there is no free lunch. In this chapter, I get down to the nitty-gritty and you will begin to see the additional things that you must do to make your software components work with the COM software bus.

At some point in this chapter, you are soon going to realize that writing COM classes is much more complicated than writing C++ classes. If you find yourself wondering why, refer back to the notion of COM as a software bus. Like the hardware bus on your computer, COM provides sockets that you can plug components into. However, when you build your software components for the COM software bus, you must—in addition to building the application-specific logic of your component—build a plug that fits into the socket the software bus provides. This is not unlike what a PC sound card manufacturer has to do if it's building a new sound card. It has to build the card in such a way that it plugs properly into the hardware bus of

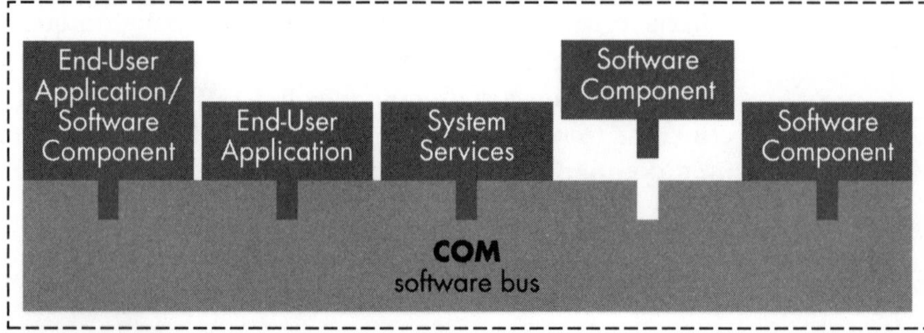

FIGURE 3.1 COM Software Bus.

a PC. Building this plug is extra work, but if you do the extra work, your component is endowed with the attributes that the software bus provides: location transparency and programming-language independence.

Software Bus Problems

I mentioned earlier that globally unique identifiers, interfaces, reference counting, marshaling, and interface description language are a part of COM because they solve specific problems related to implementing a software bus. What exactly are those problems? To be useful and robust, a software bus has to provide a solution for each of these problems:

- Naming
- Life-Cycle Management
- Programming-Language Independence
- Location Transparency
- Extensibility
- Versioning

I already talked about programming-language independence and location transparency when I defined COM. These two features represent the essence of COM. The other items on this list are there because they are either by-products of these two major goals (naming and life cycle management fall into this category) or can be considered less essential (but still important) goals of COM (extensibility and versioning). By considering each of these problems individually and examining the COM solution, I think you can make sense of COM's vaunted complexity and hopefully keep from giving up on this book after 200 pages.

Naming

It's simple to characterize the naming problem in a distributed environment. You only need two things:

- A way to assign unique names to your software components
- A way to discover the components that are currently installed on a host

To understand the need for unique names, consider what would happen if two companies created spell checking software components (with completely different interfaces) and both decided to assign their components the imaginative name of SpellChecker. People would write software that used these components and everything would work okay as long as only one of the company's spell checkers was installed on a particular host. What do you think would happen if both spell checkers were installed on the same machine? Client software that uses the spell checker and expects to get company A's component might instead receive company B's component with unpredictable results. This issue is bad enough when considered in the context of a single host. It's of far greater concern in a networked environment.

To understand the need to discover the software components that are currently installed on a host, refer back to Chapter 1 where you built a compound document by inserting an Excel chart into a Word document as shown in Figure 3.2.

When you select the `Object...` item from the `Insert` menu in Word, Word discovers all of the compound document objects that reside on your machine and presents them so you can choose one as shown in Figure 3.3.

As you will soon learn, the list of objects shown in Figure 3.3 is coming from an area in the Windows registry that is set aside for COM.

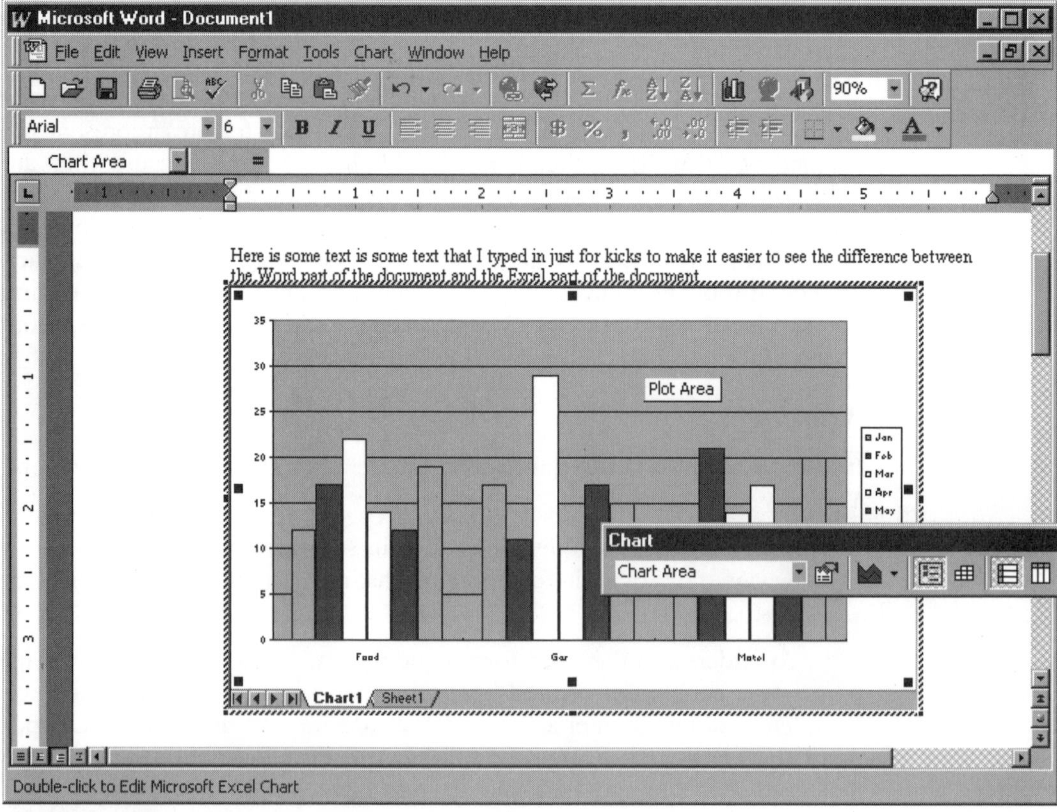

FIGURE 3.2 A Compound Document.

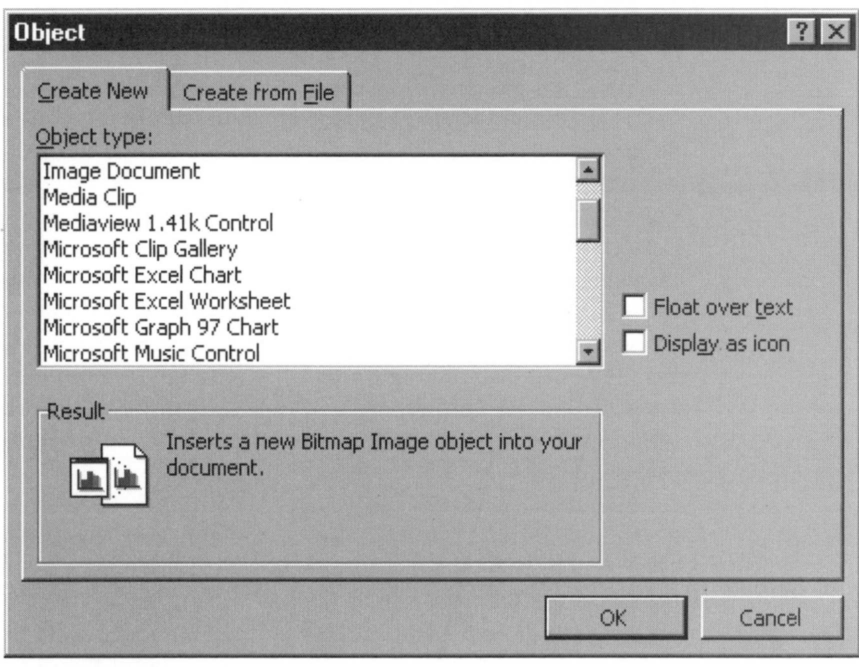

FIGURE 3.3 MS Word Discovers the Compound Document Objects Installed on Your Machine.

GUIDS: THE COM SOLUTION

So, what's the solution to the naming problem? What you really need is a way to assign a name to a component that you can guarantee to be unique. The unique name that is used for COM components is a Globally Unique Identifier or GUID.

Some people pronounce GUID so that it rhymes with squid, some people pronounce it so that it rhymes with druid. Which one is right? It doesn't matter. I have seen authoritative resources that argue for each pronunciation. After spending more than half an hour arguing over the correct pronunciation of GUID with a coworker, I finally decided it is a waste of time to argue over something so trivial. Pick a pronunciation and stick with it, or adopt the pronunciation the majority of your coworkers are using.

A GUID is a 16-byte (128-bit) integer. GUIDs are used to identify COM classes in which case they are called class IDs or CLSIDs. GUIDs are also used to identify COM interfaces in which case they are called interface IDs or IIDs. The CLSIDs for two well-known COM classes are shown below as they appear in the registry:

```
Microsoft Excel Worksheet:      00020820-0000-0000-C000-000000000046
Microsoft Word Document:        00020906-0000-0000-C000-000000000046
```

You can understand GUIDs by thinking about social security numbers. Social security numbers are unique identifiers for people. You need them because the name given to you by your parents is not guaranteed to be unique. In fact, the last time I went to vote, I discovered there is an Alan C. Gordon who lives right around the corner from me. You may not be able to distinguish between the other Alan Gordon and me by our names, but you can tell us apart using our social security numbers. Social security numbers are guaranteed to be unique because they are given out by a central agency that gives out each number only once. GUIDs are not given out by a central agency, but they are created using an algorithm that creates a particular GUID only once. So GUID's are like social security numbers for COM objects.

To understand why GUIDS are guaranteed to be unique consider first that a GUID is 128 bits. This many bits allows an essentially infinite number of possible combinations. To put it in perspective, 32 bits allows four billion possible combinations. That means that 128 bits allow 4 billion × 4 billion × 4 billion × 4 billion possible combinations. That's enough unique GUIDs so that every man, woman, and child on planet Earth (all six billion of them) could create a new GUID every second for 100 years and would still have used only $1/(10^{19})$ of the possible GUIDs. Having an essentially infinite number of possible numbers is a start, but actually generating unique sequences is another. You still need a GUID creation algorithm that will create a given number sequence only once.

THE GUID CREATION ALGORITHM

To ensure uniqueness, you must guarantee uniqueness in both time and space. In other words, you must guarantee that two GUIDs created at the same time in different places will be different and that two GUIDs created at different times in the same place will also be different. The GUID creation algorithm uses the following information when creating a GUID:

- The current date and time
- A machine identifier from a network card
- A forcibly-incremented counter to deal with high-frequency allocations

Making the GUID creation algorithm a function of the date and time provides uniqueness in time. Using a forcibly incremented counter ensures that uniqueness is maintained even if multiple GUIDs are created within an infinitesimally small unit of time. The unique identifier in your network provides uniqueness in space. If the machine on which a GUID is created does not have a network card, then the GUID creation algorithm synthesizes a unique identifier for the machine using hardware state information. The statistically insignificant probability that the same GUID may be created more than once does rise slightly when GUIDs are created on a machine that does not have a network card.

CREATING GUIDS

You can use the GUID creation algorithm by calling the `CoCreateGuid` function in the Windows API. Or you can use the GUIDGEN utility that lives in the `common\tools\directory` beneath your Visual Studio root directory. Figure 3.4 shows what the GUIDGEN utility looks like when you run it. It can generate GUIDs in four different formats.

Once the GUID is created, you can copy it to the clipboard using the copy button. Try it out. Choose one of the formats, click the `Copy` button, then open `Notepad` and select `Paste` from the `Edit` menu. Try repeating this a few times to see how the generated GUID changes each time. Try all of the formats so you can see what each of them looks like. You may need to create GUIDs manually like this on occasion, but Visual C++ generates most of your GUIDs for you automatically.

If you must create a GUID manually, never create a GUID by just typing in a sequence of letters and digits. GUIDs created in this manner are not guaranteed to be unique. Always use COM's GUID creation algorithm, either by using GUIDGEN or the `CoCreateGuid` function.

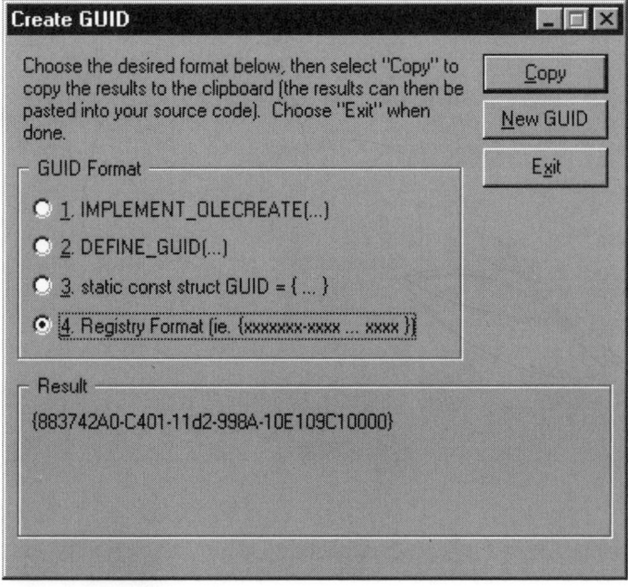

FIGURE 3.4 GUIDGEN.

WHERE GUIDS LIVE

GUIDs reside in the COM area within the registry, but COM probably should have its own repository that is separate from the system configuration information in the registry.

COM+ was originally supposed to include its own repository that was maintained outside of the registry. The version of COM+ that will be delivered with Windows 2000 will still use the registry, but some COM-related information will reside in its own repository.

For now, all of the COM-related information resides beneath the `HKEY_CLASSES_ROOT` key in the registry. To see this information in the registry, perform the following steps:

1. Click the `Start` button on the task bar.
2. Select `Run` from the `Start` menu.
3. Enter `regedit` on the `Run` window.
4. Click the `OK` button.

The registry editor should appear as shown in Figure 3.5. The first folder shown is `HKEY_CLASSES_ROOT`. If you click the "+" symbol next to the `HKEY_CLASSES_ROOT` folder and scroll down a little bit, you should see a key called CLSID. If you open this folder, you will see all the CLSIDs currently registered on your system. Let's take a look at a CLSID that most of you probably

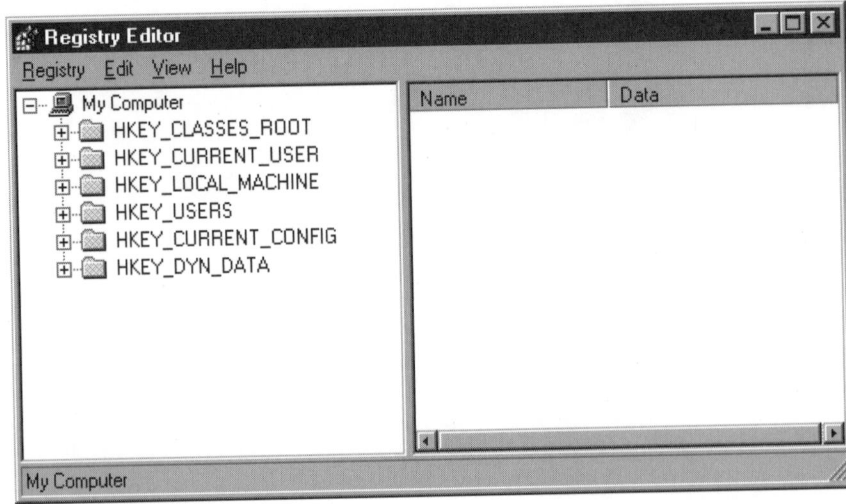

FIGURE 3.5 The Registry Editor.

have on your computer: the CLSID for Microsoft Word. To view this information, navigate to `HKEY_CLASSES_ROOT\CLSID\00020906-0000-0000-C000-000000000046`. You should see the list of keys shown in Figure 3.6.

The most important subkey within the Microsoft Word Document key is the one called `LocalServer32`. This key contains the path to the server that implements the `Microsoft Word Document` class. If you click on this entry in the left pane of the registry editor and then double-click on the default value on the right pane in the registry editor, you should see the path to Microsoft Word on your computer. When you want to use the `Microsoft Word Document` object, you can request it using the CLSID. The registry contains all the information required to start up the server for the `Microsoft Word Document` object.

There are other important subkeys beneath the CLSID for the `Microsoft Word Document` class. The insertable key is important because the presence of this key indicates that the COM class can be used as a compound document server. When you clicked the `Object...` item

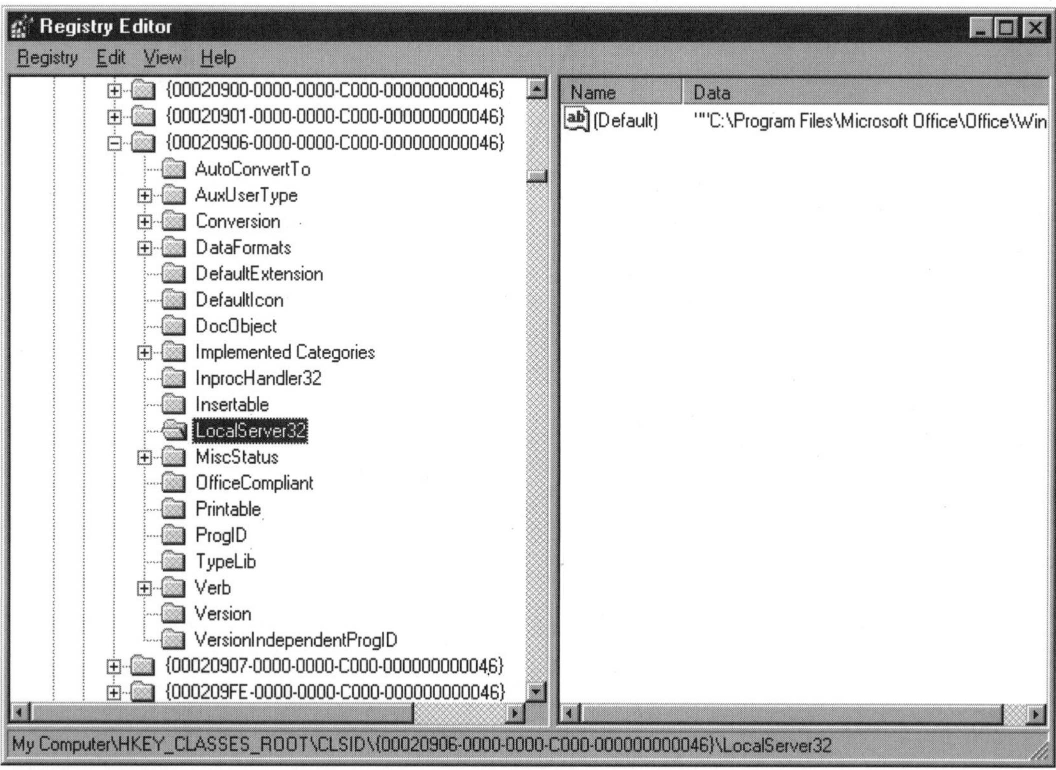

FIGURE 3.6 The CLSID Key for the Microsoft Word Document.

from the Insert menu of a compound document client application like Word, the list that is displayed contains the human-readable identifier (I explain what this is soon) for all COM classes that have the insertable subkey. Two other important subkeys are the ProgID and VersionIndependentProgID keys. It would be tedious to use COM objects if you had to remember the CLSID of a COM class before you could use it. Imagine what a pain it would be if you had to remember that the CLSID for the Microsoft Word Document class was 00020906-0000-0000-C000-000000000046 before you could create an instance of the class. The problem here is not unlike trying to use the Internet without a domain name server. Imagine having to remember the IP address for Microsoft's Web site every time you wanted to surf to it. It's so much easier to remember www.microsoft.com.

Programmer's Identifiers or ProgIDs provide an easy-to-remember name for a COM class. Each COM class can (they are not required) have a ProgID and a Version-Independent ProgID associated with it. If you click the ProgID key in the left pane of the registry editor, you will see the ProgID for the Microsoft Word Document class in the right pane. The ProgID for Microsoft Word is word.document.8. If you click on VersionIndependentProgID in the left pane of the registry, you will see that the Version-Independent ProgID for Microsoft Word is Word.Document. The naming convention is servername.objectname.version. In most cases, when you are using a COM class you can simply use this name and not concern yourself with the CLSID. The ProgID is not guaranteed to be unique like a CLSID. This is okay because if you end up with two COM classes on your machine that happen to have the same ProgID, you can still identify the one you want using its CLSID. CLSIDs are required and are guaranteed to be unique.

Another name associated with each COM class is the human-readable identifier. You can see this identifier by clicking on HKEY_CLASSES_ROOT\CLSID\00020906-0000-0000-C000-000000000046 in the left pane of the registry editor. In the right pane you should see the string "Microsoft Word Document." This is the same string that you see in the dialog that appears when you select Object... from the Insert menu of Microsoft Word. Try it out. Select Object... from the Insert menu of Microsoft Word and notice that one of the choices is "Microsoft Word Document." The human-readable name is the name you should display to an end-user when you present them with a list of objects.

Now that we understand how COM uniquely identifies COM classes, it's time to explore the next topic in our list of software bus problems: lifecycle management. In the process, you learn about the IUnknown interface.

Life Cycle Management

To understand the life-cycle management problem, it's important to understand one key point: to use a COM object, the server for that COM object must be loaded into memory. If the COM object is implemented in an in-process server, then the DLL for the server must be loaded into the process of its client. If the COM object is implemented in an out-of-process server, then the executable for the server must be started and a communication link between the client and the server must be established.

If you load your COM object's server into memory and instantiate COM objects, then you also need some means to destroy these COM objects when they are no longer needed and thereby free the resources (memory, file handles, and so on) used by the COM object. You also need some means to unload a COM object's server when there are no objects that are implemented within the server being used. Without some way to unload our COM servers, the servers would consume all of their host's memory until the machine crashed.

The life-cycle management problem in a nutshell is really a series of problems: How do you instantiate a COM object in a location and implementation independent way? How do you start/load a COM server when its services are required? And how do you (1) destroy a COM object when it is no longer needed, (2) sense that a COM object's server is no longer needed, and (3) shut down the server once it is determined that the server is no longer needed?

INSTANTIATING A COM OBJECT

At the lowest level, you instantiate a COM object using the COM API function `CoCreateInstanceEx`. There are other functions you can call to create a COM object, but `CoCreateInstanceEx` is the quintessential COM object creation function. You can think of it as COM's equivalent of the C++ new function. There is a simplified version of this function called `CoCreateInstance`, but it just delegates to `CoCreateInstanceEx` with defaults for some of the parameters. The `CoCreateInstanceEx` is defined as follows:

```
HRESULT CoCreateInstanceEx( REFCLSID  rclsid,IUnknown *  punkOuter,
                            DWORD * dwClsCtx,COSERVERINFO* pServerInfo,
ULONG  cmq,MULTI_QI  rgmqResults   );
```

The first parameter, `rclsid`, lets you specify the CLSID of the COM class that you wish to use. The second parameter lets you specify that the object being created is part of an aggregate (I explain what this is later). The third parameter has one of the following values: `CLSCTX_INPROC_SERVER`, `CLSC-TX_INPROC_HANDLER`, `CLSCTX_LOCAL_SERVER`, `CLSCTX_REMOTE_SERVER`, `CLSCTX_SERVER`, or `CLSCTX_ALL`. It lets you restrict the form of the implementation. For instance, if you specify CLSCTX_INPROC_SERVER, then you are specifying that you only want a DLL-based implementation. In most cases, you will want to specify CLSCTX_ALL, which performs a search to determine the implementation to use. It checks the registry first for a DLL-based implementation. If that's not found, it looks for an executable-based implementation on the local machine, and if that's not found, it checks the local registry to see if the object is registered to run remotely. The fourth parameter lets you specify a remote server on which to instantiate the COM object. You can specify an IP address, a Domain Name System (DNS) name like www2.alangordon.com, or a Universal Naming Convention (UNC) name like \\machinename. If this parameter is NULL, then the registry is used to determine where to instantiate the COM object. The last two parameters lets you specify an array of interface GUIDs (IIDs) that you would like to receive from the server. This lets you receive several interfaces from the server with one round trip over the network.

The key point for you to understand here is that you can setup your call to CoCreateInstanceEx in such a way (using CLSCTX_ALL for instance) that it works regardless of whether the server is a DLL or an executable or whether it resides locally or remotely. To make this work, there must be some piece of software that figures out what type of server is being used, where the server is located, and then either starts or loads the server.

STARTING/LOADING THE SERVER

The piece of software that finds the server for a COM object and starts/loads it is called the Service Control Manager. The Service Control Manager is affectionately known to COM programmers as the SCUM. The SCUM is a part of the Windows operating system. If you go to your Windows system directory (\winnt\system32 on most Windows 2000 machines and \windows\system on most Windows 95/98 machines), you can see the SCUM. It is an executable called rpcss. On Windows NT it runs as a service, on Windows 95/98 it runs as a user process.

Most other distributed object systems (CORBA for instance) call their equivalent of the Service Control Manager an Object Request Broker or ORB.

When you instantiate a COM object by specifying its CLSID, the SCUM consults the registry and finds the key associated with the CLSID. If the COM object is implemented within an executable, there's a LocalServer32 subkey beneath the CLSID key. The value for that key contains the path to the server executable. The SCUM starts the executable passing in a `/embedding` or `/automation` parameter to the server so it knows it was started on behalf of a COM client instead of an end-user. If the COM object is implemented in a DLL, there's a `InprocServer32` subkey beneath the CLSID key. The value for that key contains the path to the server DLL. The SCUM loads the DLL into the client process.

The client never has to concern itself with how the COM class is implemented. The SCUM figures out what to do based on the registry entries for the server. From the client side, the process of instantiating a COM object is exactly the same whether the server is a DLL or an executable.

SHUTTING DOWN/UNLOADING THE SERVER

Let's explore how a COM server gets unloaded. There are three elements to this problem: (1) how do you destroy/deallocate COM objects when they are no longer needed? (2) how do you determine that a COM object's server is no longer needed? (3) how do you shut down the server once you determine that it is no longer needed? The solution to all of these problems is the `IUnknown` interface.

COM object clients must participate in the management of the lifecycle of the COM objects they are using. The COM objects themselves control the lifecycle of their server. Unless the user specifies otherwise (and you will see later on how the user may specify otherwise), a COM server should be shut down when there are no COM objects that are implemented within that server being used. The logic for doing this is not difficult to implement (you will see how to do it in the next chapter).

The client helps control the lifetime of a COM object using a programming idiom called reference counting. Reference counting is done through the `IUnknown` interface. You never have to worry about a COM object not supporting the `IUnknown` interface. Support for the `IUnknown` is part of the definition of a COM object. You can think of the `IUnknown` interface as part of the plug you have to build for your software components so they can plug into the software bus. So what is the `IUnknown` interface?

IUnknown • The actual definition of IUnknown is shown here:

```
struct IUnknown
{
    virtual HRESULT QueryInterface(IID& iid,void **ppv)=0;
    virtual ULONG AddRef(void)=0;
    virtual ULONG Release(void)=0;
};
```

I extracted this definition from the file `Unknwn.h` that you can find in the include directory of your Visual C++ installation. The `AddRef` and `Release` are the key methods for this discussion; they implement reference counting.

The `QueryInterface` method in `IUnknown` lets you ask a COM object if it supports a particular interface. If the COM object implements the requested interface, it returns a valid interface pointer.

REFERENCE COUNTING • Reference counting is a programming idiom that pre-dates COM. It can be used to manage the lifetime of any dynamically allocated resource such as a file handle, memory, or a COM object. Consider the following code in Listing 3.1.

LISTING 3.1 *MULTIPLE REFERENCES TO A CHARACTER BUFFER*

```
#include <iostream.h>
#include <string.h>
int main(int argc, char* argv[])
{
   char *buf1, *buf2, *buf3;
   buf1=new char[20];
   strncpy(buf1,"reference counting",20);
   buf2=buf1;
   buf3=buf1;
// do something here...

   cout << buf1 << endl;
   cout.flush();
   delete[] buf1;                // we no longer need buf1

   cout << buf2 << endl;
   cout.flush();
   delete[] buf2;                // we no longer need buf2

   cout << buf3 << endl;
   cout.flush();
   delete[] buf3;                // we no longer need buf3
   return 0;
}
```

If you compiled and ran this code, you'd get garbage in the console after the line that writes `buf2` to the output stream:

```
cout << buf2 << endl;
```

and the following line causes a GP fault:

```
delete[] buf2;
```

What happened? Well, after you assign the `buf2` and `buf3` pointers to `buf1`, you have the situation shown in Figure 3.7.

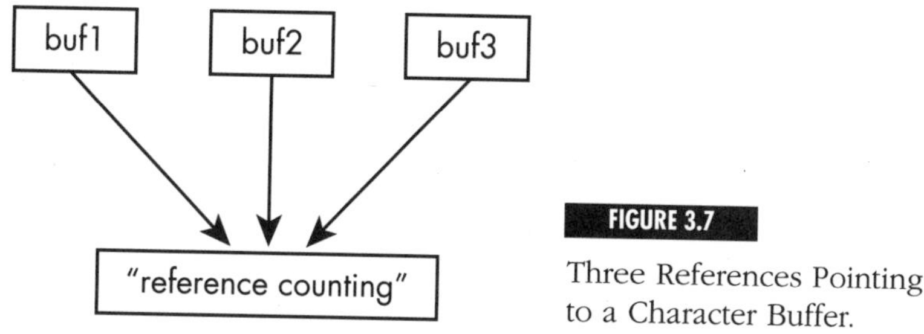

FIGURE 3.7

Three References Pointing to a Character Buffer.

You have three references all pointing to the same character buffer. The problem is that it is not safe to delete the character buffer until you are sure it's no longer being accessed through any of those references. In other words, you shouldn't delete the character buffer until there are zero references still pointing to it. So what you really need is a way to track the number of references that are pointing to the character buffer. You can do this using reference counting. Consider the code in Listing 3.2.

LISTING 3.2 *AN EXAMPLE OF REFERENCE COUNTING*

```
#include <iostream.h>
#include <string.h>
struct charbuffer
{
  charbuffer()
  {
    mbuf=new char[20];
    mrefCount=1;
  }
  ~charbuffer()
  {
    delete[] mbuf;
  }
  char *mbuf;
  int mrefCount;
};
int main(int argc, char* argv[])
{
  charbuffer *buf1, *buf2, *buf3;
  buf1=new charbuffer;
  strncpy(buf1->mbuf,"reference counting",20);
  buf2=buf1;
  buf2->mrefCount++;
  buf3=buf1;
  buf3->mrefCount++;
// do something here...

  cout << buf1->mbuf << endl;
```

```
29.    if (--buf1->mrefCount==0) // you no longer need buf1
30.      delete buf1;
31.
32.    cout << buf2->mbuf << endl;
33.    if (--buf2->mrefCount==0) // you no longer need buf2
34.      delete buf2;
35.
36.    cout << buf3->mbuf << endl;
37.    if (--buf3->mrefCount==0) // you no longer need buf3
38.      delete buf3;
39.    return 0;
40. }
```

In this new version of the code, you have bundled the character buffer and an integer reference count into a structure. The constructor for the structure allocates the buffer and sets the reference count to 1 as shown in lines 5–9. Notice also that each time you assign a new reference to the character buffer, you increment the reference count. The reference count keeps track of the number of references that are pointing to the character buffer. So if you assign a pointer to the character buffer, more than one reference will be pointing to the buffer and you have to increment the reference count as shown on lines 22 and 23. When you no longer need to use a particular reference, you decrement the reference count. This indicates that you have one less reference pointing to the character buffer. If the reference count is zero after you decrement it, that means there are no references pointing to the character buffer and you are free to delete it as shown on lines 32–34.

By now you're probably wondering what all of this has to do with COM. Well, COM objects use reference counting to control their life cycle in a manner similar to the character buffer. The reference count is maintained internally within the COM object. The `AddRef` and `Release` methods in the `IUnknown` interface are used respectively to increment and decrement the reference count.

You never have to worry about a COM object not implementing the `IUnknown` interface. Every COM object must implement the `IUnknown` interface and every interface that you define must derive from `IUnknown` either directly or indirectly. Because every interface must derive from `IUnknown`, you can call the `AddRef` and `Release` methods on any COM interface. You increment the reference count using the `AddRef` method in `IUnknown`. When you are done using a COM interface pointer, you indicate that you are no longer using the pointer by calling the `Release` method through the pointer. The COM object destroys itself when it's reference count is equal to zero. Moreover, the server for the COM object should be implemented so that it shuts itself down when all the COM objects that reside in the server have been destroyed. In the next chapter, you can implement your own COM object from scratch and see how the `AddRef` and `Release` are implemented and how to implement your server so that it shuts itself down properly.

Someday the Windows operating system will contain an implementation of the `IUnknown` interface and you won't have to worry about life cycle management at all. Managing the life cycle of COM objects and their servers will be a system-level detail that application developers won't have to concern themselves with. This is the universal runtime that was supposed to be implemented in COM+. Unfortunately, the universal runtime will have to wait for a later release of Windows 2000 or COM+.

Now that you understand how the COM software bus manages the life cycle of our COM objects, you are ready to move on to our next software bus issue: programming language independence.

Programming Language Independence

To implement a programming language-independent software bus, you need two things:

- A way to describe our software components in a programming language independent way.
- A binary standard that specifies how to call our software components at runtime.

DESCRIBING COMPONENTS IN A LANGUAGE-INDEPENDENT WAY

Think about C++ header files for a moment. If you're a Visual C++ programmer, you are familiar with header files. These files have the extension ".h" and they usually contain type information. You put your class definitions (the name of the class, the list of methods in the class, and the parameter list and return type for each method in the class) in a header file. To utilize a header file, you use the `#include` keyword to include the "`.h`" file into your source code. The compiler uses the information in the header file to perform type and syntax checking for you. For instance, if you call a method on an object variable that is not a member of the class to which the object belongs, the compiler complains. Also, if you call a method that is a member of the class, but you call it with the wrong number or type of parameters, the compiler also complains. The compiler uses the information in the header file to generate the correct binary code to call the methods in the object.

Header files do a lot of work for you and they make software development with C++ much easier. Header files, to a degree, also serve as documentation. In fact, when you are dealing with classes developed in-house, a header file may be the only documentation you have.

Even if you are not using C++, it is desirable to have a file that contains all of the information that is in a C++ header file. You can use this programming language independent equivalent of a C++ header file to do compile-time syntax and type checking and other things that can only be done with apriori knowledge of the classes and interfaces in a software component. COM's programming language-independent header file is called a type library. A type library is a binary file that contains the same sort of type information that you would find in a C++ header file. It contains the names of the classes and interfaces that are implemented within your server and the number and type of the parameters for each method in your server's interfaces. It also contains the GUIDs for each class and interface.

To create a type library, you must first describe the interfaces and classes in your COM server using a language called Interface Description Language (IDL). You then take this IDL file and compile it using a tool called MIDL.

MIDL is bundled with Visual C++. You can find it in the bin directory of your Visual C++ installation.

MIDL generates the type library file. You typically create one type library file for each server DLL or executable.

IDL

IDL is a declarative language (it contains no control structures such as "for" and "while" loops or "if" statements). It is used to describe COM classes and interfaces in a programming language-independent way. Learning IDL is not a significant stretch if you already know C++. The main differences between C++ and IDL are the latter's use of attributes. Each element that you define in IDL may have one or more attributes associated with it.

I mentioned that COM is similar to CORBA and if you know a little about CORBA, or if you follow my advice and learn about it, you will discover that CORBA also has a language called IDL. The only thing the two languages share is their name. COM IDL and CORBA IDL serve the same purpose, but they are completely different syntactically.

Listing 3.3 shows some example IDL.

LISTING 3.3 *EXAMPLE IDL*

```
// spellchecker.idl
import "unknwn.idl";
[
  object,
  uuid(02D819CD-AFF9-11D2-998A-78DC09C10000),
  helpstring("ISpellChecker Interface")
]
interface ISpellChecker : IUnknown
{
  [helpstring("method CheckSpelling")] HRESULT
  CheckSpelling([in,string] char *word,[out,retval] BOOL *isCorrect);
  [helpstring("method UseCustomDictionary")] HRESULT
  UseCustomDictionary([in,string] char *filename);
}

[
  object,
  uuid(DA881F40-E576-11d0-818D-444553540000),
  helpstring("IGrammarChecker Interface")
]
interface IGrammarChecker : IUnknown
{
  [helpstring("method CheckGrammar")] HRESULT
  CheckGrammar([in,string] char *sentence,[out,retval] BOOL
  *isCorrect);
}

[ uuid(99A9E580-E4E0-11d0-818D-444553540000) ]
library SpellcheckerLib
{
  [
    uuid(57B7A8A0-E4D7-11d0-818D-444553540000),
    version(1.0),
    helpstring("spellgrammar component 1.0 Type Library")
  ]
  coclass CSpellChecker
  {
    [default] interface ISpellChecker;
    interface IGrammarChecker;
  }
};
```

Hopefully, you can see the similarities to C++. As the first line shows, IDL uses C++ style comments. Just like a C++ header file, you can include one IDL file within another; you use the `import` keyword to do this. The `import` keyword in IDL is similar to the C++ `#include` as shown on line 2. This particular import statement imports the definition of the `IUnknown` interface. Lines 3–12 contain the definition of a COM interface called `ISpellChecker`. Lines 3–7 contain the attributes for the interface. The attributes for an interface, or any other IDL element, are always placed right before the element that they are associated with and they are enclosed within square brackets. The first attribute, object, identifies the interface as a COM interface instead of an RPC interface.

COM is built on Remote Procedure Calls (RPC). RPC uses a version of IDL that does not support objects. Microsoft enhanced RPC IDL to include support for objects. The object keyword in Microsoft's IDL is used to identify the interface as a COM object interface and not a standard RPC interface.

The next attribute contains the GUID for the interface.

```
uuid(02D819CD-AFF9-11D2-998A-78DC09C10000)
```

I used GUIDGEN and chose the registry format to create this GUID. All interface definitions must contain the `uuid` attribute. The last attribute, `helpstring`, contains a string that may be displayed when someone requests help information about the interface. The `helpstring` attribute may be associated with interface methods also.

```
helpstring("ISpellChecker Interface"),
```

Lines 8–12 in the IDL file contain the actual definition of the interface. The interface definition begins with the use of the `interface` keyword. In IDL, the `interface` keyword is used similar to the class keyword in C++. Next comes the name of the interface (`ISpellChecker`) followed by a colon and then the name of the interface that `ISpellChecker` inherits from—`IUnknown`. With IDL, you can only inherit from one interface. Multiple interface inheritance is not allowed. When you inherit from an interface, you are declaring that the current interface is composed of all the methods declared directly within the interface plus all the methods in the base interface. In this example, the `ISpellChecker` interface is composed of the `CheckSpelling` and `UseCustomDictionary` methods, plus the methods in the `IUnknown` interface: `AddRef`, `Release`, and `QueryInterface`. If you are implementing the `ISpellChecker` interface, you must implement all five of these methods. Following the declaration of the interface and its base interface, are the definitions of each method in the interface. Methods also may have attributes associated with them. In this case, the only attribute used is the aforementioned `helpstring` attribute. Attributes can also be associated with each parameter of a method. The first parameter of the `CheckSpelling` method has two attributes:

in and string. The in attribute specifies that this parameter is used as an input to the method. Other possible values for this attribute are out or in,out. Development environments can use this information to help map COM interface methods into native programming language calls. For instance, in C++, parameters that are inputs are usually passed by value, as shown below:

```
Void Func1(float inputArg)
```

Parameters that are outputs, however, must be passed by reference.

```
Void Func1(float * outputArg)
```

These per-method attributes are also used to generate a more efficient marshaling DLL (I define what this is later).

The string attribute is used with parameters that are character pointers. A pointer can point to a single value of a particular type, or to an array of that type. The string or size_is attributes can be used to specify the number of elements in the array if the pointer points to an array. If the string attribute is used, you are declaring that the character array is a null terminated string so the number of characters that are to be passed through the interface is determined at runtime. If you use the size_is attribute, you can specify the number of elements in the array explicitly. For instance, if you know that the CheckSpelling method in the ISpellChecker interface will always be used with strings that are 50 characters or less, you could have declared the CheckSpelling method as follows:

```
[helpstring("method CheckSpelling")] HRESULT
CheckSpelling([in,size_is(50)] char *word,[out,retval] BOOL *isCorrect);
```

The second parameter to the CheckSpelling method is declared using the out and retval attributes. Using out specifies that the second parameter is an output. The retval keyword indicates that this parameter is not just any output, it is to be interpreted as the application-specific return value for the function. You must do this because the literal return value of the CheckSpelling method is an HRESULT. You can have several output parameters (parameters that use the out attribute), but you can only have one return value. Return values and output parameters must be passed by reference. Note that the second parameter to the CheckSpelling method is a pointer to a BOOL.

HRESULTS

All member methods of COM interfaces must have a literal return value that is an HRESULT.

For now, think of an HRESULT as a handle to a result structure. I discuss HRESULTs in more detail in the next chapter when I implement the first COM object. There you will see how to create, use, and interpret HRESULTs.

The HRESULT is used to return error information. You can create HRESULTs and return them explicitly in the implementation of a method, but an HRESULT may also be created and returned by the COM runtime. For instance, if you are using a COM object that is running on a remote machine on your network and someone unplugs your network connection, the next time you call a method on that COM object the COM runtime will—without any help from you—return an error code through the method's HRESULT return value.

In some situations, you need to write IDL manually. In most situations though, you use Visual C++ to create your COM objects. You can simply define your methods using a point-and-click user interface and Visual C++ generates the IDL for you.

TYPE LIBRARIES

After you create a description of your classes and interfaces in IDL, you can use a tool called MIDL to compile the IDL into a type library. If you save the IDL shown above into a file called `spellcheck.idl`, then run the following command:

```
midl spellcheck.idl
```

you will generate the files shown in Table 3.1.

TABLE 3.1 Files Generated by MIDL

Filename	Contents
Spellcheck.tlb	The type library
Spellcheck.h	C and C++ definitions of the ISpellchecker and IGrammarChecker interfaces
Spellcheck_i.c	C/C++ GUID Declarations
Spellcheck_p.c	Marshaling support code
Dlldata.c	Marshaling support code

If you have trouble running MIDL, you may need to run the `VCVARS32.BAT` file in the bin directory of your Visual C++ installation.

Right now you are only concerned with the type library file; I'll talk about the other files later. A type library is a binary file that contains the same information as the IDL file. The COM runtime contains a function called `LoadTypeLib` that you can use to import and parse a type library file. The `LoadTypeLib` function returns an interface called `ITypeLib` that you can use to retrieve type information from the file. This type information includes the names and GUIDs of all the interfaces in the type library, the types of the parameters for each method in those interfaces, the name and GUID of each class, and the list of interfaces that are implemented by each class. Here are three examples of how type libraries are used:

- Some development environments, like Visual Basic, use type libraries to do syntax and type-checking.
- Visual C++ and Java (oops! Visual J++) uses type libraries to generate wrapper classes that make it easy to use COM components.
- The COM runtime uses type-libraries to make cross-process function calls more efficient (see the description of marshaling in the Location Transparency section below).

Every COM server executable or DLL should have a type library associated with it. The type library can either be in a separate file (with the extension .tlb or .olb), or it can actually be embedded into the resource area of the servers exe or DLL. However, it is not a strict requirement that every COM server have a type library. Some development environments don't need them. You can use a COM server from Visual C++ without having a type library for the server. It is, however, much easier to use the COM server if you have the type library because Visual C++ can generate a wrapper class for you that hides most of the low level details required to use the COM server. To see an illustration of this last point, compare Chapter 4 and Chapter 5. In Chapter 4, a COM server is used without using its type library. In Chapter 5, the type library is used to simplify the process of using the server. With Visual Basic, you can also use a COM server without having its type library, but your function calls will be slower and syntax and type-checking will be performed at runtime instead of compile time.

Let's take a look at a couple of type library files. If you have Visual Studio 6.0 installed, perform the following steps to use the OLE/COM Object Viewer to view a type library file:

1. Click the `Start` menu.
2. Select `Programs\Microsoft Visual Studio 6.0\Microsoft Visual Studio 6.0\Tools\OLE View`.

The OLE/COM Object Viewer should appear as shown in Figure 3.8.

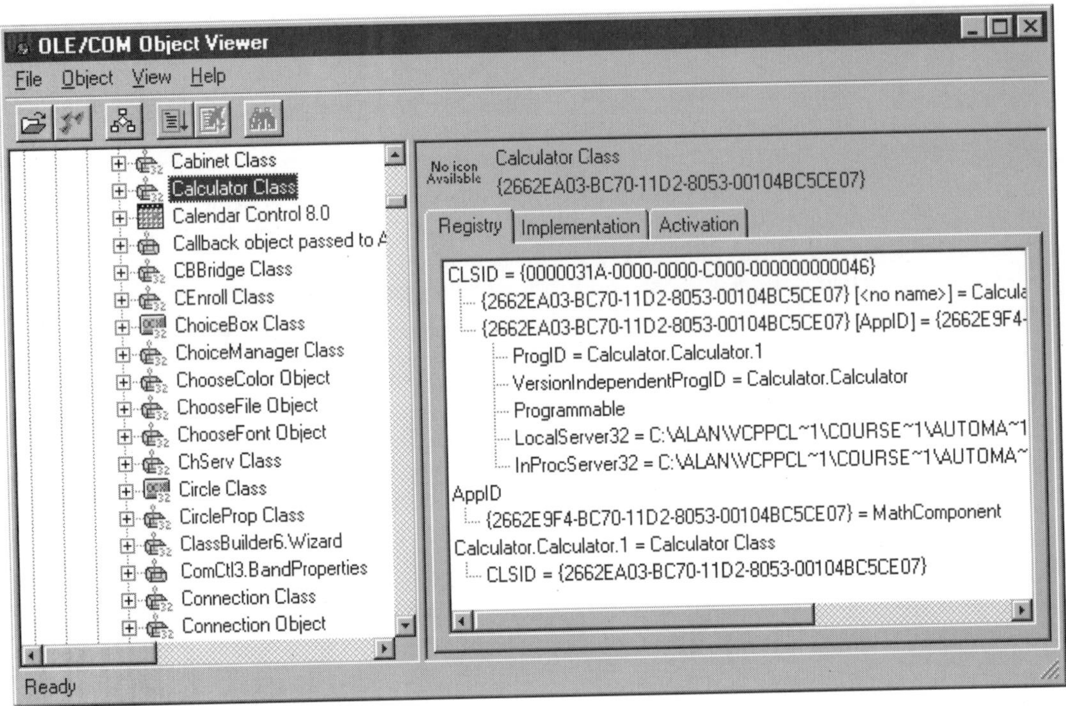

FIGURE 3.8 The OLE/COM Object Viewer.

Let's look first at the type library for Microsoft Excel. In addition to being an excellent office-productivity application, Microsoft Excel is also a first-class COM component and like all good components it has a type library. To view Excel's type library, perform the following steps:

1. Select `View Type Library` from the `File` menu in the OLE/COM Object Viewer. A file open dialog should appear.
2. In the file open dialog navigate to the Excel type library file. The filename for the Excel 97 type library is `excel8.olb`. On most machines, you should find it in the Office directory beneath your Microsoft Office installation. On my machine, the full path is: `C:\Program Files\Microsoft Office\Office\Excel8.olb`.
3. Double-click the file to open it. This is a rather large type library, so it may take a few seconds to load it. You should see the window shown in Figure 3.9.

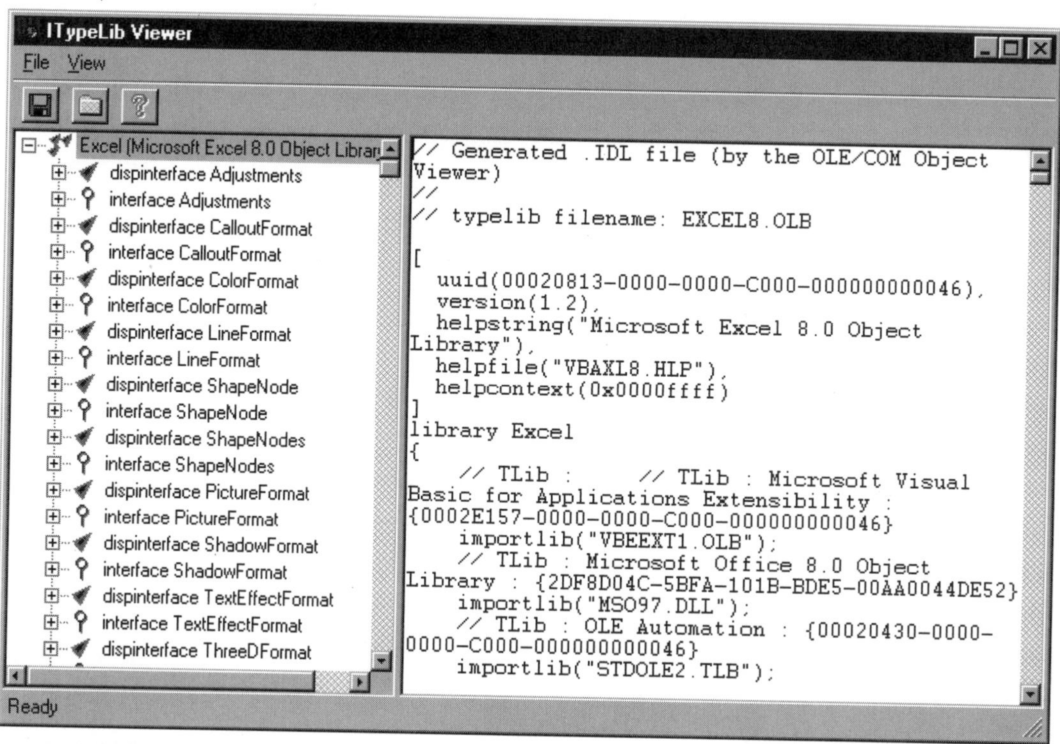

FIGURE 3.9 The Microsoft Excel Type Library Displayed in the OLE/COM Object Viewer.

In the left pane, you can see a list of the interfaces in the type library. If you scroll down to the bottom of the left pane, you can see the classes defined in the type library. If you click on a class or interface in the left pane, you can see the IDL definition of the class or interface in the right pane. Look around a little and then close the type library viewer by selecting `Close` from the `File` menu. Next, let's look at a type library that is embedded in an ActiveX control. In the main window of the OLE/COM Object Viewer, perform the following steps:

1. Select `View Type Library` from the `File` menu in OLEVIEW. A file open dialog should appear.
2. In the file open dialog navigate to the Common Dialog control. The filename for the Common Dialog control is `comdlg32.ocx`. On most machines you should find it in the Windows system directory. On my machine, the full path is: `C:\Windows\System\comdlg32.ocx`.
3. Double-click the file to open it.

This is an example of a type library file that is embedded in a binary file (a .ocx file is a DLL). All ActiveX controls have their type library embedded inside the .ocx file. You can open any .ocx file in the Windows system directory and see the type library for the control.

In Microsoft's original vision for COM+, both IDL and type libraries were to become obsolete. Instead, you would define your classes and interfaces using native programming language constructs and then your compile would use the class definition to generate a meta-data file. This meta-deta file was described by Mary Kirtland in her MSJ articles (November and December 1997) as a "type library on steroids." Unfortunately, you will have to wait a while for these buffed out type libraries. The initial release of COM+ will still use IDL and type libraries but a later release will use meta-data files and will not require IDL.

A BINARY STANDARD FOR CALLING COM COMPONENTS

It's not enough to describe your COM components in a programming language independent way. You must also be able to call them in this way. This requires a binary-level calling convention for COM objects. COM's binary-level calling standard specifies that a COM interface is an array of function pointers. There is one pointer for each method in the interface. These function pointers must use the Pascal calling convention, which means that the called function cleans up the stack.

With this standard in place, compiler vendors can map COM interfaces to some native programming language construct. In C++, a pure abstract class like the one shown below maps to a COM interface:

```
class Employee
{
public:
   virtual float GetGrossPay()=0;
   virtual float GetHourlyRate()=0;
   virtual int GetHoursWorked()=0;
   virtual void BeginPayPeriod()=0;
   virtual void Work(short numHours)=0;
   virtual short GetNumDependents()=0;
   virtual void SetNumDependents(short numDeps)=0;
   virtual string GetName()=0;
   virtual float GetSalary()=0;
};
```

A pure abstract class in C++ generates something called a vtable that is just an array of function pointers. Visual Basic has a class type that maps to a COM interface and in J++ the native language interfaces are mapped to COM interfaces.

A programming language independent type description mechanism and a programming language independent method calling convention combine to make the COM software bus programming language independent. You get to prove this to yourself when you build your first COM object in the next chapter.

Location Transparency

Location transparency is arguably the most important (and difficult to implement) thing that the COM software does. Think about it for a minute. What location transparency means is the ability to use a software component in the exact same way regardless of whether it is implemented as a DLL, an executable, or whether the software component is running on the same machine as its client or on a different machine. That's a tall order. And as you can imagine, there is a significant amount of complex code that must be written to make this work. Fortunately, you don't have to write this code yourself. The MIDL compiler can be used to generate all the code required to implement location transparency. The only thing you have to do is to describe your interfaces in IDL.

The key to implementing location transparency is a process called marshaling. Marshaling is necessary because you cannot directly call a method in a COM interface (or any software procedure for that matter) if the COM interface is implemented in another process. You can call a COM interface method directly if the interface is implemented in a DLL-based server. This is because most programming languages implement method calls as a jump to the address in memory where the method resides. Memory addresses are only valid within a single process. So if the calling software resides in the same process as the procedure being called, a direct method call is simple. If a COM object is implemented in a separate process (in other words, it is implemented as a local or remote executable), then a client that wishes to call a method in the object cannot implement a jump to the memory address of the method. COM uses marshaling to simulate a cross-process method call.

MARSHALING

With marshaling, a proxy is created in the address-space of the client. This proxy looks exactly like the COM interface that you are trying to call; it has the same methods, parameters, and return values. This proxy is created automatically for you by the COM runtime when you instantiate a COM object that is implemented as a local or remote executable. When the client calls one of the methods in this proxy, the proxy packages the method call into an InterProcess Communication (IPC) message. This message contains an identifier that specifies the method in the server that is to be called; it also contains the parameters that are being passed to the method. This message is sent via Remote Procedure Calls (RPC) to the server. Local RPC (LRPC) is used if the server resides locally and Distributed Computing Environment (DCE) RPC (which includes support for network security) is used if the executable resides on a remote machine. The message is received in the server by a piece of software called a *stub*. The stub unpacks the IPC message, calls the requested method—passing in the parameters—and then sends the return value back as another IPC message. Once you have created the DLL that implements the proxy and the stub, this process happens seamlessly. The only thing you will notice is that a method call on a local executable server is about an order of magnitude slower than a method call on a DLL-based server, and a method call on a remote server is about an order of magnitude slower than a method call on a local executable server.

Only the cost of the method invocation itself is slower. As an example, consider a computationally intensive method that has 10 arguments. It may take 10 milliseconds to complete the invocation of this method if it is implemented in a DLL (most of this time will be sent setting up the stack frame). After the method call is made, it may then take 10 seconds to run the computationally intensive algorithm. If the method is implemented in a local executable, it may take 100 milliseconds to invoke the method (most of this time is spent on marshaling) but it will still take 10 seconds to run the algorithm. If the server is implemented as a remote server, it may take a full second to invoke the method (marshaling is even slower because the IPC messages must be sent over the network) but it will still take 10 seconds to run the algorithm (assuming that the remote machine has the same performance characteristics as the local machine).

So, how do you create the DLL that implements the proxy and the stub? The answer once again is IDL. Refer back to Table 3.1. The source code files that were generated by MIDL: `dlldata.c`, `spellcheck_i.c`, `spellcheck_p.c`, and `spellcheck.h` contain all the code required to implement a marshaling DLL. All you have to do is create a makefile that compiles these files and links with the RPC runtime: `rpcrt4.lib`, `rpcndr.lib`, and `rpcns.lib`. The marshaling DLL must be present on both the client and the server machines if you are using an out-of-process COM server that has custom interfaces.

Custom interfaces are COM interfaces that you define yourself with IDL. There are literally hundreds of interfaces that have been defined already by Microsoft. These are called standard interfaces. If you are only implementing standard interfaces, then you don't need a marshaling DLL because the COM runtime already includes a marshaling DLL that works for all of the standard interfaces.

The entire marshaling process looks like that shown in Figure 3.10.

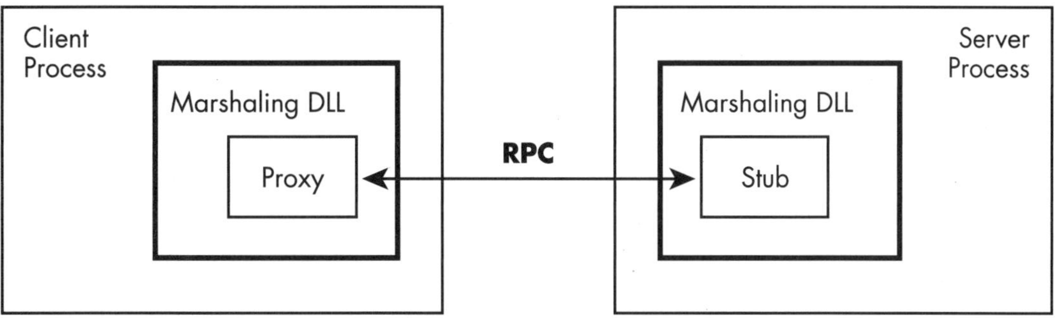

FIGURE 3.10 Marshaling for Out-of-Process Servers.

MARSHALING FOR IN-PROCESS SERVERS • I mentioned earlier that marshaling is required only when you have a COM server that is implemented in an out-of-process server (either a local or remote executable); this is a simplification. Some in-process (DLL) servers also require marshaling support. To understand why, you need to understand COM threading, which is the topic of a later chapter. So I'll defer further discussion of this point until then.

IMPLEMENTING CUSTOM MARSHALING • Now if you are a true glutton for punishment, you can implement your marshaling DLL from scratch. You have to implement a standard interface called `IMarshal` to make this work. There are only a few sources out there that show you how to do this. Chapter 5 of the Don Box book, *Essential COM*, contains a discussion and an example implementation of custom marshaling. Also, Chapter 6 of *Inside OLE* by Craig Brockschmidt demonstrates how to implement a custom marshaling DLL (yes, I eventually did get past page 200 in this book). Why would you want to make the extra effort required to implement a custom marshaling DLL? One example would be if you were creating an out-of-process COM server that is to be used in performance-critical applications. You could implement client-side caching so that an IPC message is not required for each method invocation.

Extensibility

If you are an experienced software developer, you know that no matter how feature-packed the software that you write is, your users will always want more. Rather than praising you for the great work that you have already done, most users (this includes other developers) gripe non-stop about the features that you have not implemented. With C++ class libraries (the Microsoft Foundation Classes [MFC] for instance), you can easily extend a class using implementation inheritance. I talked in Chapter 2 about why you probably need the source code if you want to do this safely. But, MFC does ship with complete source code so there's no problem using implementation inheritance with MFC. COM objects, however, are distributed in binary form. If you buy a COM object (an ActiveX control for instance), you won't get the source code for it. So how can you enhance a COM object that you have just bought that does almost everything you want it to do, but is missing that one feature you must have for your application? The COM software bus gives you two choices for extending a COM object: aggregation and containment.

CONTAINMENT

Containment is the simplest, but least elegant, extensibility mechanism in COM. Imagine that I have a COM component that implements our `ISpellChecker` interface as shown in Figure 3.11.

You want to extend this COM component so it also implements the `IGrammarChecker` interface. Remember you don't have the source code for the component. If you were using containment, you would create a new COM class and in the IDL for this COM class you would specify that the class implements both the `IGrammarChecker` and `ISpellChecker` interfaces. You would next implement this COM class using your favorite programming language Within the implementation of this new component you would create an instance of the spellchecker component shown in Figure 3.11 and implement the `ISpellChecker` interface in this new component (let's call it the outer object from now on) by delegating all calls to this internal spellchecker object (let's call it the inner object from now on). So whenever someone calls the `CheckSpelling` method in the outer object, you simply forward the call to the `CheckSpelling` method in the inner object. The situation is as shown in Figure 3.12.

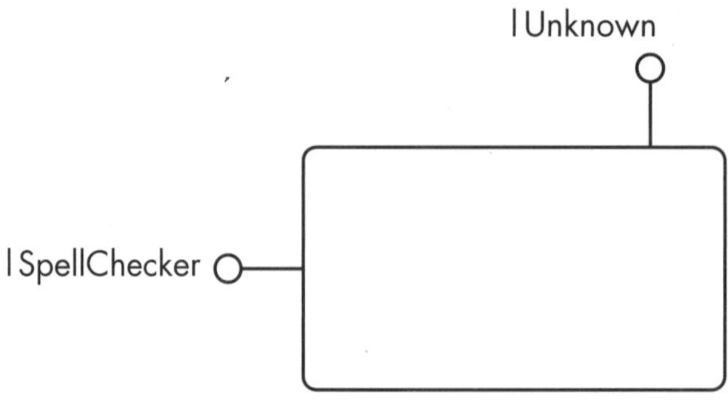

FIGURE 3.11 A Simple COM Object.

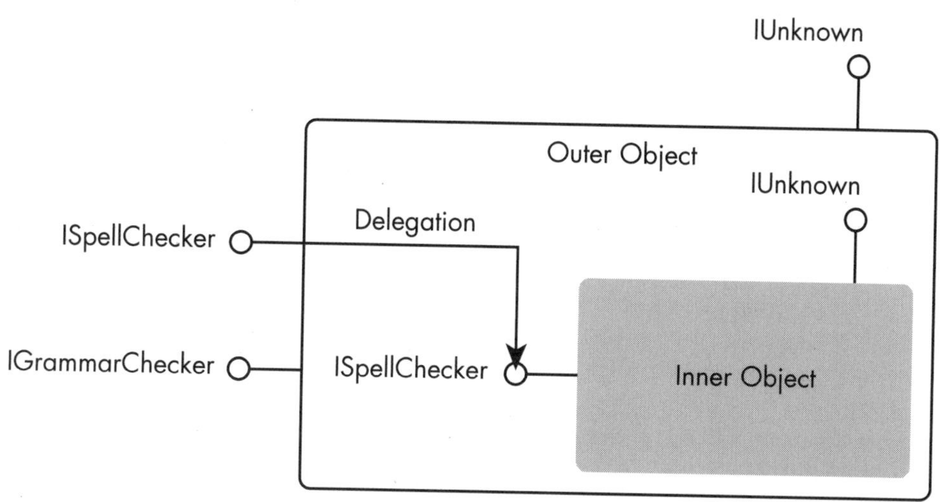

FIGURE 3.12 Extending the Simple COM Object Using Containment.

Of course, you're on your own when it comes to implementing the `IGrammarChecker` interface. This is functionality that is not already present in the simple COM object.

AGGREGATION

It requires quite a bit of code to make containment work. You have to write code to instantiate the inner object and to delegate method calls from the outer object to the implementation in the inner object. You could save some of this work if you did not have to delegate these method calls. You could simply return the inner object's `ISpellChecker` interface when the user of your COM object asks for the `ISpellChecker` interface. There's a problem with this though. The `QueryInterface` function in the `IUnknown` interface (which is used to ask a COM object for its implementation of a particular interface) must be symmetric. This means that if I have an `IGrammarChecker` interface and use the `QueryInterface` method in this interface to ask for the `ISpellChecker` interface, then if this call succeeds, I should also be able to call the `QueryInterface` method in the `ISpellChecker` interface and retrieve `IGrammarChecker`. The first part of this is easy. When I code up the `IGrammarChecker` interface I know that my COM object also supports the `ISpellChecker` interface, so I can implement its `QueryInterface` function in such a way that it returns the `ISpellChecker` interface from the inner object. But the inner object was implemented before the `IGrammarChecker` interface was ever defined, so how can its implementation of `QueryInterface` return a valid `IGrammarChecker` interface? It can't. The solution to this problem is that the inner object must have a way of forwarding all calls to `QueryInterface` to the `IUnknown` implementation in the outer object. Only the outer object knows about all the interfaces that the aggregate supports. The second parameter for the `CoCreateInstanceEx` function (remember this is COM's equivalent of C++'s new operator) allows you to pass a so-called Outer Unknown to a COM object when it is instantiated. A COM object that supports aggregation (it's not a requirement) must contain logic to forward all calls to this outer unknown if a non-zero Outer Unknown is passed to it when it is created as shown in Figure 3.13.

Aggregation is more complicated to understand than containment, but it does yield a more elegant solution.

I think most COM experts make far too big a deal about aggregation. If you didn't understand the preceding discussion, don't worry about it. Keep reading and it will probably make more sense later. Even if it doesn't, you can use COM quite successfully without using aggregation.

Versioning

Any environment that utilizes binary software components must address the software component versioning problem. Everybody who uses the Windows platform is well aware of this problem. It occurs when you install an application and suddenly some other application stops working. The

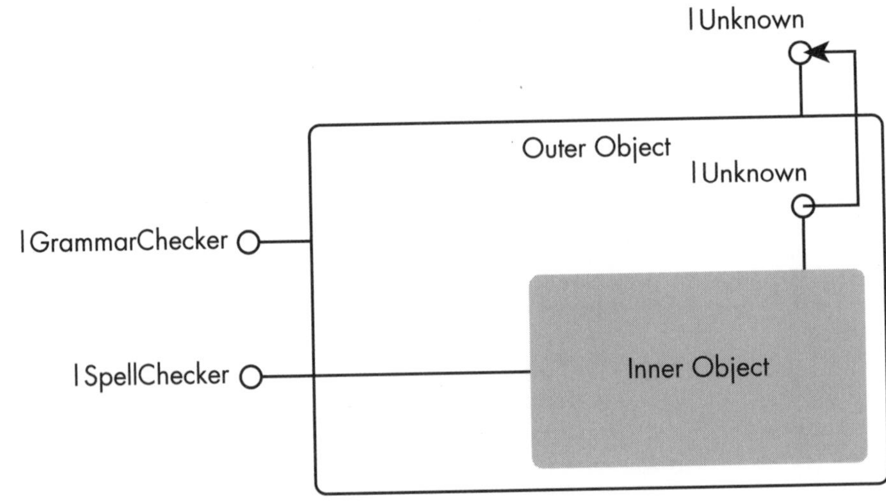

FIGURE 3.13 Extending the Simple COM Object Using Aggregation.

problem is usually caused by DLLs that are shared by several applications. The MFC runtime DLL, `mfc42.dll`, is a good example. It is used by all applications that are built with Visual C++. The versioning problem occurs when you install an application that uses a particular version of a shared DLL and then you install some other application that uses an earlier version of the same DLL. If the second application installs an older version of the shared DLL the first application will probably stop working. If the second application senses that there is a newer DLL already resident on the system and does not install its older version (a correctly written setup program should do this) the second application will not work unless the new version of the DLL is backwardly compatible. Usually, newer versions of a DLL are backwardly compatible with older versions, but there are no guarantees. So how do you fix this problem?

First let's look at this problem in the context of COM. A COM class, whether it resides in an in-process or out-of-process server, may be shared by several client applications. So COM components can potentially cause the same versioning problems as "regular" DLLs. Let's say a word processing application was built with version 1 of a spell-checking component. This spell-checking component implements the `ISpellChecker` interface shown in Listing 3.3. After the word processing application ships, the company that builds the spell checking component releases version 2 of their product. This component supports an additional interface called `ISpellChecker2` that allows a client to receive a suggested spelling for an incorrectly spelled word as shown here:

```
[ object,uuid(2550AFC0-E31C-11d2-998A-94DD09C10000) ]
interface ISpellChecker2 : ISpellChecker
{
   HRESULT CheckSpelling2([in,string] char *word,[out,size_is(100)]
char * suggestion,[out,retval] BOOL *isCorrect);
}
```

Another company uses version 2 of the spell checker component to build a spreadsheet application. This spreadsheet application uses the `ISpellChecker2` interface extensively. Now let's say that an end-user installs the word processing application and the spreadsheet application on her machine. Let's consider 2 scenarios: In scenario 1, the setup programs for both applications have worked properly and the latest version of the spell checking component (version 2) resides on the user's machine after she has installed the word processor and the spreadsheet. In scenario 2, the user installed the spreadsheet application first (which installs version 2 of the spellchecker). The user then installed the word processing application, which misbehaved and overwrote version 2 of the spellchecker with version 1.

In the first scenario, both applications will work properly as long as version 2 of the spell checker still supports the ISpellChecker interface that the word processor expects and this interface has not been altered. In the second scenario, as long as the spreadsheet application is implemented properly, it can degrade gracefully thanks to the QueryInterface method in IUnknown. The QueryInterface method allows a COM client to determine the functionality of a COM component at runtime. The spreadsheet application can request the IUnknown interface on the SpellChecker component when it instantiates the component. (All COM components support this interface). It can then call QueryInterface on the IUnknown interface pointer to obtain an ISpellChecker2 interface. This call will fail if version 1 of the SpellChecker component is installed. The spreadsheet application can then request the ISpellChecker interface and gray-out the menu item that allows the user to retrieve a suggested spelling.

You can see that there are 2 elements to this versioning solution: (1) once a COM interface is published you should never change it. If you want to add additional functionality to a COM component, you must define new interfaces and continue to support the older interfaces so you don't break clients that were built with previous versions of your component. (2) the QueryInterface method in IUnknown allows COM clients to determine the capabilities of a COM component at runtime. Even if a host does not have the correct version of a COM component installed, a client application can use the QueryInterface method to degrade gracefully.

I have found from teaching my class that some people misunderstand this immutable interface rule. During development you may change your COM interfaces as you please. You may anger the other developers on your project, but such is life! The immutable interface rule applies once you publish the interface, for example, you ship a piece of software that implements the interface.

Summary

In this chapter, you explored COM at a lower level technically. The metaphor of a software bus was used to provide a unifying framework around which to understand some of COM technical details. In the process, you learned about GUIDs, IDL, reference counting, the IUnknown interface, marshaling, type libraries, aggregation, and containment.

When I was learning COM, I read a number of different explanations of what COM is and how it worked. I soon learned that you can only comprehend so much from reading and studying. To truly understand something, you must also *do*. That's why this book contains example problems that are structured so you can follow along. I can honestly say that I didn't truly understand COM until I started from scratch and created my own COM object. You now have enough background knowledge of COM, that you are primed for this task. In Chapter 4, you will use the knowledge you have gained in the first three chapters of this book to create your first COM object. And you will create it without the help of ATL, MFC, or any of the Visual C++ wizards.

FOUR

Building Your First COM Object

So now you've learned about classes, objects, and interfaces in the context of COM. You've also learned about GUIDs, IDL, type libraries, location transparency, and versioning. In short, you've learned all that you need to know to create and use your first COM object. In practice, you use a tool like the Active Template Library (ATL) to create your COM objects. But, in this chapter you create your first COM object from scratch. I've always believed that if you want to understand something, you have to learn it from the inside out, at its most elemental level. Once you've done that, you are then ready to learn about all the tools and wizards in your favorite development environment that make the process easier. Learning this way quickly makes you a power user of your development tool. You will understand the code generated for you by the wizard and will know how to change or alter your code when it doesn't do exactly what you want it to do. You will be using Visual C++ 6.0 in this chapter to create your COM object.

The Simple Spell Checker

The COM object that you will create is a simple spell checker. This spell checker will implement a single interface called `ISpellChecker` that will have two methods: `CheckSpelling` and `UseCustomDictionary`. `CheckSpelling` will take a null-terminated, ASCII character string as input and compare this string to a list of words in a dictionary. If the word is found in the dictionary (which indicates the word is spelled correctly), the `CheckSpelling` method returns true. If the input string is not found in the dictionary, then `CheckSpelling` returns false. The spell checker's dictionary is filled with a few words when it is created, but a user may want to add custom words to the dictionary. This can be done with the `UseCustomDictionary` method that takes as input the path to a custom dictionary file. The dictionary file contains words organized one per line. The `UseCustomDictionary` method adds the contents of the custom dictionary file to the spell checker's dictionary. A diagram of our COM object is shown in Figure 4.1.

A Summary of the Steps

The steps that you will perform to build your COM object are as follows:

1. Create a new DLL project using Visual C++.
2. Create a custom interface using IDL.
3. Declare a C++ class that implements the COM interface.
4. Implement the SpellChecker Interface.
5. Create a class object.
6. Create the required DLL entry-points.
7. Create the registration functions.
8. Create a client.

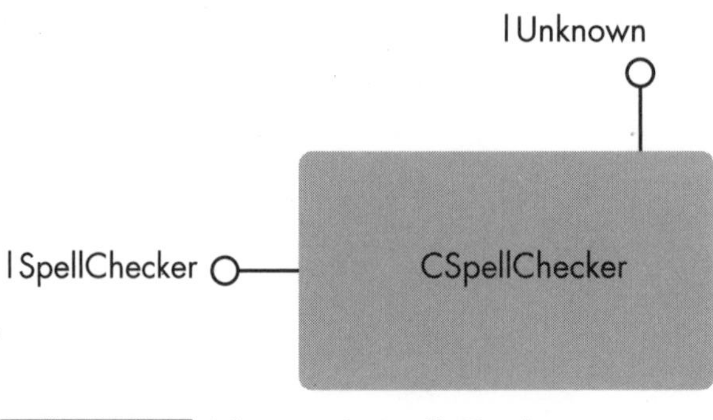

FIGURE 4.1 The Simple Spell Checker.

Creating a New DLL Project Using Visual C++

Like most development tools, Visual C++ uses a project metaphor. A project contains all the files needed to build a binary (DLL or Executable) and it also stores all the compiler and linker settings required to build the files correctly. Visual C++ has a number of wizards you can use to generate various types of projects. There are wizards for generating projects to build MFC applications and DLLs, for building ActiveX controls using MFC, and for building COM components using ATL. You will use many of these wizards later (in fact, you will use the ATL wizard in the next chapter). But for right now, we want to build an empty project that contains all the compiler and linker settings required to build a Win32 DLL from scratch (without MFC or ATL). Perform the following steps to build such a project:

1. Select `New...` from the `File` menu (the New dialog appears as shown in Figure 4.2).
2. Click the `Projects` tab.
3. Select `Win32 Dynamic Link Library` from the presented list of project types.

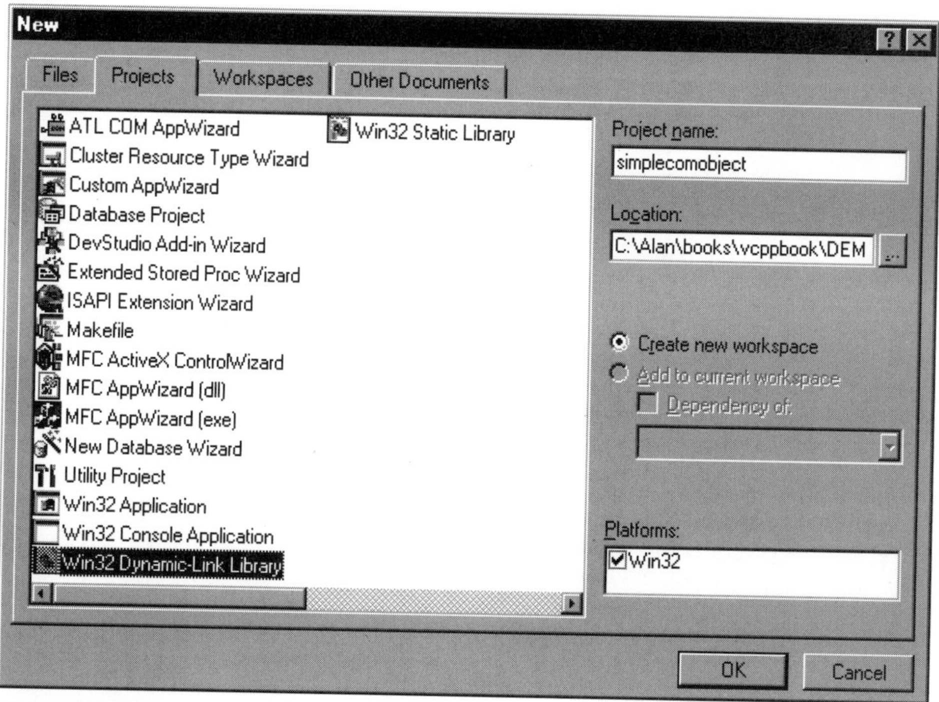

FIGURE 4.2 The New Dialog Projects Tab.

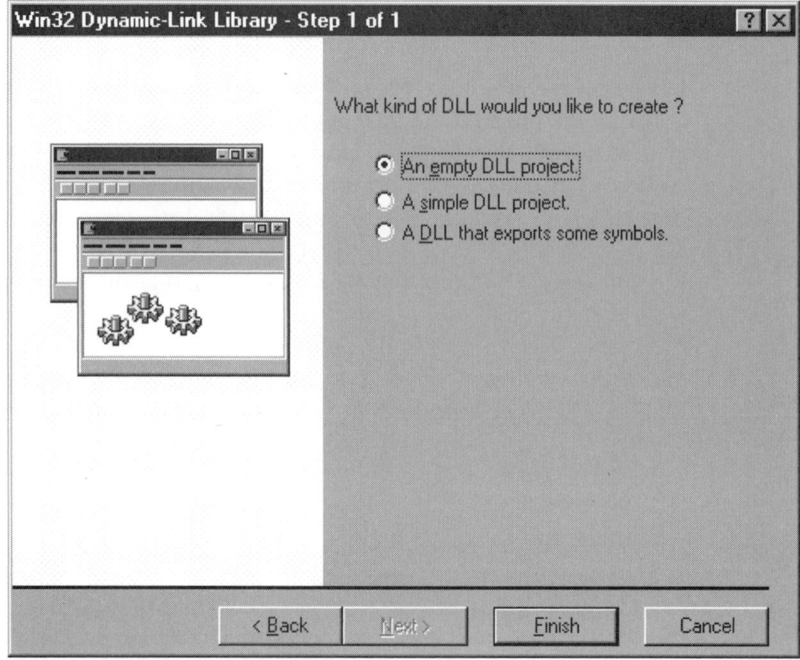

FIGURE 4.3 The DLL Project Wizard.

4. Enter `simplecomobject` in the `Project` name field.
5. Click `OK` (the DLL project wizard appears as shown in Figure 4.3).
6. Click the radio button labeled: `An empty DLL project`.
7. Click `Finish` (the New Project Information dialog appears).
8. Click `OK`.

Creating a Custom Interface Using IDL

Now that you have created your empty project, you will need to add an IDL file to it. In this IDL file, you will define a custom interface and a COM class that implements the interface. Later, you will modify your project so that it will compile the IDL using MIDL.

Adding an IDL File to Your Project

Perform the following steps to add an empty IDL file to your project:

1. Select New... from the `File` menu (the New dialog appears as shown in Figure 4.4).
2. Select `Text` File from the list of file types.
3. Enter `spellcheck.idl` in the `File` name field (make sure you include the file extension).
4. Click `OK`.

Creating GUIDs for Your Component

You will need several GUIDS for your IDL file. You will need an IID for the `ISpellChecker` interface, a CLSID for the COM class that will implement the `ISpellChecker` interface, and a LIBID for our server's type library. You will of course use Guidgen to create these GUIDs. If you're going to be a COM developer, you will often find yourself needing to create GUIDs. To make it simpler to create GUIDs, you can add Guidgen to Visual C++'s Tool menu:

1. Select `Customize` from the `Tools` menu (the Customize window appears).
2. Click the `Tools` tab.

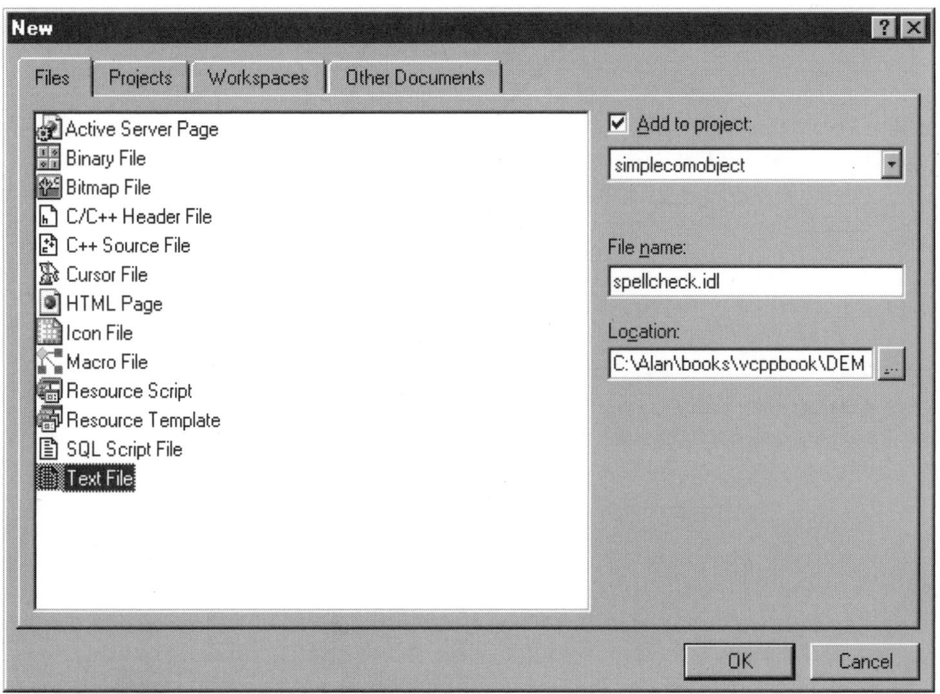

FIGURE 4.4 The New Dialog Files Tab.

3. Click the New button (the first button on the window from the left).
4. Click on the new entry in the Menu Contents list and type "Guid Generator".
5. Making sure that this new entry is still selected, click the Browse button next to the Command edit box.
6. Navigate to where GuidGen is located on your machine (it should be at c:\program files\Microsoft Visual Studio\Common\Tools\Guidgen.exe.
7. Double-click guidgen.exe.
8. Click Close.

Now you should see an item in the Tools menu called GUID Generator. Select it. Choose Registry format from the list of registry formats. Click the Copy button and then go back to Visual C++ and enter the following two lines of text into the idl file.

```
Import "unknwn.idl";
[object,uuid( )]
```

Paste the GUID that you just generated between the parentheses (remember to get rid of the curly brackets around the GUID after you paste it between the parantheses). Here's what the final result should look like:

```
Import "unknwn.idl";
[object,uuid(704A8520-E4E9-11d0-BCCE-00A024BD9ECC)]
```

Obviously your GUID will look completely different from mine. My GUID was generated at a different time and in a different place than yours. The GUID creation algorithm should ensure that your GUID is different. The two lines added above are the attributes for our spell checker interface. Now, let's define the interface itself. Add the following five lines of code:

```
interface ISpellChecker : IUnknown
{
   HRESULT CheckSpelling([in,string] char *word,[out,retval] BOOL
   *isCorrect);
   HRESULT UseCustomDictionary([in,string] char *filename);
}
```

Now that your interface is defined, you need to define a GUID and a name for your type library. Remember that the type library is generated automatically from the IDL using MIDL. MIDL embeds both the library name and the GUID into the type library file it creates. To define the GUID and the name for the type library, add the following four lines to the spellcheck.idl file:

```
[ uuid(99A9E580-E4E0-11d0-818D-444553540000) ]
library SpellcheckerLib
{

};
```

Use GUIDGEN with the registry format to generate the GUID.

You now need to define a COM class. Remember a COM class is essentially just a name—and a GUID—that identifies an implementation of one or more interfaces. In this case, I recommend that you use the GUID shown here instead of generating your own. In practice you would, of course, create a GUID using GUIDGEN for your new class. But this is an academic exercise and because this GUID is used in several places in upcoming code, if you generated your own GUID here you would have to remember to change all of this other code too. Save yourself the trouble, just use the GUID shown here. Insert the four bolded lines inside the library statement like this:

```
[ uuid(99A9E580-E4E0-11d0-818D-444553540000) ]
library SpellcheckerLib
{
   [ uuid(57B7A8A0-E4D7-11d0-818D-444553540000) ]
   coclass CSpellChecker
   {
      interface ISpellChecker;
   }
};
```

Now you need to setup Visual C++ so you can compile the IDL. If you click the compile button in Visual C++ 6.0, it compiles the IDL, but it only generates the type library. You need all the files that MIDL generates. To change the default MIDL settings for this IDL file, perform the following steps:

1. Select `Settings` from the `Project` Menu (the Project Settings dialog appears).
2. Select `All Configurations` in the `Settings For` dropdown list.
3. Click the + symbol next to the project name.
4. Click the + symbol next to the Source Files folder.
5. Select `spellcheck.idl`.
6. Click the `MIDL` tab.
7. Clear the `Mktyplib compatible` checkbox.
8. Enter `spellcheck.h` in the `Output header file` name field.

The `project settings` dialog should look as shown in Figure 4.5.

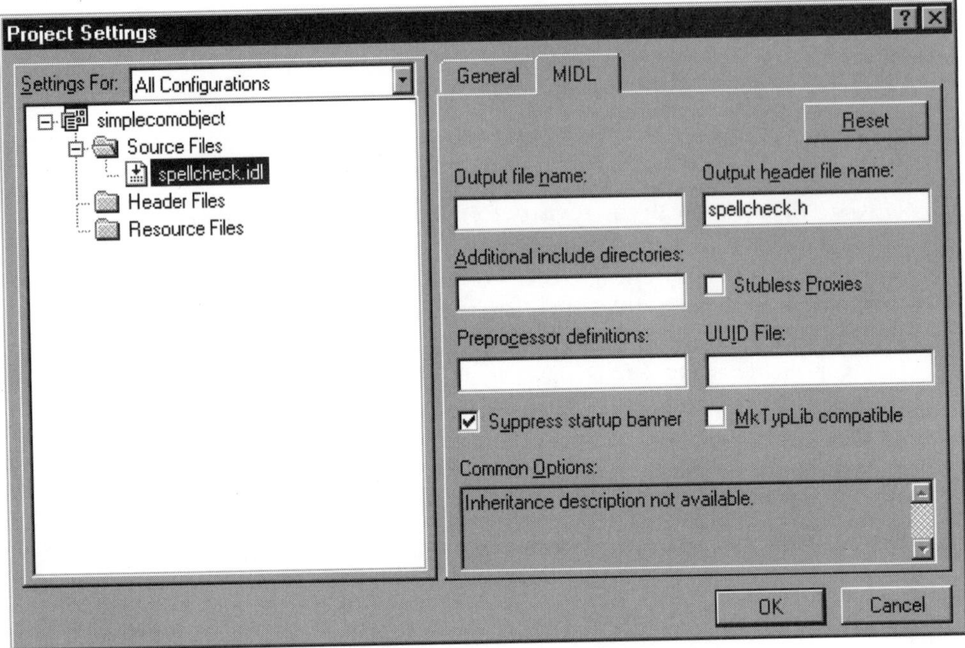

FIGURE 4.5 The Correct Settings to Compile `SpellCheck.idl`.

Now click the `Compile` button in Visual C++ or press `CTRL F7`. Table 4.1 lists the five files that MIDL generates.

TABLE 4.1 Files Generated by MIDL

Filename	Contents
Spellcheck.tlb	The type library.
Spellcheck.h	C and C++ definitions of the ISpellchecker and IGrammarChecker interfaces.
Spellcheck_i.c	C/C++ GUID Declarations.
Spellcheck_p.c	Marshaling support code.
Dlldata.c	Marshaling support code.

For this exercise, you are only interested in two of these files: `spellcheck.h` and `spellcheck_i.c`. You will use these files in both the implementation of your COM server and its client. These files contain interface declarations and GUID definitions, respectively. The compile-able, interface declaration for the `ISpellChecker` interface is contained in the file `spellcheck.h`, and is shown in the code below:

```
MIDL_INTERFACE("704A8520-E4E9-11d0-BCCE-00A024BD9ECC")
   ISpellChecker : public IUnknown    {    public:
      virtual HRESULT STDMETHODCALLTYPE CheckSpelling(
         /* [string][in] */ unsigned char __RPC_FAR *word,
         /* [retval][out] */ BOOL __RPC_FAR *isCorrect) = 0;
      virtual HRESULT STDMETHODCALLTYPE UseCustomDictionary(
         /* [string][in] */ unsigned char __RPC_FAR *filename) = 0;
   };
```

Don't let the use of the MIDL_INTERFACE macro throw you. If you look in the file rpcndr.h in your Visual C++ include directory, you will see that this macro is defined essentially as follows:

```
#define MIDL_INTERFACE(x)   struct
```

So the code shown in the previous listing is just a pure, virtual class declaration.

Structs and classes are essentially the same in C++. The only difference is that the default access specifier is public for structs and private for classes. So a struct declaration is for all intents and purposes the same as a class declaration.

A COM interface is defined in the COM specification as an array of function pointers. Each programming language is free to map this COM interface to a programming-language-specific construct. In Visual Basic, a COM interface maps to a class. In Java (oops J++), a COM interface maps nicely to a Java interface. In C++, a COM interface maps to a class or struct that has only pure virtual methods (methods that are declared as virtual with "=0" at the end of the method declaration). In other words, the code just shown defines a C++ specific construct that maps to a COM interface.

The file spellcheck_i.c contains GUID variable definitions. If you look in this file, you will see the following code:

```
const IID IID_ISpellChecker =
{0x704A8520,0xE4E9,0x11d0,{0xBC,0xCE,0x00,0xA0,0x24,0xBD,0x9E,0xCC}};

const IID LIBID_SpellcheckerLib =
{0x99A9E580,0xE4E0,0x11d0,{0x81,0x8D,0x44,0x45,0x53,0x54,0x00,0x00}};

const CLSID CLSID_CSpellChecker =
{0x57B7A8A0,0xE4D7,0x11d0,{0x81,0x8D,0x44,0x45,0x53,0x54,0x00,0x00}};
```

These variables are defined primarily for your convenience (thanks MIDL). You can refer to the GUID for the ISpellChecker interface as IID_SpellChecker instead of having to remember the actual GUID.

Declaring a C++ Class that Implements the COM Interface

Now that you have defined your interface, it is time to implement it. How you will implement a COM interface depends on the programming language you are using. For example, to implement a COM interface in Visual Basic, you first add a reference to your project that points to the type library that contains the interface definition. You then have to create a class and use the implements keyword to specify that the class will implement the interface. In C++, you first create a C++ class that inherits from the interface class—`ISpellChecker` in this example. You must then provide an implementation (in the C++ class) for all the methods declared in the interface. You can add an implementation class to your project by performing the following steps:

1. Select `New...` from the `File` menu (the `New` dialog appears).
2. Select `C/C++ Header File` from the list of file types.
3. Enter `spellcheckimpl` in the `File` name field.
4. Click `OK`.

Add the code in Listing 4.1 to this new file.

LISTING 4.1 *SPELLCHECKIMPL.H*

```
#include "spellcheck.h"
#include <list>
using namespace std;
class CSpellCheckImpl  : public ISpellChecker {
public:
    CSpellCheckImpl();
    ~CSpellCheckImpl();
    STDMETHOD(QueryInterface) (REFIID,void ** );
    STDMETHOD_(ULONG,AddRef) (void);
    STDMETHOD_(ULONG,Release) (void);
    STDMETHOD(CheckSpelling) (unsigned char *word,
                BOOL *isCorrect);
    STDMETHOD(UseCustomDictionary) (unsigned char *filename);
private:
    ULONG               m_ref;
    list<string>        m_dictionary;
};
```

The first line of this code includes the MIDL-generated header file that contains the declaration of the `ISpellChecker` interface. Lines 2 and 3 are related to your use of the C++ standard library. The C++ Standard library is a powerful, albeit complex, library of built-in classes. These classes include collections, strings, and algorithms to do searching and sorting. You are going to use the standard library list collection to hold the words that define the dictionary for our spell checker. Lines 4 and 5 contain the declaration of the implementation class. There is a constructor and a destructor in lines 6 and 7.

In lines 8–12, you have the three methods in the `IUnknown` interface: `AddRef`, `Release`, and `QueryInterface`. The `ISpellChecker` interface inherits from `IUnknown`. So this interface includes both the two methods that are declared directly within the `ISpellChecker` interface and the three methods that are inherited from `IUnknown`. To implement the `ISpellChecker` interface, your implementation class must provide an implementation of all five methods.

Finally, the private data of your class is shown in lines 14 and 15. In this case, there are two pieces of private data: the reference count, and the list that will be used to hold the words in your dictionary.

Implementing the SpellChecker Interface

The next step in building your COM component is to implement all the methods declared in the `CSpellCheckImpl` class. The first thing you must do is to add a C++ source file to your project. To do this, perform the following steps:

1. Select `New...` from the `File` menu (the New dialog appears).
2. Select `C/C++ Source File` from the list of file types.
3. Enter `spellcheckimpl` in the `File` name field.
4. Click `OK`.

Add the code in Listing 4.2 to this file.

LISTING 4.2 *SPELLCHECKIMPL.CPP*

```
#include <string.h>
#include <fstream>
#include <iterator>
#include "spellcheckimpl.h"
```

```
extern LONG gObjectCount;
const E_DICTIONARYFILENOTFOUND=MAKE_HRESULT(SEVERITY_ERROR,
FACILITY_ITF,0x200+25);
CSpellCheckImpl::CSpellCheckImpl()
{
   string str;
   str="Alan";
   m_dictionary.push_back(str);
   str="Gordon";
   m_dictionary.push_back(str);
}
CSpellCheckImpl::~CSpellCheckImpl()
{
   gObjectCount–;
}
STDMETHODIMP_(ULONG) CSpellCheckImpl::AddRef(void)
{
   return ++m_ref;
}
STDMETHODIMP_(ULONG) CSpellCheckImpl::Release(void)
{
   if (0L!=–m_ref)
      return m_ref;
   delete this;
   return 0;
}
STDMETHODIMP CSpellCheckImpl::QueryInterface(REFIID riid,void** ppv)
{
   if (IID_IUnknown==riid || IID_ISpellChecker==riid)
   {
      *ppv=this;
      AddRef();
      return S_OK;
   } else
   {
      *ppv=NULL;
      return E_NOINTERFACE;
   }
}
```

```

STDMETHODIMP  CSpellCheckImpl::CheckSpelling(unsigned char *word,BOOL *isCorrect)
{
    string str;
    vector< string >::iterator iter;
    *isCorrect=FALSE;
    for (iter=m_dictionary.begin();iter!=m_dictionary.end();iter++) {
       str=*iter;
       if (stricmp(str.c_str(),(const char *)word)==0) {
          *isCorrect=TRUE;
          break;
       }
    }
    return NOERROR;
}

STDMETHODIMP  CSpellCheckImpl::UseCustomDictionary(unsigned char *filename)
{
    string str;
    char tempBuffer[255];
    ifstream dictionaryFile;
    dictionaryFile.open((const char *)filename);
    if (!dictionaryFile.is_open())
       return E_DICTIONARYFILENOTFOUND;
    while (!dictionaryFile.eof())  {
       dictionaryFile.getline(tempBuffer,255);
       str= tempBuffer;
       m_dictionary.push_back(str);
    }
    return NOERROR;
}
```

At the beginning of the file there are several `#includes` and the declaration of a user-defined HRESULT. The include file, `string.h`, is required because you will use the case-insensitive string comparison function: `stricmp`. The file `fstream` is required because you will be using C++ I/O streams to read the custom dictionary. The include for Iterator is required because iterators are used with the standard library collections to allow you to visit (or iterate over) each of the words in the dictionary to compare it with the word that is being spell checked.

Next is the declaration of a global variable called `gObjectCount`:

```
extern LONG gObjectCount;
```

This variable keeps track of the number of objects that have been created within this server. Notice that the variable is decremented in the destructor of your implementation class:

```
gObjectCount--;
```

You will see where this variable is incremented when you create the class object for this COM class. You will also see how this variable is used to implement the life-cycle management for your server when you talk about the `DllCanUnloadNow` function.

Remember there are two types of life-cycle management that you must worry about when implementing a COM server: (1) The life-cycle of each COM object that is created within the server (this is managed by the client via the `IUnknown` interface), and (2) the life-cycle of the server itself (you'll have to wait until I talk about the `DllCanUnloadNow` function to find out more about this).

On line 6, you define a custom handle to a result (HRESULT):

```
const E_DICTIONARYFILENOTFOUND=MAKE_HRESULT(SEVERITY_ERROR,
FACILITY_ITF,0x200+25);
```

All methods that you declare in your COM interfaces should have a literal return value that is an HRESULT. There are many standard HRESULTS that are defined in the COM headers. Some examples are `E_NOERROR`, that you will return to indicate that a method call succeeded; `E_NOINTERFACE`, that you will return when a user requests an interface that your object does not support; and `E_NOTIMPL`, that you will return when you are not providing an implementation of a particular method in an interface. In addition to these generic error HRESULTS, you may also need interface-specific HRESULTs. For example, the `UseDictionary` method in the `ISpellChecker` interface allows a user to specify a file that will contain a custom dictionary for the spell checker to use. A common mistake a user might make is to specify a file that does not exist. You will need a custom HRESULT that you can return to indicate that this was the cause of the failure.

In Chapter 5 you will see how you can return rich error information, i.e., a textual description of the error.

In lines 7–20, you have the constructor and destructor for your implementation class. These methods are not contained in any of the COM interfaces that this class implements. So they are not exposed to the outside world. The constructor for our implementation class adds two words: Alan and Gordon to your dictionary. I have already discussed the destructor when I talked about the `gObjectCount` global variable.

Lines 22–48 contain the implementation of the functions in the `IUnknown` interface. In Chapter 3, I talked about reference counting as an idiom that pre-dated COM. The private member variable, `m_ref`, in the implementation class contains the reference count. `AddRef` should be called whenever an interface pointer is assigned to our COM object. In this function, you simply need to increment the reference count. In the `Release` function, you decrement the reference count. If the reference count is greater than zero after the count is decremented, then you simply return the current value of the count. If the reference count is zero, then you destroy the COM object by calling the delete operator on the pointer and return zero.

Many people have problems at first with the use of the delete operator on the "this" pointer. It is okay for a method to call "delete this" as long as the state of the object is not referenced after the call to delete.

Lines 50–79 contain the most important part of your code. It contains the implementation of the two value-added methods for the `ISpellChecker` interface: `CheckSpelling` and `UseCustomDictionary`. I call `CheckSpelling` and `UseCustomDictionary` the value-added methods for the interface because the `AddRef`, `Release`, and `QueryInterface` methods are there so you can plug your component into the COM software bus. The `CheckSpelling` and `UseCustomDictionary` methods are the methods you will call once your software is plugged into the software bus.

In the `CheckSpelling` method, you initially set the logical return value, isCorrect, to false and then iterate over the list of words in the dictionary, comparing each to the word that was passed in to be spellchecked. If the word that is being spellchecked is found in the dictionary, then you set the logical return value to true and break out of the iteration. Finally, you return the physical return value, which is the pre-defined HRESULT: NOERROR.

You're probably thinking that you are done at this point. Unfortunately you are not. There are still several other things to do to make your COM component work. The first of these is to create a class object.

Creating a Class Object

I have found during my teaching that the concept of a class object is difficult to understand. Java and Smalltalk have integrated support for class objects, but most COM programmers have a background in C++ or Visual Basic. Neither of these languages have native support for class objects. So for most beginning COM programmers, class objects are a completely new concept they must learn.

It took me a long time to understand class objects when I first started learning COM. So before I show you how to create a COM class object, I wanted to explain the concept first. If you don't understand class objects right away, don't get discouraged. Read my sidebar about the Java class object. Also, try reading about the `DECLARE_DYNCREATE` macro in the Visual C++ Help. They both provide the same functionality—primarily dynamic object creation—as COM class objects do, but they do it in a programming language dependent way. COM class objects are designed to be programming language independent.

The Java Class Object

In Java, class objects are instances of a class called `Class`. Every Java class, interface, or primitive type has an object of type Class associated with it. Consider the following Java class:

```
Public class Employee
{
private int mID;
private float mSalary;
private String mName;
private int mHoursWorked;
public Employee(int id,String name,float salary)
{
  mID=id;
  mName=name;
  mSalary=salary;
}
public void Work(int numHours)
{
  mHoursWorked+=numHours;
}
public float Pay()
{
  return mHoursWorked*mSalary/40;
}
}
```

I can get the class object for the Employee class using the following code:

```
Class cls=Class.forName("Employee")
```

The forName method is a static method that returns the Class instance associated with the named class (in this case, Employee). Table 4.2 shows some of the methods in the Java class called Class.

The most important of these methods is newInstance. You can use it to create generic code that would not be possible otherwise. Let's say you want to create a Java framework for developing Graphical User Interface (GUI) applications. In your framework, you have defined interfaces called Document, View, and Frame. Your users will need to create classes that implement each of these interfaces to build applications with your framework as shown here:

```
public class MyDocument implements Document
{
...
}
public class MyView implements View
{
...
}
Public class  MyFrame implements Frame
{
...
}
```

The Document, View, and Frame objects must be created and then attached to each other in a certain order. You don't want your users to concern themselves with how this is done, so you will instead require them to pass the name of their Document, View, and Frame classes to a method that will create instances of these classes, and attach them to each other. The code to instantiate the Document, View, and Frame objects might look like this:

```
Public void CreateDocViewFrame(String docClassName,String
viewClassName,String frameClassName)
{
  Class docCls, viewCls, frameCls;
  // Get the Class object for the view, document, and frame classes
Class viewCls=Class.forName(viewClassName);
Class docCls=Class.forName(docClassName);
Class frameCls=Class.forName(frameClassName);
// Instantiate the document and view objects and attach the
   document to the view
Document docObj=(Document)docCls.newInstance();
View viewObj=(View)viewCls.newInstance();
viewObj.AttachDocument(docObj);
```

```
// Create a frame and attach the view object to the frame
Frame frameObj=(Frame)frameCls.newInstance();
FrameObj.AttachView(viewObj);
}
```

The `CreateDocViewFrame` method can then be called as shown here:

```
CreateDocViewFrame("MyDocument","MyView","MyFrame");
```

Notice that the `CreateDocViewFrame` method is truly generic because the `Document`, `View`, and `Frame` classes are never referred to explicitly in the code. You only pass in the stringified name of each class. This code works with any classes that are assignment compatible with `View`, `Document`, and `Frame`. The key here is that you do not use the Java new keyword to create your instances. The syntax of the new keyword requires that you specify the name of the class that you will be creating an instance of at compile time.

The preceeding explanation outlines exactly how MFC works in regard to creating and establishing the connections between your `Document`, `View`, and `Frame` objects. In MFC, the `DECLARE_DYNCREATE` macro is used to add a static member to your class that contains a class object. The class object is an instance of an MFC class called `CRuntimeClass`. The Class object for your `Document`, `View`, and `Frame` classes is passed to the constructor of a document template class in the `InitInstance` method of your `Application` class. The document template is then added to the application using a method called `AddDocTemplate`. If you want to see all of this for yourself, use the MFC App Wizard (choose `New` from the `File` Menu in Visual C++, select the `Projects` tab, and then choose `MFC AppWizard` (exe) to invoke the App Wizard) to create a Single Document Interface (SDI) application. Then find the call to `AddDocTemplate` in the `InitInstance` method of the `Application` class.

TABLE 4.2 Java Class Methods

Method Name	Method Purpose
NewInstance	Creates a new instance of the class from which the Class object was obtained.
ToString	Returns the name of a class as a string.
ForName	A static method that returns a Class object given the name of the class.
IsInterface	Returns true if the Class object refers to an interface.
IsPrimitive	Returns true if the Class object refers to an instance of a primitive type.
GetSuperClass	Returns the Class object of the superclass of a class.

The Java class called `Class` contains more methods than the ones shown here, but there is no need to give an exhaustive list. See Gary Cornell's *Core Java* book or the Java documentation for a complete list of the methods in `Class`.

Understanding Class Objects

A class object is an object that implements the functionality of a class that is not instance dependent. Examples of this type of functionality are: a method to count the total number of instances of a class that have been created, or a method that will return the name of a class, or a method that you can use to create an instance of a class. All of these methods are functions of this class itself, they are not dependent on the state of a specific instance of the class. If you take this per-class functionality and bundle it into a class and then attach an object of this class to all other classes, then you have a class object. Some object-oriented languages, like Java and Smalltalk, have integrated support for class objects (see my sidebar on Java class objects). C++ does not have a built-in class object feature, but you can implement class object-like functionality using static member variables and functions. All create-able COM classes are required to have a class object.

A create-able COM class is a class that you can create an instance of by passing its CLSID to a COM API function like `CoCreateInstance`. If a class is not create-able, you have to call a method on an object of a create-able class to create an instance of the class.

UNDERSTANDING CLASS FACTORIES

COM class objects are sometimes referred to as class factories; this is not accurate. A class factory is really just a behavior that a COM class object may implement. I said that a COM interface is a set of methods that together define a behavior. So you would expect there to be a standard interface that you can implement to provide this class factory functionality. Actually, there are two class factory interfaces: `IClassFactory` and `IClassFactory2`. Class objects for COM classes should implement one of these interfaces. A COM class object can do more if it wants to. You can define and implement, in your class object, user-defined interfaces that allow you to keep track of the number of instances of the class that have been created, or get the class name, or any other functionality that is not instance dependent.

The class factory interfaces, like many COM technologies, are badly named. As you will see, class factories do not create/manufacture classes they actually create/manufacture objects, instances of classes. The class factory interfaces should be called `IObjectFactory` and `IObjectFactory2`. Microsoft (or at least the MFC group within Microsoft) has tacitly acknowledged this error. The MFC class that implements the `IClassFactory` interfaces is called `COleObjectFactory`.

The IClassFactory interface is shown here:

```
struct IClassFactory : public IUnknown
{
   virtual HRESULT STDMETHODCALLTYPE CreateInstance(IUnknown
*pUnkOuter,REFIID riid,void **ppv) = 0;
   virtual HRESULT STDMETHODCALLTYPE LockServer(BOOL fLock) = 0;
}
```

It has two methods: `CreateInstance` and `LockServer`. `CreateInstance` does exactly what its name implies; it allows you to create an instance of the COM class that the class object is associated with. The first parameter, `pUnkOuter` is only non-NULL if the object being created is the inner object in an aggregate. In this case, `pUnkOuter` contains the `IUnknown` interface of the outer object (see the section on extensibility in Chapter 3). The second parameter is an IID that identifies the interface that you want to obtain on the new object. And the third parameter is an output parameter that (if the `CreateInstance` call is successful) contains an interface pointer.

The `LockServer` method allows you to prevent a server from shutting down or unloading. It lets you lock a server into memory. The COM specification says that a COM server should shutdown if it is an executable or indicate that it can be unloaded if it is a DLL, when all the objects that are implemented in the server have been released by its client. You may want to keep the server in memory because you know that you will need to create more objects shortly. The `LockServer` method in `IClassFactory` lets you do this. It has a single parameter called `fLock`. You call it with the `fLock` parameter set to TRUE to lock the server into memory (prevent it from shutting down/unloading). You call `LockServer` with an `fLock` paramter of `FALSE` to unlock the server (allow it to shutdown/unload). You must call `LockServer` as many times with a `FALSE` parameter as you called it with a `TRUE` parameter to actually unlock it. In other words, if you lock the server twice, you must unlock it twice.

`IClassFactory2` is similar to `IClassFactory` (in fact, it inherits from `IClassFactory`) but it contains additional methods to support run-time licensing:

```
struct IClassFactory2 : public IClassFactory
{
        virtual HRESULT STDMETHODCALLTYPE GetLicInfo( LICINFO
*pLicInfo) = 0;
        virtual HRESULT STDMETHODCALLTYPE RequestLicKey( DWORD
dwReserved,BSTR *pBstrKey) = 0;
        virtual HRESULT STDMETHODCALLTYPE CreateInstanceLic( IUnknown
*pUnkOuter,
                          IUnknown *pUnkReserved,REFIID riid,BSTR
bstrKey,void **ppvObj) = 0;
};
```

The GetLicInfo function returns a LICINFO structure that describes the licensing behavior of the class factory. You call the RequestLicKey method to get the license key on the machine. This method fails if the machine does not contain a valid license. Finally, you pass a key to CreateInstanceLic method and it creates an instance of a COM class only if the license key is correct. The technology that you use to implement these licensing methods is entirely up to you, but both MFC and ATL provide rather pedestrian implementations of IClassFactory2 in the COleObjectFactory and CComClassFactory2 classes, respectively.

The class factory interfaces exists—and you should implement at least one of them in your class object—so there is a standard protocol for creating COM objects. The COM runtime and certain applications like development environments use this protocol. For instance, the COM API function, CoCreateInstance, uses the CreateInstance method in IClassFactory when it creates an instance of a COM class. It instantiates the class object, requesting the IClassFactory interface, calls the CreateInstance function on the IClassFactory interface, and then releases the IClassFactory interface.

Calling CoCreateInstance is actually not the best way to create COM objects if you are doing high-frequency allocations. You incur the cost of instantiating and then destroying the class object each time you create an object. Instead, you can get the IClassFactory interface on a classes class object using the CoGetClassObject function in the COM API. You can then call the CreateInstance as many times as you like. When you are done, you can release the class factory interface. Creating instances this way is faster because you are not creating and destroying a class object each time you create an object.

If a COM class has a runtime license, you cannot use CoCreateInstance to create an instance of the class because CoCreateInstance uses IClassFactory; IClassFactory will not work for classes that have a runtime license.You must instead invoke a COM API function called CoGetClassObject and request the IClassFactory2 interface on the class object for the COM class. You can then get the license key using the RequestLicKey method of the IClassFactory2 interface. Then pass this key to the CreateInstanceLic method to instantiate an object.

You are not limited to the object creation protocols defined in the IClassFactory and IClassFactory2. You may also add additional interfaces to your class object that support custom object creation protocols. One such protocol may allow you to pass parameters to a creation function. One big problem with the COM class factory interfaces is that you cannot pass parameters to an object when it is being created (as you can with a C++ constructor). So you could define your own class factory interface for an employee class that allows you to initialize the ID, name, and salary of a new employee. Defining interfaces for and implementing this functionality is entirely up to you.

Creating a Class Object for the SpellChecker

Enough talk about class objects, let's create one for your writers component. Since `IClassFactory` (like all COM interfaces) inherits from `IUnknown`, your class object must also implement the `IUnknown` methods: `AddRef`, `Release`, and `QueryInterface`. You will perform these steps to create your COM class factory:

1. Declare a C++ class that implements the `IClassFactory` interface.
2. Implement the `IUnknown` methods.
3. Implement the `IClassFactory` methods.

Declaring a C++ Class that Implements the IClassFactory Interface

We can add the declaration of the implementation class to our project by performing the following steps:

1. Select `New...` from the `File` menu (the New dialog appears).
2. Select `C/C++ Header File` from the list of file types.
3. Enter `spellfactoryimpl` in the `File` name field.
4. Click OK.

Add the code shown in Listing 4.3 to the new file.

LISTING 4.3 *SPELLFACTORYIMPL.H*

```
#include <ole2.h>
class CSpellFactoryImpl :  public IClassFactory {
public:
       CSpellFactoryImpl();
       ~CSpellFactoryImpl();
       STDMETHOD(QueryInterface) (REFIID, void**ppv);
       STDMETHOD_(ULONG,AddRef) (void);
       STDMETHOD_(ULONG,Release) (void);
       STDMETHOD(CreateInstance) (LPUNKNOWN, REFIID,
                    void **ppv);
       STDMETHOD(LockServer) (BOOL);
private:
       ULONG           m_ref;
};
```

Next, you implement the methods in the class. Perform the following steps:

1. Select New... from the `File` menu (the New dialog appears).
2. Select `C/C++ Source File` from the list of file types.
3. Enter `spellfactoryimpl` in the `File` name field.
4. Click `OK`.

A file called `spellfactoryimpl.cpp` is added to your project.

Implementing the IUnknown methods

Your class object is a COM object. That means it must implement the `IUnknown` interface. Add the code shown in Listing 4.4 to the `spellfactoryimpl.cpp` file. The logic is the same as the `IUnknown` implementation in the C++ class that implements the `ISpellChecker` interface.

LISTING 4.4 *SPELLFACTORYIMPL.CPP*

```
#include "spellfactoryimpl.h"
#include "spellcheckimpl.h" // spellchecker implementation
extern LONG gLockCount, gObjectCount;
CSpellFactoryImpl::CSpellFactoryImpl()
{
   m_ref=0;
}

CSpellFactoryImpl::~CSpellFactoryImpl()
{
}

STDMETHODIMP_(ULONG) CSpellFactoryImpl::AddRef(void)
{
   return ++m_ref;
}

STDMETHODIMP_(ULONG) CSpellFactoryImpl::Release(void)
{
   if (0L!=—m_ref)
      return m_ref;

   delete this;
   return 0;
}

STDMETHODIMP CSpellFactoryImpl::QueryInterface(REFIID riid,void** ppv)
{
```

```
    if (IID_IUnknown==riid || IID_IClassFactory==riid) {
        *ppv=this;
        AddRef();
        return S_OK;
    }
    else {
        *ppv=NULL;
        return E_NOINTERFACE;
    }
}
```

These methods are implemented the same way as the `CSpellCheckImpl` class so I will not repeat my explanation. I will draw your attention to the two global variables: `gLockCount` and `gObjectCount` (they are bolded in Listing 4.5) that are declared, but not defined, in this file. These variables are used to help manage the life-cycle of the server.

You are probably thinking that since the `IUnknown` methods are going to be implemented twice for each COM class that you build, it would probably make sense to create a C++ base class that you could reuse to provide an implementation of this interface. Don't do it. The Active Template Library (ATL) contains an implementation of `IUnknown` (and `IClassFactory` also) that you can reuse to your heart's content. You will learn all about it in the next chapter.

Implementing the IClassFactory Methods

Now that you have implemented the `IUnknown` interface in your class object, you need to implement the methods in the `IClassFactory` interface. `IClassFactory` has two methods: `CreateInstance` and `LockServer`. Add the code in Listing 4.5 to the `spellfactoryimpl.cpp` file to implement these two methods.

LISTING 4.5 *SPELLFACTORYIMPL.CPP*

```
STDMETHODIMP CSpellFactoryImpl::CreateInstance(LPUNKNOWN pUnkOuter,
REFIID riid, void** ppv)
{
    HRESULT hr;
    CSpellCheckImpl              *pSpellChecker;
    pSpellChecker=new CSpellCheckImpl();
    hr=pSpellChecker->QueryInterface(riid, ppv);
    if (SUCCEEDED(hr)) {
        gObjectCount++;
        return NOERROR;
    }
    else {
```

```
12.         delete pSpellChecker;
13.         *ppv=NULL;
14.         return E_NOINTERFACE;
15.     }
16. }
17.
18. STDMETHODIMP CSpellFactoryImpl::LockServer(BOOL fLock)
19. {
20.     if (fLock)
21.         gLockCount++;
22.     else
23.         gLockCount—;
24.     return NOERROR;
25. }
```

The implementation of the `CreateInstance` method is straight forward. On lines 5 and 6, you instantiate the `CSpellCheckImpl` class and then call `QueryInterface` on the new object to get the interface the user requested.

Remember that the constructor for `CSpellCheckImpl` sets the reference count to 0 and the `QueryInterface` function calls `AddRef` if it is successful. So there is no need to do an `AddRef` within `CreateInstance`. Notice that if the call to `QueryInterface` succeeded (the object supports the interface the user requested), you increment the global variable `gObjectCount` on line 8. If the call to `QueryInterface` failed (the object does not support the interface that the user requested), you delete the `CSpellCheckImpl` object you created, set the output parameter to NULL, and return an error code that indicates the object does not support the requested interface (see lines 12 thru 14). The implementation of the `LockServer` method manipulates the `gLockCount` global variable. Each time the user calls `LockServer` with `fLock` equal to `TRUE`, you increment `gLockCount`. Each time the user calls `LockServer` with `fLock` equal to `FALSE`, you decrement `gLockCount`. With this implementation (and if you initialize `gLockCount` to 0), you can easily determine if the server is locked: If `gLockCount` is greater than 0, the server is locked. If `gLockCount` is equal to 0, the server is not locked and can be unloaded.

In the next section, you will see where `gLockCount` and `gObjectCount` are defined and how the server actually is unloaded.

Creating the Required DLL Entry-Points

At this point, you should have two questions: (1) Since you must have a class object to create an instance of a COM class, how do you instantiate the class object to begin with? You have written a class, `CSpellFactoryImpl`, that implements your class object, but have not written any code yet that creates an instance of that class; (2) The `LockServer` method in `IClassFactory` lets you lock and unlock the server, but how does a DLL server actually get unloaded? All COM in-process (DLL) servers are required to implement and export two global functions: `DllGetClassObject` and `DllCanUnloadNow`. Understanding these functions answers both of these questions.

Instantiating the Class Object

Whether you call `CoCreateInstance` to instantiate a COM object or `CoGetClassObject` to retrieve the `IClassFactory` interface on a class object and then call its `CreateInstance` method, an instance of a COM classes class object must be created before you create a COM object. In COM, it is the Service Control Manager (the SCUM) that serves as an object broker. Both functions pass to the SCUM the CLSID of the COM class that you are trying to instantiate. The SCUM is responsible for finding the implementation of that class. When an instantiation request arrives, the SCUM performs the following steps (for an in-process server):

1. Using the CLSID, it consults the registry to find the path to the DLL that implements the class.
2. It calls `CoLoadLibrary` to load the DLL.
3. It calls the exported `DllGetClassObject` method in the DLL to instantiate the class object for the desired COM class.

At this point, one of two things could happen: if you called `CoCreateInstance`, the SCUM would request the `IClassFactory` interface on the class object when it called `DllGetClassObject`. `CoCreateInstance` would call `CreateInstance` on the `IClassFactory` interface. Finally, it would release the class factory interface (thereby destroying the class object) and then return the interface you requested. If you called `CoGetClassObject`, the SCUM would request, in its call to `DllGetClassObject`, whatever interface you specified when you called `CoGetClassObject`. The SCUM would then simply return this class object interface to you. Hopefully you see that the answer to the question of where does your class object get instantiated is (for an in-process server) in a function called `DllGetClassObject` that must be exported by all COM server DLLs. Let's create the `DllGetClassObject` function for your COM component.

Implementing DllGetClassObject for the SpellChecker

To create the `DllGetClassObject` function for the SpellChecker, you must first perform the following steps to add a new file to your project:

1. Select New... from the `File` menu (the New dialog appears).
2. Select `C/C++ Source File` from the list of file types.
3. Enter `spelldllfuncts` in the `File` name field.
4. Click `OK`.

You have now created a new file called `spelldllfuncts.cpp`. Add all the code shown in Listings 4.6 and 4.7 to this new file. Next, add the following code to the `spelldllfuncts.cpp` file.

LISTING 4.6 *DLLGETCLASSOBJECT*

```
#include "spellcheckimpl.h"
#include "spellfactoryimpl.h"
LONG gObjectCount=0;
LONG gLockCount=0;
STDAPI DllGetClassObject(REFCLSID rclsid, REFIID riid,void** ppv)
{
   HRESULT             hr;
   CSpellFactoryImpl *pObj;
   pObj=new CSpellFactoryImpl();
   hr=pObj->QueryInterface(riid, ppv);
   if (FAILED(hr)) {
      *ppv=NULL;
      delete pObj;
   }
   return hr;
}
```

This function is so simple there is little point in explaining it. You simply instantiate the class that implements your class object and then call `QueryInterface` to obtain the requested interface. As before, the `AddRef` is done within `QueryInterface`. Notice that the `gObjectCount` and `gLockCount` variables are defined and initialized in this file. The variable `gLockCount` is used in the `DllCanUnloadNow` function that is explained next.

Unloading the Server

Let's tackle the question of how a COM in-process server gets unloaded. The answer is that the server's client must use a COM API function called `CoFreeUnusedLibraries`. `CoFreeUnusedLibraries` will enumerate the list of DLL servers that have been loaded by COM and call the `DllCanUnloadNow` function (if the server exports it) to ask if it is okay to unload the server. If the server returns a `TRUE` reply, then the DLL will be unloaded. MFC applications and the Visual Basic runtime call CoFreeUnusedLibraries in their message loops.

To allow a client to free your server when it is not needed, you must implement and export the DllCanUnloadNow function. It must return TRUE (actually S_OK) if the server can be unloaded, FALSE otherwise. It is because of this implementation of this function that you have defined the gObjectCount and gLockCount variables. You will use them in your implementation of DllCanUnloadNow.

Implementing DllCanUnloadNow for the SpellChecker

To implement DllCanUnloadNow add the code in Listing 4.7 to the spelldllfuncts.cpp file.

LISTING 4.7 *DLLGETCLASSOBJECT*

```
STDAPI DllCanUnloadNow(void)
{
    if (gObjectCount==0 && gLockCount==0)
        return S_OK;
    else
        return S_FALSE;
}
```

As you can see, the implementation of this function is simple. If there are no objects implemented in this DLL that are still being used (gObjectCount==0) and the server is not locked (gLockCount==0), then the server can be freed, and you return S_OK. If either of these conditions is not met, then the server should not be unloaded and you return S_FALSE.

Creating the Registration Functions

As you learned in Chapter 3, all COM classes must contain registry entries that (among other things) allow the COM runtime to find the server that implements the class.

Only create-able COM classes need registry entries.

How do you get these entries into the registry? The answer is COM supports protocols that let both in-process (DLL) and out-of-process (Executable) servers to register themselves. By forcing the server to do its own registration, no one else has to worry about the exact entries the server contains. For an out-of-process server if you invoke the server and pass in the parameter `/regserver`, the server is supposed to insert into the registry all the entries it needs and then terminate. You could type the following at a command prompt:

```
Servername.exe /regserver
```

To unregister the server, you need only invoke the server again and pass the parameter `/unregserver`. To support self-registration, an in-process server must implement and export two well-known entry points: `DllRegisterServer` and `DllUnregisterServer`. To register the server, you need only load the DLL—using either the `LoadLibrary` or `CoLoadLibrary` API functions—and then get a pointer to `DllRegisterServer` using the `GetProcAddress` function, and then invoke `DllRegisterServer`. To unregister the server, call the `DllUnregisterServer` function. You don't have to implement the logic to load the server and call the register server functions yourself, Microsoft provides a utility called `regsvr32` that does all of this. You can find `regsvr32` in your Windows system directory. On Windows 2000, your system directory will most likely be `c:\winnt\system32`. On Windows 95, you will likely find it at `c:\windows\system`. You can register a server by entering the following command at a command prompt (Windows 2000) or DOS prompt (95):

```
Regsvr32 servername.dll
```

You can unregister the server by passing a /u parameter to regsvr32 as follows:

```
Regsvr32 /u servername.dll
```

The `regsvr32` command will work if your in-process server implements and exports the `DllRegisterServer` and `DllUnregisterServer` functions. In these functions you will use the registry API to write the required entries into the registry.

The Registry API

Table 4.3 summarizes the key functions in the registry API (key in this case means you will be using them).

TABLE 4.3 Registry API functions

Method Name	Method Purpose
RegCreateKey	Creates the specified key. If the key already exists in the registry, the function opens it.
RegSetValueEx	Sets the data and type of a specified value under a registry key.
RegCloseKey	Releases a handle to the specified key.
RegDeleteKey	Function deletes the specified subkey. The subkey to be deleted must not have subkeys.

You can read the online Help if you would like to find out more about these functions.

Implementing DllRegisterServer and DllUnregisterServer

You should now implement the `DllRegisterServer` function so it will add the following keys:

```
\HKEY_CLASSES_ROOT\CLSID\{57B7A8A0-E4D7-11d0-818D-
444553540000}="Spellchecker Object"
\HKEY_CLASSES_ROOT\CLSID\{57B7A8A0-E4D7-11d0-818D-
444553540000}\InprocServer32=[path of the server DLL ]
\HKEY_CLASSES_ROOT\CLSID\{57B7A8A0-E4D7-11d0-818D-
444553540000}\ProgID="Spellchecker.Object.1"
\HKEY_CLASSES_ROOT\Spellchecker.Object.1="Spellchecker Object"
\HKEY_CLASSES_ROOT\Spellchecker.Object.1\CLSID="{57B7A8A0-E4D7-11d0-
818D-444553540000}"
```

The `DllUnregisterServer` function should remove these keys. To implement the registration functions, begin by performing the following steps to add a new file to your project:

1. Select `New...` from the `File` menu (the New dialog appears).
2. Select `C/C++ Source File` from the list of file types.
3. Enter `regfuncts` in the `File` name field.
4. Click `OK`.

Next, add the code in Listing 4.8 to this file.

LISTING 4.8 *REGISTRY-RELATED FUNCTIONS*

```
#include <olectl.h>
HINSTANCE g_hinstDll;
const char *g_RegTable[][2] = {
```

```
    { "CLSID\\{57B7A8A0-E4D7-11d0-818D-444553540000}","Spellchecker
    Object"},
       { "CLSID\\{57B7A8A0-E4D7-11d0-818D-
       444553540000}\\InprocServer32",(const char*)-1},
       { "CLSID\\{57B7A8A0-E4D7-11d0-818D-
       444553540000}\\ProgID","Spellchecker.Object.1"},
       { "Spellchecker.Object.1","Spellchecker Object"},
       { "Spellchecker.Object.1\\CLSID","{57B7A8A0-E4D7-11d0-818D-
       444553540000}"}
};

STDAPI DllRegisterServer()
{
    HRESULT hr = S_OK;
    char szFileName[MAX_PATH];
    HKEY hkey;
       GetModuleFileName(g_hinstDll,szFileName,MAX_PATH);
       int nEntries = sizeof(g_RegTable)/sizeof(*g_RegTable);
    for (int i=0; SUCCEEDED(hr) && i < nEntries; i++ )  {
          const char *pszKeyName   = g_RegTable[i][0];
          const char *pszValue     =g_RegTable[i][1];
          if (pszValue==(const char *)-1)
             pszValue=szFileName;
          long err=RegCreateKey(HKEY_CLASSES_ROOT,pszKeyName,&hkey);
       if (err == ERROR_SUCCESS) {
          err = RegSetValueExA(hkey,0,0,REG_SZ,(const BYTE *)pszValue,
          (strlen(pszValue)+1));
          RegCloseKey(hkey);
       }
       if (err != ERROR_SUCCESS) {
          DllUnregisterServer();
          hr = SELFREG_E_CLASS;
       }
    }
    return hr;
}

STDAPI DllUnregisterServer()
{
       HRESULT hr=S_OK;
       int nEntries = sizeof(g_RegTable)/sizeof(*g_RegTable);
    for (int i = nEntries-1; i >= 0 ; i– )
    {
          const char *pszKeyName   = g_RegTable[i][0];
```

```
42.             long err = RegDeleteKeyA(HKEY_CLASSES_ROOT,pszKeyName);
43.             if (err != ERROR_SUCCESS)
44.         hr = S_FALSE;
45.     }
46.     return hr;
47. }
48.
49. BOOL APIENTRY DllMain(HINSTANCE hDLLInst, DWORD fdwReason, LPVOID
    lpvReserved)
50. {
51. switch (fdwReason)
52.     {
52.         case DLL_PROCESS_ATTACH :
53.             g_hinstDll = hDLLInst ;
54.     }
55.     return TRUE ;
56. }
```

When I first started teaching my class, I had an implementation of `DllRegisterServer` and `DllUnregisterServer` that was far more complicated than the one here. After reading Don Box's *Essential COM* book, I liked his implementation of `DllRegisterServer` and `DllUnregisterServer` much better than mine. So I started using it. What you are actually seeing here is a slightly modified version of his code. The first two lines contain an include file for the registry functions and a global instance handle that you will use later.

Lines 3 through 9 contain the declaration of an Nx2 array of strings. Compare this array of strings with the list of registry keys that you want to add. Each row in the array corresponds to one of the registry keys that you want to add. The first element in each row is the name of the registry key. The keys are specified relative to the `HKEY_CLASSES_ROOT` root key. The second element in each row is the value that will be entered at that key, although the following line does not adhere to this rule:

```
{ "CLSID\\{57B7A8A0-E4D7-11d0-818D-444553540000}
\\InprocServer32",(const char*)-1}
```

The value at this key should be the path of the server DLL. You must, however, execute some logic to determine the path of the server DLL. So for now, you have inserted the place holder –1. Later when you process the array of strings to insert the values into the registry, you can substitute the path of the server DLL for the row whose value is –1.

On line 16, you use the Windows API function, `GetModuleFileName`, to determine the path of the DLL server. On the next line, you pass the global instance handle, `g_hinstDLL`, as the first parameter to this function. You will see shortly where this instance handle comes from. Next you determine the number or rows in the string array: The code in lines 18-27 loops over all the rows in the array of strings and extracts the name and value for each key from the character array and calls `RegSetValueExA` to insert the key into the registry. If the value for the key is –1, you substitute the path of the server module (remember this was your place holder that I mentioned earlier). If any of the preceeding code fails, lines 28–31 will immediately unregister the server.

The implementation of the `DllUnregisterServer` function is straightforward (see lines 36–47 in Listing 4.8) in comparison to `DllRegisterServer`. You simply walk the array backward and delete each key. It is important that you walk the array backward because you must delete all the subkeys of a key before you can delete the key. Notice that the array of strings is arranged starting with parent keys and then progressing to the lowest-level child keys; this was intentional.

The only remaining issue concerning the registry functions is how do you get the global instance handle, `g_hinstDll`? The answer is that Windows passes it to you when your application is first loaded. DLLs have a main function that operates exactly like the classic main function in a console application. The DLL function is called `DllMain` and Windows calls it right after a DLL is loaded. The `DllMain` is shown on lines 49–56 of Listing 4.8. The first parameter function to this function is the instance handle for the DLL. The `DllMain` function saves this instance handle in the global variable `g_hinstDll` so you can use it to determine the filename of the server.

Only one more thing is needed to make your server work and that is to create a definition (DEF) file to export the `DllGetClassObject`, `DllCanUnloadNow`, `DllRegisterServer`, and `DllUnregisterServer` functions. To do this, perform the following steps to add a new file to your project:

1. Select `New...` from the `File` menu (the New dialog appears).
2. Select `Text File` from the list of file types.
3. Enter `spellcheck.def` in the `File` name field.
4. Click `OK`.

Now add the code in Listing 4.9 to this file.

LISTING 4.9 *SPELLCHECK.DEF*

```
EXPORTS
    DllGetClassObject       PRIVATE
    DllCanUnloadNow         PRIVATE
    DllRegisterServer       PRIVATE
    DllUnregisterServer     PRIVATE
```

In this file, you name the functions that will be exported from this DLL. The PRIVATE keyword indicates that the functions are being exported only to system-level software like the COM runtime. Now you can build your server. Press `F7` or select `Build simplecomobject.dll` from the `Build` menu. After the server is compiled and linked, select `Register Control` from the `Tools`. This runs `regsvr32` on your DLL to register it. You are now ready to create a client.

Creating a Client

The client for your COM server will be a dialog-based application that you will build using MFC. This is an application whose main window is a dialog box that you can build using the Visual C++ resource editor. To build your client application, you will perform the following steps:

1. Create a dialog-based project using the MFC AppWizard.
2. Create the user interface.
3. Add the code needed to enable COM support.
4. Implement the client.
5. Instantiate the Spell Checker COM Object and Set the Interface Pointer.

Creating a Dialog-Based Project Using the MFC AppWizard

Start Visual C++ and then execute the following steps:

1. Select `New...` from the `File` menu (the `New` dialog appears).
2. Click the `Projects` tab.
3. Select `MFC AppWizard` (exe) from the presented list of project types.
4. Enter `simplecomclient` in the `Project` Name field.
5. Click `OK` (the MFC App Wizard appears).
6. Click the radio button labeled: `Dialog-based`.
7. Click `Finish` (the New Project Information dialog appears).
8. Click `OK`.

You will have created a project that will build an application whose main window is a dialog that you can draw using the Visual C++ resource editor. To implement the application, you first need to create the user interface using the Visual C++ resource editor.

Creating the User Interface

The user interface for our COM client application will look like the one shown in Figure 4.6.

If you are reading this book, you most likely know how to build a user interface like this without my describing it to you in detail. Using the MFC class wizard, map button clicked (`BN_CLICKED`) message handlers to the three buttons on the main window dialog as specified in Table 4.4.

TABLE 4.4 Message Handler Methods

Button Caption	Message Handler for Button
Check Spelling	OnSpellcheckerButton
Ellipsis (...)	OnBrowseButton
Load Dictionary	OnLoadDictionary

If you gave your client project the name I specified (`simplecomclient`), the message handlers shown in Table 4.4 should be member functions of a class called `CSimplecomclientDlg`.

Next, use the MFC ClassWizard to map variables to the two edit boxes on the main window dialog. The edit box closest to the top of the dialog allows the user to enter a string that will be spell checked. The edit box closer to the bottom of the dialog is where the user can enter the path to a custom dictionary for the spell checker to use. Map these edit boxes as shown in Table 4.5.

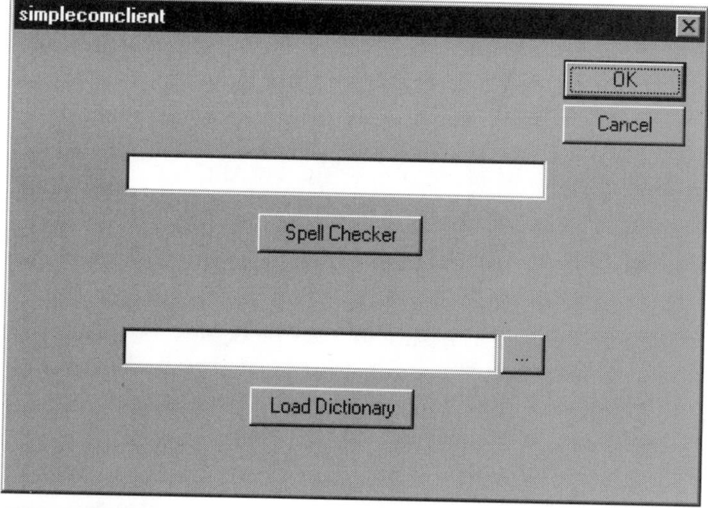

FIGURE 4.6 The `Simplecomclient` User Interface.

TABLE 4.5 Mapping of Member Variables to Controls

Edit Box Purpose	Map to member variable	Member variable type
Word to be spell checked	m_word	CString
Path to a custom dictionary for the spell checker	m_dictionaryFile	CString

Adding the Code Needed to Initialize COM

This section is very important. If you do not add the code shown in this section to your client project, nothing else will work. There is a simple explanation and a complicated explanation for what you are about to do. The complicated (and more accurate) explanation is that before a thread instantiates or uses any COM objects, it must enter an apartment. Before the thread terminates, it should leave the apartment. The simple explanation is that you must call an initialization function before you use COM and you should call a termination function when you are done using COM. If you do not understand the complicated explanation, don't worry. I discuss apartments when I talk about COM threading in Chapter 9. For the purposes of this chapter, the simple explanation will suffice.

Apartments are a conceptual construct in COM that are used to isolate the threading requirements of a COM object from the threading environment provided by its client. For instance, a COM object that is not thread-safe should only be called by a single threaded client. But you may want to use this COM object from both single-threaded and multi-threaded clients. Apartments make this possible.

To initialize COM (enter an apartment) you must call the `CoInitialize` method in the COM API. If `CoInitialize` is successful, it returns a key that you should pass to the `CoUninitialize` method before you terminate. MFC has a single method called `AfxOleInit` that does both. It calls `CoInitialize` and if the call to `CoInitialize` is successful, it calls `CoUninitialize` for you when the application shuts down. `AfxOleInit` should be called only once and it should be called before you do anything else with COM. The best place to call `AfxOleInit` is in MFC's equivalent of main, the `InitInstance` method of your `Application` class. Add the following two lines of code at the very top of the `InitInstance` method of your `Application` class:

```
BOOL CSimplecomclientApp::InitInstance()
{
   if (!AfxOleInit())
        AfxMessageBox("Could not initialize COM");
// the rest of the code in this function is omitted for clarity
}
```

If you named your project `simplecomclient`, the `Application` class is called `CSimplecomclientapp` and you will find the implementation of this class in a file called `CSimplecomclient.cpp`.

Implementing the Client

To complete the implementation of your COM client, you need to do the following:

1. Copy MIDL-generated files from the server to the client.
2. Add a COM interface pointer to the main window dialog.
3. Instantiate the spell checker COM object and set the interface pointer.
4. Implement the check spelling, browse, and load dictionary buttons.
5. Release the interface pointer when the main window dialog is destroyed.

COPYING MIDL-GENERATED FILES FROM THE SERVER TO THE CLIENT

There are two MIDL-generated files your client will need: (1) `spellcheck_i.c` and (2) `spellcheck.h`. `Spellcheck.h` contains the compile-able COM interface declarations. `Spellcheck_i.c` is needed primarily for convenience; it contains variable declarations for your server's GUIDs.

In practice, these files will either be included with a COM server, or you can reverse engineer them using the servers type library. You can always count on having a type library for a COM server.

Copy both of these files from the directory of your server project to the directory of your client project.

ADDING A COM INTERFACE POINTER TO YOUR MAIN WINDOW DIALOG

The main window dialog of your application will contain the interface pointer for your spell checker COM object. You can instantiate the COM object right before the main window dialog is shown, and release it when the dialog is destroyed. Add only the bolded lines to the main window dialog in your project:

```
#include "spellcheck.h"
class CSimplecomclientDlg : public CDialog
{
// All other code in this class is not shown for clarity
private:
   ISpellChecker* pSpeller;
};
```

If you named the project `simplecomclient`, the main window dialog class is the class called `CSimplecomclientDlg`.

Instantiating the SpellChecker COM Object and Setting the Interface Pointer

The `OnInitDialog` method is called after the main window dialog is created and right before it is shown. This is the perfect place to instantiate your spell checker COM object. To instantiate the COM object, add only the bold lines to the `OnInitDialog` method of your `Main Window Dialog` class:

```
#include "spellcheck.h"   // add at the top of CSimplecomclientDlg.cpp
#include "spellcheck_i.c" // add at the top of CSimplecomclientDlg.cpp
BOOL CSimplecomclientDlg::OnInitDialog()
{
   CDialog::OnInitDialog();

   // All other code in this file is omitted for clarity

   // TODO: Add extra initialization here
HRESULT hRes;
hRes=CoCreateInstance(CLSID_CSpellChecker,NULL,CLSCTX_ALL,
IID_ISpellChecker,(void**)&pSpeller);
   if (FAILED(hRes))
   {
      AfxMessageBox("Could not instantiate object");
   }
   return TRUE;  // return TRUE  unless you set the focus to a control
}
```

The key line here is the call to CoCreateInstance. CoCreateInstance is COM's equivalent of the C++ new operator. You call this function when you want to create a new instance of a COM class. The first parameter is the GUID of the COM class that you wish to instantiate. The second parameter is the controlling unknown of an outer object. It is only non-null if the object is being instantiated as part of an aggregate. The third parameter is a so-called class context. With this parameter you can specify the type(s) of server implementation that you will accept. For instance, you could have set this parameter to CLSCTX_INPROC_SERVER. This value means that you want the call to fail unless the COM class has an in-process server. You can also pass CLSCTX_LOCAL_SERVER to specify a local, out-of-process implementation, or CLSCTX_REMOTE_SERVER to specify a remote, out-of-process implementation. CLSCTX_ALL will search for an in-process implementation first. If this fails, it will attempt to find a local executable. If it does not find that either, it will search for a remote implementation. CLSCTX_ALL is the most flexible value that you can input for this parameter and it is the value you should use most of the time. The fourth argument to CoCreateInstance is the GUID of the initial interface you wish to receive on the spell checker object. The fifth argument is an output and it will contain the requested interface pointer if the call to CoCreateInstance is successful. Notice you are setting the interface pointer that was added to the main window dialog class.

IMPLEMENTING THE CHECKSPELLING, BROWSE, AND LOAD DICTIONARY BUTTONS

Add the code in Listing 4.10 to the message handler for the CheckSpelling button.

LISTING 4.10 *MESSAGE HANDLER FOR THE CHECKSPELLING BUTTON*

```
void CSimplecomclientDlg::OnSpellcheckerButton()
{
   BOOL isCorrect;
   HRESULT hRes;
   UpdateData(TRUE);

   char *str=m_word.GetBuffer(80);

   hRes=pSpeller->CheckSpelling((unsigned char *)str,&isCorrect);
   if (FAILED(hRes))
   {
      AfxMessageBox("Could not invoke CheckSpelling method");
   }
      if (isCorrect)
      AfxMessageBox("Spellcheck complete");
   else
      AfxMessageBox("The word is misspelled");
}
```

The key line of code in this method is the call to the CheckSpelling method through the interface pointer. Notice how the return value is passed back as an output parameter.

Add the code in Listing 4.11 to the message handler for the browse (ellipsis) button.

LISTING 4.11 *MESSAGE HANDLER FOR THE BROWSER BUTTON*

```
void CSimplecomclientDlg::OnBrowseButton()
{
   CFileDialog dlg(TRUE);
   if (dlg.DoModal()==IDOK)
   {
      m_dictionaryFile=dlg.GetPathName();
      UpdateData(FALSE);
   }
}
```

This code has nothing to do with COM. It is simply code to instantiate and show the common file open dialog. This is done so the user can easily select a custom dictionary. When Listing 4.12 is added to the message handler for the load custom dictionary button it will cause the dictionary to actually be loaded into the spell checker.

LISTING 4.12 *MESSAGE HANDLER FOR THE LOAD DICTIONARY BUTTON*

```
void CSimplecomclientDlg::OnLoaddictionaryButton()
{
   HRESULT hr;
   UpdateData(TRUE);
   hr=pSpeller->UseCustomDictionary((unsigned char *)
   m_dictionaryFile.GetBuffer(80));
   if (FAILED(hr))
      AfxMessageBox("Cannot load dictionary");
}
```

RELEASING THE INTERFACE POINTER WHEN THE MAIN WINDOW DIALOG IS DESTROYED

Finally, you need to Release the spell checker interface pointer when the main window dialog is destroyed. If the reference count is zero after Release is called, the spell checker COM object will be destroyed. Add a message handler for the WM_DESTROYED windows message and add the code in Listing 4.13 to the message handler.

LISTING 4.13 *MESSAGE HANDLER FOR WM_DESTROYED*

```
void CSimplecomclientDlg::OnDestroy()
{
   if (pSpeller!=0)
      pSpeller->Release();
   CDialog::OnDestroy();
}
```

At last you are done. Compile the client by pressing F7 and test. You should be able to type in any of the words that have been added to the dictionary. Notice that the spell checker only interprets a word as correct if there is a match for the word in the dictionary. Try out the custom dictionary functionality. You should be able to create a file that has several words in it (one on each line), select it using the `Browse` button and then click the `Load Custom Dictionary` method. This causes the words in the file to be added to the dictionary.

Summary

So there you have it. You have successfully (I hope) built your first COM object. In the process, you have learned how the `IUnknown` interface is implemented, what a class object is, what functions are required of all DLL-based COM servers, and how to write registry update functions. Pretty good for one chapter. In practice, you will not build COM objects this way. Visual C++ has the Active Template Library (ATL) and associated wizards to make developing COM servers easier and it now has native support for COM in its C++ compiler to make it easier to write COM clients. In the next chapter, I use these technologies to build a similar server and a client in a far more efficient manner.

FIVE

Making It Simple with ATL and Visual C++ COM Native Support

In this chapter, you will learn how to use the Active Template Library (ATL) to make it easier to build a COM component. ATL is a little difficult to use. It does not hide all of COM's details from you. You will need to understand COM, IDL, and C++ templates fairly well to use ATL effectively. Fortunately, Visual C++ 6.0 also contains the ATL Object Wizard, which makes it much easier to use ATL than if you were trying to write ATL code from scratch. You will also learn how to use this wizard in this chapter.

ATL is primarily used for developing COM servers. Microsoft realized that it was important to simplify the creation of COM clients. Not everyone wants to understand the intricacies of the `CoCreateInstance` function, and many programmers have a hard enough time remembering to free memory let alone release interface pointers. To simplify the development of COM clients, Microsoft added several non-standard extensions to its C++ compiler. These language extensions include the ability to auto-magically generate wrapper classes from a type library and associate a GUID with a class or struct. Microsoft's COM-enabling extensions try to make it as easy for you to use COM classes as it is to use plain C++ classes. These language extensions, which are collectively called Visual C++ native COM support, are also a precursor to Microsoft's ultimate vision for COM+: a Universal COM runtime that will make it as easy to build and use COM classes as it is to use the native classes of any programming language. In this chapter, you will also learn how to use native COM support to build a COM client.

In practice, ATL, the ATL Object Wizard, and Native COM Support are the tools you will use most of the time when you are building COM components and clients with Visual C++.

A Quick Introduction to ATL

I don't intend to give an exhaustive introduction to ATL in this section. That would require an entire book. In fact, an excellent introduction to ATL has been written: *ATL Internals* by Brent Rector and Chris Sells is my ATL reference book of choice and one of the best COM books ever written. In this chapter, I will give you enough ATL basics so you can follow along with the example I will present in this chapter.

The `CheckSpelling` and `UseCustomDictionary` methods in your spell checker implementation class in Chapter 4 contained the only value-added logic in your component. The rest of the code in your spell checker component was required so your component would work with COM. Metaphorically speaking, you had to create a connector so your component could plug into the COM software bus. Fortunately, most of this COM-specific code is generic. The implementation of `IUnknown` is essentially the same for any COM class. Similarly, class objects, `DllGetClassObject`, `DllCanUnloadNow`, and the registration functions all have fairly standard implementations. Microsoft recognized this and created a C++ library that encapsulates most of the COM-specific code that you need to write to build a COM server. This library is called the Active Template Library (ATL). Although ATL can be somewhat difficult to use, using it allows you to concentrate on the business logic of your COM components rather than having to concern yourself with low-level, COM details.

Version 3.0 of ATL is bundled with Visual C++ 6.0.

The word Template is used in the name of ATL because it depends heavily on the use of C++ templates. Although you don't have to be an expert with C++ templates to use ATL, the more you know about C++ templates, the easier time you will have.

The Key ATL Classes

The key classes in ATL are: CComObjectRootEx, CComCoClass, and CComModule. ATL contains dozens more classes, but these, in my opinion, are the classes that represent the essence of ATL.

CCOMOBJECTROOTEX

CComObjectRootEx contains an implementation of IUnknown. All of the logic required to implement reference counting via the AddRef and Release methods is implemented in this class. An implementation of QueryInterface is also provided. The implementation of QueryInterface in CComObjectRootEx requires you to specify the interfaces that your COM class is implementing using COM_MAP macros. These macros use a table-driven scheme similar to MFC message maps. The CComObjectRootEx class takes template parameters that let you specify the threading model of the COM class.

Specifying the threading model for a COM class is your way of indicating the threading requirements of the COM class. You can specify that the COM class is safe to use in a multi-threaded environment, or you can ask COM to guarantee that instances of the COM class will only be accessed by a single thread. I talk about COM's threading support and Apartments, which are used to implement COM's threading support, in Chapter 9.

CCOMCOCLASS

CComCoClass implements the class object for your COM class. Remember in Chapter 4 that the IClassFactory interface, which should be implemented by your class object, provides the link between a COM class and the code that implements the COM class. It should be obvious then why the template parameters for CComCoClass are the CLSID of the COM class you are implementing and the name of the C++ class that is used to implement the COM class. The overall logic of a class object is fairly generic, but the implementation must work with your CLSIDs and your implementation classes. The template parameters let you make this generic code work with your COM classes and implementation classes.

CCOMMODULE

The CComModule class in ATL implements the server-level logic of a COM component. This class contains an implementation of the DllGetClassObject and DllCanUnloadNow functions that you implemented in the previous chapter. It also contains an implementation of the registration functions: DllRegisterServer and DllUnregisterServer. The implementation is conceptually similar to the implementation you developed in Chapter 4.

CComModule has a string of registry entries that DllRegisterServer and DllUnregisterServer read to register and unregister the server, respectively. The only difference is that the string is a Windows resource instead of a static string that is compiled into your source code.

How It All Fits Together

To implement a COM class with ATL, you define an implementation class that inherits from CComObjectRootEx, CComCoClass, and the interfaces that you are planning to implement. The implementation of a COM class that implements the ISpellChecker interface from Chapter 4 and a new IGrammarChecker interface is shown in Listing 5.1.

LISTING 5.1 *AN EXAMPLE ATL CLASS*

```
// CDocumentChecker implements the COM class defined as follows in IDL
//     coclass CDocumentChecker {
//         interface ISpellChecker;
//         interface IGrammarChecker;
// };
//
class CDocumentChecker :
       public CComObjectRootEx<CComSingleThreadModel>,
       public CComCoClass<CDocumentChecker, &CLSID_DocumentChecker>,
       public ISpellChecker,
       public IGrammarChecker
{
// The constructors and destructors for CDocumentChecker go here...
BEGIN_COM_MAP(CSpellChecker)
       COM_INTERFACE_ENTRY(ISpellChecker)
       COM_INTERFACE_ENTRY(IGrammarChecker)
END_COM_MAP()
// The methods in the ISpellChecker and IGrammarChecker interfaces go here...
}
```

Notice that this class inherits from CComObjectRootEx and CComCoClass. Because of this, there is no need to define the IUnknown methods: AddRef, Release, and QueryInterface, or to implement a separate class object. Through the magic of C++ multiple inheritance, any calls to IUnknown methods through either the ISpellChecker or IGrammarChecker interfaces (they, like all COM interfaces, inherit from IUnknown) will be routed to the implementation of IUnknown in CComObjectRootEx. This implementation class also inherits from the interfaces that you are implementing (ISpellChecker and IGrammarChecker in this case). The COM map entries list the interfaces that this class is implementing and are required if the QueryInterface method in CComObjectRootEx is to function correctly. The only thing you need to do to complete the implementation of this COM class is to redeclare and implement those methods that are contained in the ISpellChecker and IGrammarChecker interfaces.

Thanks to ATL, implementing the server for your COM class is also easy. You still have to create the usual COM entry points for an in-process server: DllGetClassObject, DllCanUnloadNow, DllRegisterServer, and DllUnregisterServer. But your implementations of these functions can simply delegate to ATL's CComModule class as shown in Listing 5.2.

LISTING 5.2 *ATL'S IMPLEMENTATION OF THE REQUIRED ENTRY POINTS*

```
CcomModule Module;
STDAPI DllCanUnloadNow(void)
{
   return (_Module.GetLockCount()==0) ? S_OK : S_FALSE;
}

STDAPI DllGetClassObject(REFCLSID rclsid, REFIID riid, LPVOID* ppv)
{
   return _Module.GetClassObject(rclsid, riid, ppv);
}

STDAPI DllRegisterServer(void)
{
   return _Module.RegisterServer(TRUE);
}

STDAPI DllUnregisterServer(void)
{
   return _Module.UnregisterServer(TRUE);
}
```

The implementation of the DllRegisterServer and DllUnregisterServer functions depends on a registry script file. CComModule reads this script file and either inserts or deletes the registry entries it contains. This file has the extension .rgs. Listing 5.3 shows an example registry script file.

LISTING 5.3 *A REGISTRY SCRIPT FILE*

```
HKCR
{
   FirstATLObject.DocumentChecker.1 = s 'DocumentChecker Class'
   {
      CLSID = s '{02D819CE-AFF9-11D2-998A-78DC09C10000}'
   }
   FirstATLObject.DocumentChecker = s 'DocumentChecker Class'
   {
      CLSID = s '{02D819CE-AFF9-11D2-998A-78DC09C10000}'
      CurVer = s 'FirstATLObject.DocumentChecker.1'
   }
   NoRemove CLSID
   {
      ForceRemove {02D819CE-AFF9-11D2-998A-78DC09C10000} = s
 'DocumentChecker Class'
      {
         ProgID = s 'FirstATLObject.DocumentChecker.1'
         VersionIndependentProgID = s 'FirstATLObject.DocumentChecker'
         InprocServer32 = s '%MODULE%'
         {
            val ThreadingModel = s 'Apartment'
         }
         'TypeLib' = s '{02D819C1-AFF9-11D2-998A-78DC09C10000}'
      }
   }
}
```

Using ATL is even easier than I have shown so far. Visual C++ provides two wizards that make using ATL much easier: the ATL COM AppWizard and the ATL Object Wizard. These wizards actually save you from having to write any of the code just presented. With the help of these wizards, building a COM server is simply a matter of selecting what server type you want (in-process or out-of-process) in the AppWizard and then adding COM classes to the server using the Object Wizard. The only code that you have to write is the business logic of your component. Let's build an improved version of the component that you built in Chapter 4 so you can see how easy it is to build COM servers with ATL.

The Writer's Component

You will create a COM component called the Writer's Component. This will implement a single COM class called `DocumentChecker` that implements spell checking and grammar checking. This COM class will implement the `ISpellChecker` interface that was defined in Chapter 4. It will also implement a simple grammar checking interface called `IGrammarChecker` and support rich error information.

The DocumentChecker COM Class

`DocumentChecker` implements a total of four interfaces (3 + `IUnknown`). It will implement `ISpellChecker` in the same manner as it was used in Chapter 4. It will also support a new interface called `IGrammarChecker`. `IGrammarChecker` has a single method called `CheckGrammar`. `CheckGrammar` takes a null-terminated, wide character string as input and checks to see if the string contains both a comma and a period. If it contains both, the string is considered to have correct grammar. If either is missing, then the string contains incorrect grammar. (I said it was a simple grammar checker.) Your server will also use an interface called `ISupportsErrorInfo`, which indicates to a client that your server supports rich error information (see the sidebar in this section about Rich Error Information). A diagram of your document checker COM class is shown in Figure 5.1.

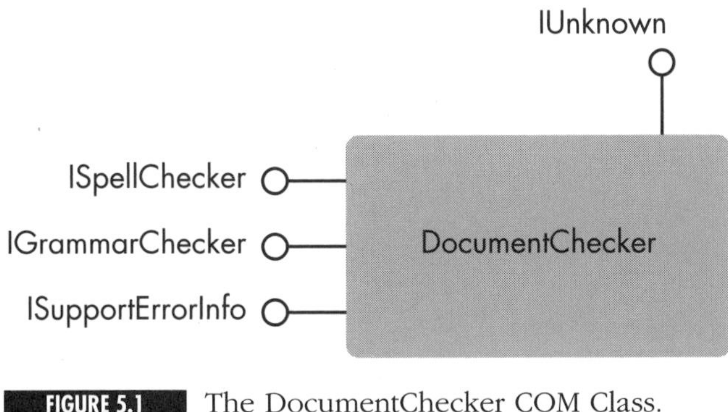

FIGURE 5.1 The DocumentChecker COM Class.

Rich Error Information

The simple spell checker returns a user-defined handle to a result (HRESULT) if the user enters a non-existent path for the custom dictionary. This is the standard COM way of returning error information. For many kinds of errors, just returning an error code is enough. But in some situations, a server may want to return additional error information like a textual description of the error, or a description of the source of the error.

If you have used an object-oriented language like C++ or Java, you have probably used their language-specific exception mechanisms. The exception mechanism in most object-oriented languages allows you to create and throw exception objects that contain information about the error that occurred. This information usually includes a textual description of the error, but it can include other things, like the filename and context ID of help information related to the error. The following code shows the skeleton of a C++ method that throws an exception when a division by zero error occurs and a client that catches the exception:

```
#include <iostream>
#include <string>
using namespace std;
class MyException {
public:
   MyException(const char *desc) : mDescription(desc) { }
   string Description() { return mDescription; }
private:
   string mDescription;
};

int Divide(int arg1,int arg2)
{
   if  (arg2==0) {
      throw MyException("divide by zero");
   }
   else {
      return arg1/arg2;
   }
}

int main()
{
   try {
      Divide(3,0);
   }
   catch (MyException e) {
      cout << e.Description() << endl;
   }
   catch (...) {
      cout << "An unknown exception was caught";
   }
   return 0;
}
```

In this example, you first declared a class, `MyException`, that contains a textual description of an error. If a numerator equal to zero is passed to the Divide function, it throws a `MyException` object to its calling routine. The calling routine indicates that it wishes to catch any exceptions the `Divide` method throws by enclosing the call to Divide in a "try" block. Each try block has one or more "catch" blocks associated with it. If an exception of the type specified in a catch block occurs, the code in that catch block is executed. So if a `MyException` is thrown by the `Divide` method, the calling routine will write the error description to cout. If an exception object of any other type is caught (that's what catch(...) means), the calling routine writes the string, "An unknown exception was caught", to cout. The syntax for using Java exceptions is virtually the same as the syntax for using C++ exceptions.

The problem with Java and C++ exceptions is that they are language-specific. You cannot, easily generate an exception in a Java method and catch it in a calling C++ method. In fact, because the C++ standard does not specify how exceptions should be implemented, you cannot easily pass exceptions between C++ code that was compiled with different compilers.

COM has a mechanism that is conceptually similar to C++ or Java exceptions, but it is implemented in a programming-language independent way. A COM class indicates to its clients that it supports rich error information by implementing the `ISupportErrorInfo` interface. When an error occurs, a COM object that implements `ISupportErrorInfo` can send rich error information to its client by first calling the `CreateErrorInfo` function in the COM API to create a COM exception object. The `CreateErrorInfo` function returns an interface called `ICreateErrorInfo`. The COM object can use the `ICreateErrorInfo` interface to populate the COM exception object with the source, description, help file, and help context ID for the error that just occurred. Once the exception object is populated with all the necessary error information, the COM object can send the exception object to its client by first using `QueryInterface` to obtain the `IErrorInfo` interface on the exception object and then passing this interface to the `SetErrorInfo` function as shown here.

```
STDMETHODIMP CSpellChecker::UseCustomDictionary(unsigned char
        *filename) {
// code omitted for clarity
    if (!dictionaryFile.is_open()) {
        ICreateErrorInfo *pCreateErrorInfo;
        HRESULT hr=CreateErrorInfo(&pCreateErrorInfo);
        hr=pCreateErrorInfo->SetGUID(IID_ISpellChecker);
        hr=pCreateErrorInfo->SetDescription(
            OLESTR("Dictionary file not found"));
        IErrorInfo *pErrorInfo;
        hr=pCreateErrorInfo->QueryInterface(IID_IErrorInfo,
                (void**)&pErrorInfo);
        hr=SetErrorInfo(0,pErrorInfo);
        pCreateErrorInfo->Release();
        pErrorInfo->Release();
        return E_DICTIONARYFILENOTFOUND;
```

```
    }
// code omitted for clarity
}
```

The client can then call the GetErrorInfo function in the COM API to retrieve this error information as shown here.

```
void CComclientDlg::OnLoadDictionaryButton()
{
  HRESULT hRes;
  ISpellChecker *pSpellChecker;
  IErrorInfo *pErrInfo;
  BSTR bstrErrorDesc;

  UpdateData(TRUE);
  hRes=::CoCreateInstance(CLSID_CDocumentChecker,NULL,CLSCTX_ALL,
      IID_ISpellChecker,(void **)&pSpellChecker);
  if (SUCCEEDED(hRes))
  {
    BSTR bstrDictionaryPath=m_dictionaryFile.AllocSysString();
    hRes=pSpellChecker->UseCustomDictionary(bstrDictionaryPath);
    if (FAILED(hRes))
    {
      hRes=::GetErrorInfo(0,&pErrInfo);
      if (SUCCEEDED(hRes))
      {
        pErrInfo->GetDescription(&bstrErrorDesc);
        AfxMessageBox(CString(bstrErrorDesc));
      }
    }
    ::SysFreeString(bstrDictionaryPath);
  }
}
```

If you are using ATL to develop your COM objects, you can use ATL's Error function and it will call `CreateErrorInfo` and `SetErrorInfo` for you. On the client-side, most COM-enabled development environments, map COM exceptions to the native exception mechanism of their programming language. For instance, the native COM support in Visual C++, maps COM exceptions to C++ exceptions. Visual Basic maps COM exceptions to its horrid "on error goto" error handling mechanism.

Highlighting the Steps

The steps that you perform to build the Writer's Component are as follows:

1. Create an ATL project using the ATL/COM AppWizard.
2. Add the document checker object to the project using the ATL object wizard.
3. Implement the `ISpellChecker` interface.
4. Implement the `IGrammarChecker` interface.
5. Create a client using Visual C++ native COM support.

Creating an ATL Project Using the ATL/COM AppWizard

Start Visual C++ and then execute the following steps:

1. Select `New...` from the `File` menu (the `New` dialog appears).
2. Click the `Projects` tab.
3. Select `ATL COM AppWizard` from the presented list of project types.
4. Enter `WritersComponent` in the `Project Name` field.
5. Click the `OK` button (the ATL/COM AppWizard will appear).
6. Select `Dynamic Link Library` under `Server Type`.
7. Click `Finish`.

Visual C++ will create a new project for you. The project will contain no classes, but it will have a global `CComModule` object and all the COM entry points required to implement an in-process COM server. If you named the project as I specified, you can view this code in a file called `WritersComponent.cpp`. The essential portions of this file are shown in Listing 5.4.

LISTING 5.4 *WRITERSCOMPONENT.CPP*

```
CComModule _Module;

STDAPI DllCanUnloadNow(void)
{
   return (_Module.GetLockCount()==0) ? S_OK : S_FALSE;
}

STDAPI DllGetClassObject(REFCLSID rclsid, REFIID riid, LPVOID* ppv)
{
```

```
    return _Module.GetClassObject(rclsid, riid, ppv);
}

STDAPI DllRegisterServer(void)
{
    // registers object, typelib and all interfaces in typelib
    return _Module.RegisterServer(TRUE);
}

STDAPI DllUnregisterServer(void)
{
    return _Module.UnregisterServer(TRUE);
}
```

These functions simply delegate to the implementation provided by the `CComModule` object. Right now, you have all the boiler plate code required for your COM server, but you have no COM classes. Let's add one.

Adding the Document Checker COM Class Using the ATL Object Wizard

You use the ATL Object Wizard to create a new COM class.

The ATL Object Wizard does not create objects; it creates classes. You create an object when you create an instance of the class that the Wizard generates. People (even people who should know better) often refer to COM objects when they really mean COM classes. The Visual C++ group at Microsoft is apparently no different. Just remember that the ATL Object Wizard should be called the ATL Class Wizard.

The ATL Object Wizard

The ATL Object Wizard is a tool that lets you create new COM classes using a simple-to-use GUI. Figure 5.2 shows the main window of the ATL Object Wizard.

In the wizard, you can select from a wide variety of COM classes including various types of ActiveX controls, Microsoft Transaction Server (MTS) components, Microsoft Management Console SnapIns, OLEDB Consumers and Providers, and simple classes. After selecting the type of COM class that you want, the ATL Object Wizard lets you specify COM-specific properties for your new COM class. You can specify these properties using the Properties dialog that appears as soon as you click the `Next` button in the ATL Object Wizard. On the `Names` tab of the Properties dialog

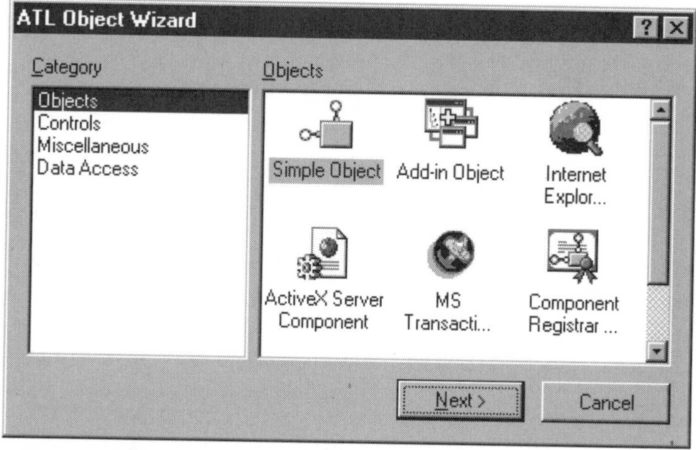

FIGURE 5.2 The Main Window of the ATL Object Wizard.

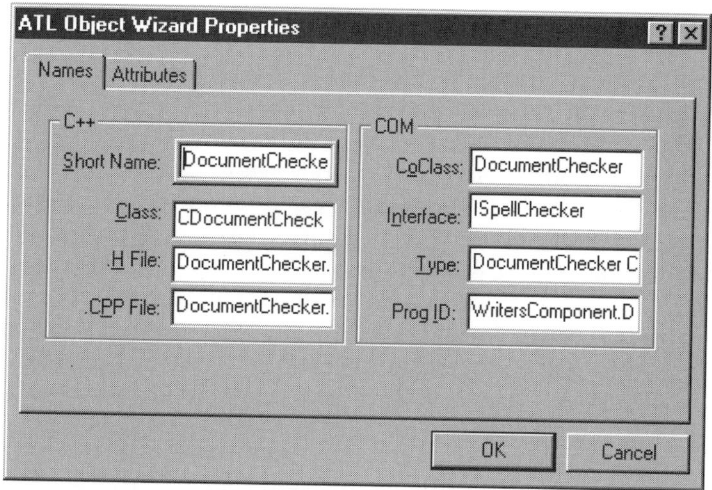

FIGURE 5.3 The Names Tab of the ATL Object Wizard Properties Dialog.

you can enter the name of the C++ class that will implement your COM class. You can also enter the programmers ID for the COM class, and the name of the interface that the COM class will implement. Figure 5.3 shows the `Names` tab of the ATL Object Wizard Properties dialog.

On the `Attributes` tab of the ATL Object Wizard Properties dialog you can specify more advanced features of your COM class such as its threading model, whether it supports events, dual or custom interfaces, aggregation, or rich error information. Figure 5.4 shows the `Attributes` tab of the ATL Object Wizard Properties dialog.

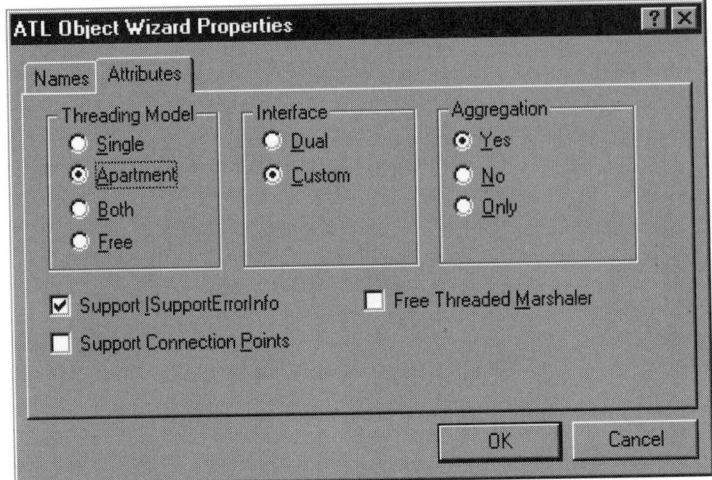

FIGURE 5.4 The Attributes tab of the ATL Object Wizard Properties Dialog.

Events in this context are callbacks that are sent from a COM object back to its client. They are implemented using a set of standard COM interfaces that are collectively called Connection Points. The interfaces you have looked at so far are called custom interfaces. You will learn later that there are two types of COM interfaces: `IDispatch` (or Automation) interfaces and custom interfaces. Dual interfaces can function as both. I explore `IDispatch` interfaces in Chapter 7.

Common defaults are provided for all of these parameters, so you don't have to change anything on the `Attributes` tab if you don't want to.

To add a Document Checker COM class to your Writer's Component using the ATL Object Wizard, perform the following steps:

1. Select `New ATL Object...` from the `Insert` menu (the ATL Object Wizard will appear as shown in Figure 5.2).
2. Under `Category`, select `Object` and under `Object` select `Simple Object`.
3. Click the `Next` button (the ATL Object Wizard Properties dialog will appear as shown in Figure 5.3).
4. On the `Names` tab enter `DocumentChecker` in the `Short Name` field under C++ (see Figure 5.3).
5. Under COM, change the interface to `ISpellChecker` (see Figure 5.3).
6. Click the `Attributes` tab.
7. Change the interface type to `custom`.
8. Set the `ISupportErrorInfo` checkbox (see Figure 5.4).
9. Click `OK`.

The ATL Object Wizard generates the code in Listing 5.5 in a file called CDocumentChecker.h.

LISTING 5.5 *THE CDOCUMENTCHECKER ATL CLASS*

```
1.  class ATL_NO_VTABLE CDocumentChecker :
2.      public CComObjectRootEx<CComSingleThreadModel>,
3.      public CComCoClass<CDocumentChecker, &CLSID_DocumentChecker>,
4.      public ISupportErrorInfo,
5.      public ISpellChecker
6.  {
7.  public:
8.      CDocumentChecker()
9.      {
10.     }
11.
12. DECLARE_REGISTRY_RESOURCEID(IDR_DOCUMENTCHECKER)
13.
14. DECLARE_PROTECT_FINAL_CONSTRUCT()
15.
16. BEGIN_COM_MAP(CDocumentChecker)
17.     COM_INTERFACE_ENTRY(ISpellChecker)
18.     COM_INTERFACE_ENTRY(ISupportErrorInfo)
19. END_COM_MAP()
20.
21. // ISupportsErrorInfo
22.     STDMETHOD(InterfaceSupportsErrorInfo)(REFIID riid);
23.
24. // ISpellChecker
25. public:
26. };
```

Notice that the generated class inherits from ATL's CComObjectRootEx class. CComObjectRootEx provides the implementation of the IUnknown interface for your COM class. The template parameter passed to this class is CComSingleThreadModel (see line 2 of Listing 5.5). This indicates that the class is not thread-safe. COM will serialize all method calls on objects of this class. You will learn how in chapter 9. Your class is not thread-safe (or at least it is telling COM that it is not thread safe) because you chose the default threading model (*Apartment*) on the Attributes tab of the ATL Object Wizard. Had you selected either *Free* or *Both* for the Threading model, the template parameter for CComObjectRootEx would have been CComMultiThreadModel as shown below, and you would have to make sure that all the methods of this class are thread-safe.

```
CComObjectRootEx<CComMultiThreadModel>
```

CDocumentChecker also inherits from CComCoClass with CDocumentChecker (the implementation class) and CLSID_DocumentChecker (the CLSID for the COM class that you are implementing) as the two template parameters (see line 3 of Listing 5.5). CComCoClass implements the class object for your COM class; it implements the IClassFactory interface.

CDocumentChecker also inherits from the ISpellChecker and ISupportErrorInfo interfaces. ISpellChecker is your user-defined, custom interface. Implementing ISupportErrorInfo is your way of indicating to your clients that you can return COM exception objects.

Lines 16–19 of Listing 5.5 contain the COM map for your COM class. The COM map contains entries for the two interfaces that you currently support: ISpellChecker and ISupportErrorInfo. CComObjectRootEx uses the COM map in its implementation of the QueryInterface method. Each COM map entry adds the specified interface to a table which QueryInterface looks up when you request an interface. So, every time you add a new interface to an ATL-based COM implementation, you must add the interface to the COM map.

In addition to creating this implementation class, the ATL Object Wizard also added code to your IDL file. The new IDL code is shown in Listing 5.6.

LISTING 5.6 *WRITERSCOMPONENT.IDL*

```
import "oaidl.idl";
import "ocidl.idl";
    [
        object,
        uuid(9497426D-777B-11D3-998A-50E64AC10000),
        helpstring("ISpellChecker Interface"),
        pointer_default(unique)
    ]
    interface ISpellChecker : IUnknown
    {
    };
[
    uuid(94974261-777B-11D3-998A-50E64AC10000),
    version(1.0),
    helpstring("WritersComponent 1.0 Type Library")
]
library WRITERSCOMPONENTLib
{
    importlib("stdole32.tlb");
    importlib("stdole2.tlb");
    [
```

```
23.         uuid(9497426E-777B-11D3-998A-50E64AC10000),
24.         helpstring("DocumentChecker Class")
25.     ]
26.     coclass DocumentChecker
27.     {
28.         [default] interface ISpellChecker;
29.     };
30. };
```

The ATL Object Wizard uses several IDL keywords that you did not use when you built your COM class from scratch; I discuss all of these new IDL keywords below.

The ATL Object Wizard has added an interface definition, for `ISpellChecker`, to our IDL file and it has added a COM class declaration for `DocumentChecker`. The attributes for `ISpellChecker` include the familiar *object* keyword, which indicates that the interface is a COM interface and not a DCE RPC interface. The attributes also contain a GUID for the interface. This GUID was generated for us by Visual C++ (by way of the `CoCreateGUID` API function). You can change the GUID if you like as long as the new GUID is created using the GUID creation algorithm. Notice on line 7 of Listing 5.6 that the IDL file contains an attribute that you have not seen before: `pointer_default`.

The `pointer_default` attribute is harder to understand. Remember that one of the reasons you specify COM interfaces in IDL is so the IDL compiler, MIDL, can generate the code required to do marshaling for your interface.

Marshaling is required if your server is implemented in an out-of-process server or, as you'll see in Chapter 9, in certain multi-threading scenarios.

The `pointer_default` attribute is your way of telling MIDL how a pointer will be used so it can optimize the proxy and stub that it will create in the marshaling DLL. The `pointer_default` attribute of an interface defines the default behavior of pointers when they are used as input or output parameters in methods of that interface. You can override the default for a particular method in the interface, or for one parameter of a method, by specifying the `pointer_default` keyword again as one of the attributes of the method or parameter. The `pointer_default` attribute has three possible values.

- *Ref*—When this value is chosen, MIDL assumes that the pointer always points to a valid location. A pointer defined with this attribute cannot be NULL and it should point to the same memory location before and after the function call. Only one pointer can point to the memory address that this pointer points to.
- *Unique*—Pointers declared with this value are allowed to be NULL, they also can point to different memory locations before and after the function call. Only one pointer can point to the memory address that this pointer points to.
- *Ptr*—Behaves the same as unique pointers, except more than one pointer can point to a particular memory address.

The ATL Object Wizard specifies *unique* as the `pointer_default` for all interfaces it creates. But you can, and should, change this value if pointers used in your interface's methods will not adhere to the rules for unique pointers.

The IDL file also contains a library specification (see line 17 of Listing 5.6). A library specification defines the name and GUID for the type library that MIDL will generate. Notice the `importlib` statements on lines 19 and 20 of Listing 5.6. This statement imports all the classes, interfaces, and other types declared in the type library. Finally, you have the COM class specification.

Notice that this COM class specification uses the default keyword. The use of the default keyword indicates that the `ISpellChecker` interface best represents the functionality that the COM class is providing. Some environments, like Visual Basic, let you access the default interface as though it were a method on an instance of the COM class.

There's one more file that you should look at before you begin implementing our COM class, and that's the registry file. If you click the `FileView` tab in the Visual C++ workspace and then open the `Resource Files` folder, you should see a file called `DocumentChecker.rgs`. The contents of this file are shown in Listing 5.7.

LISTING 5.7 *DOCUMENTCHECKER.RGS*

```
HKCR
{
   WritersComponent.DocumentChecker.1 = s 'DocumentChecker Class'
   {
      CLSID = s '{9497426E-777B-11D3-998A-50E64AC10000}'
   }
   WritersComponent.DocumentChecker = s 'DocumentChecker Class'
   {
      CLSID = s '{9497426E-777B-11D3-998A-50E64AC10000}'
      CurVer = s 'WritersComponent.DocumentChecker.1'
   }
   NoRemove CLSID
```

```
    {
        ForceRemove {9497426E-777B-11D3-998A-50E64AC10000} = s
'DocumentChecker Class'
        {
            ProgID = s 'WritersComponent.DocumentChecker.1'
            VersionIndependentProgID = s
'WritersComponent.DocumentChecker'
            InprocServer32 = s '%MODULE%'
            {
                val ThreadingModel = s 'Apartment'
            }
            'TypeLib' = s '{94974261-777B-11D3-998A-50E64AC10000}'
        }
    }
}
```

This file is used to register your component. ATL's implementation of `DllRegisterServer` reads the contents of this file and inserts the entries it finds into the registry. ATL's implementation of `DllUnregisterServer` reads the contents of this file and deletes the entries it finds from the registry.

Implementing ISpellChecker

Now you can start adding methods to the `ISpellChecker` interface. You need to make three changes to your project for each method that you add: (1) add the new method to your IDL, (2) add a prototype for the method to the header file for your implementation class, (3) implement the method in the

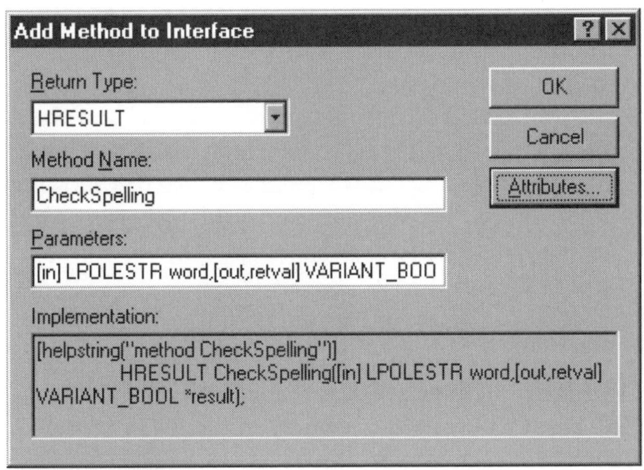

FIGURE 5.5 The Add Method to Interface Dialog.

source file for the implementation class. Thankfully, Visual C++ includes a tool that does all this in one simple step. You can use this tool by right-clicking on the ISpellChecker interface in the ClassView tab of the Visual C++ workspace. From the Context menu that appears, select Add Method... The dialog box shown in Figure 5.5 appears.

You are going to add a CheckSpelling method that takes a string as input and returns a Boolean that indicates whether the string contains correct spelling. In the Add Method to Interface dialog, perform the following steps:

1. Enter CheckSpelling in the Method Name field.
2. Enter [in] LPOLESTR word,[out,retval] VARIANT_BOOL *result in the Parameters field.
3. Click the OK button.

You can view the changes to your project by double-clicking on the ISpellChecker interface to view the IDL file for the project. Note the addition of the CheckSpelling method to the ISpellChecker interface:

```
interface ISpellChecker : IUnknown
{
    [helpstring("method CheckSpelling")] HRESULT CheckSpelling([in]
LPOLESTR word,[out,retval] VARIANT_BOOL *result);
};
```

If you go to the file named DocumentChecker.h, you will see that the CheckSpelling method has been added to the CDocumentChecker implementation class. And if you go to the DocumentChecker.cpp, you will see that an empty skeleton for the CheckSpelling method has been added to the file. Within the Visual C++ environment, you can navigate to this skeleton by clicking the "+" symbol next to the CDocumentChecker class in the ClassView tab of the Visual C++ workspace. In the expanded tree beneath the CDocumentChecker class, you should see the ISpellChecker interface. If you click the "+" symbol next to the ISpellChecker interface, you should see the CheckSpelling method. If you double-click on the CheckSpelling method, Visual C++ will take you to the empty skeleton for the CheckSpelling method. Your Visual C++ window should look like that shown in Figure 5.6.

Perform the following steps to add the UseCustomDictionary method to the ISpellChecker interface:

1. Right-click on the ISpellChecker interface in the ClassView tab of the Visual C++ workspace.
2. Select Add Method... from the Context menu.
3. Enter UseCustomDictionary in the Method Name field.
4. Enter [in] LPOLESTR path in the Parameters field.
5. Click the OK button.

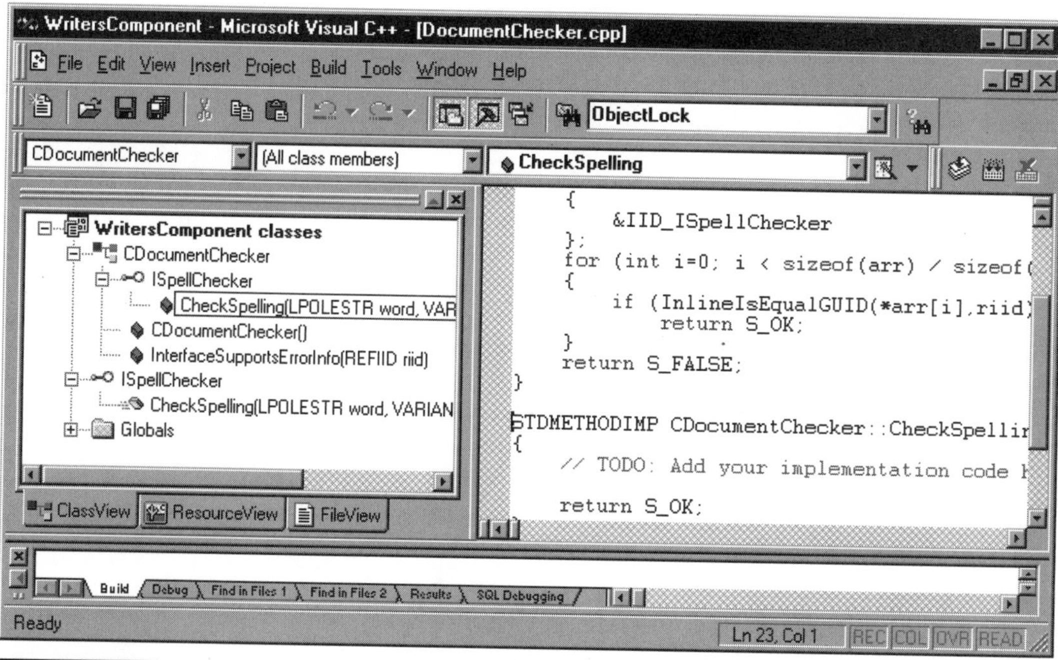

FIGURE 5.6 Viewing the CheckSpelling Method in the Visual C++ Workspace.

Before you implement the `CheckSpelling` method, you need to add the bolded code shown in Listing 5.8 to the header file for `CDocumentChecker`, `DocumentChecker.h`.

LISTING 5.8 *COMPLETING DOCUMENTCHECKER.H*

```
//////////////////////////////////////////////////////////////////////
// CDocumentChecker
#include <vector>
#include <string>
using namespace std;
class ATL_NO_VTABLE CDocumentChecker :
   public CComObjectRootEx<CComSingleThreadModel>,
   public CComCoClass<CDocumentChecker, &CLSID_DocumentChecker>,
   public ISupportErrorInfo,
   public ISpellChecker
{
public:
   CDocumentChecker()
   {
       m_dictionary.push_back(OLESTR("Alan"));
       m_dictionary.push_back(OLESTR("Gordon"));
```

```
        m_dictionary.push_back(OLESTR("COM"));
        m_dictionary.push_back(OLESTR("ActiveX"));
        m_dictionary.push_back(OLESTR("OLE"));
        m_dictionary.push_back(OLESTR("COM+"));
    }
// Code omitted for clarity...
private:
    vector<wstring> m_dictionary;
};
```

Here you are using the vector and string classes from the C++ standard library just as you did in Chapter 4. You are also using the push_back method in the vector class to add several strings to your spell checker's dictionary. With the preceeding code added, the implementation of the CheckSpelling method is straightforward. Add the bolded lines in Listing 5.9 to the CheckSpelling method in the CDocumentChecker class. You can find the empty skeleton for this method in the file DocumentChecker.cpp.

LISTING 5.9 *THE IMPLEMENTATION OF THE CHECKSPELLING METHOD*

```
STDMETHODIMP CDocumentChecker::CheckSpelling(LPOLESTR word,
VARIANT_BOOL *result)
{
    wstring str;
    vector< wstring >::iterator iter;
    *result=VARIANT_FALSE;
    for (iter=m_dictionary.begin();iter!=m_dictionary.end();iter++) {
        str=*iter;
        if (_wcsicmp(str.c_str(),word)==0) {
            *result=VARIANT_TRUE;
            break;
        }
    }
    return S_OK;
}
```

In Listing 5.9 you compare each word in the dictionary to the word that is being spell checked. If a match is found, then the word is spelled correctly. This is exactly the same as the implementation in Chapter 4.

Before you implement the UseCustomDictionary method, you must add the following code near the top of the DocumentChecker.cpp file:

```
#include <fstream>
const E_DICTIONARYFILENOTFOUND=MAKE_HRESULT(SEVERITY_ERROR,
FACILITY_ITF,0x200+99);
```

Put these lines right below the include statements that are already present in the file. Both of these lines should be familiar from Chapter 4. They are an include statement for the standard library header file that contains the file-based streams, and the definition of a custom HRESULT. With this code added to the file, the implementation of the `UseCustomDictionary` method is as shown in Listing 5.10. Add the bolded lines in Listing 5.10 to the file `DocumentChecker.cpp`.

LISTING 5.10 *THE IMPLEMENTATION OF THE USE CUSTOMDICTIONARY METHOD*

```
1.  STDMETHODIMP CDocumentChecker::UseCustomDictionary(LPOLESTR path)
2.  {
3.      wstring str;
4.      char sz_path[255];
5.         wifstream dictionaryFile;
6.      size_t bufsize;
7.      bufsize=wcstombs(sz_path,path,255);
8.      if (bufsize==sizeof(sz_path) || bufsize == -1) {
9.         return Error(_T("Invalid or excessively long path specified"),
           IID_ISpellChecker,E_INVALIDARG);
10.     }
11.     dictionaryFile.open(sz_path);
12.        if (!dictionaryFile.is_open()) {
13.        return Error(_T("Dictionary file not found"),IID_ISpellChecker,
           E_DICTIONARYFILENOTFOUND);
14.     }
15.        while (!dictionaryFile.eof()) {
16.        dictionaryFile >> str;
17.        m_dictionary.push_back(str);
18.        }
19.        return S_OK;
20. }
```

The code for this function looks almost exactly as it did in Chapter 4. The only difference is that you call the ATL Error function if the client passes an invalid string, or a string that is too long instead of just returning an HRESULT (see line 9 of Listing 5.10). If the specified dictionary file cannot be found, you again call the `Error` function (see line 13 of Listing 5.10). The ATL error function calls the `CreateErrorInfo` and `SetErrorInfo` functions in the COM API to create and send a COM exception to the client. COM exceptions typically include an error description and a handle to a result as you have here. But you can also include a string that tells what the source of the error is. And if you want to be really slick, include the name of a Help file and a context ID that contains information about the error. Many development environments (Visual Basic for instance) let the user click a button and jump straight to this Help topic when an error occurs. There are several overloaded versions of `Error` that allow you to specify as much, or as little, information as you would like to send with your COM exception. See the ATL documentation online if you would like to learn more.

Implementing IGrammarChecker

One problem I mentioned with the ATL Object Wizard is that it does not let you create a COM class that implements multiple user-define interfaces. It's important, then, to know how to add an interface after you have initially created a COM class with the Wizard. That's why you are implementing the `IGrammarChecker` interface. The steps to implement the `IGrammarChecker` interface are as follows:

1. Add an empty interface definition to the IDL file.
2. Add the new interface to the COM class definition.
3. Compile the IDL.
4. Add the new interface to our implementation class.
5. Add the `CheckGrammar` method to the `IGrammarChecker` interface.
6. Implement the `CheckGrammar` method.

Adding an Empty Interface Definition to the IDL file

Visual C++ 6.0 includes tools that let you add additional user-defined interfaces to your implementation class. Before you can use these tools, you must manually add the new interface to your IDL. Add the bolded code shown in Listing 5.11 to the IDL file in your project, `WritersComponent.idl`.

LISTING 5.11 *ADDING IGRAMMARCHECKER TO WRITERSCOMPONENT.IDL*

```
import "oaidl.idl";
import "ocidl.idl";
    [
        object,
        uuid(9497426D-777B-11D3-998A-50E64AC10000),
        helpstring("ISpellChecker Interface"),
        pointer_default(unique)
    ]
    interface ISpellChecker : IUnknown
    {
        [helpstring("method CheckSpelling")] HRESULT CheckSpelling([in]
        LPOLESTR word,[out,retval] VARIANT_BOOL *result );
        [helpstring("method UseCustomDictionary")] HRESULT
        UseCustomDictionary([in] LPOLESTR path );
```

```
13.     };
14.
15.     [
16.        object,
17.        uuid(6C1ED360-0BFC-11d3-998A-0CE109C10000),
18.        helpstring("IGrammarChecker Interface"),
19.        pointer_default(unique)
20.     ]
21.     interface IGrammarChecker : IUnknown
22.     {
23.     };
24.
25. [
26.     uuid(94974261-777B-11D3-998A-50E64AC10000),
27.     version(1.0),
28.     helpstring("WritersComponent 1.0 Type Library")
29. ]
30. library WRITERSCOMPONENTLib
31. {
32.     importlib("stdole32.tlb");
33.     importlib("stdole2.tlb");
34.     [
35.        uuid(9497426E-777B-11D3-998A-50E64AC10000),
36.        helpstring("DocumentChecker Class")
37.     ]
38.     coclass DocumentChecker
39.     {
40.        [default] interface ISpellChecker;
41.        interface IGrammarChecker;
42.     };
43. };
```

Notice that I first added the declaration of the `IGrammarChecker` interface (lines 15–23) and then added the interface to the `coclass` declaration (line 41). The GUID for the `IGrammarChecker` interface should be created by GUIDGEN as always.

Compiling the IDL

You can now compile the IDL. Compiling the IDL will create the type library for your server. You need an updated type library or the next step, adding the interface to our implementation class, will not work. To compile the IDL, make the IDL file the current window by double-clicking the `ISpellChecker` interface in the `ClassView` tab of the Visual C++ workspace and press `CTRL F7`.

Adding the New Interface to the Implementation Class

Next, you will use the Implement Interface command in Visual C++ to quickly add the `IGrammarChecker` interface to your implementation class. To do this, perform the following steps:

1. Right-click on `CDocumentChecker` in the `ClassView` tab of the Visual C++ workspace.
2. Select `Implement Interface` (the Implement Interface dialog appears as shown in Figure 5.7).
3. Set the `IGrammarChecker` checkbox.
4. Click `OK`.

Listing 5.12 shows the changes (in bold face type) that Visual C++ made to the header file for the implementation class.

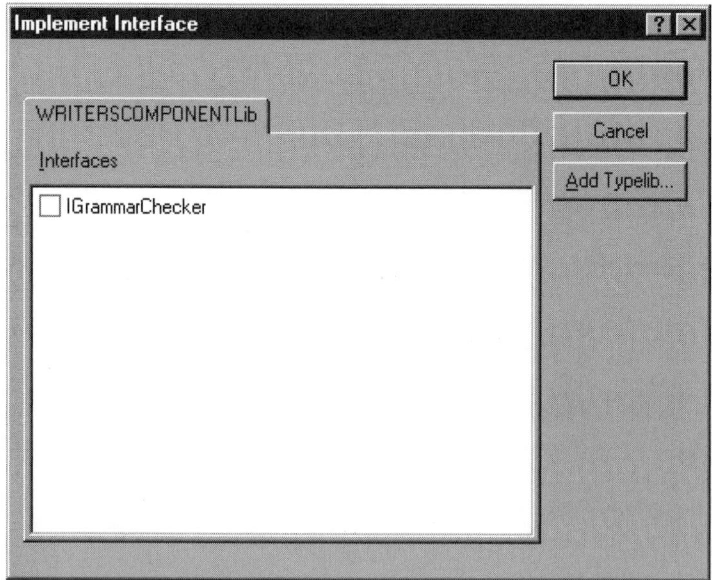

FIGURE 5.7 The Implement Interface Dialog.

LISTING 5.12 *THE CHANGES VISUAL C++ MADE TO YOUR IMPLEMENTATION CLASS*

```
class ATL_NO_VTABLE CDocumentChecker :
   public CComObjectRootEx<CComSingleThreadModel>,
   public CComCoClass<CDocumentChecker, &CLSID_DocumentChecker>,
   public ISupportErrorInfo,
   public ISpellChecker,
   public IGrammarChecker
{
public:
// code omitted for clarity...
BEGIN_COM_MAP(CDocumentChecker)
   COM_INTERFACE_ENTRY(ISpellChecker)
   COM_INTERFACE_ENTRY(ISupportErrorInfo)
   COM_INTERFACE_ENTRY(IGrammarChecker)
END_COM_MAP()
// ISupportsErrorInfo
   STDMETHOD(InterfaceSupportsErrorInfo)(REFIID riid);
// ISpellChecker
public:
   STDMETHOD(UseCustomDictionary)(/*[in]*/ LPOLESTR path);
   STDMETHOD(CheckSpelling)(/*[in]*/ LPOLESTR word,/*[out,retval]*/
VARIANT_BOOL *result);
private:
   vector<wstring> m_dictionary;
// IGrammarChecker
};
```

Visual C++ added `IGrammarChecker` to the inheritance list for your implementation class. It also added the `IGrammarChecker` interface to the COM map for your implementation class. It also inserted a comment showing where it intends to place any methods that you add to the `IGrammarChecker` interface. The only thing that it did not do was to add the `IGrammarChecker` interface to the list of interfaces that support rich error information. The `InterfaceSupportsErrorInfo` method in the `ISupportsErrorInfo` interface allows the COM class that implements the interface to specify which of its interfaces support rich error information. Right now the only interface that is so specified is `ISpellChecker`:

```
STDMETHODIMP CDocumentChecker::InterfaceSupportsErrorInfo(REFIID riid)
{
   static const IID* arr[] =
   {
      &IID_ISpellChecker
   };
   for (int i=0; i < sizeof(arr) / sizeof(arr[0]); i++)
   {
```

```
        if (InlineIsEqualGUID(*arr[i],riid))
            return S_OK;
    }
    return S_FALSE;
}
```

To indicate that the `IGrammarChecker` interface also implements rich error information, add the bolded line shown below to the `InterfaceSupportsErrorInfo` method.

```
STDMETHODIMP CDocumentChecker::InterfaceSupportsErrorInfo(REFIID riid)
{
    static const IID* arr[] =
    {
        &IID_ISpellChecker,
        &IID_IGrammarChecker
    };
    for (int i=0; i < sizeof(arr) / sizeof(arr[0]); i++)
    {
        if (InlineIsEqualGUID(*arr[i],riid))
            return S_OK;
    }
    return S_FALSE;
}
```

You added the GUID for the `IGrammarChecker` interface to the list of interfaces for which you will return a positive response when asked if the interface supports rich error information.

Adding the CheckGrammar Method to the IGrammarChecker Interface

Now we can use the Visual C++ environment to add a method called `CheckGrammar` to the `IGrammarChecker` interface. Perform the following steps:

1. Right-click on the `IGrammarChecker` interface in the `ClassView` tab of the Visual C++ Workspace.
2. Select `Add Method to Interface...` from the `Context` menu that appears.
3. Enter `CheckGrammar` for the Method Name.
4. Enter [in] LPOLESTR sentence, [out,retval] VARIANT_BOOL *result in the `Parameters` field.
5. Click `OK`.

Implementing the CheckGrammar Method

Add the following implementation for the `CheckGrammar` method:

```
STDMETHODIMP CDocumentChecker::CheckGrammar(LPOLESTR sentence, VARI-
ANT_BOOL *result)
{
    *result=VARIANT_FALSE;
        if (wcschr(sentence,',') && wcschr(sentence,'.'))
        *result=VARIANT_TRUE;

        return S_OK;
}
```

This uses the `wcschr` method to check if the sentence contains both a comma and a period. If the sentence contains both, the grammar is correct; if either is missing, the grammar is incorrect. Now let's build a client for your server using Visual C++ Native COM support.

Creating a Client with Visual C++'s Native COM Support

Here are steps you should perform to create your client:

1. Create a dialog-based project using the MFC AppWizard.
2. Create the user interface.
3. Add the code needed to enable COM support.
4. Import the type library for your server.
5. Add a smart pointer instance to your dialog class.
6. Instantiate a COM object.
7. Implement the user interface.
8. Test.

Creating a Dialog-Based Project Using the MFC AppWizard

Start Visual C++ and then execute the following steps:

1. Select New... from the `File` menu (the New dialog appears).
2. Click the `Projects` tab.
3. Select MFC AppWizard (exe) from the presented list of project types.
4. Enter `nativecomclient` in the `Project` Name field.
5. Click OK (the MFC App Wizard will appear).
6. Click the radio button labeled "`Dialog-based`".
7. Click `Finish` (the New Project Information dialog appears).
8. Click `OK`.

Creating the User Interface

The user interface for your COM client application will look like the one shown in Figure 5.8. Draw this dialog using the resource editor in Visual C++.

Using the MFC class wizard, map button clicked (`BN_CLICKED`) message handlers to the three buttons on the main window dialog as specified in Table 5.1.

TABLE 5.1 Message Handler Methods

Button Caption	Message Handler for Button
Check Spelling	OnSpellcheckerButton
Check Grammar	OnGrammarcheckerButton
Ellipsis (...)	OnBrowseButton
Load Dictionary	OnLoadDictionary

Next, use the MFC ClassWizard to map variables to the two edit boxes on the main window dialog. The edit box closest to the top of the dialog lets the user enter a string that will be spell checked. The edit box closer to the bottom of the dialog is where the user can enter the path to a custom dictionary for the spell checker to use. Map these edit boxes to member variables as shown in Table 5.2.

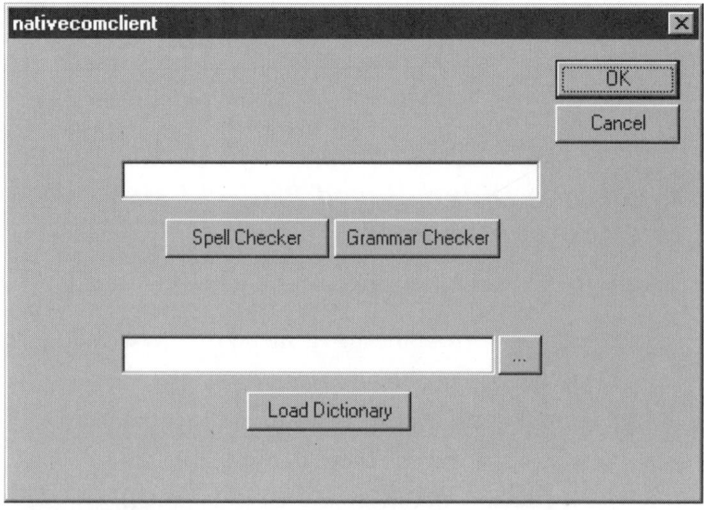

FIGURE 5.8 The Nativecomclient User Interface.

TABLE 5.2 Mapping of Member Variables to Controls

Edit Box Purpose	Map to member variable	Member variable type
Word to be spell checked	m_word	CString
Path to a custom dictionary for the spell checker	m_dictionaryFile	CString

Adding the Code Needed to Enable COM Support

To enable COM support, you need to add a single line to the `InitInstance` method of your `Application` class. As explained in Chapter 4, you have to enter a COM apartment before you can do anything else with COM. Add the bolded lines of code shown below at the beginning of the `InitInstance` of the `CNativecomclientApp` class:

```
BOOL CNativecomclientApp::InitInstance()
{
   if (!AfxOleInit())
       AfxMessageBox("Could not initialize COM");
// the rest of the code in this function is omitted for clarity
}
```

So far you haven't done anything unusual or different. Essentially, you have repeated the steps used to create your client in Chapter 4. Now things get interesting.

Importing the Type Library for Your Server

To use Visual C++'s native COM support, you must first import the type library for your server. Add the following line of code to the `stdafx.h` file in the native COM client project:

```
#import "c:\alan\books\vcppbook\demos\chapter5\writerscomponent\
writerscomponent.tlb"
```

The path shown here is valid on my machine. If you are following along and wish to compile your client, you will need to change this path to be the path where you built the server on your machine.

If you don't like having a hard-coded path like this in your code, then you can add the directory that contains the type library to the default list of directories that Visual C++ will search for include files. (Visual C++ searches these directories for type libraries also). To add a directory to the search path for include files, perform the following steps in the Visual C++ Workspace.

1. Select `Options...` from the `Tools` menu (the `Options` dialog appears as shown in Figure 5.9).
2. Click the `Directories` tab (shown in Figure 5.9).
3. Make sure `Include files` is selected under `Show directories for`.
4. Click the `New` button.
5. Enter the directory path where your type library resides.
6. Click `OK`.

This code uses the `import` keyword which is a key component of Visual C++'s native COM support. Using the `#import` keyword and then specifying a type library file causes Visual C++ to load the type library and generate wrap-

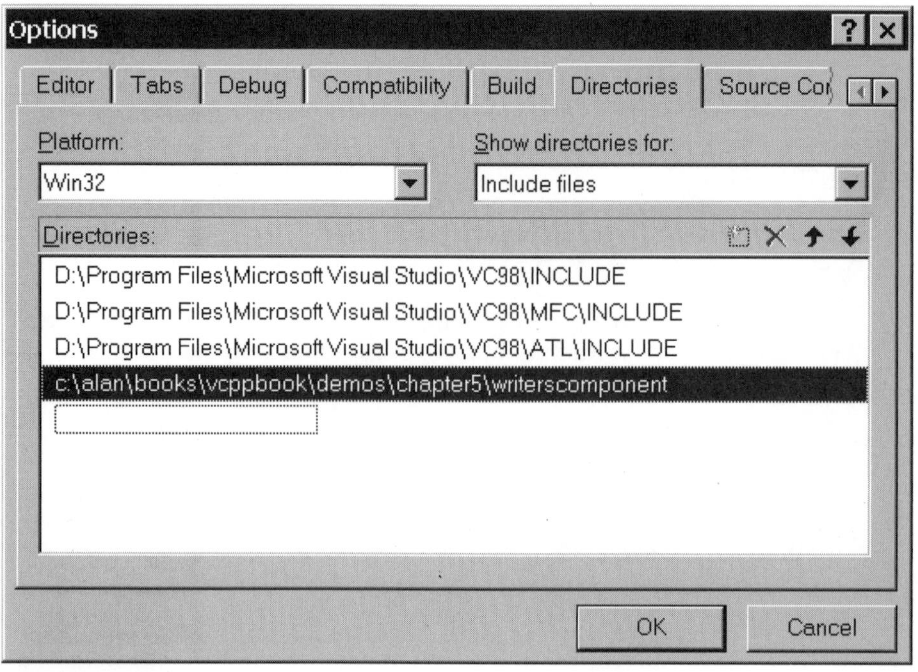

FIGURE 5.9 The Directories tab of the Options Dialog.

per classes that make it relatively simple to use COM. If you build the project now and then look in the debug directory of your project, you will see two files generated by these statements: `writerscomponent.tlh` and `writerscomponent.tli`. The essential contents of writerscomponent.tlh are shown in Listing 5.13. I have eliminated some code for clarity.

LISTING 5.13 *WRITERSCOMPONENT.TLH*

```
#include <comdef.h>
namespace WRITERSCOMPONENTLib {

_COM_SMARTPTR_TYPEDEF(ISpellChecker, __uuidof(ISpellChecker));
_COM_SMARTPTR_TYPEDEF(IGrammarChecker, __uuidof(IGrammarChecker));

struct __declspec(uuid("2ce8270e-0ad5-11d3-998a-0ce109c10000"))
DocumentChecker;

struct __declspec(uuid("2ce8270d-0ad5-11d3-998a-0ce109c10000"))
ISpellChecker : IUnknown  {
   // Wrapper methods for error-handling
   VARIANT_BOOL CheckSpelling (LPWSTR word );
   HRESULT UseCustomDictionary (LPWSTR path );

   // Raw methods provided by interface
   virtual HRESULT __stdcall raw_CheckSpelling (LPWSTR word,
   VARIANT_BOOL * result ) = 0;
   virtual HRESULT __stdcall raw_UseCustomDictionary (LPWSTR path ) = 0;
};

struct __declspec(uuid("6c1ed360-0bfc-11d3-998a-0ce109c10000"))
IGrammarChecker : IUnknown  {
   // Wrapper methods for error-handling
   VARIANT_BOOL CheckGrammar (LPWSTR sentence );

   // Raw methods provided by interface
   virtual HRESULT __stdcall raw_CheckGrammar (LPWSTR sentence,
   VARIANT_BOOL * result ) = 0;
};

// Wrapper method implementations
#include "c:\alan\books\vcppbook\demos\chapter5\nativecomclient\debug\
writerscomponent.tli"
} // namespace WRITERSCOMPONENTLib
```

The first thing you should notice is the #include for the file comdef.h on line 1. Comdef.h contains a variety of smart pointer definitions (see the sidebar "Smart Pointers" in this chapter for more details) and declarations of several helper classes, including a _com_error class that greatly simplifies error handling in COM. The code shown in Listing 5.13 also uses C++ namespaces. All of the code in this file is enclosed in a namespace called WRITERSCOMPONENTLib. (See the sidebar on "C++ Namespaces" in the chapter.) If you decide that you really don't like namespaces, and there are no naming clashes between declarations in the "tlh" file and other code in your project, you can use the no_namespace qualifier on your import statement as shown in the following code:

```
#import "d:\alan\writerscomponent\writerscomponent.tlb" no_namespace
```

This suppresses the generation of a namespace in the "tlh" file. Notice the two smart pointer definitions on lines 4 and 5 in listing 5.13. A smart pointer is created for each interface in the type library and its definitions create two classes—ISpellCheckerPtr and IGrammarCheckerPtr—that you will use in your client.

The next line of code, line 7, uses Visual C++'s native COM support to associate the CLSID of your DocumentChecker COM class with the name DocumentChecker. The __declspec keyword is a non-standard addition to the Microsoft C++ compiler. It lets you associate an attribute with a struct or class. In this case, the use of uuid(...) indicates that you are associating a GUID with this struct. You can now return the CLSID for DocumentChecker (DocumentChecker was the name of your COM class) using the following syntax:

```
__uuidof(DocumentChecker)
```

The lines 9 through 18 contain the declaration of the wrapper class for the ISpellChecker interface. Line 9 uses __declspec to associate a GUID with the ISpellChecker interface. You can retrieve the IID for ISpellChecker at a later time using the following code:

```
__uuidof(ISpellChecker)
```

The wrapper class next has duplicate definitions for each method in the interface that it is wrapping. Notice that there is a CheckSpelling and a raw_CheckSpelling method. These duplicate methods map COM exceptions to native C++ exceptions. All methods in a COM interface have a physical return value that is an HRESULT. Error information is returned in this value. Each method may also have a logical return value, which is declared in the idl using [out,retval]. If you were creating a regular C++ class, you would return the logical return value for a method in the actual return value for the method and then use language-specific exceptions to catch error information as shown here:

```
Try {
   Boolean isCorrect=anObject.CheckSpelling(word);
}
catch (ExceptionClass *err){
   cout <<   err->Description();
}
```

The raw_CheckSpelling and CheckSpelling methods work together to make your COM class behave like a C++ class. The raw_CheckSpelling method maps to the CheckSpelling method in the ISpellChecker interface. The CheckSpelling function is not virtual so it is not a part of the COM interface. It is actually a convenience function. The implementation of the CheckSpelling method is contained in the writerscomponent.tli file and looks like this:

```
inline VARIANT_BOOL ISpellChecker::CheckSpelling ( LPWSTR word ) {
   VARIANT_BOOL _result;
   HRESULT _hr = raw_CheckSpelling(word, &_result);
   if (FAILED(_hr)) _com_issue_errorex(_hr, this, __uuidof(this));
   return _result;
}
```

Notice that when you call CheckSpelling on an instance of this wrapper class it calls the raw CheckSpelling method in the ISpellChecker interface. It gets the HRESULT from the physical return value of raw_CheckSpelling and checks to see if the call failed. If the call failed, it passes the HRESULT to a method called _com_issue_errorex, which throws a C++ exception. CheckSpelling also fetches the logical return value from raw_CheckSpelling and returns it as the physical return value from CheckSpelling. If you use the CheckSpelling method in the wrapper class, there is no need to check an HRESULT to see if the method succeeded or failed. If the method fails, it throws an exception. Given an instance of the ISpellChecker smart pointer class, you can now call the CheckSpelling method using this code:

```
try {
   VARIANT_BOOL result=mSpellChecker.CheckSpelling(word);
}
catch (_com_error err) {
   cout << err.Description()'
}
```

This code looks exactly like the code that you would write if you were using a CheckSpelling method implemented in a regular C++ class. This is not an accident. The whole idea behind the native COM support is to make it as simple to use COM classes as it is to use the native classes in a programming language such as C++.

Smart Pointers

A smart pointer is a C++ class that overrides the C++ pointer dereference operator:"->". A class that overrides this operator behaves like a pointer, but because it's a class, it can manage the resource that it points to in a more intelligent way than a raw pointer. That's why it's called a *smart* pointer.

A smart pointer class typically contains a real pointer that points to some resource such as memory, a file, or in this case a COM object. It also has a constructor or other member functions that initialize the resource that the real pointer points to and a destructor that makes sure that the resource is cleaned up properly. The smart pointers that Visual C++ generates contain a COM interface pointer internally. Each smart pointer class contains a `CreateInstance` function that calls `CoCreateInstance` for you (you don't have to remember all the intricacies of this complicated method). These COM smart pointers also call the `Release` method on the internal interface pointer in their destructor.

To use one of these smart pointers, just instantiate an object of the smart pointer class and call the `CreateInstance` method using either a `ProgID` or a call to `__uuidof`. You can then call methods in the COM interface that the smart pointer is associated with through the pointer dereference operator, "->". When you are done with the object, you don't have to worry about calling `Release`. When the object goes out of scope, the `Release` method is called automatically in the destructor of the smart pointer class. The following code shows how to use the COM smart pointer classes that Visual C++ generates:

```
#include <iostream.h>
#import "d:\alan\writerscomponent\writerscomponent.tlb" no_namespace
// using namespace WRITERSCOMPONENTLib;
void testspellchecker()
{
    HRESULT hr;
    ISpellCheckerPtr pSpellChecker;

hr=pSpellChecker.CreateInstance("WritersComponent.DocumentChecker");
// Or you can instantiate the object as shown on the following line
// hr=pSpellChecker.CreateInstance(__uuidof(DocumentChecker));
    if (FAILED(hr)) {
        _com_error err(hr);
        cout << err.ErrorMessage() << endl;
    }
    bstr_t word=L"Alan";
    try {
```

```
        VARIANT_BOOL isCorrect=pSpellChecker->CheckSpelling(word);
        if (isCorrect==VARIANT_TRUE)
            cout << "spellcheck complete" << endl;
        else
            cout << "word misspelled" << endl;
    }
    catch (_com_error err) {
        cout << err.Description();
    }
    return;
}
```

Once you get used to them, using these smart pointers in your COM clients is far easier than working with COM interface pointers directly.

Adding a Smart Pointer Instance to Your Dialog

Armed with your smart pointer classes, you are ready to begin implementing your client. To use the smart pointer classes, you need to add the bold lines of code to the header file for the main window class, `CNativecomclientDlg` of your project. If you named your project as I instructed, this file should be called `nativecomclientdlg.h`. Add the code directly above the class declaration for `CnativecomclientDlg` like this:

```
using namespace WRITERSCOMPONENTLib;
class CNativecomclientDlg : public CDialog {
// The rest of the code for this class is omitted for clarity...
private:
    ISpellCheckerPtr mSpellChecker;
};
```

If you used the no_namespace qualifier on your #import statement, you don't need the using namespace declaration shown here.

Instantiating a COM Object

Next, you need to use the `CreateInstance` method on your smart pointer to instantiate a COM object. The best place to do this is in the

OnInitDialog method of CNativecomclientDlg. OnInitDialog is called right after the dialog is created, but before it is shown. Add the bolded lines shown in the following code to OnInitDialog:

```
BOOL CNativecomclientDlg::OnInitDialog()
{
   // The rest of the code in this method is omitted for clarity...

   // TODO: Add extra initialization here
   HRESULT
hr=mSpellChecker.CreateInstance("WritersComponent.CDocumentChecker");
   if (FAILED(hr)) {
      _com_error err(hr);
      AfxMessageBox(err.ErrorMessage());
   }
   return TRUE;  // return TRUE  unless you set the focus to a control
}
```

You passed the ProgID for your COM class to the CreateInstance method of your smart pointer. CreateInstance determines the CLSID that goes with our ProgID using the CLSIDFromProgID API function. You could also use the GUID for CDocumentChecker directly: HRESULT hr=mSpellChecker.CreateInstance(__uuidof(CDocumentChecker));

Implementing the User Interface

Now you can finish off your client by implementing the logic for the CheckSpelling and CheckGrammar Buttons. Implement the OnSpellCheckerButton method as shown here:

```
void CNativecomclientDlg::OnSpellcheckerButton()
{
   UpdateData(TRUE);
   bstr_t word=m_word;
   VARIANT_BOOL isCorrect=mSpellChecker->CheckSpelling(word);
   if (isCorrect==VARIANT_TRUE) {
      AfxMessageBox("Spell check complete");
   }
   else {
      AfxMessageBox("Word misspelled");
   }

}
```

Next implement the OnBrowseButton as shown here:

```
void CSimplenativecomclientDlg::OnBrowseButton()
{
   CFileDialog dlg(TRUE);
   if (dlg.DoModal()==IDOK) {
      m_dictionaryFile=dlg.GetPathName();
      UpdateData(FALSE);
   }
}
```

In this button, you create an instance of the MFC class that maps to the Windows common file dialog. If the user selects a dictionary file and clicks OK, you set the variable that is mapped to the dictionary file edit box and call UpdateData(FALSE) to cause the path that was selected to be shown in the dictionary file edit box. Next you have the OnLoadDictionaryButton method. This method causes an exception if the user enters an invalid path. So you are using C++ exception handling to catch the exception:

```
void CNativecomclientDlg::OnLoaddictionaryButton()
{
   UpdateData(TRUE);
   bstr_t dictionaryFile=m_dictionaryFile;
   try {
      mSpellChecker->UseCustomDictionary(dictionaryFile);
   }
   catch(_com_error err) {
      AfxMessageBox(err.ErrorMessage());
}
   }
```

Finally, you have the OnGrammarcheckerButton() method. While this function looks simple, something really important is happening here. The mSpellChecker variable contains an ISpellChecker smart pointer. To use the grammar checking functionality of your COM object, you have to get the IGrammarChecker interface. You're probably thinking that you need to call QueryInterface on mSpellChecker. Well, thanks to smart pointers and Visual C++'s native COM support, you don't have to. Take a look at the implementation of the OnGrammarCheckerButton message handler shown in Listing 5.14.

LISTING 5.14 *THE MESSAGE HANDLER FOR THE CHECKGRAMMAR BUTTON*

```
1. void CNativecomclientDlg::OnGrammarcheckerButton()
2. {
3.     VARIANT_BOOL isCorrect;
4.     UpdateData(TRUE);
5.     bstr_t word=m_word;
6.     IGrammarCheckerPtr grammarChecker;
7.     try {
8.        grammarChecker=mSpellChecker;
9.        isCorrect=grammarChecker->CheckGrammar(word);
10.       if (isCorrect)
11.          AfxMessageBox("Grammar check complete");
12.       else
13.          AfxMessageBox("Incorrect grammar");
14.    }
15.    catch (_com_error err) {
16.       AfxMessageBox(err.Description());
17.    }
18.}
```

On line 6, you declare an `IGrammarChecker` smart pointer. On line 8, you assign this smart pointer to the `ISpellChecker` smart pointer. The `QueryInterface` was performed for you on line 8. Remember that each of these smart pointer classes has the IID of the interface they are associated with stored with them (thanks to `__declspec`). The assignment operator for COM smart pointers checks the IIDs of the smart pointers on each side of the equal sign. If the IIDs are different, it calls `QueryInterface` on the pointer on the right-hand side and passes the IID of the smart pointer on the left-hand side. It is effectively asking the smart pointer on the right-hand-side if it implements the interface that the smart pointer on the left-hand-side works with. If the object that the smart pointer on the right-hand side points to does not support this interface, the assignment operator throws an exception.

Notice that there are no calls to `Release` in any of my client. The smart pointers have taken care of this for you. When the destructor for a smart pointer is called, it calls `Release` on the interface that it is associated with.

C++ Namespaces

C++ namespaces let you prevent naming clashes. If you have two classes called `Employee`, you can put them each in their own namespace as follows:

```
namespace ThirdPartyLib {
    class Employee {
    //...
    };
}
namespace HomegrownLib {
    class Employee {
    };
}
```

You can then use both `Employee` classes in the same source file without causing a naming clash by appending the Namespace that each class belongs to as shown here:

```
ThirdPartyLib::Employee emp1(...);
HomegrownLib::Employee emp2(...);
```

In this way, you can disambiguate the two classes, if you need to use both. If you are writing code that is using only one of the `Employee` classes, you can add all the classes in its namespace to the global namespace with this statement:

```
using namespace HomegrownLib;
```

After inserting this statement into a source file, you can use the `Employee` class in the `HomegrownLib` namespace without prepending its namespace:

```
Employee emp1(...);
```

Test

Build your client and test it out. You should be able to type in any of the words that you initially added to your dictionary: `Alan`, `Gordon`, `COM`, `ActiveX`, `OLE`, `COM+`. You should also be able create a dictionary file that contains additional words—one per line—and load this file. After the dictionary file is loaded, the spell checker will recognize all the words in the file.

■ Summary

It was much easier to build both your client and your server when you used ATL and the Visual C++ native COM support. Using ATL and the ATL Object Wizard freed you from having to implement the boiler plate logic required of a COM server. You did not have to implement the IUnknown interface, a class object, the DllGetClassObject and DllCanUnloadNow functions, or the registry functions. The only thing you had to do was to implement the "business logic" of your server.

The native COM support dramatically simplified the development of your client. By using the smart pointer classes that the #import statement generates, you are freed from having to use the CoCreateInstance function, nor did you have to call Release on any of your interface pointers. Using these COM, smart pointer classes was almost as easy as using regular C++ classes.

So far, you have only built in-process (DLL-based) COM servers. In the next chapter, you will see how to build an out-of-process server.

PART TWO

Digging Deeper

In This Part

In this section we will start "digging deeper" into COM. The objective of this section is to teach you enough COM so that you are primed to begin learning COM+. In chapter 6 you will learn how to build a COM server that runs in a separate process from its client. In chapter 7 you will learn about Automation, which makes COM accessible to simpler programming languages. In chapter 8 you will learn about Connection Points, which allow COM components to send callbacks to their clients. In chapter 9 we will talk about threading and you will tackle the dreaded topic of COM Apartments. Finally in chapter 10 we will discuss Distributed COM (DCOM), which allows COM clients and components to communicate across a network.

By the time you are done with this section you should have all the knowledge you need to begin learning COM+.

SIX

Creating an Out-of-Process Server

So far, you have created only in-process servers. An in-process server is implemented on the Microsoft Windows platform as a DLL. The COM objects in an in-process server execute in the same process as their client (hence the name). In this chapter, you will explore the creation of an out-of-process server, which is implemented in an executable server (an "exe" file) and runs in a separate process from its client. The trade-off between an in-process server and an out-of-process server is one of robustness and fault-tolerance versus speed and performance.

An in-process server offers the best speed and performance. Threading issues aside, a method call on an object that is implemented in an in-process server is almost as fast as a virtual method call on a C++ class. The downside is that because an in-process server runs in the same process as its client, if its internal code crashes, it will also crash its client.

An out-of-process server is more fault-tolerant. An out-of-process server can crash its own process, but as long as you have implemented proper error handling in your client code (so that you don't use an invalid interface pointer for instance), the client process continues to run. The client can even restart the server if it senses that the server has crashed. Another potential advantage of an out-of-process server is that multiple clients can share a single instance of the server. If a server is running in the same process as its client, then each client, by definition, has its own instance of the server.

The big disadvantage of using out-of-process servers is performance. A method call on an object implemented in an out-of-process server is about an order of magnitude slower (as you will see in this chapter) than a method call on an object implemented in an in-process server. This is because an out-of-process method call must be *marshaled* from the client process to the server process. Out-of-process servers also introduce new issues that you did not have to deal with when building an in-process server, such as the choice between single-use or multi-use instancing. In this chapter, you will see how to create an out-of-process server using ATL and explore the differences between in-process and out-of-process servers.

Marshaling

The key to making an out-of-process server work is marshaling. You will learn in Chapter 9 that because of threading issues, an in-process-server *sometimes* requires marshaling. But an out-of-process *always* requires marshaling. What is marshaling? The simple answer is that marshaling is a technique that allows method calls to be made across contexts. For now you can think of a context as a process, but later I give a more precise definition of a context. Marshaling is handled by two pieces of software called a proxy and a stub. Both the proxy and stub are COM objects that are implemented in an in-process server that is referred to as a marshaling DLL or proxy/stub DLL. The proxy runs in the client process and the stub runs in the server process as shown in Figure 6.1.

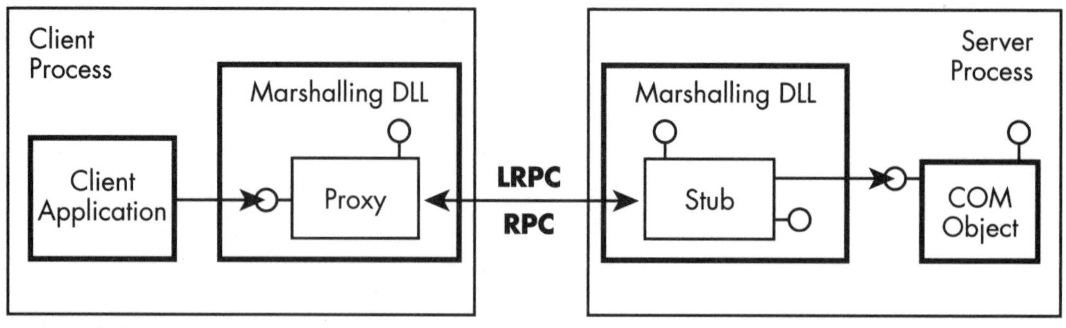

FIGURE 6.1 Marshaling via a Proxy and Stub.

Each COM interface that is implemented in an out-of-process server requires a proxy and a stub. All of the proxies and stubs for a particular COM server are usually implemented in a single marshaling DLL that can be either embedded into the COM server that it is associated with or distributed as a separate file.

To the client, the proxy for an interface looks exactly like the interface itself; it has the same methods. Because it looks and behaves exactly like the interface it represents, the COM runtime can sneakily return a proxy whenever you request an interface on an object that is implemented in an out-of-process server. When the client makes a method call on the proxy, the proxy translates the method call into an InterProcess Communication (IPC) message. This message contains the name of the method that the client wishes to call and all the parameters that the client is passing to the method.

If the client and server processes reside on the same machine, COM uses Local Remote Procedure Calls (LRPC) as the transport mechanism between the client and server process. If you are using Distributed COM (DCOM), then Distributed Computing Environment (DCE) RPC is used as the transport mechanism.

This message is sent to the stub in the server process. The stub interprets the message, determines which method the client wants to call, and calls the method passing in the parameters that were sent along with the message. When the method call is complete, the stub sends the return value and any output parameters back to the proxy. The proxy returns the return value it received to the client and sets all the output parameters.

From the client-side, what you see is that you called a method and the return values came back and the output parameters were set with the values that were assigned in the method. This is exactly the result you would expect if the method were implemented in the same process as the client. The proxy and the stub handle all of the additional complexity associated with making the call across processes. The only difference you will notice is that the method call takes longer.

Providing a marshaling DLL for your servers is simpler than you might think. In many cases, the operating system provides a marshaling DLL for you and you don't have to build a server-specific marshaling DLL. If your server implements only standard interfaces (interfaces that have been defined by Microsoft already), marshaling support is provided by the operating system in the file ole32.dll. If your server implements only automation-compatible interfaces, marshaling support is provided by the universal marshaler, which is implemented in the oleaut.dll system DLL. Only if your COM server implements custom interfaces (interfaces that you define yourself in IDL like `ISpellChecker`) are you required to create and distribute a specific marshaling DLL for your server.

For reasons that have to do with threading (which I discuss in Chapter 9), you may also need to create a server-specific marshaling DLL if you also implement custom interfaces in an in-process server.

If you have to create a server-specific marshaling DLL, you can either use the MIDL-generated marshaler or create a custom marshaling DLL. In most cases, you will use the MIDL-generated marshaler.

Using the MIDL-Generated Marshaler

Given an IDL description of the COM interfaces that will be implemented in a COM server, MIDL generates all the source code you need to implement a marshaling DLL for the server. To use the MIDL-generated marshaler, you have to compile the source files that are generated by MIDL and link them with the RPC runtime. Figure 6.2 shows schematically the steps you must go through to create a marshaling DLL using the files generated by MIDL.

Given an IDL file called `spellcheck.idl`, MIDL generates the following source files: `spellcheck.h`, `spellcheck_i.c`, `spellcheck_p.c`, and `dlldata.c`. These files contain all the server-specific code you need to build your marshaling DLL. To build your marshaling DLL, you have to link with the RPC runtime and the other libraries shown in Figure 6.2 and provide a ".def" file that exports the standard COM entry for an in-process server: `DllGetClassObject`, `DllCanUnloadNow`, `DllRegisterServer`, and `DllUnregisterServer`. When you create a COM server project using the ATL AppWizard, it creates a makefile for you that automates this build process. If you don't use ATL, you have to either create a makefile yourself or enter the build commands manually. After building the marshaling DLL, you must register it using `regsvr32` just like any other in-process server.

Creating a Custom Marshaling DLL

In some situations, the MIDL-generated marshaler may not be sufficient for your needs. In those situations, you can create a custom marshaling DLL. To implement custom marshaling, both the COM object and the proxy that you create for the COM object must implement the `IMarshal` interface. You must write your own IPC code to implement this interface, which isn't easy. The big advantage of using custom marshaling is that you can implement performance optimizations that the MIDL-generated code does not do. You can implement client-side caching for instance and eliminate some of the

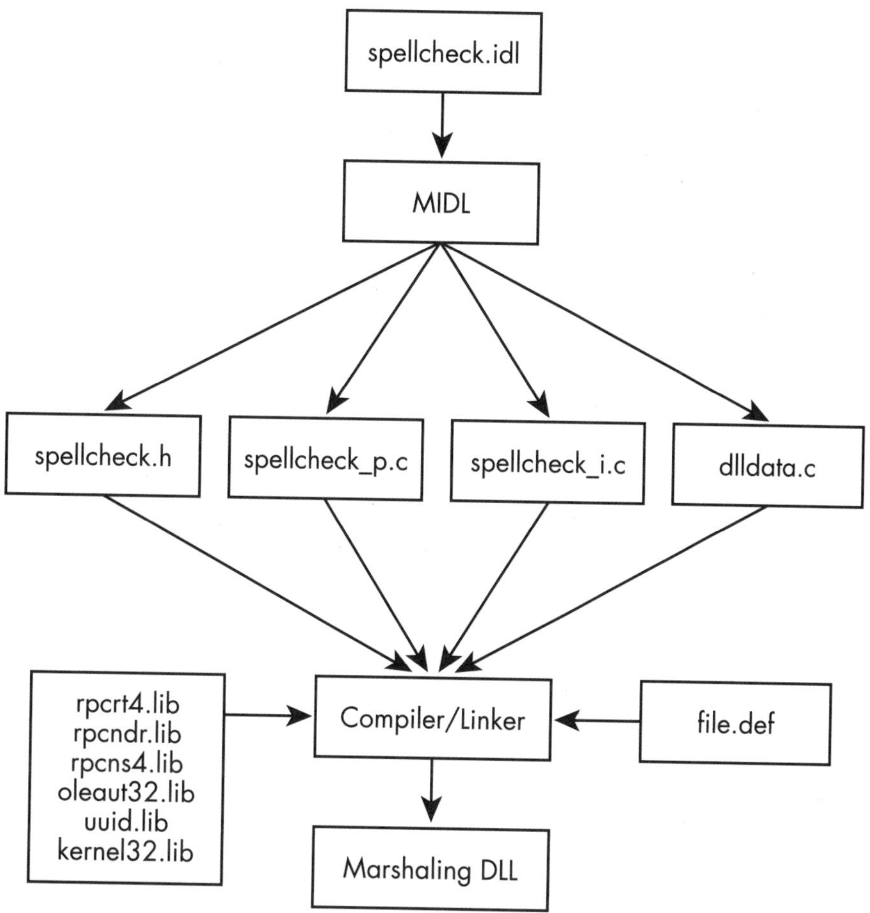

FIGURE 6.2 Building a Marshaling DLL from the Files Generated by MIDL.

communication between the proxy and stub. You can also reduce interprocess communication by combining several remote calls into one. This is definitely an advanced topic and way out of scope for a primer book, so I'll refer you to Chapter 5 of *Essential COM* by Don Box or Chapter 6 of *Inside OLE* by Craig Brockschmidt for further discussion.

How COM Finds a Marshaling DLL

As I mentioned earlier, if the COM runtime sees that the object you are attempting to instantiate lives in an out-of-process server, it returns a proxy instead of a direct interface pointer. How does the COM runtime know that an object is implemented in an out-of-process server? It knows this by looking beneath the following key in the registry:

```
HKEY_CLASSES_ROOT\CLSID\{CLSID_FOR_SERVER}
```

All out-of-process servers have a `LocalServer32` subkey beneath this key. The default value of this subkey contains the path to the server executable. Figure 6.3 shows the `LocalServer32` entry for the Microsoft Word Document COM class, which is implemented in an out-of-process server: Microsoft Word.

Remember, in-process servers have an `InprocServer32` entry that contains the path to the server DLL.

Whenever you instantiate a COM object (using `CoCreateInstance` or some other function), the COM runtime eventually contacts the Service Control Manager (the SCUM), passes it a CLSID, and asks it to activate the COM object identified by that CLSID. The SCUM searches the local registry and once it sees the `LocalServer32` entry, it knows that the server for this object will run out-of-process. The COM runtime then starts the server executable and uses the interface ID (IID) that the client requested on the COM object to locate the marshaling DLL for the requested interface. It does this by searching for the following key in the registry:

```
HKEY_CLASSES_ROOT\interface\{IID_OF_REQUESTED_INTERFACE}
```

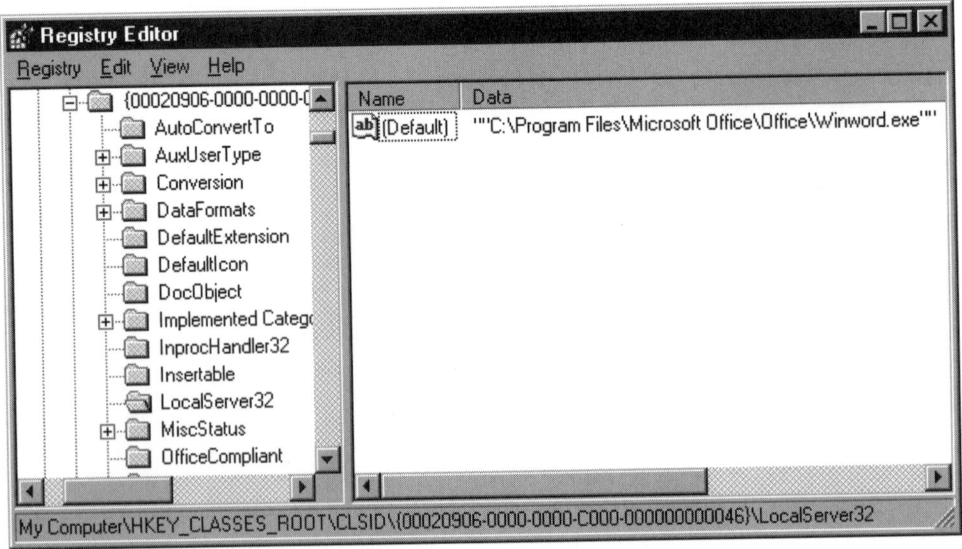

FIGURE 6.3 LocalServer32 Subkey for the Microsoft Word Document Object.

Let's explore the HKEY_CLASSES_ROOT\interface\ key a little more to help our understanding. Fire up the registry editor by performing these steps:

1. Click the Start button on the task bar.
2. Select Run from the Start menu.
3. Enter regedit on the Run window.
4. Click the OK button.

Then, take a look at the entries beneath HKEY_CLASSES_ROOT\interface\. Figure 6.4 shows a sample entry.

The subkey ProxyStubCLSID32 contains the CLSID of the proxy stub DLL for an interface. The GUID you see there corresponds to a CLSID key under HKEY_CLASSES_ROOT\CLSID\. The HKEY_CLASSES_ROOT\CLSID\ registry key contains the path to the marshaling DLL. Many of the entries that you see beneath HKEY_CLASSES_ROOT\ interface have a ProxyStubCLSID32 equal to {00000320-0000-0000-C000-000000000046}. If you check HKEY_CLASSES_ROOT\CLSID\, you see this is the CLSID for a DLL called ole32.dll. Remember I said earlier that marshaling support is already provided for all standard COM interfaces. Ole32.dll (among other things) is the marshaling DLL for the standard COM interfaces. The other popular ProxyStubCLSID32 value is {00020420-0000-0000-C000-000000000046}. You'll notice that all of the interface entries that have this key also have a typelib key. These are automation-compatible interfaces. If you search for the GUID, {00020420-0000-0000-C000-000000000046}, beneath

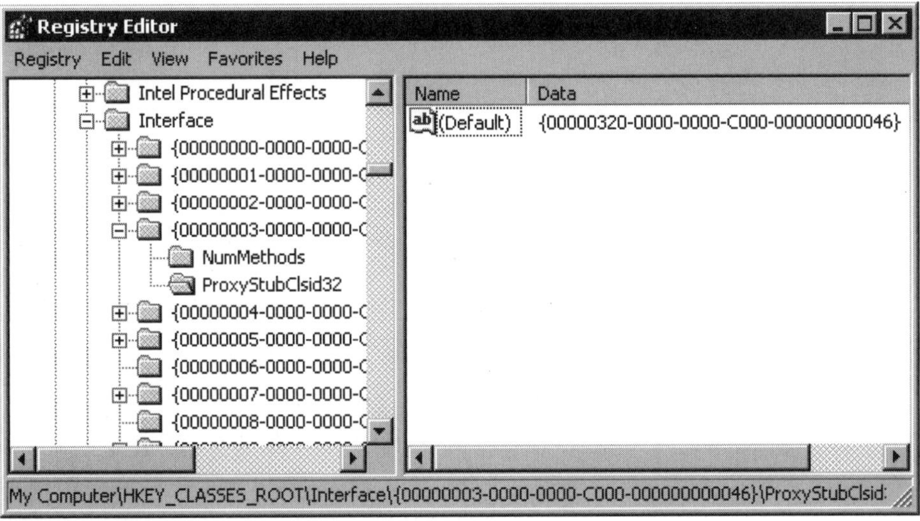

FIGURE 6.4 Interface Keys in the Registry.

HKEY_CLASSES_ROOT\CLSID\, you will see it points to a DLL called oleaut32.dll. This DLL implements marshaling support for automation-compatible interfaces. To work properly, oleaut32.dll needs the type library for the interfaces it is marshaling. That's why HKEY_CLASSES_ROOT\interface\ entries that use oleaut32.dll include a typelib subkey. If your server uses a server-specific marshaler, then the HKEY_CLASSES_ROOT\interface\{IID} entry for each interface in the server will contain the CLSID for your marshaling DLL and the HKEY_CLASSES_ROOT\CLSID\ registry key for this CLSID will contain the path to the marshaling DLL that you registered.

Instancing

An in-process server always runs in the process of its client. Therefore, the process that a particular object runs in is pre-determined; it runs in the process of its client. But an out-of-process server runs in its own process. But how many of these server processes should there be? Should each object run in its own server process? Or should all the objects of a particular type run in a single process? The answer to these questions is that the choice is up to you, the developer of the COM class. You can decide on a class-by-class basis whether each object of a COM class will have its own process or if all the instances will share a single process. This is called the *Instancing* property of a COM class. A COM class can have either *single-use* or *multi-use* instancing. A single-use class provides a separate process for each object. A multi-use class runs all of its objects in one process.

Although you can set this property for each COM class individually, in practice you should set the same value for all of the classes in a server. That's why I usually refer to instancing as a server-level property (i.e., I refer to a single-use or multi-use *server*.)

Figure 6.5 shows three objects running in a single-use server. Notice that each object has its own server process.

Figure 6.6 shows three objects running in a multi-use server. Notice that there is only one instance of the server process. All objects instantiated by any clients run in that one instance of the server process.

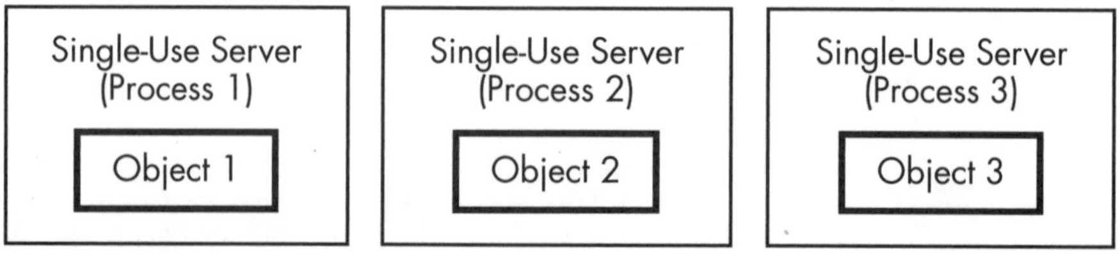

FIGURE 6.5 Three Objects in a Single-Use, Out-of-Process Server.

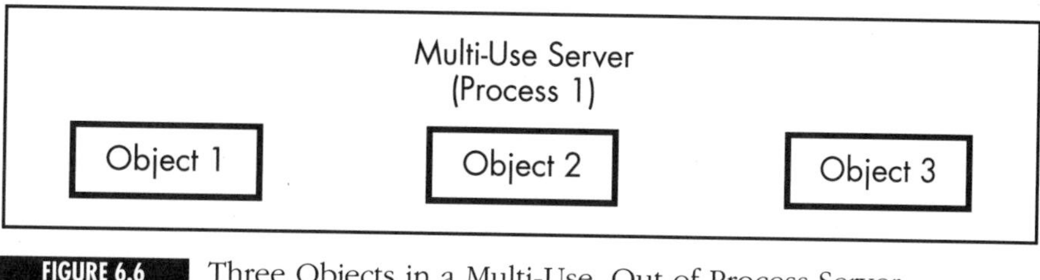

FIGURE 6.6 Three Objects in a Multi-Use, Out-of-Process Server.

Whether you choose to make a server single-use or multi-use depends on the requirements of your application and its expected use pattern. A single-use server offers the greatest possible fault-tolerance. An object in a single-use server can crash its own server without affecting any of the other instances. A single-use server also lets you have multiple instances of an object executing simultaneously without having to worry about threading issues. The operating system schedules the primary thread in each process and because each object is running in its own process, you won't have to worry about any nasty thread-synchronization issues. And therein lies one of the biggest problems with a single-use server; because each object runs in its own process, it is difficult for each object to share in-memory information. Another big problem is resource usage. The overhead of creating a process for each object can become intolerable if a large number of objects will be used.

Using a multi-use server solves both of these problems. If all objects of a particular type share the same server process, they can share in-memory information. Also, because a new process does not have to be created for each object, you can potentially have more active objects without bogging down a particular machine. However, there are a number of problems with multi-use servers. If several objects are to run concurrently, you have to create a multi-threaded server. Because these objects run in the same process, you have to worry about thread-synchronization when objects in a multi-threaded server access shared memory or other shared resources. Also, if one object crashes the server process, it also destroys all the other objects currently running in the server process. So a multi-use server is also less fault-tolerant than a single-user server.

Class Object Registration

The choice of whether a COM class server is single-use or multi-use is made when the class object for the COM class is registered. Visual Basic hides this detail from you, but you can see how it really works in C++.

You register COM classes using a COM API function that is appropriately named CoRegisterClassObject. An out-of-process server should register the class objects for all its COM classes immediately after it is started. The COM runtime will timeout and return an error code if it starts a server process and a class object is not registered within 5–10 minutes. The prototype for the CoRegisterClassObject function is shown here:

```
HRESULT CoRegisterClassObject(
   [in] REFCLSID rclsid,         // Identifier (CLSID) of that class that
                                    is being registered
   [in] IUnknown *pUnk,          // Pointer to the class object
   [in] DWORD dwClsContext,      // This parameter is usually
                                    CLSCTX_LOCAL_SERVER
   [in] DWORD dwFlags,           // REGCLS_MULTIPLEUSE or
                                    REGCLS_SINGLEUSE1
   [out] DWORD *dwCookie);       // This parameter is an output, it
                                    contains an ID for this registration
```

When you call this function, you are effectively telling the COM runtime that the server executable for the COM class identified by the first argument has been started. You are also passing to the COM runtime (in the second argument) an IUnknown interface pointer for the class object of the COM class. The COM runtime stores the class object interface pointer in a table (call it the class table from now on). The COM runtime creates a new object by calling the CreateInstance method on the IClassFactory interface of this class object if you call CoCreateInstance, or it returns an interface on this class object if the user calls CoGetClassObject.

You can remove an entry from the class table using the COM API function, CoRevokeClassObject. The prototype for this function is shown here:

```
HRESULT CoRevokeClassObject( [in] DWORD dwReg);
```

CoRevokeClassObject has a single argument, which is the output (the cookie) that you received from the CoRegisterClassObject function.

The key to understanding how instancing is implemented is to realize that COM only starts a new server process if it does not find an entry for the requested COM class in the class table. If the fourth argument to CoRegisterClassObject is REGCLS_SINGLEUSE, the class table entry for that class is used to service a single-object instantiation request only. After the class object is used to service this request, it is removed from the class table. COM then starts a new server process when the next activation request is received. This new server process calls CoRegisterClassObject with a REGCLS_SINGLEUSE parameter and the whole process starts again. If the fourth argument passed to CoRegisterClassObject is REGCLS_MULTIPLEUSE, the COM runtime maintains the entry in the class object table for the specified class until you call CoRevokeClassObject. So a new server process is never started, all object instantiation requests flow to the process that called CoRegisterClassObject with REGCLS_MULTIPLEUSE.

An in-process server does not have to call CoRegisterClassObject because the COM runtime obtains the class objects for all the class objects implemented in the server using the DllGetClassObject function. The COM runtime can call this well-known entry point in the server DLL to get the class object for a particular COM class any time it wants.

In ATL, the class object registration process works slightly different from the raw case. The ATL class, CComModule has a method called RegisterClassObjects that is called from the WinMain function that ATL generates for your server. The RegisterClassObjects method calls CoRegisterClassObject for all the classes implemented by a server. The code below was taken from an ATL executable server project:

```
hRes = _Module.RegisterClassObjects(CLSCTX_LOCAL_SERVER,
REGCLS_MULTIPLEUSE);
```

Notice that ATL moves the single-use/multi-use specification up to the server level. You can easily get around this and specify the property on a per-class level if you want to. But this illustrates the point that you should think of instancing as a server-level property and register all of the classes in a server as either single-use or multi-use in a server and not mix them. By default, all executable projects that you build with ATL are multi-use servers. If you want to change your server to be single-use, you can simply change the code shown above to look as follows:

```
hRes = _Module.RegisterClassObjects(CLSCTX_LOCAL_SERVER, REGCLS_SINGLEUSE);
```

Registering an Out-of-Process Server

Another key difference between an in-process server and an out-of-process server is the way that their required entries are inserted or removed from the registry. This is called registering and unregistering the server. You register an out-of-process COM server by starting the server and passing "regserver" on the command line shown below:

```
servername.exe /regserver
```

When the server sees this command line, it should insert its required entries into the registry and then shut down. You unregister an out-of-process server by passing "unregserver" on the command line shown below:

```
servername.exe /unregserver
```

When the server sees this command line, it should remove all of its entries from the registry and shut down. Using these command-line arguments is the equivalent of using `regsvr32 servername.dll` and `regsvr32 /u servername.dll` to register and unregister an in-process server.

You are responsible for creating the logic to parse the command line and update the registry. If you build an out-of-process COM server using the ATL AppWizard, it will build all of this logic for you, as you will see in the next section.

Building an Out-of-Process Server

It's time to provide an example that illustrates all the concepts that you have learned so far. From the server-development side, the main differences between developing an out-of-process server compared to developing an in-process server are that you need to:

- Choose between a single-use or multi-use server.
- Build a marshaling DLL if any of the server's classes implement custom interfaces.

From the client-side, the biggest difference you will see between an out-of-process and an in-process server is performance. An out-of-process server is much slower. The example used in this chapter lets you explore these differences further. You can build your server with ATL and then test it using a dialog-based project, as you did in the previous chapter. Your server will contain a single COM class called `TestClass`. `TestClass` supports a single interface called `ITestClass`. This interface will have two rather sarcastically named methods: `LongOperation` and `LongOperationArgs`. These methods are sarcastically named because both methods do nothing. `LongOperation` takes no arguments, does nothing with those arguments, and returns nothing. `LongOperationArgs` takes several arguments, does nothing with those arguments, and also returns nothing. So why are you going to implement these methods that do nothing? So you can explore the overhead of making a method call across process boundaries. By not having these methods do anything it makes it easy to see the overhead associated with making a method call; it's all overhead.

Listing 6.1 shows the IDL for the out-of-process server that you (with the help of Visual C++) will build.

LISTING 6.1 *IDL FOR OUR OUT-OF-PROCESS SERVER*

```
1.  [
2.         object,
3.         uuid(B296C34D-1307-11D3-998A-74EE08C10000),
4.
5.         helpstring("ITestClass Interface"),
6.         pointer_default(unique)
7.      ]
8.      interface ITestClass : IUnknown
9.      {
10.        [helpstring("method LongOperation")] HRESULT
           LongOperation([out,retval] long *millisecs);
11.        [helpstring("method LongOperationArgs")] HRESULT
           LongOperationArgs([in,string] LPOLESTR arg1,[out] double
12.        *arg2,[out,size_is(2048)] unsigned char *arg3,[out,retval]
           long *milliSecs);
13.     };
14.
15. [
16.     uuid(B296C341-1307-11D3-998A-74EE08C10000),
17.     version(1.0),
18.     helpstring("svroutofprocess 1.0 Type Library")
19. ]
20. library SVROUTOFPROCESSLib
21. {
22.     importlib("stdole32.tlb");
23.     importlib("stdole2.tlb");
24.
25.     [
26.        uuid(B296C34E-1307-11D3-998A-74EE08C10000),
27.        helpstring("TestClass Class")
28.     ]
29.     coclass TestClass
30.     {
31.        [default] interface ITestClass;
32.     };
33. };
```

The only thing new in this IDL file is the use of the `size_is` attribute in the `LongOperationArgs` method on line 12. The `size_is` attribute in IDL lets you specify the number of elements of the associated type that will be sent when the method is marshaled. The code shown above indicates that 2048 unsigned characters will be sent to the server when this method is called. The `LongOperationArgs` method also has three output parameters: `arg2`, `arg3`, and the return value, `milliSecs`. I added this method so you could see the effects that changing the number and size of the parameters had on performance. Your client will exercise the `LongOperation` and `LongOperationArgs` methods and let you gather performance data and perform comparisons with an in-process version of your server. After you test the performance of your server, you will explore changing from a multi-use to a single-use server.

A Summary of the Steps

You will build this application using the ATL/COM AppWizard. The only difference between what you do in this chapter and what you did in Chapter 5 is that you will build both executable and in-process versions of your server (so you can compare their performance). You will then use the Visual C++ native COM support to create a client. A summary of the steps to build this demonstration is as follows:

1. Create an Executable ATL project using the ATL/COM AppWizard.
2. Add a `Test` Class COM class to the project using the ATL object wizard.
3. Implement the `ITestClass` interface.
4. Create an in-process version of our server.
5. Create a client using Visual C++ native COM support.
6. Run Performance Tests.
7. Change the server to single-use.

Creating an ATL Executable Project Using the ATL AppWizard

Start Visual C++ and then execute the following steps:

1. Select `New...` from the `File` menu (the New dialog appears).
2. Click the `Projects` tab.
3. Select `ATL COM AppWizard` from the presented list of project types.
4. Enter `svroutofprocess` in the `Project` Name field.
5. Click `OK` (the ATL/COM AppWizard appears).
6. Select `Executable` under `Server Type`.
7. Click `Finish`.

Before we go any further, let's take a look at some of the code in this new project (Listing 6.2). As was the case with the in-process server, most of the server-specific logic is implemented in `CComModule`. If you build an out-of-process server with ATL it adds a new class to your project that derives from `CComModule`. This class is called `CExeModule`. The class declaration for `CExeModule` can be found in the `stdafx.h` file in your project.

LISTING 6.2 *CXEXEMODULE CLASS IN STDAFX.H*

```
class CExeModule : public CComModule
{
public:
    LONG Unlock();
    DWORD dwThreadID;
    HANDLE hEventShutdown;
    void MonitorShutdown();
    bool StartMonitor();
    bool bActivity;
};
extern CExeModule _Module;
```

The implementation of the CExeModule's methods is shown in Listing 6.3; it can be found in svroutofprocess.cpp.

LISTING 6.3 *IMPLEMENTING THE CEXEMODULE CLASS IN SVROUTOFPROCESS.CPP*

```
const DWORD dwTimeOut = 5000; // time for EXE to be idle before shutting down
const DWORD dwPause = 1000;  // time to wait for threads to finish up

// Passed to CreateThread to monitor the shutdown event
static DWORD WINAPI MonitorProc(void* pv)
{
    CExeModule* p = (CExeModule*)pv;
    p->MonitorShutdown();
    return 0;
}

LONG CExeModule::Unlock()
{
    LONG l = CComModule::Unlock();
    if (l == 0)
    {
        bActivity = true;
        SetEvent(hEventShutdown); // tell monitor that we transitioned to zero
    }
```

```
    return 1;
}

//Monitors the shutdown event
void CExeModule::MonitorShutdown()
{
    while (1)
    {
        WaitForSingleObject(hEventShutdown, INFINITE);
        DWORD dwWait=0;
        do
        {
            bActivity = false;
            dwWait = WaitForSingleObject(hEventShutdown, dwTimeOut);
        } while (dwWait == WAIT_OBJECT_0);
        // timed out
        if (!bActivity && m_nLockCnt == 0) // if no activity let's really bail
        {
#if _WIN32_WINNT >= 0x0400 & defined(_ATL_FREE_THREADED)
                CoSuspendClassObjects();
                if (!bActivity && m_nLockCnt == 0)
#endif
                    break;
        }
    }
    CloseHandle(hEventShutdown);
    PostThreadMessage(dwThreadID, WM_QUIT, 0, 0);
}

bool CExeModule::StartMonitor()
{
    hEventShutdown = CreateEvent(NULL, false, false, NULL);
    if (hEventShutdown == NULL)
        return false;
    DWORD dwThreadID;
    HANDLE h = CreateThread(NULL, 0, MonitorProc, this, 0, &dwThreadID);
    return (h != NULL);
}
```

This code is there so the server will shut down correctly even if it has multiple threads executing within it.

The key piece of code that the ATL/COM AppWizard created is the `_tWinMain` function in `svroutofprocess.cpp`. Most of you already know that the `WinMain` function is the equivalent of the standard C/C++ main function. It is the entry point for a process, the first piece of code called by the operating system. The WinMain function that was generated by the ATL AppWizard is shown in Listing 6.4.

LISTING 6.4 *IMPLEMENTING* _tWinMain *IN* svroutofprocess.cpp

```
extern "C" int WINAPI _tWinMain(HINSTANCE hInstance,
    HINSTANCE /*hPrevInstance*/, LPTSTR lpCmdLine, int /*nShowCmd*/)
{
    lpCmdLine = GetCommandLine(); //this line necessary for _ATL_MIN_CRT

#if _WIN32_WINNT >= 0x0400 & defined(_ATL_FREE_THREADED)
    HRESULT hRes = CoInitializeEx(NULL, COINIT_MULTITHREADED);
#else
    HRESULT hRes = CoInitialize(NULL);
#endif
    _ASSERTE(SUCCEEDED(hRes));
    _Module.Init(ObjectMap, hInstance, &LIBID_SVROUTOFPROCESSLib);
    _Module.dwThreadID = GetCurrentThreadId();
    TCHAR szTokens[] = _T("-/");

    int nRet = 0;
    BOOL bRun = TRUE;
    LPCTSTR lpszToken = FindOneOf(lpCmdLine, szTokens);
    while (lpszToken != NULL)
    {
        if (lstrcmpi(lpszToken, _T("UnregServer"))==0)
        {
            _Module.UpdateRegistryFromResource(IDR_Svroutofprocess,
            FALSE);
            nRet = _Module.UnregisterServer(TRUE);
            bRun = FALSE;
            break;
        }
        if (lstrcmpi(lpszToken, _T("RegServer"))==0)
        {
            _Module.UpdateRegistryFromResource(IDR_Svroutofprocess,
            TRUE);
            nRet = _Module.RegisterServer(TRUE);
            bRun = FALSE;
            break;
        }
        lpszToken = FindOneOf(lpszToken, szTokens);
    }

```

```
38.     if (bRun)
39.     {
40.         _Module.StartMonitor();
41. #if _WIN32_WINNT >= 0x0400 & defined(_ATL_FREE_THREADED)
42.         hRes = _Module.RegisterClassObjects(CLSCTX_LOCAL_SERVER,
43.             REGCLS_MULTIPLEUSE | REGCLS_SUSPENDED);
44.         _ASSERTE(SUCCEEDED(hRes));
45.         hRes = CoResumeClassObjects();
46. #else
47.         hRes = _Module.RegisterClassObjects(CLSCTX_LOCAL_SERVER,
48.             REGCLS_MULTIPLEUSE);
49. #endif
50.         _ASSERTE(SUCCEEDED(hRes));
51.
52.         MSG msg;
53.         while (GetMessage(&msg, 0, 0, 0))
54.             DispatchMessage(&msg);
55.
56.         _Module.RevokeClassObjects();
57.         Sleep(dwPause);        //wait for any threads to finish
58.     }
59.
60.     _Module.Term();
61.     CoUninitialize();
62.     return nRet;
63. }
```

The code on line 4 gets the command line that was passed to the process, so you can see if `regserver` or `unregserver` was passed as an argument. The lines 6 thru 10 enter the multi-threaded apartment if you are running on either Windows 98 or Windows NT 4.0 and the symbol `_ATL_FREE_THREADED` is defined (it's not), or a single-threaded apartment otherwise.

Don't let my use of the word apartment throw you off here. For now you can think of a call to `CoInitialize` as simply initializing COM. I discuss apartments in Chapter 9 when I talk about threading. Also, the symbol `_ATL_APARTMENT_THREADED` is defined in the `stdafx.h` file of your project. If you want to create a free-threaded server, you can change the code that defines `_ATL_APARTMENT_THREADED` to `_ATL_FREE_THREADED`. I talk about why you may want to do this and what the implications are in Chapter 9.

The code in lines 18 through 36 parses the command line and looks for the symbols `UnregServer` or `RegServer`. If `UnregServer` is passed on the command line to the process, then the code unregisters the server. If

RegServer is passed on the command line to the server, then the code registers the server.

The calls that you make to the UpdateRegistryFromResource method instantiate the ATL Registry Component. The calls to RegisterServer and UnRegisterServer, insert and remove, respectively, all of the CLSID's implemented in the server beneath the HKEY_CLASSES_ROOT key in the registry.

Lines 18 thru 36 implement the COM standard for registering an executable server. To register this server, execute the following at a command prompt or in a batch file:

```
svroutofprocess.exe /RegServer
```

To unregister this server, use this command:

```
Servername.exe /UnregServer
```

Lines 40 through 57 register the class objects for all of the COM classes implemented in the server with the COM runtime. Line 40 calls the StartMonitor function in the CExeModule class. The next nine lines of code call the RegisterClassObjects method on the _Module object, passing in REGCLS_MULTIPLEUSE | REGCLS_SUSPENDED for the second parameter if _ATL_FREE_THREADED is defined, or REGCLS_MULTIPLEUSE if it isn't. RegisterClassObjects calls the CoRegisterClassObject function for each COM class implemented in the server. You can see that the server is multi-use by default. If you wish to change the server to be single-use, you need only change REGCLS_MULTIPLEUSE to REGCLS_SINGLEUSE.

Lines 52 through 54 implement a windows message loop. Any server that implements objects that do not handle their own concurrency protection need to have a message loop to make COM's concurrency protection (Single Threaded Apartments) work. If this sentence makes no sense to you, just keep reading, I explain apartments in Chapter 9. Finally, when the message loop terminates, the server revokes all the class objects using the CoRevokeClassObject function and then sleeps for one second to give the server a chance to cleanup before it exits the apartment by calling the CoUninitialize function.

At this point you probably know more about this server than you want to know. Let's add a COM class to the server.

Adding a Test Class to the Server

To add a COM class to your out-of-process server, perform the following steps:

1. Select New ATL Object... from the Insert menu (the ATL Object Wizard appears).

2. Under Category, select Object and under Object, select Simple Object.
3. Click the Next button (the ATL Object Wizard Properties dialog appears).
4. On the Names tab enter TestClass in the Short Name field under C++.
5. Click the Attributes tab.
6. Change the interface type to custom.
7. Check the ISupportErrorInfo checkbox.
8. Click OK.

Implementing the ITestClass Interface

Your test class will have only the one interface that was defined by the ATL Object Wizard, ITestClass.

To implement the LongOperation method, perform these steps:

1. Right-click on the ITestClass interface in the ClassView tab of the Visual C++ Workspace.
2. Select Add Method to Interface... from the Context menu that appears.
3. Enter LongOperation for the Method Name.
4. Click OK.

To implement the LongOperationArgs method, perform the following steps:

1. Right-click on the ITestClass interface in the ClassView tab of the Visual C++ Workspace.
2. Select Add Method to Interface... from the Context menu that appears.
3. Enter LongOperationArgs for the Method Name.
4. Enter [in,string] LPOLESTR arg1,[out] double *arg2, [out,size_is(2048)] unsigned char *arg3,[out,retval] long *returnValue in the Parameters field.
5. Click OK.

You won't bother looking at these methods, because they are not going to do anything. Compile your project. Notice that Visual C++ registers your server for you. There is one more thing you have to do to make your server work. Do you remember what it is? You need to compile and register your marshaling DLL. As long as your server has custom interfaces—which ours does—you have to build and register this DLL. Had you elected to create Dual Interfaces (which is the default) instead of custom interfaces for your COM class on the Attributes tab of the ATL Object Wizard, you could use the universal marshaler, but the universal marshaler will not work for custom interfaces like yours. For now though, let's pretend that you forgot to do this and you'll see the effects shortly. Let's build a client for your server.

Creating an In-Process Version of Your Server

The only way to assess the performance impact of implementing a COM class in an out-of-process server is to compare its performance with a similar COM class implemented in an in-process server. So you'll build a version of your server that runs in-process. To do this, perform the following steps in Visual C++ to create an in-process server project:

1. Select `New...` from the `File` menu (the `New` dialog appears).
2. Click the `Projects` tab.
3. Select `ATL COM AppWizard` from the presented list of project types.
4. Enter `svrinprocess` in the `Project` Name field.
5. Click `OK` (the ATL/COM AppWizard appears).
6. Select `Dynamic Link Library` (DLL) under `Server` Type (accept the defaults for the other settings on this window).
7. Click `Finish`.

Now follow the steps outlined above under the headings "Add a Test Class to the Server" and "Implement the `ITestClass` Interface." Make sure you compile the server.

Creating a Client

The client uses high-resolution timing to record the amount of time it takes to call the `LongOperation` and `LongOperationArgs` methods in both the out-of-process and in-process servers. If you want to learn more about high-resolution timing, see the *High Resolution Timing* sidebar in this chapter. To build your client, you will perform the following steps:

1. Create a dialog-based project using the MFC AppWizard.
2. Create the user interface.
3. Add the code needed to enable COM support.
4. Import the type library for your servers.
5. Add smart pointer instances for the out-of-process and in-process COM classes to our dialog class.
6. Instantiate our COM objects.
7. Get the high-resolution timer frequency.
8. Implement the user interface.

CREATING A DIALOG-BASED PROJECT USING THE MFC APPWIZARD

Start Visual C++ and then execute the following steps:

1. Select `New...` from the `File` menu (the New dialog appears).
2. Click the `Projects` tab.
3. Select `MFC AppWizard (exe)` from the presented list of project types.
4. Enter `Timingclient` in the `Project` Name field.
5. Click `OK` (the MFC App Wizard appears).
6. Click the radio button labeled "`Dialog-based`".
7. Click `Finish` (the New Project Information dialog appears).
8. Click `OK`.

CREATING THE USER INTERFACE

The client for your server will look like the one shown in Figure 6.7.

Using the MFC class wizard, map button clicked (`BN_CLICKED`) message handlers to the four buttons on the main window dialog as specified in Table 6.1.

TABLE 6.1 Message Handler Methods

Button Caption	Message Handler for Button
TestArgs (Out of Process Frame)	OnTestArgsOutOfProcessButton
Test (Out of Process Frame)	OnTestOutOfProcessButton
TestArgs (In Process Frame)	OnTestArgsInProcessButton
Test (In Process Frame)	OnTestInProcessButton

If you gave your client project the name that I specified (`Timingclient`), the message handlers shown in Table 6.1 should be member functions of a class called `CTimingclientDlg`.

Next, use the MFC ClassWizard to map variables to the three edit boxes on the main window dialog. The edit box closest to the top of the dialog lets the user enter the number of times the selected COM object method will be called. The two edit boxes closer to the bottom of the dialog show the total time required to make the method calls and the average time of each call. Map these edit boxes as shown in Table 6.2.

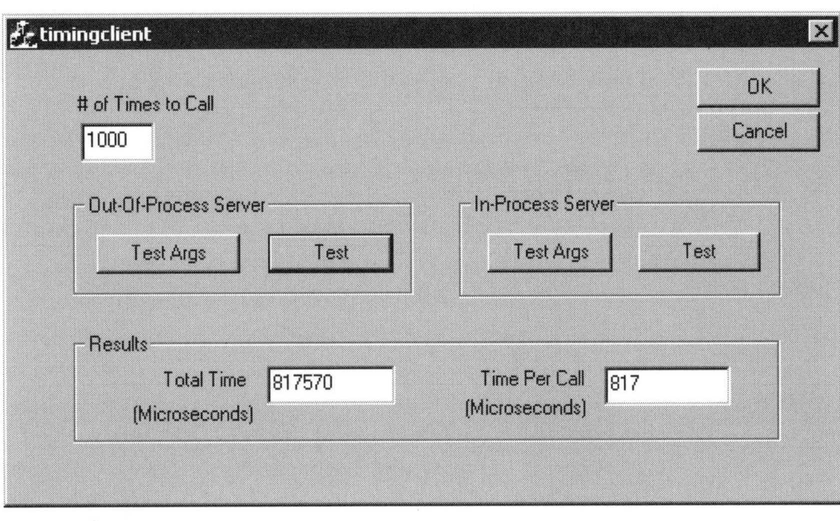

FIGURE 6.7 Test Client.

TABLE 6.2 Mapping of Member Variables to Controls

Edit Box Purpose	Map to Member Variable	Member Variable Type
Number of times to call method	M_timesToCall	Long
Total time required to make method calls	M_totalTime	Long
Average time per call	M_timePerCall	Long

ADDING THE CODE NEEDED TO ENABLE COM SUPPORT

To enable COM support, you need to add a call to `AfxOleInit` to the `InitInstance` method of your `Application` class. Add the bolded lines of code to the `InitInstance` of the `CTimingclientApp` class:

```
BOOL CTimingclientApp::InitInstance()
{
    if (!AfxOleInit())
        AfxMessageBox("Could not initialize COM");
// the rest of the code in this function is omitted for clarity
}
```

IMPORTING THE TYPE LIBRARY FOR YOUR SERVERS

You now need to import the type libraries for both of your servers. Add the following two lines to the `stdafx.h` file in your client project:

```
#import "c:\alan\books\vcppbook\demos\chapter6\svroutofprocess\
   svroutofprocess.tlb"
#import "c:\alan\books\vcppbook\demos\chapter6\svrinprocess\
   svrinprocess.tlb"
// Add the import statements directly above the AFX_INSERT_LOCATION comment
//{{AFX_INSERT_LOCATION}}
```

If you are following along, you must change these paths to match the location of the `svroutofprocess` and `svrinprocess` projects on your machine. Or add the directories to the default search path.

ADDING SMART POINTER INSTANCES TO YOUR DIALOG CLASS

To use the smart pointer class, you need to add these bold lines of code to the main window dialog class of your project:

```
class CTimingclientDlg : public CDialog {
// The rest of the code for this class is omitted for clarity...
private:
   SVROUTOFPROCESSLib::ITestClassPtr mServerOutOfProcess;
   SVRINPROCESSLib::ITestClassPtr mServerInProcess;
};
```

INSTANTIATING YOUR COM OBJECTS

Next you need to instantiate your out-of-process and in-process COM object. To do so, call the `CreateInstance` method on both of your smart pointer classes. Add the bolded code shown below to the `OnInitDialog` of the `CTimingclientDlg` class:

```
BOOL CTimingclientDlg::OnInitDialog()
{
   // The rest of the code in this method is omitted for clarity...

   // TODO: Add extra initialization here
   HRESULT hRes;
   hRes=mServerOutOfProcess.CreateInstance("svroutofprocess.testclass");
   if (FAILED(hRes))
```

```
    {
        _com_error err(hRes);
        AfxMessageBox(err.ErrorMessage());

    }
    hRes=mServerInProcess.CreateInstance("svrinprocess.testclass");
    if (FAILED(hRes))
    {
        _com_error err(hRes);
        AfxMessageBox(err.ErrorMessage());

    }
    return TRUE;    // return TRUE unless you set the focus to a control
}
```

GETTING THE HIGH-RESOLUTION TIMER FREQUENCY

You need to get and store the frequency of the high-resolution counter so you can convert your timings that you will obtain later into microseconds. The frequency of this counter varies from machine to machine. To store the frequency, add the bolded code below to the CTimingclientDlg class:

```
class CTimingclientDlg : public CDialog {
// The rest of the code for this class is omitted for clarity...
private:
    __int64 m_highResFrequency;

};
```

The frequency of the high-resolution timer is returned as a 64-bit integer, hence the compiler specific type __int64 is used to hold the frequency. To get the frequency, add the bolded code shown below to the OnInitDialog method of CtimingclientDlg:

```
BOOL CTimingclientDlg::OnInitDialog()
{
    // The rest of the code in this method is omitted for clarity...

    // TODO: Add extra initialization here
    if (FALSE==QueryPerformanceFrequency((LARGE_INTEGER*)
            &m_highResFrequency))
    {
        AfxMessageBox("Could not get high resolution timer");
        return FALSE;
```

```
    }

    HRESULT hRes;
    return TRUE;  // return TRUE  unless you set the focus to a control
}
```

High Resolution Timing

It was more difficult than I initially thought it would be to gather timing data for your servers. Most of you are probably familiar with the `GetTickCount` and `GetCurrentTime` methods (they both do the same thing). They let you gather timings with millisecond resolution. Because the calls to the DLL server are so fast, you really need microsecond resolution timing. The only way to do this is with the high-resolution timing functions in the Windows API: `QueryPerformanceFrequency` and `QueryPerformanceCounter`. `QueryPerformanceFrequency` lets you determine the frequency of the high-resolution timer on your system. The prototype for this function is shown below:

```
BOOL QueryPerformanceFrequency( LARGE_INTEGER * lpFrequency);
```

If your system supports a high-resolution timer (most do) the output parameter, `*lpFrequency`, will contain the frequency in counts per second and the return value will be `TRUE`. If your machine does not support a high-resolution timer, then the return value will be `FALSE` and `*lpFrequency` will be zero. The frequency is returned as a 64-bit integer (`LARGE_INTEGER`). `QueryPerformanceCounter` returns the current value of the high-resolution timer; its prototype is shown below:

```
BOOL QueryPerformanceCounter( LARGE_INTEGER *lpHighResCount);
```

You use this function just like `GetTickCount`. You call it at the start of an operation and record the count, and then you call it again at the end of the operation. The difference between these two counts is the elapsed time of the operation. You can turn this elapsed time into microseconds by multiplying the elapsed time by 1,000,000 and then dividing by the frequency you get from `QueryPerformanceFrequency`.

IMPLEMENTING THE USER INTERFACE

Now you can finish off your client by implementing the logic for the `Test` and `Test Args` buttons for both servers. The message handlers for the `Test` and `Test Args` buttons for the out-of-process server are shown here:

```
void CTimingclientDlg:: OnTestOutOfProcessButton ()
{
    long i;
    __int64 startTime, stopTime;
    UpdateData(TRUE);
```

```
    if (FALSE==QueryPerformanceCounter((LARGE_INTEGER*)&startTime)) {
        AfxMessageBox("Count not get start counter");
        return;
    }

    for (i=0;i<m_timesToCall;i++) {
        mServerOutOfProcess->LongOperation();
    }

    if (FALSE==QueryPerformanceCounter((LARGE_INTEGER*)&stopTime)) {
        AfxMessageBox("Count not get start counter");
        return;
    }
    m_totalTime=((stopTime-startTime)*1000000)/m_highResFrequency;
    if (m_timesToCall > 0)
        m_timePerCall=m_totalTime/m_timesToCall;
    else
        m_timePerCall=0;
    UpdateData(FALSE);
}

void CTimingclientDlg:: OnTestArgsOutOfProcessButton ()
{
    long i, returnValue;
    __int64 startTime, stopTime;

    double arg2;
    unsigned char arg3[2048];
    UpdateData(TRUE);

    if (FALSE==QueryPerformanceCounter((LARGE_INTEGER*)&startTime)) {
        AfxMessageBox("Count not get start counter");
        return;
    }

    for (i=0;i<m_timesToCall;i++) {
        returnValue=mServerOutOfProcess-
>LongOperationArgs(OLESTR("ALAN"),&arg2,arg3);
    }

    if (FALSE==QueryPerformanceCounter((LARGE_INTEGER*)&stopTime)) {
        AfxMessageBox("Count not get start counter");
        return;
    }
```

```
   m_totalTime=((stopTime-startTime)*1000000)/m_highResFrequency;
   if (m_timesToCall > 0)
      m_timePerCall=m_totalTime/m_timesToCall;
   else
      m_timePerCall=0;
   UpdateData(FALSE);
}
```

In both cases, you call QueryPerformanceCounter to get the start time. Next, you call the method on your object, either LongOperation or LongOperationArgs, and finally call QueryPerformance counter again to get the ending time. You next calculate the total time in microseconds to make the specified number of method calls and then divide the total time by the number of method calls to get the time per method call.

The message handlers for the in-process methods are implemented in similar fashion. The only difference is that the method calls are made on the mServerInProcess smart pointer instead of mServerOutOfProcess.

```
void CTimingclientDlg:: OnTestInProcessButton ()
{
   long i;
   __int64 startTime, stopTime;
   UpdateData(TRUE);

   if (FALSE==QueryPerformanceCounter((LARGE_INTEGER*)&startTime)) {
      AfxMessageBox("Count not get start counter");
      return;
   }

   for (i=0;i<m_timesToCall;i++) {
      mServerInProcess->LongOperation();
   }

   if (FALSE==QueryPerformanceCounter((LARGE_INTEGER*)&stopTime)) {
      AfxMessageBox("Count not get start counter");
      return;
   }

   m_totalTime=((stopTime-startTime)*1000000)/m_highResFrequency;
   if (m_timesToCall > 0)
      m_timePerCall=m_totalTime/m_timesToCall;
   else
      m_timePerCall=0;
   UpdateData(FALSE);
}
```

```
void CTimingclientDlg:: OnTestInProcessArgsButton()
{
   long i, returnValue;
   __int64 startTime, stopTime;
   double arg2;
   unsigned char arg3[2048];
   UpdateData(TRUE);

   if (FALSE==QueryPerformanceCounter((LARGE_INTEGER*)&startTime)) {
       AfxMessageBox("Count not get start counter");
       return;
   }
   for (i=0;i<m_timesToCall;i++) {
       returnValue=mServerInProcess-
>LongOperationArgs(OLESTR("ALAN"),&arg2,arg3);
   }

   if (FALSE==QueryPerformanceCounter((LARGE_INTEGER*)&stopTime)) {
       AfxMessageBox("Count not get start counter");
       return;
   }

   m_totalTime=((stopTime-startTime)*1000000)/m_highResFrequency;
   if (m_timesToCall > 0)
       m_timePerCall=m_totalTime/m_timesToCall;
   else
       m_timePerCall=0;
   UpdateData(FALSE);
}
```

Compile the client and now you are ready to explore the differences between an in-process and an out-of-process server.

Performance Testing

Run the client. If you have not registered the marshaling DLL, you should see the error shown in Figure 6.8.

FIGURE 6.8

Without the Marshaling DLL, You Should Receive the Following Error.

You receive this error when you attempt to create an instance of COM class that is implemented in an out-of-process server if the COM runtime cannot locate a marshaling DLL for the COM class. On seeing that the server is out-of-process, COM attempts to locate a marshaling DLL for the requested `ITestClass` interface. It searches the `Registry` key shown below:

```
HKEY_CLASSES_ROOT\interface\"IID"
```

Where IID is the GUID for `ITestClass`. Beneath this key should be the CLSID of the marshaling DLL for the `ITestClass` interface. Right now this registry key does not exist. Because `ITestClass` is a custom interface, you have to build and register the MIDL-generated marshaler to create this registry key.

When you create a project with the ATL/COM AppWizard, it generates a makefile that you can use to build the marshaling DLL. This makefile has the name `projectnameps.mk`. If you look in the directory where you just built your server project, you should see a file called `svroutofprocessps.mk`. This makefile compiles all the source code generated by MIDL from your project's IDL file and it links with the RPC runtime. Type the following at a command prompt to build the marshaling DLL:

```
nmake svroutofprocessps.mk
```

If your system does not recognize the nmake command, you need to run vcvars32.bat which you can find in the bin directory of your Visual C++ installation. On a Windows machine, enter the following command in the bin directory: vcvars32 /x86.

Register the marshaling DLL with is:

```
regsvr32 svroutofprocessps.mk
```

Now try running the client again; it should work this time.

Remember to change directories to the directory where you are building your project.

PERFORMANCE DATA

Now that your client is working, let's gather some numbers. Table 6.3 summarizes the results I found running the client on a Pentium 200 with 96MB of memory.

TABLE 6.3 Performance Results for 1000 Method Calls

Server Type and Method Call	Total Time (microseconds)	Time per Call (microseconds)
Out-of-process without arguments	817839	817
Out-of-process with arguments	1272632	1272
In-Process without arguments	975	1
In-Process with arguments	1015	1

Pretty startling results. It takes 817 microseconds (.8 milliseconds) to call the `LongOperation` method in the out-of-process server. Adding arguments makes the method call about 50% slower. It takes 1272 microseconds (1.27 milliseconds) to call `LongOperationArgs`. Most of this is time spent marshaling the method call across processes.

The proxy is taking the method call turning it into an IPC and sending the IPC message to the out-of-process server via Local RPC. The stub is interpreting the messaging, calling the method, and sending the result back to the stub. You didn't have to write the software to do all of this, but that does not mean that you won't pay the price in performance. You could make this faster if you wanted by implementing a custom marshaling DLL, but that is beyond the scope of this book. See Chapter 5 of *Essential COM* by Don Box or Chapter 6 of *Inside OLE* by Craig Brockschmidt for a discussion of writing a custom marshaling DLL.

To be fair, most of the 50% slow down for the arguments is caused by argument 3, the 2K string. If you reduce the size of this string to 1K, the time for making the method drops almost down to that for the method call without arguments. By playing around with this parameter, I was able to summize that LRPC (Local RPC is used for this case, because you are not going across machines) sends messages in blocks of approximately 2K. Increasing the size of the arguments so that the total size of the arguments was greater than 2K caused a significant slow down.

The call to the in-process server is, for all intents and purposes, instantaneous. All that is needed to make a method call on a COM object in an in-process server is a pointer dereference.

Remember, a COM interface is an array of function pointers.

De-referencing a pointer is a fast operation. Adding arguments to the method does not make this call significantly slower. The additional parameter only requires the additional time to set up a larger stack frame. Again, this does not take much time.

PERFORMANCE IMPLICATIONS

What does this mean? It means that method calls on an object implemented in an out-of-process server are an expensive operation. On my machine, it takes approximately a millisecond to call such a method. That may not seem like a long time, but it is an eternity to a computer. You should always keep this in mind when you are designing an out-of-process server. Design your server to minimize the number of method calls that a client must make. For instance, if there are three values that need to be initialized in your server, rather than having three separate methods the user must call to set each value separately, create one method the user can call to set all three. Also, where it makes sense, you may have to let a user call one method that performs several operations at once. This problem becomes even more accute if your client and server are running on separate machines. I talk about DCOM in Chapter 10.

Single-Use Versus Multi-Use Revisited

Before you leave this chapter, let's explore the difference between a single-use and a multi-use server one last time. Run two instances of the timing client. Check the task manager if you are using Windows NT or Windows 2000, or press CTRL-ATL-DEL and look at the task list if you are using Windows 95/98. You should see one instance of `svroutofprocess.exe` running. This is exactly the behavior to expect from a multi-use server. All objects implemented within a multi-use server run in a single instance of the server process. To convert your server to a single-use server, open the out-of-process server project and go to the file `svroutofprocess.cpp`. Change the following code:

```
#if _WIN32_WINNT >= 0x0400 & defined(_ATL_FREE_THREADED)
   hRes = _Module.RegisterClassObjects(CLSCTX_LOCAL_SERVER,
      REGCLS_MULTIPLEUSE | REGCLS_SUSPENDED);
   _ASSERTE(SUCCEEDED(hRes));
   hRes = CoResumeClassObjects();
#else
   hRes = _Module.RegisterClassObjects(CLSCTX_LOCAL_SERVER,
      REGCLS_MULTIPLEUSE);
#endif
```

It should look like this:

```
#if _WIN32_WINNT >= 0x0400 & defined(_ATL_FREE_THREADED)
   hRes = _Module.RegisterClassObjects(CLSCTX_LOCAL_SERVER,
      REGCLS_SINGLEUSE | REGCLS_SUSPENDED);
```

```
   _ASSERTE(SUCCEEDED(hRes));
   hRes = CoResumeClassObjects();
#else
   hRes = _Module.RegisterClassObjects(CLSCTX_LOCAL_SERVER,
      REGCLS_SINGLEUSE);
#endif
```

Compile the server and run two instances of the timing client. You should see two instances of the server process running now. Each object you instantiate runs in its own process. Which one is better? The trade-off here is between fault isolation and data isolation for a single-use server and efficient use of server resources and data sharing for the multi-use server. Which one is better depends on your application and which of these attributes is most important.

Summary

In this chapter, you learned about out-of-process (executable) COM servers. You learned that out-of-process servers provide greater fault isolation and, if the server is multi-use, sharing of data between objects servicing multiple clients. The principle negative of out-of-process servers is that they require marshaling support. This means that if your server implements custom interfaces, you must build a marshaling DLL. This can be easily built from code that is generated by MIDL from the IDL for the server. You also learned there is a substantial performance difference between making method calls in an out-of-process server as compared to an in-process server. Performance tests on my machine showed that it took approximately one millisecond to make a method call on an out-of-process server. It took approximately one microsecond to make the same call on an in-process server. In the next chapter, I explore Automation.

SEVEN

Automation

All the interfaces you have created so far are custom or vtable interfaces. When you call a method in one of those interfaces, your compiler (which has a priori knowledge of the interface through either a header file or type library) determines the offset of the method in the vtable and generates code to call the method. There are several problems with this approach. One problem is that this approach *does* require a priori knowledge of the interfaces supported by a COM server. This information may not always be available. Sometimes, you may want to write code that calls a method in a COM interface assuming that the interface supports the method. If the interface does not support the method, you want to handle the error at runtime. Interpreted languages, in particular, need this functionality. Another problem is that many programming languages do not work well with pointers, let alone pointers to functions, or arrays of function pointers. Also, many programming languages do not have a data model rich enough to work with all COM interfaces. It is easy to define a COM interface that cannot be called from Visual Basic. You cannot, for instance call OLEDB interfaces directly from Visual Basic; that's one of the reasons that Active Data Objects (ADO) exist.

OLEDB is a data-access API that is defined as a set of COM interfaces.

Automation and the `IDispatch` interface are the solution to all of these problems. They allow COM to be easily useable by simple scripting languages and interpreters.

Defining Automation

Automation is using the `IDispatch` interface to enable communication between a COM client and a server. A client that talks to a COM server through `IDispatch` is called an Automation controller. A COM server that implements `IDispatch` is called an Automation server. Microsoft created the `IDispatch` interface because they wanted to expose the functionality of Microsoft Office applications via COM interfaces. But they wanted to make these interfaces accessible to the kinds of simple scripting languages (Visual Basic for instance) that power users and Information Technology (IT) personnel like to use. Microsoft's goal was to let these kinds of programmers *automate* common business processes using Microsoft Office applications. One example is using Microsoft Excel to generate a chart from data that it queried from a database, embed the chart into a report that is written in Word, and then e-mail the report to a group of people. The name Automation derived from this goal of allowing people to *automate* business processes.

The Visual Basic group at Microsoft designed the `IDispatch` interface. Because of this, Automation servers are easiest to use from Visual Basic and similar 4GL languages such as `PowerBuilder`. If you are using C++, it is actually easier to use vtable interfaces.

More Naming Confusion

The World of Automation within COM forms yet another minefield of confusing and altered names. Back in the days when COM was still called OLE, Automation was called OLE Automation. OLE Automation meant the same thing as Automation as I have defined it: using the `IDispatch` interface to communicate between a COM client and server. Recently, Microsoft has attempted to change the meaning of Automation. The new definition of Automation is that it is a technology that allows an application to expose its features as services that can be programmed using scripting languages. An application exposes its features as COM objects that are officially called `ActiveX` objects. These `ActiveX` objects can implement dual interfaces or even custom, vtable interfaces. The use of dispinterfaces and the `IDispatch` interface is no longer a requirement. Unfortunately (or fortunately depending on how you look at it) most people don't seem to be "buying into" this changed definition. Most COM-related books and articles that I have seen recently are still using the word Automation to refer only to communication via the `IDispatch` interface. In this chapter, I use the popular (and original) meaning of the word Automation and eschew the party line.

IDispatch

I have said that Automation is using the `IDispatch` interface to communicate between clients and servers. That begs the question, what is `IDispatch`? `IDispatch` is a COM interface. The code below shows the declaration of the `IDispatch` interface, which can be found in the file `oaidl.idl`:

```
interface IDispatch : IUnknown
{
    HRESULT GetTypeInfoCount(
                [out] UINT * pctinfo
            );
    HRESULT GetTypeInfo(
                [in] UINT iTInfo,
                [in] LCID lcid,
                [out] ITypeInfo ** ppTInfo
            );
    HRESULT GetIDsOfNames(
                [in] REFIID riid,
                [in, size_is(cNames)] LPOLESTR * rgszNames,
                [in] UINT cNames,
                [in] LCID lcid,
                [out, size_is(cNames)] DISPID * rgDispId
            );
HRESULT Invoke(
                [in] DISPID dispIdMember,
                [in] REFIID riid,
                [in] LCID lcid,
                [in] WORD wFlags,
                [in, out] DISPPARAMS * pDispParams,
                [out] VARIANT * pVarResult,
                [out] EXCEPINFO * pExcepInfo,
                [out] UINT * puArgErr
            );
}
```

The two most important functions in `IDispatch` are `GetIDsOfNames` and `Invoke`.

GetIDsOfNames

When using the `IDispatch` interface, you must associate an integer ID with each method in your interface (you'll see how to do this shortly). This integer ID is called a Dispatch ID or DISPID. `GetIDsOfNames` lets you retrieve this integer ID given a textual name for a function. This works well for interpreted languages. With a compiled language, the development environment has information about the methods supported by a particular interface (the name of its methods, type and number of arguments to the method, and the return type of the method). This information either comes from a type library or from a header file. With an interpreted language, like Visual Basic Script or JavaScript, such a priori knowledge of an interface is not available. For instance, a Web browser interprets Visual Basic Script and Java Script as the HTML file is parsed. Or, if the Visual Basic code is in an Active Server Page, a Visual Basic runtime in the Web server interprets the script when the Active Server Page is requested. In either case, if the script uses a COM object, the calls to the object need to be interpreted at runtime. The `GetIDsOfNames` method in `IDispatch` lets an interpreter ask a server at runtime if it supports a method and returns an ID that the interpreter can use to make the method call.

Using IDispatch to Build a Dynamic Client Application

`IDispatch` and Automation lets you create certain kinds of applications that would be difficult or impossible to create without it. For instance, you may want to create an application that can work with any server. The application first lets the user select a COM server from a list. This application then presents to the user a list of methods and properties that the server supports and lets the user invoke a method or manipulate a property. If you want to see an application of this type, check out the ActiveX Control Test Container in Visual C++. If you have installed Visual C++ on your system, you'll find the ActiveX Control Test Container on the `Start` Menu under `\Programs\Microsoft Visual Studio 6.0\Microsoft Visual Studio 6.0 Tools\`. If you run it, you will see the Window shown in Figure 7.1.

The ActiveX Control Test Container is a COM client (an Automation controller) that can be used to test ActiveX Controls while they are in development.

You can import the Calendar ActiveX control into the ActiveX Control Test Container with the following steps:

1. Select `Insert New Control` from the `Edit` menu.
2. Choose `Calendar Control 8.0` from the list that appears.
3. Click `OK`.

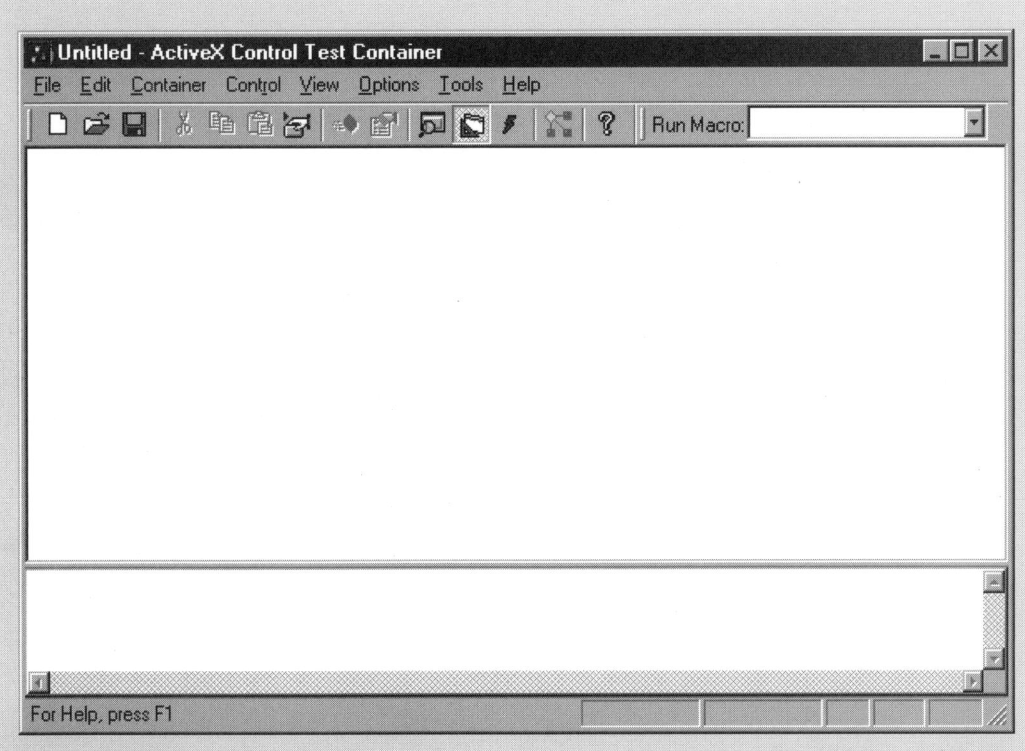

FIGURE 7.1 The ActiveX Control Test Container.

You can see a list of the methods and properties the control supports by selecting `Invoke` Methods from the `Control` menu. This brings up the `Invoke` Methods dialog shown in Figure 7.2.

You can change the background color of the calendar to a rather annoying red by performing the following steps:

1. Select `BackColor` (PropPut) from the `Method Name` drop-down.
2. Select `VT_UI4` from the `Parameter` Type drop-down.
3. Type 255 into the Parameter Value edit box.
4. Click the `Set Value` Button.
5. Click the `Invoke` Button.

The ActiveX Control Test Container is an Automation controller; it can invoke the methods of the Calendar Control and, indeed any control, without having information about the control compiled into the application. The ActiveX Control Test Container constructs its

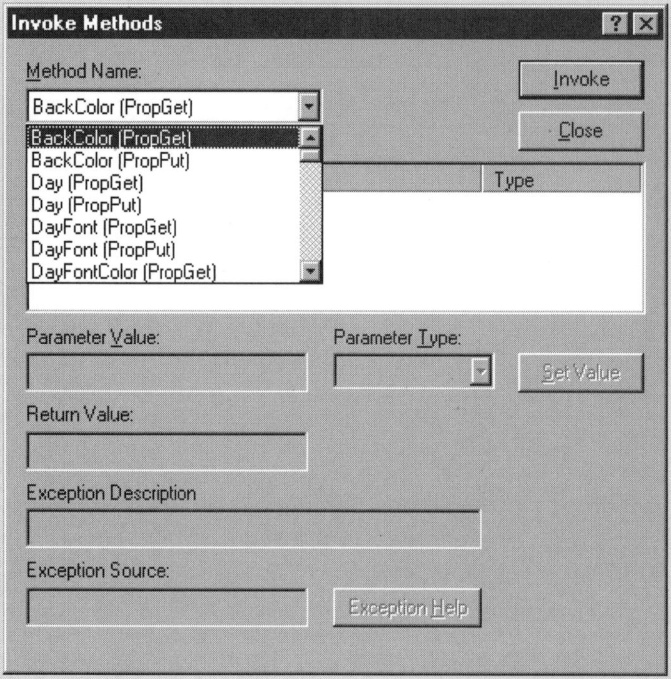

FIGURE 7.2

The Invoke Methods Dialog in the ActiveX Control Test Container.

method calls at runtime using `IDispatch`. It reads the type library information for the control through the `GetTypeInfoCount` and `GetTypeInfo` methods of `IDispatch`, uses `GetIDsOfNames` to find the DISPID for a method or property, and then uses `Invoke` to actually call the method or property. It would be difficult to build an application like the ActiveX Control Test Container without `IDispatch`. There are other kinds of applications you can build with `IDispatch` that would be difficult to build without it. For instance, you can develop an application that searches your network for an object that implements certain functionality and then dynamically constructs and issues a method call to use that functionality.

ActiveX controls are COM components that implement a defined set of interfaces and obey a set of rules outlined in the ActiveX control standard.

Invoke

The `Invoke` method is the real key to the `IDispatch` interface. I like to call it a gateway method because it acts as a gateway through which you can call other methods supported by a server. `Invoke` is a complex method that has eight arguments. Table 7.1 summarizes the arguments and their purpose.

TABLE 7.1 Arguments for the Invoke Method of IDispatch

Argument Name	Argument Purpose
dispIdMember	The dispatch identifier (DISPID) of the method that you wish to call.
riid	Reserved, and should always be null (actually IID_NULL).
locale ID	The location ID. Applications that do not support multiple languages can ignore this argument. In most cases you can pass the result of the GetUserDefaultLCID function.
wFlags	The kind of procedure you wish to Invoke: property get, property put, or method. The four possible values you can pass are: DISPATCH_METHOD, DISPATCH_PROPERTYGET, DISPATCH_PROPERTYPUT, DISPATCH_PROPERTYPUTREF.
pDispParams	A pointer to a structure that contains the input arguments for the method or property that you are calling. The structure essentially contains an array of Variants.
pVarResult	A pointer to a Variant that contains the return value from the method or property. You can pass NULL if you do not expect a return value. This argument is ignored if DISPATCH_PROPERTYPUT or DISPATCH_PROPERTYPUTREF is specified for wFlags.
pExcepInfo	Pointer to a structure that contains exception information. This structure should be filled in if DISP_E_EXCEPTION is returned. Can be Null.
PuArgErr	The index within *rgvarg* of the first argument that has an error. Arguments are stored in *pDispParams->rgvarg* in reverse order, so the first argument is the one with the highest index in the array. This parameter is returned only when the resulting return value is DISP_E_TYPEMISMATCH or DISP_E_PARAMNOTFOUND.

The `Invoke` method lets you call (invoke) a method in an Automation server by specifying the DISPID of the method (`dispIDMember`), the type of method (`wFlags`), and the set of input parameters (`pDispParams`). The return value of the method call stored in the `pVarResult`. And if the method call fails, exception information is stored in the `pExcepInfo` parameter.

GetTypeInfo and GetTypeInfoCount

A client can call GetIDsOfNames to retrieve the DISPID for a method in an IDispatch interface, but that isn't enough information to dynamically build a call for that method. The GetTypeInfo and GetTypeInfoCount methods in IDispatch let you retrieve type information about a particular IDispatch interface. This type of information includes the names and return type of each method in the interface, and the number and types of the parameters for each method. GetTypeInfo and GetTypeInfoCount are optional and you should always call GetTypeInfoCount before calling GetTypeInfo. If GetTypeInfoCount returns 0, then type library information is unavailable. If GetTypeInfoCount returns a value greater than zero, you can call GetTypeInfo to retrieve an ITypeInfo interface that contains information about the methods and properties (I discuss properties shortly) supported by the IDispatch interface pointer. Don't get bogged down by any of this. You will see at the end of this chapter when you build your example project, that it is unlikely you will ever need to call these two methods.

Using IDispatch

IDispatch is unlike any COM interface that we have seen so far because it defines a new type of communication protocol between a COM client and server. When you define a custom (vtable) interface, you are defining a communication protocol between a COM client and server. That communication protocol is defined by the set of methods in the interface. So, when you define your ISpellChecker interface:

```
interface ISpellChecker : IUnknown
{
   HRESULTCheckSpelling([in,string]char*word,[out,retval]BOOL *isCorrect);
   HRESULT UseDictionary([in,string] char *filename);
}
```

you are defining a protocol that consists of the five methods shown in Figure 7.3.

When a client calls the CheckSpelling function in ISpellChecker, the protocol works as follows:

1. Find the function at the Fourth position in the ISpellChecker vtable.
2. In the first argument to the function, pass a string that is to be spell checked.
3. On output, the second argument to the function contains a Boolean that indicates whether the first argument is spelled correctly.
4. The physical return value contains an HRESULT that has error information if there are errors, or S_OK if there are no errors.

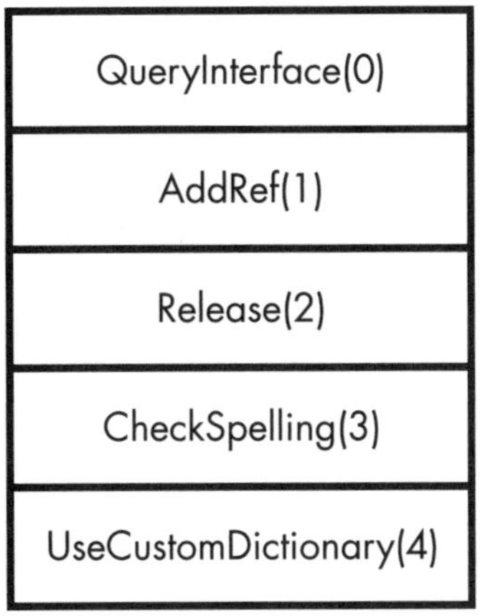

QueryInterface(0)
AddRef(1)
Release(2)
CheckSpelling(3)
UseCustomDictionary(4)

FIGURE 7.3

The ISpellChecker Vtable.

This protocol is language independent, but that doesn't mean that it works for all languages. There are a number of potential problems. One problem is the string that is passed to the `CheckSpelling` method is represented as a single-byte, null-terminated, character array. This works great for C++, but Visual Basic represents strings as length-prefixed, wide-character arrays. Also, many languages do not work well with pointers, let alone pointers to functions, or arrays of function pointers. Moreover, some programming languages do not have a data model rich enough to handle some COM interfaces. So how do you fix all of these problems? What is needed is a different protocol. The `IDispatch` interface defines a protocol that is friendlier to languages that don't have the flexibility of C++. With `IDispatch`, the protocol for calling a `CheckSpelling` method is as follows:

1. Call `GetIDsOfNames` to find the integer ID of the `CheckSpelling` method.
2. Package the arguments that you wish to pass to `CheckSpelling` into an array of self-describing data structures called Variants (we'll talk more about Variants shortly).
3. Pass the ID and the array of Variants to the `Invoke` method of `IDispatch`.
4. The implementation of the `Invoke` method in the server uses the integer ID to determine the right method to call. It unpacks the Variant array and passes these parameters to an internal function that implements the `CheckSpelling` logic.
5. The return value from this internal function is then packaged as a Variant and returned to the client as one of the output parameters from `Invoke`.
6. If anything went wrong, the seventh argument to the `Invoke` method, which is an output argument, contains error information.

So, what's the advantage of this protocol? Well, notice that all communication between the client and server goes through the `IDispatch` interface. This makes it much easier for pointer-challenged programming languages to use this interface. It is much easier for a programming language vendor to add support for a well-defined and documented COM interface like `IDispatch` then it is to let users create their own COM interfaces. Also, because all arguments to methods must be packaged into Variants, a programming language vendor only has to add support for the types you can put in a Variant to allow their language to work with any `IDispatch`-based interface. Unfortunately, a developer who is designing an `IDispatch`-based interface is also limited to arguments and return values that can be packaged into a Variant. You are losing some flexibility, but this restriction is consistent with the goal of Automation and `IDispatch`: to make COM accessible to simpler programming languages.

If you use Visual Basic, you will probably see mention of a technology called Remote Automation. Remote Automation was introduced with Visual Basic 4.0 as a means of enabling distributed application development. This was just prior to the release of NT 4.0, which included the first release of Distributed COM (DCOM). Remote Automation is a legacy technology. Anything you can do with Remote Automation can be done with DCOM. Only use Remote Automation if you have legacy code that you have to maintain. For all new development, you should be using DCOM.

Defining IDispatch Interfaces

`IDispatch` interfaces are defined in a different way than vtable interfaces. You still use IDL and MIDL to define `IDispatch` interfaces, but you use a slightly different syntax. Not that long ago, COM had two interface definition languages: Interface Description Language (IDL) and Object Description Language (ODL). ODL was used to define `IDispatch`-based interfaces. The ODL code was then compiled using a compiler called `mktyplib`. The only thing `mktyplib` did with the ODL was to make a type library. It didn't create header files (they are not needed because you are always communicating through `IDispatch`) and it didn't create a marshaling DLL (a marshaling DLL is not needed because `IDispatch` is a standard interface so it can use the standard marshaler). Starting with Visual C++ 5.0, Microsoft enhanced IDL and the MIDL compiler so it subsumed all the functionality of ODL, thus obviating the need for `mktyplib`. Now, you can think of ODL as a dialect of IDL. Listing 7.1 shows a spell checking, `IDispatch` interface, and a COM class defined in the ODL dialect of IDL.

LISTING 7.1 *EXAMPLE ODL*

```
1.  [uuid(4D9FFA38-B732-11CD-92B4-08002B291EED),Version(1.0),help
    string("Demonstration automation server")]
2.  library AutoSvr {
3.     importlib("stdole32.tlb");
4.
5.     [uuid(4D9FFA39-B732-11CD-92B4-08002B291EED),
6.     helpstring("Dispatch interface for autospell server")]
7.     dispinterface SpellChecker {
8.     properties:
9.        [id(1)]  BSTR Dictionary;
10.    methods:
11.       [id(2)] boolean CheckSpelling(BSTR word);
12.       [id(3)] boolean SuggestSpelling(BSTR word);
13.    };
14.    [uuid(4D9FFA40-B732-11CD-92B4-08002B291EED),helpstring("Auto
       spell Server")]
15.    coclass AutoSpell {
16.       [default] dispinterface SpellChecker;
17.    }
18. };
```

The definition of the type library, `AutoSvr`, and its GUID are exactly the same as that for a vtable interface. But the rest of the code is different from an equivalent vtable interface. The most important section of the code is lines 5 through 13 where I define a dispinterface called `SpellChecker`.

Dispinterfaces

An implementation of `IDispatch` (what I've been calling an `IDispatch`-based interface) is called a `dispinterface`. A `dispinterface` defines the set of methods and properties that can be called through the `Invoke` method of a *particular* `IDispatch` interface pointer. Each `dispinterface` has a GUID associated with it so it can be unambiguously identified. Each method and property (I define properties shortly) in a `dispinterface` has a DISPID associated with it.

The `dispinterface` declaration starts with the attributes for the interface, which can be seen on lines 5 and 6 of listing 7.1. Next, comes the `dispinterface` declaration on lines 7 through 13. A `dispinterface` contains separate sections for properties and methods. Notice how you can assign a DISPID to each method and property. The DISPID only has to be unique within a particular `dispinterface`. The same DISPID can be used more than once within a server if the server has multiple `dispinterfaces`—and most do. A `dispinterface` is conceptually similar to a vtable interface in that it lets you define a set of methods that together define a behavior. Dispinterfaces are grouped together into a COM class, in the same way as vtable interfaces, using the coclass keyword as shown on lines 14 through 17.

Properties

A dispinterface can contain both methods and properties. The use of properties is an area of significant difference between Automation and vtable interfaces. Properties are used to define attributes for your dispinterface. There are certain methods that you may define that are attributes rather than actions. An example is a width, height, font, or color. It is usually easy to tell when you define a method, that it should be a property instead. If the method has or it would be natural to append *Get* or *Set* to its name, it probably should be a property. If you have a method in an interface with a name like GetFont, SetFont, SetWidth, or GetWidth, it should be a property instead. Methods should be reserved for verbs like Run, Start, Stop, and so on. A property maps to a GetPropertyName/SetPropertyName method pair if the property is read/write and to a GetPropertyName method if the property is read-only. Although they are rare, there are write-only properties and these have only a SetPropertyName method. Even though read/write properties map to two methods, both methods share the same DISPID—the DISPID assigned to the property. You disambiguate the methods using the fourth parameter to Invoke. You pass DISPATCH_PROPERTYGET for this parameter to get the Dictionary property, and DISPATCH_PROPERTYPUT to set it.

If you are creating a C++ client, the distinction between defining functionality as a property and defining it as a method is largely one of semantics. You still have to make a method call to read or write the property. If you are using Visual Basic, the distinction between a property and a method is more important. If you have an interface that contains a property called Dictionary, you can read and write the property using the code shown below:

```
Dim server as Object
Set server=new CreateObject("autosvr.autospell")
Server.Dictionary="c:\mydictionary.txt" 'Set the dictionary
```

Notice that the Dictionary property appears to be a public member variable of the COM class called AutoSpell. This is just syntactic sugar provided by the Visual Basic interpreter. When you execute the following line:

```
Server.Dictionary=="c:\mydictionary.txt"
```

Visual Basic calls the Invoke method in the IDispatch interface specifying the Dispatch ID for the Dictionary property.

Variants

All the parameters that are passed to an `IDispatch` interface are passed as Variants. A Variant is a data type that can represent almost anything. You can think of it as a universal type. A Variant can hold a string, a floating-point number (of either single or double precision), a Boolean, a currency, a color, or a 2- or 4-byte integer. If you have used Visual Basic, then you are familiar with Variants. In Visual Basic, you can declare a variable to be a Variant and then assign it to anything. You can start using a variable without even declaring it and Visual Basic automatically types the variable as a Variant.

The option explicit keyword in Visual Basic disables the capability to use variables without explicitly declaring them. Most Visual Basic programmers use it.

A Variant is a structure that contains two fields: a byte that contains the type of the Variant and a union that contains the data for the Variant.

Understanding Unions

When I'm explaining Variants in my class, a significant number of students have no idea what a union is. At first, this surprised me, but then as I thought about it more, I realized that most modern programming languages emphasize type-safety. If you are using an object-oriented language (and using it correctly), there is little need for unions. Outside of using them in Variants, I can count on the fingers of one hand the times I have used unions.

To understand unions, think about C/C++ structures (structs). If I defined the struct shown below, how large is it?

```
struct MyStruct {
   float m_realNumber;
   short m_cardinalNumber;
   char m_name[12];
};
```

To find the correct answer, sum the size of its fields. The correct answer is 18 bytes, 4 bytes for the `m_realNumber` field, 2 bytes for the `m_cardinalNumber` field, and 12 bytes for the `m_name` field. Each instance of `MyStruct` contains a value for each of the three fields. So I can write code like that shown here:

```
MyStruct data;
data.m_realNumber=3.5;
```

```
data.m_cardinalNumber=2;
Strcpy(data.m_name,"whatever");
```

Now if you declare a union that had the same fields as shown below:

```
union MyUnion {
   float m_realNumber;
   short m_cardinalNumber;
   char m_name[12];
};
```

how large is this data structure? The correct answer is 12 bytes. The size of a union is the size of its largest member, in this case the 12-byte string m_name. With a union, I can assign to only one of the fields in each instance, like this:

```
MyUnion data1, data2, data3;
data1.m_realNumber=3.5;
data2.m_cardinalNumber=2;
strcpy(data3.m_name,"whatever");
```

Notice that you have assigned to only one member variable in each of the three union variables that we have declared. Unions let you create variables that can contain multiple types of data. The union that I have declared here can be either a string, a real number, or a cardinal number.

A simplified version of the declaration of a Variant is shown below:

```
typedef struct tagVariant {
   VARTYPE vt;
   union {
      LONG lVal;                    // VT_I4
         BYTE bVal;                 // VT_UI1
         SHORT iVal;                // VT_I2
         FLOAT fltVal;              // VT_R4
         DOUBLE dblVal;             // VT_R8
         VARIANT_BOOL boolVal;      // VT_BOOL
         SCODE scode;               // VT_ERROR
         CY cyVal;                  // VT_CY (currency)
         DATE date;                 // VT_DATE
         BSTR bstrVal;              // VT_BSTR
         IUnknown *punkVal;         // VT_UNKNOWN
         IDispatch *pdispVal;       // VT_DISPATCH
         SAFEARRAY *parray;         // VT_ARRAY
   };
};
```

The complete declaration, which can be found in the oaidl.h file in the include directory of your Visual C++ installation, contains more fields in the union and is more complex. What I have shown here captures the essence of a Variant. There are actually two Variant structures. One is called VARIANT and the other is VARIANTARG. The two types are the same and can be used interchangeably.

The vt field, which is a VARTYPE enumeration, is used to indicate which field in the union is set. You can find the definition of VARTYPE in wtypes.h and it looks as follows:

```
enum VARENUM
    {   VT_EMPTY    = 0,
   VT_NULL   = 1,
   VT_I2  = 2,
   VT_I4  = 3,
   VT_R4  = 4,
   VT_R8  = 5,
   VT_CY  = 6,
   VT_DATE   = 7,
   VT_BSTR   = 8,
   VT_DISPATCH      = 9,
   VT_ERROR  = 10,
   VT_BOOL   = 11,
   VT_VARIANT       = 12,
   VT_UNKNOWN       = 13,
   VT_DECIMAL       = 14,
   VT_I1  = 16,
   VT_UI1 = 17,
   VT_UI2 = 18,
   VT_UI4 = 19,
   VT_I8  = 20,
   VT_UI8 = 21,
   VT_INT = 22,
   VT_UINT   = 23,
   VT_VOID   = 24,
   VT_HRESULT       = 25,
   VT_PTR = 26,
   VT_SAFEARRAY     = 27
    };
```

Once again, I have edited the declaration for brevity. But what I have shown you here captures the essence of the enumeration. It contains an entry for each type that a Variant can be assigned to.

Creating and Using Variants

Creating a Variant is a four-step process.

1. Declare the Variant.
2. Initialize the Variant by calling `VariantInit`.
3. Set the VARTYPE of the Variant to indicate its type.
4. Set the member variable in the Variant that corresponds to that type.

For instance, if you want to create a Variant that is a single precision floating point number, you would do the following:

```
VARIANT var;
VariantInit(&var);
var.vt=VT_R4;
var.fltVal=3.5;
```

To create a Variant that is a Boolean, you would do the following:

```
VARIANT var;
VariantInit(&var);
var.vt=VT_BOOL;
var.boolVal=VARIANT_TRUE;
```

BSTRs

Different programming languages have different ways of representing strings. C/C++ uses a NULL-terminated character array and Visual Basic uses a length-prefixed wide-character array. The Variant data type uses a string representation that is identical to Visual Basic's representation, which is called a Basic String or simply a BSTR. Figure 7.4 shows how a BSTR is represented in memory.

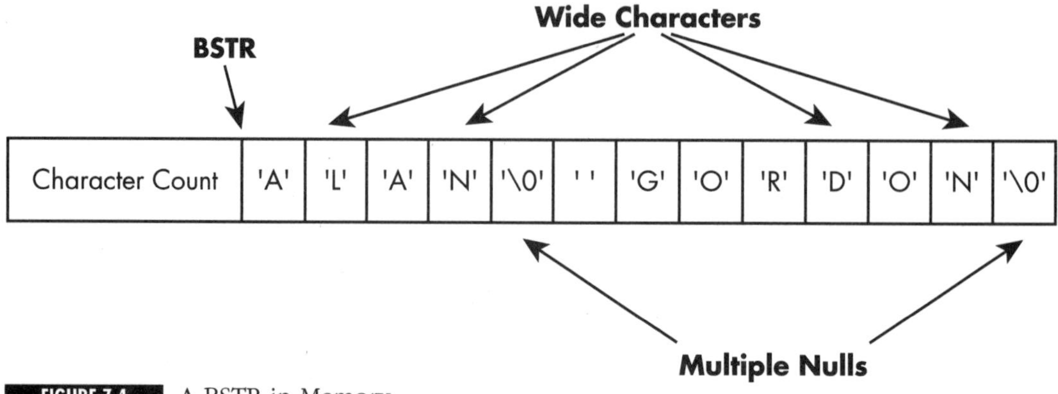

FIGURE 7.4 A BSTR in Memory.

A BSTR variable is actually a pointer that points to a wide character array. The number of wide characters in the array is stored right before the array in memory. This layout has two advantages: First, because the length of the wide character array is known from the prefixed count, you can have multiple nulls in the wide character array as I have in Figure 7.4. Second, a BSTR can be marshaled more efficiently than a null-terminated string because the marshaler can determine how many bytes need to be sent to marshal the string without having to loop through all of the characters in the string looking for a null. The major disadvantage of this layout is that you must use the `SysAllocString` function to allocate a BSTR and the `SysFreeString` function to free a BSTR. If you don't, the prefixed length will not be handled correctly. The following code shows how you would create a BSTR and then create a variant that points to the BSTR:

```
OLECHAR str[]="Here is a string";
BSTR bstr;
bstr=::SysAllocString(str);
VARIANT var;
Var.vt=VT_BSTR;
Var.bstrVal=bstr;
// Do something with the variant
::SysFreeString(bstr);
```

Currency

You can also create variants that represent currency values quite accurately. Currencies are represented as signed 64-bit integers in a Variant. The following code shows how you would create a Variant that contains a Currency value. The code initializes a floating-point variable to 1.35 and then converts the floating-point number to a currency using the `VarCyFromR4` function:

```
VARIANT varCurrency;
CURRENCY cur;
float flt;
flt=1.35;
VarCyFromR4(flt,&cur);
varCurrency.vt=VT_CY;
varCurrency.cyVal=cur;
```

Converting Variants from One Type to Another

`VarCyFromR4` is one of many type conversion functions for Variants. `VarCyFromR4` converts a single precision floating point number (R4) to a currency (CY). There are a number of type conversion functions like this one, including one called VarBstrFromCy, which converts a currency to a string. You can use this function to convert a currency to a string as shown below:

```
CURRENCY cur;
BSTR bstrCurrency;
// Initialize the currency value...
VarBstrFromCy(cur, LANG_USER_DEFAULT, 0, &bstrCurrency);
```

Usually, you will not use these functions directly like this. Instead you will use them indirectly through the VariantChangeType function. VariantChangeType allows you to perform type conversions on Variants. It has the following parameter list:

```
HRESULT VariantChangeType(VARIANTARG* pVarDest, // The converted variant
                    VARIANTARG* pVarSrc,       // The Variant to be
                                                  converted
                    Unsigned short wFlags,     // Flags
                    VARTYPE vtNew              // The type to convert to
    );
```

The following code shows how to use the VariantChangeType function to convert a floating-point number to a BSTR:

```
VARIANT varFlt, varBstr;
VariantInit(&varFlt);
VariantInit(&varBstr);
varFlt.vt=VT_R4;
varFlt.fltVal=3.5;
varBstr.vt=VT_BSTR;
varBstr.bstrVal=::SysAllocString(L"");
HRESULT hr=VariantChangeType(&varFlt,&varBstr,0,VT_BSTR);
```

Fortunately, in practice you will not have to work with Variants at this level, unless you want to. In the Microsoft Foundation Classes (MFC) there is a class called COleVariant you can use to simplify the process of using Variants. There are also classes called COleCurrency and COleDateTime that work with Currency and Date Variants. Moreover, the CString class in MFC work well with BSTRs.

The Active Template Library (ATL) contains a class called CComVariant that makes it simple to work with Variants and another class called CComBstr specifically for BSTRs. If you are using Visual C++ native COM support, there is a class called _variant_t and a class specifically for BSTRs called _bstr_t. These types make it much easier to work with Variants. Each of these classes has a constructor you can call and pass the data that you would like the Variant initialized to. They also have overloaded assignment operators and methods that make it easy to perform type conversions. For instance, you can create a Variant that contains a string using the following code with COleVariant:

```
COleVariant var("Here is a Variant");
```

The following code shows how to Create a Variant that contains a string using ATL's CComVariant class:

```
CComVariant alan1("whatever");
```

Here is the code to create a String Variant using the _variant_t class from Visual C++'s native COM library (you must include comdef.h to use this class).

```
_variant_t alan2("whatever also");
```

The following code creates two Variants, one a floating-point number, the other a string, and then it assigns the string to a different string, and changes the type of the floating point number to a string. There are three versions of the code: the first uses MFC's COleVariant class, the second uses ATL's CComVariant, the third uses _variant_t from the native COM library in Visual C++:

```
// Uses MFC's COleVariant
COleVariant varFlt(3.5);
COleVariant varStr("Here is a string");
varStr="Some other string";
varFlt.ChangeType(VT_BSTR);

// Uses ATL's CComVariant
CComVariant varFlt(3.5);
CComVariant varStr("Here is a string");
varStr="Some other string";
varFlt.ChangeType(VT_BSTR);

// Uses _variant_t from the Visual C++ native COM support
_variant_t varFlt(3.5);
_variant_t varStr("Here is a string");
varStr="Some other string";
varFlt.ChangeType(VT_BSTR);
```

With MFC, you can convert a CString to a Variant using the AllocSysString method of CString like this:

```
CString str;
str="Whatever it takes";
BSTR bstr=str.AllocSysString();
// Use the BSTR
::SysFreeString(bstr);
```

The COleVariant, CComVariant, and _variant_t convenience classes are easy to work with. Whichever tool you use, I encourage you to use them instead of trying to work with raw Variants. The MFC documentation is excellent and I encourage you to learn as much as you can about the COleVariant, COleCurrency, and COleDateTime classes. The best source of information on ATL right now is the book *ATL Internals* by Chris Sells and Brent Rector. Chapter 2 of this book has an excellent introduction to CComVariant. No one has written a book on Visual C++'s native COM support yet, but the documentation available on the Visual Studio MSDN is fair in this area. Look up _variant_t and _bstr_t.

You can see that VARIANTS effectively let you subvert the compile-time type checking of most programming languages. They can be assigned to any type of data and can easily be converted from one type to another. They make it easy to pass data of almost any type through an IDispatch interface. However, you have to perform all of your type checking at runtime (you will see the performance implications of this at the end of the chapter).

Dual Interfaces

You have learned about vtable and IDispatch/Automation interfaces. You might be thinking that it would be helpful to have an interface that could function as either. A dual interface combines a vtable interface with an IDispatch interface. A client that is developed with a scripting language like Visual Basic script, or would like the additional flexibility that comes with late binding, could use the IDispatch methods. A client that is developed with a more capable language and wants maximum performance can utilize the vtable portion of the interface. Microsoft recommends that you define all your interfaces to be dual interfaces. If you build your COM components with ATL, your only two choices for interface types are either a dual interface or a custom (vtable) interface and dual is the default. All COM objects that you build with Visual Basic have dual interfaces. In fact, the only easy way to write a COM server with IDispatch-only interfaces without starting from scratch is to use MFC. And that's because the COM support in MFC was developed before dual interfaces became the recommended way to create COM interfaces. Most of the COM servers you will use in practice will have dual interfaces and, unless you have a good reason for doing otherwise, the servers that you build should also have dual interfaces. Using dual interfaces makes your servers available to the widest possible number of clients. Listing 7.2 shows your spell checker interface defined as a dual interface.

LISTING 7.2 *A DUAL INTERFACE*

```
1.  [
2.      object,
3.      uuid(C21D693F-1DE5-11D3-998A-E0EC08C10000),
4.      dual,
5.      helpstring("ISpellChecker Interface"),
6.      pointer_default(unique)
7.  ]
8.  interface ISpellChecker : IDispatch
9.  {
10.     [propget, id(1), helpstring("property Dictionary")] HRESULT
        Dictionary([out, retval] BSTR *pVal);
11.     [propput, id(1), helpstring("property Dictionary")] HRESULT
        Dictionary([in] BSTR newVal);
12.     [id(2), helpstring("method CheckSpelling")] HRESULT
        CheckSpelling([in] BSTR word,[out,retval] VARIANT_BOOL
13. *result);
14.     [id(3), helpstring("method SuggestSpelling")] HRESULT
        SuggestSpelling([in] BSTR word,[out,retval] BSTR
15. *result);
16. };
```

Compare this definition, both to the Custom interface that was defined at the beginning of the chapter under the heading *Using IDispatch*, and the pure `IDispatch` interface defined later in Listing 7.1. It has elements of both. On line 4, notice the use of the *dual* keyword in the attributes. Notice on line 8 that the interface is declared like a custom interface except that it inherits from `IDispatch` instead of `IUnknown`. DISPIDs are associated with each property and method just like a dispinterface. Also notice on lines 10 and 11 the way that properties are declared. Instead of a properties section, you have a `propget` and a `propput` method for each property. This is so you can access the properties even if you are not going through the `Invoke` method of `IDispatch`.

Like a pure Automation interface, a dual interface must have arguments and return values that are compatible with Variants. This is probably the biggest drawback to using dual interfaces. The vtable for this interface will look like that shown in Figure 7.5.

As defined, this interface contains all the methods in `IUnknown` (`IDispatch` derives from `IUnknown`) and all the methods in `IDispatch`.

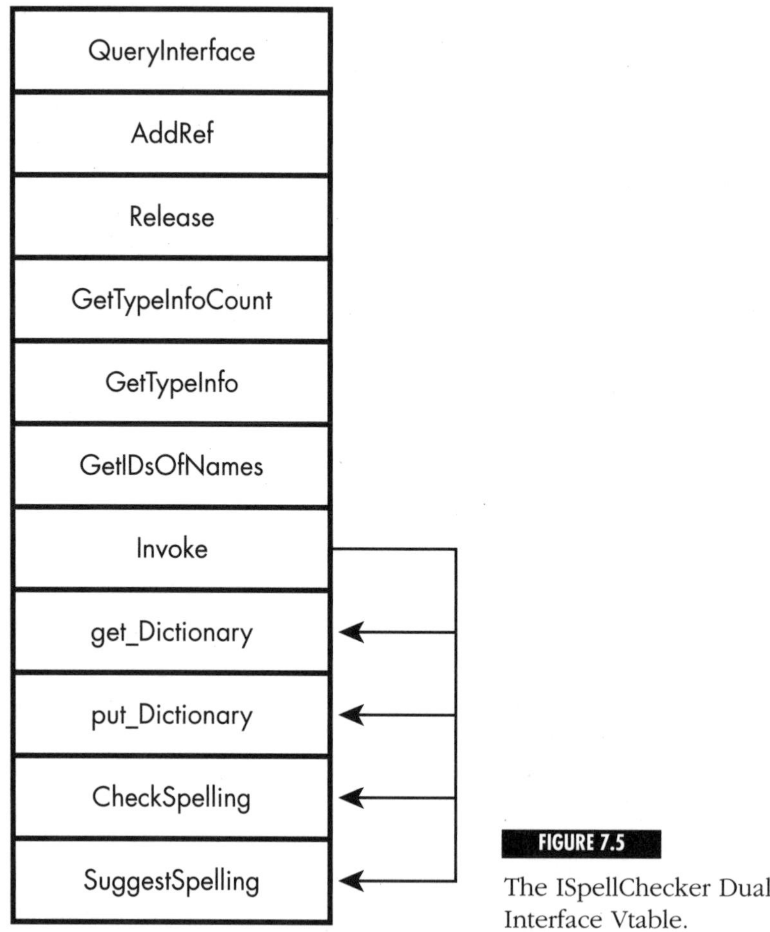

FIGURE 7.5

The ISpellChecker Dual Interface Vtable.

It also contains all the methods that were declared in the `ISpellChecker` interface, including a get and set method for the Dictionary property.

Early- and Late-Bound Clients

You can call the get and set methods for the Dictionary property or the `CheckSpelling` or `SuggestSpelling` methods through `Invoke` using the Dispatch IDs. In a dual interface, the implementation of Invoke l delegates calls on `Invoke` to the corresponding vtable methods as shown in Figure 7.5. You can also call the vtable methods directly if you want. Clients that go through `Invoke` are called late-bound clients; clients that go through the vtable are called early-bound clients.

USING VISUAL BASIC TO CREATE EARLY- AND LATE-BOUND CLIENTS

In Visual Basic, you can create both kinds of clients easily. To create a late-bound client, type your object reference as an Object and then call your methods. The method calls that you are making are not checked at runtime.

```
Dim server as Object
Dim result as boolean
Set server=createobject("dualserver.spellchecker")
Result=server.CheckSpelling("whatever")  '
Server.DoSomething        'This method is not supported by our
server, the call will fail at runtime
```

To create an early-bound client, you must first import the type library for the server. In Visual Basic, you can do this by selecting `References` from the `Project` menu and then checking the checkbox beside the server's type library and then clicking `OK`. Importing the type library, means that the client will have *a priori* knowledge of the layout of the server's interfaces, so it can bind directly to the `CheckSpelling` method in the interface's vtable. Now you can write the following code:

```
Dim server as dualserver.spellchecker
Dim result as Boolean
Set server=new dualserver.spellchecker
Result=server.CheckSpelling("whatever")
Server.DoSomething    'This method is not supported by our
server, it will fail at compile time
```

USING VISUAL C++ TO CREATE EARLY- AND LATE-BOUND CLIENTS

In Visual C++, there are three ways that you can use an Automation Server. You can use MFC to generate a `COleDispatchDriver`-derived wrapper class. Another approach is to use the native COM support in Visual C++ and the import keyword. The third approach is to use the `IDispatch` interface directly. This last approach is the most time-consuming and difficult approach and is rarely done.

USING MFC'S COLEDISPATCHDRIVER CLASS • The MFC ClassWizard in Visual C++ has a feature that lets you generate a wrapper class from a type library. This functionality is similar to, but not the same as, the Visual C++ native COM support. The MFC Class Wizard reads a type library and generates a wrapper class for each interface in the type library. The wrapper class derives from a COM support class in MFC called `COleDispatchDriver`. `COleDispatchDriver` does exactly as its name implies—it makes it simple to drive a Dispatch interface. The wrapper class contains a method for each method supported by the dispatch interface, and Get/Set methods for each property supported by the interface. The following code shows a class that was generated by the MFC ClassWizard for your server:

```
class ISpellChecker : public COleDispatchDriver
{
public:
   ISpellChecker() {}     // Calls COleDispatchDriver default constructor
   ISpellChecker(LPDISPATCH pDispatch) : COleDispatchDriver(pDispatch) {}
   ISpellChecker(const ISpellChecker& dispatchSrc) :
COleDispatchDriver(dispatchSrc) {}

// Attributes
public:

// Operations
public:
   CString GetDictionary();
   void SetDictionary(LPCTSTR lpszNewValue);
   BOOL CheckSpelling(LPCTSTR word);
   CString SuggestSpelling(LPCTSTR word);
};
```

The implementation of the CheckSpelling method in the wrapper class is shown below.

```
BOOL ISpellChecker::CheckSpelling(LPCTSTR word)
{
   BOOL result;
   static BYTE parms[] =
      VTS_BSTR;
   InvokeHelper(0x2, DISPATCH_METHOD, VT_BOOL, (void*)&result, parms,
      word);
   return result;
}
```

This method delegates to an MFC method called InvokeHelper. InvokeHelper takes the parameters that are passed to CheckSpelling and packages them into a DISPPARAMS structure and then calls the Invoke method in IDispatch. The MFC Class Wizard encoded the DISPID of the CheckSpelling method into the wrapper class (see the first parameter that is passed to InvokeHelper in ISpellChecker::CheckSpelling). The Class Wizard determined the DISPID for the CheckSpelling method from the type library.

This approach lies somewhere between late-binding and early-binding and is sometimes called dispid-binding. The client does not have to call

GetIDsOfNames to get the DISPID of the CheckSpelling method before it calls the method. The code in the wrapper class that calls the Get/SetDictionary properties is shown below:

```
CString ISpellChecker::GetDictionary()
{
   CString result;
   InvokeHelper(0x1, DISPATCH_PROPERTYGET, VT_BSTR, (void*)&result, NULL);
   return result;
}

void ISpellChecker::SetDictionary(LPCTSTR lpszNewValue)
{
   static BYTE parms[] =
      VTS_BSTR;
   InvokeHelper(0x1, DISPATCH_PROPERTYPUT, VT_EMPTY, NULL, parms,
      lpszNewValue);
}
```

The main difference between these methods and the method that calls CheckSpelling is the second parameter to InvokeHelper. InvokeHelper is a member function of COleDispatchDriver. For SetDictionary, the second parameter passed to InvokeHelper is DISPATCH_PROPERTYPUT. For GetDictionary the second parameter is DISPATCH_PROPERTYGET. The Dictionary property has a single DISPID associated with it, and the server is told whether to get or set the property depending on this second parameter. CheckSpelling uses DISPATCH_METHOD for the second parameter to InvokeHelper.

The implementation of COleDispatchDriver::InvokeHelper is interesting and it is a good example of how to write code to use a Dispatch interface at the lowest level. You can find this method in the file OLEDISP2.CPP that can be found in the \VC98\MFC\SRC\ directory of your Visual Studio installation.

A major disadvantage of using the MFC COleDispatchDriver-derived wrapper classes is that they do not support early binding. Even if the server has dual interfaces, these wrapper classes will always go through Invoke via the InvokeHelper method. These classes are more efficient than pure late binding because they have pre-wired DISPIDs for each method. However, this isn't nearly as efficient as early binding.

Using Visual C++ Native COM Support • If you want to use early binding, the best approach is to use Visual C++'s native COM support and the import keyword. You have used this before, but were using a vtable interface. You can use the import keyword with an Automation or dual interface also. If the interface is an IDispatch-only interface, using the import keyword will generate a smart pointer class that uses DISPID binding similar to the COleDispatchDriver class. To import a type library, add a #import statement similar to the following line of code somewhere in your project, typically in stdafx.h:

```
#import "c:\alan\books\vcppbook\demos\chapter7\dualserver\dispatchonly.tlb"
```

The following code shows part of a smart pointer class that was generated by adding this statement. In this case, you are using an IDispatch-only server:

```
struct __declspec(uuid("5b1e1fb5-7c77-11d0-bc9c-00a024bd9ecc"))
ISpellChecker : IDispatch
{
   // Property data
   __declspec(property(get=GetDictionary,put=PutDictionary))
   _bstr_t Dictionary;
   // Methods:
   VARIANT_BOOL CheckSpelling (_bstr_t word );
   // Properties:
   _bstr_t GetDictionary ( );
   void PutDictionary ( _bstr_t _val );
};
```

The implementation of these methods shows that it uses the same technique of DISPID binding as COleDispatchDriver.

```
inline VARIANT_BOOL ISpellChecker::CheckSpelling ( _bstr_t word )
{
   VARIANT_BOOL _result;
   _com_dispatch_method(this, 0x2, DISPATCH_METHOD, VT_BOOL,
(void*)&_result, L"\x0008", (BSTR)word);
   return _result;
}

inline _bstr_t ISpellChecker::GetDictionary ( )
{
   BSTR _result;
   _com_dispatch_propget(this, 0x1, VT_BSTR, (void*)&_result);
   return _bstr_t(_result, false);
}

inline void ISpellChecker::PutDictionary ( _bstr_t _val )
{
   _com_dispatch_propput(this, 0x1, VT_BSTR, (BSTR)_val);
}
```

If the server has dual interfaces, then the server will generate a class that binds to the vtable portion of the interface. The following code shows a smart pointer class that was generated from a similar server that has dual interfaces:

```
struct __declspec(uuid("5a40064d-2197-11d3-998a-e0ec08c10000"))
ISpellChecker : IDispatch
{
   // Property data
   __declspec(property(get=GetDictionary,put=PutDictionary),_bstr_t
   Dictionary;
   // Wrapper methods for error-handling
   _bstr_t GetDictionary ( );
   void PutDictionary (_bstr_t pVal );
   VARIANT_BOOL CheckSpelling (_bstr_t word );
   _bstr_t SuggestSpelling (_bstr_t word );
   // Raw methods provided by interface
   virtual HRESULT __stdcall get_Dictionary (BSTR * pVal ) = 0;
   virtual HRESULT __stdcall put_Dictionary (BSTR pVal ) = 0;
   virtual HRESULT __stdcall raw_CheckSpelling (BSTR word,VARIANT_BOOL
* isCorrect ) = 0;
   virtual HRESULT __stdcall raw_SuggestSpelling (BSTR word,BSTR *
result ) = 0;
};
```

The implementation of these methods is shown below. Notice there isn't a DISPID in sight.

```
inline _bstr_t ISpellChecker::GetDictionary ( )
{
   BSTR _result;
   HRESULT _hr = get_Dictionary(&_result);
   if (FAILED(_hr)) _com_issue_errorex(_hr, this, __uuidof(this));
   return _bstr_t(_result, false);
}

inline void ISpellChecker::PutDictionary ( _bstr_t pVal )
{
   HRESULT _hr = put_Dictionary(pVal);
   if (FAILED(_hr)) _com_issue_errorex(_hr, this, __uuidof(this));
}

inline VARIANT_BOOL ISpellChecker::CheckSpelling ( _bstr_t word )
{
   VARIANT_BOOL _result;
```

```
    HRESULT _hr = raw_CheckSpelling(word, &_result);
    if (FAILED(_hr)) _com_issue_errorex(_hr, this, __uuidof(this));
    return _result;
}

inline _bstr_t ISpellChecker::SuggestSpelling ( _bstr_t word )
{
    BSTR _result;
    HRESULT _hr = raw_SuggestSpelling(word, &_result);
    if (FAILED(_hr)) _com_issue_errorex(_hr, this, __uuidof(this));
    return _bstr_t(_result, false);
}
```

Using IDispatch From Scratch • You can also use the `IDispatch` interface without going through a wrapper class. Only in this way can you do true late binding in C++. This technique has the most flexibility. You can even change the DISPID of a method or property in your server without having to rebuild your client, but it is also the slowest. The following code shows how to construct a method call using the Invoke method of an `IDispatch` interface pointer:

```
DISPID dispid;
BSTR bWord;
OLECHAR *methodName=L"CheckSpelling";
bWord=m_word.AllocSysString();
VARIANT vargs[1], vresult;
::VariantInit(&vresult);
vresult.vt=VT_BOOL;
::VariantInit(&vargs[0]);
vargs[0].vt=VT_BSTR;
vargs[0].bstrVal=bWord;

DISPPARAMS param;
param.cArgs=1;
param.rgvarg=vargs;
param.cNamedArgs=0;
param.rgdispidNamedArgs=NULL;

EXCEPINFO errorInfo;
UINT intArg;
hRes=pDisp-
>GetIDsOfNames(IID_NULL,&methodName,1,GetUserDefaultLCID(),&dispid);
hRes=pDisp-
>Invoke(dispid,IID_NULL,GetUserDefaultLCID(),DISPATCH_METHOD,&param,&v
result,&errorInfo,&intArg);
```

You can check for errors using the following code:

```
if (FAILED(hRes))
{
   if (hRes==DISP_E_EXCEPTION)
   {
      if (errorInfo.pfnDeferredFillIn != NULL)
      {
         (*(errorInfo.pfnDeferredFillIn))(&errorInfo);
      }
      AfxMessageBox(CString(errorInfo.bstrDescription));
      }
      else
      {
         _com_error err(hRes);
         AfxMessageBox(err.ErrorMessage());
      }
   }
}
```

As I'm sure you can see, you'll only use your Automation servers this way if you are a true glutton for punishment.

Building an Automation Server

It's time to do an example to bring it all together. By now you are probably sick of spell checkers, so to make it interesting, I'm going to build a financial component. Your financial component will allow you to calculate a loan payment given an interest rate, the loan amount, and the amortization period of the loan (you can use this to calculate the monthly payment required for a new car or house). It will also let you calculate the amount you can borrow given an interest rate, a monthly payment, and the amortization period of the loan (you can use this to figure out how much house or car you can afford). Because taxes are as much a part of life as breathing, your financial component will also perform simple tax calculations.

A Summary of the Steps

The steps that you perform to build your financial component are as follows:

1. Create a new ATL DLL project using the ATL/COM AppWizard.

2. Add a COM class with a dual interface to the project using the ATL Object Wizard.
3. Add a second interface to the COM class.
4. Add properties and methods to the COM class.
5. Implement the COM class.
6. Create a late-bound client using Visual Basic.
7. Create an early-bound client using Visual Basic.

Creating an ATL Project Using the ATL/COM AppWizard

Start Visual C++ and then execute the following steps:

1. Select `New...` from the `File` menu (the New dialog appears).
2. Click the `Projects` tab.
3. Select `ATL COM AppWizard` from the presented list of project types.
4. Enter `FinancialComponent` in the `Project` Name field.
5. Click the OK button (the ATL COM AppWizard will appear).
6. Select `Dynamic Link Library` under Server Type.
7. Click `Finish`.

Visual C++ will create an empty project for you. The next step is to add your financial COM class.

Adding a COM Class with a Dual Interface

1. Select `New ATL Object...` from the `Insert` menu (the ATL Object Wizard appears).
2. Under `Category` select `Object` and under `Object` select `Simple Object`.
3. Click the `Next` button (the ATL Object Wizard Properties dialog appears).
4. On the `Names` tab enter `TimeValue` in the `Short Name` field under C++.
5. Under COM, change the interface to `ISpellChecker`.
6. Click the `Attributes` tab.
7. Make sure the interface type is dual (this is the default).
8. Check the `ISupportErrorInfo` checkbox.
9. Click `OK`.

After creating our new COM class, the IDL for your financial component will look like that shown below:

```
import "oaidl.idl";
import "ocidl.idl";
    [
        object,
        uuid(EB47FA0D-22EE-11D3-998A-E0EC08C10000),
        dual,
        helpstring("ITimeValue Interface"),
        pointer_default(unique)
    ]
    interface ITimeValue : IDispatch
    {
    };

[
    uuid(EB47FA01-22EE-11D3-998A-E0EC08C10000),
    version(1.0),
    helpstring("financialcomponent 1.0 Type Library")
]
library FINANCIALCOMPONENTLib
{
    importlib("stdole32.tlb");
    importlib("stdole2.tlb");

    [
        uuid(EB47FA0E-22EE-11D3-998A-E0EC08C10000),
        helpstring("TimeValue Class")
    ]
    coclass TimeValue
    {
        [default] interface ITimeValue;
    };
};
```

Notice that `ITimeValue` is a dual interface. The ATL Object Wizard also generated the implementation class shown in Listing 7.3.

LISTING 7.3 *IMPLEMENTATION CLASS FOR YOUR FINANCIAL COMPONENT*

```
1.  class ATL_NO_VTABLE CTimeValue :
2.      public CComObjectRootEx<CComSingleThreadModel>,
3.      public CComCoClass<CTimeValue, &CLSID_TimeValue>,
4.      public ISupportErrorInfo,
5.      public IDispatchImpl<ITimeValue, &IID_ITimeValue,
        &LIBID_FINANCIALCOMPONENTLib>
6.  {
7.  public:
8.      CTimeValue()
9.      {
10.     }
11.
12. DECLARE_REGISTRY_RESOURCEID(IDR_TIMEVALUE)
13.
14. DECLARE_PROTECT_FINAL_CONSTRUCT()
15.
16. BEGIN_COM_MAP(CTimeValue)
17.     COM_INTERFACE_ENTRY(ITimeValue)
18.     COM_INTERFACE_ENTRY(IDispatch)
19.     COM_INTERFACE_ENTRY(ISupportErrorInfo)
20. END_COM_MAP()
21.
22. // ISupportsErrorInfo
23.     STDMETHOD(InterfaceSupportsErrorInfo)(REFIID riid);
24.
25. // ITimeValue
26. public:
27. };
```

In line 5, the implementation class derives from an ATL class called `IDispatchImpl` instead of deriving directly from the `ITimeValue` interface. `IDispatchImpl` is a template class that implements the `IDispatch` interface. It has three template parameters: the interface that it will be working with, the IID of the interface, and the LIBID for the server's type library. `IDispatchImpl` implements all the methods in the `IDispatch` interface: `GetIDsNames`, `Invoke`, `GetTypeInfo`, and `GetTypeInfoCount`. In this case, it implements the `Invoke` method to call the methods in the `ITimeValue` vtable. The LIBID for our type library is needed for the implementation of the `GetTypeInfo` and `GetTypeInfoCount` methods in `IDispatch`.

Your implementation class includes entries in its COM map for both `ITimeValue` and `IDispatch` (see lines 16 through 20).

If an Automation server implements multiple `IDispatch`-based interfaces, whether they are dual or not, one of the interfaces must be returned when the client requests `IDispatch`. The interface that is designated as the default interface in the IDL file is the one that should be returned. Right now, your server has only one `IDispatch`-based interface, `ITimeValue`, but you will see shortly how ATL handles the situation where you have multiple `IDispatch` interfaces.

Adding a Second Interface to the COM Class

To add a second interface to the financial component, perform the following summarized steps:.

1. Add an empty interface to the IDL for the project.
2. Compile the IDL.
3. Use the Implement Interface Command in Visual C++ to add the interface to your COM class.

ADDING AN EMPTY INTERFACE TO THE IDL

Add the bolded lines shown below to the IDL file for your project. Remember to use GUIDGEN to create the IID for the new interface:

```
import "oaidl.idl";
import "ocidl.idl";
   [
      object,
      uuid(EB47FA0D-22EE-11D3-998A-E0EC08C10000),
      dual,
      helpstring("ITimeValue Interface"),
      pointer_default(unique)
   ]
   interface ITimeValue : IDispatch
   {
   };

   [
      object,
      uuid(1C208680-22F2-11d3-998A-E0EC08C10000),
      dual,
      helpstring("ITaxCalculator Interface"),
      pointer_default(unique)
   ]
```

```
    interface ITaxCalculator : IDispatch
    {
    };

[
    uuid(EB47FA01-22EE-11D3-998A-E0EC08C10000),
    version(1.0),
    helpstring("financialcomponent 1.0 Type Library")
]
library FINANCIALCOMPONENTLib
{
    importlib("stdole32.tlb");
    importlib("stdole2.tlb");

    [
        uuid(EB47FA0E-22EE-11D3-998A-E0EC08C10000),
        helpstring("TimeValue Class")
    ]
    coclass TimeValue
    {
        [default] interface ITimeValue;
        interface ITaxCalculator;
    };
};
```

COMPILING THE IDL

To quickly implement the interface we must first compile the IDL so that our type library reflects the new interface. Perform the following steps to compile the IDL file.

1. Double-click `ITimeValue` in the `ClassView` tab of the Visual C++ workspace.
2. Click the `Compile` button or press `CTRL-F7`.

USING THE IMPLEMENT INTERFACE COMMAND

The implement interface command gives you a fast way to implement a second interface. You used this command in Chapter 5, but it behaves slightly different when you are working with a dual interface. To use the Implement Interface command to implement the `ITaxCalculator` interface, perform the following steps:

1. Right-click on `CTimeValue` in the `ClassView` tab of the Visual C++ workspace.
2. Select `Implement Interface` (the Implement Interface dialog appears).
3. Click the `ITaxCalculator` checkbox.
4. Click `OK`.

If you go back to the header file for the implementation class you will see the changes shown in bold in Listing 7.4.

LISTING 7.4 *YOUR IMPLEMENTATION CLASS AFTER YOU HAVE ADDED THE ITAXCALCULATOR INTERFACE*

```
class ATL_NO_VTABLE CTimeValue :
    public CComObjectRootEx<CComSingleThreadModel>,
    public CComCoClass<CTimeValue, &CLSID_TimeValue>,
    public ISupportErrorInfo,
    public IDispatchImpl<ITimeValue, &IID_ITimeValue,
    &LIBID_FINANCIALCOMPONENTLib>,
    public IDispatchImpl<ITaxCalculator,&IID_ITaxCalculator,
    &LIBID_FINANCIALCOMPONENTLib>
{
public:
    CTimeValue()
    {
    }

DECLARE_REGISTRY_RESOURCEID(IDR_TIMEVALUE)

DECLARE_PROTECT_FINAL_CONSTRUCT()

BEGIN_COM_MAP(CTimeValue)
    COM_INTERFACE_ENTRY(ITimeValue)
//DEL COM_INTERFACE_ENTRY(IDispatch)
    COM_INTERFACE_ENTRY(ISupportErrorInfo)
    COM_INTERFACE_ENTRY2(IDispatch, ITimeValue)
    COM_INTERFACE_ENTRY(ITaxCalculator)
```

```
23. END_COM_MAP()
24.
25. // ISupportsErrorInfo
26.     STDMETHOD(InterfaceSupportsErrorInfo)(REFIID riid);
27.
28. // ITimeValue
29. public:
30. // ITaxCalculator
31. };
```

On line 6, you see that the implement interface command added an additional entry to the inheritance list for the implementation class. This entry is an `IDispatchImpl` class that is parameterized with the `ITaxCalculator` interface and the IID for the `ITaxCalculator` interface. Now that you have two `IDispatch`-based interfaces, which one should you return when your client requests `IDispatch`? The answer to this question can be found in lines 17 through 23 in the altered COM map. Visual C++ deleted the original `COM_INTERFACE_ENTRY` for `IDispatch` and replaced it with a call to `COM_INTERFACE_ENTRY2`. When you have multiple `IDispatch` interfaces, the default interface (the one that you return when the user requests `IDispatch`) should be added to the COM map using a `COM_INTERFACE_ENTRY2` entry. Since `ITimeValue` was added to the COM map using `COM_INTERFACE_ENTRY2`, this interface is returned when the user requests `IDispatch`.

Adding Properties and Methods to the COM Class

You will add a property to your COM class that will contain the interest rate to be used by the time-value of money methods in the `ITimeValue` class. You will also add methods to the `ITimeValue` class to calculate a monthly payment given a purchase price and a number of payments. You will also add a method to the `ITaxCalculator` class that lets you calculate the taxes owed given the earnings of an individual. Perform the following steps to add the required properties and methods to your COM class:

1. Add the interest rate property to `ITimeValue`.
2. Add the `MonthlyPayment` and `LoanAmount` methods to `ITimeValue`.
3. Add the `Calculate tax` method to `ITaxCalculator`.

ADDING THE INTEREST RATE PROPERTY TO ITIMEVALUE

To add the Interest Rate Property to `ITimeValue`, perform the following steps:

1. Right-click on the `ITimeValue` in the `ClassView` tab of the Visual C++ Workspace and select `Add Property...` from the `Context` menu (the Add Property to Interface dialog appears).
2. Select `double` in the `Property Type` combo box (I won't complicate this by using the Currency type).
3. Enter `InterestRate` in the `Property` Name field.
4. Click `OK`.

Visual C++ makes the bolded additions to your IDL file.

```
interface ITimeValue : IDispatch
{
   [propget, id(1), helpstring("property InterestRate")] HRESULT
InterestRate([out, retval] double *pVal);
   [propput, id(1), helpstring("property InterestRate")] HRESULT
InterestRate([in] double newVal);
};
```

It also makes the additions shown in bold in the following code to your implementation class:

```
class ATL_NO_VTABLE CTimeValue :
   public CComObjectRootEx<CComSingleThreadModel>,
   public CComCoClass<CTimeValue, &CLSID_TimeValue>,
   public ISupportErrorInfo,
   public IDispatchImpl<ITimeValue, &IID_ITimeValue,
&LIBID_FINANCIALCOMPONENTLib>,
   public IDispatchImpl<ITaxCalculator, &IID_ITaxCalculator,
&LIBID_FINANCIALCOMPONENTLib>
{
// The rest of the class declaration is omitted for clarity
public:
   STDMETHOD(get_InterestRate)(/*[out, retval]*/ double *pVal);
   STDMETHOD(put_InterestRate)(/*[in]*/ double newVal);
};
```

ADDING THE MONTHLYPAYMENT AND LOANAMOUNT METHODS TO ITIMEVALUE

To add the LoanAmount and MonthlyPayment methods to the ITimeValue interface, perform the following steps:

1. Right-click on the ITimeValue in the ClassView tab of the Visual C++ Workspace and select Add Method... from the Context menu (the Add Method to Interface dialog appears).
2. Enter MonthlyPayment in the Method Name field.
3. Enter [in] short numMonths,[in] double loanAmount, [out, retval] double *monthlyPayment in the Parameters field.
4. Click OK.
5. Right-click on the ITimeValue in the ClassView tab of the Visual C++ Workspace and select Add Method... from the Context menu (the Add Method to Interface dialog appears).
6. Enter LoanAmount in the Method Name field.
7. Enter [in] short numMonths,[in] double monthlyPayment, [out,retval] double *loanAmount in the Parameters field.
8. Click OK.

Visual C++ makes the following bolded additions to your IDL file:

```
interface ITimeValue : IDispatch
{
   [propget, id(1), helpstring("property InterestRate")] HRESULT
InterestRate([out, retval] double *pVal);
   [propput, id(1), helpstring("property InterestRate")] HRESULT
InterestRate([in] double newVal);
   [id(2), helpstring("method MonthlyPayment")] HRESULT
MonthlyPayment([in] short numMonths,[in] double loanAmount, [out,ret-
val] double *result);
   [id(3), helpstring("method LoanAmount")] HRESULT LoanAmount([in]
short numMonths,[in] double monthlyPayment,[out,retval] double *
loanAmount);
};
```

It has also made these additions to your implementation class:

```
class ATL_NO_VTABLE CTimeValue :
   public CComObjectRootEx<CComSingleThreadModel>,
   public CComCoClass<CTimeValue, &CLSID_TimeValue>,
   public ISupportErrorInfo,
   public IDispatchImpl<ITimeValue, &IID_ITimeValue,
&LIBID_FINANCIALCOMPONENTLib>,
```

```
   public IDispatchImpl<ITaxCalculator, &IID_ITaxCalculator,
&LIBID_FINANCIALCOMPONENTLib>
{
// The rest of the class declaration is omitted for clarity
public:
   STDMETHOD(LoanAmount)(/*[in]*/ short numMonths,/*[in]*/ double
monthlyPayment,/*[out,retval]*/ double * loanAmount);
   STDMETHOD(MonthlyPayment)(/*[in]*/ short numMonths,/*[in]*/ double
loanAmount, /*[out,retval]*/ double *result);
};
```

ADDING THE CALCULATETAX METHOD TO ITAXCALCULATOR.

To add the dreaded `CalculateTax` method to the `ITaxCalculator` interface in your server, perform the following steps:

1. Right-click on the `ITaxCalculator` in the `ClassView` tab of the Visual C++ Workspace and select `Add Method...` from the `Context` menu (the Add Method to Interface dialog appears).
2. Enter `CalculateTax` in the `Method` Name field.
3. Enter `[in] double earnings, [out,retval] double *tax` in the `Parameters` field.
4. Click `OK`.

Visual C++ adds the code shown in bold to your IDL file:

```
   interface ITaxCalculator : IDispatch
   {
      [id(1), helpstring("method CalculateTax")] HRESULT
CalculateTax([in] double earnings,[out,retval] double *tax);
};
```

Visual C++ also adds these bolded lines to your implementation class:

```
class ATL_NO_VTABLE CTimeValue :
   public CComObjectRootEx<CComSingleThreadModel>,
   public CComCoClass<CTimeValue, &CLSID_TimeValue>,
   public ISupportErrorInfo,
   public IDispatchImpl<ITimeValue, &IID_ITimeValue,
&LIBID_FINANCIALCOMPONENTLib>,
   public IDispatchImpl<ITaxCalculator, &IID_ITaxCalculator,
&LIBID_FINANCIALCOMPONENTLib>
{
```

```
// The rest of the class declaration is omitted for clarity
public:
   STDMETHOD(CalculateTax)(/*[in]*/ double earnings,/*[out,retval]*/
double *tax);
};
```

Implementing the COM class

To implement the methods and properties in your COM class, add the lines shown in bold to the `timevalue.h` file in your project:

```
class ATL_NO_VTABLE CTimeValue :
   public CComObjectRootEx<CComSingleThreadModel>,
   public CComCoClass<CTimeValue, &CLSID_TimeValue>,
   public ISupportErrorInfo,
   public IDispatchImpl<ITimeValue, &IID_ITimeValue,
&LIBID_FINANCIALCOMPONENTLib>,
   public IDispatchImpl<ITaxCalculator, &IID_ITaxCalculator,
&LIBID_FINANCIALCOMPONENTLib>
{
public:
   CTimeValue()
   {
      mInterestRate=8.0;
   }
private:
   double mInterestRate;
};
```

The implementation of the `MonthlyPayment` method uses the following equation to calculate the monthly payment required for a loan of a specified amount and duration:

$A=P*(1+i)^n/((1+i)^n-1)$

Where,

P=Loan Amount
A=Monthly Payment Amount
I =The interest rate per loan period (months in this case)
N=The number of periods (months)

The implementation of the `LoanAmount` method uses the following equation to calculate the present value of a series of uniform payments:

$P=A*((1+i)^n-1)/(i*(1+i)^n)$

You can find these equations and probably more than you ever wanted to know about compounded interest and time value of money calculations in *Engineering Economy* by DeGarmo et al.

The `CalculateTax` method uses the rate table shown in Table 7.2 to calculate taxes.

TABLE 7.2 Rate Table for the CalculateTax Method

Tax Rate	Income Range
.15	0–$25350.00
.28	$25350.00–$61400.00
.33	$61400.00–$128700.00
.396	>$128700.00

With the preceding section as background, add the bolded lines of code below to complete the implementation of the financial component:

```
#include "stdafx.h"
#include "Financialcomponent.h"
#include "TimeValue.h"
#include <math.h>
struct TaxBracket {
   double minIncome;
   double taxRate;
};

STDMETHODIMP CTimeValue::get_InterestRate(double *pVal)
{
   *pVal=mInterestRate;
   return S_OK;
}

STDMETHODIMP CTimeValue::put_InterestRate(double newVal)
{
   mInterestRate=newVal;
   return S_OK;
}

STDMETHODIMP CTimeValue::MonthlyPayment(short numMonths, double
loanAmount, double *monthlyPayment)
{
   double monthlyRate, tempVal;
```

```
   monthlyRate=mInterestRate/1200;  // Convert A.P.R. to decimal,
monthly rate
   tempVal=pow((1+monthlyRate),(double)numMonths);
   *monthlyPayment=loanAmount*monthlyRate*tempVal/(tempVal-1);
   return S_OK;
}

STDMETHODIMP CTimeValue::LoanAmount(short numMonths, double
monthlyPayment, double *loanAmount)
{
   double monthlyRate, tempVal;
   monthlyRate=mInterestRate/1200;  // Convert A.P.R. to decimal,
monthly rate
   tempVal=pow((1+monthlyRate),(double)numMonths);
   *loanAmount=monthlyPayment*(tempVal-1)/monthlyRate*tempVal;
   return S_OK;
}

STDMETHODIMP CTimeValue::CalculateTax(double earnings, double *tax)
{
   static TaxBracket
taxBrackets[4]={{128700.0,.396},{61400.0,.33},{25350.0,.28},{0.0,.15}}
;
   double taxAmount, incomeInBracket;
   int i;
   TaxBracket aTaxBracket;
   taxAmount=0.0;
   for (i=0;i<4;i++)
   {
      aTaxBracket=taxBrackets[i];
      if (earnings >= aTaxBracket.minIncome)
      {
         incomeInBracket=earnings-aTaxBracket.minIncome;
         taxAmount+=incomeInBracket*aTaxBracket.taxRate;
         earnings=aTaxBracket.minIncome;
      }
   }
   *tax=taxAmount;
   return S_OK;
}
```

Now you are ready to compile. Click the `Compile` button or press F7.

Creating a Late-Bound and Early-Bound Client

You can create a client in the simplest way possible by using Visual Basic. With Visual Basic, it is easy to create both late-bound and early-bound clients. You can then compare the performance of using `IDispatch` as compared to using the vtable directly.

To build your Visual Basic client, perform the following steps:

1. Create a new Standard Exe project.
2. Draw the user interface.
3. Add a Reference to the Financial Component.
4. Instantiate a late-bound and an early-bound financial object.
5. Implement the button handlers.

CREATING A NEW STANDARD EXE PROJECT

To create a standard Exe Project, start Visual Basic 6.0 on your system and perform these fsteps:

1. If it is not up already, select `New` from the `File` menu to bring up the new project dialog.
2. Select `Standard Exe` in the list of projects.
3. Click the `Open` button.

DRAWING THE USER INTERFACE

Draw the user interface shown in Figure 7.6.

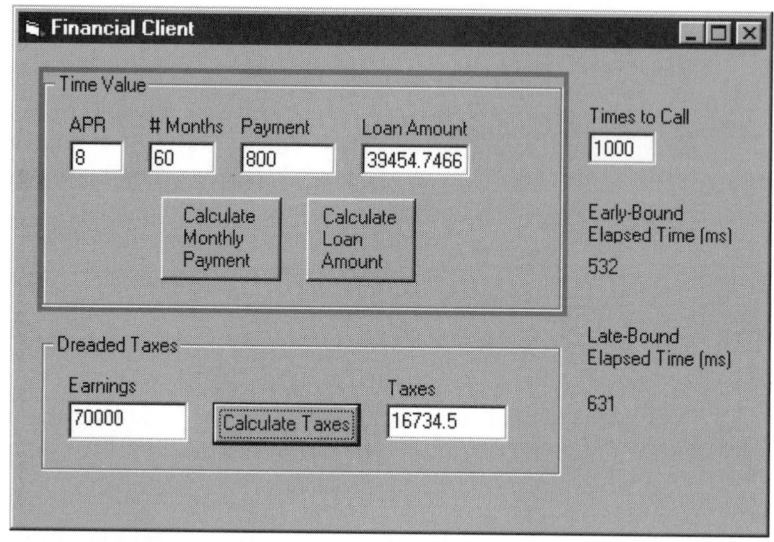

FIGURE 7.6 The Visual Basic Financial Client

The control description, control type, and control name for each control are listed in Table 7.3.

TABLE 7.3 Controls for the Financial Client

Control Description	VB Control Type	Control Name in VB Project
APR	TextBox	txtInterestRate
#Months	TextBox	txtNumMonths
Payment	TextBox	txtPayment
Loan Amount	TextBox	TxtLoanAmount
Calculate Monthly Payments	Command Button	CmdPayment
Calculate Loan Amount	Command Button	cmdCalculateLoanAmount
Times to Call	TextBox	txtTimesToCall
Early-Bound Elapsed Time	Label	lblEarlyElapsedTime
Late-Bound Elapsed Time	Label	lblLateElapsedTime
Earnings	TextBox	txtEarnings
Calculate Tax	Command Button	cmdCalculateTax

ADDING A REFERENCE TO THE FINANCIAL COMPONENT

Adding a reference in Visual Basic is equivalent to using the `import` keyword in Visual C++. In Either case, you are providing your development environment with a priori knowledge of the COM classes and interfaces supported by your server. This allows our development environment to do early binding. To add a reference to the financial component, perform the following steps:

1. Select `References...` from the `Project` menu.
2. Check the checkbox next to `Financial Component 1.0` Type Library.
3. Click `OK`.

You will not see the Financial Compliment's type library in the References dialog until you either build the DLL for the financial component or register the DLL if you downloaded it from the website.

INSTANTIATING A LATE-BOUND AND AN EARLY-BOUND FINANCIAL OBJECT

Double-click the form to add the following code to the Load handler on the form. The Load event is fired after the form is created but before it is shown:

```
Private mLateBound As Object
Private mEarlyBound As TimeValue
Private Sub Form_Load()
   On Error GoTo errHandler
   txtTimesToCall = 100
   txtInterestRate = 8#
   txtNumMonths = 60
   Set mLateBound =
CreateObject("Financialcomponent.TimeValue")
   Set mEarlyBound = New TimeValue
   Exit Sub
errHandler:
   MsgBox (Err.Description)
End Sub
```

IMPLEMENTING THE BUTTON HANDLERS

Add the following code to the project's main form:

```
Private mElapsedTime As Long
Private Sub cmdCalculateLoanAmount_Click()
   On Error GoTo errHandler
   Dim lngSavedTime As Long
   Dim intTimesToCall As Integer
   Dim i As Integer
   mEarlyBound.InterestRate = CDbl(txtInterestRate.Text)
   lngSavedTime = GetTickCount()
   For i = 1 To CInt(txtTimesToCall)
      txtLoanAmount.Text = mEarlyBound.loanAmount(CInt(txtNumMonths.Text),
CDbl(txtPayment.Text))
   Next
   lblEarlyElapsedTime.Caption = GetTickCount() - lngSavedTime

   mLateBound.InterestRate = CDbl(txtInterestRate.Text)
   lngSavedTime = GetTickCount()
   For i = 1 To CInt(txtTimesToCall)
      txtLoanAmount.Text = mLateBound.loanAmount(CInt(txtNumMonths.Text),
CDbl(txtPayment.Text))
   Next
   lblLateElapsedTime.Caption = GetTickCount() - lngSavedTime
   Exit Sub
errHandler:
   MsgBox (Err.Description)
End Sub

Private Sub cmdCalculateTax_Click()
   On Error GoTo errHandler
   Dim taxCalculator As ITaxCalculator
   Set taxCalculator = mEarlyBound
   txtTaxes = taxCalculator.CalculateTax(CDbl(txtEarnings.Text))
   Exit Sub
errHandler:
   MsgBox (Err.Description)
End Sub

Private Sub cmdPayment_Click()
   On Error GoTo errHandler
   Dim lngSavedTime As Long
   Dim intTimesToCall As Integer
   Dim i As Integer

   mEarlyBound.InterestRate = CDbl(txtInterestRate.Text)
   lngSavedTime = GetTickCount()
   For i = 1 To CInt(txtTimesToCall)
      txtPayment.Text =
mEarlyBound.MonthlyPayment(CInt(txtNumMonths.Text),
CDbl(txtLoanAmount.Text))
   Next
```

```
    lblEarlyElapsedTime.Caption = GetTickCount() - lngSavedTime
    mLateBound.InterestRate = CDbl(txtInterestRate.Text)
    lngSavedTime = GetTickCount()
    For i = 1 To CInt(txtTimesToCall)
        txtPayment.Text =
mLateBound.MonthlyPayment(CInt(txtNumMonths.Text),
CDbl(txtLoanAmount.Text))
    Next
    lblLateElapsedTime.Caption = GetTickCount() - lngSavedTime
    Exit Sub
errHandler:
    MsgBox (Err.Description)
End Sub
Notice that the logic is written so that I can enter the number of
times that the selected method will be called.
For i = 1 To CInt(txtTimesToCall)
    txtPayment.Text = mEarlyBound.MonthlyPayment(CInt(txtNumMonths.Text),
CDbl(txtLoanAmount.Text))
Next
```

Running the client on a 200 MHz Pentium machine with 96MB of RAM produced the results shown in Table 7.4. I used the button that calculates the loan amount to generate these numbers.

TABLE 7.4 Performance Test Results

Times the Method was Called	Elapsed Time (Average of 5 runs) (Early Bound)	Elapsed Time (Average of 5 runs) (Late Bound)
1000	680 ms	841 ms
500	260 ms	315 ms
100	47 ms	66 ms

Notice that the late-bound client is about 19% slower.

Summary

In this chapter you explored the concept of Automation and learned that Automation means using the `IDispatch` interface to communicate between COM clients and servers. `IDispatch` is interface that enables indirect calls of methods through a single interface. This property together with the requirement that all arguments to `IDispatch` must be Variants means that Automation and `IDispatch` are perfect for COM-enabling simpler pointer-challenged programming languages and interpreted languages such as VB script. You also learned that using `IDispatch` is slower than using a vtable interface but the difference isn't nearly as great as that between an in-process and out-of-process server.

EIGHT

COM Callbacks and Connectable Objects

The COM objects that you have developed so far have provided functionality to their clients as implemented interfaces. When a client wishes to use a piece of functionality provided by an object, it simply requests from the object the interface that implements the functionality and then calls the methods in the interface. Interfaces like these are called incoming interfaces because they allow an object to receive messages (as method invocations) from their clients. This is okay for about 90% of the scenarios that you will encounter.

There are, however, certain situations where instead of calling a method on an object's interface, a client would like the object to notify them when something interesting has happened. These object-to-client notifications are called *events* or *callbacks* (I use both names interchangeably in this chapter). In order for a client to receive callbacks from an object, you must establish a bi-directional communication link between the client and the object. Since clients communicate with a COM object by calling a method in one of the object's interfaces, it is natural to have the object call back to its client using a COM interface that is implemented by the client. These interfaces are called *outgoing* interfaces, because they allow an object to *send* messages (as method invocations) to their clients. By implementing these outgoing interfaces using COM, your callbacks gain the attributes that COM provides: location transparency and programming-language independence. You can send callbacks across processes and—subject to security constraints—even across machines. You can also use send and receive callbacks between a client and an object regardless of what programming language each is implemented in.

In this chapter you will learn how to implement callbacks using COM. You'll also learn about Connection Points, which are a set of COM interfaces that provide a standard way to setup and tear-down a bi-directional communication link between a client and server. You'll also learn how to implement COM callbacks without using Connection Points and why you may want to avoid Connection Points in some situations. In the process you will build your most interesting (and challenging) example program to date. The example program in this chapter is a multi-threaded, stock monitor that sends notifications of price changes on a specified stock. The example is interesting because it shows how to implement a multi-threaded COM server, even though you won't dive deeply into COM threading until Chapter 9.

Understand COM Callbacks/Events

Imagine that you want to implement a server application that provides stock prices. You might implement an `IStockQuote` interface that looks like this:

```
interface IStockQuote
{
   [id(1), helpstring("method GetPrice")] HRESULT GetPrice([in] BSTR
ticker,[out,retval] float *price);
}
```

And then define a COM class that implements the interface as follows:

```
coclass StockQuoter
{
      [default] interface IStockQuote;
};
```

Whenever people want to know the price of a stock, they have to obtain an `IStockQuote` interface pointer on a `StockQuoter` object. They must then pass the ticker symbol for the stock to the `GetPrice` method to retrieve the current price of the stock. This is a typical usage scenario for an *incoming* interface. But likely, they will want to monitor the price of the stock. In other words, they would like to receive some sort of notification when the price of a stock changes. Or, maybe they would like to be notified when the price crosses a certain price threshold, or if the price increases by more than a certain delta. You could implement this functionality by requiring the client to poll the `IStockQuote` interface, but that would waste a lot of CPU cycles, and if the client and server were on different machines and were communicating across a network, it would also consume a great deal of network bandwidth. A better solution is to have the server notify the client whenever the price of a stock changes. Instead of the client calling the server to retrieve the price of a stock, the server calls a method on an outgoing interface that the client implements. You could define an outgoing interface called `IStockEvent` as follows:

```
interface IStockEvent : IDispatch
{
   [id(1), helpstring("method PriceChange")] HRESULT PriceChange([in]
BSTR ticker,[in] float newPrice,[in] float oldPrice);
};
```

A client must now do a couple of things to receive price change notifications through this interface:

- Implement the `IStockEvent` interface. The client's implementation of this interface might update a chart or display a message box.
- Pass its implementation of the `IStockEvent` interface to the server so that the server may callback to the client when a stock's price changes.

The second bullet puts a requirement on the `StockQuoter` class to also implement an interface that the client can use to pass its `IStockEvent` interface to the `StockQuoter` object when it wants to begin receiving callbacks. To satisfy this requirement, the `StockQuoter` class could implement an interface called `IStockMonitor` that is defined as follows:

```
interface IStockMonitor : IDispatch
{
   [id(1), helpstring("method Advise")] HRESULT Advise([in] BSTR
ticker,[in] IStockEvent *evt,[in] float delta,[out,retval] short *cookie);
   [id(2), helpstring("method Unadvise")] HRESULT Unadvise([in] short
*cookie);
};
```

The most important method in this interface is the `Advise` method, which has four parameters. Table 8.1 summarizes the purpose of each parameter.

TABLE 8.1 Arguments for the Advise method of IStockMonitor

Argument Name	Argument Purpose
Ticker	The name of the stock that you wish to monitor.
Evt	The outgoing interface pointer. This is the interface that the object will callback on when it wants to send notifications.
Delta	The change in price that will trigger a notification.
Cookie	An identifier that represents this monitor that can be passed to the Unadvise method to remove the monitor.

When a client wants to receive price change callbacks for a stock, it has to pass to the `Advise` method of `IStockMonitor`, the ticker symbol for the stock, its implementation of the `IStockEvent` interface, and the price delta that will trigger the event. The `Advise` method will return an ID, a "cookie," that represents this callback request. The client can store this cookie and when it no longer wishes to receive callbacks, it can pass this cookie to the `Unadvise` method of `IStockMonitor`. Figure 8.1 shows the objects and interfaces involved in this client/server relationship.

Notice that it's hard to tell which is the client and which is the server in this picture. Outgoing interfaces blur the distinction between a client and a server. When a `StockQuoter` object calls the `PriceChange` method in the `IStockEvent` interface to notify your client, it effectively becomes a client. The client, which implements `IStockEvents`, becomes a server for this method call.

With all of the interfaces in place, you can summarize the protocol that the client must follow to receive stock notifications like this:

1. Create a class that implements the `IStockEvent` interface.
2. Instantiate an instance of the `StockQuoter` COM class requesting the `IStockMonitor` interface.
3. Pass the `IStockEvent` interface from the class that you created in Step 1 to the `Advise` method of `IStockMonitor` along with the ticker symbol for the stock that you wish to receive price change callbacks on and the price delta that will trigger a notification.
4. When the price delta has been exceeded the `StockQuoter` calls the `PriceChange` method on the interface that was passed in Step 3.

Interfaces like `IStockMonitor` and `IStockEvent` are called custom event/callback interfaces or proprietary event/callback interfaces. Unfortunately, implementing events/callbacks this way is not as simple as it may seem.

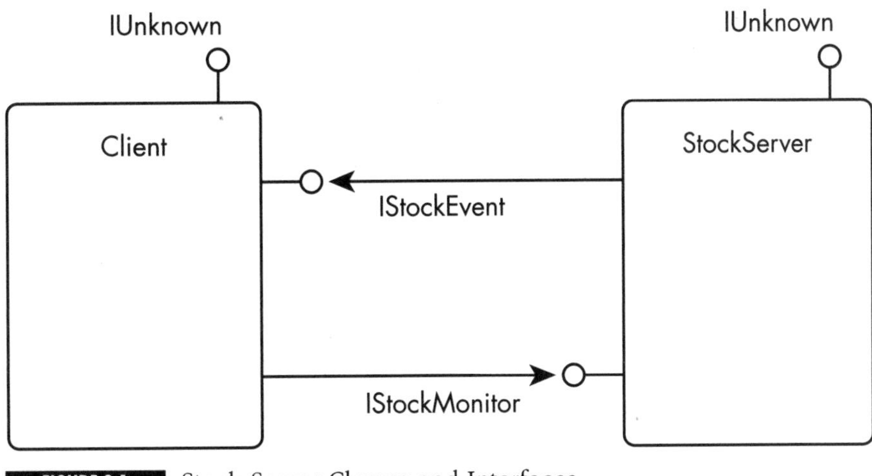

FIGURE 8.1 Stock Server Classes and Interfaces.

Problems with Proprietary Outgoing Interfaces

There are several problems with implementing callbacks using proprietary interfaces.

- The client is required to have a priori knowledge of the proprietary outgoing interface (`IStockEvent`).
- You have to create a COM class on your client to receive callbacks from the `StockQuoter`.
- The client is required to have a priori knowledge of the interface, `IStockMonitor`, that is used to register outgoing interfaces.

OUTGOING INTERFACES

Proprietary outgoing interfaces like `IStockEvent` make it difficult for development environments to create event handlers. Ideally, you would want the events/callbacks that are fired from your COM objects to be as easy to use as the events that are fired from GUI controls, such as edit boxes and list boxes. If you have used a Visual Development, like Visual Basic, you know what I'm talking about. In Visual Basic, you can drop a text box or a list box onto a form and then click a drop-down list to see the list of events that the control will fire to the form. You can then select which events you would like to handle. You want your COM objects to work the same way. In theory, you should be able to import your COM objects into a project and view all of the callbacks it supports and then click a button to add a handler for one of the callbacks. Unfortunately, `IStockEvent` presents some problems in this regard. Since it is a vtable interface, an implementation class built by the client to receive the methods in the interface will need to implement all of the methods in the interface or your compiler will complain. `IStockEvent` only has one method, but you could have an outgoing interface that had 2, 3, or even 6 methods. If you want to catch one of the callbacks in an outgoing interface, you would have to implement all of them. You could put blank implementations for the methods that you don't want to handle, but that's still extra work.

REGISTERING CALLBACK INTERFACES

Even if your development tool is smart enough to implement `IStockEvent` auto-magically, how can it know that it needs to register its implementation of `IStockEvent` with the server using the `Advise` method of the `IStockMonitor` before it starts receiving callbacks? There is no way for the development tool to figure this out without a priori knowledge of the semantics of the `IStockMonitor` interface. Instead of the proprietary `IStockMonitor` interface, you need a standard interface that performs the same function.

Connectable Objects

What is needed to solve all of these problems is an architecture that includes a set of well-known, standard interfaces and a protocol that clients and servers can use to establish a bi-directional relationship. These interfaces should allow a server to:

- Advertise the fact that it supports outgoing interfaces (callbacks).
- Advertise the outgoing interfaces that it does support.
- Provide a generic means for the client to register and unregister its implementation of the outgoing interfaces with the server.

There exists a set of standard COM interfaces that implement this functionality, and collectively these interfaces are called Connectable Objects or Connection Points. Connectable Objects are a set of COM interfaces that establish a known protocol for constructing and tearing down bi-directional communication relationships between COM clients and servers. There are four main interfaces in the Connectable Objects architecture: `IConnectionPointContainer`, `IConnectionPoint`, `IEnumConnections`, and `IEnumConnectionPoints`, and one minor interface: `IProvideClassInfo`. Supporting the `IConnectionPointContainer` interface allows a COM object to advertise that it supports outgoing interfaces and to advertise the outgoing interfaces that it supports. `IConnectionPoint` provides a generic means for a client to register and unregister its implementation of a particular outgoing interface. `IEnumConnectionPoints` and `IEnumConnections` are enumerations (COM's word for collections) that contain connection points and connections-to-connection points, respectively.

IProvideClassInfo is used to return type library information, such as the parameter list, for the methods in an outgoing interface.

IConnectionPointContainer

A COM object that supports the IConnectionPointContainer interface is advertising to all interested parties that it supports one or more IConnectionPoint interfaces that a client can use to register outgoing interfaces to receive callbacks (events). IConnectionPointContainer has a method called EnumConnectionPoints that allows a client to enumerate all the IConnectionPoint interfaces that a connectable object supports. It has another method called FindConnectionPoint that a client can use to find a particular IConnectionPoint implementation if it knows the GUID of the outgoing interface associated with the IConnectionPoint implementation. IConnectionPointContainer is defined as shown here:

```
interface IConnectionPointContainer : IUnknown
{
   HRESULT EnumConnectionPoints ( [out] IEnumConnectionPoints **
ppEnum );
   HRESULT FindConnectionPoint( [in] REFIID riid, [out]
IConnectionPoint ** ppCP );
}
```

You can find this declaration in the file ocidl.idl that resides in the include directory of your Visual C++ installation.

IConnectionPoint

IConnectionPoint is an interface that a client can connect itself to when it wishes to receive callbacks. In the stock monitor example, the IStockMonitor interface is similar to a connection point. However, with connection points you do not use a custom interface like IStockMonitor to let clients register themselves to receive callbacks. Instead you provide a distinct implementation of IConnectionPoint for each outgoing interface (like IStockEvent) that your server supports. IConnectionPoint has methods called Advise and Unadvise that perform the same function as the Advise and Unadvise methods in IStockMonitor. The difference with IConnectionPoint is that it is a standard interface. That means development environments can know ahead of time how to establish the link between a COM object that wants to send callbacks and a piece of client code that wants to receive them. An object that implements the IConnectionPoint interface is often called a *source* because it produces events. The client's implementation of an outgoing interface is called a *sink* because it receives (consumes) the events produced by the connection point object. The `IConnectionPoint` interface is defined as shown below. You can also find this definition in `ocidl.idl`:

```
interface IConnectionPoint : IUnknown
{
   HRESULT GetConnectionInterface([out] IID * pIID);
   HRESULT GetConnectionPointContainer([out] IConnectionPointContainer
** ppCPC);
   HRESULT Advise([in] IUnknown * pUnkSink,[out] DWORD * pdwCookie);
   HRESULT Unadvise( [in] DWORD dwCookie);
   HRESULT EnumConnections([out] IEnumConnections ** ppEnum);
}
```

A description of each method in this interface is shown in Table 8.2.

TABLE 8.2 IConnectionPoint Interface

IConnectionPoint Methods	Description
GetConnectionInterface	Returns the IID of the outgoing interface that is associated with this connection point.
GetConnectionPointContainer	Returns the parent container of this connection point.
Advise	Creates a connection between a connection point and a client's sink, where the sink implements the outgoing interface supported by this connection point.
Unadvise	Terminates a notification previously set up with Advise.
EnumConnections	Returns an object to enumerate the current advisory connections for this connection point.

Notice that the client passes its implementation of an outgoing interface to the `Advise` method of `IConnectionPoint` just like we passed an implementation of `IStockEvent` to the `Advise` method of `IStockMonitor`. For maximum flexibility, outgoing interfaces used with connection points are almost always `dispinterfaces`. Using `dispinterfaces` for the outgoing interfaces makes connection points accessible to the widest possible number of languages. Figure 8.2 shows the relationships between the various objects and interfaces in the connectable objects architecture.

IEnumConnections and IEnumConnectionPoints

`IEnumConnections` and `IEnumConnectionPoints` are *enumerations* (which are COM's equivalent of collections). An IEnumConnections interface is returned from the `EnumConnections` method in `IConnectionPoint`. It allows a client to iterate over all the outgoing interfaces that are currently connected to a connection point. Connection points support multi-casting (the ability of a server to send a callback to multiple clients at once).

An `IEnumConnectionPoints` interface is returned from the `EnumConnectionPoints` method in `IConnectionPointContainer`. It allows a client to iterate over all the connection points supported by a connectable object. Both enumerations support the standard enumeration methods: `Next`, `Skip`, `Reset`, and `Clone`.

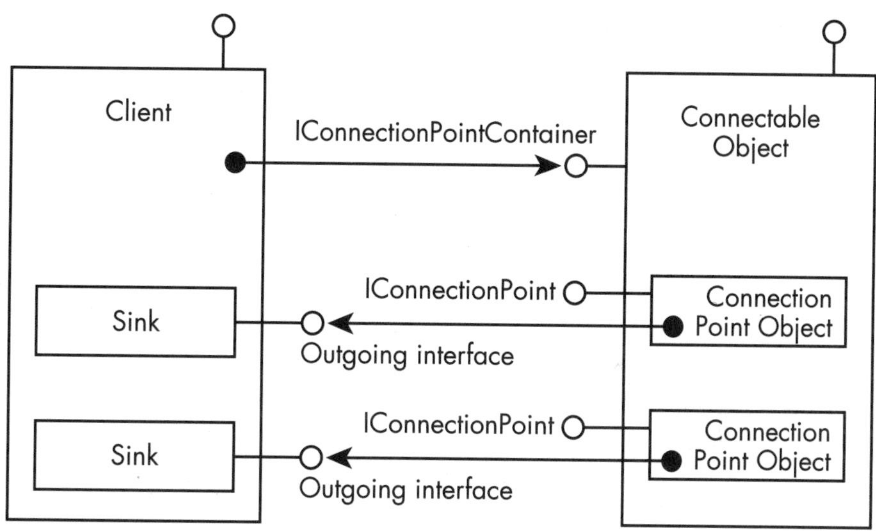

FIGURE 8.2 Connectable Object Architecture.

Enumerations

Enumerations are COM's equivalent of collections. In implementing your COM objects, you will often need to define methods that return collections of objects. With connection points, for instance, there are two places where you have to return collections of objects. In one case, you need to return a collection of all the connection points supports by a particular object (the `EnumConnectionPoints` method in `IConnectionPointContainer`). In another case, you want to get all the outgoing interfaces that are associated with a particular connection point (the `EnumConnections` method in `IConnectionPoint`). In both cases, the method involved returns an enumeration interface. Enumeration interfaces are always given the name `IEnumXXX` where XXX is the name of the type that the enumerations hold. So the enumerations that hold `IConnectionPoints` is called `IEnumConnectionPoints`. There are a number of standard enumeration interfaces that hold other COM-related types like `IEnumUnknown`, `IEnumDispatch`, and `IEnumVariant`. All enumeration interfaces have four key methods: `Next`, `Skip`, `Reset`, and `Clone` that are specialized for the type that the enumeration holds. The (simplified) IDL for `IEnumConnectionPoints` is shown in the following example:

```
[
   object,
   uuid(B196B285-BAB4-101A-B69C-00AA00341D07),
   pointer_default(unique)
]
interface IEnumConnectionPoints : IUnknown
{
   HRESULT Next( [in] ULONG cConnections, [out, size_is(cConnections),
length_is(*pcFetched)]
                        LPCONNECTIONPOINT * ppCP, [out] ULONG *
pcFetched);
   HRESULT Skip( [in] ULONG cConnections);
   HRESULT Reset( void);
   HRESULT Clone( [out] IEnumConnectionPoints ** ppEnum);
}
```

The purpose of each of the four methods in the `IEnumXXX` interfaces is described in Table 8.3.

TABLE 8.3 The IConnectionPoint Interface

Methods	Description
Next	Retrieves a specified number of items in the enumeration.
Skip	Skips over a specified number of items in the enumeration sequence.
Reset	Resets the enumeration sequence to the beginning.
Clone	Creates a new enumeration with the same items but an independent index.

IProvideClassInfo

Although it's not a requirement, many connectable objects implement an interface called IProvideClassInfo. IProvideClass is defined as shown here in ocidl.idl:

```
[
   object,
   uuid(B196B283-BAB4-101A-B69C-00AA00341D07),
   pointer_default(unique)
]

interface IProvideClassInfo : IUnknown
{
   HRESULT GetClassInfo( [out] ITypeInfo ** ppTI);
}
```

IProvideClassInfo has one method called GetClassInfo that returns an ITypeInfo interface. ITypeInfo contains type information from the server's type library. Using ITypeInfo, you can find the outgoing interfaces supported by a server. A server marks an interface as an outgoing interface using the *source* keyword in IDL as shown here:

```
coclass StockMonitor
   {
      [default] interface IStockMonitor;
      [default, source] dispinterface _IStockEvents;
   };
```

After it identifies the source interfaces supported by its server, a client can use the information in the type library (via the ITypeInfo interface pointer obtained from IProvideClassInfo) to dynamically construct an implementation of the outgoing interface. This is easier to do if the outbound interface is a dispinterface (which is usually the case).

Implementing Connection Points

If you implement your stock monitor using connection points, you would first define your outgoing interface as a pure dispinterface as shown here:

```
dispinterface _IStockEvents
{
   properties:
   methods:
```

```
        [id(1), helpstring("method PriceChange")] HRESULT
PriceChange([in] BSTR ticker,[in] float newPrice,[in] float oldPrice);
};
```

By convention, outgoing connection point interfaces are usually declared with an underscore in front. This causes the interface to be hidden by most object browsers.

Next, you provide an implementation of the `IConnectionPoint` interface that works with the `IStockEvents` interface. You must also implement the `IConnectionPointContainer` interface. Because you only have one connection point, your implementation of `IConnectionPointContainer` will be fairly simple: `EnumConnectionPoints` return an enumeration with one item and `FindConnectionPoint` only returns your connection point when you specify the IID for `IStockEvents` as the first parameter. Unfortunately, if a client wants to use your connection points, there is a complicated protocol it must go through and therein lies a problem.

The Connection Point Protocol

The protocol for establishing bi-directional communication between a client and an object using connection points is as follows:

1. Use `QueryInterface` to request the `IConnectionPointContainer` interface from the connectable object.
2. Call `FindConnectionPoint` specifying the IID for the outgoing interface (`IStockEvents`) to get the `IConnectionPoint` associated with `IStockEvents`.
3. Call the `Advise` method on `IConnectionPoint` passing in the client's implementation of `IStockEvents`.
4. Since you must pass an `IUnknown` point to `Advise`, the connectable object must `QueryInterface` the `IUnknown` pointer that it receives to get an `IStockEvents` interface pointer.
5. Release the `IConnectionPoint` interface pointer.

It took a total of five round trips between the client and server to setup your callback.

You need to keep one interface pointer on the object to keep it alive so it won't count a release of the `IConnectionPointContainer` interface pointer as a sixth round trip.

If your server is in-process, this is not a problem. A call on a method in an in-process server is no slower than making a normal (non-COM) function call. But, as you saw in Chapter 6, if your server is out-of-process, method calls are slow. If your object resides on a remote host, they are slower. Making five method calls can be prohibitively expensive. Compare the five step, connection point protocol to the protocol you used to setup callbacks with our proprietary interface.

1. Use `QueryInterface` to request the `IStockMonitor` interface from the stock monitor object.
2. Call the `Advise` method on `IConnectionPoint` passing in the client's implementation of `IStockEvents`.

Once again, I won't count a release on `IStockMonitor` because you do need to keep one reference to the object.

The lesson is that you should use Connection Points with in-process COM objects such as ActiveX controls. But for callbacks that need to be sent across processes or even across machines, consider implementing custom callback interfaces.

Your Multithreaded Stock Monitor Example

For your example, you will implement a stock monitor similar to the one discussed in this chapter. Your stock monitor will use connection points to send stock price change notifications to its clients. It will be multithreaded; it will have a worker thread that monitors the price of a group of stocks (actually, it will use a random number generator to simulate stock price changes) and sends callbacks to the client when a price changes. You will build a Visual Basic client so you can see how easy it is to receive events from a visual development environment that knows how to work with connection points.

A Summary of the Steps

The steps that you perform to build your stock monitor component are as follows:

1. Create a new ATL executable project using the ATL AppWizard.
2. Make the server free-threaded.
3. Add a free-threaded, connection point-enabled class using the ATL Object Wizard.
4. Implement the connection point interface.
5. Add Methods to the COM classes' main interface.
6. Complete the implementation of your server.
7. Create a client using Visual Basic.

Create a New ATL Project Using the ATL/COM AppWizard

Start Visual C++ and then execute these steps:

1. Select `New...` from the `File` menu (the New dialog appears).
2. Click the `Projects` tab.
3. Select `ATL COM AppWizard` from the presented list of project types.
4. Enter `StockServer` in the `Project` Name field.
5. Click `OK` (The ATL COM AppWizard will appear).
6. Select `Executable` under `Server Type`.
7. Click `Finish`.

Visual C++ creates a project that contains the entire infrastructure required for a COM executable server. By default, the ATL/COM AppWizard makes the server apartment threaded. If you are not sure what an apartment threaded server is, don't worry. In Chapter 9, I discuss COM threading and it should be clear. For now, think of it this way: the ATL/COM AppWizard assumes that you are creating your COM classes in the simplest way possible, in other words, you let COM handle the threading issues for you. If your intention is to implement a server that has worker threads, then your server must be multi-threaded. You have to make an alteration to your project if you want to build a server that works efficiently with multiple threads.

Make the Server Free-Threaded

To make your server free-threaded, go into the file `stdafx.h` and change the line of code that reads like this:

```
#define _ATL_APARTMENT_THREADED
```

to this:

```
#define _ATL_FREE_THREADED
```

To see the effect that making this change has, go to the _tWinMain function in the file, stockserver.cpp. At the beginning of this function, you should see this code:

```
#if _WIN32_WINNT >= 0x0400 & defined(_ATL_FREE_THREADED)
   HRESULT hRes = CoInitializeEx(NULL, COINIT_MULTITHREADED);
#else
   HRESULT hRes = CoInitialize(NULL);
#endif
```

The first line uses conditional compilation to check if _ATL_FREE_THREADED is defined; and the operating system the code is being compiled on is NT 4.0 or later. This is necessary because free-threaded servers were not supported on versions of Windows prior to NT 4.0. Notice that if _ATL_FREE_THREADED is defined and the operating system is NT 4.0 or later, then your code calls the CoInitializeEx function to initialize COM and passes a second parameter of COINIT_MULTITHREADED. If either of these conditions is false, your code calls CoInitialize. In COM lingo, you are entering the Multi-Threaded Apartment (MTA) if ATL_FREE_THREADED is defined and entering the Single-Threaded Apartment (STA) if it is not. I explain this more in Chapter 9. For now, just remember that a free-threaded server must initialize COM in a different way than a single-threaded one.

Add a Free-Threaded, Connection Point-Enabled COM Class

Next, you need to add a free-threaded COM class that supports connection points. To do this, perform the following steps in Visual C++:

1. Select New ATL Object... from the Insert menu (the ATL Object Wizard appears).
2. Under Category select Object and under Object select Simple Object.
3. Click the Next button (the ATL Object Wizard Properties dialog appears).
4. On the Names tab, enter StockMonitor in the Short Name field under C++.
5. Click the Attributes tab (see Figure 8.3).
6. Select Free under Threading Model.

7. Leave the interface type as dual.
8. Set the `Support Connection Points` checkbox.
9. Set the `Support ISupportErrorInfo` checkbox.
10. Click `OK`.

Setting the `Support Connection Points` check box made several changes to the generated COM class. The bolded code below shows the lines that were added.

LISTING 8.1 *THE STOCK MONITOR IMPLEMENTATION CLASS*

```
class ATL_NO_VTABLE CStockMonitor :
   public CComObjectRootEx<CComMultiThreadModel>,
   public CComCoClass<CStockMonitor, &CLSID_StockMonitor>,
   public ISupportErrorInfo,
   public IConnectionPointContainerImpl<CStockMonitor>,
   public IDispatchImpl<IStockMonitor, &IID_IStockMonitor,
&LIBID_STOCKSERVERLib>
{
public:
   CStockMonitor() { }
```

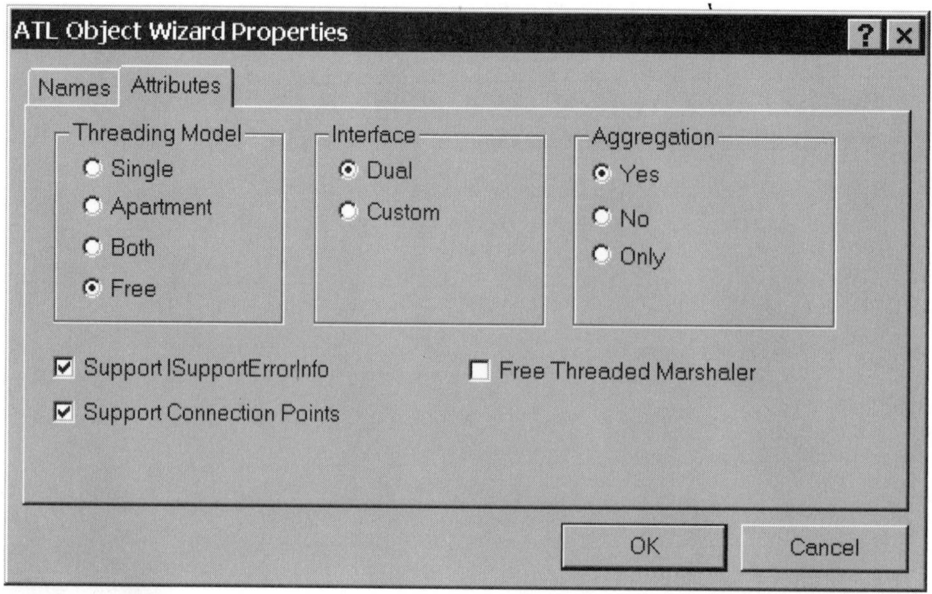

FIGURE 8.3 Creating a Free-Threaded, Connection Point–Enabled Class.

```
BEGIN_COM_MAP(CStockMonitor)
    COM_INTERFACE_ENTRY(IStockMonitor)
    COM_INTERFACE_ENTRY(IDispatch)
    COM_INTERFACE_ENTRY(ISupportErrorInfo)
    COM_INTERFACE_ENTRY(IConnectionPointContainer)
END_COM_MAP()
BEGIN_CONNECTION_POINT_MAP(CStockMonitor)
END_CONNECTION_POINT_MAP()

// ISupportsErrorInfo
    STDMETHOD(InterfaceSupportsErrorInfo)(REFIID riid);

// IStockMonitor
public:
};
```

The ATL Object Wizard has added support for the `IConnectionPointContainer` interface to your COM class by adding the `IConnectionPoint ContainerImpl` class to your list of base classes and adding a `COM_INTERFACE_ENTRY` for `IConnectionPointContainer`. The ATL Object Wizard also added a connection point map to your COM class:

```
BEGIN_CONNECTION_POINT_MAP(CStockQuote)
END_CONNECTION_POINT_MAP()
```

Much like the `COM_MAP` is used to implement `QueryInterface` to return the list of interfaces supported by the COM class, the `CONNECTION_POINT_MAP` is used to implement the `EnumConnectionPoints` and `FindConnectionPoint` methods in `IConnectionPointContainer`. Selecting `Support Connection Points` also added an outgoing interface to your IDL as shown here:

```
[
    uuid(4506CE8F-2A84-11D3-998A-E0EC08C10000),
    helpstring("_IStockMonitorEvents Interface")
]
dispinterface _IStockMonitorEvents
{
    properties:
    methods:
};
```

Notice that this is a pure `dispinterface` and not a `dual` interface. As mentioned earlier, `dispinterfaces` are usually used as the outgoing interface with connection points. In the `stockserver.idl` file, also notice that _IStockMonitorEvents has been added to the StockMonitor coclass as a source interface:

```
coclass StockMonitor
{
   [default] interface IStockMonitor;
   [default, source] dispinterface_IStockMonitorEvents;
      };
```

One more difference between this class and the other classes that you have generated using the ATL Object Wizard is that this class is multi-threaded as shown by the second line in Listing 8.1:

```
public CComObjectRootEx<CComMultiThreadModel>
```

The classes that we have generated previously using the ATL Object Wizard use the CComObjectRootEx as shown below:

```
public CComObjectRootEx<CComSingleThreadModel>
```

This change was made because you selected Free for the threading model. I will defer further discussion of this until Chapter 9.

Implement the Connection Point Interface

The ATL Object Wizard added the IConnectionPointContainer interface to your COM class, but it did not add any IConnectionPoint interfaces to our COM class. To add a connection point to your class, perform the following summarized steps:

1. Add PriceChange and MonitorInitiated methods to your _IStockMonitorEvents outgoing interface.
2. Compile the IDL.
3. Use the Implement Connection Point Command in Visual C++ to add a connection point interface to your COM class.

ADD PRICECHANGE AND MONITORINITIATED METHODS

To add the PriceChange and MonitorInitiated methods to the _IStockMonitorEvents interface, perform the following steps:

1. Right-click on the _IStockMonitorEvents interface in the ClassView tab of the Visual C++ Workspace as shown in Figure 8.4.
2. Select Add Method... from the Context menu (the Add Method to Interface dialog appears).
3. Enter PriceChange in the Method Name field.

4. Enter [in] BSTR ticker,[in] float newPrice,[in] float oldPrice in the Parameters field.
5. Click OK.
6. Repeat steps 1–5, but enter MonitorInitiated in the Method name field on step 3 and [in] BSTR ticker, [in] float currentPrice in the parameters field on step 4.

Visual C++ adds the PriceChange and MonitorInitiated methods to the IDL for the _IStockMonitorEvents interface as shown here:

```
dispinterface _IStockMonitorEvents
{
properties:
methods:
    [id(1), helpstring("method PriceChange")] HRESULT
PriceChange([in] BSTR ticker,[in] float newPrice,[in] float oldPrice);
    [id(2), helpstring("method MonitorInitiated")] HRESULT
MonitorInitiated([in] BSTR ticker,[in] float currentPrice);
};
```

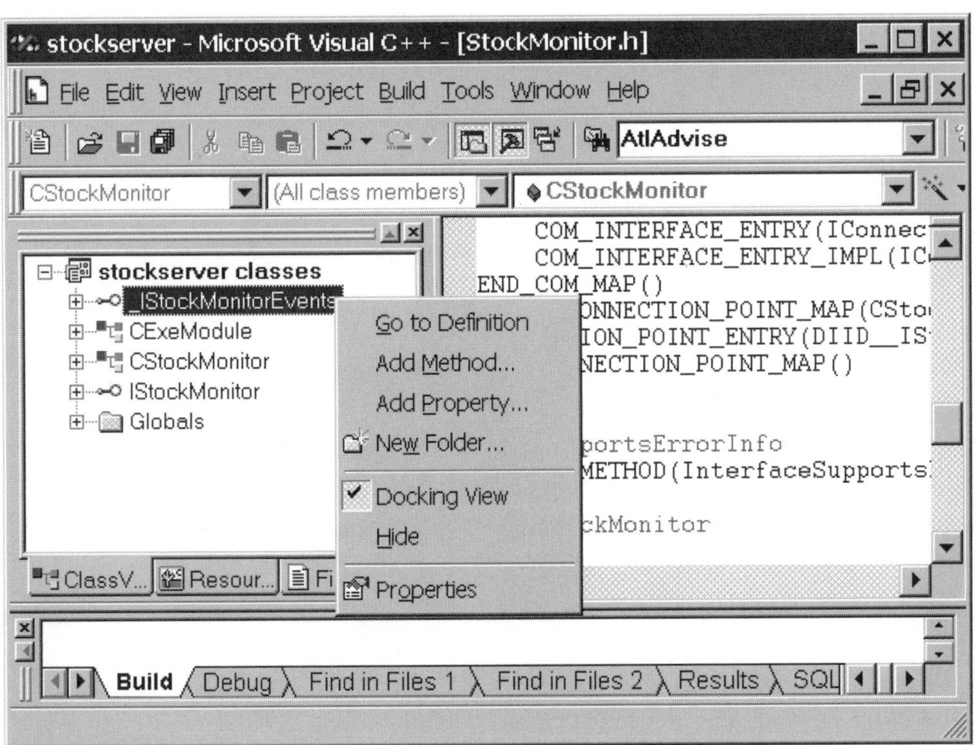

FIGURE 8.4 Adding Methods to the _IStockMonitorEvents Interface.

COMPILE THE IDL

To implement the connection point interface, you must first compile the IDL so that your type library reflects the updated outgoing interface. Perform the following steps to compile the IDL file:

1. Make `StockMonitor.idl` the current file by double-clicking the `IStockMonitor` interface in the `ClassView` tab of the Visual C++ workspace.
2. Click the `Compile` button or Press `CTRL-F7`.

USE THE IMPLEMENT CONNECTION POINT COMMAND

The implement connection point command in Visual C++ gives you a fast way to implement a connection interface. To use the Implement connection point command on `_IStockEvents`, perform the following steps:

1. Right-click on the `CStockMonitor` class in the `ClassView` tab of the Visual C++ workspace as shown in Figure 8.5.
2. Select `Implement Connection Point` from the `Context` menu (the Implement Connection Point dialog appears as shown in Figure 8.6).
3. Set the `_IStockMonitorEvents` checkbox.
4. Click `OK`.

This command adds a new class to your project that implements `IConnectionPoint`. It also adds this connection point class to the list of base classes for the `CStockMonitor` implementation class. So the methods in this new class now become part of the `CStockMonitor` class and can be called from any of this class's methods. The new connection point class can be found in a file called `stockserverCP.h`. The contents of this file are shown here:

```
template <class T>
class CProxy_IStockMonitorEvents : public IConnectionPointImpl<T,
&DIID__IStockMonitorEvents, CComDynamicUnkArray>
{
public:
   HRESULT Fire_PriceChange(BSTR ticker, FLOAT newPrice, FLOAT
oldPrice)
   {
       CComVariant varResult;
       T* pT = static_cast<T*>(this);
       int nConnectionIndex;
       CComVariant* pvars = new CComVariant[3];
       int nConnections = m_vec.GetSize();
```

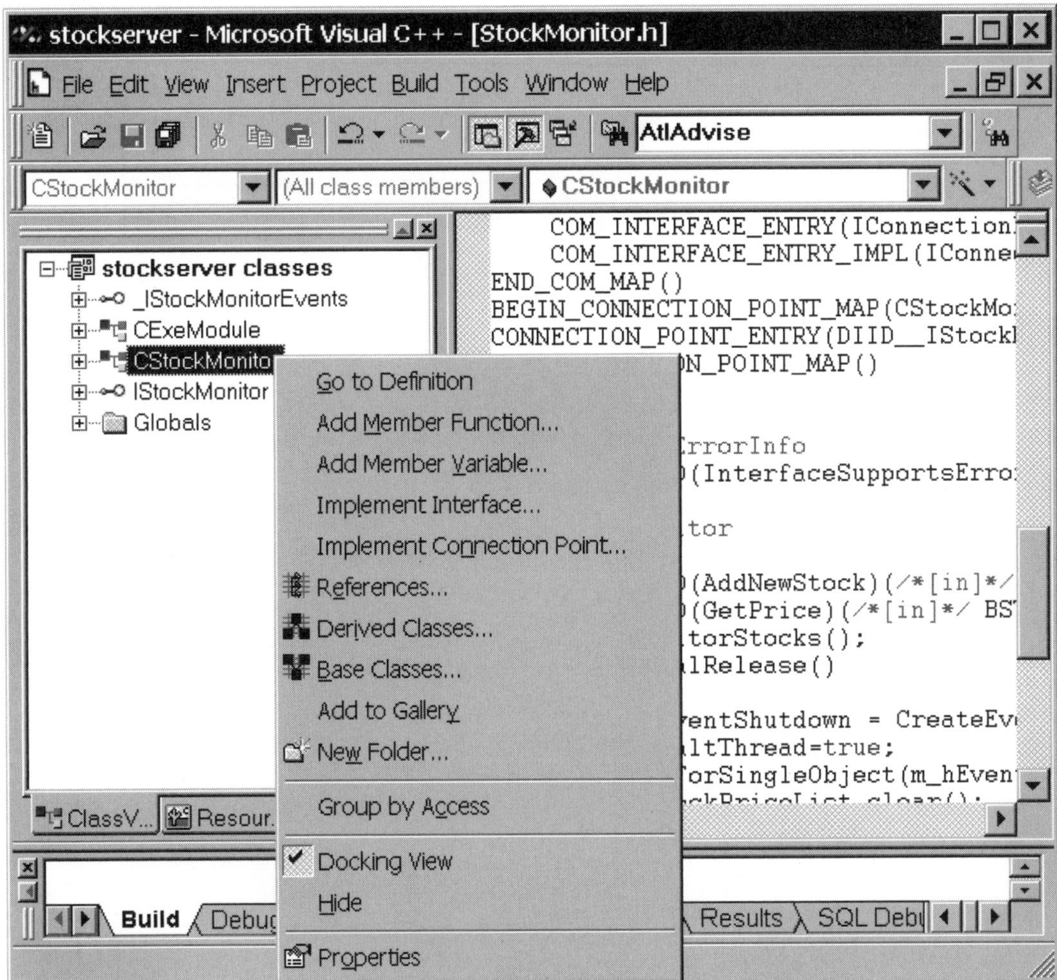

FIGURE 8.5 Implementing Connection Points in the CStockMonitor Class.

```
      for (nConnectionIndex = 0; nConnectionIndex < nConnections;
nConnectionIndex++)
      {
         pT->Lock();
         CComPtr<IUnknown> sp = m_vec.GetAt(nConnectionIndex);
         pT->Unlock();
         IDispatch* pDispatch = reinterpret_cast<IDispatch*>(sp.p);
         if (pDispatch != NULL)
         {
```

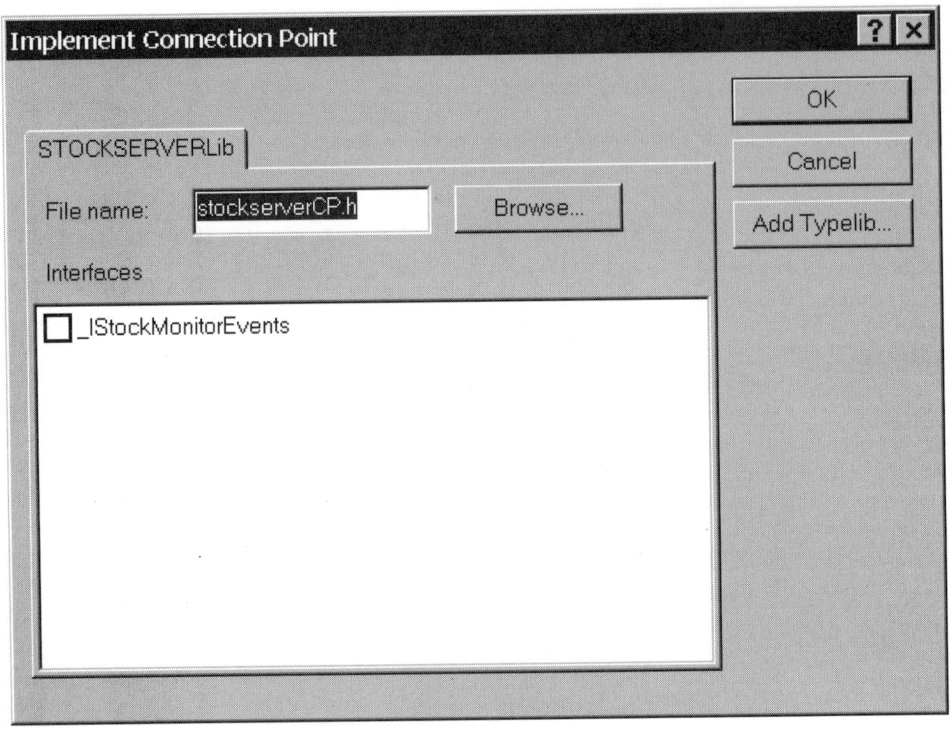

FIGURE 8.6 The Implement Connection Point Dialog.

```
            VariantClear(&varResult);
            pvars[2] = ticker;
            pvars[1] = newPrice;
            pvars[0] = oldPrice;
            DISPPARAMS disp = { pvars, NULL, 3, 0 };
            pDispatch->Invoke(0x1, IID_NULL, LOCALE_USER_DEFAULT, DIS-
PATCH_METHOD, &disp, &varResult, NULL, NULL);
         }
      }
      delete[] pvars;
      return varResult.scode;

   }
// The fire Fire_Notification method is abbreviated here for clarity
   HRESULT Fire_MonitorInitiated(BSTR ticker, FLOAT currentPrice)
   {
   //Similar to Fire_PriceChange …
   }
};
```

Notice that this new class, `CProxy_IStockMonitorEvents`, derives from the ATL class `IConnectionPointImpl` and contains `Fire` methods for both of the methods that you define in your outgoing interface, `_IStockMonitorEvents`. You call these methods when you wish to send a callback to a client. This generated class does all the work for you in setting up a call to your outgoing dispinterface.

In addition to this connection point implementation, if you go back to the header file for the implementation class, `CStockMonitor`, you will see the changes shown in bold (Listing 8.2).

LISTING 8.2 *THE STOCK MONITOR IMPLEMENTATION CLASS AFTER IMPLEMENTING YOUR CONNECTION POINT*

```
#include "stockserverCP.h"

///////////////////////////////////////////////////////////////////
// CStockMonitor
class ATL_NO_VTABLE CStockMonitor :
    public CComObjectRootEx<CComMultiThreadModel>,
    public CComCoClass<CStockMonitor, &CLSID_StockMonitor>,
    public ISupportErrorInfo,
    public IConnectionPointContainerImpl<CStockMonitor>,
    public IDispatchImpl<IStockMonitor, &IID_IStockMonitor,
    &LIBID_STOCKSERVERLib>,
    public CProxy_IStockMonitorEvents< CStockMonitor >
{
public:
CStockMonitor() { }

DECLARE_REGISTRY_RESOURCEID(IDR_STOCKMONITOR)

DECLARE_PROTECT_FINAL_CONSTRUCT()

BEGIN_COM_MAP(CStockMonitor)
    COM_INTERFACE_ENTRY(IStockMonitor)
    COM_INTERFACE_ENTRY(IDispatch)
    COM_INTERFACE_ENTRY(ISupportErrorInfo)
    COM_INTERFACE_ENTRY(IConnectionPointContainer)
    COM_INTERFACE_ENTRY_IMPL(IConnectionPointContainer)
END_COM_MAP()
BEGIN_CONNECTION_POINT_MAP(CStockMonitor)
CONNECTION_POINT_ENTRY(DIID__IStockMonitorEvents)
END_CONNECTION_POINT_MAP()

// ISupportsErrorInfo
```

```
32.     STDMETHOD(InterfaceSupportsErrorInfo)(REFIID riid);
33.
34. // IStockMonitor
35. public:
36.
37. };
```

Notice on line 1 that Visual C++ has added the header file for your new connection point implementation class to the header file for CStockMonitor. On line 11 you can see that it has added the connection point implementation class to the base class list for CStockMonitor. On line 25 you can see that Visual C++ has added a COM_INTERFACE_ENTRY_IMPL entry to our COM map and it has added a new connection point entry to our connection point map.

Visual C++ has a bug, which may be fixed by the time you read this book. The error causes Visual C++ to insert IID_IStockMonitorEvents **instead of** DIID_IStockMonitorEvents **in the** CONNECTION_POINT_ENTRY. **If you get a compile error that says that** IID_IStockMonitorEvents **is an undeclared identifier, change the** CONNECTION_POINT_ENTRY **so that it reads as follows:** CONNECTION_POINT_ENTRY(DIID_IStockMonitorEvents).

Add Methods to the Main Interface

In addition to its connection point interfaces, your StockMonitor class has a regular (incoming) COM interface called IStockMonitor. You can add two methods to this interface: GetPrice, which takes a stock ticker as its only parameter and returns the price of the stock identified by that ticker, and AddNewStock that a user can call to add a new stock. To add the GetPrice and AddNewStock methods to your StockMonitor COM class, perform the following steps:

1. Right-click on the IStockMonitor interface in the ClassView tab of the Visual C++ Workspace as shown in Figure 8.7.
2. Select Add Method... from the Context menu (the Add Method to Interface dialog appears).
3. Enter GetPrice in the Method Name field.
4. Enter [in] BSTR ticker,[out,retval] float *price in the Parameters field.
5. Click OK.
6. Repeat steps 1–5 but enter AddNewStock for the method name on step 3 and [in] BSTR ticker, [in] float price, [in] short propensityToRise for the parameter list on step 4.

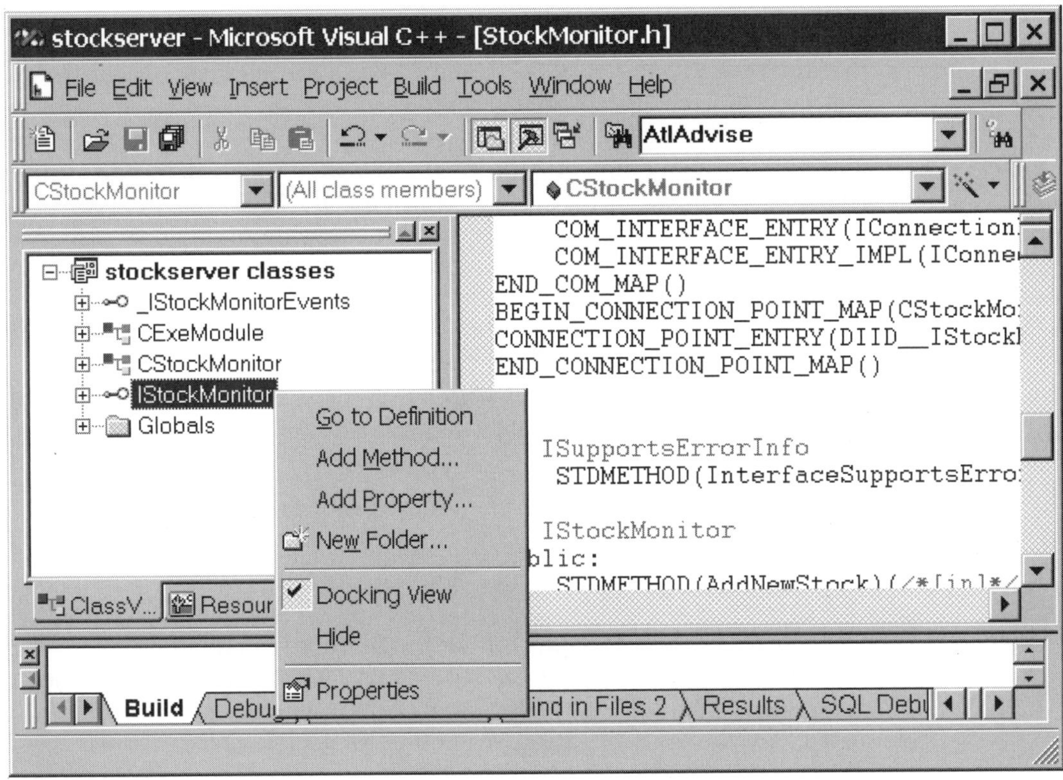

FIGURE 8.7 Adding Methods to the IStockMonitor Interface.

Visual C++ adds the `GetPrice` and `AddNewStock` methods to the IDL for your project and adds a prototype for the methods to the header file for the `CStockMonitor` and an empty implementation for the methods to the source file for the `CStockMonitor` class.

Complete the Implementation of Your Server

Now you are ready to complete the implementation of your server. This will be by far the most complicated example code so far, because it does involve some multi-threading. A summary of the steps to complete the implementation, are as follows:

1. Add a public, implementation-only `MonitorStocks` method.
2. Add a thread procedure for your worker thread.
3. Add code to the header file for the `CStockMonitor` class.
4. Implement all the methods in the `CStockMonitor` class.

ADD THE MONITORSTOCKS METHOD

The `MonitorStocks` method in the `CStockMonitor` class uses a random number-generator to simulate price changes in a number of stocks. It then fires the price change events through the `Fire_PriceChange` method in your connection point implementation. `MonitorStocks` method is not a part of the COM interface for the `StockMonitor` class. It exists only in the `CStockMonitor` implementation class. To add this method to the `CStockMonitor` class, perform these steps:

1. Right-click on the `CStockMonitor` class in the `ClassView` tab of the Visual C++ workspace as shown in Figure 8.5.
2. Select `Add Member Function...` from the `Context` menu (the Add Member Function dialog appears as shown in Figure 8.8.
3. Enter `void` in the `Function Type` field.
4. Enter `MonitorStocks` in the `Function Declaration` field.
5. Select `public` under `Access`.
6. Click `OK`.

Visual C++ adds a declaration for the `MonitorStocks` function to the header file for the `CStockMonitor` class and adds an empty implemenation to the source file for `CStockMonitor`. Before we implement this method we need to talk about the thread procedure that your worker thread will use.

ADD A THREAD PROCEDURE

The threading mechanism in the Windows API works as follows: You first define a thread procedure, which is just a function with a prescribed para-

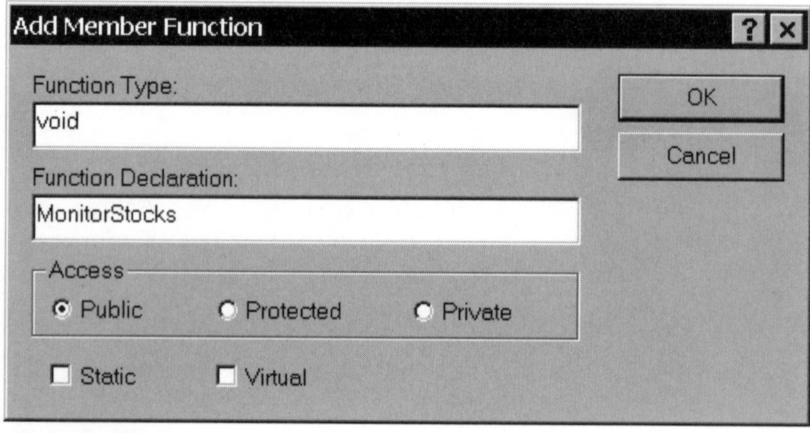

FIGURE 8.8 The Add Member Function Dialog.

meter list. You next call the CreateThread Windows API function and pass a pointer to this thread procedure in the third parameter to CreateThread. This thread procedure is the starting point for the new thread. You may also pass a pointer to a data structure or class in the fourth parameter to `CreateThread`. This data is passed to the thread procedure by the operating system after it creates the new thread. So, if you are to have a worker thread in your COM server, you must first define a thread procedure. To do this, add the following function declaration to the header file for the `CStockMonitor` class, `stockmonitor.h`:

```
DWORD WINAPI threadProc(void *pv);
```

Next, add the following implementation (Listing 8.3) for the thread procedure to the source file for the `CStockMonitor` class, `stockmonitor.cpp`:

LISTING 8.3 *THE THREAD PROCEDURE FOR YOUR WORKER THREAD*

```
1.  DWORD WINAPI threadProc(void *pv)
2.  {
3.      DWORD retval;
4.      CStockMonitor *stockMonitor;
5.      HRESULT hRes;
6.      hRes = CoInitializeEx(NULL, COINIT_MULTITHREADED);
7.      if (SUCCEEDED(hRes))
8.      {
9.          stockMonitor=(CStockMonitor*)pv;
10.         while (!stockMonitor->m_bHaltThread)
11.         {
12.             stockMonitor->MonitorStocks();
13.             ::Sleep(3000);
14.         }
15.         CoUninitialize();
16.         SetEvent(stockMonitor->m_hEventShutdown);
17.         retval=0;
18.     }
19.     else
20.         retval=2;
21.     return retval;
22. }
```

I've already talked about the `CoInitializeEx` function. For now, you should think of this function as initializing COM. Every thread in a particular server must initialize COM. So, your new worker thread must call `CoInitializeEx` also. The first thing that your thread procedure does is to call `CoInitializeEx` (see line 6 of Listing 8.3). The second parameter that you pass to this method

COINIT_MULTITHREADED indicates that you are entering the Multi-Threaded Apartment (MTA). Again, if you are not sure what this means, don't worry; it should be clear after Chapter 9. If the call to CoInitializeEx succeeds you cast the pointer that was passed to the thread procedure to a CStockMonitor pointer (you will pass the "this" pointer of a CStockMonitor instance as the fourth parameter to CreateThread. Next, on line 10, you enter a while loop that does not terminate until the m_bHaltThread member variable in CStockMonitor is set to true. Inside this while loop, you call the MonitorStocks method of CStockMonitor and then it sleeps for three seconds. When m_bHaltThread is set to true, the thread procedure exits the while loop, calls CoUnitialize and then on line 16 calls the Windows API function, SetEvent, to signal the worker thread has successfully shut down. This last step is important because the CStockMonitor object must wait until the thread is shut down before it is destroyed. You will see later that CStockMonitor uses the WaitForSingleObject Windows API function to wait until the worker thread calls SetEvent.

ADD CODE TO THE HEADER FILE FOR THE CSTOCKMONITOR CLASS

To complete the CStockMonitor class, you need to add quite a bit of code to the header file for this class. Add the bold code in Listing 8.4 to the header file for the CStockMonitor class, stockmonitor.h.

LISTING 8.4 *CODE ADDED TO THE CSTOCKMONITOR CLASS*

```
#ifndef __STOCKMONITOR_H_
#define __STOCKMONITOR_H_
#include "resource.h"       // main symbols
#include "stockserverCP.h"
#include <map>
#include <vector>
#include <time.h>
using namespace std;
/////////////////////////////////////////////////////////////////////////
// CStockMonitor
DWORD WINAPI threadProc(void *pv);
class ATL_NO_VTABLE CStockMonitor :
    public CComObjectRootEx<CComMultiThreadModel>,
    public CComCoClass<CStockMonitor, &CLSID_StockMonitor>,
    public ISupportErrorInfo,
    public IConnectionPointContainerImpl<CStockMonitor>,
    public IDispatchImpl<IStockMonitor, &IID_IStockMonitor,
    &LIBID_STOCKSERVERLib>,
    public CProxy_IStockMonitorEvents< CStockMonitor >
{
```

```
public:
    CStockMonitor()
    {
        DWORD threadID;
        HANDLE hThreadHandle;
        srand( (unsigned)time( NULL ) );
        m_bHaltThread = false;
        AddNewStock(CComBSTR("MSFT"), 95, 67);
        AddNewStock(CComBSTR("NOC"), 57, 45);
        AddNewStock(CComBSTR("IBM"), 67, 55);
        AddNewStock(CComBSTR("COKE"), 78, 44);
        AddNewStock(CComBSTR("EMLX"), 190, 34);
        hThreadHandle=CreateThread(0,0,threadProc,this,0,&threadID);
    }

DECLARE_REGISTRY_RESOURCEID(IDR_STOCKMONITOR)
DECLARE_PROTECT_FINAL_CONSTRUCT()

BEGIN_COM_MAP(CStockMonitor)
    COM_INTERFACE_ENTRY(IStockMonitor)
    COM_INTERFACE_ENTRY(IDispatch)
    COM_INTERFACE_ENTRY(ISupportErrorInfo)
    COM_INTERFACE_ENTRY(IConnectionPointContainer)
    COM_INTERFACE_ENTRY_IMPL(IConnectionPointContainer)
END_COM_MAP()
BEGIN_CONNECTION_POINT_MAP(CStockMonitor)
CONNECTION_POINT_ENTRY(DIID__IStockMonitorEvents)
END_CONNECTION_POINT_MAP()

// ISupportsErrorInfo
    STDMETHOD(InterfaceSupportsErrorInfo)(REFIID riid);

// IStockMonitor
public:
    STDMETHOD(AddNewStock)(/*[in]*/ BSTR ticker, /*[in]*/ float price,
    /*[in]*/ short propensityToRise);
    STDMETHOD(GetPrice)(/*[in]*/ BSTR ticker,/*[out,retval]*/ float
    *price);
    void MonitorStocks();
    void FinalRelease()
    {
        m_hEventShutdown = CreateEvent(NULL, false, false, NULL);
        m_bHaltThread=true;
        WaitForSingleObject(m_hEventShutdown, INFINITE);
```

```
62.         m_StockPriceList.clear();
63.         m_StockPropensityList.clear();
64.         m_StockTickerList.clear();
65.     }
66.     bool m_bHaltThread;
67.     HANDLE m_hEventShutdown;
68. private:
69.     map<CComBSTR,float> m_StockPriceList;
70.     map<CComBSTR,short> m_StockPropensityList;
71.     vector<CComBSTR> m_StockTickerList;
72. };
73. #endif //__STOCKMONITOR_H_
```

On lines 5 and 6 of Listing 8.4 you've added header files for two Standard Template Library (STL) collection classes that you will be using: vector and map (a map is an associative array in STL). On line 7, you include `time.h` so you can use the `time` function to initialize the random number generator (see line 25). On line 8, you have a `using namespace std` statement. You have added this statement so you don't have to prefix the names of classes in the standard library with the `std` namespace. On lines 23–32, you have implemented the constructor for the `CStockMonitor` class. On lines 23 and 24, you have variable declarations. On line 25, you initialize the random number generator using the current time. On line 26, you set the private member variable, `m_bHaltThread` to false. Just as its name implies, this variable is used to halt your worker thread. On lines 27 to 31 you add an initial group of five stocks to be monitored: Microsoft (MSFT), IBM, Northrop Grumman (NOC), COKE, and Emulex (EMLX). On line 32, you call the Windows API function, `CreateThread`, to create your worker thread. Notice that you pass the `threadProc` that you declared on line 11 as the third parameter to this function and pass the this pointer for the current object as the fourth parameter. The third parameter is the thread procedure for the new thread. The fourth parameter contains a data pointer that is passed to the thread procedure. The fifth parameter is an output parameter—it contains the ID for the new thread.

If you now go down to line 57 of Listing 8.4, you see the `FinalRelease` method. When the last client calls the `Release` method on one of this object's interfaces, the reference count goes to zero and the object is destroyed. But before the object is destroyed, the `FinalRelease` method is called. In this method, you need to shut down your worker thread and clear the collections that you were using. On line 59, you begin the process of shutting down the worker thread by calling the `CreateEvent` Windows API function to create a new event object.

An Event is a Windows Kernel object that can be used to synchronize multiple threads. One thread can wait on an Event object until another thread sets the Event's state to signaled using the SetEvent function.

Next, set the `m_bHaltThread` member variable to true. This causes the worker thread to exit the next time it gets a chance to run. Unfortunately, you have no idea when that will be and you do not want the process to terminate until the worker thread is shutdown properly. So, use the `WaitForSingleObject` Windows API method to cause the current thread to halt until the Event object becomes signaled. The `Event` object becomes signaled when the worker thread shuts down. Once the worker thread is shut down, on lines 62–64, you clear the collections that you used in the implementation of `CStockMonitor`. In the last few lines of this header file (lines 66–71), you declare the private member variables needed in your implementation of the Stock Monitor.

IMPLEMENT THE METHODS IN THE CSTOCKMONITOR CLASS

Finally, you are ready to implement the methods in the `CStockMonitor` class. You will implement three methods: `MonitorStocks`, `GetPrice`, and `AddNewStock`. The implementation of these methods is shown in Listing 8.5.

LISTING 8.5 *THE IMPLEMENTATION OF THE METHODS IN CSTOCKMONITOR*

```
void CStockMonitor::MonitorStocks()
{
   map<CComBSTR,float>::iterator iter;
   short propensityValue, numStocks, randomNumber, index;
   CComBSTR ticker;
   float oldPrice, newPrice;
   ObjectLock lock(this);
   numStocks=m_StockPriceList.size();
   if (numStocks > 0)
   {
      randomNumber=rand();
      index=randomNumber % numStocks;
      ticker=m_StockTickerList[index];
      oldPrice=m_StockPriceList[ticker];
      propensityValue=m_StockPropensityList[ticker];
      if ((randomNumber % 100) < propensityValue)
         newPrice=oldPrice+4.0;
      else
      {
```

```
         if (oldPrice > 2.0)
            newPrice=oldPrice-2.0;
      }
      m_StockPriceList[ticker]=newPrice;
      Fire_PriceChange(ticker,newPrice,oldPrice);
   }
}

STDMETHODIMP CStockMonitor::GetPrice(BSTR ticker, float *price)
{
   map<CComBSTR,float>::iterator iter;
   ObjectLock lock(this);
   iter=m_StockPriceList.find(ticker);
   if (iter!=m_StockPriceList.end())
      *price=m_StockPriceList[ticker];
   else
   {
      *price=-1.0;
      return Error(_T("This stock does not exist"),IID_IStockMonitor,
         E_STOCKNOTFOUND);
   }
   return S_OK;
}

STDMETHODIMP CStockMonitor::AddNewStock(BSTR ticker, float price, short propensityToRise)
{
   map<CComBSTR,float>::iterator iter;
   ObjectLock lock(this);
   iter=m_StockPriceList.find(ticker);
   if (iter==m_StockPriceList.end())
   {
      m_StockPriceList[ticker]=price;
      m_StockPropensityList[ticker]=propensityToRise;
      m_StockTickerList.push_back(ticker);
      Fire_MonitorInitiated(ticker,price);
   }
   else
      return Error(_T("This stock exists already"),IID_IStockMonitor,
         E_STOCKEXISTSALREADY);
   return S_OK;
}
```

The `MonitorStocks` method is implemented on lines 1–26 of Listing 8.5. On lines 3–6, you have local variable declarations. Line 7 is an interesting line of code. Remember that your COM is free-threaded. That means multiple threads potentially may call it. If an object may be called by multiple threads simultaneously, you should use one of the thread-synchronization primitives provided by the operating system to make sure that only one thread is allowed within one of the object's methods at a time. By far the easiest thread synchronization primitive to use is a critical section. You create a critical section by declaring a variable of type `CRITICAL_SECTION` and then passing the variable, by reference, to the `InitializeCriticalSection` API function. You then enter a critical section by calling the `EnterCriticalSection` API function. If another thread is already in the critical section, this call blocks until the other thread leaves the critical section by calling `LeaveCriticalSection`. You declare an ATL implementation class using a `CComMultiThreadModel` template parameter to `CComObjectRootEx` as shown below:

```
CComObjectRootEx<CComMultiThreadModel>
```

ATL adds a critical section member variable to your implementation class (see the `ATLCom.h` file in the `ATL\include\` directory of your Visual C++ installation for details).

The ATL Object Wizard uses the `CComMultiThreadModel` template parameter if you choose `Free` or `Both` for your threading model on the `Attribute` tab of the ATL Object Wizard (see Figure 8.3).

The ATL class, `ObjectLock`, enters this critical section in its constructor and leaves the critical section in its destructor. So line 7 of Listing 8.5 makes sure that only one thread is executing within your classes' method at any time.

I will talk more about the `ObjectLock` class and the `CComMultiThread` template parameter in Chapter 9.

On line 8 of Listing 8.5, you retrieve the number of stocks in your stock list. If the number of stocks is greater than 0, then on line 11 you get a random number and take the modulus of the random number with the number of stocks and get a random number between 0 and 1 (the number of stocks). Use this number to retrieve a stock ticker from the list of stock tickers on line 13. On lines 14 and 15, you retrieve the price and propensity-to-rise for the stock.

On line 16, you check if the propensity-to-rise is greater than the modulus of the random number you received on line 11 with 100. If the propensity is greater than the random number, then on line 17 you set the new price of the stock equal to the old price plus four. If the propensity is less than the random number, you decrease the value of the stock by two unless the price is already less than two. On lines 23, you assign the new price to the stock, and on line 24 you fire the `PriceChange` event back to your clients.

You are now ready to compile, press `F7`. If you receive a warning telling you that C++ Exception Handling was used but unwind semantics are not enabled, perform the following steps in the Visual C++ Workspace to enable exception handling and then select `Rebuild All` from `Build` menu.

1. Select `Settings`... from the `Project` menu (the Project Setting dialog will appear).
2. Click the `C/C++` tab.
3. Select `C++ Language` in the `Category` drop-down.
4. Set the `Enable Exception Handling` checkbox.
5. Click `OK`.

CREATE A NEW STANDARD EXE PROJECT

To create a standard Exe Project, start Visual Basic 6.0 on your system and perform these steps:

1. If the new project dialog is not already visible, select `New` from the `File` menu to bring up the new project dialog.
2. Select `Standard Exe` in the list of projects.
3. Click the `Open` button.

DRAW THE USER INTERFACE

Your project will contain a form called `form1`. Draw the user interface shown in Figure 8.9 on this form.

You have used an UpDown (Spinner) control to let the user specify the propensity for a new stock. To use the spinner control, you first need to reference the Microsoft Windows Common Control type library. Perform the following steps in your Visual Basic project to do this:

1. Select `Components` from the `Project` menu.
2. Set the checkbox next to the Microsoft Windows Common Controls—2 6.0 entry.
3. Click `OK`.

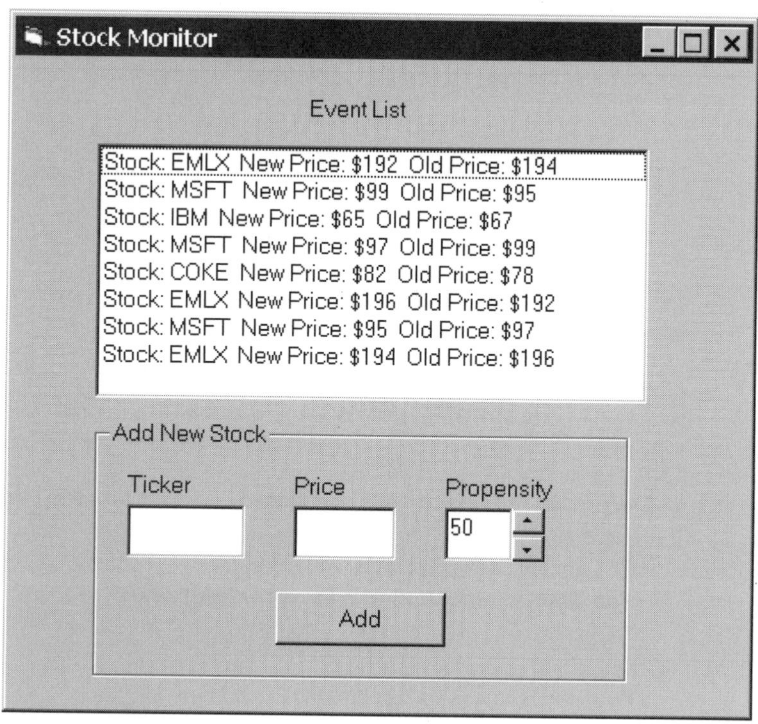

FIGURE 8.9 The Visual Basic EventClient.

The control description, control type, and control name for all the controls on the `EventClient` main window are listed in Table 8.4.

TABLE 8.4 The Controls on the Event Client Main Window

Control Description	Control Type	Control Name in VB Project
Event List	List Box	LstEvents
Ticker text box	Text Box	TxtTicker
Price text box	Text Box	TxtPrice
Propensity text box	Text Box	TxtPropensity
Propensity Spinner	Up Down (spinner)	UpdPropensity
Add button	Command Button	CmdAdd

Now you need to add a reference to your stock server component.

ADD A REFERENCE TO THE STOCKSERVER COMPONENT

To add a reference to the `stockserver` component, perform these steps:

1. Select `References...` from the `Project` menu.
2. Check the checkbox next to stockserver 1.0 Type Library.
3. Click `OK`.

INSTANTIATE AN EARLY-BOUND STOCKSERVER OBJECT USING WITHEVENTS

Double-click the form in the project and add the following code to the Load handler for the form. The Load event is fired after the form is created but before it is shown.

```
Private WithEvents mStockServer As StockMonitor
Private Sub Form_Load()
   On Error GoTo errHandler
   Set mStockServer = New StockMonitor
   Exit Sub
errHandler:
   MsgBox (Err.Description)
End Sub

Private Sub Form_Unload(Cancel As Integer)
   Set mStockServer = Nothing
End Sub
```

WITHEVENTS • Notice that you have declared your object using the `WithEvents` keyword. The `WithEvents` keyword is Visual Basic's way of working with Connection Point events. When you declare an object using `WithEvents`, Visual Basic checks the server's type library for source interfaces, then it presents each method in the source interface as an event that can define a handler. Figure 8.10 shows the `MonitorInitiated` and `PriceChange` events as they are presented in the Visual Basic environment.

ADD HANDLERS FOR THE STOCKSERVER EVENTS

To add handlers for the `PriceChange` and `MonitorInitiated` events, you need only select `mStockServer` in the left-hand drop down in the Visual Basic environment and then choose the event you wish to add a handler for in the right-hand drop down. Refer to Figure 8.10 to see how you select these events in the Visual Basic environment. After you add empty handlers for the `PriceChange` and `MonitorInitiated` events, add the bolded code to the empty handlers.

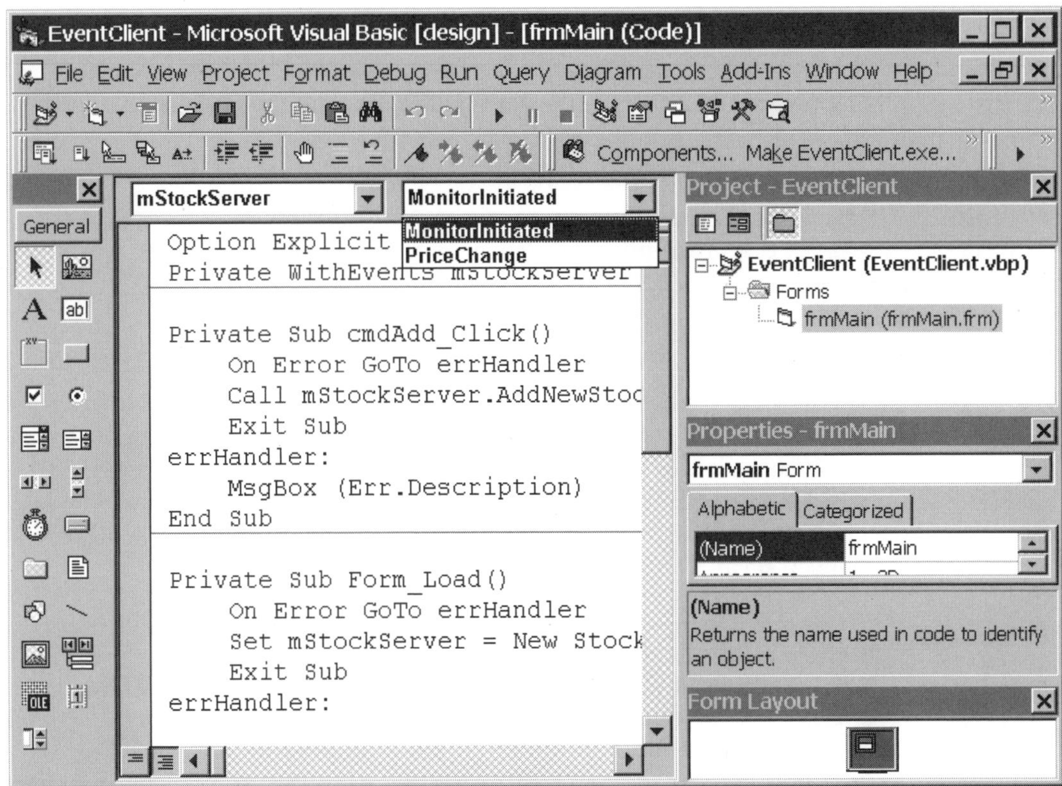

FIGURE 8.10 Handling Events with Visual Basic.

```
Private Sub mStockServer_MonitorInitiated(ByVal ticker As String,
ByVal currentPrice As Single)
   Dim strMessage As String
   strMessage = "Monitor initiated for " & ticker & vbCrLf & _
                "Current price $" & CStr(currentPrice)
   Call MsgBox(strMessage, vbInformation, "Monitor Initiated")
End Sub

Private Sub mStockServer_PriceChange(ByVal ticker As String, ByVal
newPrice As Single, ByVal oldPrice As Single)
   Dim strMessage As String
   strMessage = "Stock: " & ticker & "  New Price: $" & CStr(newPrice) & _
               "  Old Price: $" & CStr(oldPrice)
   lstEvents.AddItem (strMessage)
   lstEvents.TopIndex = lstEvents.NewIndex
End Sub
```

IMPLEMENT THE BUTTON HANDLERS

Finally, you need to add a handler for the Add button on your event client window. Double-click on the Add button and add the code shown in bold below:

```
Private Sub cmdAdd_Click()
   On Error GoTo errHandler
   Call mStockServer.AddNewStock(txtTicker.Text, txtPrice.Text,
txtPropensity.Text)
   Exit Sub
errHandler:
   MsgBox (Err.Description)
End Sub
```

You can now test your client. Select `start with full compile` from the `Run` menu in Visual Basic. After the client starts, you should begin seeing price change events appearing in the main window of the event client. You can also add new stocks to be monitored.

I decided this project had enough step-by-step instructions and did not want to go through the process of creating a Visual C++ client in this text. Instructions to create a Visual C++ client are included on the web site that accompanies this book.

■ Summary

In this chapter, you saw how to implement callbacks/events using COM. These callbacks can be sent across processes and using DCOM, even across machines. There are two ways of setting up events in COM. You can use Connection Points, which are a set of standard interfaces that define a protocol for setting up COM callbacks, or you can define custom callback interfaces. The main advantage of Connection Points is that they work well with Visual Development environments. Both Visual Basic and Visual C++ make it simple to define callbacks using Connection Points and then receive callbacks at a client. With custom callback interfaces, you have to do a little more work to setup your callbacks. The advantage of custom callback interfaces is performance. The `ConnectionPoint` protocol requires five round trips to set up a callback—using the custom callback interfaces only requires two. If the server is running in-process with its client, this is no problem. If the server is running out-of-process on the same machine, it is a small problem. If the server is running remotely via DCOM, five round trips could present a serious problem. So basically, when it comes to implementing bi-directional communication (callbacks) in COM, the choice is yours. You can have maximum performance by defining custom callback interfaces, or you can use connection points for ease-of-use. In the example for this chapter, you only used the connection point interface approach.

Later in this book you will learn about a new technology that is a part of COM+ called COM+ events that you can also use to send events between a client and server. There are a few more things to learn before I can discuss this, so let's keep going. In the next chapter, I talk about COM threading models.

NINE

COM Threading

At least a dozen times in this book I have said: "I'll discuss that more in Chapter 9." Well, you are finally here. Threading is one of the most difficult concepts to understand in COM. In my class, whenever I mention the words *COM apartments,* I can see that "deer caught in the headlights" look from my students. As you go through this chapter, remember that COM apartments exist to make your life easier, not harder. In a nutshell, COM apartments make it possible for you to write components that are not thread-safe and use them in a multi-threaded environment. If you are not sure what apartment, thread-safe, or multi-threading means, then you'll definitely want to read on.

Definitions and Background

I'll begin by defining some terms and providing background information. There are certain concepts *processes*, *threads*, *multi-threading*, and *thread-safe* that you must understand before I can begin a discussion of COM apartments. Most people assume that anyone who's trying to learn COM already understands these concepts. I have found from teaching classes that many people do not have a firm grasp on these concepts and that makes it difficult, if not impossible, to understand COM apartments. If you already understand all of these concepts, you can skip this section. If not, let's begin by defining processes.

Processes

A process is an instance of a running program. If you click the `Start` button and then select an application in Windows 2000, Windows NT, or Windows 98, you are starting a process. The running processes on your system can be viewed using the task manager if you are running Windows 2000 or NT. You can also view the processes on a Windows 98 machine by pressing `CTRL-ATL-Delete`, which brings up the task list. Figure 9.1 shows the running processes on my machine in the Windows 2000 task manager.

A process defines a 4GB-address space that contains executable code and data. A process also owns certain resources such as files and dynamic memory. You create a process using the `CreateProcess` API function. All resources created during a process's life are destroyed when the process is

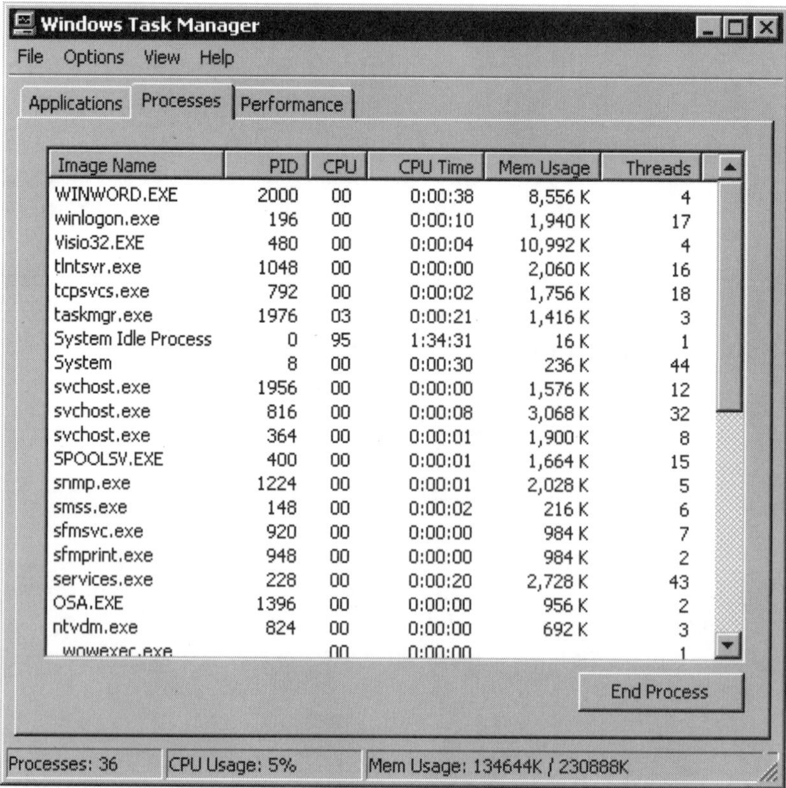

Windows Task Manager
File Options View Help
Applications Processes Performance
Image Name PID CPU CPU Time Mem Usage Threads
WINWORD.EXE 2000 00 0:00:38 8,556 K 4
winlogon.exe 196 00 0:00:10 1,940 K 17
Visio32.EXE 480 00 0:00:04 10,992 K 4
tlntsvr.exe 1048 00 0:00:00 2,060 K 16
tcpsvcs.exe 792 00 0:00:02 1,756 K 18
taskmgr.exe 1976 03 0:00:21 1,416 K 3
System Idle Process 0 95 1:34:31 16 K 1
System 8 00 0:00:30 236 K 44
svchost.exe 1956 00 0:00:00 1,576 K 12
svchost.exe 816 00 0:00:08 3,068 K 32
svchost.exe 364 00 0:00:01 1,900 K 8
SPOOLSV.EXE 400 00 0:00:01 1,664 K 15
snmp.exe 1224 00 0:00:01 2,028 K 5
smss.exe 148 00 0:00:02 216 K 6
sfmsvc.exe 920 00 0:00:00 984 K 7
sfmprint.exe 948 00 0:00:00 984 K 2
services.exe 228 00 0:00:20 2,728 K 43
OSA.EXE 1396 00 0:00:00 956 K 2
ntvdm.exe 824 00 0:00:00 692 K 3
End Process
Processes: 36
CPU Usage: 5%
Mem Usage: 134644K / 230888K

FIGURE 9.1 Processes in the Task Manager.

terminated. A process by itself does not *do* anything. For a process to do something, it must have at least one thread.

Threads

A thread is a path of execution through the code in a process and has its own call stack and CPU-state. Because each thread has its own stack, variables that reside on the stack are private to that thread.

Variables that are declared locally within a function (whether it is a global function or a member function of a class) reside on the stack.

As an example, if you have a function that is defined as shown here:

```
int gCounter1;                    // This variable is declared globally
void DoSomething(int arg1, float arg2)
{
// This variable is declared on the stack so each thread will have its
own copy
    int counter2;
// …
}
```

all threads in this function's process see the same value for `gCounter1`, but each thread has its own value for `counter2`.

Modern operating systems like Windows 2000 and Windows 98 can juggle dozens (even hundreds) of threads to create the illusion that these threads are running simultaneously, even on a machine that has a single CPU. The operating system does this by assigning a quantum of time to each thread. When this unit of time is complete, the operating system saves the state of the CPU associated with that thread and then gives another thread a chance to run for a quantum of time. When this time has expired, another thread gets a chance to run, and so on.

The situation is somewhat more complicated than described here because threads can have different priorities. Threads with lower priorities only run when there are no threads with higher priorities waiting to run.

Switching between threads like this is called a context switch. It happens so often (and fast) and the unit of time involved is so small that it creates the illusion that multiple programs are running at the same time.

Multi-Threading

All processes are initially created with one thread, the so-called primary thread. In a C or C++ program, this thread executes some initialization code in the C/C++ runtime and then calls the main routine in the code for the process. If this is the only thread your application has, writing applications and COM components is fairly simple. You never have to worry about problems that may arise from having more than one thread in the process simultaneously executing a piece of code. There are many good reasons why people like to create additional threads in a process. As an example, many of you may remember the Windows 3.0/3.1 days when applications like word processors would get hung up while printing. If you had to print a long document, you might as well go and get a cup of coffee because several minutes would elapse before you could get back to work. Now, you can click the print button on most applications and go right back to work while the application creates a separate thread that prints the document.

On the Windows platform you can create additional threads using the `CreateThread` API function. `CreateThread` is declared as shown here:

```
HANDLE CreateThread(
   LPSECURITY_ATTRIBUTES pSecurityAttributes,
   DWORD stackSize,
   LPTHREAD_START_ROUTINE pStartAddr,
   LPVOID pThreadParm,
   DWORD createFlags,
LPDWORD pThreadID)
```

On successful return, this function returns a `HANDLE` to the new thread. The purpose of each of the parameters to this function is summarized in Table 9.1.

TABLE 9.1 Arguments for the CreateThread Method

Argument Name	Argument Purpose
PSecurityAttributes	A pointer to a SECURITY_ATTRIBUTES structure. In most cases, you can pass NULL for this argument. If you want child processes to inherit a handle to this thread object, you must pass a valid SECURITY_ATTRIBUTES structure whose bInheritHandles member variable is set to TRUE. For more information, see *Advanced Windows* by Jeffrey Richter.
StackSize	Specifies the size of the stack for the new thread. If you pass zero for this parameter, the stack size for the new thread is the same as the calling threads. The default size is 1MB.
PStartAddr	A pointer to a function that will be the starting point for the new thread. This thread procedure or threadproc must have the following prototype: DWORD WINAPI ThreadProc(LPVOID pThreadParameter).
PThreadParm	A 32-bit parameter value that is passed to the thread. Usually the value that is passed here is a pointer to a structure.
CreateFlags	Additional flags that control the creation of the thread. If the value is 0, the thread starts executing immediately. If the value is CREATE_SUSPENDED, the thread does not start executing immediately. You must call ResumeThread to start the thread executing.
PThreadID	An output parameter that on return contains the thread ID for the new thread.

Thread-Safe

Now you know *why* you might want to create multiple threads within a process and *how* to create multiple threads in a process. The question is *should* you create multiple threads in a process? The answer to that depends on the code that your process will be executing. Code can be either safe or unsafe for use by multiple threads. Code that is safe to be used by multiple threads is often referred to as simply being *thread-safe*. Here is an example of code that is *not* thread-safe:

```
long gCounter;
void NotSafe()
{
   gCounter++;
}
```

The problem here is that `gCounter` is a global variable; all the threads in a process share it. Imagine that thread 1 in your process is currently executing. It gets to the `NotSafe` function and reads the value of `gCounter` (let's say the value is 3) into a CPU register in preparation to increment the value. Suddenly, the operating system decides that it's time to give thread 2 a chance to run. So the operating system saves the state of the CPU and the stack for thread 1 and then swaps in the CPU state and stack for thread 2, and thread 2 will start executing. Now let's say that thread 2 gets to the `NotSafe` function and it also reads in the value of `gCounter` (which is still 3). It increments the value and writes it back to the global variable `gCounter`, whose value now is 4. Thread 2 has used its time quantum and the operating system does a context switch back to thread 1. Thread 1 picks up where it left off. It increments the value in its CPU register to 4 and writes it back to `gCounter`. The problem is that the code `gCounter++` has been executed twice starting with a value of 3 and the value of the variable is 4; it should be 5. You're probably thinking what are the odds of something like this actually happening. While you are testing and debugging your application by yourself, it's almost nil: when your boss and all of your customers are watching a demo you are conducting, it's almost 100%.

So how would you make this code thread-safe? In general, you would use a thread-synchronization primitive like a critical section to prevent two threads from executing the code in the `NotSafe` function simultaneously.

```
CRITICAL_SECTION gCritSec;
// We must initialize this critical section using InitializeCriticalSection
before we use it
long gCounter;
void NotSafe()
{
    EnterCriticalSection(&gCritSec);
    gCounter++;
    LeaveCriticalSection(&gCritSec);
}
```

Once one thread calls `EnterCriticalSection`, the other thread blocks at the call to `EnterCriticalSection` until the first thread calls `LeaveCriticalSection`. The code shown here works for even more complicated pieces of code. For the case of a simple call to increment a variable, you could also use the following code:

```
long gCounter;
void NotSafe()
{
    InterLockedIncrement(&gCounter);
}
```

The `InterLockedIncrement` function increments the counter as an atomic call. In other words, it guarantees that a context switch does not occur while the variable is being incremented.

Object-Oriented Thread-Safety

There is some new terminology that must be introduced when discussing threading in object-oriented programming languages. Object-orientation centers on the use of classes as the building blocks of an application. Let's return to Chapter 2 and the `Employee` class used as an example in that chapter. The declaration of this class is repeated in Listing 9.1.

LISTING 9.1 *THE EMPLOYEE CLASS FROM CHAPTER 2*

```
#include<string>
using namespace std;
class Employee {
public:
   Employee(int id,const char *nm,float sal);
   virtual ~Employee();
   virtual float GetGrossPay() {
      return GetHoursWorked() * GetHourlyRate();
   }
   int GetHoursWorked() {
      return m_hoursWorked;
   }
   float GetHourlyRate() {
      return m_salary/40;
   }
   void BeginPayPeriod() {
      m_hoursWorked = 0;
   }
   void Work(short numHours) {
      m_hoursWorked += numHours;
   }
   short GetNumDependents() {
      return m_numDependents;
   }
   void SetNumDependents(short numDependents) {
      m_numDependents=numDependents;
   }
   string GetName() {
      return m_name;
   }
   float GetSalary() {
      return m_salary;
   }
```

```
private:
   int m_id;
   string m_name;
   float m_salary;
   short m_hoursWorked;
   short m_numDependents;
};
```

The state of an Employee object is the values in the member variables of the Employee class: m_id, m_name, m_salary, m_hoursWorked, and m_numDependents. Each instance of Employee that you create contains an instance of each of these member variables. These variables are sometimes referred to as the *per-instance state* of the Employee class. One strategy you could use to make the Employee class thread-safe is to add a thread-synchronization primitive as a member variable of the class as follows:

```
#include<string>
using namespace std;
class Employee {
public:
   Employee(int id,const char *nm,float sal);
   virtual ~Employee();
// The other methods in the class are omitted for clarity...

private:
   int m_id;
   string m_name;
   float m_salary;
   short m_hoursWorked;
   short m_numDependents;
   CRITICAL_SECTION m_critSec;
};
```

The constructor for the Employee class should initialize the critical, and the destructor of the class should delete it as shown here:

```
#include "employee.h"
Employee::Employee(int id,const char *nm,float sal)
{
   ::InitializeCriticalSection(&m_critSec);
   ::EnterCriticalSection(&m_critSec);
   m_id=id;
   m_name=nm;
   m_salary=sal;
   ::LeaveCriticalSection(&m_critSec);
```

```
}

Employee::~Employee()
{
    ::DeleteCriticalSection(&m_critSec);
}
```

Each member function in the class could then enter the critical section on entry and leave the critical section on exit as shown here:

```
void BeginPayPeriod()
{
    ::EnterCriticalSection(&m_critSec);
    m_hoursWorked = 0;
    ::LeaveCriticalSection(&m_critSec);
}
void Work(short numHours)
{
    ::EnterCriticalSection(&m_critSec);
    m_hoursWorked += numHours;
    ::LeaveCriticalSection(&m_critSec);
}
void SetNumDependents(short numDependents)
{
    ::EnterCriticalSection(&m_critSec);
    m_numDependents=numDependents;
    ::LeaveCriticalSection(&m_critSec);
}
```

In this way, you can guarantee that only one thread executes within any instance of the Employee class. A scheme like this is not the best for maximizing concurrency, however. One thread may be trying to call the Work method on a particular instance of Employee (which writes to m_hoursWorked) while another thread may be trying to call the SetNumDependents method on an Employee (which writes to m_numDependents). There is no reason that these threads should block each other since they are using different elements of the Employee's state. To maximize concurrency, you could create a critical section for each member variable. Unfortunately, this approach opens the door to another problem, deadlock. Imagine that you did create a critical section for each member variable and thread 1 enters the critical section for m_numDependents and then tries to enter the critical section for m_hoursWorked. Now imagine further that thread 1 blocks trying to enter the critical section for m_hoursWorked because thread 2 is in this critical section, but thread 2 is also blocked because it is waiting for thread 1 to leave the critical section for m_numDependents. Neither thread will be able to continue.

See the book *Win32 Multi-Threaded Programming* by Aaron Cohen for information on how to detect and prevent deadlock.

In addition to per-instance state, classes can have a state that is shared by all of its instances. In C++, you define this *per-class state* using static member variables. You could, for instance, add a static variable to the Employee class that tracks the total number of Employees that have been created as follows:

```
#include<string>
using namespace std;
class Employee {
public:
   Employee(int id,const char *nm,float sal);
   virtual ~Employee();
// The other methods in the class are omitted for clarity...

private:
   int m_id;
   string m_name;
   float m_salary;
   short m_hoursWorked;
   short m_numDependents;
   CRITICAL_SECTION m_critSec;
   static short m_numEmployees;
};
```

If you declare a static member variable like this in a class. You must add a definition of the variable to the source (.cpp) file for the class as follows:

```
short Employee::m_numEmployees=0;
```

You can increment this variable in the constructor for the Employee class and decrement it in the destructor for the class like this:

```
Employee::Employee(int id,const char *nm,float sal)
{
   ::InitializeCriticalSection(&m_critSec);
   ::EnterCriticalSection(&m_critSec);
   m_id=id;
```

```
    m_name=nm;
    m_salary=sal;
    m_numEmployees++;
    ::LeaveCriticalSection(&m_critSec);
}

Employee::~Employee()
{
    m_numEmployees—;
    ::DeleteCriticalSection(&m_critSec);
}
```

You can also declare a member function that returns the value of this variable. Typically, this function can also be static.

```
static short NumEmployees()
{
    return m_numEmployees;
}
```

For your Employee class to be truly thread-safe, you need to protect both its per-instance state and its per-class state. You cannot use the CRITICAL_SECTION member variable that you declared earlier to synchronize access to a static variable like m_numEmployees because each instance has a separate critical section. You need to create another critical section and declare it as a static variable as shown here:

```
#include<string>
using namespace std;
class Employee {
public:
    Employee(int id,const char *nm,float sal);
    virtual ~Employee();
// The other methods in the class are omitted for clarity...

private:
    int m_id;
    string m_name;
    float m_salary;
    short m_hoursWorked;
    short m_numDependents;
    CRITICAL_SECTION m_critSec;
    static CRITICAL_SECTION m_classCritSec;
    static short m_numEmployees;
};
```

Each instance can then enter this shared critical section before it increments or decrements `m_numEmployees`.

Multi-Threading and COM

You are now getting the point that the whole idea of COM is to enable reuse. I said in Chapter 1, COM's main purpose in life is to make it easy for you to create programming-language independent and location-transparent software components. You *should* want to do this because these components are easy to reuse. A developer who is using a software component with these attributes does not have to be concerned with knowing what programming language the component is implemented in and will use the component in the exact same way whether it is a DLL or an executable. But what about threading? Software developers encounter problems if they attempt to use a component that is not thread-safe in a multi-threaded application.

To prevent this problem, each COM software component could come with a sticker that says whether it's thread-safe or not. But that really isn't a good solution. A lot of software is distributed electronically (someone downloads it from a Web site) and few people actually read readme files. Just as a client can use a COM component in the same way regardless of whether it resides in an in-process server or an out-of-process server. You would like your COM components to be usable by a multi-threaded client or a single-threaded client in the same way regardless of whether the component is thread-safe. You want your COM components to not only be programming-language independent and location-transparent, you also want them to be threading-transparent.

As a component developer, you should be able to specify whether your component is thread-safe, not by putting a sticker on a box, but by making a function call or writing to the registry. If you indicate that your component is not thread-safe and a software developer tries to use your object in a multi-threaded application, the COM runtime should step in and *serialize* all calls to the object. If the object is thread-safe, then the COM runtime has no need to intervene.

In this context, Serialize ensures that only one thread is ever executing a method on an object at any given time.

Conceptually, this sounds easy but you must have an answer for each of the following questions before you can implement this scheme.

- How can the COM runtime determine if an application is multi-threaded?
- How can a COM object indicate whether it is thread-safe?
- How will the COM runtime serialize method calls if you attempt to call a COM that is not thread-safe from an application that is multi-threaded?

Determine if an Application is Multi-Threaded

For your object synchronization scheme to work, a COM client must have some way of indicating whether it is multi-threaded. A COM client indicates whether it is multi-threaded when it calls the `CoInitialize`, `CoInitializeEx`, or `OleInitialize` functions. Until now, I have been saying that an application calls `CoInitialize` or `CoInitializeEx` to initialize COM, but it's actually more complicated than that. An application isn't just initializing COM, it is indicating what type of threading environment it is establishing; it is in the lingua of COM, *entering an apartment*. Also, I said that the *application* is initializing COM. That was a simplification; each *thread* in the application's process must enter an apartment. Each thread effectively represents a runtime environment for COM objects and through `CoInitializeEx` (or `CoInitialize` or `OleInitialize`) you can indicate if that runtime environment consists of one thread or multiple threads. In the MFC clients that you created, you called `AfxOleInit` (which calls `CoInitialize`) only once because your client applications were single-threaded. But if your application has multiple threads, you must call `CoInitialize` (or a similar function) for each thread. I will discuss apartments shortly. For now, here's the skinny: Think of an apartment as the threading environment that one or more COM objects runs in. All COM objects in a process must belong to an apartment; only threads that have entered an object's apartment can call methods directly on that COM object. All other threads can only call methods on that object indirectly by sending a message to a thread in the object's apartment. An apartment can be a Single-Threaded Apartment (STA), in which case all objects in the apartment are accessed by a single thread, thus freeing those objects from most (but not all) problems associated with multi-threading. Or an apartment can be a Multi-Threaded Apartment (MTA). Multiple threads may call the methods on an object in the MTA simultaneously. So an object must be thread-safe if it is to run in the MTA.

Each process may have several STAs, but each process can only have one MTA. So, the wrong question was being asked at the beginning of this section. The question isn't: How can the COM runtime determine if an application is multi-threaded? It should be: How can the COM runtime determine if the thread that is accessing a COM object is part of a single-threaded environment or is one thread in a multi-threaded environment? And the answer is that each thread must indicate whether it is part of a single-threaded or multi-threaded environment by entering an STA or the MTA.

How an Object Indicates if It Is Thread-Safe

The answer to this question depends on whether the object resides within an in-process server or an out-of-process server. If the object resides within an out-of-process server, then the server has its own process and creates its own apartments by calling `CoInitialize` or `CoInitializeEx` for each thread it creates. If an object resides in an in-process server, the client has called `CoInitialize`, `CoInitializeEx`, or `OleInitialize` before the call to instantiate the COM object. Another way to think of it is that with an out-of-process server, the server owns its process and establishes the correct threading environment for the objects it exports. With an in-process server, the client "owns" the process that the objects run in, so the client will define the threading environment. The COM objects within an in-process server need some way to indicate whether they are compatible with the threading environment the client has established. COM objects that reside in an in-process server indicate their threading requirements using `ThreadingModel` registry keys. The `ThreadingModel` registry keys can be found in the registry at these locations:

```
HKEY_CLASSES_ROOT\CLSID\CLSID_FOR_A_COM_CLASS\ThreadingModel
```

An example entry is shown here:

```
HKEY_CLASSES_ROOT\CLSID\ {06637330-314D-11D3-998A-E0EC08C10000}
\ThreadingModel=Apartment
```

The possible values for the `ThreadingModel` key are summarized in Table 9.2.

TABLE 9.2 Possible Values for the ThreadingModel Registry Key

ThreadModel Value	Interpretation
Single	Objects of this class are pathologically unthread-safe. Not only are the objects not thread-safe, the class factory for the class and the DllGetClassObject and DllCanUnloadNow functions for the server are not thread-safe. A single thread must call *all* the code in this server.
Apartment	Objects of this class do not protect their per-instance state from multi-threading problems. Access to each instance must be limited to a single thread. But, the per-class state for this class and the class factory and the DllGetClassObject and DllCanUnloadNow functions in the classes' server *are* thread-safe.
Free	COM Objects of this class protect their per-instance state and per-class state from multi-threading problems using thread synchronization primitives, such as critical sections or mutexes. These objects are safe to use in a multi-threaded environment.

Both	Object of this class are instantiated in the same apartment as their client so they can, for maximum performance, execute on their caller's thread. Because they may run in a multi-threaded environment, these classes should protect their per-instance state and per-class state from multi-threading problems.
Neutral	Objects of this class also execute on their caller's thread, but they reside in their own apartment, the Thread Neutral Apartment (TNA), rather then residing in their caller's apartment. Because any thread (STA or MTA) in a process can enter the TNA at any time, objects marked as Neutral must either use thread-synchronization primitives internally to make themselves thread-safe or they can use the thread synchronization service provided by the COM+ runtime. I talk more about this in Chapter 11.

More Naming Problems

Microsoft's COM naming problems raise their ugly head again when talking about apartments. The possible values for the `ThreadingModel` registry keys shown in Table 9.2 are poorly named. The `ThreadingModel=Apartment` value implies this is the only Threading model that use apartments; this is untrue. All COM Threading Models use apartments, they just use different types of apartments. Objects that have a `ThreadingModel` registry key with the value `Apartment`, use Single-Threaded Apartments just as objects that have a `ThreadingModel` registry key of `Free` use Multi-Threaded Apartments. The `Both` threading model is poorly named because starting with Windows 2000, there are three types of apartments: Single-Threaded Apartments (STAs), Multi-Threaded Apartments (MTAs) and Thread-Neutral Apartments (TNAs). The Both threading model should really be called Any because objects with this threading model can reside in any of these apartments.

A better name for the `ThreadingModel` registry key would be `ApartmentType;` the translation between the poorly named `ThreadingModel` registry key and the `ApartmentType` registry key is shown in Table 9.3.

TABLE 9.3 Translating Between the ThreadingModel Key and the Mythical ApartmentType Key

Threading Model	Apartment Type
Single	PrimarySTA
Apartment	STA
Free	MTA
Both	ANY
Neutral	TNA

If a COM class does not contain a `ThreadingModel` registry key (like the first COM class you built in Chapter 4), then its `ThreadingModel` is assumed to be Single. Remember, you, the developer of a COM class must decide what the threading requirements are of your class (based on how you have implemented it) and make sure the class registers the correct `ThreadingModel` entry. Most COM-enabled development environments make this easy for you. If you are using Visual C++ and the ATL Object Wizard, you can select the `ThreadingModel` for your object on the `Attributes` tab of the ATL Object Wizard as shown in Figure 9.2.

Notice that you cannot select the Neutral threading model in Visual C++ 6.0. The Neutral threading model is a feature of COM+ and you have to wait for Visual C++ 7.0 (2000?) to see wizard support for it. If you are building an in-process server, the threading model you select is reflected in the registry in the `ThreadingModel` key. If you are building an out-of-process server, the `ThreadingModel` key is not entered into the registry. In either case, your choice of threading model does influence how your ATL implementation class is defined. If you select `Single` or `Apartment`, the implementation class is defined using `CComSingleThreadModel` as the template parameter to the `CComObjectRootEx` parameterized class as follows:

```
CComObjectRootEx<CComSingleThreadModel>
```

If you select `Free` or `Both` for the threading model, `CComMultiThreadModel` is used as the template parameter for `CComObjectRootEx`:

```
CComObjectRootEx<CComMultiThreadModel>
```

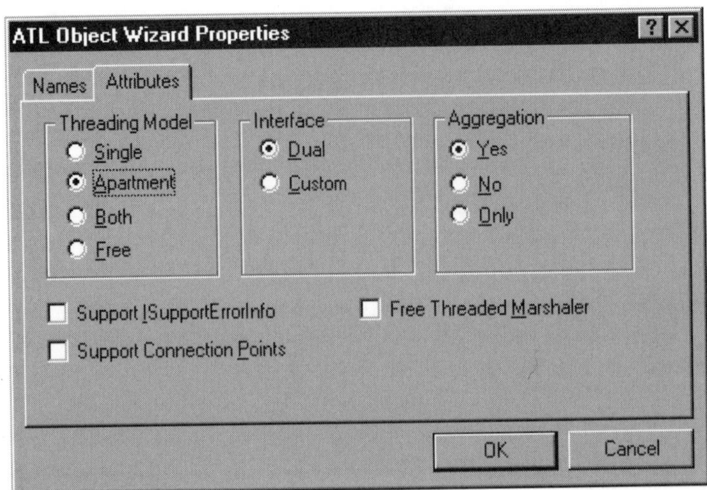

FIGURE 9.2 The Attributes Tab of the ATL Object Wizard Properties Dialog.

Using a template parameter of CComMultiThreadModel causes a CRITICAL_SECTION member variable to be added to your implementation class, which you can use to make the class thread-safe.

How the COM Runtime Serializes Method Calls

The COM runtime serializes method calls using a logical construct called an apartment.

APARTMENTS

Each process that is using or contains COM objects has one or more apartments, and each apartment contains one or more COM objects. Both the threads and the COM objects that reside in a process must indicate in which apartment they will reside. You have already seen how COM objects specify which apartment they will reside in via the ThreadingModel registry key. A thread enters an apartment by calling CoInitializeEx (or a similar function such as CoInitialize or OleInitialize). If a thread calls CoInitializeEx with COINIT_APARTMENTTHREADED as the second parameter as follows:

```
HRESULT hRes = CoInitializeEx(NULL, COINIT_APARTMENTTHREADED);
```

the thread has entered a Single-Threaded Apartment (STA). Only one thread can enter an STA (hence, the name) and each process can have multiple STAs, so each thread that calls CoInitializeEx with COINIT_APARTMENTTHREADED as its second parameter creates a new STA.

If a thread calls CoInitializeEx with COINIT_MULTITHREADED as the second parameter as follows:

```
HRESULT hRes = CoInitializeEx(NULL, COINIT_MULTITHREADED);
```

then the thread has entered the Multi-Threaded Apartment (MTA). Each process only has one MTA, so each thread that calls CoInitializeEx with COINIT_MULTITHREADED as the second parameter resides in the same apartment. There is a third apartment type that is new to COM+ called the Thread-Neutral Apartment (TNA). Threads do not specifically enter the TNA through CoInitializeEx. Either STA or MTA threads can call objects in the TNA and when one of these threads calls an object in the TNA, they enter that apartment and leave when they are done. The relationship between processes, apartments, threads, and COM objects is as shown in Figure 9.3.

Once the objects and the threads in a process have indicated which apartments they belong to, the COM runtime can make sure the concurrency requirements for each object are adhered to by restricting which threads are allowed to call methods on a particular COM object. Any thread that

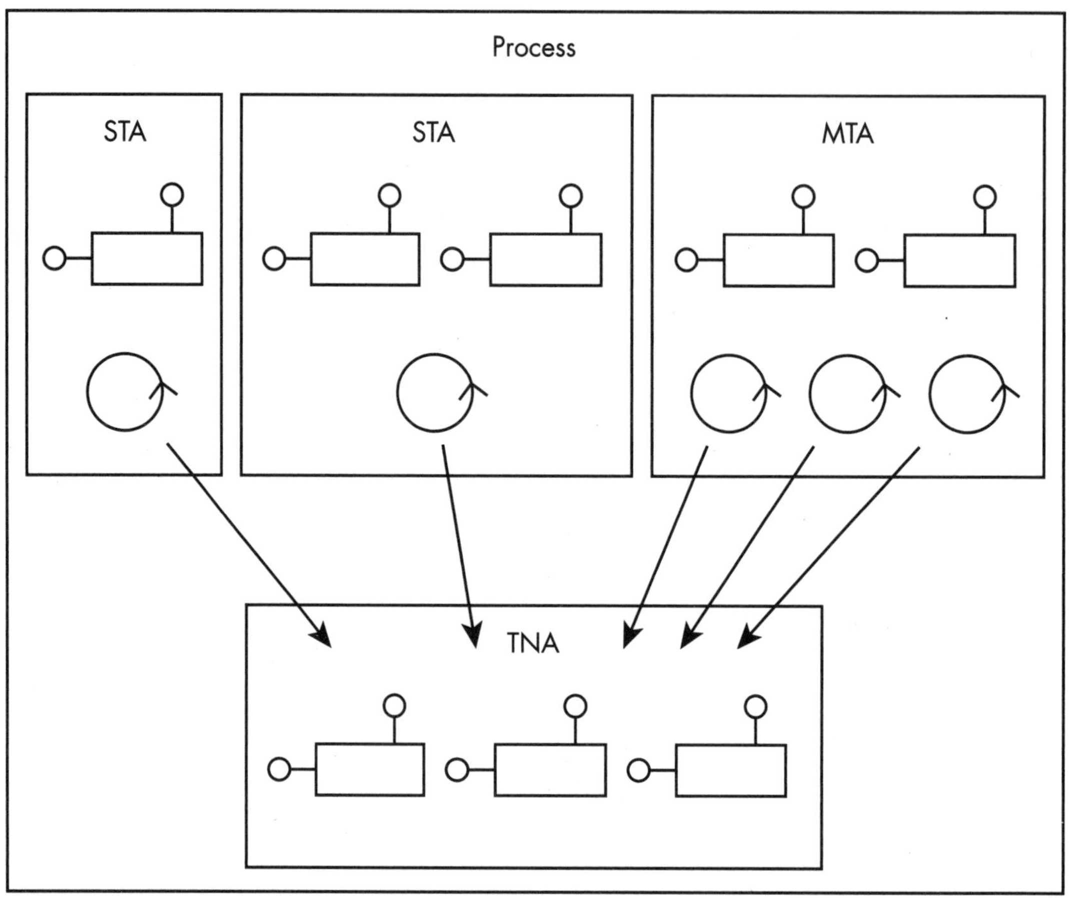

FIGURE 9.3 Processes, Apartments, Threads, and COM Objects.

enters the MTA can call methods on objects that reside in the MTA; therefore, COM objects that reside in the MTA must be thread-safe. Only one thread is allowed to invoke methods on an object in an STA. This means that objects that run in an STA do *not* have to be thread-safe. In this way, thread-safe COM objects and COM objects that are not thread-safe can happily co-exist in a multi-threaded process. Think of COM apartments as a thread barrier you can place around your COM objects. The `ThreadingModel` registry entry and the `CoInitializeEx` functions are just our way of setting up the barriers. After the barriers are set up, the COM runtime does all the work.

HOW THE COM RUNTIME USES APARTMENTS

If a COM object indicates it is thread-safe (`Threading-Model=Free`), then the COM runtime sees that this object runs in the MTA. If the object is instantiated by an MTA thread, the COM runtime does not have to do anything. If the object is instantiated by an STA thread, then the COM runtime creates a new MTA thread for the object. The creating STA thread receives a marshaled interface pointer (you'll learn what that is shortly). Multiple threads can enter the MTA, and any thread that enters the MTA can invoke methods on any COM object in the MTA. This is permissible because objects whose threading model is `Free` use a critical section, mutex, or some other thread synchronization primitive to synchronize these threads.

If a COM object indicates that it is *not* thread-safe, (`Threading Model=Apartment or Single`), then the COM runtime sees that this object runs in an STA. If the object's threading model is `Apartment`, and the object is instantiated by an STA thread, then the object resides in the same apartment as its creating thread. If the object is instantiated by an MTA thread, then the COM runtime creates a new thread and an STA for the object and returns a marshaled interface pointer to the MTA thread. If the thread model of the object is `Single`, then the object always resides in the Primary STA of the process. The primary STA is just the first STA that is created in the process. If the creating thread *is* the primary STA, then the object resides in its creator's apartment. In any other case, the COM runtime instantiates the object in the primary STA and returns a marshaled interface to the calling apartment.

INTER–APARTMENT METHOD CALLS

Remember I said the entire idea behind apartments is to restrict which threads are allowed to call the methods of a COM object. Although you want to allow only one thread to call the methods in an STA object directly, that doesn't mean you want to shut the other threads in the process completely off from being able to call methods on the STA object. The other threads simply have to make an indirect method call. If a thread in one apartment wants to make a method call on an object in another apartment, the COM runtime has to make sure this method call is made using a thread in the called object's apartment. This is the only way the COM runtime can guarantee that the threading requirements of the object are met. If the calling thread is an MTA thread, for instance, and the object is an STA object, then the MTA thread must send a message to the lone thread in the COM object's STA instructing it to call the method on behalf of the MTA thread. The STA calls the method (parameters are included in the message) and then sends a message back with the output parameters and return value. If this sounds like the same marshaling process that was used to enable out-of-process components it's because it is. The same mid-generated proxy and stub is used to do this intra-process marshaling as shown in Figure 9.4.

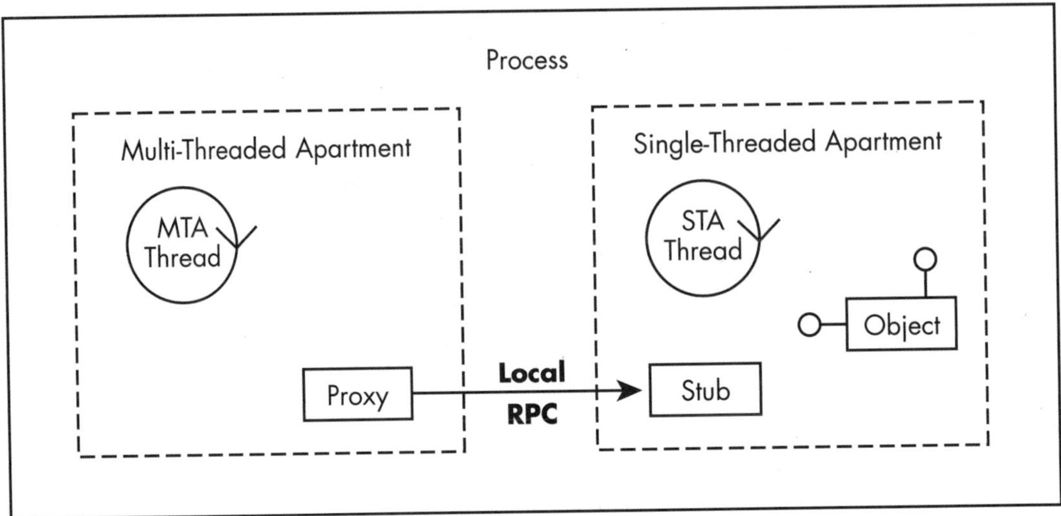

FIGURE 9.4 Intra-Process Marshaling.

Intra-Process marshaling is sometimes called a *thread switch* because the only reason that marshaling is required is to make sure that a method call occurs on a thread in the object's apartment.

If the called apartment (where the stub and the COM object reside) is an MTA, the method call is dispatched using a thread from the Remote Procedure Call (RPC) thread cache. Threads in the RPC thread cache can enter the MTA.

Remember from Chapter 6 that the proxy and stub use RPC to communicate with each other.

If the called apartment is an STA, the situation is more complicated. The method call must occur on the lone thread that resides in the STA. So, an RPC thread uses the `PostMessage` API function to post a Windows message to the STA that tells the STA thread which method to call. The lone thread in the STA must have a Windows message loop, similar to the code here, to receive these messages.

```
MSG msg;
while (GetMessage(&msg, 0, 0, 0))
    DispatchMessage(&msg);
```

You studied the negative performance implications of inter-process marshaling in Chapter 6. Unfortunately, intra-process marshaling is almost as slow. See Chapter 5 of *Essential COM* by Don Box for a more detailed discussion of inter-apartment method calls.

MARSHALING INTERFACE POINTERS BETWEEN APARTMENTS

If a thread running in one apartment is to call a method on an object that resides in a different apartment, then the interface pointer through which the calling thread makes the method call must be marshaled between the two apartments. An interface pointer is marshaled between two apartments if a stub has been setup in the apartment where the object resides and a proxy is returned to the calling apartment as shown in Figure 9.4. All method calls made through this interface pointer are marshaled to the calling apartment as explained in the previous section. Whether an interface pointer is correctly marshaled into a thread's apartment depends on how the thread acquired the interface pointer. If a thread acquires an interface pointer on an object running in a different apartment through a COM API function, like `CoCreateInstanceEx` or `CoGetClassObject`, then the interface pointer is correctly marshaled. One example where this occurs is if an MTA thread calls `CoCreateInstanceEx` to create an instance of an STA object (`ThreadingModel=Apartment`). Another example where an interface pointer is correctly marshaled between apartments is when a COM object receives an interface pointer through a method call (like when an object passes an interface pointer to the `Advise` method of `IConnectionPoint`).

What happens if a thread in an apartment acquires an interface pointer through some other means than a COM API function or a method call on a COM object? There are two answers to this question: If the interface pointer was manually marshaled between the two apartments, then the method call proceeds as normal using inter-apartment marshaling. If the interface pointer was not marshaled at all, then the calling thread receives a `RPC_E_WRONG_THREAD` HRESULT when it makes the method call. This is the thread barrier at work. When a thread enters an apartment (which it must do before it calls any COM-related method), information is stored in Thread Local Storage (TLS) that indicates which apartment the thread resides in. The COM runtime checks this information whenever the thread tries to do anything that is related to COM.

Do you see now why the example program (the Stock Monitor) that you built in Chapter 8 used Free threading for its COM objects? Each Stock Monitor object had two threads: the main thread that is used to service method calls and a worker thread that monitors stocks. The main thread acquires outgoing interface pointers that are passed to it through the `Advise` method of `IConnectionPoint` (the logic to do this is hidden in

ATL code). This interface pointer is correctly marshaled between an apartment that resides in the client process and the main thread of the stock monitor server. The problem is the worker thread; it calls methods through this outgoing interface pointer to send callbacks to the client. The outgoing interface pointer is not marshaled properly between the main thread and the worker thread. The main thread simply places the interface pointer on a collection that is maintained by ATL. The worker thread then comes along and uses the interface pointer later. If the main thread and the worker thread were in different STAs, you would receive the RPC_E_WRONG_THREAD HRESULT when you tried to send your callback. This is a classic situation where manual marshaling is required. I solved this problem by having both the main thread and the worker thread enter the multi-threaded apartment. By adding the following `#define` to `stdafx.h`, you caused the main thread to enter the MTA:

```
#define ATL_FREE_THREADED
```

and the bolded code shown below (see Listing 8.3) caused the worker thread to also enter the MTA:

```
DWORD WINAPI threadProc(void *pv)
{
    DWORD retval;
    CStockMonitor *stockMonitor;
    HRESULT hRes;
    hRes = CoInitializeEx(NULL, COINIT_MULTITHREADED);
    if (SUCCEEDED(hRes))
    {
        stockMonitor=(CStockMonitor*)pv;
        while (!stockMonitor->m_bHaltThread)
        {
            stockMonitor->MonitorStocks();
            ::Sleep(3000);
        }
        CoUninitialize();
        SetEvent(stockMonitor->m_hEventShutdown);
        retval=0;
    }
    else
        retval=2;
    return retval;
}
```

It's easy to see what would have happened had you not made the Stock Monitor free-threaded. Go back to the Stock Monitor example that you built in Chapter 8. Go to the file `stdafx.h` and comment out the line that reads:

```
#define ATL_FREE_THREADED
```

and either uncomment the original `#define` or add a new `#define` that reads as follows:

```
#define _ATL_APARTMENT_THREADED
```

This causes the main thread of your Stock Monitor object to be an STA thread. Now compile the stock server application and run the Event client. Nothing should happen; no events arrive. The worker thread is failing when it tries to `Fire` the `PriceChange` event through the outgoing interface pointer that was passed to the `Advise` method of `IConnectionPoint`. To see what's going on, you need to modify the Wizard-generated `Fire_PriceChange` method. Add the following bolded lines of code to the `Fire_PriceChange` method in the file `stockserverCP.h`:

```
HRESULT Fire_PriceChange(BSTR ticker, FLOAT newPrice, FLOAT oldPrice)
{
    HRESULT hRes;
    CComVariant varResult;
    T* pT = static_cast<T*>(this);
    int nConnectionIndex;
    CComVariant* pvars = new CComVariant[3];
    int nConnections = m_vec.GetSize();

    for (nConnectionIndex = 0; nConnectionIndex < nConnections;
nConnectionIndex++)
    {
        pT->Lock();
        CComPtr<IUnknown> sp = m_vec.GetAt(nConnectionIndex);
        pT->Unlock();
        IDispatch* pDispatch = reinterpret_cast<IDispatch*>(sp.p);
        if (pDispatch != NULL)
        {
            VariantClear(&varResult);
            pvars[2] = ticker;
            pvars[1] = newPrice;
            pvars[0] = oldPrice;
            DISPPARAMS disp = { pvars, NULL, 3, 0 };
            hRes=pDispatch->Invoke(0x1, IID_NULL, LOCALE_USER_DEFAULT,
DISPATCH_METHOD, &disp, &varResult, NULL, NULL);
            if (RPC_E_WRONG_THREAD==hRes)
                ::MessageBox(NULL,"Wrong Thread","Stock Server",MB_OK);
```

```
        }
    }
    delete[] pvars;
    return varResult.scode;
}
```

Now try running the Event client again. The wrong thread message box should pop up every three seconds. By having both the main thread and the worker thread use the MTA, you avoid this problem.

MANUALLY MARSHALING INTERFACE POINTERS

If, for whatever reason, you could not use the MTA in Chapter 8, then you would have had to manually marshal the interface pointers. It is not terribly difficult to do this. The COM API provides two functions: `CoMarshalInterThreadInterfaceInStream` and `CoGetInterfaceAndReleaseStream`. These function names are so long it's almost comical. But they are actually quite descriptive. `CoMarshalInterThreadInterfaceinStream` turns a COM interface pointer into an apartment-neutral stream of bytes that can be accessed through an `IStream` interface pointer. This apartment-neutral stream can be passed to another apartment to marshal the interface pointer into that apartment. `CoGetInterfaceAndReleaseStream` is called from the receiving apartment to reconstitute the stream into a marshaled interface pointer and release the `IStream` interface pointer. So the steps to marshal an interface between thread A in apartment one and thread B in apartment two are as follows:

1. Thread A calls `CoMarshalInterThreadInterfaceInStream` passing in the interface pointer and the IID for the interface. The return value for `CoMarshalInterThreadInterfaceInStream` is an `IStream` interface pointer.
2. The `IStream` interface pointer must then be passed to thread B either by passing it as the argument to the thread procedure for thread B, or by placing the interface pointer in a data structure that thread B can access.
3. Thread B calls `CoGetInterfaceAndReleaseStream` passing in the `IStream` interface pointer and the IID for the interface. The return value for the function is the marshaled interface pointer.

For instance, the following method call causes the outgoing interface pointer to be marshaled into an apartment-neutral stream:

```
IStream *pStream;
IDispatch *pOutgoing.
::CoMarshalInterThreadInterfaceInStream(IID__IDispatch,pOutgoing,&pStream);
```

From the worker thread, you would need to add the following code to reconstitute the stream into a valid interface pointer:

```
IStream *pStream;
IDispatch *pMarshaledOutgoing;
::CoGetInterfaceAndReleaseStream(pStream,IID_IDispatch,(void
**)&pMarshaledOutgoing);
```

Since you are using the ATL connection point implementation, you would have to add this logic to ATL code which would get complicated. So instead, on the Web site, you can find a version of the Stock Monitor server that uses STAs and manual marshaling. This example program uses a proprietary callback interface called `IStockEvent` that the client of the stock monitor must implement. The client then registers its implementation of `IStockEvent` to receive callbacks by passing the interface pointer to the `Advise` method of `IStockMonitor`. The situation is exactly like the example I discussed at the beginning of Chapter 8 (see Figure 8.1 and the section entitled "Understanding COM Callbacks/Events" in Chapter 8).

Use the Global Interface Table

One problem with the approach you used to do manual marshaling is that after you call `CoMarshalInterThreadInterfaceInStream`, you can only call `CoGetInterfaceAndReleaseStream` once. That means that if your process contains many apartments, you have to call `CoMarshalInterThreadInterfaceInStream` and `CoGetInterfaceAndReleaseStream` once for each apartment that you wish to marshal an interface pointer to. Fortunately, there is another way to do manual interface marshaling. You can marshal interface pointers between apartments using the Global Interface Table (GIT). Think of the GIT as a way to store an interface pointer in an apartment-neutral form so you can share it among multiple apartments. A thread in an apartment can store an interface pointer in the GIT and receive an apartment-neutral cookie. Any thread in any apartment in the process can use this cookie to retrieve from the GIT an interface pointer that is marshaled for its use as shown in Figure 9.5.

The GIT is implemented as a COM object that supports an interface called `IGlobalInterfaceTable`. `IGlobalInterfaceTable` supports three methods: `RegisterInterfaceInGlobal`, `RevokeInterfaceFromGlobal`, and `GetInterfaceFromGlobal` whose argument lists and purpose are summarized in Table 9.4.

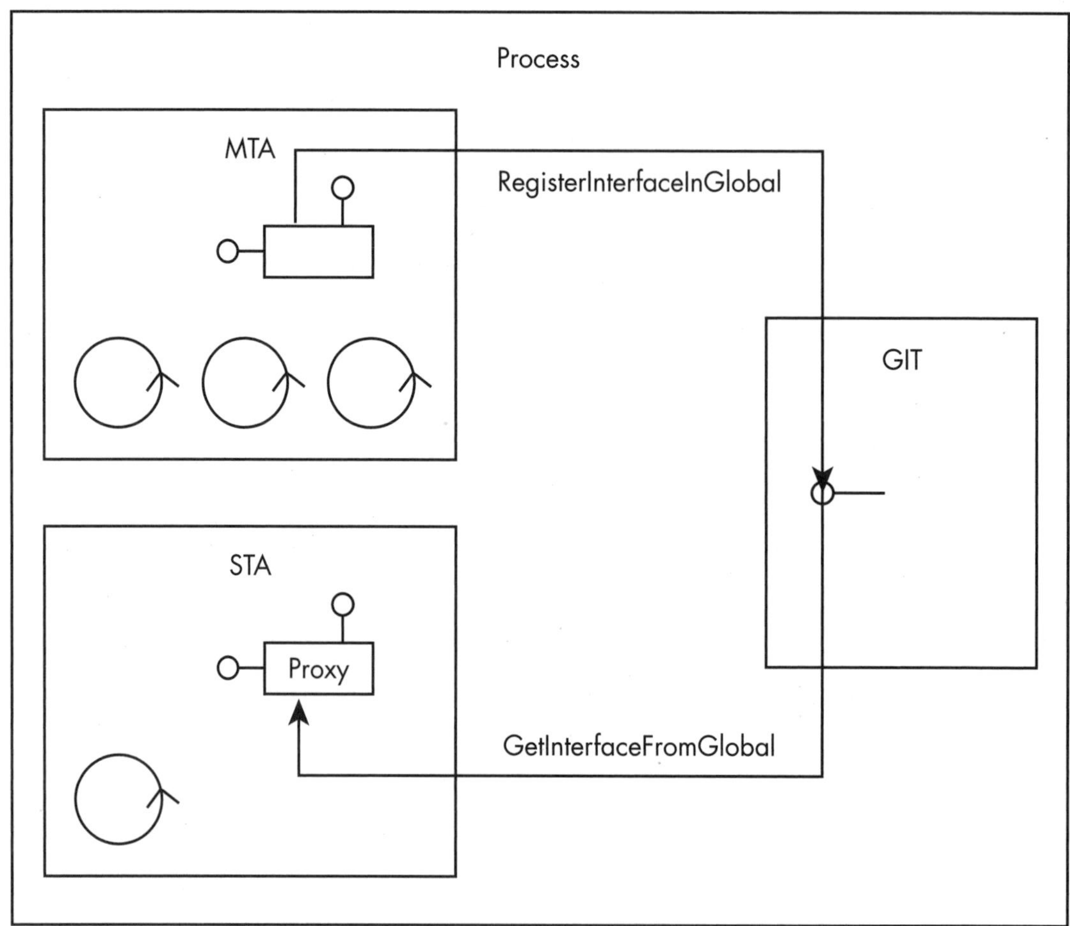

FIGURE 9.5 Intra-Process Marshaling Using the GIT.

TABLE 9.4 IGlobalInterfaceTable Methods

Method Name	Description
HRESULT RegisterInterfaceInGlobal(IUnknown *pUnk, REFIID riid, DWORD *pdwCookie)	Register the interface pointer pUnk with IID riid for use by all apartments in a process. The return value, pdwCookie, contains an apartment-neutral cookie that can be shared between apartments.
HRESULT RevokeInterfaceFromGlobal(DWORD dwCookie)	Revokes the interface pointer identified by dwCookie from the global interface table.
HRESULT GetInterfaceFromGlobal(DWORD dwCookie, REFIID riid, Void **pv)	Retrieves the interface pointer identified by dwCookie in a form that is usable by the calling apartment. The argument riid is the IID for the interface and pv is the interface pointer.

On the Web site for this book, I have created a version of the Stock Server that uses Single-Threaded Apartments and the GIT. The main thread of the Stock Monitor stores the outgoing interface in the GIT and then the worker thread retrieves the interface pointer from the GIT when it is going to make its callback. This example also uses the `IStockEvent` proprietary callback interface just like the example you used to demonstrate the `CoMarshalInterThreadInterfaceInStream` and `CoGetInterfaceAndReleaseStream` functions. I don't want to go through the code in this example line-by-line because it is complicated, but I have highlighted the key lines of code here.

Because the GIT is a COM object, to use it you must first create a GIT instance using `CoCreateInstance` as follows:

```
IGlobalInterfaceTable *m_pGIT;
CoCreateInstance(CLSID_StdGlobalInterfaceTable,0,CLSCTX_INPROC_SERV-
ER,IID_IGlobalInterfaceTable,(void **)&m_pGIT);
```

After you have created the GIT instance, you can add an interface pointer from any apartment to the GIT with this code:

```
HRESULT hResult;
DWORD dwGITCookie;
IStockEvent *pOutgoing;
hResult=m_pGIT-
>RegisterInterfaceInGlobal(pOutgoing,IID_IStockEvent,&dwGITCookie);
```

Another apartment can then use the GIT cookie to get an interface pointer marshaled for its purposes using the following code:

```
IStockEvent *pOutgoing;
DWORD dwGITCookie
m_pGIT->GetInterfaceFromGlobal(dwGITCookie,IID_IStockEvent,(void
**)&pOutgoing);
pOutgoing->PriceChange(ticker,newPrice,oldPrice);
```

Finally, when you no longer need the interface pointer, or when the process is shutting down, you can remove your apartment-neutral interface pointer from the GIT using this code:

```
DWORD dwGITCookie;
m_pGIT->RevokeInterfaceFromGlobal(dwGITCookie);
```

Take a look at the code on the Web site for this book and see Chapter 5 in *Essential COM* by Don Box if you would like to learn more about manual marshaling and the Global Interface Table. But don't get bogged down on this topic, especially if you're just starting out with COM. It's not critical that you understand manual marshaling or the GIT to use COM.

THE BOTH AND NEUTRAL THREADING MODELS

So far, I have conveniently avoided the `Both` and `Neutral` threading models. This was intentional because you needed to have some background before you can understand these threading models. The `Both` and `Neutral` threading models are similar yet different. They are similar because they both exist to accomplish the same goal: to avoid the expensive thread-switch that occurs when a method call must be made across apartments. Both of these threading models cause a COM object to always execute on their caller's thread. They are different because they accomplish this goal in different ways.

The `Both` threading model is poorly named, especially now that the Neutral apartment has been added under COM+. Instead of only two possible apartment types (STA and MTA), there are three (STA, MTA, and TNA). A better name for this threading model would be `Any`. When a component has `Both` for its threading model, the COM runtime instantiates the object in the apartment of its creator. Because this component may be instantiated in the MTA or TNA, it must be thread-safe.

It might seem that instantiating an object in the same apartment as its creator would accomplish the goal of the `Both` threading model, avoiding an expensive thread switch, but there are still situations where a thread switch is required. An object that uses the `Both` threading model is instantiated in the apartment of its creating thread, but if an interface pointer on the object is marshaled into another apartment, then marshaling still occurs. For instance, imagine that an MTA thread calls CoCreateInstanceEx to create an instance of an object with Threading Model `Both`. The object resides in the MTA. Now imagine that an STA thread in the same process attempts to call a method on this object as shown in Figure 9.6.

The interface pointer through which the STA thread is making the method call still has to be marshaled into the STA and any method calls made through that interface pointer will use inter-apartment marshaling. This goes against the stated goal of the `Both` threading model, to avoid such thread switches. Do you also see that this thread switch is unnecessary? After all, if an object has a Threading Model of `Both`, it must be thread-safe; there is no reason that both the MTA and STA threads could not call this object directly. The strict rules of COM apartments, which in most cases make life easier, are actually hurting us here.

To avoid thread switches in this situation, a COM component must aggregate the Free-Threaded Marshaler (FTM) as shown in Figure 9.7.

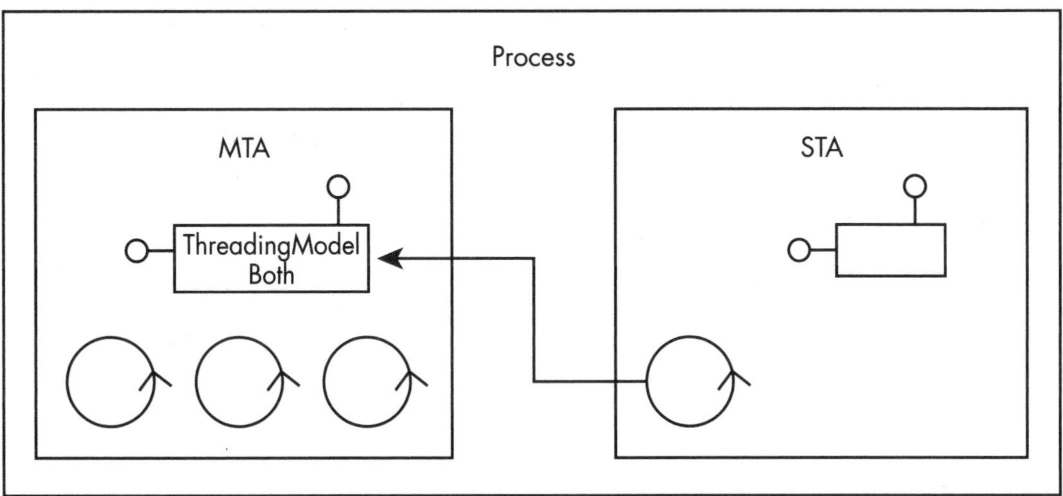

FIGURE 9.6 An MTA and an STA Thread and an Object Whose Threading Model is Both.

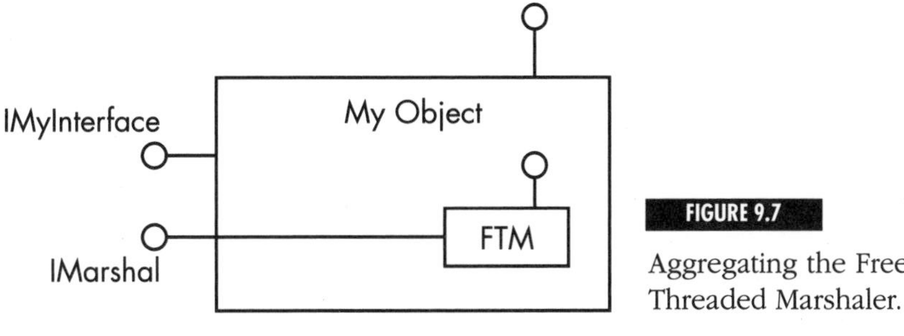

FIGURE 9.7 Aggregating the Free Threaded Marshaler.

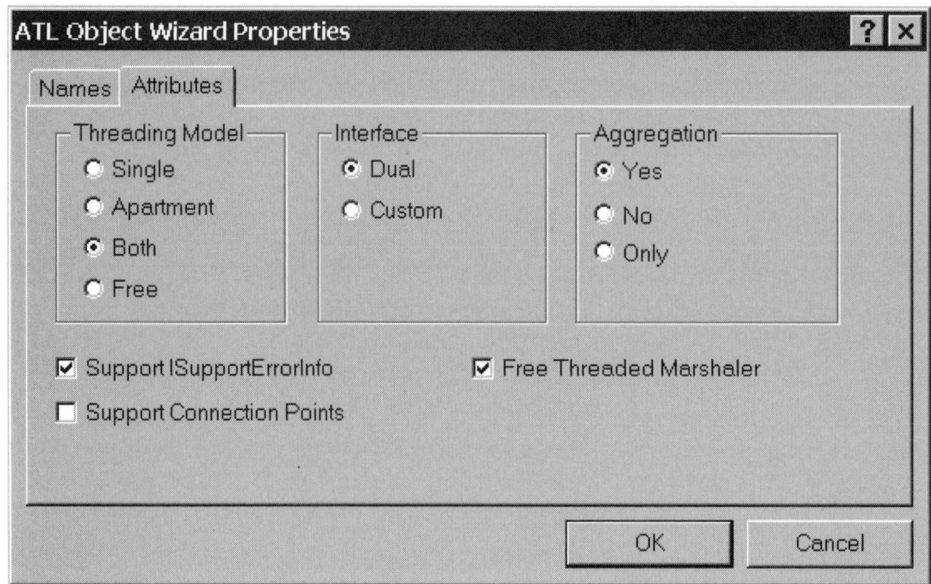

FIGURE 9.8 Selecting the FTM Using the ATL Object Wizard Properties Dialog.

You can aggregate the FTM when you first create a COM using the ATL Object Wizard. On the `Attributes` tab of the ATL Object Wizard Properties dialog you can select the `Free Threaded Marshaler` as shown in Figure 9.8.

The ATL object wizard adds the code shown below in bold to your implementation class when you elect to aggregate the free-threaded marshaler.

```
class ATL_NO_VTABLE CStockMonitor :
   public CComObjectRootEx<CComMultiThreadModel>,
   public CComCoClass<CStockMonitor, &CLSID_StockMonitor>,
   public ISupportErrorInfo,
   public IDispatchImpl<IStockMonitor, &IID_IStockMonitor,
&LIBID_BOTHSTOCKSERVERLib>
{
public:
   CStockMonitor()
   {
      m_pUnkMarshaler = NULL;
   }

DECLARE_REGISTRY_RESOURCEID(IDR_STOCKMONITOR)
DECLARE_GET_CONTROLLING_UNKNOWN()
```

```
DECLARE_PROTECT_FINAL_CONSTRUCT()

BEGIN_COM_MAP(CStockMonitor)
   COM_INTERFACE_ENTRY(IStockMonitor)
   COM_INTERFACE_ENTRY(IDispatch)
   COM_INTERFACE_ENTRY(ISupportErrorInfo)
   COM_INTERFACE_ENTRY_AGGREGATE(IID_IMarshal, m_pUnkMarshaler.p)
END_COM_MAP()

   HRESULT FinalConstruct()
   {
      return CoCreateFreeThreadedMarshaler(
         GetControllingUnknown(), &m_pUnkMarshaler.p);
   }
   void FinalRelease()
   {
      m_pUnkMarshaler.Release();
   }

   CComPtr<IUnknown> m_pUnkMarshaler;

// ISupportsErrorInfo
   STDMETHOD(InterfaceSupportsErrorInfo)(REFIID riid);

// IStockMonitor
public:
};
```

To understand what's going on here it would probably be worthwhile for you to re-read the section in Chapter 3 entitled *Aggregation*. The whole idea behind aggregation is that an object (the outer object) wants to either extend the functionality of an existing component (the inner object) or to use the services of the inner object to implement a portion of its (the outer object's) functionality as shown in Figure 9.8. To accomplish this, the outer object delegates the implementation of one or more of its interfaces to the inner object. In the case of an object that is aggregating the Free-Threaded Marshaler, the outer object delegates the implementation of the IMarshal interface to the Free-Threaded Marshaler. The IMarshal interface is used by the COM runtime to marshal interface pointers from one apartment to another. If an object does not implement IMarshal (which is usually the case), then the COM runtime searches for the proxy stub (marshaling) DLL that has been registered for the interface. If an object does implement IMarshal, then the COM runtime instead calls the MarshalInterface method in IMarshal to marshal the interface pointer between apartments. As long as the calling apartment is in the same process, the implementation of `IMarshal::MarshalInterface` in the Free-Threaded Marshaler always returns a direct pointer to the calling apartment.

If an object and its caller reside in different processes, marshaling is always used.

Do you see that this amounts to a slick way of bypassing the rules of COM Apartments? When an interface pointer on an object that aggregates the FTM is marshaled from one apartment to another (for example from the MTA where it was created to a calling STA), the calling apartment receives a direct pointer (assuming that the calling apartment and the apartment of the COM object are running in the same process). This is all right in most situations, but bypassing the rules of COM apartments can cause problems in some situations. For instance, consider the situation where you have an object (object 1) whose threading model is `Both` and aggregates the FTM. Let's say this object was instantiated by thread 1 in STA1. In addition, let's say that object 1 instantiates object 2, which uses the apartment threading model as shown in Figure 9.9.

Since STA1 is a single threaded apartment, the COM runtime assumes that only the lone thread running in the STA (thread 1) will ever directly call a method on object 2. So object 1 (which is running in STA1) will receive a direct interface pointer (instead of a proxy) when it instantiates object 2. Unfortunately, because object 1 has aggregated the FTM, STA2 will receive a direct interface pointer on object 1 when an interface pointer on object 1 is marshaled into STA2. So, thanks to the FTM, thread 2 is also allowed to call methods directly on object 1. This is okay for object 1; it is thread-safe and has elected to circumvent the threading rules of COM apartments by aggregating the FTM. There is a problem, however, if thread 2 calls a method on object 1 and that method subsequently invokes a method on object 2. Object 2 is not thread-safe. COM objects that use `Apartment` for their threading model aren't required to be thread-safe. It is now possible for either thread 1 and thread 2 to invoke methods on object 2 simultaneously. Moreover, if object 2 has thread affinity, it will likely suffer a failure when it is invoked by thread 2 because thread 2 is not the creating thread for object 2. So how do you fix this problem?

You should know that in this example you violated two of the basic rules of the `Both` ThreadingModel: (1) objects that use the `Both` threading model should not hold apartment-relative resources like interface pointers, (2) objects that use the `Both` threading model should only make callbacks to a client on the same thread that received the outgoing interface.

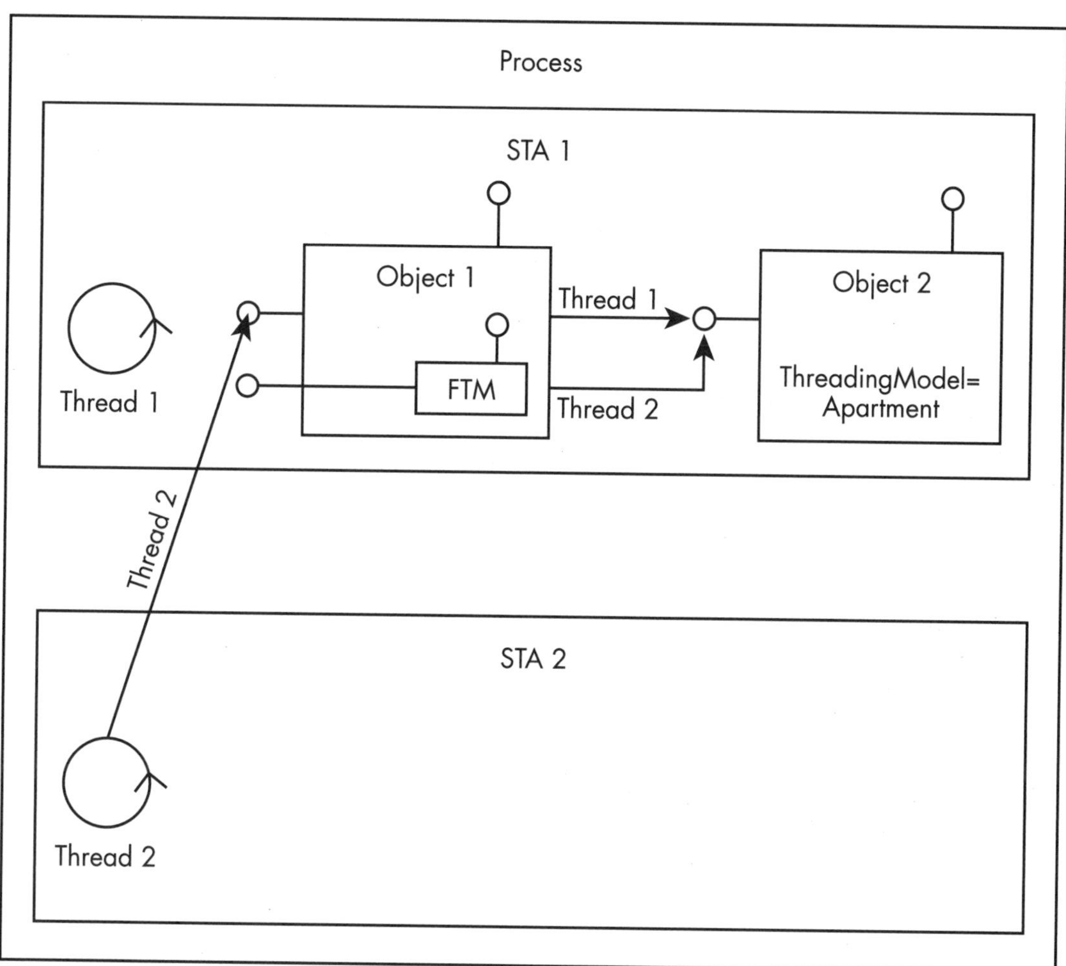

FIGURE 9.9 Problems Caused by the FTM.

You can always satisfy the first rule by using the GIT to hold your interface pointers. Your `Both` threading model object can then retrieve an interface pointer marshaled for the current apartment when a method call must be made through that interface pointer. The second rule must be enforced through careful coding. As you can see, using the `Both` threading model can be complicated. Typically, when you use the `Both` threading model you aggregate the FTM and use the GIT.

The `Neutral` threading model was created as a way to get the performance benefits of the `Both` threading model without the complexity of aggregating the FTM and using the GIT. Objects with `ThreadingModel=Neutral` always execute on their caller's thread, just like objects that use the `Both` ThreadingModel. The key difference is that the `Neutral` threading model has an associated apartment: the Thread Neutral Apartment (TNA). Using the `Both` threading model means that an object can exist in any apartment; the `Both` threading model does not have an associated apartment type. No threads are explicitly bound to the TNA, but threads in either the MTA or the STA can call methods on objects that reside in the TNA. When an STA or MTA thread makes a call on an object in the TNA, it does so through a lightweight proxy as shown in Figure 9.10.

This lightweight proxy never does a thread switch although it does adhere to the other rules of apartments. In particular, `Neutral` threading

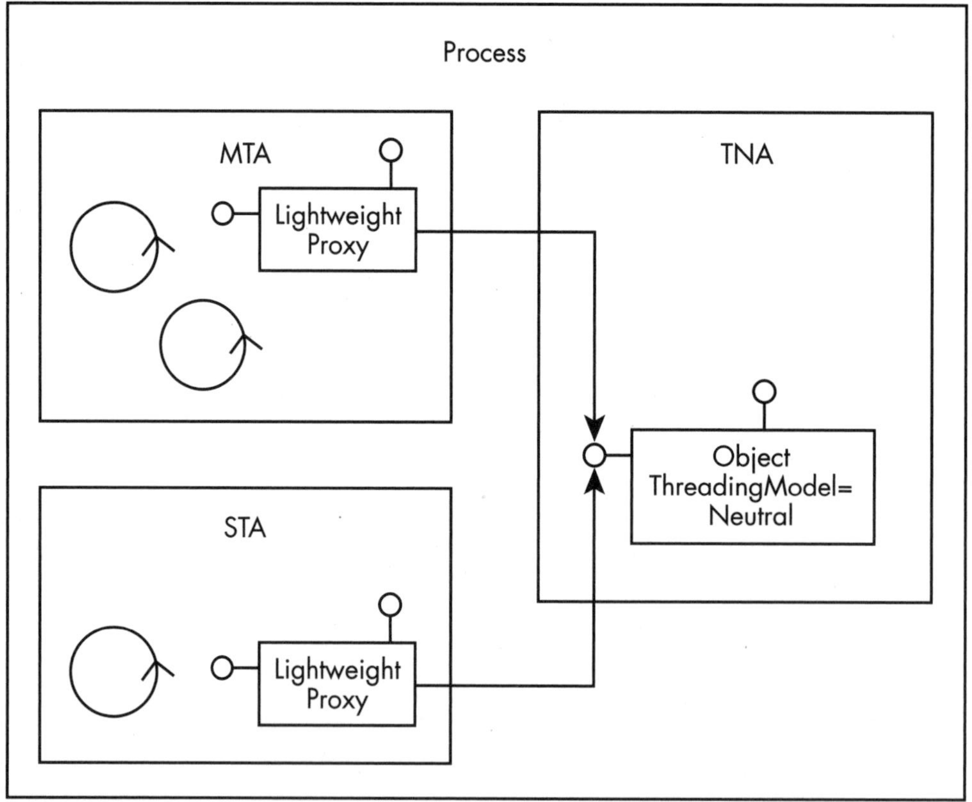

FIGURE 9.10 STA and MTA Apartments Calling Objects Running in the TNA.

model objects can store apartment-relative resources because any interface pointers that the `Neutral` object acquires are marshaled into the `Neutral` apartment. So if object 1, which has threading model `Neutral`, instantiates an STA object (object 2), any thread that is calling object 1 can make a method call safely on object 2.

Because objects that use the `Neutral` threading model can be called by MTA or STA threads, an object that uses the `Neutral` threading model must be thread-safe. In most cases, `Neutral` COM objects are configured to use the COM+ services, which include system-provided thread-synchronization, so you will not have to write this thread-synchronization code yourself.

You will learn more about the thread-synchronization provided by COM+ in Chapters 11–13.

Because the `Neutral` threading model gives you maximum performance without the complexity of the `Both` threading model, it is the preferred threading model for creating non-visual components with COM+. Components that have a user interface or for other reasons have *thread affinity* should still use the `Apartment` (STA only) threading model. A component has thread affinity if, because of its design, it should only be accessed by a single thread. A component might have thread-affinity because it stores information in Thread-Local Storage (TLS) or because it has a user-interface. Components that have a user interface have thread affinity because Windows Handles should only be accessed by the thread that created them. In addition, STAs have built-in logic to prevent a user-interface from hanging when they are servicing outbound COM method calls. An STA creates a COM-managed message loop to service Windows messages while an outbound method call is being processed. If a COM component with a user interface uses the MTA, it does not get this benefit. I talk more about thread affinity and apartments in Chapter 11 when I discuss a new-to-COM+ abstraction called Contexts.

Implement Objects That Will Run in Any STA

By now you're probably thinking that as long as your COM classes use STAs (`ThreadingModel` registry key = `Apartment`), you never have to worry about problems associated with multi-threading because your object will always be called by a single thread. Unfortunately, it's not quite that simple. For a COM object to be safely used in an STA, all the code in the object and its server that is shared between instances such as the class factory (and in the case of an in-process server), and the server entry points like `DllGetClassObject` and `DllCanUnloadNow` need to be thread-safe. Figure 9.11 should make this clear.

In Figure 9.11, object 1 and object 2 reside in STA 1. To create these objects, thread 1 must go through the class factory and the `DllGetClassObject` method. Thread 2 creates object 3 and this object resides in STA 2. To create object 3, thread 2 must also go through the class factory and `DllGetClassObject`. As you can see, object 1 and object 2 are only called by a single thread but, depending on how it is implemented, the class factory may be called simultaneously by both threads. Also, both

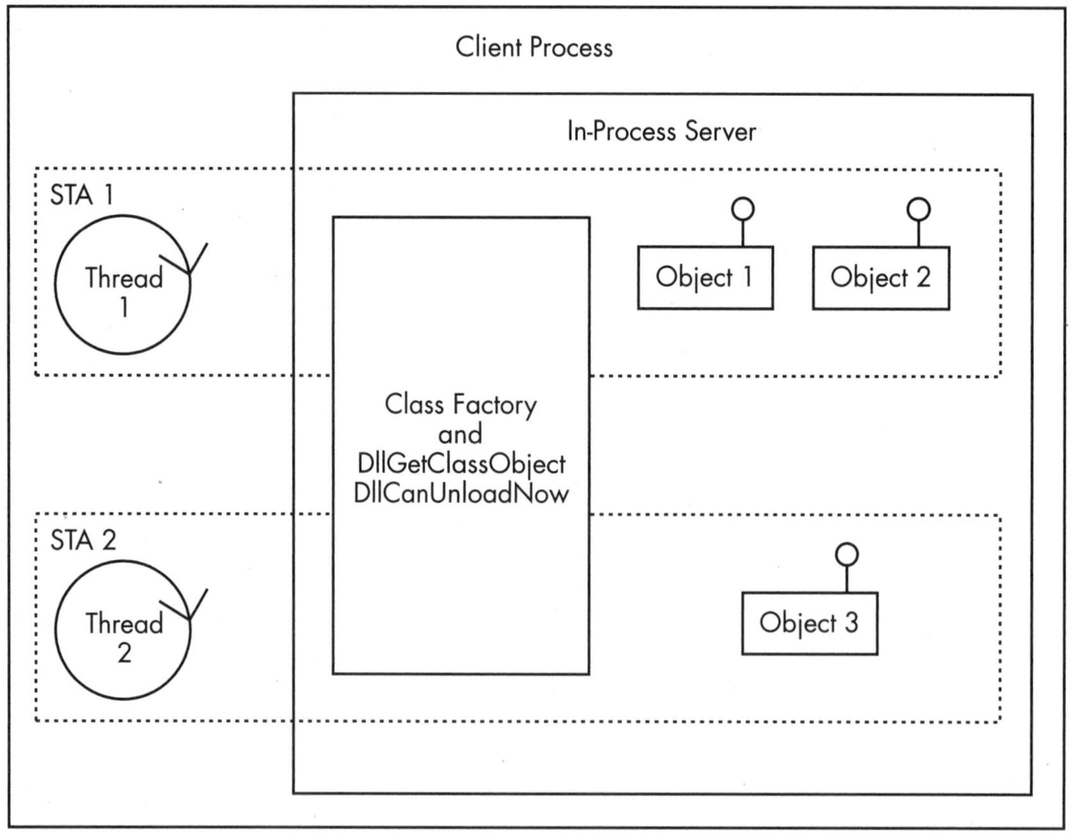

FIGURE 9.11 Multiple STAs in a Process.

threads may call the `DllGetClassObject` at the same time. Moreover, either thread can call `CoFreeUnusedLibraries` at any time, which will call `DllCanUnloadNow`.

Whether the class factory causes a problem in this scenario depends on how it is implemented. A class factory can be implemented so that a new instance of the class factory is created for each instantiation request, or there could be a single instance of the class factory that is used for all instantiation requests. You will have fewer problems with multiple threads if a new instance of the class factory is created for each instantiation request. *But* this implementation approach is less efficient in terms of memory usage and performance.

The Golden Rule regarding objects that can run in any STA (`ThreadingModel=Apartment`) is that they do not have to protect their per-instance state from concurrent access by multiple threads, but they do have to protect their per-class state, their class factory, and their DLL entry methods from multiple threads.

Implement Objects That Will Run in the Primary STA

Unfortunately, some COM servers have class factories and DLL entry points that are not thread-safe. Also, some COM classes do not protect their per-instance state or their per-class state from multiple threads. These COM classes should have `ThreadingModel=Single` or no `ThreadingModel` at all. The COM runtime makes sure that all objects of this class run in the Primary STA (the first STA created in a process). Because *all* instances of a class with `ThreadingModel=Single` run in the same STA, and hence the same thread, you don't have to worry about making the DLL entry points, the class factory, or the per-class state for these objects thread-safe. Obviously, this threading model also has the worst concurrency and performance and should be avoided in most situations.

Implement Objects That Will Run in the MTA

Multiple threads can make simultaneous method calls on COM objects that run in the MTA (`ThreadingModel=Free`). These objects must protect both their per-instance state and their per-class state from concurrent access by multiple threads. In addition, they must have a thread-safe class factory and DLL entry points. So, for instance, the reference counting methods in `IUnknown` must use the thread-safe, `InterlockedIncrement` and `InterlockedDecrement` methods instead of the ++ and – operators to increment and decrement the reference count. All other per-instance and per-class state is usually protected from multiple threads using a thread synchronization object, such as a critical section or mutex. Typically, you add a mutex or a critical section as a member variable of the implementation class and each method in the class that reads or writes the classes state locks the thread-synchronization object before it accesses the classes state and unlocks it when it is done.

COM+ provides a thread-synchronization service that you can use to make your class thread-safe without writing code like this yourself. You learn more about this in Chapters 11-13.

ATL makes locking the per-instance state relatively simple. The ATL class `CComObjectRootEx`, which all COM implementation classes must derive from, has a critical section member variable as shown here:

```
class CComObjectRootEx : public CComObjectRootBase
{
public:
// The rest of the class is omitted for clarity.

   void Lock() {m_critsec.Lock();}
   void Unlock() {m_critsec.Unlock();}
private:
   _CritSec m_critsec;
};
```

Notice that `CComObjectRootEx` contains a method called `Lock` that locks the critical section and a method called `Unlock` that unlocks the critical section. So you could write your thread-safe methods in your multithreaded class as follows:

```
STDMETHODIMP CStockMonitor::Unadvise(long cookie)
{
// Don't do this!!!
   map<DWORD,DWORD>::iterator iter;
   long lCookie;
   Lock();
   iter=m_outgoingCookies.find(cookie);
   if (iter!=m_outgoingCookies.end())
   {
      lCookie=(*iter).second;
      m_pGIT->RevokeInterfaceFromGlobal(lCookie);
      m_outgoingCookies.erase(lCookie);
```

```
    }
    else
       return Error(_T("There is no pointer in the GIT with this cookie"),
                      IID_IStockMonitor,E_NOINTERFACEWITHTHISCOOKIE);
    Unlock();
    return S_OK;
}
```

There is a problem with this code. If you look closely at the code above, you can see that Unlock is not going to be called if the user passes in an invalid cookie. Luckily, ATL includes a class called ObjectLockT that is declared as follows:

```
template <class ThreadModel>
class CComObjectLockT
{
public:
   CComObjectLockT(CComObjectRootEx<ThreadModel>* p)
   {
      if (p)
         p->Lock();
      m_p = p;
   }

   ~CComObjectLockT()
   {
      if (m_p)
         m_p->Unlock();
   }
   CComObjectRootEx<ThreadModel>* m_p;
};
```

Notice that the constructor for this class calls the Lock method on the CComObjectRootEx instance that is passed to it and the destructor calls Unlock. CComObjectRootEx contains a typedef called ObjectLock that is an alias for CComObjectLockT. With this class, you can write your thread-safe methods as follows:

```
STDMETHODIMP CStockMonitor::Unadvise(long cookie)
{
   map<DWORD,DWORD>::iterator iter;
   long lCookie;
   ObjectLock lock(this);
   iter=m_outgoingCookies.find(cookie);
   if (iter!=m_outgoingCookies.end())
```

```
    {
        lCookie=(*iter).second;
        m_pGIT->RevokeInterfaceFromGlobal(lCookie);
        m_outgoingCookies.erase(lCookie);
    }
    else
        return Error(_T("There is no pointer in the GIT with this cookie"),
                        IID_IStockMonitor,E_NOINTERFACEWITHTHISCOOKIE);
    return S_OK;
}
```

Now you are guaranteed that the critical section object is unlocked regardless of how the method returns. The destructor of all stack variables (and the `ObjectLock` variable is a stack variable) is called when the `Unadvise` method returns.

If you are writing a thread-safe COM object for use in the multi-threaded apartment, make sure that your implementation class does not derive from `CComObjectRootEx` using a template parameter of `CComSingleThreadModel`. The file `ATLCOM.h` contains a special declaration of `CComObjectRootEx` that looks as follows:

```
template <>
class CComObjectRootEx<CComSingleThreadModel> : public CComObjectRootBase
{
public:
// The rest of the code in this class is omitted for clarity…

    void Lock() {}
    void Unlock() {}
};
```

No, that's not a typo. If your implementation class contains `CComObjectRootEx<CComSingleThreadModel>` as one of its base classes, then the `Lock` and `Unlock` methods do absolutely nothing. The goal of this class is noble: to make it possible to write code that is thread-safe or code that is not thread-safe by changing a template parameter. The problem is that it is too easy to write code that you think is thread-safe, but really isn't. Just remember that if your COM class is to be used in the MTA (it has a `ThreadingModel` of `Free` or `Both`), it must derive from `CComObjectRootEx` with `CComMultiThreadModel` as its template parameter as shown here:

```
class ATL_NO_VTABLE CStockMonitor :
    public CComObjectRootEx<CComMultiThreadModel>,
    public CComCoClass<CStockMonitor, &CLSID_StockMonitor>,
    public ISupportErrorInfo,
    public IDispatchImpl<IStockMonitor, &IID_IStockMonitor,
```

```
&LIBID_STOCKSERVERLib
{
public:
};
```

See pages 99 throughout 109 in *ATL Internals* if you want to learn more about `CComObjectRootEx` and writing thread-safe code.

Implement Objects That Will Run in the TNA

COM classes that have the value `Neutral` for their `ThreadingModel` registry key run in the Thread Neutral Apartment (TNA). These classes have the same requirements as classes that run in the MTA. Any thread may access instances of these classes, so they must be thread-safe and cannot have thread-affinity. Because the `Neutral` threading model is new to COM+, it is likely that most people who use this threading model will use the thread synchronization provided by COM+. With COM+ you can configure a component and then use the COM+ thread synchronization service to make your class thread-safe. You can also use the thread-synchronization service to make classes that run in the MTA thread-safe.

You will learn what it means to configure a COM+ class in Chapter 11–12.

Keep in mind that whether you need to make a class that uses the `Neutral` Threading Model thread-safe depends on how you plan to use it. If you plan to configure the class and take advantage of the COM+ thread synchronization service, you do *not* need to write internal thread synchronization code for the class. If you plan to use the object without configuring it, then you need to write the same thread-synchronization code that you would write for an object that runs in the MTA.

Out-of-Process Servers and Apartments

So far the discussion has centered on apartments as they relate to in-process COM objects. I would be remiss if I went into the example for this chapter without talking about COM Apartments and how they relate to objects implemented in out-of-process servers. All method calls on an object in an out-of-process server are marshaled. The stub in the server receives the method call from the client proxy and it dispatches a thread to make the method call on behalf of the client. How this call is dispatched depends on whether the server is an apartment threaded (STA) server or a free-threaded (MTA) server. If the server is a free-threaded server, then a thread is dispatched from the RPC thread cache. This cache actually grows and shrinks as the amount of activity within the server increases or decreases. More than one of these threads may be executing within an object simultaneously.

If the object resides within an STA, then a thread from the thread cache is dispatched to call the object. But instead of calling the object directly, this thread calls the `PostMessage` API function to send a message to the thread that resides within the object's STA. This thread receives the message in its message loop and invokes the desired method.

Out-of-process servers built with ATL are apartment threaded by default. The server type is set in the `stdafx.h` file with this line:

```
#define _ATL_APARTMENT_THREADED
```

Defining the `_ATL_APARTMENT_THREADED` variable causes the server's main thread to call `CoInitialize` on startup, thus entering an STA. All objects within the server run in this STA. If you change the line in `stdafx.h` to read as follows:

```
#define _ATL_FREE_THREADED
```

then the server calls `CoInitializeEx` with `COINIT_MULTITHREADED`, thus entering the MTA. All objects within the server will now run in the MTA.

Compare the Different Threading Models: An Apartment Study

The example for this chapter is an apartment study. You will build five COM classes using the ATL object wizard. Your COM classes will have each of the five threading models: `Single`, `Apartment`, `Free`, `Both`, and `Neutral`. The COM classes will reside in an in-process server. Each of the classes will support a single interface called `IThreadView`. `IThreadView` has a read-only property called `GetThreadID`. `GetThreadID` returns the

ID of the thread that the COM object is running on. The client for your server allows the user to create new client (UI) threads and have them enter either an STA or an MTA. By running this demo, you can see which thread each type of object runs on when it is instantiated from either an MTA or an STA. I built a program just like this for myself several years ago when I was struggling to understand apartments. It helped me to gain valuable insight. Hopefully, it will do the same for you. The steps that you perform to build your server are as follows:

1. Create a new ATL DLL project using the ATL/COM AppWizard.
2. Add five COM classes using the ATL Object Wizard.
3. Remove duplicate `IThreadView` interfaces from the IDL.
4. Implement the `IThreadView` interface in all five COM classes.
5. Create a client.
6. Test your work.

Create an ATL Project Using the ATL/COM AppWizard

Start Visual C++ and then execute these steps:

1. Select New... from the `File` menu (the New dialog appears).
2. Click the `Projects` tab.
3. Select `ATL COM AppWizard` from the presented list of project types.
4. Enter `threaddemo` in the `Project` Name field.
5. Click `OK` (The ATL/COM AppWizard appears).
6. Select `Dynamic Link Library` under `Server Type`.
7. Click `Finish`.

Visual C++ creates an empty project for you. The next step is to add your five COM classes.

Add Five COM Classes Using the ATL Object Wizard

Adding COM classes for each of the four threading models supported by the ATL Object Wizard (`Single`, `Apartment`, `Free-Threaded`, and `Both`) is fairly simple; everything can be done through the Wizard. Unfortunately, you have to take a slightly different approach when creating a COM class that uses the `Neutral` threading model because Visual C++ 6.0 does not support this Threading Model.

ADD CLASSES WITH THREADING MODELS SUPPORTED BY THE WIZARD

To add the COM classes that use the `Single`, `Apartment`, `Free`, and `Both` threading models to your project, perform the following steps:

1. Select `New ATL Object...` from the `Insert` menu (the ATL Object Wizard appears).
2. Under `Category` select `Objects` and under `Objects` select `Simple Object`.
3. Click the `Next` button (the ATL Object Wizard Properties dialog appears).
4. On the `Names` tab, enter `SingleThreaded` in the `Short` Name field in the `C++` section. In the `COM` section, change the interface name to `IThreadView` (see Figure 9.12).
5. Click the `Attributes` tab.
6. Change the Threading Model entry to `Single` and the interface type to `Custom` (see Figure 9.13).
7. Click OK.
8. Repeat steps 1–7, but on step 4 enter `ApartmentThreaded` for the `Short Name`, and on step 6, change the `ThreadingModel` to `Apartment`. Remember to change the interface name to `IThreadView` and select `Custom` for the interface type.
9. Repeat steps 1–7, but on step 4 enter `FreeThreaded` for the `Short Name`, and on step 6, change the `ThreadingModel` to `Free`. Remember to change the interface name to `IThreadView` and select `Custom` for the interface type.
10. Repeat steps 1–7 but on step 4 enter `BothThreaded` for the `Short Name`, and on step 6, change the `ThreadingModel` to `Both`. Remember to change the interface name to `IThreadView` and select `Custom` for the interface type.

The ATL Object Wizard adds four COM implementation classes to your project: `CSingleThreaded`, `CApartmentThreaded`, `CFreeThreaded`, and `CBothThreaded`.

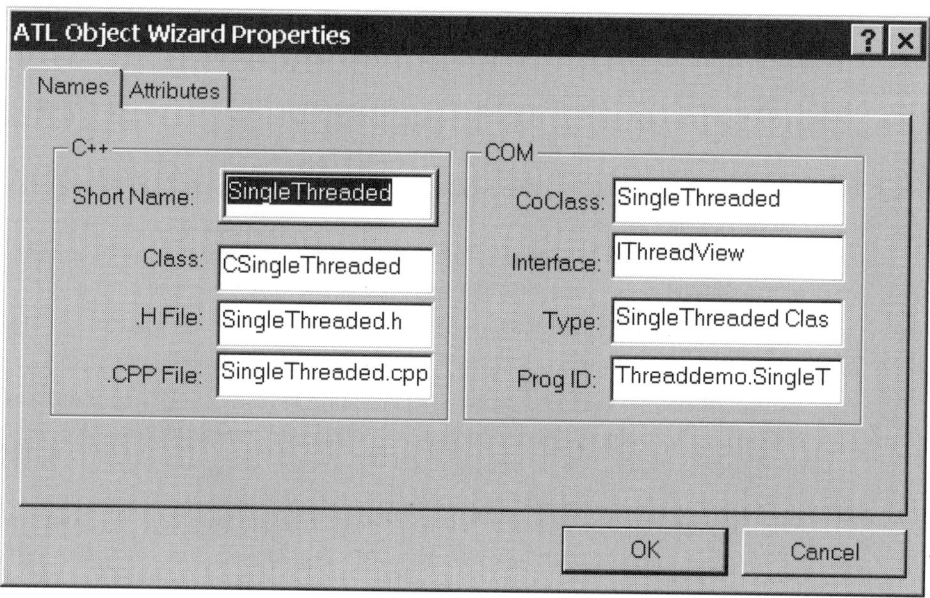

FIGURE 9.12 The Names Tab of the ATL Object Wizard Properties Dialog.

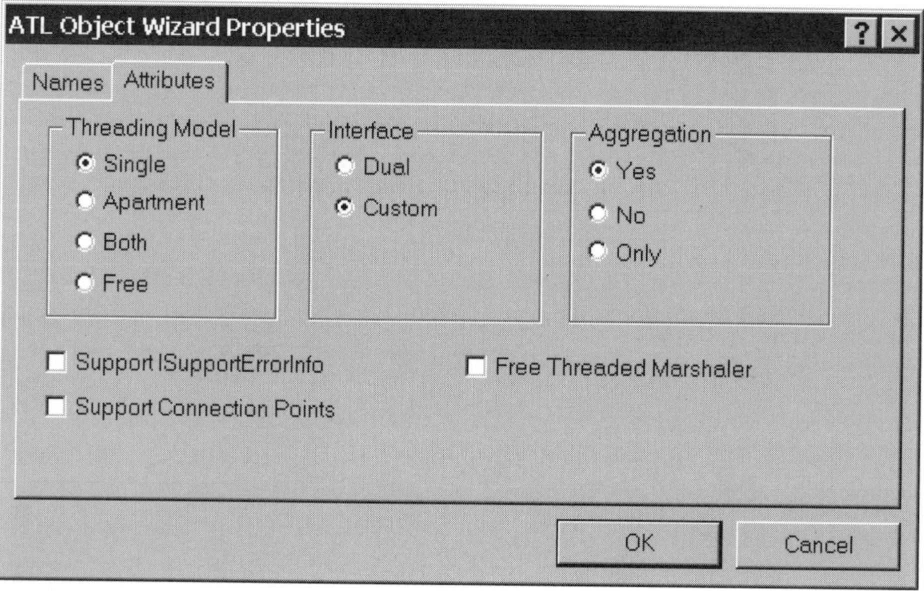

FIGURE 9.13 The Attributes Tab of the ATL Object Wizard Properties Dialog.

ADD A NEUTRAL-THREADING MODEL CLASS

To add the `Neutral-threaded` class, first create the class as a `Free-threaded` class and then manually alter its registry setting to make it `Neutral-threaded`. To do this, perform the following steps:

1. Repeat steps 1–7 in the previous section, but on step 4 enter `NeutralThreaded` for the `Short Name`, and on step 6, change the `ThreadingModel` to `Free`. Remember to change the interface name to `IThreadView` and select `Custom` for the interface type.
2. Open the `Resource Files` folder in the `File View` tab of the Visual C++ Workspace as shown in Figure 9.14.
3. In the file `NeutralThreaded.rgs`, change the string that reads as follows: `val ThreadingModel = s 'Free'` so that it reads: `val ThreadingModel = s 'Neutral'` as shown in Figure 9.14.

The registry entries that are entered for each class are contained in the .rgs file for that class. Changing the `ThreadingModel` entry in the `.rgs`

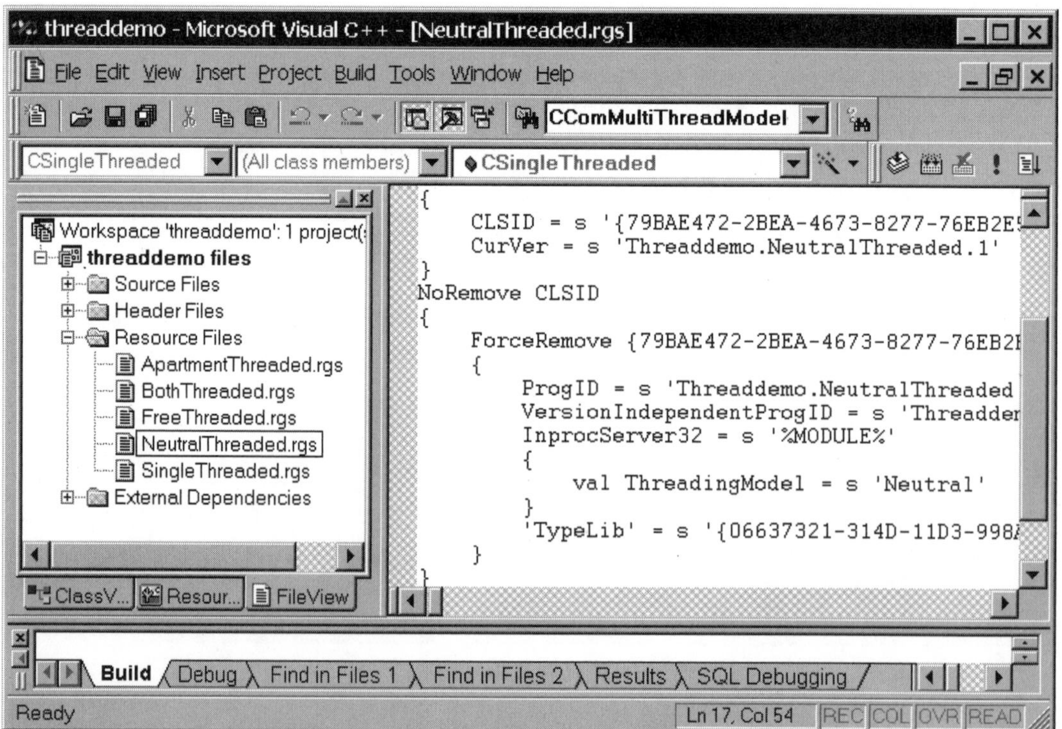

FIGURE 9.14 Changing the Registry File to Make Your Class Neutral-Threaded.

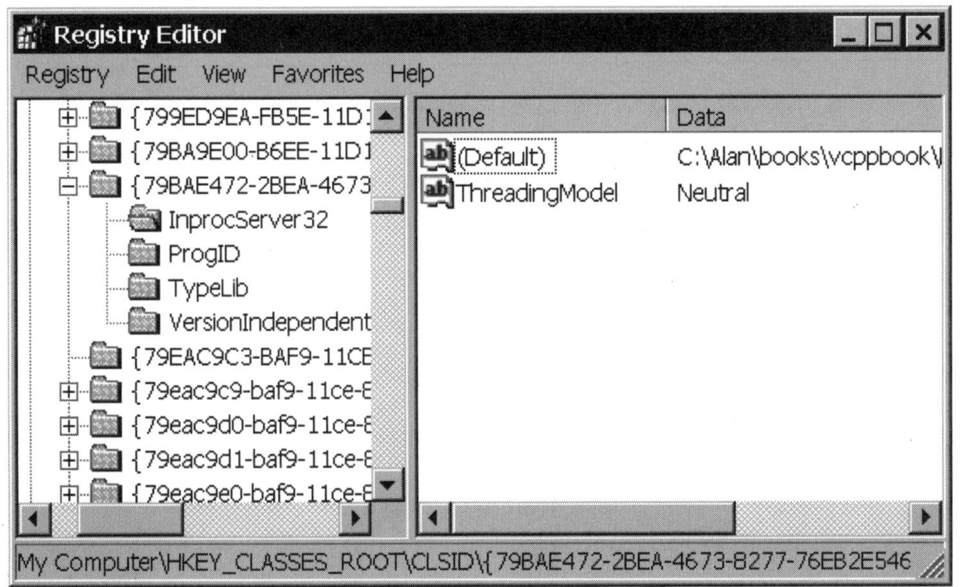

FIGURE 9.15 The Neutral-Threaded Class in the Registry.

file for a COM class to `Neutral` causes that class to be registered with the `Neutral` threading model as shown in Figure 9.15.

The COM runtime then makes sure that this class always runs in the Thread Neutral Apartment (TNA).

Remove Duplicate IThreadView Interfaces from the IDL

Unfortunately, the ATL Object Wizard is not smart enough to realize that you want all five of your COM classes to implement the same `IThreadView` interface. It creates five instances of the `IThreadView` interface in the IDL file for the `threaddemo` project. To fix this, go to the file `threaddemo.idl` by clicking on one of the `IThreadView` interfaces in the `ClassView` of the Visual C++ workspace and remove all but one of the declarations for `IThreadView`. When you are finished, the `threaddemo.idl` file should look as follows (of course your GUIDs will be different):

```
import "oaidl.idl";
import "ocidl.idl";
   [
      object,
      uuid(0663732D-314D-11D3-998A-E0EC08C10000),
```

```
      helpstring("IThreadView Interface"),
      pointer_default(unique)
   ]
   interface IThreadView : IUnknown
   {
      [propget, helpstring("property ThreadID")] HRESULT
ThreadID([out, retval] long *pVal);
   };

[
   uuid(06637321-314D-11D3-998A-E0EC08C10000),
   version(1.0),
   helpstring("threaddemo 1.0 Type Library")
]
library THREADDEMOLib
{
   importlib("stdole32.tlb");
   importlib("stdole2.tlb");

   [
      uuid(0663732E-314D-11D3-998A-E0EC08C10000),
      helpstring("SingleThreaded Class")
   ]
   coclass SingleThreaded
   {
      [default] interface IThreadView;
   };
   [
      uuid(06637330-314D-11D3-998A-E0EC08C10000),
      helpstring("ApartmentThreaded Class")
   ]
   coclass ApartmentThreaded
   {
      [default] interface IThreadView;
   };
   [
      uuid(06637332-314D-11D3-998A-E0EC08C10000),
      helpstring("FreeThreaded Class")
   ]
   coclass FreeThreaded
   {
      [default] interface IThreadView;
   };
   [
```

```
        uuid(06637334-314D-11D3-998A-E0EC08C10000),
        helpstring("BothThreaded Class")
    ]
    coclass BothThreaded
    {
        [default] interface IThreadView;
    };
    [
        uuid(79BAE472-2BEA-4673-8277-76EB2E546BB8),
        helpstring("NeutralThreaded Class")
    ]
    coclass NeutralThreaded
    {
        [default] interface IThreadView;
    };
};
```

Implement the IThreadView Interface in All Five COM Classes

Now you need to implement the `IThreadView` interface in each of your COM classes. To do this, perform the following steps in the Visual C++ development environment:

1. Right-click on the `IThreadView` interface in the `ClassView` tab of the Visual C++ Workspace (as shown in Figure 9.16).
2. Select `Add Property` from the `Context` menu (the Add Property to Interface dialog appears as shown in Figure 9.17).
3. Under `Property Type` select `Long`.
4. Enter `ThreadID` for the `Property` Name.
5. Clear the `Put Function` checkbox (you are creating a read-only property).
6. Click `OK`.

Visual C++ creates the following method to the `IThreadView` interface in the `threaddemo.idl` file as shown here:

```
interface IThreadView : IUnknown
    {
        [propget, helpstring("property ThreadID")] HRESULT
ThreadID([out, retval] long *pVal);
};
```

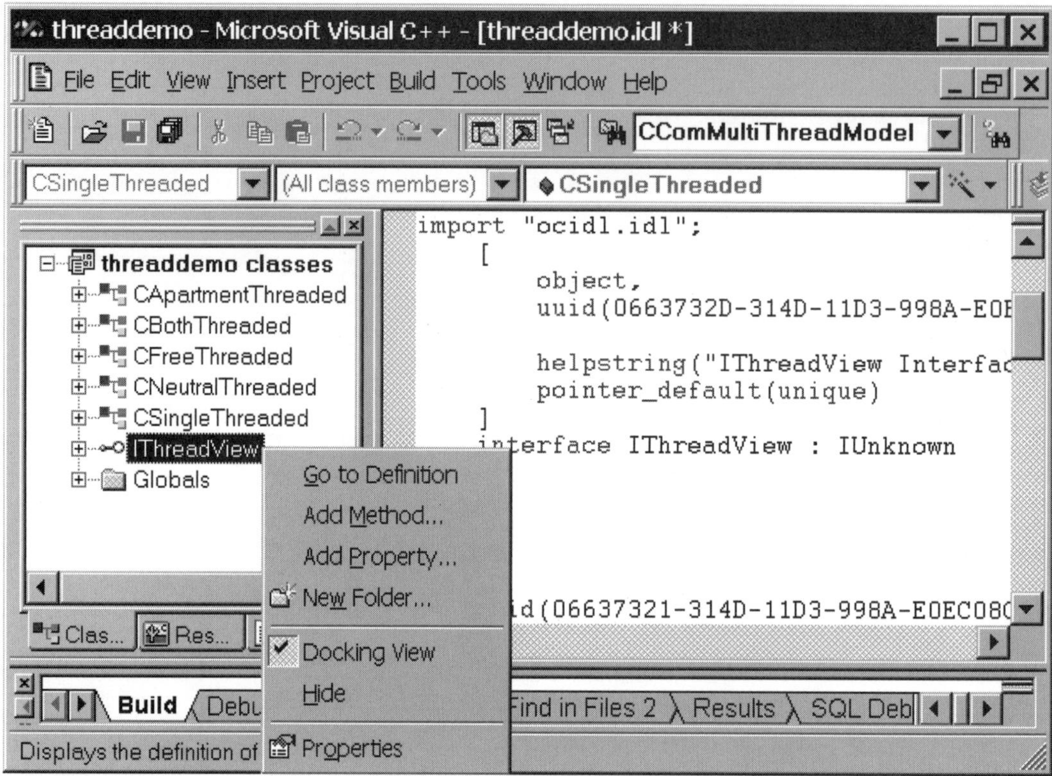

FIGURE 9.16 The IThreadView interface in the ClassView tab of Visual C++.

It also adds the following empty definition of the method to each implementation class as shown here:

```
STDMETHODIMP CApartmentThreaded::get_ThreadID(long *pVal)
{
   // TODO: Add your implementation code here

   return S_OK;
}
```

For each of the implementation classes, change the implementation so that it looks as follows:

```
STDMETHODIMP CSingleThreaded::get_ThreadID(long *pVal)
{
   *pVal=::GetCurrentThreadId();
   return S_OK;
}
```

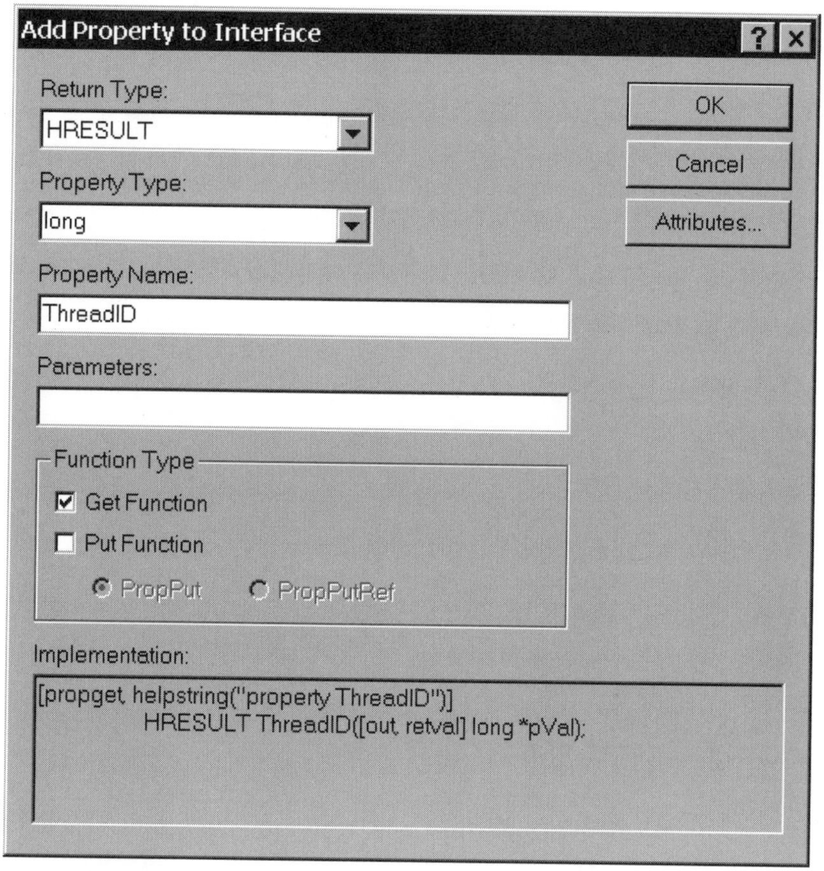

FIGURE 9.17 The Add Property to Interface Dialog.

Your implementation calls the `::GetCurrentThreadId` API function to retrieve the ID of the thread that is calling the COM object's method. You are now done with your server, so you can compile by pressing F7 and now build a client.

Create a Client

To create a client, you can perform these steps that are detailed in the following sections:

1. Create a dialog-based project using the MFC AppWizard.
2. Create the user interface.
3. Add a new object-creation dialog.
4. Import the type library for your server.

5. Implement the Create Object button.
6. Add the declaration needed to use `CoInitializeEx`.
7. Add an STA user-interface thread class.
8. Add an MTA user-interface thread class.
9. Implement the buttons on the main window dialog.

CREATE A DIALOG-BASED PROJECT USING THE MFC APPWIZARD

Start Visual C++ and perform the following steps:

1. Select `New...` from the `File` menu (the New dialog appears).
2. Click the `Projects` tab.
3. Select `MFC AppWizard` (exe) from the presented list of project types.
4. Enter `threaddemoclient` in the `Project` Name field.
5. Click `OK` (the MFC App Wizard will appear).
6. Click the radio button labeled: "`Dialog-based`".
7. Click `Finish` (the New Project Information dialog will appear).
8. Click `OK`.

CREATE THE USER INTERFACE

Your project will contain a dialog resource called `IDD_THREADDEMO-CLIENT_DIALOG` that will be used as the main window for your application. Using the Visual C++ resource editor, draw the two buttons shown in Figure 9.18 on this dialog.

Using the MFC class wizard, map button clicked (BN_CLICKED) message handlers to the two buttons on the main window dialog as specified in Table 9.5.

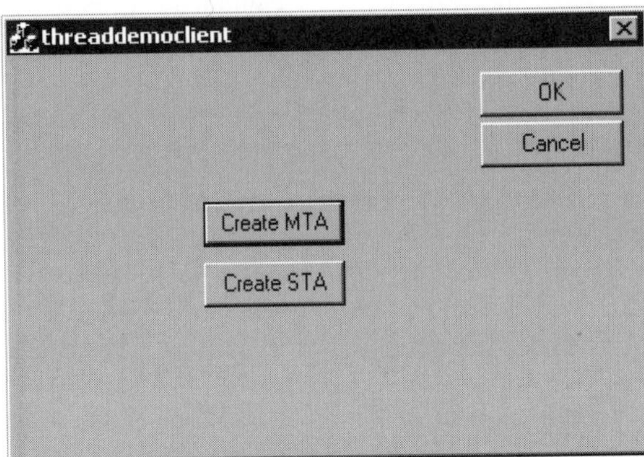

FIGURE 9.18

The Main Window of Your Client.

TABLE 9.5 Message Handler Methods

Button Caption	Message Handler for Button
Create MTA	OnCreateMtaButton
Create STA	OnCreateStaButton

If you gave your client project the name that I specified (`threaddemo-client`), the message handlers shown in Table 9.5 should be member functions of a class called `CThreaddemoclientDlg`.

ADD A NEW OBJECT-CREATION DIALOG

When you click either the Create MTA or Create STA buttons on the main window dialog, a second dialog appears that allows you to create either a `Single`, `Apartment`, `Free`, `Both`, or `Neutral-Threaded` object. To create this second dialog—the object-creation dialog—perform the following summarized steps:

1. Add a new dialog resource.
2. Draw the user interface.
3. Add a class for the new dialog resource.
4. Map message handlers and member variables to controls.
5. Add a Caption member variable.
6. Add a `WM_INITDIALOG` handler.

Add a New Dialog Resource • To create a new dialog resource, perform the following steps in the Visual C++ workspace:

1. Select `Resource...` from the `Insert` menu (the Insert Resource dialog appears as shown in Figure 9.19).
2. Select `Dialog` for the `Resource Type` and click the `New` button.

Drawing the User Interface • Double-click the new dialog in the resource tab of the Visual C++ workspace. Draw the user interface shown in Figure 9.20.

Static text controls with their sunken style property set are used to display the thread ID for the COM object and for the client window. Remove the default caption "static" from both of these controls. To map these static text controls to member variables you must change their resource ID from the default value, `IDC_STATIC`. Change the resource ID of the static text control that displays the window thread ID to `IDC_WINDOW_THREAD_STATIC`. Change the resource ID of the static text control that displays the object thread ID to `IDC_OBJECT_THREAD_ID_STATIC`. Also, for the threading model radio buttons to function correctly, you must select the Group property on the first radio button (the one labeled `Single`).

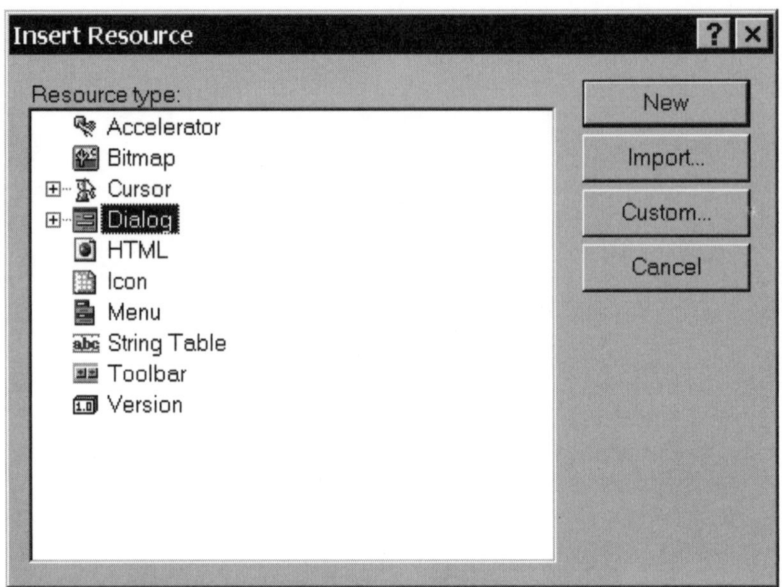

FIGURE 9.19 The Insert Resource Dialog.

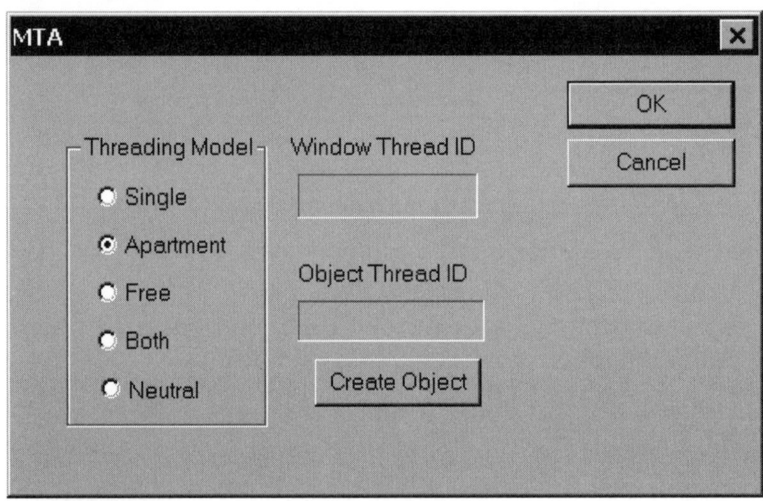

FIGURE 9.20 The Object Creation Dialog

Adding a Class for the Dialog Resource • To use your dialog, map a new CDialog-derived class to the dialog resource. To do this, perform the following steps:

1. While the dialog is displayed in the resource editor, press CTRL-W to bring up the ClassWizard (the Adding a class dialog appears).

2. Make sure that `Create a new class` is selected, and click `OK` (the New Class dialog appears).
3. Enter `CObjectCreationDialog` in the name field.
4. Click `OK`.

Mapping Message Handlers and Member Variables • Using the ClassWizard, map button clicked (BN_CLICKED) message handlers to the Create Object button and map member variables to controls on the window as outlined in Table 9.6.

TABLE 9.6 Mapping of Member Variables to Controls

Control Purpose	Map to member variable	Member variable type
Static text that displays the window thread ID	m_windowThreadID	CString
Static text that displays the object thread ID	m_objectThreadID	CString
Radio button for the object type	m_objectType	Int

Adding a Caption Member Variable • This dialog is displayed from either an STA or an MTA thread. You want the caption on the dialog to indicate which type of apartment the thread belongs to (STA or MTA). To do this, you need to add a member variable to the object creation dialog. Add the bolded lines of code to `objectcreationdialog.h` like this:

```
class CObjectCreationDialog : public CDialog
{
public:
   CObjectCreationDialog(CWnd* pParent = NULL);
void SetCaption(const char *caption);
// Code omitted for clarity...
private:
   CString m_caption;
};
```

Next, add the following code to `objectcreationdialog.cpp`:

```
void CObjectCreationDialog::SetCaption(const char *caption)
{
   m_caption=caption;
}
```

ADDING A WM_INITDIALOG HANDLER • Perform the following steps to add a handler for the WM_INITDIALOG Windows message that is fired right after a dialog is created, but before it is shown:

1. Press CTRL-W to bring up the ClassWizard.
2. Click the Message Maps tab.
3. Make sure that CObjectCreationDialog is selected under Class name.
4. Click CObjectCreationDialog under Object IDs.
5. Scroll down in the Messages list to WM_INITDIALOG and select this entry.
6. Click the Add Function button.
7. Click the Edit Code button.

Add the bolded lines to the OnInitDialog method in CObject-CreationDialog.

```
BOOL CObjectCreationDialog::OnInitDialog()
{
   CDialog::OnInitDialog();

   // TODO: Add extra initialization here
   SetWindowText(m_caption);
   m_windowThreadID.Format("%ld",::GetCurrentThreadId());
   UpdateData(FALSE);
   return TRUE;
}
```

The call to SetWindowText sets the titlebar of the dialog to the value that is passed to the SetCaption method. In this case, it is either MTA or STA. The next two lines cause the ID of the thread that the window is running to be displayed in the window thread ID static text control.

IMPORT THE TYPE LIBRARY FOR YOUR SERVER

You can use the native COM support in Visual C++ to build this client. To do this, you must import the type library of your server. Add the import statement to the stdafx.h file in your client project, then add the bolded code shown here to stdafx.h:

```
#import "..\threaddemo\threaddemo.tlb" no_namespace
```

The path shown above is correct on my machine. If you are following along with the steps in this example, you may need to change the path to the correct path on your machine.

IMPLEMENT THE CREATE OBJECT BUTTON

Add the following code to the handler for the create object button. Notice that you set a string variable equal to the programmer's ID of the selected object and then pass the programmer's ID to the `CreateInstance` method of your `IThreadViewPtr` smart pointer class. This works because all of your COM classes support the `IThreadView` interface. Add the following code to `CObjectCreationDialog::OnCreateObjectButton`:

```
void CObjectCreationDialog::OnCreateObjectButton()
{
   HRESULT hRes;
   CString objectType;
   long threadID;
   IThreadViewPtr threadView;
   UpdateData(TRUE);
   switch (m_objectType)
   {
   case 0:
      objectType="threaddemo.singlethreaded";
      break;
   case 1:
      objectType="threaddemo.apartmentthreaded";
      break;
   case 2:
      objectType="threaddemo.freethreaded";
      break;
   case 3:
      objectType="threaddemo.boththreaded";
      break;
   case 4:
      objectType="threaddemo.neutralthreaded";
      break;
   default:
      ASSERT(FALSE);
   }
   hRes=threadView.CreateInstance(objectType);
   if (FAILED(hRes))
   {
      _com_error err(hRes);
```

```
            AfxMessageBox(err.ErrorMessage());
            return;
        }
        try {
            threadView->get_ThreadID(&threadID);
            m_objectThreadID.Format("%ld",threadID);
            UpdateData(FALSE);
        }
        catch (_com_error err)
        {
            AfxMessageBox(err.ErrorMessage());
            return;
        }
    }
```

This logic instantiates the correct COM class (`Single`, `Apartment`, `Free`, `Both`, or `Neutral` threaded) based on the selection the user has made on the `Object Type` radio buttons in the `Object Creation` dialog.

ADD THE DECLARATION NEEDED TO USE CoInitializeEx

You can call `CoInitializeEx` to create your apartments. To use `CoInitializeEx`, you must be using a machine that is running Windows 2000, Windows NT 4, Windows 98, or Windows 95 with the DCOM add-on. The version of MFC in Visual C++ does not assume that you are on such a machine. Assuming that you are on a machine with one of these operating systems, you must add the bolded line shown here to `stdafx.h` before you can call the `CoInitializeEx` method:

```
#define VC_EXTRALEAN    // Exclude rarely-used stuff from Windows headers
#define _WIN32_DCOM
#include <afxwin.h>     // MFC core and standard components
#include <afxext.h>     // MFC extensions
#include <afxdisp.h>    // MFC Automation classes
#include <afxdtctl.h> // MFC support for Internet Explorer 4 Common
Controls
#ifndef _AFX_NO_AFXCMN_SUPPORT
#include <afxcmn.h>
```

ADD AN STA USER-INTERFACE THREAD CLASS

MFC's lets you create User Interface (UI) threads. These are threads that have a Windows message loop and display a GUI. You can use MFC's user interface threads to create a multi-threaded client that has a separate thread and apartment for each CreateObject dialog that is displayed. To create an STA, UI thread class, perform the following steps:

1. Create a CWinThread-derived class.
2. Implement the InitInstance method to enter an STA and then show the create object dialog.
3. Implement the ExitInstance method to call CoUninitialize.

Creating a CWinThread-Derived Class • To create a CWinThread-derived class, perform the following steps:

1. Press CTRL-W to bring up the ClassWizard.
2. Click the Add Class... drop-down button and select New (the New Class dialog appears).
3. Select CWinThread for the Base class.
4. Enter CSTAThread in the Name field.
5. Click OK.
6. Click OK again to close the ClassWizard.

Implementing the InitInstance Method • First, add the include file for the object creation dialog, objectcreationdialog.h near the top of the file stathread.cpp as shown here:

```
// STAThread.cpp : implementation file
//

#include "stdafx.h"
#include "threaddemoclient.h"
#include "STAThread.h"
#include "objectcreationdialog.h"
```

Next, add the bolded code shown here to the InitInstance method of CSTAThread:

```
BOOL CSTAThread::InitInstance()
{
    CObjectCreationDialog dlg;
    CoInitializeEx(0,COINIT_APARTMENTTHREADED);
    dlg.SetCaption("STA");
    m_pMainWnd=&dlg;
    dlg.DoModal();
    return TRUE;
}
```

In this code, you create an instance of the object creation dialog. Then you enter an STA and set the caption of the object creation dialog to STA. Next, set the main window of the UI thread to the object creation dialog and then display the dialog modally. This does not hang the main window because it is running in its own thread (that's the whole point of UI threads).

Implementing the ExitInstance Method • Add the bolded lines of code shown here to the `ExitInstance` method of `CSTAThread`:

```
int CSTAThread::ExitInstance()
{
   // TODO:  perform any per-thread cleanup here
   CoUninitialize();
   return CWinThread::ExitInstance();
}
```

ADD AN MTA USER-INTERFACE THREAD CLASS

Implementing an MTA, UI thread class is similar to implementing an STA UI thread class. The summarized steps are as follows:

1. Create a `CWinThread`-derived class.
2. Implement the `InitInstance` method to enter an MTA and then show the create object dialog.
3. Implement the `ExitInstance` method to call `CoUninitialize`.

Creating a CWinThread-Derived Class • To create a `CWinThread`-derived class, perform the following steps:

1. Press `CTRL-W` to bring up the ClassWizard.
2. Click the `Add Class...` drop-down button and select `New` (the New Class dialog appears).
3. Select `CWinThread` for the Base class.
4. Enter `CMTAThread` in the `Name` field.
5. Click `OK`.
6. Click `OK` again to close the ClassWizard.

Implementing the InitInstance Method • Add the include file for the object creation dialog, `objectcreationdialog.h` near the top of the file `mtathread.cpp` as shown here:

```
// MTAThread.cpp : implementation file
//

#include "stdafx.h"
#include "threaddemoclient.h"
#include "MTAThread.h"
#include "objectcreationdialog.h"
```

Next, add the bolded code shown here to the InitInstance method of CMTAThread.

```
BOOL CMTAThread::InitInstance()
{
   CoInitializeEx(0,COINIT_MULTITHREADED);
   CObjectCreationDialog dlg;
   dlg.SetCaption("MTA");
   m_pMainWnd=&dlg;
   dlg.DoModal();
   return TRUE;
}
```

In this code, you create an instance of the object creation dialog. Then enter the MTA and set the caption of the object creation dialog to MTA. Next, set the main window of the UI thread to the object creation dialog and then display the dialog modally. This won't hang the main window because it is running in its own thread (that's the whole point of UI threads).

Implementing the ExitInstance Method • Add the bolded lines of code shown here to the `ExitInstance` method of `CMTAThread`:

```
int CMTAThread::ExitInstance()
{
   CoUninitialize();
   return CWinThread::ExitInstance();
}
```

IMPLEMENT THE BUTTONS ON THE MAIN WINDOW DIALOG

To complete your server, you need to implement the buttons on your main window dialog, the `CThreaddemoclientdlg` class. First, you need to add the header files for your UI thread classes as shown here:

```
// threaddemoclientDlg.cpp : implementation file
//

#include "stdafx.h"
#include "threaddemoclient.h"
#include "threaddemoclientDlg.h"
#include "stathread.h"
#include "mtathread.h"
```

Add the bolded code shown here to threademoclientdlg.cpp:

```
void CThreaddemoclientDlg::OnCreateMtaButton()
{
   CWinThread* pThread=AfxBeginThread(RUNTIME_CLASS(CMTAThread));
}

void CThreaddemoclientDlg::OnCreateStaButton()
{
   CWinThread* pThread=AfxBeginThread(RUNTIME_CLASS(CSTAThread));
}
```

AfxBeginThread creates an instance of either the CMTAThread or CSTAThread class and creates a new thread and message loop.

Now your client is complete. Press F7 to compile.

Testing

With this application, you create an STA thread by clicking the Create STA button on the main window. You create an MTA thread by clicking the Create MTA button on the main window. Both buttons bring up the object creation dialog. The static text at the top of the object creation dialog contains the thread ID of the STA or MTA that the client thread is running in. To create an object with a particular threading model, select the desired threading model and then click the Create Object button. The static text above the create object button shows the ID of the thread that the object is running in. In this way, you can quickly see if an object is running on the same thread as its client. Because you only create 1 MTA thread in all of your tests, if the client and the object are running on different threads that indicates they are in different apartments.

For your first test, start the client and bring up three windows: 1 MTA and 2 STAs. Make sure you remember which STA window you created first, because this is the primary STA. Do not build or register the marshaling DLL yet. Now, try to create an object of each type from each window. You should see the results shown in Table 9.7.

TABLE 9.7 Test 1 Results

Threading Model	MTA Window	Primary STA Window	Second STA Window
Single	Marshaling Error	Object has the same thread ID as the client window.	Marshaling error
Apartment	Marshaling Error	Object has the same thread ID as the client window.	Object has the same thread ID as the client window.
Free	Object has the same thread ID as the client window.	Marshaling Error	Marshaling Error
Both	Object has the same thread ID as the client window.	Object has the same thread ID as the client window.	Object has the same thread ID as the client window.
Neutral	Marshaling Error	Marshaling Error	Marshaling Error

If the result for a particular threading model and thread type says: object has the same thread ID as the client window, that means the calling thread and the COM object are running in the same apartment. If the result shows a marshaling error, that means the client thread and the object are running in different apartments. Marshaling is required whenever an inter-apartment method call is made. To perform this marshaling, the COM runtime needs the marshaling DLL. If the marshaling DLL has not been built and registered, you will see the message box that is shown in Figure 9.21.

You receive the same message if you attempt to use an out-of-process server before you build and register its marshaling DLL. This demonstration should convince you that marshaling is required, even for an in-process server, if method calls are made across apartment boundaries. Notice the key difference between the `Neutral` and `Both` threading models. The `Both` threading model always works even when a marshaling DLL is not

FIGURE 9.21 Message Indicating that a Marshaling DLL is Required.

present because the `Both` threading model causes the object to be instantiated in the apartment of its creator. In contrast, the `Neutral` threading model always requires a marshaling DLL because a neutral object always runs in a different apartment (the TNA) than its calling thread. The lightweight proxy used by the TNA requires a marshaling DLL to work.

For your second test, build the marshaling DLL by executing the following command at a command prompt:

```
nmake threaddemops.mk
```

Then register the marshaling DLL by executing this command:

```
regsvr32 threaddemops.dll
```

Now rerun the same test you did above. You should see the results shown in Table 9.8.

TABLE 9.8 Test 2 Results

Threading Model	MTA Window	Primary STA Window	Second STA Window
Single	Object has the same thread ID as the primary STA window.	Object has the same thread ID as the client window.	Object has the same thread ID as the primary STA window.
Apartment	The Object has a different thread ID than all client windows.	Object has the same thread ID as the client window.	Object has the same thread ID as the client window.
Free	Object has the same thread ID as the client window.	The Object has a different thread ID than all client windows.	The Object has a different thread ID than all client windows.
Both	Object has the same thread ID as the client window.	Object has the same thread ID as the client window.	Object has the same thread ID as the client window.
Neutral	Object has the same thread ID as the client window.	Object has the same thread ID as the client window.	Object has the same thread ID as the client window.

Once again, if the result for a particular threading model and thread type says the object has the same thread ID as the client window, that means the client thread and the object are running in the same apartment. If the result says that object has a different thread ID than all client windows, that means the COM runtime had to create a new apartment for that object. This occurs, for instance, if you instantiate an object with `ThreadingModel=Apartment` from an MTA thread. The object with `ThreadingModel=Single` will always have the thread ID of the primary STA.

With this information and Table 9.8, you can summarize all the cases where direct or marshaled access is used for a COM object in Table 9.9.

TABLE 9.9 Apartment/Object Interactions

Threading Model	MTA	Primary STA	Other STA
Single	Marshaled	Direct	Marshaled
Apartment	Marshaled	Direct	Direct
Free	Direct	Marshaled	Marshaled
Both	Direct	Direct	Direct
Neutral	Marshaled	Marshaled	Marshaled

Summary

I'm sure that the preceding chapter was a lot to digest. As I mentioned earlier, most people don't understand COM apartments the first time they try to. If you are confused right now, the key is not to become discouraged. Read this chapter a second time. Yes, I know it's long, but read it again anyway. Also, read any other magazine articles or books that talk about apartments. Tom Armstrong has an excellent chapter on COM threading in Chapter 10 of his book *Active Template Library: A Developer's Guide*. George Sheperd wrote a fine pair of articles on apartments in the February/March and April/May 1999 editions *of Visual C++ Developers Journal*, http://www.vcdj.com. Read them all. Now it's time to move on to Distributed COM.

TEN

Distributed COM

I, at one time, recall seeing a review on Amazon's Web site of a Distributed COM (DCOM) book. The reader lamented that "90% of this book is about COM" and gave the book a fairly low score. The book was probably better than the reader gave it credit for, because 90% of DCOM *is* COM. If you understand the previous nine chapters of this book (okay, chapters 1-8, since many of you will be chewing on Chapter 9 for a while), then you understand 90% of DCOM. This chapter is about teaching you the other 10%. Most of that 10% is concerned with security. If a COM client is using a COM object that is located on the same machine, there is little need for security beyond the operating-system level security enforced when you login. But if you make a COM server available to a client connecting over a network, then you make all of the information that the server may return available to anyone who contacts the server. You most likely need some way to validate the identity of the client who is making the request and bar completely or restrict the things that certain users are allowed to do. If you are developing a client who will use a COM object located on a different machine then you will be sending potentially sensitive information over a network—possibly a wide-area network—where it can be viewed or altered by hackers. You need some way of keeping that information secure. Distributed COM provides you with this functionality and more.

In this chapter you will first learn about the importance of DCOM. While DCOM is important, it only addresses some of the problems associated with building distributed applications. Next, you will revisit the related topics of location transparency and marshaling. DCOM does introduce some changes and additional complexity in these areas. Then, you will tackle the subject of security. This section is—by far—the largest in this chapter. Finally, you can create your example for this chapter, see how to configure a COM server for distributed use, and explore the performance penalty associated with using a COM server from across a network.

The Importance of DCOM

Distributed COM (DCOM) is that part of COM concerned with enabling COM-based software components to be used over a network. In a nutshell, this means that DCOM lets you put a COM server on one machine and have it used by a client on a different machine. At first that may not seem like a big deal, but it actually represents a fundamental change. Until Windows NT 4.0 was released, COM was a desktop, application integration technology. NT 4.0 contained the first release of DCOM, and with the release of this new technology COM became a distributed technology. This prompted a fundamental shift in the entire focus of COM. Before DCOM, most of the focus of COM was on ActiveX Controls (which were called OLE Custom Controls at that time) and Compound Documents. Most books and magazine articles written about COM covered these topics (especially controls). After DCOM was introduced, most of the books and magazines about COM discussed distributed processing. The reason is simple, once you allow COM clients and servers to communicate with each other across a network, a whole new world opens up. There is only so much you can do with one PC but when you can get two, three, four, or even dozens of PCs to work together and share information, you can begin to consider problems that you could not tackle before. You can start building enterprise-class applications that people can use to run their businesses, the kinds of applications that in the not too distant past could only run on mainframe or midrange computers.

Unfortunately, building enterprise class applications introduces new problems, some of which are addressed by DCOM and some are not. Let's take security as an example. Most businesses do not want just anyone to have access to their business-related information: customer and employee information for instance. So if you want this data to be easily shared among the people in your organization who *should* have access to it, then you need security. You need the ability to restrict certain individuals from accessing the information while allowing others to use it. DCOM provides this functionality.

However, distributed processing and building enterprise-class applications (which is the main, but not the only, goal of distributed processing) also requires scalability and data-integrity. Scalability means the application should be able to handle simultaneous use by hundreds or even thousands of users. Data-integrity means that updates to data-stores must be made in a consistent way (data must not be corrupted, updates must not be lost, and invalid intermediate states must not be allowed to propagate through the system) even in the face of simultaneous use by numerous users. DCOM does not provide this functionality; COM+ and Microsoft Transaction Server (MTS) do. These technologies are built on top of DCOM. Understanding DCOM, therefore, is important if you are to understand COM+ and MTS. The good news is that everything you have learned about COM so far carries forward into DCOM. DCOM adds two additional complexity factors to COM: security and performance. These two factors, especially security, are responsible for the additional complexity that arises once I start talking about DCOM.

Location Transparency Revisited

In Chapter 6, I discussed location transparency and you learned that COM has a piece of software called the Service Control Manager (SCM), which is affectionately referred to as the SCUM. The SCUM is the key to implementing location transparency. When a client makes an object activation request (via the `CoCreateInstance` function, for instance), the SCUM is called to locate the object. The SCUM takes the CLSID that is passed to `CoCreateInstance` and searches for its key beneath `HKEY_CLASSES_ROOT\CLSID\` in the system registry. When the SCUM finds the key in the registry it searches for either an `InprocServer32` or a `LocalServer32` key. If it finds `InprocServer32`, it loads the DLL identified in the default value for the key into the client process. If it finds a `LocalServer32` key, it starts up the executable and establishes an Inter-Process Communication (IPC) link between the client and the server. In the case of a remote server, there is neither a `LocalServer32` or `InprocServer32` key. Finding neither of these, the SCUM next searches for the following key in the registry:

```
HKEY_CLASSES_ROOT\AppID\
```

AppID

This registry key is called an application ID, or simply an AppID. There is one AppID per server. Even if a server has multiple COM classes, all those classes share a single AppID. Beneath this AppID is stored security-related information for a server and a key called `RemoteServerName`. The

`RemoteServerName` key identifies a remote machine where the server can be found. The value at this key can be either an IP address or the Domain name of the remote machine on which the server is resident. An example AppID is shown below:

```
HKEY_CLASSES_ROOT\AppID\{B296C342-1307-11D3-998A-74EE08C10000}
\RemoteServerName="MyServer"
```

This key indicates that the COM class with CLSID `{B296C342-1307-11D3-998A-74EE08C10000}` may be instantiated on the server called `MyServer`. If the SCUM finds this key, it contacts the SCUM on the remote machine and requests that this machine start the server and return a proxy. The SCUM on the remote machine first verifies that the requesting user is authorized to use this server (I talk about how this works in the section entitled Security). It then starts up the remote server (assume that it is an executable for now, but it doesn't have to be), sets up a stub in the server process, and returns a proxy to the client. After the client has the proxy, all further communication occurs directly between the proxy and the stub as shown in Figure 10.1.

Because both the client machine and the server machine require marshaling support, the marshaling DLL must be installed and registered on both machines if the COM server implements custom interfaces. If the serv-

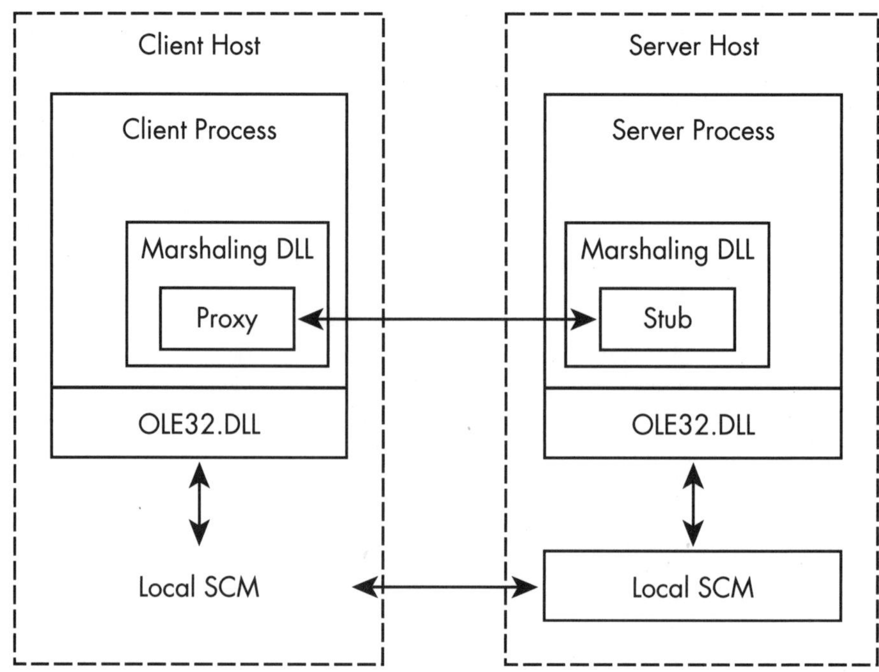

FIGURE 10.1 DCOM's Implementation of Location Transparency.

er only implements standard interfaces, marshaling support is provided by `ole32.dll`. If the server implements only Automation interfaces, marshaling support is provided by `oleaut32.dll`. In both of these cases, you do not need a server-specific marshaling DLL.

You can also start a server on a remote machine by calling CoCreateInstanceEx, which accepts a COSERVERINFO structure that lets you specify either the domain name or IP address of a remote server. You can learn how to use this function when you implement your example for this chapter.

Marshaling

In Chapter 6, I discussed marshaling. Marshaling lets you make function calls across processes. The idea is that you have a piece of software that runs in the client process called a proxy and a piece of software that runs in the server process called a stub as shown in Figure 10.1.

When you call a COM Instantiation method like `CoCreateInstance` or `CoGetClassObject` or pass a COM interface pointer to a COM method, the COM runtime sets up a stub in the server process and returns a proxy to the client if it determines that marshaling is required. The COM runtime makes this determination by looking at the implementation of the server. If the server is a remote or local out-of-process server or if the client and the server have incompatible threading models, marshaling is required.

The proxy that the COM runtime returns to the client looks exactly like the interface pointer the client requested from the server. When the client calls methods in the proxy, the proxy takes the method call and turns it into a stream of bytes. Encoded in this stream of bytes is the name of the method the client wishes to call and the parameters it wishes to pass to the method. This stream of bytes is then sent to the stub, which interprets the message, calls the requested method, and sends the return value back to the client.

The only thing that has to change to enable COM to be distributed is that you must be able to send the stream of bytes across machines. When the COM runtime sets up a proxy for a local, out-of-process server, COM uses Local Remote Procedure Calls (LRPC) to send this stream of bytes across processes on the same host. When you are using a remote server, COM instead uses Distributed Computing Environment (DCE) Remote Procedure Calls (RPC). DCE RPC lets you send the stream of bytes that represents the method call across machine boundaries. It also has built-in support for security that DCOM leverages.

DCE RPC is a standardized, distributed application development technology that pre-dates COM.

Security

The single most important issue that DCOM adds to COM is security. Before I talk about security in the context of COM, it is useful to give a quick introduction to Windows NT/2000 security in general.

NT Security

One of the main differences between Windows 95/98 and Windows NT/2000 is the latter's support for security. NT's security support centers on its use of user accounts and groups.

USER ACCOUNTS AND GROUPS

To log on to Windows NT/2000, you must have a user account. Each user account has a user name, a password, and a Security IDentifier (SID) associated with it. A SID is similar to a GUID in that it is a unique identifier. Instead of identifying a COM class or interface, a SID identifies a user account. Two different user accounts may have the same user name, agordon for instance, but each account has a unique SID. User accounts can be created or removed, and passwords for user accounts can be changed using the User Manager in Windows. Figure 10.2 shows the Windows 2000 User Manager.

Often a system administrator wants to refer to a group of users as one. User groups lets you collect users together into a single entity you can assign permissions to. For instance, you may want to give everyone working on a certain project the right to read from a particular directory. Rather than having to give each user one-by-one the necessary permissions, you can add all the users to a group and then grant permissions to the entire group. You also create and maintain groups with the user manager.

You must be logged on as an administrator to create or change a user account or group.

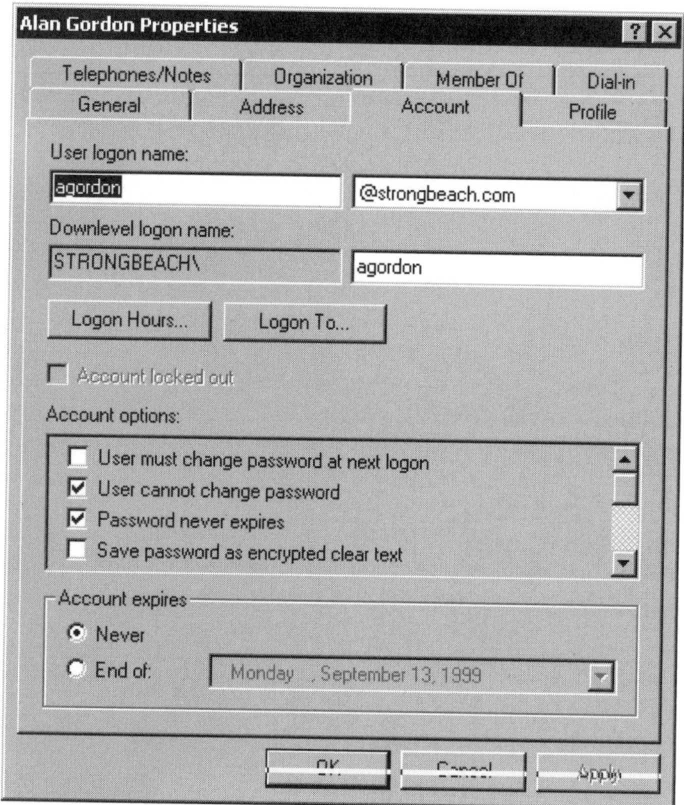

FIGURE 10.2 The Windows 2000 User Manager.

DOMAINS

If you have a network with several machines, you may want to log on to any of those machines using the same user name and password. If you didn't know any better, you could create accounts on each machine and assign the same user name and password to each account thus allowing you to log onto your machines with the same user name and password for a while. But, each of these accounts is considered to be a separate account by the operating system (each account has a unique SID). So if you decide to change your password, you would have to change it on each of those machines. Obviously, this is an unworkable situation. Over time it's difficult to keep the information in each of these accounts consistent. What you really need is to have one machine on your network act as a central repository for user account information. Then, when you attempt to log onto any machine on your network, the local machine would contact this central repository machine and request that it validate your user name and password. If this machine is able to validate you as a user, it would instruct the local machine to grant you access. With this scheme, you could log onto any machine on your network using a single account. If you ever need to change your password, you simply change it in one place.

Windows 2000 and Windows NT lets you designate one machine on your network to be a central repository for user account information; this machine is called a *Primary Domain Controller*, or *PDC*. A *Domain* is a logical grouping of machines that share a PDC; this allows them to be managed as a unit. Many of you may have a single Windows NT or Windows 2000 machine that is not connected to a network. A single standalone machine defines a domain by itself. If you have a real domain (more than one machine), you can configure a machine on your network to be a Backup Domain Controller (BDC) and a client on your network can use the BDC if the PDC is down or busy.

A machine must be running Windows 2000 Server, Windows NT Server, or higher to be a PDC or a BDC. With Windows NT 4.0, you had to configure your server as a PDC or BDC when you first installed the operating system. With Windows 2000, you can promote a machine to a PDC, BDC, or demote it at any time.

DEFINE RELATIONSHIPS BETWEEN DOMAINS

Large organizations typically have multiple domains. If an organization has several geographically dispersed offices they may have a separate domain for each location. This makes it easy for local administrators to manage the local network. It's quite possible that users in one domain may need access to shared directories, printers, or even machines on another domain so trust relationships can be established between these domains. If Domain A trusts Domain B, then a person with a user account in Domain B may be able to log onto a machine or use other resources in Domain A.

ACTIVE DIRECTORY

Designing the Domain topology for a large organization can be complicated and that's why Active Directory exists. Active Directory is a Directory Service that organizes user information and shared resources, such as printers, into a tree-like hierarchy in much the same way that information is organized on the Internet. You can run the Active Directory Service on Windows NT 4.0, but it is an integrated part of Windows 2000. I won't talk a great deal about Active Directory in this chapter. Entire books can—and will—be written about it. I discuss the Active Directory more in Chapter 11 when I begin talking about COM+.

Security Tokens

When a user logs into a Windows 2000/NT machine, the user gets a security token. This token contains the SID of the user's account and the SID of all the group accounts the user belongs to. Every process the user starts after they login carries this security token. Whenever a process that the user has started attempts to use some resource (this resource may be a file, directory, or COM component), the operating system uses the security token to verify that the user has permission to use that resource. The operating system does this by comparing the SIDs in the security token with a Discretionary Access Control List (DACL) that is associated with the resource.

DACL

A DACL contains a list of Access Control Entries (ACEs). An ACE contains the SID of a user or group and some type of access that is either granted to

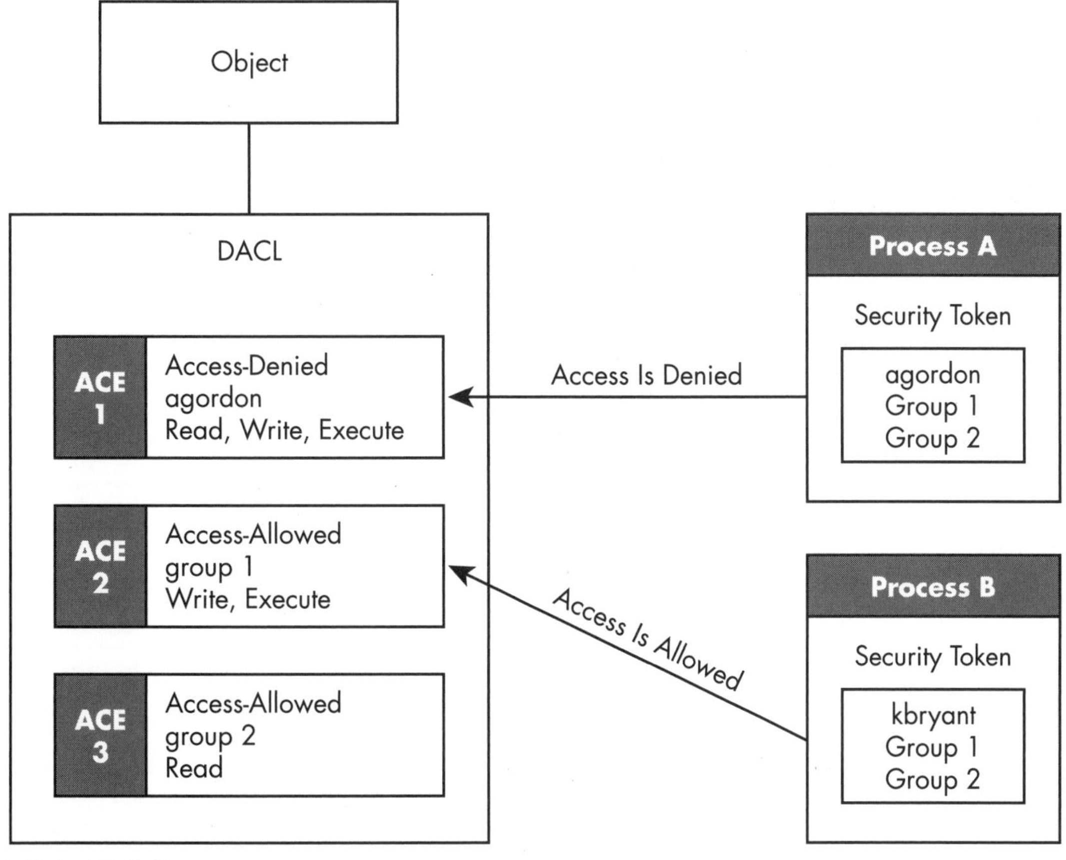

FIGURE 10.3 A DACL.

that SID in the case of an access-allowed ACE, or denied in the case of an access-denied ACE. An example DACL is shown in Figure 10.3. Notice that this DACL contains three ACEs. ACE 1 is an access-denied ACE that denies read, write, and execute access to the user agordon.

Access-denied ACEs always appear first in a DACL.

ACE 2 allows write and execute access to any user in group 1. ACE 3 allows read access to any user in group 2. When process A attempts to access the object associated with this DACL, access is denied because the security token for Process A contains the SID for the user agordon and the DACL for the object contains an access-denied ACE for agordon. Process B, however, is allowed access to the object. The security token for process B contains the SID for group 1. The DACL for the object has an access-allowed entry that grants access to group 1.

The read, write, and execute privileges shown here are not the only kinds of access rights that are available. There are dozens of generic access rights that are defined in the Windows API and you can also define custom ones. Table 10.1 shows a small sampling of the generic access rights available.

TABLE 10.1 Example Access Control Entries

Access Right	Description
GENERIC_READ	Read Access
GENERIC_WRITE	Write Access
GENERIC_EXECUTE	Execute Access
GENERIC_ALL	Read, write, and execute Access

A DACL is created and modified in various dialogs. Figure 10.4 shows the DACL associated with a file on my computer displayed on the Security tab of the property sheet that appears when you elect to view the properties of the file.

The access rights that you can grant or deny for a file are: Full Control, Modify, Read and Execute, Read, and Write. Later in this chapter you will see there are DACLs associated with a DCOM server. You can define which users are allowed to Launch, Access, and Configure your DCOM server through these DACLs. You can view and edit these DACLs using a tool called `dcomcnfg` or you can view or edit the DACLs programmatically.

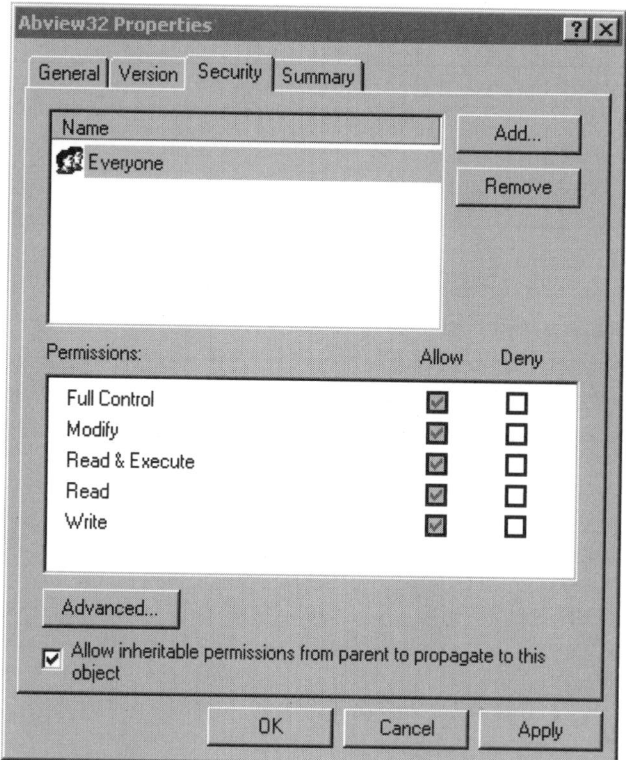

FIGURE 10.4 The DACL for an NTFS File.

Security Support Providers

Much of the security support provided by Windows NT/2000 depends on the operating system being able to accurately determine the identity of a user. This is called *authentication*. With Windows 2000 or NT, a user typically sits down at a client machine that is part of a Domain and types in his user name and password. The operating system must now send this information to the PDC so the user can be authenticated. This is not as simple as you might think. You certainly would not want the user's password to be sent as clear text over the network, and you would like the authentication algorithm to impose a minimum amount of network bandwidth and processing overhead.

Windows 2000/NT delegates the job of authenticating a user (and all other security-related checks) to a piece of software called a Security Support Provider (SSP). The `Win32` API defines a security API called the Security Support Provider Interface (SSPI) that the SSP implements. The SSP is simply a DLL that provides the methods specified in the SSPI. The idea was that third parties could create their own specialized SSPs that implement the SSPI. NT 4.0 comes with one SSP, either the NT LAN Manager or NTLM. Under NTLM, the authentication of a user is carried out as follows:

1. The PDC sends a large random number to the client. This is called a *challenge.*
2. The client uses the encoded password of the user to encrypt the challenge.
3. The encrypted challenge is sent back to the PDC. This is called the *response.*
4. The server uses what it believes is the encoded password of the client user to encrypt the original challenge. If the server's encrypted challenge matches the response sent by the client, the user is authenticated.

Notice in this scheme that authentication is performed using the user's password, but the password is never sent over the network.

Windows 2000 gives you a choice of SSPs and each of these uses a different algorithm for authentication. New SSPs available in Windows 2000 include: Kerberos, SChannel, and DCE. The default SSP is actually a pseudo-SSP called Simple GSS-API Negotiation Mechanism (Snego). Snego is not an SSP itself; it is a protocol that allows the client and server to negotiate with each other to choose either NTLM or Kerberos for their SSP. The snego protocol chooses Kerberos if it is supported by both the client and the server, otherwise it chooses NTLM. You can explicitly select an SSP using either the `CoInitializeSecurity` API function or the `SetBlanket` method of the `IClientSecurity` interface. You will learn more about these later in this chapter.

COM Security

Now that you have a basic understanding of the security features that Windows 2000 and Windows NT provide, I can bring this discussion back to DCOM. When you are running a COM client and server on the same machine, the only security needed is that which is required to prevent unauthorized users from logging into the machine. Once you start running your clients and servers on separate machines, you need several different forms of protection. First you need *authentication*. That means you must be able to determine in an accurate and un-subvertible way, the identity of the user who is attempting to use your COM server. Once that is determined, the next thing you need is *access control* based on identity. You may want to give some users full access to your COM server, others may have access to only certain features, but would be restricted from using others, and to other users you would want to deny access completely. You also need *security token management*. Some of the issues involved here are: with whose security token should a COM server process run? Should it run with the client's security token, the security token of whomever is logged in to the server at the moment, or perhaps some other token? You also may or may not want the server to be allowed access to the security token of the client.

There are other security-related issues that you must handle and many of these are communications related. They are issues that arise because you are sending information over a public wire. For instance, if a COM client is sending information to you from across a network, you may want to verify that someone hasn't intercepted the network packets along the way and altered their contents. In other words, you need some way to guarantee the *integrity* of the data that is sent to and from the server.

You may also want *privacy*. There is some information that a client either sends to a server or receives from a server that you do not want anyone who may be snooping on the network to see. You want to encrypt the information being sent from the client to the server and vice versa. DCOM's security features let you do all of these things. You can configure the level of authentication for your server, control access to it, manage the security tokens associated with your server, and decide whether you want DCOM to guarantee the integrity and privacy of all communications between the client and server in two ways: via the registry or programmatically.

DCOM SECURITY CONFIGURATION VIA THE SYSTEM REGISTRY

The registry contains both a system-wide default value for each security-related configuration setting and a server-specific value. The system-wide defaults can be found at the following registry key:

```
HKEY_LOCAL_MACHINE\Software\Microsoft\Ole\
```

Figure 10.5 shows the values at this registry key on the machine that I am currently writing on. These registry values are usually configured using a tool called `dcomcnfg`.

DCOMCNFG • You can find `dcomcnfg` in the system directory on a Windows 2000 or Windows NT machine (on most machines the system directory is `c:\winnt\system`). You must be a system administrator to use `dcomcnfg`. This should make sense to you. You wouldn't want any user to be able to alter security-related information. You can run dcomcnfg by performing these steps:

1. Click the `Windows Start` button.
2. Select `Run...` (the Run dialog appears).
3. Type `dcomcnfg` into the `Open edit` box.
4. Click `OK`.

The default (Applications) tab of `dcomcnfg` looks like that shown in Figure 10.6.

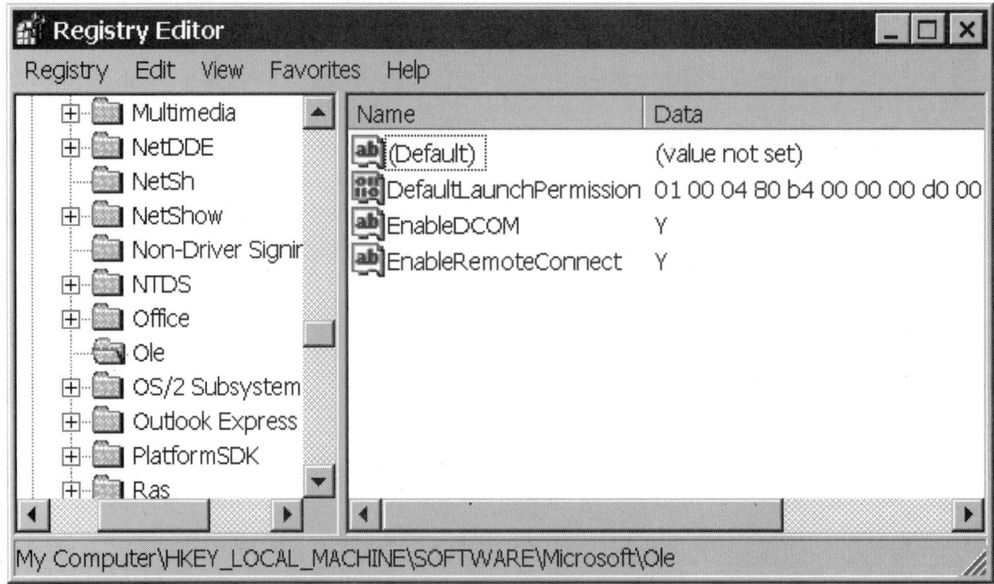

FIGURE 10.5 The DCOM-Related, System-Wide Defaults.

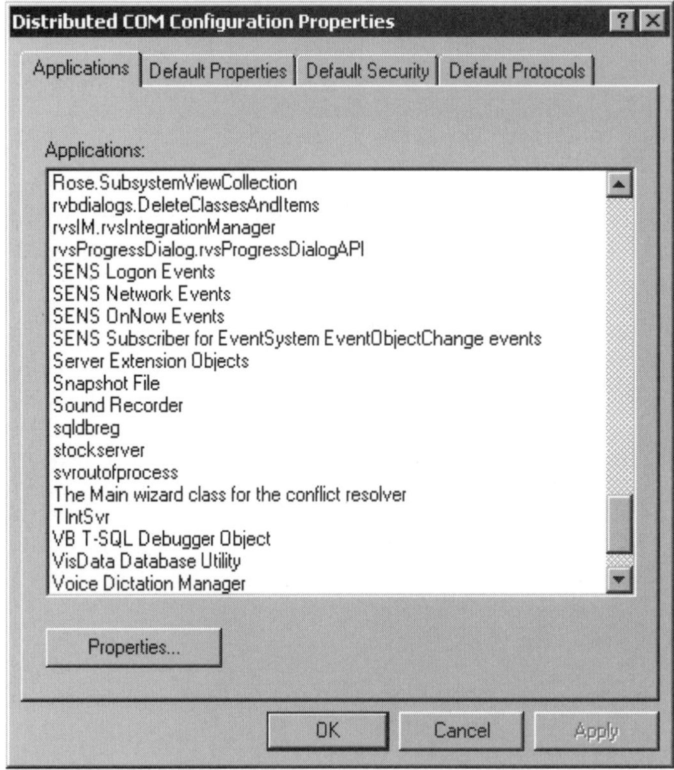

FIGURE 10.6

The Applications Tab of Dcomcnfg.

If you are not an administrator, you will see a dialog that warns you that you must be an administrator to run `dcomcnfg`. The listbox on the Applications tab displays the human-readable identifier for each COM server that is registered on your machine. You can configure server-specific DCOM parameters by selecting a server in this listbox and then clicking the `Properties...` button. You will then see a tabbed dialog that allows you to configure DCOM-related parameters for a specific server as shown in Figure 10.7.

Server-specific settings override system-wide default settings. You can configure the system-wide defaults on the Default Properties and Default Security tabs of `dcomcnfg`. A major weakness of `dcomcnfg` is that the finest granularity at which you can configure security settings is per server. This is because `dcomcnfg` writes to the AppID for a server, it does not

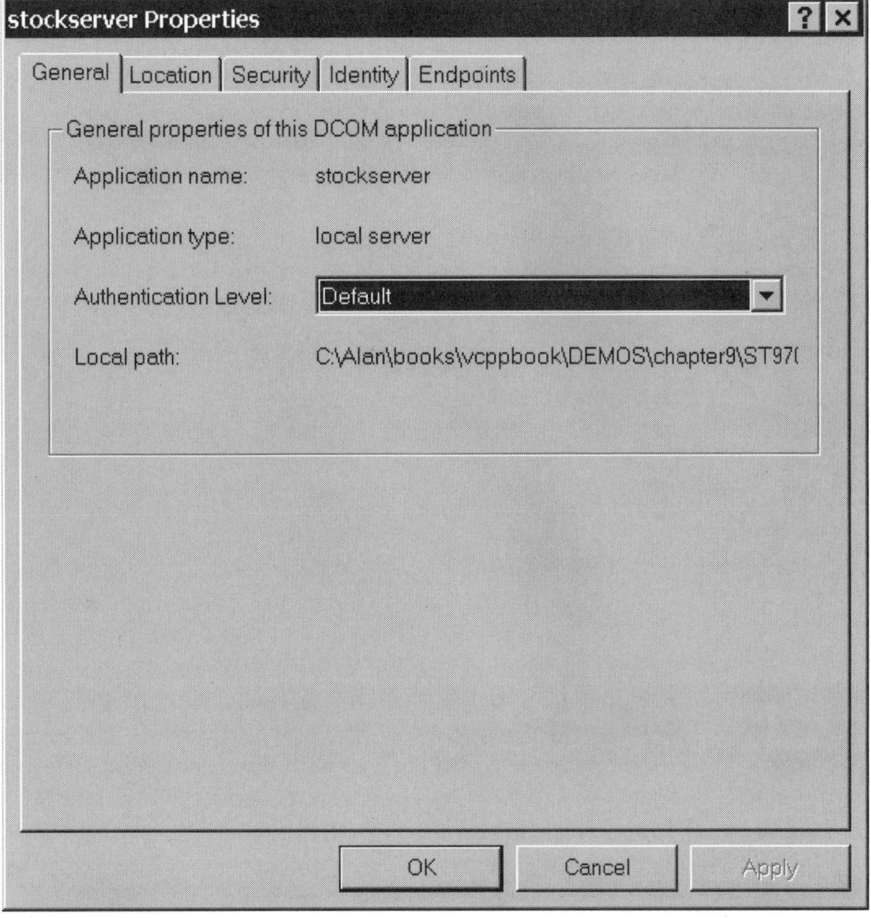

FIGURE 10.7 The Server-Specific Properties Dialog in Dcomcnfg.

write to the CLSID for each class in the server. If you want to configure different security settings for each class or even each method in a server, you must use programmatic security. I discuss the specific steps required to set both the system-wide, default DCOM configuration and the server-specific DCOM configuration as I discuss authentication, access control, security token management, integrity, and privacy in the following sections.

PROGRAMMATIC DCOM SECURITY CONFIGURATION

You can also configure security for a DCOM server programmatically. The keys to this are the `CoInitializeSecurity` COM API function, security blankets, and the `IClientSecurity` and `IServerSecurity` interfaces. `CoInitializeSecurity` lets you set programmatically all the parameters you can configure with `dcomcnfg`. You do not have to call `CoInitializeSecurity` if you don't want to, but if you don't, the COM runtime will read the DCOM-related security settings in the registry and call `CoInitializeSecurity` for you, passing in the registry settings. A security blanket is COM's name for the set of security-related parameters that are being used by a client or server. The `IServerSecurity` interface lets you adjust the security settings (the security blanket) for a server on a per-interface or per-method basis. `IClientSecurity` lets you adjust the security blanket for a client on a per-interface or per-method basis. I talk more about programmatic security later in this chapter, I first need to discuss exactly how one goes about setting the authentication, access control, security token management, integrity, and privacy configuration both at a system-wide level and for a specific server using `dcomcnfg`.

Authentication

In the context of this discussion, authentication basically means verifying that the users are who they say they are. How this verification is done depends on the Security Support Provider that is in use. The COM runtime uses the services of the SSP to authenticate the user. In most cases, both the client and the server machine must have access to the client user's account information (remember under the challenge and response algorithm both the client and the server encrypt a large random number using the user's password). That means that to perform authentication, you must be running on a network with a Domain and a PDC. It is not sufficient to have one account on the server with a particular name like jsmith and then have another account on the client with the same name. These two accounts are considered to be different accounts and have different SIDs. For authentication to work, you must be able to share user account information between the client and server. This should make sense; you cannot authenticate users unless you have access to their account information.

You cannot perform authentication with DCOM unless you have a domain controller. That does not mean you cannot use DCOM without a domain controller. Later in this section I discuss how you can use a DCOM server either on a network without a domain controller, or where the client is not logged in to a domain account. Essentially, you have to turn off authentication.

DCOM supports different levels of authentication. These levels affect how often the system authenticates the user. You can only validate users when they first connect to the server. But there is a danger that someone could start spoofing the server after the connection is made. At the most secure level, you can perform authentication on each network packet that is sent between the client and server. The more authentication you perform, the higher the price you pay in terms of performance. There are five authentication levels that can be set. Table 10.2 summarizes these and gives a description for each of them.

TABLE 10.2 DCOM Authentication Levels

Authentication Level	Description
None	No authentication will be done. You can use this setting for performance reasons, but usually you use this setting if you want to allow users who cannot be authenticated to use a DCOM server; for instance, if you are on a network that does not have a domain controller or if users who do not have domain accounts want to use the server.
Call	Authentication is performed on the first packet of each COM request or response.
Connect	Authentication is performed only when the client first connects to the server.
Default	Same as Connect.
Packet	Authentication is performed on each packet that is sent between the client and server.
Packet Integrity	Everything Packet level does, plus DCOM verifies using a checksum that the packet has not been altered in transit.
Packet Privacy	Everything Packet Integrity level does, plus DCOM encrypts each packet that is sent between the client and the server.

The last two authentication settings provide the means to guarantee the *Integrity* and the *Privacy* of all communication between the client and the server. They also significantly degrade the performance of your application because they require that the SSP perform operations on the data in every packet that is sent between the client and server.

You can set the system-wide default authentication level on the default properties tab of dcomcnfg as shown in Figure 10.8. You can configure the authentication level for a particular server by selecting a server on the Applications tab of dcomcnfg and then clicking the Properties... button. The General tab of the server properties dialog allows you to set the authentication level for a particular server as shown in Figure 10.9.

The authentication level can be configured on both a client machine and a server machine. Neither a client nor its server has complete control of the authentication level that is used between them. The authentication level that a particular client uses when it talks to a particular server must be negotiated. To understand why this is so, consider what would happen if the server could unilaterally decide the authentication that should be used. Imagine that you had a client whose system-wide authentication level was set to packet privacy. A server that was satisfied with Connect level authentication could overrule the client's request for encrypted communication. The same thing works in the other direction. If the client had complete control over the authentication level, a client whose authentication level was

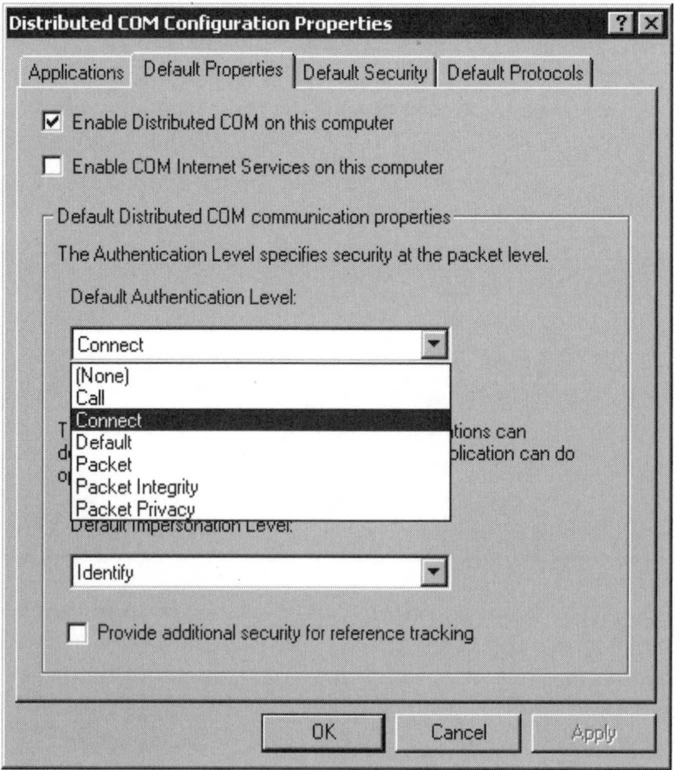

FIGURE 10.8 Setting the Default Authentication Level.

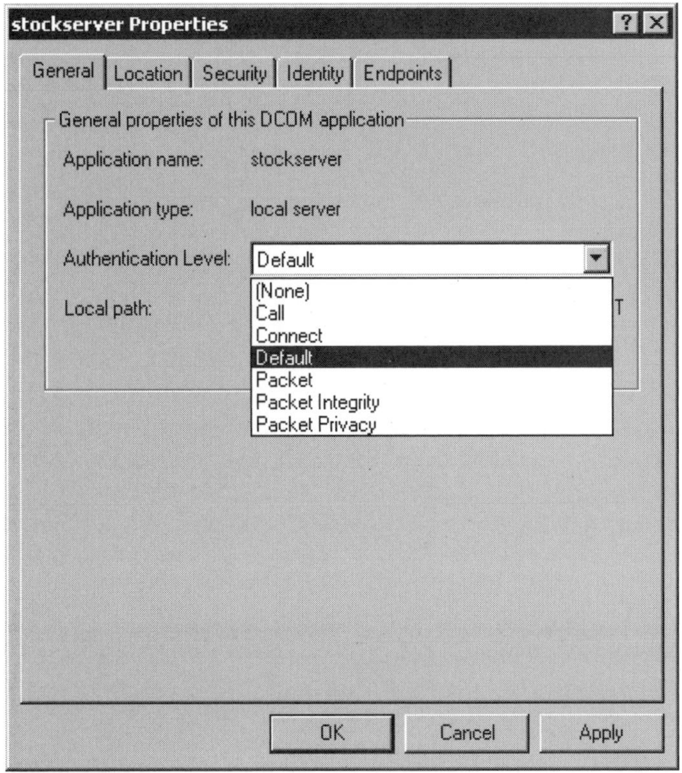

FIGURE 10.9 Setting the Authentication Level for a DCOM Server.

Connect could override a server that desired packet privacy. The DCOM authentication level that is set on any machine is called its *low-water mark*. The authentication level on a client and server is treated by the COM run-time as the lowest authentication level that the host accepts. The actual authentication level that is used between a DCOM client and server is:

```
Max(client,server)
```

So, if the client is configured for Connect level authentication and the server is configured for Packet level authentication, Packet level is used.

Access Control

Once you determine who the user of a COM server *is*, the next thing needed is the ability to restrict the things that a user is allowed to *do*. Some users can be allowed to do almost anything with the COM server. Others may have very limited access. You can set a system-wide set of default access permissions or you can set the access permissions on a per-server basis.

Using `dcomcnfg`, you can configure the system-wide access control default using the Default Security tab of `dcomcnfg`. On this tab, you can set permissions for Access, Launch, and Configuration as shown in Figure 10.10.

ACCESS

The access permission specifies who can use the services of a COM server assuming that the server process has been already launched. In other words, who is allowed to use a COM server that is already running. If you click the `Edit Default...` button on the Default Security tab of `dcomcnfg` as shown in Figure 10.10, you see a DACL similar to the one shown in Figure 10.11.

Using the DACL editor window shown in Figure 10.11, you can add users to, or remove users from the list of users authorized to Access a COM server. The type of access drop-down allows you to specify that a user is allowed or denied access. Each user that you add in this list either adds an access-allowed or access-denied ACE to the Access DACL. You can add individual users or groups to the DACL. As with all permissions, the default is

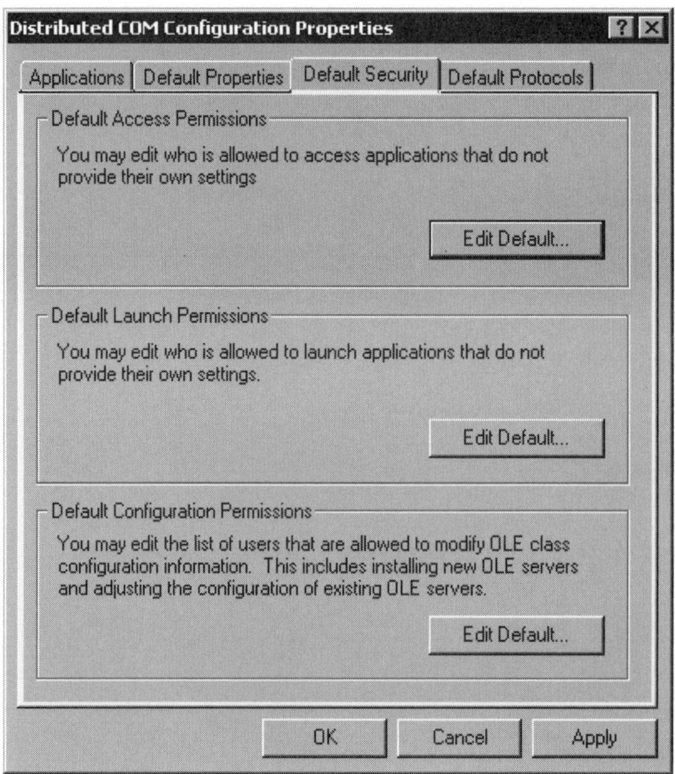

FIGURE 10.10 Setting the Access Control Permissions Using Dcomcnfg.

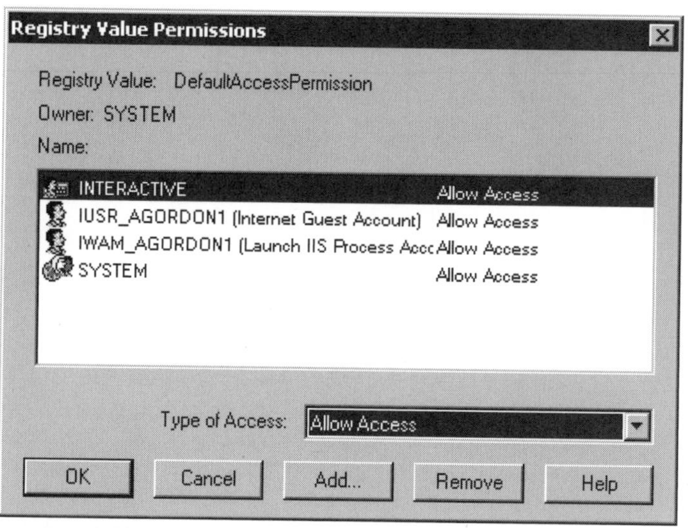

FIGURE 10.11 The DACL for Access Permissions.

only used if you do not specify permissions for a specific server. The default access permissions can be found in the registry under the following key:

```
HKEY_LOCAL_MACHINE\software\Microsoft\OLE\DefaultAccessPermission
```

You can configure the access permissions for a specific server by performing the following steps:

1. Start `dcomcnfg` (you should see the window shown in Figure 10.6).
2. Select the server in the `Applications` tab of `dcomcnfg`.
3. Click the `Properties...` button (the server properties dialog appears see Figure 10.7).
4. Click the `Security` tab (your window should look like that shown in Figure 10.12).
5. Click the `Use custom access permissions` radio button (the edit... button should enable).
6. Click the `Edit...` button (the DACL editor appears see Figure 10.11).
7. Add and remove users using the DACL editor.

Server-specific access permissions can be found under the following key in the registry.

```
HKEY_CLASSES_ROOT\AppID\{ServerAppID}\AccessPermission.
```

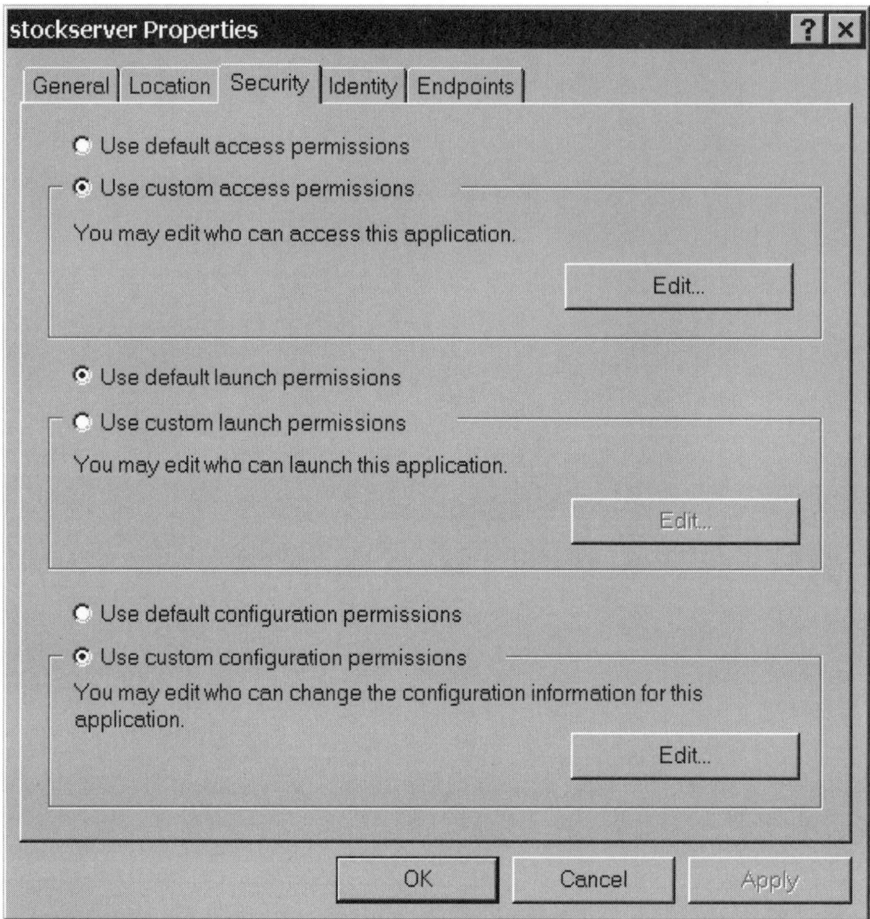

FIGURE 10.12 The Security Tab of the Server-Specific DCOM Properties Dialog.

When you bring up the DACL editor for either the access, launch, or configuration permissions you will see 2 interesting users: the Network user and the System user. In the DACL editor, if you click the `Add...` button you will see the Add Users and Groups dialog and there you can see the description of both of these users as shown in Figure 10.13.

The description for the Network user is "Users accessing this object remotely." The description for the System user says "The operating System." You have to add the System user to the list of users allowed access to a server for the server to be accessible remotely. This is necessary because the Service Control Manager must have access permission to start and use the server.

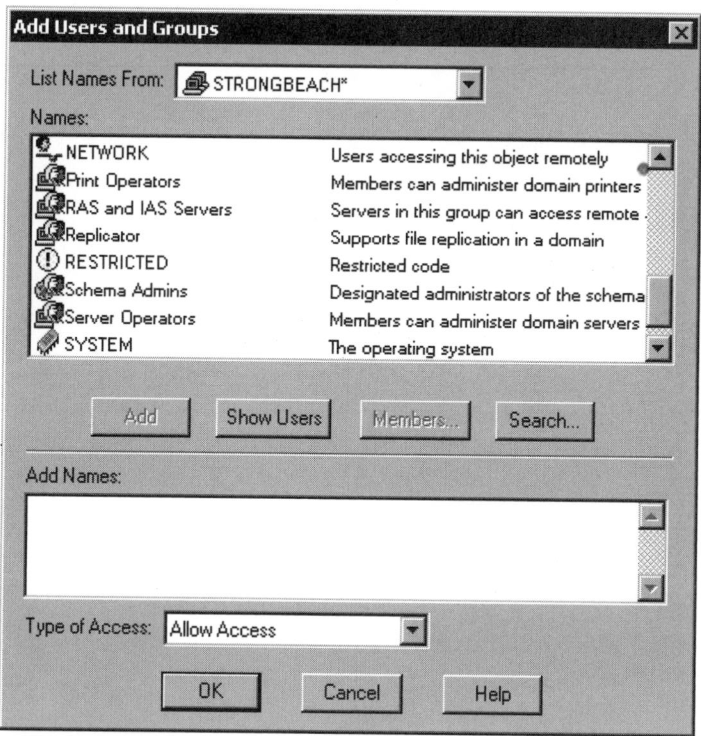

FIGURE 10.13 The System and Network Users.

LAUNCH

The launch permission specifies who can cause an instance of the server process to be launched. It's a little difficult to understand why there are separate Access and Launch permissions, but consider the case of a multi-use COM class. All instances of this class run in the same instance of the server process, assuming you haven't selected Launching User for the RunAs setting (more on this later). If the server process is not already running, an activation request causes the server process to be started and then a COM object is created and accessed. In this scenario, a user must have both Launch and Access permissions to use the server. However, if the server is already running, then an activation request does not cause the server process to be launched. So the user only requires Access permission. I actually tried this out while I was writing this chapter. I created a server with a multi-use class and installed and registered it on a remote machine. I configured one user (Alan) to have both Access and Launch permissions. I configured a second user (Mike) to have only Access permissions. Sure enough, Mike could create an object only if Alan created one first (thus launching the server process). If Alan had not launched the server process, Mike would receive an Access Denied error. A COM class that is Single-Use starts up a new server process each time an Activation request is received. You must grant both Access and Launch Permissions to users for them to use this type of COM class.

In most practical situations, the list of users that you give Access permissions to will be the same as the list of users that you give Launch permissions to. If you are using Authentication (i.e., both the client and server have something other than "None" for their Authentication setting), I recommend that you grant Access Permission to the system user and all the individual users and groups that wish to use your server. Then add the same users and groups to the Launch permissions. If you are not using Authentication, you can simply grant Access Permissions to the System user and Launch Permissions to the Network user. The default launch permissions can be found in the registry under the following key:

```
HKEY_LOCAL_MACHINE\software\Microsoft\OLE\DefaultLaunchPermission
```

You can edit this key using `dcomcnfg` by performing these steps:

1. Start `dcomcnfg`.
2. Select the `Default Security` tab.
3. Click the `Edit Default...` button under Default Launch Permissions (the DACL editor appears).
4. Add and remove users using the DACL editor.

You can configure the launch permissions for a specific server by performing the following steps:

1. Start `dcomcnfg`.
2. Select the server in the `Applications` tab of `dcomcnfg`.
3. Click the `Properties...` button (the properties dialog appears).
4. Select the `Security` tab on the server properties dialog.
5. Click the `Use custom launch permissions` radio button.
6. Click the `Edit...` button (the DACL editor appears).
7. Add and remove users using the DACL editor.

Server-specific launch permissions can be found under the following key in the registry:

```
HKEY_CLASSES_ROOT\AppID\{ServerAppID}\LaunchPermission.
```

CONFIGURATION

The configuration permission specifies who is allowed to perform system administration procedures (such as changing the Access and Launch permissions) on a DCOM server. You can edit the default configuration permissions using `dcomcnfg` by performing these steps:

1. Start `dcomcnfg`.
2. Select the `Default Security` tab.
3. Click the `Edit Default...` button under Default Configuration Permissions (the DACL editor appears).
4. Add and remove users or change the type of access using the DACL editor.

The type of access drop-down on the DACL editor for Configuration Permissions contains three possible settings: Read, Full Control, or Special Access... The read permission specifies that a particular user is only allowed to see the configuration for a server. Full Control means the user can read or write the security settings. Special Access... brings up the dialog shown in Figure 10.14 that allows a system administrator to configure permissions in a more selective way. You can set the configuration permissions for a specific server by performing the following steps:

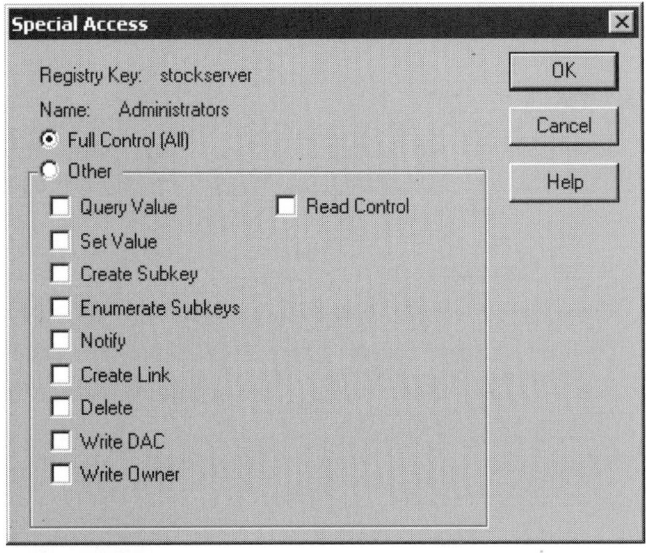

FIGURE 10.14 Special Access Configuration Permissions.

1. Start `dcomcnfg`.
2. Select the server in the `Applications` tab of `dcomcnfg`.
3. Click the `Properties...` button (the server properties dialog appears).
4. Select the `Security` tab on the properties dialog.
5. Click the `Use custom configuration permissions` radio button.
6. Click the `Edit...` button (the DACL editor appears).
7. Add and remove users or change the type of access using the DACL editor.

Security Token Management

There are several DCOM configuration-related parameters that are related to identity. This is sometimes referred to as security token management or just token management. Token management is concerned with the who in regard to DCOM. I mentioned earlier in this chapter when I talked about NT security that every process must run with the security token of some user. If a server process is running on a remote machine on behalf of a user on a client machine, under whose security token should this server process run? And if that server process has to use a resource, such as a file, whose security token should the process use to open the file? There are two DCOM settings that address these issues: Identity and Impersonation. The Identity setting specifies whose security token a server process runs with. The Impersonation setting specifies whether the server is allowed to use the client's security token to gain access to system resources.

IDENTITY

The identity setting is configured only on a per-server basis in dcomcnfg. There is no system-wide default. You can configure the identity that a server will run by performing the following steps:

1. Start `dcomcnfg`.
2. Select the server in the `Applications` tab of `dcomcnfg`.
3. Click the `Properties...` button (the properties dialog appears).
4. Select the `Identity` tab on the properties dialog (the dialog appears as shown in Figure 10.15).
5. Select a user.

There are three possible identity settings: Interactive User, Launching User, or This User. These values are stored in the registry under the following key:

```
HKEY_CLASSES_ROOT\AppID\{ServerAppID}\RunAs\
```

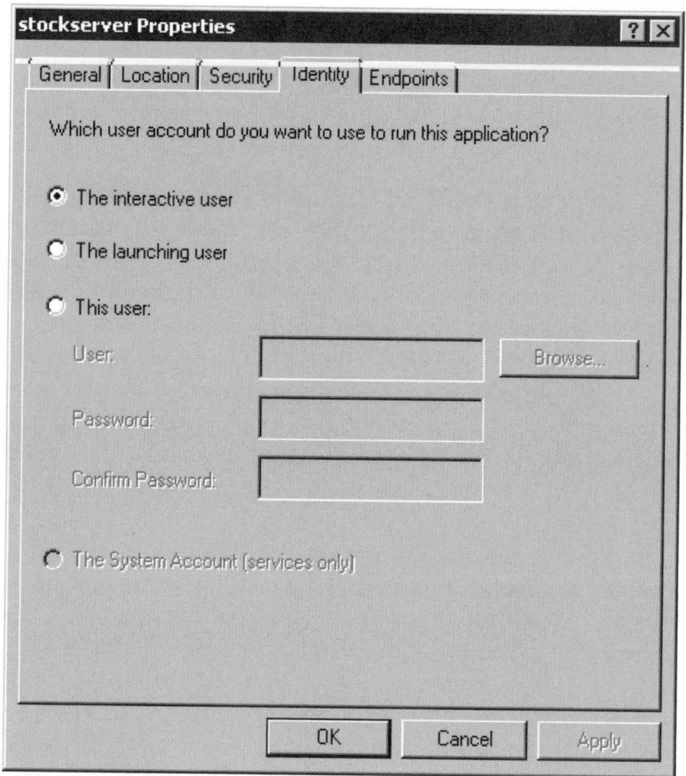

FIGURE 10.15 Configuring Identity Using Dcomcnfg.

If the Interactive User setting is selected, the RunAs registry key contains the value Interactive User. If This User is selected, the key contains the user name of the selected user. If Launching User is selected, the key is empty.

INTERACTIVE USER • The Interactive User setting specifies that the DCOM server will run using the security token of the user who is currently logged in on the server machine. In most cases, this is not a good setting to use. The biggest problem with this setting is that it will not work if someone is not currently logged in. Using this setting also means that you won't know the permissions that the DCOM server runs with; it runs with the permissions of whoever is logged in. If the logged-in user is a system-administrator, the server could do some potentially dangerous things. There is one big advantage to using the Interactive User setting. Only with this setting can you cause a window to appear on a remote machine. Usually this is not a big deal because in most cases it really doesn't make sense to bring up a window on a remote machine. But there are some cases where you want to do this—a chat application is a good example. Another example is for pedagogical purposes. When I am covering DCOM in my class, I usually pre-install and configure a DCOM server that has a user interface on several of my students machines. I then surprise the students by popping up windows on their machines as I discuss the topic. This certainly isn't a practical use for this setting, but it is a use nonetheless.

LAUNCHING USER • The Launching User setting causes the server to run with the security token of the client user. In most cases Launching User is also a bad setting. There are a number of problems with this setting. First, the server must actually be able to authenticate the client. This may not be possible if the client and server are not on the same domain. Second, since the server is running with the client's identity, the client user must have permissions to access any resources that the server may use. This is not necessarily a bad thing, but it does make system administration more complicated. Third, using the Launching User also causes problems with classes that are multi-use. If a COM server is configured to run as the Launching User, the server process for an object runs with the security token of the user who activated the object. Imagine that user agordon creates an instance of a multi-use class. If this is the first instance that agordon created, then a server process is started and that server process runs with the security token for agordon. Now imagine that user kbryant comes along and attempts to create an instance of this multi-use class and the existing process is running with agordon's security token. The Launching User setting means that kbryant's object must run in a process with kbryant's security token, so a new server process must be started. This runs counter to the intended operation of a multi-use class (all instances should share the same process) but it is consistent with the Launching User Identity setting.

THIS USER • In most cases, you want to use This User as the Identity setting for your DCOM servers. Under this setting you explicitly specify the name of a user whose security token the DCOM server will run with. To use this setting, you must have the password of the specified user to enter it into dcomcnfg. The advantages of this setting are that: (1) You always know the identity that the server will run with, so it is easy to configure access for the resources (files etc...) that the server will use, and (2) Multi-use classes will work as expected (all instances of the class will run within the same server process).

IMPERSONATION

Another permission that is related to security token management is impersonation. Unlike the other settings, which are really specified for the server, this setting is specified on the client, and states what things the server can do with the security token of the client. You specify this setting on the default properties tab of `dcomcnfg` as shown in Figure 10.16.

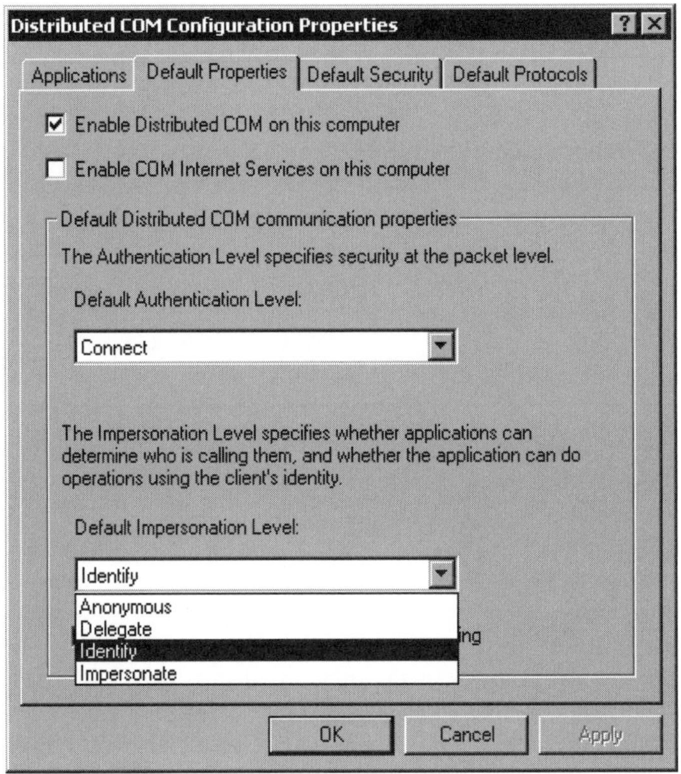

FIGURE 10.16 Configuring Impersonation Using Dcomcnfg.

There are four possible values for this setting: Anonymous, Delegate, Identify, and Impersonate. The anonymous setting means that the server cannot determine the identity of the client. The delegate setting means the server can use the client's security token to make a connection to another remote machine. This setting is not supported under Windows NT 4.0. It is supported under Windows 2000 thanks to the Kerberos Security Support Provider. The Identify setting allows the server to use the client's security token only to determine the identity of the client. The Impersonate setting allows the server to impersonate the client. This means that the server can assume the client's identity before it accesses a particular resource to check if the user has the required permissions to use that resource.

Miscellaneous Security Settings

There are three other security settings you can configure using `dcomcnfg`. These settings do not fall neatly into any category so it makes sense to group them together under miscellaneous. These three settings can all be found on the default properties tab of dcomcnfg (see Figure 10.16). There you will find three checkboxes: (1) enable Distributed COM on this computer, (2) enable COM Internet Services on this computer, and (3) provide additional security for reference tracking. Enable Distributed COM on this computer is self-explanatory. You have the option of disabling DCOM on any machine by clearing this checkbox. Enable COM Internet Services lets a client communicate with a server using HTTP as the network protocol. This is useful to get around firewalls, at least until firewall manufacturers figure out how to thwart it. Provide additional security for reference tracking is an interesting setting. It is possible—unlikely, but still possible—that someone could attempt to thwart a DCOM client and server by forcing a call to the server's Release function, potentially causing the server to deactivate. When you enable reference tracking, you are requesting that distributed AddRef and Release calls be authenticated by COM. COM keeps track of per-user reference counts so a user can call Release only on objects that he previously called AddRef on.

Programmatic Security

In most situations, you can configure a COM server that you wish to run remotely using dcomcnfg. Some situations may arise where dcomcnfg is not sufficient, however. Perhaps the biggest problem with dcomcnfg is that it only allows you to configure security on a per-server basis. You cannot configure the security for your server on a per-class, per-interface, or a per-method basis.

The ability to configure the security settings for a server on a per-class, per-interface, or per-method basis is called fine-grained security.

For instance, the PKT_PRIVACY authentication setting should be used when you need to encrypt all the information to be sent between a DCOM client and server. Unfortunately, this setting causes your server to run slowly. Imagine that you were using a DCOM server that has three interfaces with a total of 20 methods. Imagine that 19 of those methods do not accept sensitive information, but one does. Suppose you have an EnterInfo method in an interface called ICreditCard that allows you to enter the credit card number and expiration date of a credit card. You probably want this information to be encrypted when it is sent over the wire, but there is no need to incur the performance penalty associated with encrypting the other 19 methods. If you were using dcomcnfg to setup this server, you would have no choice but to set the Authentication level for the entire server to packet privacy. Another example where using dcomcnfg alone is not sufficient is if the server wishes to impersonate the client user for the length of a method call. I talked about how you could get the server to run as the client all the time using the Launching User setting under dcomcnfg. I also said that in most cases using this setting is a bad idea. Even though you may not want your server to run as the client *all* the time, you may want the server to run using the client's security token *some* of the time. If you wish to do something like this, you must use programmatic security.

The keys to the COM programmatic security API are the CoInitializeSecurity function, Security Blankets, and the IServerSecurity and IClientSecurity interfaces.

COINITIALIZESECURITY

CoInitializeSecurity is a COM API function that lets you specify the same settings that you configured using dcomcnfg. A DCOM client or a server that wishes to use programmatic security may call CoInitializeSecurity. CoInitializeSecurity should be called only once per process. It should be called after you call CoInitialize, but before you make any other interesting COM API call—for example, a call to CoCreateInstance qualifies as interesting.

If you do not call CoInitializeSecurity explicitly, the COM runtime calls the function when you make your first interesting COM function call. COM passes the values in the registry to CoInitializeSecurity. If server-specific values are configured in the registry for things such as authentication and access control, then the COM runtime passes these values to CoInitializeSecurity. If not, the COM runtime reads the system-wide defaults from the registry and passes these to CoInitializeSecurity.

CoInitializeSecurity is declared as shown below:

```
HRESULT CoInitializeSecurity(
[in] PSECURITY_DESCRIPTOR pSecDec,
[in] LONG cAuthSvc,
[in] SOLE_AUTHENTICATION_SERVICE *rgAuthSvc,
[in] void *pReserved1,
[in] DWORD dwAuthLevel,
[in] DWORD dwImpLevel,
[in] void *pReserved2,
[in] DWORD dwCapabilities,
[in] void *pReserved3
};
```

Table 10.3 describes the meaning of each of the function's parameters. Some of the parameters are used only if the calling application is a DCOM server and some are used if the calling application is a DCOM client. Table 10.3 also indicates which parameters are used by a client or server.

TABLE 10.3 CoInitializeSecurity Parameters

Parameter	Used by	Description
pSecDec	Server	Specifies who is allowed to use the objects exported by this server. This parameter can either be NULL, in which case all users are granted access, or you can pass an IAccessControl interface pointer. If you do pass an IAcessControl interface pointer, you must pass EOAC_ACCESS_CONTROL for the dwCapabilities parameter (see the sidebar about the IAccessControl interface below).
cAuthSvc	Server	The number of entries in the next parameter, the rgAuthSvc array. Or this value can be –1, in which case rgAuthSvc array must be NULL.
rgAuthSvc	Server	This parameter is an array SOLE_AUTHENTICATION structures that specifies which security providers are used for incoming calls. Outgoing calls may use any security provider installed on the machine.
PReserved1	Neither	Reserved for future use.
DwAuthLevel	Both	The low-water authentication level. The actual authentication level used between a client and server will be max(client,server). Possible values for this parameter are: RPC_C_AUTHN_LEVEL_DEFAULT, RPC_C_AUTHN_LEVEL_NONE, RPC_C_AUTHN_LEVEL_CONNECT, RPC_C_AUTHN_LEVEL_CALL, RPC_C_AUTHN_LEVEL_PKT, RPC_C_AUTHN_LEVEL_PKT_INTEGRITY, RPC_C_AUTHN_LEVEL_PKT_PRIVACY.
DwImpLevel	Client	Specifies what the server is allowed to do with the client's security token. Possible values for this parameter are: RPC_C_IMP_LEVEL_ANONYMOUS, RPC_C_IMP_LEVEL_IDENTIFY, RPC_C_IMP_LEVEL_IMPERSONATE, RPC_C_IMP_LEVEL_DELEGATE.
PReserved2	Neither	Reserved for future use.
DwCapabilities	Both	A bitmask that allows you to specify miscellaneous settings. Possible values are EOAC_NONE, EOAC_MUTUAL_AUTH, EOAC_SECURE_REFS, EOAC_ACCESS_CONTROL, EOAC_APPID.
PReserved3	Neither	Reserved for future use.

Use the IAccessControl Interface

`CoInitializeSecurity` allows you to programmatically specify all of the information that you would otherwise specify with `dcomcnfg`. One of the main things that `dcomcnfg` lets you specify is who is (or isn't) allowed to use a particular server. The `IAccessControl` interface lets you build a list of users and groups that will be allowed or disallowed access to a server. There is a system-provided access control object that implements the `IAccessControl` interface. You can instantiate this object by calling `CoCreateInstance` and passing in `CLSID_DCOMAccessControl` for the CLSID as follows:

```
IAccessControl *pAccess;
HRESULT
hr=CoCreateInstance(CLSID_DCOMAccessControl,0,CLSCTX_ALL,IID_IAcces
sControl,(void**)*pAccess);
```

You can now build an access control list that grants access and launch privileges to the users agordon and kbryant in the Engineering domain as follows:

```
ACTRL_ACCESS_ENTRYW pAces[] = {
{ {0, NO_MULTIPLE_TRUSTEE, TRUSTEE_IS_NAME, TRUSTEE_IS_USER,
L"Engineering\\agordon}, ACTRL_ACCESS_DENIED, COM_RIGHTS_EXECUTE,
0, NO_INHERITANCE},
{ {0, NO_MULTIPLE_TRUSTEE, TRUSTEE_IS_NAME, TRUSTEE_IS_USER,
L"Engineering\\kbryant}, ACTRL_ACCESS_DENIED, COM_RIGHTS_EXECUTE,
0, NO_INHERITANCE}
};
ACTRL_ACCESS_ENTRY_LISTW acl = { sizeof(pAces)/sizeof(*pAces),
pAces };
ACTRL_PROPERTY_ENTRYW ape = { 0, &acl, 0 };
ACTRL_ACCESSW aa = { 1, &ape };
hr=pAccess->SetAccessRights(&aa);
hr=CoInitializeSecurity(pAccess,-1,
0,0,RPC_C_AUTHN_LEVEL_PKT,RPC_C_IMP_LEVEL_IDENTIFY,0,EOAC_ACCESS_CO
NTROL,0);
```

SECURITY BLANKET

The current set of security-related settings that are in effect for a process or a particular interface proxy is called a security blanket. A security blanket consists of these settings:

- Authentication service
- Authorization service
- Principal name

- Authentication level
- Impersonation level
- Authentication identity
- Capabilities
- An ACL (servers only)

Notice that this list consists of the same parameters that can be specified in `CoInitializeSecurity`. So when you call `CoInitializeSecurity`, you are really setting the default security blanket for all COM interfaces that will be imported (in the case of a client) and exported (in the case of a server) from a process. You can alter the security blanket on a per-class, per-interface, or per-method basis using the `IClientSecurity` interface.

Obviously someone thought it was cute to use the term Security Blanket. At the risk of sounding like a curmudgeon, I think it's just another example of confusing names making it more difficult to understand an already difficult technology.

ISERVERSECURITY

The server uses `IServerSecurity` to query the security parameters in the client's security blanket or to impersonate the client. The `IServerSecurity` interface is declared as follows:

```
Interface IServerSecurity : IUnknown {
   HRESULT QueryBlanket(
      [out] DWORD  *pAuthnSvc,
      [out] DWORD  *pAuthzSvc,
      [out] OLECHAR **pServerPrincName,
      [out] DWORD  pAuthnLevel,
      [out] DWORD  pImpLevel,
      [out] void   **pPrivs,
      [out] DWORD   *pCapabilities
      );
   HRESULT ImpersonateClient(void);
   HRESULT RevertToSelf(void);
   BOOL IsImpersonating(void);
}
```

QUERYBLANKET • `QueryBlanket` lets you retrieve information about the current Security Blanket. Notice that all of the parameters to `QueryBlanket` are output parameters. If you pass a NULL for any of those parameters, that value is not retrieved.

The parameters for the `QueryBlanket` method are described in Table 10.4.

TABLE 10.4 QueryBlanket Parameters

Parameter	Description
pAuthnSvc	The authentication service currently in use. Possible values include: RPC_C_AUTHN_WINNT, RPC_C_AUTHN_GSS_NEGOTIATE, RPC_C_AUTHN_GSS_KERBEROS, RPC_C_AUTHN_DEFAULT, RPC_C_AUTHN_NONE.
pAuthzSvc	The authorization service currently in use. Possible values include: RPC_C_AUTHZ_NONE, RPC_C_AUTHZ_NAME, RPC_C_AUTHZ_DEFAULT, RPC_C_AUTHZ_DCE.
pServerPrincName	The current principle name, i.e., the name of the user who is using this server.
pAuthnLevel	The current authentication level. Possible values are: RPC_C_AUTHN_LEVEL_DEFAULT, RPC_C_AUTHN_LEVEL_NONE, RPC_C_AUTHN_LEVEL_CONNECT, RPC_C_AUTHN_LEVEL_CALL, RPC_C_AUTHN_LEVEL_PKT, RPC_C_AUTHN_LEVEL_PKT_INTEGRITY, RPC_C_AUTHN_LEVEL_PKT_PRIVACY.
pImpLevel	Must be NULL, this parameter is reserved for future use.
pPrivs	The privilege information for the client application. The format of the structure is authentication service specific.
pCapabilities	Return flags indicating capabilities of the call.

IMPERSONATECLIENT • The `ImpersonateClient` method lets a server execute using the security token of its client while it performs an operation. This method is useful if you would like to allow a server to use a particular resource only if the client user is allowed access to that resource. You can call `ImpersonateClient` to assume the identity of the client, attempt to access the resource (a file for instance), and then the server can revert back to its original identity. This approach is much better than running as the Launching User all the time. For the `ImpersonateClient` method to work, the client's Impersonate Security setting must be set to Impersonate or higher (see the section entitled Impersonation above).

REVERTTOSELF • A server reverts back to its original identity using the `RevertToSelf` method.

ISIMPERSONATING • A server can check to see if it is currently impersonating the client using the `IsImpersonating` method.

GETTING AND USING ISERVERSECURITY • The server can get an `IServerSecurity` interface by calling the `CoGetCallContext` function within a method of a COM object. `CoGetCallContext` is defined as follows:

```
HRESULT CoGetCallContext([in] REFIID riid, [out,iid_is(riid)] void **ppv);
```

The following code shows how you would use the CoGetCallContext method and the IServerSecurity interface to verify that a client is using Packet Privacy Authentication. If the client is using Packet Privacy Authentication, the server impersonates the client, obtains a secure resource, and then reverts back to its previous identity, like this:

```
HRESULT hr;
IServerSecurity *pSecurity;
DWORD AuthLevel;
hr=CoGetCallContext(IID_IServerSecurity,(void **)&pSecurity);
if (SUCCEEDED(hr))
{
    hr=pSecurity->QueryBlanket(0,0,0,&AuthLevel,0,0,0);
    if (SUCCEEDED(hr))
    {
        if (RPC_C_AUTHN_LEVEL_PKT_PRIVACY==AuthLevel)
        {
            hr=pSecurity->ImpersonateClient();
            if (SUCCEEDED(hr))
            {
                GetSecureResource(); // Implementation not shown
            }
            pSecurity->RevertToSelf();
        }
    }
    pSecurity->Release();
}
```

If you don't want to work directly with the IServerSecurity interface, COM API also provides a set of convenience functions that make using the interface simpler. Table 10.5 lists and describes these functions.

TABLE 10.5 Convenience Functions for IServerSecurity

Convenience Function	Description
CoQueryClientBlanket	Retrieves security information about the client that is using a server.
CoImpersonateClient	Allows the server process to run, temporarily, with the client's security token.
CoRevertToSelf	Returns the server to its original security token.
CoIsImpersonating	Allows the server to determine if it is currently running with the client's security token.

CoQueryClientBlanket, for instance, encapsulates the following logic:

```
CoGetCallContext(IID_IServerSecurity, (void**)&pSecurity);
pSecurity->QueryBlanket(pAuthnSvc, pAuthzSvc, pServerPrincName,
      pAuthnLevel, pImpLevel, pPrivs, pCapabilities);
pSecurity->Release();
```

You could implement the code to test for Packet Privacy and impersonate the client using the convenience functions as follows:

```
HRESULT hr;
DWORD AuthLevel;
hr=CoQueryClientBlanket(0,0,0,&AuthLevel,0,0,0);
if (SUCCEEDED(hr))
{
   if (RPC_C_AUTHN_LEVEL_PKT_PRIVACY==AuthLevel)
   {
      hr=CoImpersonateClient();
      if (SUCCEEDED(hr))
         GetSecureResource(); // Implementation not shown
      CoRevertToSelf();
   }
}
```

ICLIENTSECURITY

The IClientSecurity interface is used by a client to set or query the Security Blanket for an interface proxy. All proxies generated by the COM MIDL compiler support the IClientSecurity interface. So you can get an IClientSecurity interface pointer in a client application by calling QueryInterface on an interface proxy and specifying IID_IClientSecurity for the GUID of the requested interface. IClientSecurity is declared as follows:

```
Interface IClientSecurity : IUnknown {
   HRESULT QueryBlanket(
     [in]  IUnknown   *pProxy,
      [out] DWORD  *pAuthnSvc,
      [out] DWORD  *pAuthzSvc,
      [out] OLECHAR   **pServerPrincName,
      [out] DWORD  *pAuthnLevel,
      [out] DWORD  *pImpLevel,
      [out] void      **pAuthInfo,
      [out] DWORD     *pCapabilities
      );
```

```
    HRESULT SetBlanket(
      [in]  IUnknown   *pProxy,
       [in] DWORD   AuthnSvc,
       [in] DWORD   AuthzSvc,
       [in] OLECHAR *pServerPrincName,
       [in] DWORD   AuthnLevel,
       [in] DWORD   ImpLevel,
       [in] void    *pAuthInfo,
       [in] DWORD   Capabilities
       );
    HRESULT CopyProxy([in] IUnknown *pProxy, [out] IUnknown *ppCopy);
}
```

Most of the arguments to the QueryBlanket and SetBlanket methods in IClientSecurity are the same as the QueryBlanket method in IServerSecurity except for the first parameter, pProxy, which is an input argument that is typed as an IUnknown interface pointer, and the seventh parameter, pAuthInfo, which is a data structure that contains the identity of the client.

The first parameter, pProxy, is the interface proxy whose security blanket you are either setting or querying. To query the security blanket for an interface proxy, you QueryInterface the proxy for the IClientSecurity interface. Then you pass the interface pointer to the QueryBlanket method of the IClientSecurity interface pointer passing in output arguments for the parameters that you wish to retrieve. The following code uses the IClientSecurity interface to retrieve the authentication service that the proxy is using and the principal name (the account name) that method calls through the proxy uses.

```
BOOL CAutosvrclientDlg::QuerySecurityBlanket(IDispatch *pDisp)
{
   IClientSecurity *pClient;
   HRESULT hRes;
   OLECHAR *pPrincipalName;
   DWORD dwAuthnService;
   hRes=pDisp->QueryInterface(IID_IClientSecurity,(void **)&pClient);
   if (SUCCEEDED(hRes))
      pClient-
>QueryBlanket(pDisp,&dwAuthnService,0,&pPrincipalName,0,0,0,0);
   else
      return FALSE;
// Use the principal name and authorization service
// ...
   CoTaskMemFree(pPrincipalName);
   pClient->Release();
   return TRUE;
}
```

If you wish to set the security blanket for an interface proxy, you first QueryInterface the proxy for the IClientSecurity interface. Then you call the CopyProxy method of IClientSecurity to make a copy of the proxy and pass the copy of the proxy to the SetBlanket method of IClientSecurity as shown below:

```
IDispatch* CAutosvrclientDlg::SetSecurityBlanket(IDispatch *pDisp)
{
   IDispatch *pCopyDisp;
   IClientSecurity *pClientSecurity;
   HRESULT hr=pDisp-
>QueryInterface(IID_IClientSecurity,(void**)&pClientSecurity);
   if (SUCCEEDED(hr))
   {
      hr=pClientSecurity->CopyProxy(pDisp,(IUnknown**)&pCopyDisp);
      if (SUCCEEDED(hr))
      {
         hr=pClientSecurity->SetBlanket(pCopyDisp,RPC_C_AUTHN_WINNT,
RPC_C_AUTHZ_NONE, 0, RPC_C_AUTHN_LEVEL_CONNECT, RPC_C_IMP_LEVEL_IMPER-
SONATE, 0, EOAC_NONE);
      }
   }
   pClientSecurity->Release();
   return pCopyDisp;
}
```

IClientSecurity also has a set of convenience functions that you can use instead of using the IClientSecurity interface directory. Table 10.6 summarizes each of these functions.

TABLE 10.6 Convenience Functions for IClientSecurity

Convenience Function	Description
CoQueryProxyBlanket	Queries the security blanket for a proxy.
CoSetProxyBlanket	Sets the security blanket for a proxy.
CoCopyProxy	Copies a proxy.

CoQueryProxyBlanket wraps the QueryBlanket method of IClientSecurity. CoSetProxyBlanket wraps the SetBlanket method of IClientSecurity and CoCopyProxy wraps the CopyProxy method of IClientSecurity.

You won't build an example using programmatic security, mainly because I consider programmatic security to be part of that 10% of COM that I won't cover in-depth in this book. If you didn't understand everything in this section on programmatic security, that's okay. When you are first starting out with DCOM, you should use dcomcnfg to do your DCOM-related security configuration. Also, as you will see in Chapter 11, when you learn about COM+, there are fewer reasons now to use the low-level security API when you are developing distributed applications on the Windows platform. COM+ lets you implement fine-grained security in a much simpler way.

If you would like to learn more about programmatic security in COM, see Chapter 6 in *Essential COM* by Don Box; also see Rules 38–42 in *Effective COM* by Don Box et al, and David Chappell's excellent article on the Kerberos protocol in the August 1999 edition of *Microsoft Systems Journal* (MSJ). If you would like to learn more about encryption and authentication algorithms, see *Applied Cryptography* by Bruce Schneier. This book is the Bible of computer-based security and is so good, the National Security Agency (NSA) tried to prevent it from being published.

Example: Configuring a Server via DCOM

For this chapter's example, rather than building a server from scratch, you can instead configure one of your existing servers for distributed use via DCOM. You can then rewrite the client for this server so you can choose to instantiate the server on the default host that is configured in the `RemoteServerName` key under the AppID in the registry, or you can explicitly specify a server using the server from Chapter 6. This server was used to demonstrate out-of-process servers and it did high-resolution timing. You can configure this server to run remotely and modify the client so you can easily compare the performance of a local out-of-process call to a remote one. To follow along with all the steps in this example, you need two machines (one is your client, the other is your server) that are connected via a network. It is preferable that the network have a PDC, but if it doesn't, just remember to use None for your authentication settings.

Many of you may not have access to multiple machines connected by a network. If this is your situation, you can still follow along with this example. You obviously won't be able to compare the performance of a remote server to a local one, but you can do almost everything else, including configuring your server with dcomcnfg.

A Summary of the Steps

The steps that you will perform to build this demonstration are as follows:

1. Perform a Release, Minimum Dependency build of the server from Chapter 6.
2. Make sure the server is registered on both the client and server machine.

3. Make sure the marshaling DLL is installed and registered on both the client and server machine.
4. Configure the server to run remotely using `dcomcnfg`.
5. Configure the client so it activates the server on a remote host by default.
6. Test using your unmodified client.
7. Modify the client so you can select a server at runtime.
8. Test.

Before you begin this example, I recommend that you do a Release (Minimum Dependency) build of the server that you created in Chapter 6 and make sure the server is copied to and registered on both the client and server machines.

Perform a Release Build

A Release, Minimum Dependency build in ATL creates a server executable that has no dependencies on any runtime DLLs. This makes it easy to copy and use the server on a machine that does not have Visual C++ installed. Perform the following steps to do a Release, Minimum Dependency build:

1. Open the Chapter 6 server project in Visual C++.
2. Select `Customize...` from the `Tools` menu (the Customize dialog appears).
3. Select the `Toolbars` tab on the Customize dialog.
4. Check the Checkbox next to `Build in the Toolbars` list (the Build toolbar appears).
5. Click the `Close` button on the Customize dialog.
6. On the second drop-down from the left in the Build toolbar, select `Win32 Release MinDependency`.
7. Click the `Build` button or press `F7` (the server should build and register itself).

The new version of the server may be found in a directory called `ReleaseMinDependency` beneath the main project directory for the server. If you did not build the server in chapter 6, you can copy it from the Web site for this book.

Ensure the Server Is Registered on the Client and Server

Visual C++ automatically registers a COM server built with ATL after the DLL or executable is linked. If either the client or the server that you will use for this demonstration is *not* the build machine, perform the following steps on that machine:

1. Copy the executable in the `ReleaseMinDependency` directory to the client and/or server machine.
2. Open a command prompt by (on Windows 2000) selecting `\Programs\Accessories\Command Prompt\`.
3. Change directory to the directory where you copied the executable.
4. Type in the following command at the prompt: `svroutofprocess /regserver`.

Ensure the Marshaling DLL is Installed and Registered on the Client and Server

If a DCOM server implements custom interfaces, you must install and register the marshaling DLL on both the client and server machine. If you have not built the marshaling DLL already, build it by opening a command prompt, changing directories to the main directory for your project, and typing in the following command:

```
nmake svroutofprocessps.mk
```

Once the build is complete, you can register the server by entering this command:

```
regsvr32 svroutofprocessps.dll
```

Remember to copy the marshaling DLL to both the client and server and register it in both places.

Configure the Server to Run Remotely Using Dcomcnfg

To configure the server to run remotely using `dcomcnfg`, you must first log in as a user with administrative privilege. Next, click the `Start` button, select `Run...` from the `Start` menu, type in `dcomcnfg`, and click the `OK` button. If you see a message box that says, "you must be an administrator to run this tool" then you are not logged in as an administrator. After you have started `dcomcnfg`, you must perform the following summarized steps to configure your server to run remotely:

1. Configure the authentication level.
2. Configure the access permissions.
3. Configure the launch permissions.
4. Set the RunAs identity.

CONFIGURE THE AUTHENTICATION LEVEL

Using `dcomcnfg`, perform the following steps to configure the authentication level:

1. On the `Application`'s tab, select the entry that says "`svroutofprocess`".
2. Click the `Properties`... button (the server properties dialog appears).
3. On the `General` tab, select `Connect for the authentication level`.

If you do not see `svroutofprocess` in the Application tab of dcomcnfg, then the server is not registered. Follow the steps in the section entitled "Make Sure the Server is Registered on the Client and Server" to register the server.

CONFIGURE THE ACCESS PERMISSIONS

On the Security tab of the server properties dialog of `dcomcnfg` (see Figure 10.12), perform the following steps to configure the access permissions for your server:

1. Click the `use custom access permissions` radio button.
2. Click the `Edit`... button (the Registry Value Permissions dialog appears).
3. Click the `Add`... button (the Add Users and Groups dialog appears).
4. Select the group called `Everyone` and click the `Add` button.
5. Add the `System` user if it is not added by default.
6. Click the `OK` button.
7. Click the `OK` button in the Registry Value Permissions dialog.

If you have a specific user account that you wish to test with, you can use that instead of `Everyone`.

CONFIGURE THE LAUNCH PERMISSIONS

On the Security tab of the server properties dialog of `dcomcnfg`, perform the following steps to configure the launch permissions for your server:

1. Click the `use custom launch permissions` radio button.
2. Click the `Edit`... button (the Registry Value Permissions dialog appears).

3. Click the Add... button (the Add Users and Groups dialog appears).
4. Select the group called Everyone and click the Add button.
5. Click the OK button.
6. Click the OK button in the Registry Value Permissions dialog.

If you have a specific user account that you wish to test with, you can use that instead of Everyone.

SET THE RUNAS IDENTITY

Select the Identity tab on the server properties dialog of dcomcnfg (see Figure 10.15) and perform the following steps to configure the RunAs identity for your server:

1. Click the This User radio button.
2. Enter the user name of the user that you are currently logged in as in the User edit box.
3. Enter the password of the user that you are currently logged in as into the Password edit box.
4. Reenter the password in the Confirm Password edit box.
5. Click OK.

The server is now configured to run via DCOM. You must now configure your client to point to the server machine.

Configure the Client

You need to do two things to configure your client to use your server: (1) Tell the client machine the name of the default server machine that the client will use (you can override this default by explicitly specifying which server you want to use via the CoCreateInstanceEx function). (2) You must also configure authentication so the client uses the authentication level specified by the server.

All of the following steps must be performed on the client machine.

CONFIGURE THE SERVER LOCATION

You need to tell the client the default location of the server. To do this, start dcomcnfg on the client machine and perform these steps:

1. Select `svroutofprocess` on the `Applications` tab.
2. Click the `Properties...` button (the server properties dialog appears).
3. Click the `Location` tab (see Figure 10.17).
4. Set the `Run Application on the Following Computer` checkbox.
5. Clear the `Run Application on this computer` checkbox.

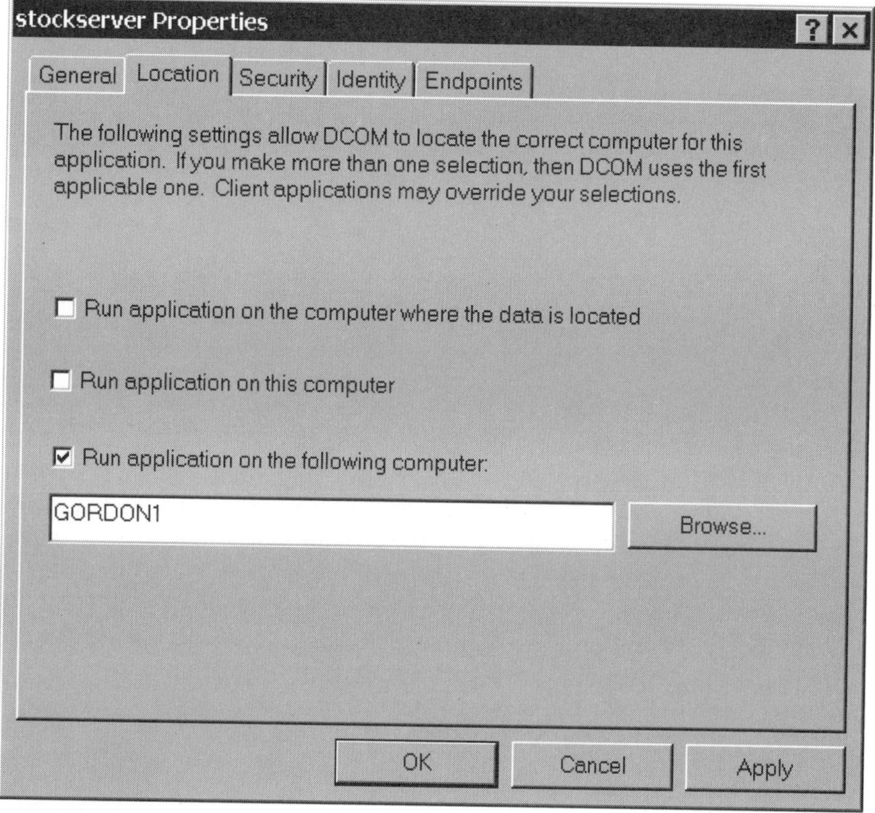

FIGURE 10.17 The Location tab of the Server Properties Dialog of dcomcnfg.

6. Click the `Browse...` button (the Select Domain dialog appears with the name of your domain).
7. Double-click the Domain name, a list of possible hosts appears.
8. Select the machine on which you configured your DCOM server.

Performing these steps sets the `RemoteServerName` subkey beneath the AppID for the server. It also effectively comments out the `LocalServer32` registry entry for the server by changing the value at the key to `_LocalServer32`.

CONFIGURE THE CLIENT TO USE THE AUTHENTICATION LEVEL

As mentioned earlier in this chapter, the authentication level used between a client and a server is negotiated. The COM runtime chooses the server's authentication or the client's authentication depending on which one is higher. Since None is the lowest authentication level possible, you can configure your client to use None as its authentication level. The server's authentication level is either equal to or greater than this setting. So the server's authentication level takes precedence.

To set the client's authentication level to None, start dcomcnfg and perform the following steps:

1. Select `svroutofprocess` on the `Applications` tab.
2. Select `svroutofprocess and click Properties...` (the server properties dialog appears).
3. On the `General` tab, set the authentication level to `None`.

Test by Using Your Unmodified Client

You are now ready to test using your timing client. Find the application called `TimingClient` on the Web site if you didn't build the demo yourself.

Run the application. The following results were obtained on a Pentium II 400 with 128MB of memory (see Table 10.7). You can switch backward and forward between running the server locally and running it on a remote machine on the Location tab of `dcomcnfg`. Select `Run Application` on `This Computer` to run locally. Select `Run application on the following computer` (and select a remote machine) to run remotely.

TABLE 10.7 Performance Results with a Remote Server

Server Type and Method Called	Total Time For 1 Thousand Method calls (microseconds)	Average Time Per Call (microseconds)
Out-of-process without arguments. Remote	911137	911
Out-of-process with arguments. Remote	2980096	2980
Out-of-process without arguments. Local	115398	115
Out-of-process with arguments. Local	191731	191

Notice a couple of interesting things. When you run locally, the method call with arguments is about 70% slower than the method call without arguments. When you run remotely, the method call with arguments is about 300% slower. Also notice that the difference between running locally without arguments and running remotely without arguments is about 8 times (911 vs. 115 microseconds). The difference between running with arguments locally and remotely is about 15 times (2,980 vs. 191 microseconds). The difference is the amount of overhead associated with sending a method call with several large parameters over the network instead of between two processes on the same machine. This overhead increases dramatically the more information you try to send over the network.

Modify the Client So You Can Select a Server at Runtime

When DCOM was introduced with NT 4.0, Microsoft added a new function to the API called `CoCreateInstanceEx` that you can use to explicitly specify a server. Calling `CoCreateInstanceEx` and specifying a server overrides what is in the registry.

COCREATEINSTANCEEX

As its name implies, this function is an extended version of the `CoCreateInstance` object instantiation function. `CoCreateInstanceEx` is defined as follows:

```
HRESULT CoCreateInstanceEx( REFCLSID  rclsid,IUnknown *  punkOuter,
                            DWORD * dwClsCtx,COSERVERINFO* pServerInfo,
                            ULONG  cmq,MULTI_QI  rgmqResults   );
```

The parameters to this function are shown in Table 10.8.

TABLE 10.8 The Parameter List for CoCreateInstanceEx

Parameter	Description
rclSID	The CLSID of the class that you wish to create an instance of.
pUnkOuter	The IUnknown interface pointer for the Outer Unknown. This parameter will be NULL unless the object you are creating is the inner object in an aggregate.
dwClsCtx	The class context for the new object. This parameter will typically be either CLSCTX_INPROC_SERVER, CLSCTX_LOCAL_SERVER, CLSCTX_REMOTE_SERVER, CLSCTX_SERVER, or CLSCTX_ALL.

`pServerInfo`	A pointer to a COSERVERINFO structure. The COSERVERINFO structure is defined as follows:
	`typedef struct _COSERVERINFO`
	`{`
	`DWORD dwReserved1;`
	`LPWSTR pwszName;`
	`COAUTHINFO __RPC_FAR *pAuthInfo;`
	`DWORD dwReserved2;`
	`} COSERVERINFO;`
	The pwszName parameter is either the domain name or the IP address of a remote server. In most cases, the pAuthInfo structure should be NULL.

cmq	The number of the MULTI_QI structures being passed in as the rgmqResults parameter.

`rgmqResults`	Contains an array of MULTI_QI structures, which is defined as:
	`typedef struct _MULTI_QI`
	`{`
	`const IID* pIID;`
	`IUnknown * pItf;`
	`HRESULT hr;`
	`} MULTI_QI;`
	Upon calling, the pIID portion contains a pointer to the IID of each interface to QueryInterface() for. Upon call return, the pItf member contains the interface pointer requested if the hr member is S_OK. If the hr member for a specified interface is E_NOINTERFACE, the pItf member is invalid, and the object doesn't support the interface requested.

To convert your client to use `CoCreateInstanceEx`, you must perform the following summarized steps:

1. Alter the GUI for the client.
2. Add a #define for `_WIN32_WINNT`.
3. Remove the code that instantiates the out of process server.
4. Using the ClassWizard, map variables to the new edit box and client buttons.

5. Add code to enable and disable the client's buttons.
6. Add code to instantiate a remote server using `CoCreateInstanceEx`.
7. Add code to instantiate a server at the default location using the registry.

ALTER THE GUI FOR THE CLIENT

Alter the GUI for the timing client so the main window dialog looks like that shown in Figure 10.18. The additions made to this window are: a new edit box (labeled `Remote Server Name`) was added. Two buttons (labeled `Use Remote Server` and `Use Default Server`) were also added.

ADD A "#DEFINE" FOR _WIN32_WINNT

You will be calling the `CoCreateInstanceEx` function in your modified client. `CoCreateInstanceEx` can only be called on a machine that is running NT 4.0 or greater, Windows 98, or Windows 95 with the DCOM upgrade. `CoCreateInstanceEx` is defined in the system include file, `objbase.h`, as follows:

```
#if (_WIN32_WINNT >= 0x0400 ) || defined(_WIN32_DCOM)
WINOLEAPI  CoInitializeEx(LPVOID pvReserved, DWORD dwCoInit);
#endif
```

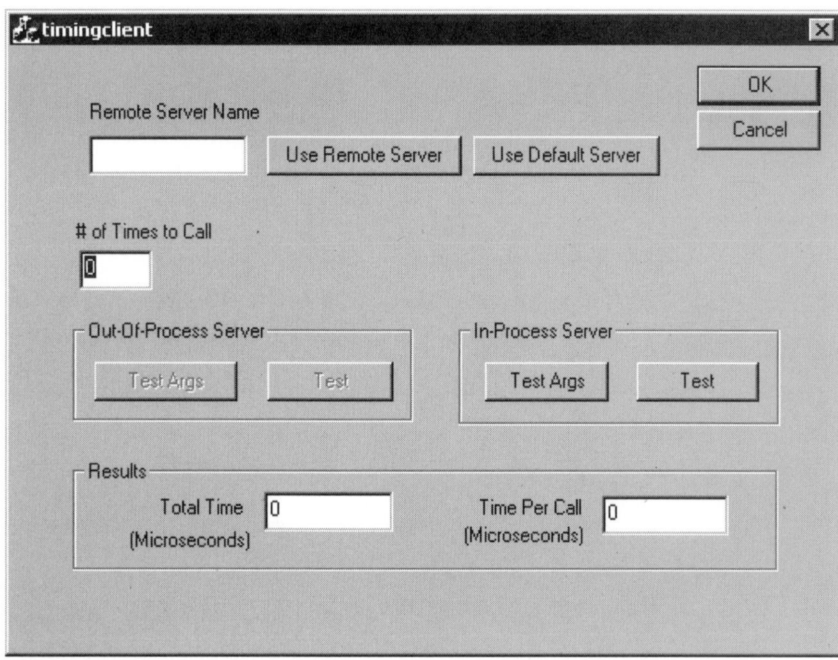

FIGURE 10.18 The Altered Main Window for the Timing Client.

To call CoCreateInstanceEx, you must (1) be on a machine with one of the operating systems specified above and (2) tell your compiler that you are on a machine with one of the operating systems specified above. You can tell your compiler that you are on such a machine by either setting the variable _WIN32_WINNT to 0x0400 or greater, by defining a variable called _WIN32_DCOM. If you are using Visual Studio 6.0, this is not done for you. If you compile without performing this step, the compiler tells you that CoInitializeEx does not exist. So add the following code to the stdafx.h file in your client project:

```
#define _WIN32_WINNT 0x0400
```

REMOVE THE CODE THAT INSTANTIATES THE OUT OF PROCESS SERVER

Remove the following code from the OnInitDialog function in the source file for the main window dialog.

```
HRESULT hRes;
hRes=mServerOutOfProcess.CreateInstance("svroutofprocess.testclass");
if (FAILED(hRes))
{
    _com_error err(hRes);
    AfxMessageBox(err.ErrorMessage());

        }
```

If you followed the recommended naming convention from Chapter 6, this file should be called timingclientDlg.cpp. Or to be sure that you are in the correct file, you can perform the following steps:

1. Click on the Resource tab in the Visual C++ workspace.
2. Open the folder that contains the resources for the client project.
3. Open the dialog folder beneath that.
4. You should find two dialogs beneath there—one is the about box, the other is the dialog you want.
5. Double-click on the dialog to bring it up in the Visual C++ environment.
6. Double-click on the dialog to bring up the editor with its code.
7. Find the OnInitDialog function.
8. Locate and delete the code.

USE THE CLASSWIZARD TO MAP VARIABLES TO THE CLIENT'S BUTTONS

Use the MFC ClassWizard to map variables to the new edit box and the two new buttons on the main window dialog as shown in Table 10.9.

TABLE 10.9 Mapping of Member Variables to Controls

Control	Map to member variable	Member variable type
Remote Server Name Edit Box	M_remoteServerName	CString
Use Remote Server Button	M_testOutOfProcessButton	CButton
Use Default Server Button	m_testOutOfProcessButtonWithArgs	CButton

You can map a member variable to a control in Visual C++ by performing the following steps:

1. Type `CTRL-W` on the keyboard to bring up the ClassWizard.
2. Click the `Member Variables` tab.
3. Make sure that the Class Name field contains the name of your main window dialog class.
4. Select the resource ID of the control that you want to map a member variable to.
5. Click the `Add Variable...` button (the Add Member Variable dialog appears).
6. Enter the name of the member variable that you would like to map to the control in the `Member variable` name field.
7. Click `OK`.

ADD CODE TO ENABLE AND DISABLE THE CLIENT'S BUTTONS

To add code to disable the client buttons, perform the following steps:

1. Click the `ClassView` tab in the Visual C++ workspace.
2. Right-click on the main window dialog class; it should be called `CTimingclientdlg`.
3. From the context menu that appears, select `Add Member Function...` (the Add Member Function dialog appears).
4. Enter `void` in the `Function Type` field.
5. Enter `DisableButtons` in the `Function Declaration` field.
6. Select `Private` under `Access`.
7. Click `OK`.

Visual C++ adds a prototype for this new function to the include file for your main window dialog class and adds a blank implementation function into the source file for the class. After you click OK you should find yourself in the editor at the blank implementation for this function. Add the following code to this function:

```
void CTimingclientDlg::DisableButtons()
{
   m_testOutOfProcessButton.EnableWindow(FALSE);
   m_testOutOfProcessWithArgsButton.EnableWindow(FALSE);
}
```

To add code to enable the client buttons, perform the following steps:

1. Click the `ClassView` tab in the Visual C++ Workspace.
2. Right-click on the main window dialog class; it should be called `CTimingclientdlg`.
3. From the `Context` menu that appears, select `Add Member Function...` (the Add Member Function dialog appears).
4. Enter `void` in the `Function Type` field.
5. Enter `EnableButtons` in the `Function Declaration` field.
6. Select `Private` under `Access`.
7. Click `OK`.

Visual C++ adds a prototype for this new function to the include file for your main window dialog class and adds a blank implementation function into the source file for the class. After you click OK, you should find yourself in the editor at the blank implementation for this function. Add the following code to this function:

```
void CTimingclientDlg::EnableButtons()
{
   m_testOutOfProcessButton.EnableWindow(TRUE);
   m_testOutOfProcessWithArgsButton.EnableWindow(TRUE);
}
```

Now add a call to the `DisableButtons` method from your `InitDialog` method as shown below:

```
BOOL CTimingclientDlg::OnInitDialog()
{
   CDialog::OnInitDialog();

   // Code is omitted here for clarity...
```

```
    // TODO: Add extra initialization here

    if
(FALSE==QueryPerformanceFrequency((LARGE_INTEGER*)&m_highResFrequency))
    {
        AfxMessageBox("Could not get high resolution timer");
        return FALSE;
    }
    hRes=mServerInProcess.CreateInstance("svrinprocess.testclass");
    if (FAILED(hRes))
    {
        _com_error err(hRes);
        AfxMessageBox(err.ErrorMessage());

    }
    DisableButtons();
    return TRUE;  // return TRUE  unless you set the focus to a control
}
```

ADD CODE TO INSTANTIATE A REMOTE SERVER USING COCREATEINSTANCEEX

Add the following code to the handler for the button whose label is Use Remote Server:

```
void CTimingclientDlg::OnRemoteServerButton()
{
    UpdateData(TRUE);
    CLSID clsid;
    HRESULT hRes;
    BSTR serverName=m_remoteServerName.AllocSysString();
    MULTI_QI multiQI={ &IID_ITestClass,NULL,NOERROR };
    COSERVERINFO serverInfo={ 0,serverName,NULL,0 };
    DisableButtons();
    hRes=::CLSIDFromProgID(L"svroutofprocess.testclass",&clsid);
    if (FAILED(hRes))
    {
        AfxMessageBox("Server not registered on remote machine");
        return;
    }
    hRes=CoCreateInstanceEx(clsid,NULL, CLSCTX_ALL,&serverInfo,1,&multiQI);
    if (FAILED(hRes))
    {
        _com_error err(hRes);
```

```
        AfxMessageBox(err.ErrorMessage());
    }
    else
    {
        mServerOutOfProcess=(ITestClass*)multiQI.pItf;
        EnableButtons();
    }
    ::SysFreeString(ServerName);
}
```

ADD CODE TO INSTANTIATE A SERVER AT THE DEFAULT LOCATION USING THE REGISTRY

Add the following code to the handler for the button whose label is Use Default Server:

```
void CTimingclientDlg::OnUseDefaultButton()
{
    HRESULT hRes;
    DisableButtons();
    hRes=mServerOutOfProcess.CreateInstance("svroutofprocess.testclass");
    if (FAILED(hRes))
    {
        _com_error err(hRes);
        AfxMessageBox(err.ErrorMessage());

    }
    else
        EnableButtons();
}
```

Except for the calls to Disable and Enable the buttons, this is the same code you originally had in the `OnInitDialog` handler.

Testing

Now you can test your new client. If you are on a network, register your server on other machines on your network, type in the name of the machine into the `Remote Server Name` edit box, and press the `Use Remote Server` button; the server is instantiated on the remote machine. The `Use Default Server` button uses whatever is currently configured as the remote server in the registry. To use the local server, bring up `dcomcnfg`, select `svroutofprocess` on the `Applications` tab, and click properties (the properties dialog appears). Click the `Location` tab. To run on this machine, set the `Run application on this computer` checkbox. To run on a remote machine, select Run application on the following computer and you can either type in the name of a computer or click the Browse... button and select a computer from your network.

Summary

DCOM is that part of COM that enables COM servers and clients to communicate over a network, thus enabling distributed processing using COM. Unfortunately, allowing clients and servers to communicate over a network exposes that information to snooping, tampering, or identity spoofing. You can set the authentication level using dcomcnfg or programmatically to prevent snooping (authentication level Packet Privacy), tampering (Packet Integrity), or identity spoofing (Connect or higher). In this chapter you also learned that you can configure who is allowed to access—and launch—your servers using dcomcnfg or the CoInitializeSecurity API function and the IAccessControl interface.

From this chapter's example, you learned that DCOM is slow. The overhead associated with a method call is approximately an order of magnitude higher than using an out-of-process server on the local machine.

With a basic understanding of DCOM under your belt, you now have a complete understanding of the COM foundation. In the next chapter, you will learn that while DCOM makes it *possible* to build distributed applications with COM, COM+ makes it *practical*.

PART THREE

COM+

In This Part

In this section we will begin our discussion of COM+. DCOM makes it *possible* to build enterprise-class, distributed applications on the Windows platform; COM+ was designed to make it *practical*. This is an important point and understanding what it means is the key to understanding, at a high-level, what COM+ is all about. DCOM provides you with a network-capable communication infrastructure and support for security but there are a number of things, that enterprise-class distributed applications need that DCOM does not provide. Among these things are: fine-grained security (the ability to configure security settings at the class, interface, or method level), distributed transactions, scalability to hundreds and even thousands of clients, and support for disconnected operation such as over a wireless network. Given the time and expertise you could implement these services yourself using DCOM, but thanks to COM+ you don't have to.

COM+ is a set of System Services that are designed to make it easy for you to develop enterprise-class distributed applications. COM+ is really just a runtime environment for COM objects. This runtime environment provides the following services to COM objects: fine-grained security, distributed transactions, thread synchronization, load balancing, asynchronous store and forward method invocation, and enhanced scalability through Just In Time (JIT) Activation and pooling of objects and database connections. In order to use this runtime environment you must implement your COM+ objects in an in-process server and then configure your server to run within the COM+ runtime environment. You can then select which of the aforementioned services that you want your object to use and configure attributes that control how the services work. Windows 2000 provides a graphical tool called the Component Services Explorer that makes this simple.

You will learn how COM+ works and how to configure your COM objects to use it in chapters 11 and 12. In chapter 13 you will learn that even though COM+ solves many of the problems that you will encounter when developing enterprise-class distributed applications, it doesn't solve all of them. Microsoft has developed an entire suite of tools and technologies including a web server (Internet Information Server), a database server (SQL Server 7/2000), and a set of universal data-access APIs (OLEDB, ODBC, and ADO) that together provide a complete solution for developing enterprise-class distributed applications. Microsoft has also developed an architectural style guide called the Windows Distributed interNet Applications Architecture (Windows DNA) that shows you how to architect your applications to best use these tools and technologies. In chapter 13 we use all of these tools and technologies to build a complete application. In chapter 14 we will discuss the COM+ Queued Components Service that enables disconnected and asynchronous operation and finally in chapter 15 we discuss COM+ Events which provide a Publish and Subscribe mechanism for sending events. COM+ Events are a more scalable and loosely coupled alternative to Connection Points.

ELEVEN

An Introduction to the COM+ Architecture

COM+ is the final step in the evolution of COM from its genesis as a desktop, application integration technology to an infrastructure for developing enterprise-class, distributed applications. The goal of COM+ is to make it easy to develop enterprise-class distributed applications with COM. COM+ is a set of system services that provides the following services to COM objects: fine-grained security, distributed transactions, thread synchronization, load balancing, asynchronous store and forward method invocation, and enhanced scalability through Just In Time (JIT) Activation and pooling of objects and database connections. COM+ also includes a number of improvements to COM that aren't necessarily related to enterprise-class application development but are still important and useful, including loosely-coupled events and asynchronous (but without store and forward) method invocation. The essence of COM+ is the improvements, which facilitate enterprise-class, distributed application development.

COM+ is not nearly as fundamental a change to COM as many people thought it would be. Everything that you have learned about COM so far applies to COM+. COM+ represents improvement by addition. Nothing that existed in COM already has been changed significantly; you now have a set of new tools and technologies that make it easier to develop distributed applications.

For those who think that COM is overwhelmingly complex, there is good news and bad news. The good news is that nothing you did before—whether you were building ActiveX Controls or using Automation to drive MS Office applications—is *harder* to do now that COM+ is here. The bad news is that unless you are building enterprise-class, distributed applications, COM+ is not going to make your life any *easier*. COM+ is only going to significantly impact the lives of developers who are building enterprise-class, distributed applications. That's going to be a disappointment to a lot of people. A pair of articles written by Mary Kirtland (one of the COM leads at Microsoft) in the November and December 1997 issues of *Microsoft Systems Journal* led many people, including yours truly, to believe that COM+ would include implementation inheritance, a universal runtime, and other improvements to make it as easy for Visual C++ programmers to develop COM objects as it is for Visual Basic programmers to develop COM objects. These improvements, if they come at all, will have to wait for future versions of COM+. Even with this scaling back of expectations, COM+ is still big stuff.

This chapter serves as an overview of the new features of COM+. There is so much to cover that you won't create a demonstration in this chapter. In the following two chapters, you can build a demonstration program that uses all the new features of COM+.

Why Do You Need COM+?

The easiest way to understand COM+ is to first understand the problems that COM+ was designed to solve. I mentioned that COM+ was designed to make it simple (or at least simpler than it was before) to develop enterprise-class distributed applications. But what exactly is an enterprise-class, distributed application? And what are the problems that must be overcome to develop one? Once you understand the inherent complexity of these problems and how much work you would have to do to build an enterprise-class distributed application on the Windows platform without COM+, you can appreciate how elegant and comparatively simple the COM+ solution actually is.

Enterprise-Class, Distributed Applications

An enterprise-class distributed application is an application that has the following attributes:

1. The correct and timely functioning of the application is critical to the operation of some business.

2. The application is used by many people throughout a business: customers, employees, suppliers, and so on.
3. The application must be Internet/Intranet-capable, i.e., someone should be able to easily adapt the application so it can be used over the Internet or Intranet.
4. The application must have some support for security. An administrator must be able to control the amount of access that individual users have to business information.

CORRECT AND TIMELY FUNCTIONING IS CRITICAL

Many companies are dependent on their information systems. Computer-based information systems are used for everything from receiving orders from customers to placing orders with suppliers. At my previous employer, we all submitted our time cards using an application that ran on the corporate Intranet. The good news is that many of these businesses can operate more efficiently with these information systems in place; the bad news is that many of these companies are now completely dependent on these information systems. That means that these systems must process data correctly. Customers cannot be charged for orders they *did not* place and they must be billed correctly for orders they *did* place. The correct type and amount of supplies must be ordered from suppliers and those suppliers must be paid correctly. Employees' hours must be recorded correctly and they must be paid accurately. This all must be done promptly. If customers are kept waiting, they will go somewhere else. Time that an employee spends looking at an hourglass is lost productivity. To meet these requirements your systems must be transactional (this is explained later in this chapter) and scalable. It's easy to write an application that performs well (and correctly) when only one person is using it. It's a lot harder to write an application that performs well (and correctly) when 100 or 1,000 people are using it simultaneously.

If the correct and timely functioning of a software system is critical to a business, then the software systems must also be *available*. By that I mean it must be relatively immune to failures that render it unusable. Think about a company such as amazon.com or Dell. Their Web sites and the underlying information systems are the life-blood of their business. If their Web sites are unavailable to their customers for even an hour, it costs them millions of dollars.

For your application to function in a correct and timely manner, it must be *transactional* (which guarantees data integrity), it must be *scalable*, and it must be *available*.

THE APPLICATION IS USED BY MANY PEOPLE

Most medium to large corporations (and many small ones, too) have offices in various locations. In many cases, these corporations have employees in the field using laptop computers or Personal Digital Assistants (PDAs) and customers who communicate with the company over the Internet. To support all of these geographically dispersed users, an enterprise-class application must not only be distributed, it must also support a wide variety of client types from native Win32 executables to Web clients communicating over the Internet and Intranet to PDAs. In addition, network bandwidth is still the most scant of computer resources right now, compared to memory and CPU processing power. To support a large number of users, an enterprise-class application must be *distributed*, and it must be architected to support a wide variety of clients and make efficient use of network resources.

THE APPLICATION MUST BE INTERNET/INTRANET CAPABLE

Doing business on the Internet is not an option, for most businesses it is a necessity. There are still some companies that have pages on their Web site that say a few things about the company and tell you what their address and stock ticker is. But most companies are doing much more than that. They are providing and purchasing products and services directly over the Internet. For some companies, like Amazon.com, selling products on the Internet is *all* they do. Any application that is being developed to support a medium to large organization must be able to send and retrieve information via the Internet and/or Intranet. This means the application must be able to send information to its clients, as HTML, and must be able to receive information from a standard Web browser.

THE APPLICATION MUST RESTRICT ACCESS

Any application that is used by a large number of users has to restrict access to some of those users. For instance, the application that I am working on now allows a field service business to store information about the markups they charge on parts and calculate the amount of profit they made on each job. This is obviously information they do not want their customers to have. On the other hand, the field service company may want to allow a customer to check, via the Web, the name and expected arrival time of the technician who will be carrying out a service call. Both users may be using the same underlying application, but they need completely different levels of access.

Application Architecture

Now that you know what an enterprise-class, distributed application is and the attributes it must have, the next question is how should you design and build one? If you are building a small desktop application, you can draw screens using Visual Basic, create COM components, and create a few tables in a database. But if you are building an enterprise-class application, you are jumping ahead of yourselves. You must first define an architecture for your application.

Software Architecture

According to Ivar Jacobson, Grady Booch, and Jim Rumbaugh from their book *The Unified Software Development Process*, you must do the following to define a software architecture:

- Partition a system into major structural elements.
- Specify the interfaces between the major structural elements.
- Specify the behavior of the structural elements and their interfaces.
- Determine how these structural and behavioral elements will be integrated into a larger subsystem.

The essence of software architecture then is the partitioning of a system into structural elements and then specifying the interfaces and behavior for each of those structural elements. Why partition a software system in the first place? There are two main reasons: (1) Applications that are partitioned into separately compilable and configurable, loosely-coupled elements are easier to design, develop, maintain, and reuse, and (2) Distributed applications can benefit even more from being partitioned into separate components because (depending on how the interfaces between the different elements in your architecture are specified) each of the elements in your architecture can execute on a separate machine. You can accomplish work that would normally require a large expensive machine on a network of smaller, cheaper machines.

Partition Business Applications

What is the best way to partition your business applications? All business applications do essentially the same thing: They *store*, *process*, and *display* information.

STORING INFORMATION

Storing information usually means writing the data into one or more *relational databases*, but in most modern businesses, important information is not just stored in relational databases.

I'm assuming that you already know what a relational database is. If not and you want to learn, I highly recommend the book *LAN TIMES Guide to SQL* by James Groff and Paul Weinberg. Another of my favorite relational database books is *An Introduction to Database System* by C. J. Date. This book is more theoretical and far more difficult to read, but is a classic in the field.

Important information may also be stored in Excel spreadsheets, in company e-mail, and now in XML documents. Corporate information also resides in non-relational databases—from homespun, proprietary databases to legacy hierarchical databases and to object-oriented or object-relational databases. Business applications must be able to work with all of these disparate forms of data.

PROCESSING INFORMATION

Processing information means performing some value-added calculation on, or transformation of, information that is entered into the business application. This may be anything from determining based on provided information, if a customer is qualified for a loan, to calculating the amount that someone owes on their income tax, to totaling up the shipping and handling costs for an online purchase.

Processing information also means that data-integrity constraints must be enforced. For instance, a rental car contract must include a valid credit card number, or all orders placed with an online retailer must include a valid delivery address. These calculations and data-integrity constraints are also called *business rules*.

BUSINESS RULES • A business rule is an algorithm or data-integrity constraint that codifies some aspect of how a business operates. Some examples of business rules are shown here:

- Sales tax for all purchases made in Los Angeles County is 8.25%.
- The shipping costs for an online purchase is $1.50 for the first item and $1.00 for each additional item.
- A 10% discount is applied on all orders over $100.00.
- To rent a car, you must have a valid credit card.
- Cheeseburgers are 39 cents on Sunday.

DISPLAY INFORMATION

Displaying information means presenting information to the user in some form they can easily understand, usually via a Graphical User Interface (GUI) but it can be through sound or other forms. On the Windows platform, an application can have a display that consists of a Win32 application with a Multiple Document Interface (MDI) or Single Document Interface (SDI) main window and a number of modal or modeless secondary windows (dialogs). The advent of the Internet has added another type of user interface that most business applications must now support, HTML. Both external users on the Internet and internal users on corporate Intranets expect to be able to view and edit important information on any platform in their favorite Web browser. HTML pages must be generated on-the-fly to support the needs of these Web clients. People also expect to execute all kinds of business transactions via the Web in a secure environment and with low latency times. The recent, explosive growth of handheld Personal Digital Assistants (PDAs) and wireless networks has added another type of client. These devices (right now) have small screens, limited input devices and low bandwidth, but they will be an increasingly important class of client that business applications must support. Often a business application needs to support all these clients: native Windows applications; cross-platform, HTML clients; and PDAs.

THE THREE-TIERED ARCHITECTURE

To maximize reuse and make your application as easy to deploy and reuse as possible, you want to make the software elements in your architecture as loosely coupled as possible. You can achieve this by packaging related functionality together. The easiest way to do this is to partition your business applications into the three layers mentioned: the information storage or *data access layer*, the information processing or *business layer*, and the information display or *presentation layer* as shown in Figure 11.1. This is referred to as a *three-tiered* architecture.

The three-tiered architecture is a logical partitioning of an application; each tier can *potentially* run on a different machine, however, each tier doesn't *have* to run on a different machine. In practice, each layer in the three-tiered architecture should be composed of a separately compilable and configurable binary (an executable or DLL), but this is not a requirement. I have seen situations where the three-tiers were simply used as a design abstraction. In other words, the application was a single, monolithic executable, but the three parts of the application, data-access, business processing, and presentation, were designed as separate code modules and then linked together.

Although it is possible to build an application that consists of three logical tiers but physically is composed of a single executable, the three-

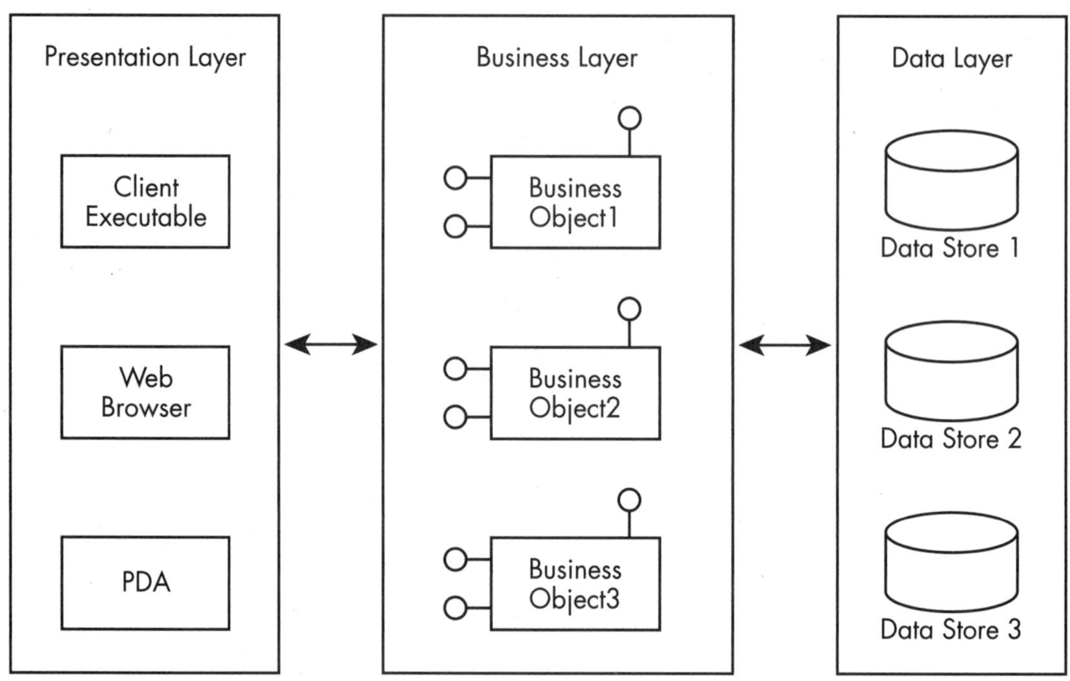

FIGURE 11.1 The Three-Tiered Architecture.

tiered architecture pays the greatest dividends when used to build enterprise-class distributed applications. In these kinds of applications, the three tiers often execute on different machines as shown in Figure 11.2.

Deploying your three-tiered architectures this way has a number of benefits. Because the business processing of your application is centered in one place, it makes it much easier to change your information system when the business rules of a corporation change. Instead of having to deploy the new software out to each client, you only need to deploy new software to the server machines that are being used to host the business layer. This architecture is also far more scalable. With the three-tiered architecture, there is no need for each client to maintain its own connection to the data store. The business layer can even cache and share a limited pool of connections. Of course, logic such as this is difficult to implement, but that's where COM+ comes into the picture. You are also dividing up the total processing of your application into more nodes. The database still performs the same functions but now your client has significantly less work to do. Now, the presentation layer only has to handle graphical display and processing of user inputs, the business logic is performed on a different machine, and you can use less powerful, inexpensive and more portable clients. This is

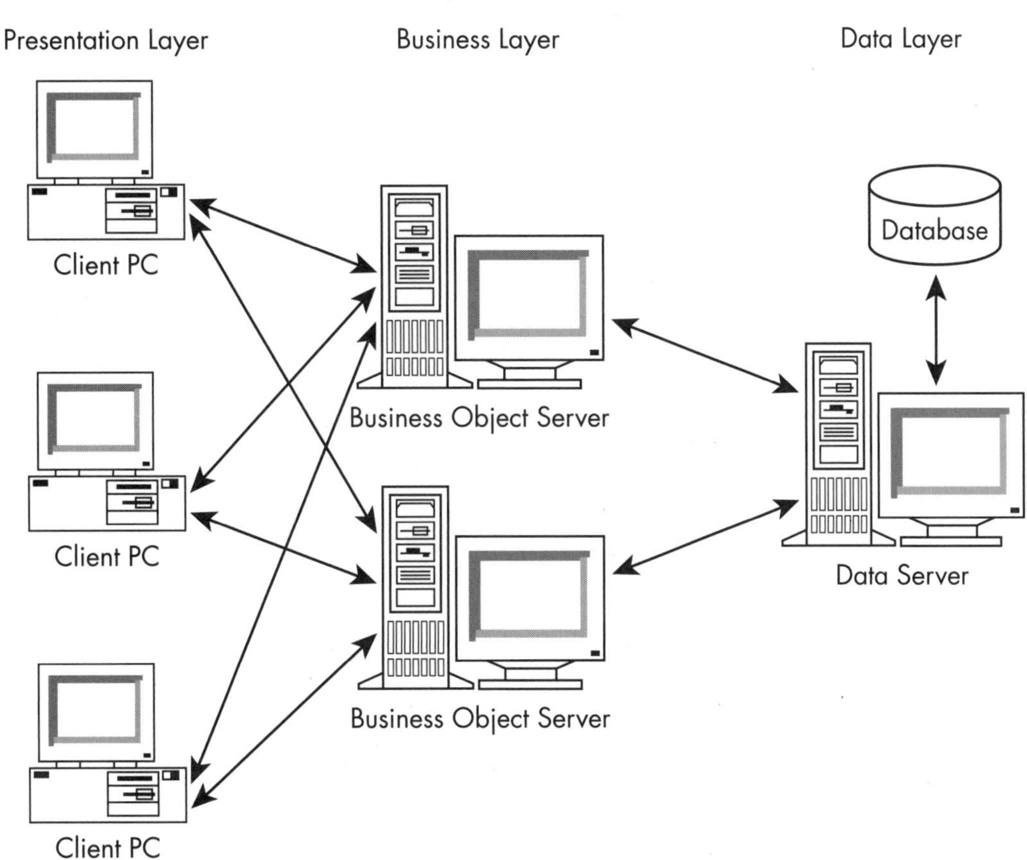

FIGURE 11.2 A Distributed 3-Tiered Architecture.

sometimes referred to as a *thin-client architecture*. The best example of a thin-client is when you use a Web browser as your presentation layer. In situations like this, there is usually little or no actual processing that is done on the client. By contrast, a *fat-client architecture* is where all of the presentation logic resides on the client. With the three-tiered architecture, you can develop your business processing using standard programming languages (C++, Visual Basic, Java) instead of limited, database-specific, stored procedure languages. There are also increased opportunities for reuse because all the client applications in your corporation can share the same business logic—you do not have to compile or recode the logic into several applications. This last benefit is made even easier to implement if you use a programming-language independent and location-transparent mechanism to implement your business layer. Can you already see how COM and DCOM are going to fit into this architecture?

Data Access Layer • The data access layer in the three-tiered architecture is typically composed of one or more Relational DataBase Management Systems (RDBMS)s and the application-specific schema (tables, stored procedures, and so on) that they contain. Although an RDBMS is the canonical data access layer, the data access layer can be composed of other kinds of data storage software, including: non-relational databases (for example, object-oriented or hierarchical databases); Enterprise Resource Planning (ERP) systems like SAP, BAAN, or PeopleSoft; or even Mainframe applications.

Business Layer • As a COM+ programmer (or someone who wants to be) the business layer, the so-called middle-tier, is of most interest to you. Although COM can—and is—used in all three layers of the three-tiered architecture, COM+ is primarily designed to simplify the development of the business layer. The business layer is where you implement the business rules of your application. Typically in this layer, you provide an object layer above your database that hides the schema and implementation of the data stores that the business layers receive information from. This object layer and the associated business rules are implemented in business objects.

Business Objects • Business objects are software components that implement logic specific to some business domain. According to Robert Orfali, Dan Harkey, and Jeri Edwards from their book *The Essential Distributed Objects Survival Guide,* a business object is:

> A representation of a thing active in the business domain, including at least its business name and definition, attributes, behavior, relationships, and constraints. A business object may represent, for example, a person, place, or concept.

You typically implement the business rules of a particular business or domain area in business objects you develop for that business or domain. As an example, if you built a business object that represented an Order, this object might have methods that allow you to retrieve an order or set of orders from a data store given a set of query criteria. It might also let you add line items to an order and save those line items and their association to an Order in some data store. An Order business object might contain methods that let you calculate the total price of an order (including taxes and shipping costs). It might also include methods that allow you to send the order off to be fulfilled. This last step might involve saving the customer and payment information for the order as well as the line items for the order in a data store, or sending this information via some communication mechanism to a third party. By encapsulating all of this logic within a software component you can reuse it from several different types of GUIs (native Windows App, HTML, PDA) in a variety of scenarios. This last sentence lets you see the connection between business objects and COM/COM+. On the Windows platform, it makes sense to implement your business objects using COM. There are a number of advantages to this approach:

- COM objects are location-transparent, so you can easily deploy your COM business objects on the client or on a separate server without changing client code.
- COM is programming-language independent, so you can implement your business objects in any programming language and then use them from clients implemented in any programming language.

THE PRESENTATION LAYER • The presentation layer is the user interface of the application and can take on several forms—from a standard Win32 executable, HTML or dynamic HTML (DHTML), to PDAs. One of the key benefits of the three-tiered architecture is that if you pull the business logic of the application out of the GUI and put it in a separate business layer, then all the different clients can share this logic. In fact, the application I am working on for my present employer has both HTML and PDA-based clients that share the same COM-based business objects.

Other Application Architectures

The three-tiered architecture is now considered the standard architecture for business applications, however, this is a relatively new development. The other types of architectures used today are the MainFrame, two-tiered client/server, and two-tiered client/server with stored procedures.

MAINFRAME

In the mainframe architecture, all the data storage and processing is done on a single, shared node. This shared node sends and receives GUI inputs from a dumb terminal that has only enough processing power to run its input/output devices; such as a keyboard, monitor, and so on. When you type in commands at the keyboard, the mainframe receives the commands, performs some processing and sends commands to update the state of the dumb terminal. Figure 11.3 schematically shows what the mainframe architecture looks like.

The main advantage of this model is that it is easy to administer because there is no client software. All of the software is installed on one node. If you need to change the software, you simply change the software on one computer. Although this may not seem like a big deal, Total Cost of Ownership (TCO) is a big thing in information technology, and having software installed on dozens or even hundreds of machines dramatically increases the TCO of an information system.

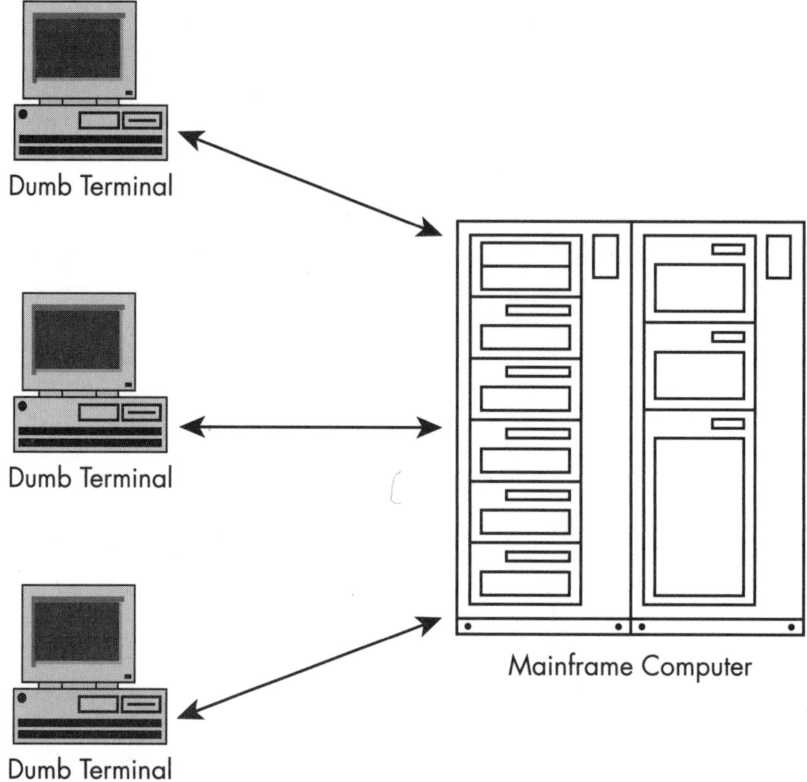

FIGURE 11.3 The Mainframe Application Model.

The disadvantages of this architecture are numerous. If you are going to run an enterprise application on one single machine, it must be quite a machine! Mainframes are large and expensive and development costs of these machines must be amortized over a much smaller number of sales than for a workstation or PC class machine. Hence, mainframe-class machines tend to be significantly more expensive in terms of processing power per dollar. The mainframe architecture also doesn't scale well because the entire processing load is borne by a single machine and that machine quickly becomes a bottleneck as the number of users grow.

Business application architectures, like clothes, go in and out of fashion. You hear so much talk about thin clients, but a mainframe is the ultimate thin-client architecture. In addition, the Application Service Provider model (discussed in Chapter 13) is a lot like the old mainframe time shares.

CLIENT/SERVER

In the client/server architecture your application is divided between a server, which is a software service that accepts commands and performs processing in response to those commands, and a client that sends commands to the server. The canonical client/server application has a RDBMS running on a server and a Graphical User Interface (GUI) application running on a client as shown in Figure 11.4.

Typically, the server is either a server-class PC, a UNIX workstation, a mid-range computer, or some times even a mainframe-class machine. In most cases, the client is either a PC or a UNIX workstation. It is not a requirement that the client and server be located on different machines. Like the three-tiered architecture, the client-server architecture is a logical partitioning of your application. The client and server are software services not machines.

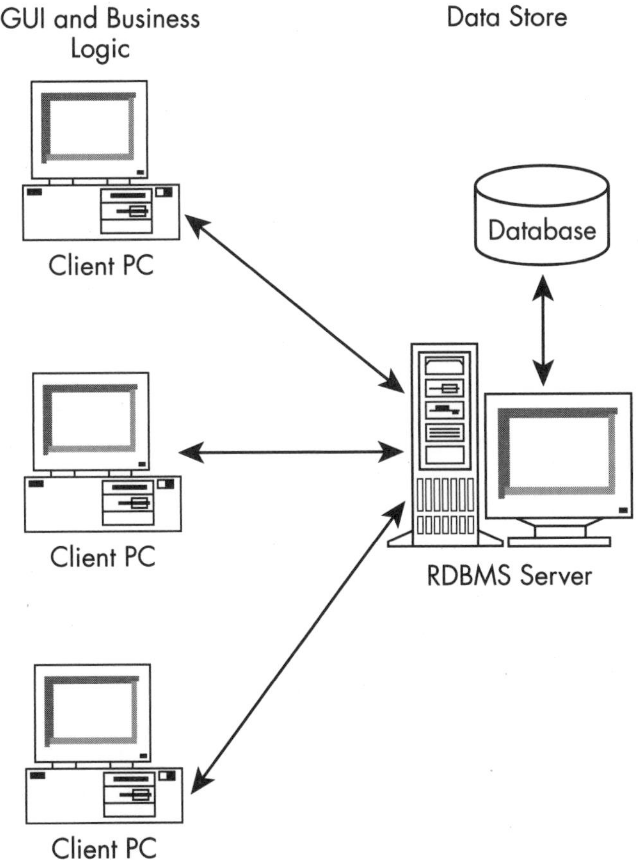

FIGURE 11.4 The Canonical Client/Server Architecture.

In the client/server architecture, the total processing required by an application is divided between the client and the server. In the canonical case (an RDBMS as the server with a GUI client), the server is responsible for optimizing and executing queries, fetching the data from physical storage and sending it out over the network to the client. Once the client receives the information, it may or may not perform some processing of the data before it is displayed in the GUI. Going the other way, when the user wishes to make updates, business rules and data-integrity constraints are enforced on the client and then the data is sent via the network to the server, which stores it in the database. The database may also enforce certain data-integrity constraints.

The advantages of this architecture, relative to the mainframe architecture, are that it is more cost effective and scalable than the mainframe architecture because instead of requiring one large, expensive machine, the client/server architecture uses several smaller, less expensive machines to accomplish the same task. You get more bang for your buck with these smaller machines (usually PCs or UNIX workstations) because they are in much wider use. The cost of developing these machines is amortized over a much larger number of sales.

The client/server architecture is also more scalable because you can easily add more client machines in this architecture. Of course, if you add too many clients, you eventually exceed the capabilities of your server. In many cases, you can replace a single server with a cluster of servers if you need to scale your system upward. Even if you have to replace the server completely, it is usually much cheaper to buy a new server-class PC or UNIX workstation than it is to buy a new mainframe-class machine.

There are some disadvantages to this architecture, however. Although the hardware costs for client/server architecture are significantly cheaper, the difference in TCO is not nearly as great. Client/server applications are harder to develop and deploy than mainframe applications.

Perhaps the biggest problem with the client/server architecture is that the only place where business processing and data integrity rules can be enforced is in client software. Business rules tend to change often. A business may offer a 10% discount on orders over $100.00 in one month, but the next month their major competitor may go out of business and there may be little reason to offer such a discount. Due to slow sales, 39-cent cheeseburger Sunday may well become 29-cent cheeseburger Saturday. It is expensive to develop and deploy new software to hundreds of clients when the business rules of an organization change. Also, by having all the business processing on the client, opportunities for reuse are hindered. An accounting application and an order-taking application may use the same business rules. If the same business logic must be coded into each application, then you have to recompile and redeploy both of these clients if you change the code that implements these business rules.

CLIENT/SERVER WITH STORED PROCEDURES

Stored procedures were created to address many of the problems with the pure client/server architecture. Most enterprise-class relational database management systems let you create stored procedures. Stored procedures are small programs that are executed by the database server. With stored procedures, you can move some of your business processing into the database itself and this is a big win on many levels. It significantly improves the performance of an application because queries that are executed in a stored procedure are pre-compiled and optimized so they run faster. Also, in many cases, instead of performing several queries to bring data to the client so it can be processed according to business rules, you can instead fetch the data in the stored procedure (the data never goes out over the network because the stored procedure executes on the server), perform the processing on the server, and return a single processed value to the client. This not only drastically improves performance it also reduces network traffic. There are, however, problems with stored procedures. The languages used to write stored procedures are not standardized. Each RDBMS has its own stored procedure language. If you use Transact SQL to write stored procedures for Microsoft SQL Server, you have to re-write all of those stored procedures if you decide to change to Oracle because Oracle uses a completely different language called PL SQL, for stored procedures. Another problem is that stored procedure languages tend to be somewhat limited and are best suited for small amounts of code, and each client still has to maintain its own connection to the database.

N-TIERED

The N-Tiered architecture is really just an extension of the three-tiered architecture. Frankly, I don't like the term N-Tiered because most of these architectures still have three logical tiers. The additional tiers tend to be purely implementation constructs. For instance, an application I recently worked on had two-tiers of business objects. There were data-centric business objects that took scalar parameters as inputs, executed queries or stored procedures, and returned disconnected ADO recordsets. These data-centric business objects also took disconnected ADO recordsets as input and performed updates. These objects ran under Microsoft Transaction Server (MTS) as originally written. The architecture also contained User Interface (UI)-centric business objects that took the recordsets from the data-centric business objects and presented the information to the presentation layer in a way that made the information easy to use. You could call this a four-tiered architecture, or N-tiered architecture, but it's still three-logical tiers. You are just implementing one of those *logical* layers with two *physical* layers of software. The application I am working on for my current employer actually has more than four tiers. The architecture includes presenter objects, data objects, meta-data objects, and interchange objects (for communicating with third-party software). These are still implementation constructs. You can group all of the objects logically into presentation, business, and data.

DCOM Alone Is Not Enough

Now that you know what an enterprise-class distributed application is and how they are architected, let's bring this discussion back to the central question of this section: why do you need COM+? In Chapter 10, you learned that DCOM enables computer-to-computer communication and it allows you to configure security, at a course-grain declaratively using `dcomcnfg`, or at a fine-grain programmatically. But there are several problems that make it difficult to develop enterprise-class distributed applications with DCOM alone. Let's understand these problems first, before talking about the COM+ solution.

Fine-Grained Security

Enterprise-class distributed applications need *fine-grained security*. Fine-grained security is the ability to configure the security settings for a server on a per-class, per-interface, or even a per-method basis. You can implement fine-grained security using the COM, programmatic security API. As you can see from Chapter 10, many business application developers may have a tough time with this API. Most of the functions and interfaces in this API cannot even be called from the 4GL languages (VB, Delphi, or Powerbuilder) that most IT shops prefer.

Scalability

Another problem is *scalability*. An enterprise-class application must be able to handle simultaneous use by hundreds and perhaps thousands of corporate employees and customers while maintaining acceptable latency and response times. What is acceptable latency or response depends on the operation in question. Usually employees and customers expect latencies and response times to be measured in seconds not minutes.

Data Integrity

Another problem that enterprise-class applications must address is *data-integrity*. This means that updates to data stores must be made in a consistent way (data must not be corrupted, updates must not be lost, and invalid intermediate states must not be allowed to propagate through the system), even in the face of simultaneous use by hundreds of users. Data-integrity is usually enforced with *transactions*. Most corporations store their important data in databases of one kind or another and most of these databases provide sophisticated transaction management tools that let you make updates while maintaining data-integrity. These transaction management mechanisms work well if you are using a single database that resides on one node in your network, however, important information may be spread throughout the enterprise on multiple servers. Also, important corporate information is also stored in other places from Microsoft Office Documents such as Excel spreadsheets, e-mail (as Microsoft found out in their anti-trust trial), and even directories like the Active Directory. Updating these various, disparate data stores requires distributed transactions.

The COM+ Solution

The easiest way to understand how COM+ works is to consider all the things you would have to do if you wanted to write an enterprise-class distributed application on the Windows platform and COM+ didn't exist.

If this is truly an enterprise-class application, you most likely have requirements that restrict how much access certain people have to the application. These may restrict some users access to parts of an application while allowing them to use other parts of it. The DCOM configuration tool, dcomcnfg, does not let you do this. So, you would probably start out by learning all about the COM programmatic security API. It may take you a while to come up to speed and you will have to write quite a bit of code, but eventually you would probably build a framework for yourself (perhaps a DLL or some reusable code) that you could reuse repeatedly in your COM objects.

If this application is like most enterprise-class applications, you need to retrieve data from and update one or more database servers. To perform updates while maintaining data-integrity, you need transactions. If the application has to update more than one database simultaneously, you need distributed transactions.

You can learn to use either the transaction management primitives (Begin, Commit, Rollback) provided by your database's native API, or you can learn how to use the transaction management features in one of the standardized data access APIs that Microsoft provides (ODBC, OLEDB). The problem isn't bad if you are interacting with only one database server. Using transactions becomes far more problematic if the data you are working on resides on multiple servers. To make transactional updates to multiple servers, you need support for distributed transactions. There are tools you can buy that let you add distributed transactions to your applications. Transarc (now owned by IBM) and Encina are just a few of the companies that make Transaction Processing (TP) monitors that can be used to enable distributed transactions. If you decide to use one of these products, you need to learn their APIs and write code to interface with them.

Assuming you solved the fine-grained security and transaction problems, once you started using your application you would probably find that it was not scalable. If you deployed your COM objects in the classical three-tiered architecture (see the section on application architecture), you may find that the server where your business objects reside is getting bogged down when more than a few dozen simultaneous users try to use it. Perhaps it is even crashing. After examining the situation, you realize that each client is creating, and then holding on to, several COM objects for the life of each user's session. Once several dozen or even a few hundred users start using the application, the amount of memory and threads being used on the business-layer server quickly grows to an intolerable level. Moreover, each business object is also creating a connection to the database and then holding on to the connection for the entire life of the business object. Soon the number of simultaneous connections to the database starts to be a problem. That's if you don't run into licensing restrictions first. Once again, you can get around these problems if you have the time and expertise. For instance, you can use several server machines to host your COM objects and then create a broker object that the client must go to first to instantiate a COM object. The broker is responsible for finding the server machine with the lightest load and instantiating the requested COM object there; this is called Load Balancing. You could also enhance the scalability of your business layer by recognizing that even though hundreds of clients may be holding references to COM objects, only a small fraction of those clients will be executing a method on an object at any given time. You can take advantage of this fact by essentially tricking the client into believing that it is holding a reference to the actual COM object when it is instead holding a wrapper object. When the client makes a method call, this wrapper object can quickly instantiate a real object, execute the requested method, and then destroy the object when you are done. In this way, you only have as many objects as you have clients currently executing methods. This is sometimes referred to as Just In Time (JIT) activation. You can make this scheme even more efficient by maintaining a pool of objects and returning the object to this pool instead of destroying it when you are done.

You can solve the problem of too many database connections by maintaining a pool of connections that all the business objects can share. When an object needs a database connection, it can obtain one from the pool. When the object is done with the connection, it can return it to the pool where it can be used by another object. Of course you'll have to write thread-synchronization code to avoid some nasty race conditions. Again, with time and expertise, you could probably implement this logic.

Even if you solve all of these problems, you are still not done. You may have to support mobile workers using PDAs, laptop computers, and wireless networking technology. The availability requirements of these users will likely exceed the typical availability of today's wireless network infrastructure. In other words, your application (or at least parts of it) have to continue to function even if they are unable to communicate with the home office at that exact moment. This is sometimes called disconnected operation. Again, with time and expertise, you could build a store and forward mechanism that would cache information on the mobile client until a connection to the home office was available and then it would forward it to the home office.

Are you starting to see a problem here? You're simply trying to build a business application and to do so, you have to write thousands of lines of infrastructure code to implement fine-grained security, distributed transactions, object and connection pooling, load balancing, and store and forward method invocation. This code has nothing to do with the business logic you are trying to implement. It's code that you have to write so your application will function in an enterprise-class distributed environment. This is where COM+ comes in. COM+ provides you with the infrastructure needed to build enterprise-class distributed applications. All you have to do is implement your business logic in an in-process (DLL-based) COM server and configure your server to run in the COM+ runtime environment. COM+ provides you with fine-grained security, transactions, load balancing, enhanced scalability through JIT activation and pooling of objects and connections, thread synchronization, and store and forward method invocation. You do your part: Implement the business logic of your application. COM+ does its part: making sure that your business logic is usable in an enterprise-class, distributed environment.

How It Works: The COM+ Architecture

The keys to understanding COM+ architecture are Attribute-Based Programming, Contexts, and Interception. If you understand these concepts, you'll understand how COM+ works.

Attribute-Based Programming

Understanding attribute-based programming should be fairly easy for you because you've already used it. In Chapter 9 I talked about threading in the context of COM. In that chapter, you learned that COM classes that are implemented in an in-process server should register a `ThreadingModel` key in the registry. This `ThreadingModel` key tells the COM runtime what threading support objects of that class expect to receive. If the `ThreadingModel` registry key contains the value `Apartment`, that tells the COM runtime that objects of the class are not thread-safe and COM should only allow one thread to call the object's methods directly. If the `ThreadingModel` registry key contains the value `Free`, then the class is telling the COM runtime that objects of the class are thread-safe and COM can allow any thread in the Multi-Threaded Apartment to access the object. The key is that the COM class indicates the threading support it needs from COM by setting the value of an attribute (the `ThreadingModel` registry key), the COM runtime then handles the rest. You don't have to write any code. This is Attribute-Based Programming.

COM+ takes this idea and runs with it. COM+ adds many new attributes that let you control such things as transaction support, fine-grained security, object pooling, and so on. Table 11.1 contains a list of the new attributes that COM+ provides. Don't let the length of this list intimidate you, since most of these attributes have defaults and I discuss each attribute in either this chapter or in Chapter 12.

TABLE 11.1 COM+ Attributes

Attribute	Possible Settings	Applies To
Must activate in activator's context	On/Off	Class
Transaction	Nonsupported, Supported, Required, Requires New	Class
Synchronization	Nonsupported, Supported, Required, Requires New	Class
Object Pooling	On/Off, Max Pool Size, Min Pool Size, Timeout	Class
Declarative Construction	A string that is passed to each object of the class when it is first created.	Class
JIT Activation	On/Off	Class
Component Supports Events and Statistics	On/Off	Class
Enforce declarative fine-grained security	On/Off	Application, Class, Interface, Method
Security Level	Perform access checks at the process level/ Perform Access Checks at the Component and Process Level.	Application
Authentication Level	None, Connect, Call, Packet, Packet Integrity, Packet Privacy	Application
Impersonation Level	Anonymous, Identify, Impersonate, Delegate	Application
Server Process Shutdown	Leave running when idle, Number of minutes until server shutdown	Application
Disable Deletion	On/Off	Application
Disable Shutdown	On/Off	Application
Launch in Debugger	On/Off	Application
Enable Compensating Resource Managers	On/Off	Application

Enable 3GB Support	On/Off	Application
Identity	Interactive User, This User (User Name and Password of Selected User)	Application
Activation	Server Application, Library Application	Application
Queueing	On/Off	Application

To add support for distributed transactions to a COM+ object, for instance, just set the appropriate value for the object's transaction attribute. The COM+ runtime takes care of either starting a transaction on the object's behalf or having the object enlist in an existing transaction. When the object is deactivated, the COM+ runtime takes care of committing the transaction. To add support for fine-grained security, set the appropriate values for the security-related attributes. The COM+ runtime ensures that the calling user is authorized to call a method or use an interface.

These new attributes do not live in the registry. They live in a new Windows 2000 configuration database called the COM+ catalog.

The COM+ catalog is composed of both the `HKEY_CLASSES_ROOT` key in the system registry and a new Windows 2000 repository called the Auxiliary Configuration Database.

Windows 2000 contains a set of Administrative interfaces that you can use to build a Catalog Manager, with an application that can administer the COM+ catalog. These interfaces are implemented in an Automation server called `COMAdmin.dll`. Figure 11.5 shows the interfaces exported by this Automation server.

Table 11.2 contains a short description of each of the COM+ administrative interfaces.

TABLE 11.2 The COM+ Administrative Interfaces

Interface	Description
COMAdminCatalog	The root interface for the server.
Root	Provides access to other collections.
Applications	COM+ applications on this machine.
ApplicationCluster	Server machines within this machine's application cluster.
ComputerList	List of all computers that this machine knows about.
DCOMProtocols	Underlying protocols to be used by DCOM.

InProcServers	All DLL Servers registered with the system.
LocalComputer	Represents properties of this machine.
TransientSubscriptions	All transient event subscriptions currently active on this machine.
Components	Components installed in a COM+ application.
Roles	All the Roles in a COM+ application.
SubscriptionsForComponent	All the persistent subscriptions to events received by this component.
InterfacesForComponent	Interfaces supported by this component.
RolesForComponent	Roles whose members are allowed to use this component.
MethodsForInterface	Methods of this interface.
RolesForInterface	Roles whose members are allowed to use this interface.
RolesForMethod	Roles whose members are allowed to use this method.

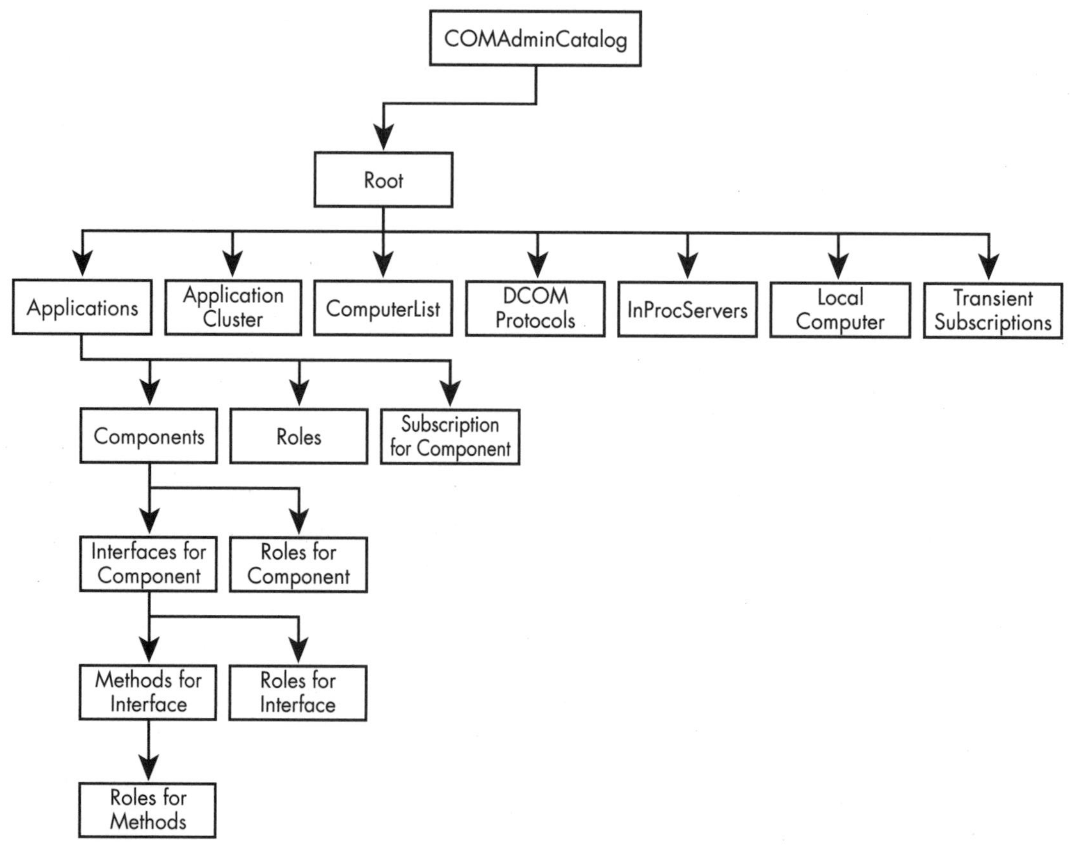

FIGURE 11.5 The COM+ Administrative Interfaces.

Windows 2000 also contains a pre-built Catalog Manager you can use to administer the new COM+ attributes. This Catalog Manager is called the Component Services Explorer. The Component Services Explorer is a snap-in for the Microsoft Management Console (MMC). The Microsoft Management Console is a common tool that is used to administer all of Microsoft's Server Applications. The latest versions of IIS, SQL Server, and Index Server are all managed using MMC. Each server application that wants to be administered via the MMC must provide a snap-in, which is a COM component that implements a set of interfaces that the MMC expects. The snap-in provides all the property sheets, menus, and displays that are particular to a given server.

You can create your own MMC snap-ins using Visual C++ and ATL. Create an ATL project and then select New ATL Object… from the Insert Menu. Notice that one of the choices listed is MMC Snap-In.

To bring up the component services explorer, perform the following steps:

1. Click the `Start` Button.
2. Select `Programs\Administrative Tools\Component Services\` (the MMC with the Component Services snap-in appear as shown in Figure 11.6).

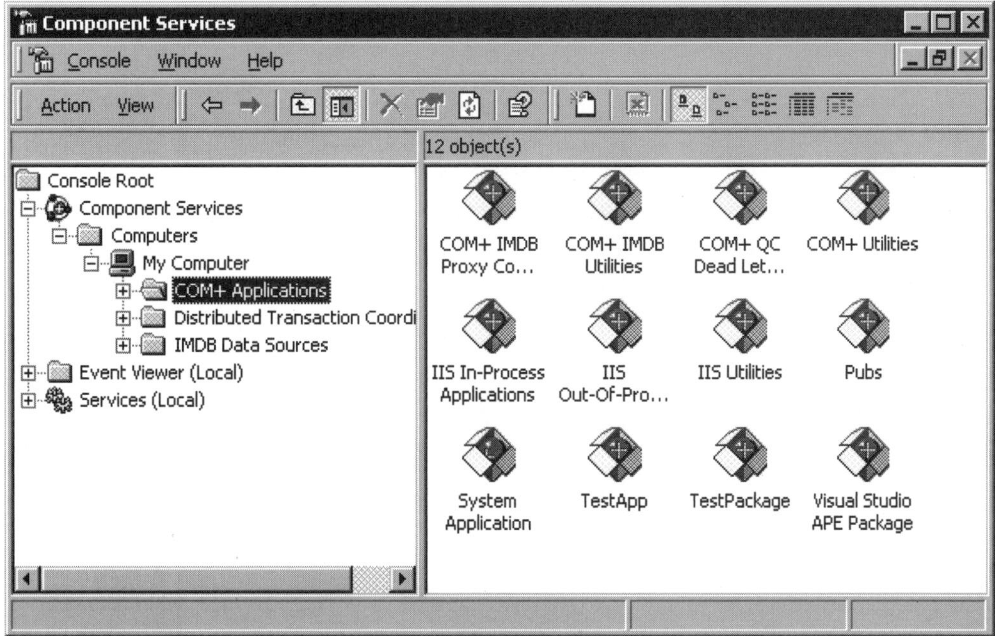

FIGURE 11.6 The Component Services Explorer.

Objects that are configured to use the new COM+ attributes are called *configured components*. You will learn a little later in this chapter how to use the Component Services Explorer to configure a component.

You do not have to configure a COM component to use it under Windows 2000. COM+ also supports *unconfigured components* that do not have entries in the auxiliary configuration database. They only have the usual entries for a COM server beneath HKEY_CLASSES_ROOT. Unconfigured components continue to work as normal and do not require recompilation to work under Windows 2000. Before you can understand the new attributes that COM+ supports, you have to understand the role of a new-to-COM+ concept called a Context.

The Importance of Context

A COM+ Context is the runtime environment in which one or more *compatible* COM+ objects in a particular process execute. Compatible objects are objects that share the same runtime requirements, i.e., they have the same settings for their COM+ attributes. For a group of COM+ objects to reside in the same context, they must share exactly the same attribute settings. If any of these settings differ, the objects are placed in different Contexts. The relationship between Processes, Contexts, and Apartments is shown in Figure 11.7.

A Context resides in an apartment within a process. Only threads in that apartment can call into a Context directly unless the Context is in the

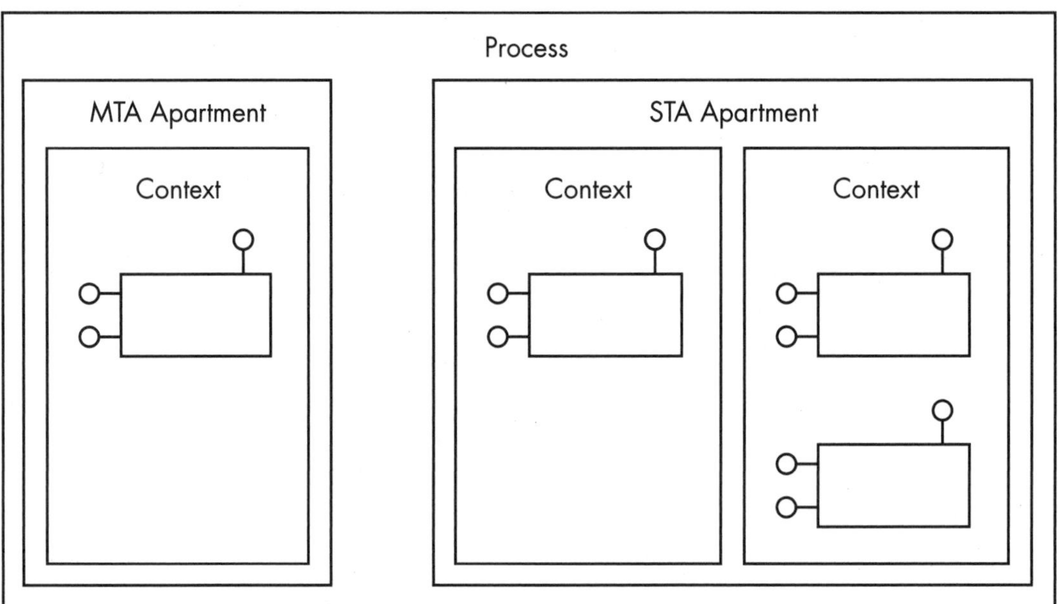

FIGURE 11.7 Processes, Apartments, and Contexts.

thread-neutral apartment. An apartment can contain one or more Contexts and a Context can contain one or more objects (you already know that a process can contain one or more apartments).

If you are like me, you may find Contexts confusing at first. Keep in mind that COM+ Contexts are largely a conceptual construct. Think of them as cozy environments where COM+ objects can execute. This environment can enforce certain security constraints; it can also guarantee that all database operations that an object performs occur within a transaction and can also guarantee thread synchronization for an object.

THE OBJECT CONTEXT

When the COM+ runtime first creates the Context for an object, it reads the settings for the COM+ attributes (security, transaction, object pooling, and so on) that are configured for the object's class from the COM+ Catalog. These settings are stored in a system-created COM object called an object context. I've also heard the object context referred to as a context object. Object context is probably a better name because, there are actually two system-created context objects that a COM+ object can access within its methods to retrieve and modify context information. There is an *Object Context* that can be used to retrieve and modify context information that is specific to an object and there is a *Call Context* that can be used to retrieve and modify context information that is specific to a particular method call on an object.

A COM+ object can retrieve its object context by calling a new Windows 2000 API function called `CoGetObjectContext`, which is defined as shown below:

```
HRESULT CoGetObjectContext(REFIID riid,LPVOID **ppv)
```

If you are using Visual Basic, you must reference the COM+ Services Type Library and then you can call the GetObjectContext method to retrieve an object context.

The context object implements a number of interfaces as shown in Figure 11.8.

In the first parameter to `CoGetObjectContext`, specify the interface you would like to receive on the object context. If the call is successful, the interface pointer is returned in the second parameter. If the call is unsuccessful, the second parameter is NULL and an error HRESULT is returned. An example call to `CoGetObjectContext` is shown below:

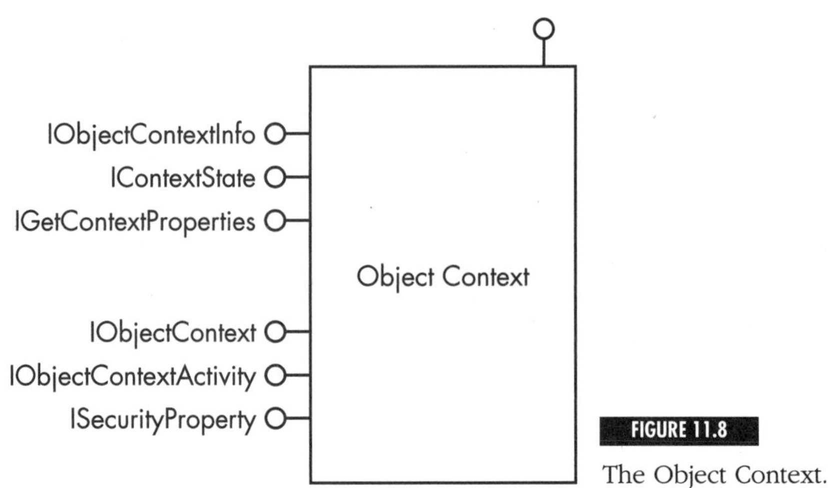

FIGURE 11.8

The Object Context.

```
HRESULT hRes;
IContextState *pContextState;
   hRes=CoGetObjectContext(IID_IContextState,(void **)&pContextState);
   if (SUCCEEDED(hRes))
   {
   // Use the object context
   }
```

Table 11.3 lists the interfaces that the context object supports and gives a short description of each one.

TABLE 11.3 Interfaces Supported by the Object Context

Interface Name	Description
IContextState	Controls object deactivation and transaction voting by manipulating context state bits. Calling the methods of this interface lets you set consistent and done bits independently of each other and get the current status of each bit.
IObjectContextInfo	Returns transaction, activity, and context information on the current context object. Using the methods of this interface, you can retrieve relevant information contained within an object context.
IGetContextProperties	Provides access to object context properties.
IObjectContext	Provides access to the current object's context.
IObjectContextActivity	Used to retrieve a unique identifier associated with the current activity. This activity identifier is a GUID, and is only valid for the lifetime of the current activity.
ISecurityProperty	Used to determine the security ID of the current object's original caller or direct caller.

With the current version of Visual C++ 6.0, you have to include comsvcs.h and link with `comsvcs.lib` to use `CoGetObjectContext`. You will see how to do this in the next chapter.

The `IObjectContext`, `IObjectContextActivity`, and `ISecurityProperty` interfaces are all deprecated under Windows 2000. Everything you may want to do with the object context can be done through the `IContextState`, `IObjectContextInfo`, and `IGetContextProperties` interfaces.

CALL CONTEXT

To retrieve method-specific Context information, you must use the `CoGetCallContext` API function, which is also new to Windows 2000. `CoGetCallContext` is defined as shown below:

```
HRESULT CoGetCallContext(REFIID riid,LPVOID **ppv)
```

This method is called in a similar manner as `CoGetObjectContext`. The Call Context implements the interfaces shown in Figure 11.9.

Table 11.4 gives a brief description of each interface implemented by the Call Context.

TABLE 11.4 Interfaces Supported by the Call Context

Interface Name	Description
ISecurityCallContext	The key interface used to control fine-grained security programmatically. It allows you to determine if fine-grained security is enabled and if the specified user is a member of a role.
IServerSecurity	Used to access and modify DCOM-related security information as opposed to COM+—related security information.
ICancelMethodCalls	Manages cancellation requests on an outbound method call and monitors the current state of that method call on the server thread.

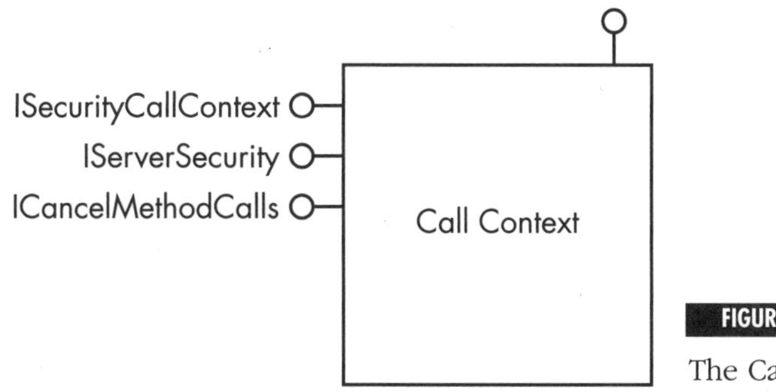

FIGURE 11.9 The Call Context.

The code shown below demonstrates how you would use the Call Context:

```
HRESULT hRes;
ISecurityCallContext *pSecurityCallContext;
hRes=CoGetCallObjectContext(IID_ISecurityCallContext,(void
**)&pSecurityCallContext);
if (SUCCEEDED(hRes))
{
// Use call context
}
```

Interception

If a client calls a COM+ object that resides in the same Context, then a direct method call can be made from the client to the COM+ object. The client in this scenario already has the exact same environment that the COM+ requires. There is no need to alter the environment in any way. If the client of a COM+ object resides in a different Context from the object, then a lightweight proxy called an interceptor is setup between the client and the COM+ object. The interceptor is responsible for performing whatever actions are required to transfer control from the client's Context to the COM+ object's Context. If the COM+ object requires a Transaction, that means a transaction may need to be started. If the COM+ object's Context enforces fine-grained access control, then the interceptor verifies that the user is authorized to call the method.

If a COM+ object runs in its own process (separate from the client), the COM+ interceptor resides between the RPC channel and the marshaling stub as shown in Figure 11.10.

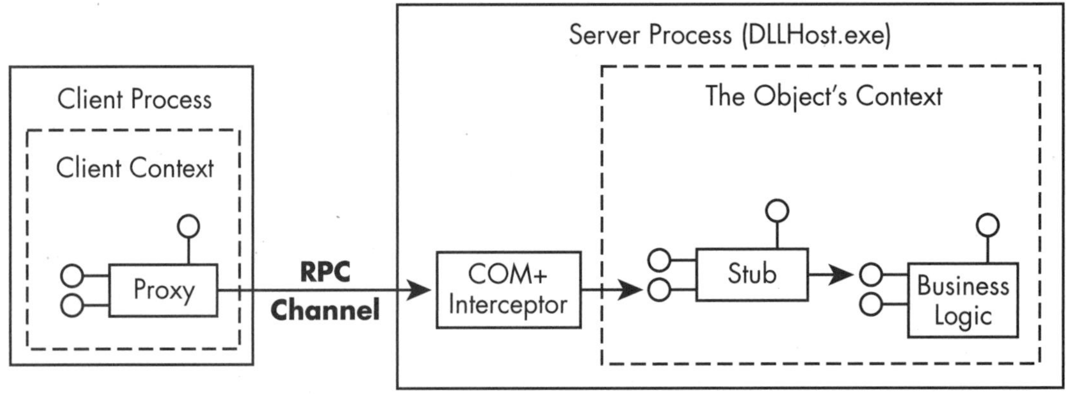

FIGURE 11.10 Interception with an Out-of-Process COM+ Object.

If a COM+ object runs in the same process as its client, the COM+ interceptor sits between the client and the object as shown in Figure 11.11.

Notice in Figure 11.11 that the object and the client are running in the same process. In Figure 11.10, they are in different processes. In either case, the COM+ interceptor has the opportunity to perform actions both before and after a method call on a COM+ object. In this way, the interceptor can enforce fine-grained security, start a transaction, perform thread synchronization, or even fetch an object from a pool of objects. This process is called *Interception* and it is the key to how COM+ can (almost) transparently provide a range of value-added services to your COM objects.

The COM+ interceptor is sometimes called a lightweight proxy. You can understand why by comparing it to the marshaling proxy talked about in Chapter 6 when I discussed out-of-process COM objects. A marshaling proxy sits between a COM object and its client and provides services that enable them to function properly. If the client and the object reside in different processes, possibly on different machines, the proxy provides InterProcess Communication (IPC) that allows the method call to transfer from a thread in the client process to a thread in the server process. If the client and the object reside in the same process, but in different apartments, the marshaling proxy does an intra-process thread switch. A COM+ interceptor also sits between a COM object and its client and provides services that enable them to function properly. But, the COM+ interceptor is a *lightweight* proxy because it never does a thread (or process) switch. It only provides whatever actions are necessary to make sure that a COM+ object always runs within its configured environment. InterProcess Communication is still provided via marshaling proxies and stubs. Thread-switching if it is needed is still provided by apartments.

COM+ CLIENTS AND CONTEXT

To understand interception, it helps if you understand the two types of clients that a COM+ object can have. A COM+ object that resides in a

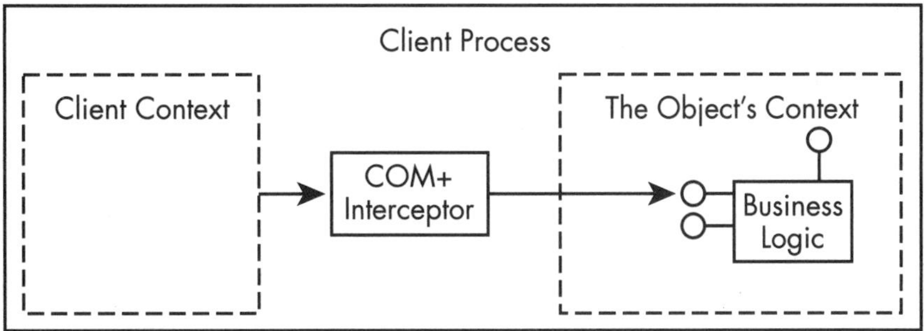

FIGURE 11.11 Interception with an In-Process COM+ Object.

Context can be accessed by two types of clients: (1) another COM+ object or (2) a client that is running outside of the COM+ runtime environment as shown in Figure 11.12.

The second type of client is called a *Base Client.* This is a piece of software that uses the services of a COM+ object but itself runs outside the COM+ runtime environment. Base clients are usually User Interface (UI) software but they don't have to be. As you write COM+ objects, you will often find yourself writing code wherein one COM+ object utilizes the services of another COM+ object. In Figure 11.12, Object A is using the services of object B. So, object A is a client of object B, but it is not base client because it is also running in the COM+ environment.

In most cases a COM+ object's base client runs in a separate process from the object itself. So by definition (a Context is process-relative) the client and the COM+ are in different Contexts and interception is required. If one COM+ object is utilizing the services of another COM+ object (a bank object is using an account object for example), then it is possible that the we objects will run in the same Context if they are configured in the exact same way.

Contexts and Apartments

The introduction of Contexts changes the role and definition of apartments from that discussed in Chapter 9. In COM+, an apartment is just a group of Contexts within a process as shown in Figure 11.13. An apartment can contain many Contexts, but each Context belongs to one and only one apartment.

Contexts replace apartments as the innermost execution environment that a COM object runs within. Apartments also determine which threads are allowed to call directly into an object within a particular Context. If you look at Figure 11.13, notice that in the case of the multi-threaded and single-threaded apartment types, only those threads in a Context's enclosing apartment can directly access objects in that Context. Threads in any apartment, however, can access objects that reside within Contexts in the thread-neutral apartment.

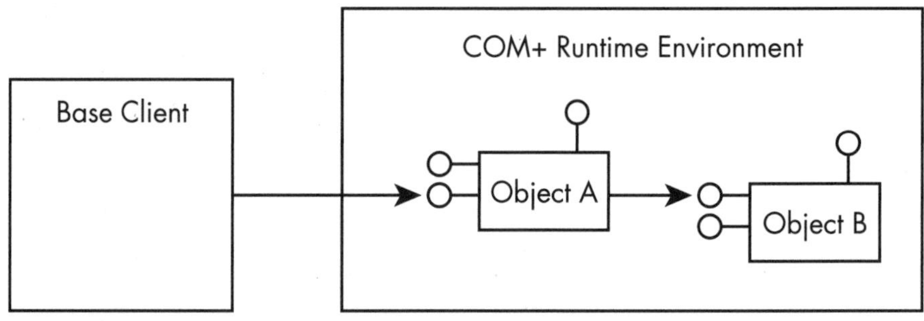

FIGURE 11.12 Two Types of COM+ Clients.

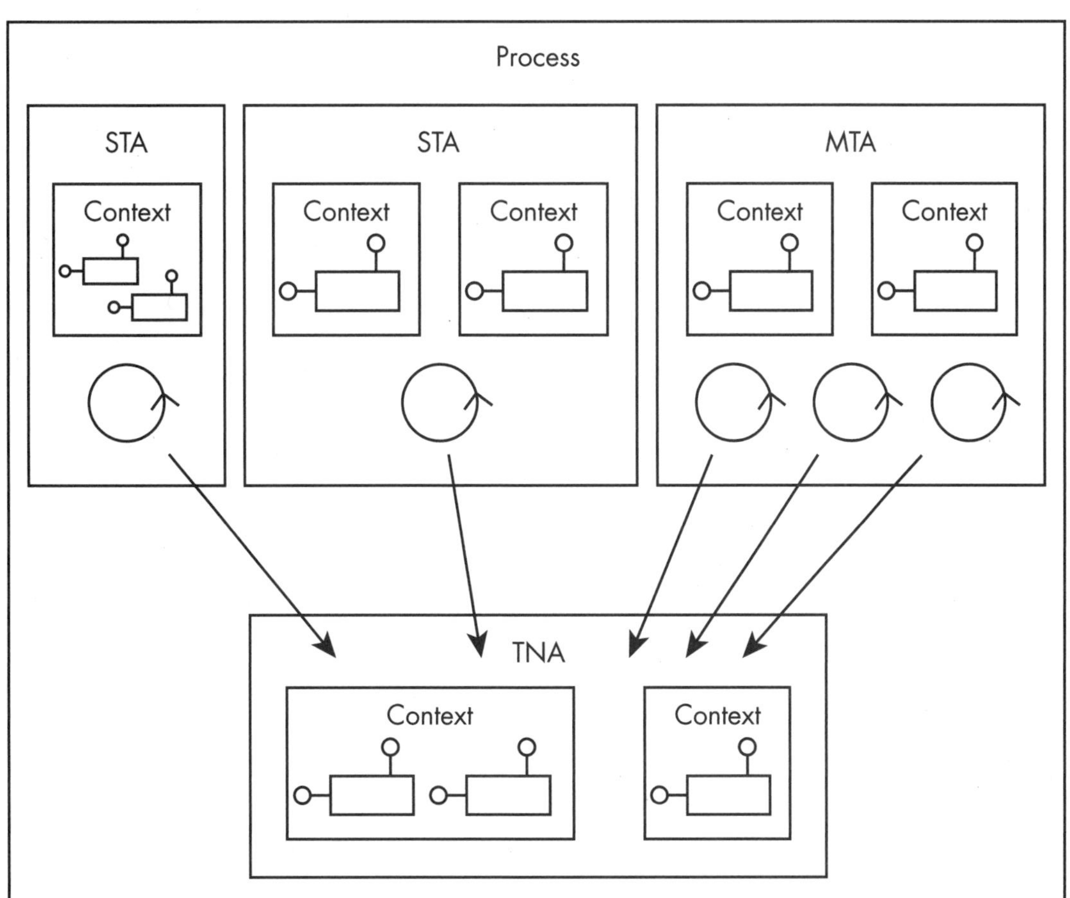

FIGURE 11.13 Apartments and Contexts.

Contexts are also capable of providing thread synchronization for COM+ objects that do not provide it themselves. In classic COM, this was always done with single-threaded apartments. So why do you even need apartments? The answer is *thread-affinity*.

As discussed in Chapter 9, COM objects that have thread affinity are objects that (because of their design) must only be accessed by one *particular* thread. An object might have thread affinity because it uses thread-local storage to store information or because it contains GUI code.

The thread synchronization provided by COM+ does not work with objects that have thread-affinity. COM+ uses locking to provide thread synchronization.

If you configure an object to use the thread synchronization provided by COM+, once one thread (any thread) invokes a method on the object, all other threads are locked out until the first thread exits the method and releases the lock. This scheme works well with the object pooling of COM+, which requires that an object be accessed by multiple threads during its lifetime. Because this scheme does not restrict *which* threads are allowed to call the object, it doesn't work well for objects that have thread affinity.

Remember you don't have to use the thread synchronization provided by COM+. You can configure your objects to use it or not use it.

Single-Threaded Apartments (STA) do not use locking to provide thread-synchronization. They allow one and only one thread (the one thread in the STA) to access a COM object for its entire life. This scheme provides protection against the problems caused by multiple threads. It also works well with COM objects that have thread-affinity because it guarantees that only one *particular* thread ever accesses the object. Unfortunately, STAs do not work well with object pooling (I discuss why shortly) and because apartment-threaded objects are so picky about the thread that they execute on, lots of thread-switching results which has negative effects on performance. The best way to understand the new relationship between Contexts and apartments is that Contexts let you control *when* threads are allowed to call methods on a COM+ object. Apartments let you control *which* threads are allowed to call methods on COM+ objects. The new rules regarding apartments with COM+ are as follows:

- Most COM+ objects should use the new Thread Neutral Apartment (TNA) discussed in Chapter 9 and should use the thread-synchronization provided by COM+.
- Only COM+ objects that have a User Interface, or for other reasons have thread-affinity should continue to use STAs.

To support legacy unconfigured components, each COM apartment contains a default Context. The default Context doesn't support any of the extended features of COM+. Components that are configured never reside in the default Context. Objects that have *not* been configured reside in the default Context if the COM object's threading model is incompatible with its client's apartment or if `CoCreateInstance` is called by a freshly-`CoInitialized` thread from a compatible apartment.

Configure an Object to Use COM+

With an understanding of the COM+ architecture under your belt, you are now ready to start talking about how to configure your COM components to use COM+. To use the extended services that COM+ provides (fine-grained security, distributed transactions, object pooling, and so on), you must first add the component's server (which must be a DLL) to a COM+ application.

A COM+ application is a group of COM+ components that are administered together and run in the same process.

Once you have added your component to a COM+ application, you can use the Component Services Explorer to select settings for each of the COM+ attributes. Most of these attributes are configured on a per-class basis. Some COM+ attributes—primarily the ones that control fine-grained security—can be configured separately for a class, interface, or method. There are also some attributes that apply to an entire COM+ application. Table 11.1 summarizes the COM+ attributes that you will need to configure for a COM+ application and the configuration unit: class, interface, method, or application, to which each attribute applies.

Preliminaries

To use the extended services that COM+ provides, you must implement your COM+ components in an in-process server. The COM+ runtime environment is a control freak and it simply cannot exercise enough control over an out-of-process server to do its job. Although your components must reside in an in-process server to work with COM+, in most cases, once a component is configured to run under COM+, it actually runs in its own process. You'll learn how when I talk about surrogate processes.

Ideally, your COM+ objects should also use the Thread Neutral Apartment (TNA). Objects that use the MTA or STA objects can be configured also, but they have limitations. For instance, your components cannot use object pooling unless they can run in the TNA or MTA.

A component must also use standard marshaling if it is to be configured. If the component is an Automation server, you can use the standard type library marshaler. Or, if your component has custom interfaces, you can build a marshaling DLL from the code generated by MIDL. But you cannot configure components that use custom marshaling.

Because Visual Basic (VB) 6.0 only lets you build apartment-threaded COM objects, it is not a good environment for creating objects to be used in COM+. VB 7.0 remedies this problem and is likely to become the easiest way to build COM+ components.

COM+ Applications

To configure a COM+ component, you must first create a COM+ application. A COM+ application is a group of one or more COM+ components that are administered as a unit and run in the same process. A COM+ application can include components from multiple servers (DLLs).

Application is such an overloaded word that I use the term COM+ application whenever I am referring to the COM+ notion of an application.

There are two types of COM+ applications: *Server Applications* and *Library Applications*.

SERVER APPLICATIONS

Each COM+ Server Application runs in its own process. Actually, the server application runs in a *surrogate process* that is provided by COM+. Each surrogate process is an instance of `DLLHost.Exe`. You can find `DLLHost.exe` in `\winnt\system32\`.

WHAT IS A SURROGATE PROCESS? • I can explain what a surrogate process is by first asking the following rhetorical question: can an in-process server run in a separate process (perhaps even on a separate machine) from its client? Although it sounds like an oxymoron, the answer to this question is actually *yes*. To run an in-process server in a separate process from its client, you simply have to load the in-process server into the address space of some process *other* than the client process. The client can then communicate with the in-process server by going through this other process as shown in Figure 11.14.

In most cases, you configure your COM+ applications to be a server application. A server application is also the default type of COM+ application.

LIBRARY APPLICATIONS

A COM+ library application runs in the same process as its client. The main reasons for choosing a library application is if two or more COM+ server applications need to use the services of a separate COM+ application. Each

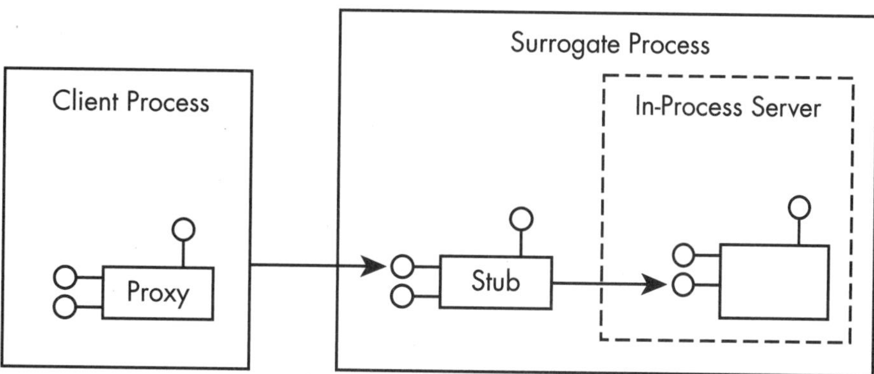

FIGURE 11.14 A Surrogate Process.

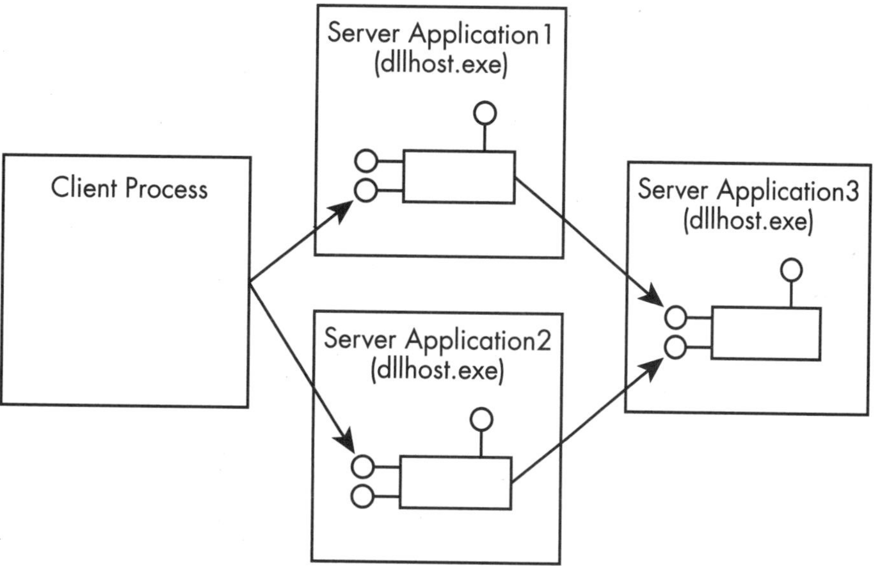

FIGURE 11.15 Two COM+ Server Applications Sharing a Third Server Application.

of the two or more COM+ server applications run in their own process. If the shared COM+ application also runs in its own process, you incur a performance hit due to marshaling each time you call a method in the shared COM+ application, as shown in Figure 11.15.

If you make the shared COM+ application a library application, then the two or more COM+ server applications can use the shared functionality of the library application more efficiently because the shared code runs in the same process as its client as shown in Figure 11.16.

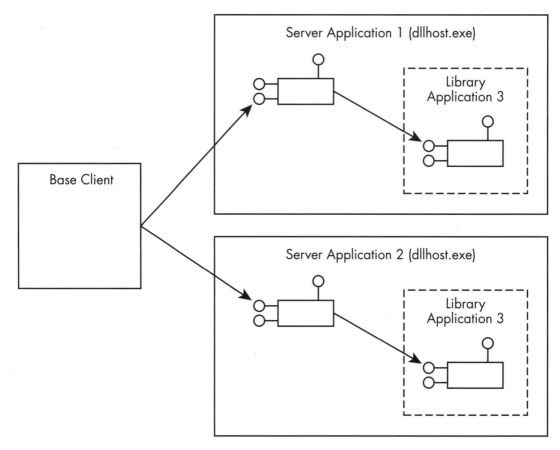

FIGURE 11.16 Two COM+ Server Applications Sharing a Library Application

You can also use library applications in objects that are accessed by a base client. For robustness reasons, this is a situation that you should avoid.

COM+ applications replace MTS Packages. For more information about MTS, see the sidebar entitled What happened to MTS and the NT Option Pack?

Here are some talking points to keep in mind when deciding how many COM+ applications you need for your business layer and which components (COM classes) should go in each COM+ application.

- In most cases, you only need one COM+ application. In this case, you can just add all of your components to this one COM+ application. You should consider this the default configuration.
- Components in *different* COM+ applications *can* run the same process by using COM+ library applications. Components in the *same* COM+ application *always* run in the same process.
- You should include in a COM+ application, components that need to work closely together; these components benefit greatly from running in the same process.
- Use COM+ library applications to group together components that need to be shared by different COM+ server applications or, for performance reasons, must run in the same process as their client.
- Components in the same COM+ application are administered together. You can configure the class-level attributes individually for each component in a COM+ application, but all components in a COM+ application share the same application-level attributes. Components that need different application level attributes, different authentication levels for instance, need separate COM+ applications.

What Happened to MTS and the NT Option Pack?

The NT Option Pack was the forerunner of COM+. The NT Option Pack was an add-on for Windows NT 4.0 that turned NT into a platform suitable for enterprise-class, distributed application development. Perhaps the most important piece of technology in the Option Pack is Microsoft Transaction Server (MTS). The NT Option Pack was (and still is as this book is going to print) available for free download from Microsoft's Web site. Go to http://www.microsoft.com and do a search on NT Option Pack to find the URL.

MTS

Like most COM-related technologies, MTS was poorly named. MTS is a runtime environment that provides COM objects with distributed transactions, fine-grained security, and enhanced scalability.

Sound familiar? MTS did most of the things that COM+ does—just not nearly as well. In fact, it's not completely incorrect to think of COM+ as MTS 3.0 (the version of MTS in the NT Option Pack is 2.0). For instance, MTS did not implement object pooling because NT 4.0 did not support Thread Neutral Apartments. MTS did not provide synchronization support for COM objects; it didn't have to because only apartment-threaded objects (objects that run in an STA) could be used with MTS.

In addition to not having all of the functionality of COM+, MTS was also harder to use than COM+. Because MTS was an add-on, it was also not nearly as well integrated with the operating system. When you configured a COM component to run under MTS, MTS took over the object's registry entry, redirecting the component's `InprocServer32` registry entry to point to MTS's surrogate process: `mtx.exe`. Because most development tools register a component—with the path to the server DLL—when they build the server DLL, you had to reregister your MTS components every time you did a build to replace MTS's registry updates. MTS's registry manipulation also reeked havok when you tried to debug using Visual Basic. Visual Basic also replaces a COM object's `InprocServer32` entry when you debug. I can tell you from experience that debugging MTS components was not fun.

COM+ fixes all of these problems. Because Windows 2000 was designed from the beginning to work with COM+, it can work without changing the `InprocServer32` registry setting. The debugging problem goes away and you don't have to reregister a component after you build it.

With Windows 2000 and COM+, both MTS and the Option Pack become obsolete. All of the functionality in MTS has been incorporated into COM+ (Microsoft merged the MTS and COM development teams to help make this happen) and all of the other technologies in the NT Option Pack have been folded into Windows 2000.

Despite this, I suspect that many organizations will still be using NT 4.0, the Option Pack and MTS well into the year 2000 and possibly into 2001. Many companies will wait until the first Service Pack for Windows 2000 is delivered.

Creating a COM+ Application

To create a COM+ application, you have to first start the Component Services Explorer, which is used to administer the COM+ catalog. The component services Explorer is the primary tool you use for configuring COM+ objects. If you don't like using the Component Services Explorer or you want to automate the process of creating or administering COM+ applications, you can build your own custom catalog manager using the COM+ Administrative interfaces.

Until you are ready to create your own catalog manager, you can use the Component Services Explorer that COM+ provides out-of-the box. To bring up the Component Services Explorer, perform the following steps:

1. Click the `Start` Button.
2. Select `Programs\Administrative Tools\Component Services\` (the MMC with the Component Services snap-in appears as shown in Figure 11.6).

To create a new COM+ application, perform the following steps in the Component Services Explorer:

1. Right-click on the folder console `root\component\services\Computers\My Computer\COM+ application\` (see Figure 11.17).
2. Select `New` from the `Context` menu that appears (The COM+ application Install Wizard appears, see Figure 11.18)

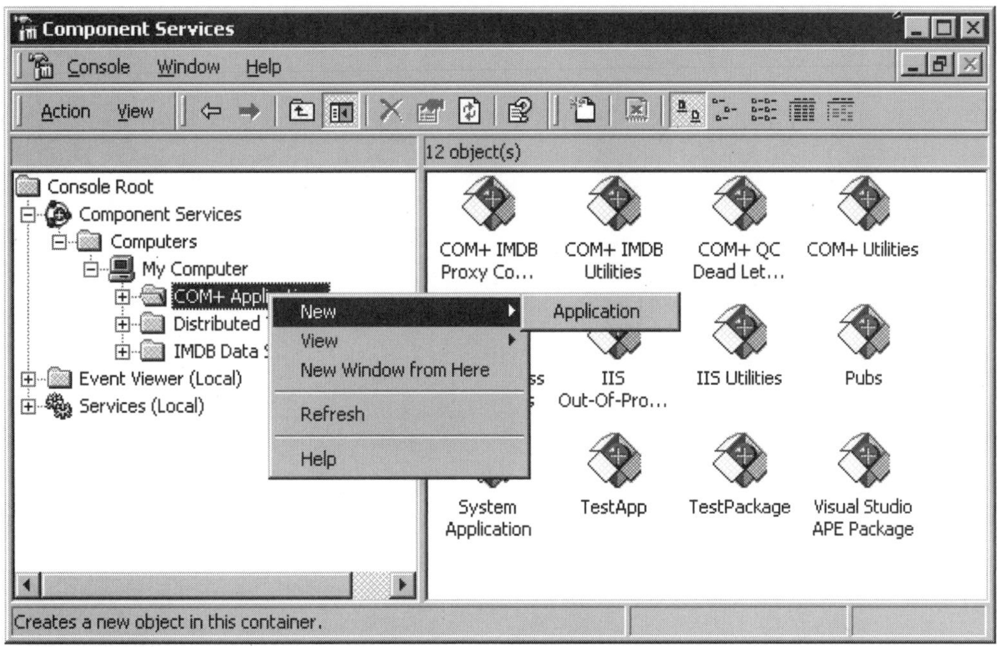

FIGURE 11.17 First Step to Create a New COM+ Application.

3. Click `Next` (step 2 of the COM+ application Install Wizard appears, see Figure 11.19).
4. Click `Create an Empty Application` (step 3 of the COM+ application Install Wizard appears, see Figure 11.20).
5. Enter `TestApp` for the application name and Accept the default activation type (Server Application).
6. Click `Next` (step 4 of the COM+ application Install Wizard appears, see Figure 11.21).
7. Accept the default Identity (Interactive User).
8. Click `Next` and then Click `Finished` on the final screen.

Notice that under Identity you weren't even allowed the option to select the much-maligned launching user Identity setting. I spoke so negatively about this setting in Chapter 10 that you might have wondered why it was even there. Microsoft must have wondered the same thing, because it doesn't exist under COM+.

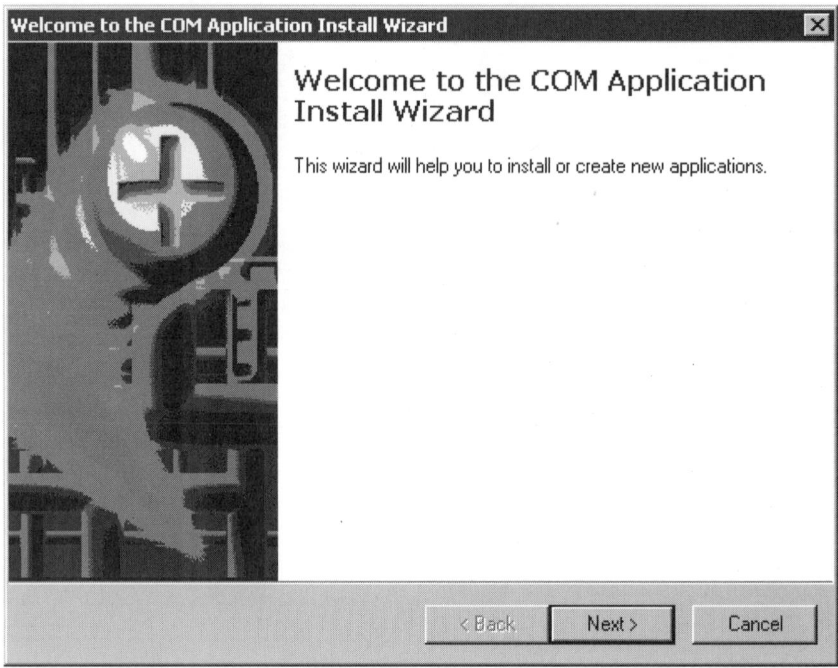

FIGURE 11.18 The Welcome Screen for the COM+ Application Install Wizard.

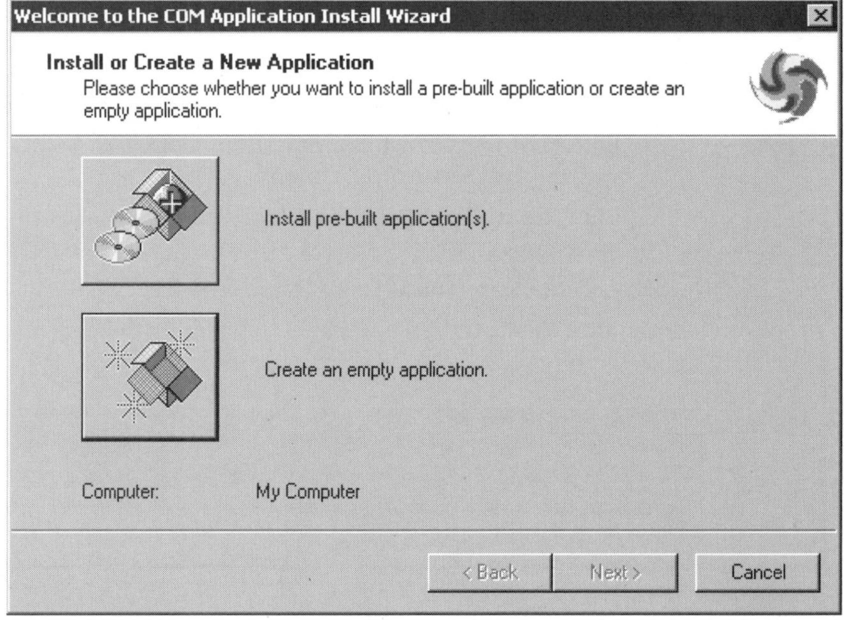

FIGURE 11.19 Installing a Pre-Built COM+ Application or Creating a New One.

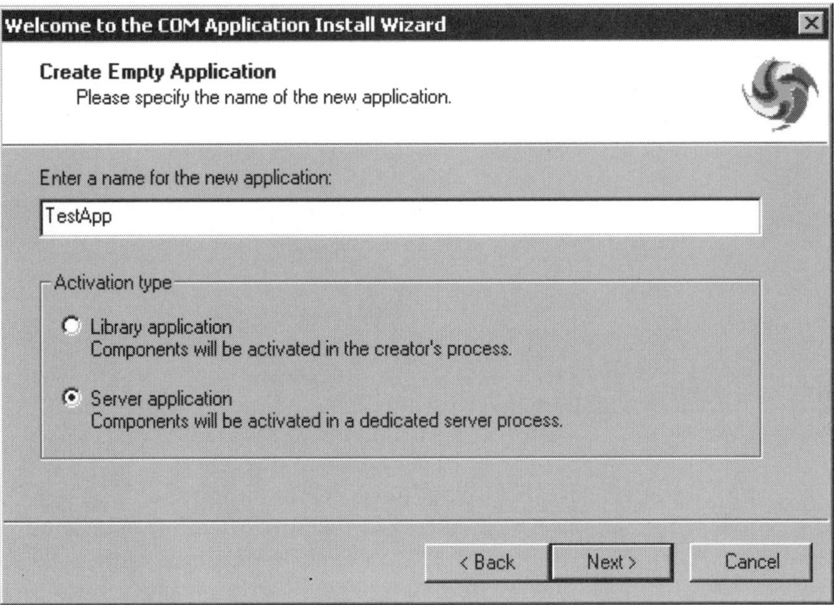

FIGURE 11.20 Choosing a Name and an Activation Type.

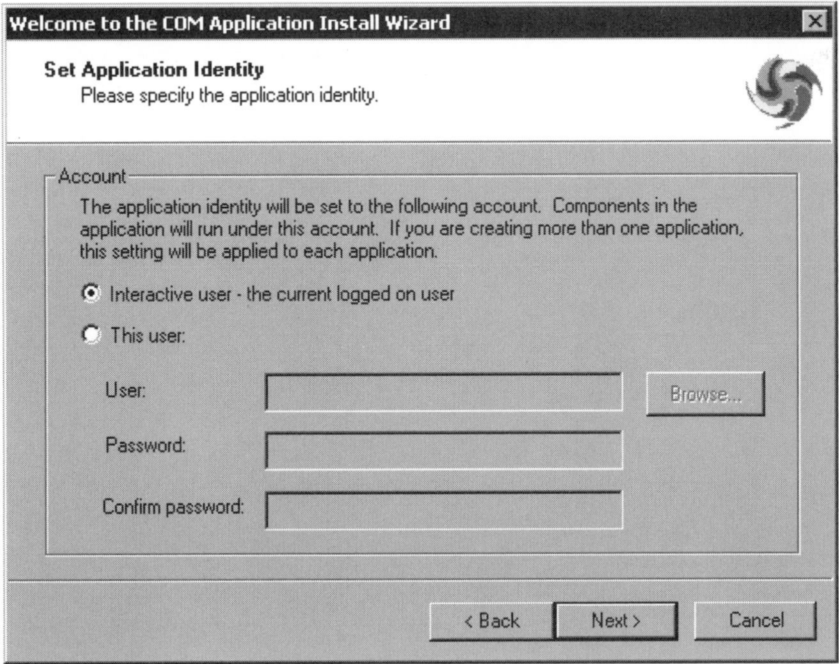

FIGURE 11.21 Choosing the Identity for the COM+ Application.

Now that you have created a new COM+ application, it appears as an icon under COM+ applications in the Component Services, as shown in Figure 11.22. Beneath the folder for your new application are two subfolders called Components and Roles. You can add components to your application using the Components folder and configure fine-grained security using a new security entity called a Role, which you will learn about shortly.

Perform the following steps in the Component Services Explorer to view the Application-Level attributes for our new COM+ application:

1. Right-click on the icon for your new COM+ application in the COM+ Applications folder.
2. Select `Properties` from the `Context` menu (the COM+ application Properties dialog appears as shown in Figure 11.23).

Notice the Application ID shown on this Window. The Application is just a GUID that identifies this COM+ application in the COM+ catalog. Take note of this GUID because you need it later when you are trying to debug your COM+ application. You can look through the other tabs now if you want to, but in the next chapter I explore the various services that COM+ offers and discuss each tab in detail there. For now, let's add a component to your Application. To convince you that old COM components work

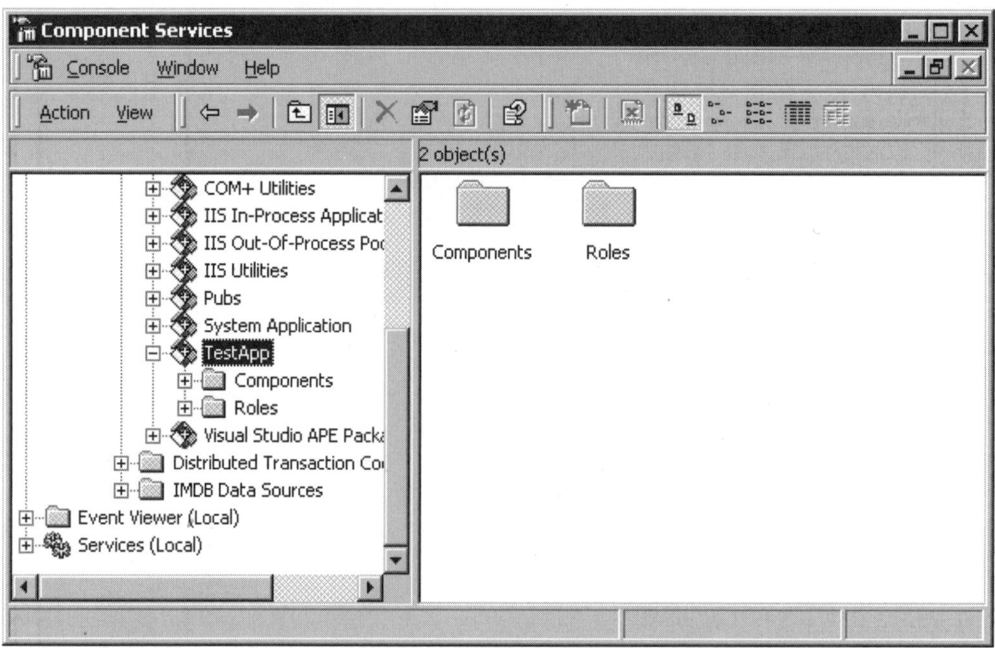

FIGURE 11.22 The Component Services Explorer with Your New Application Displayed.

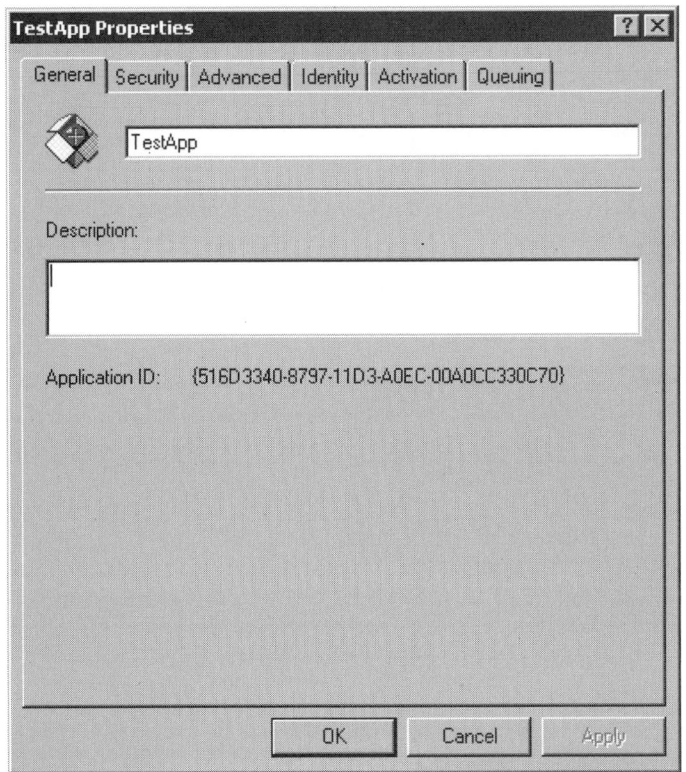

FIGURE 11.23 The General Tab of the COM+ Application Properties Window.

seamlessly with COM+, let's use the financial component created in Chapter 7. If you did not build it yourself, you can find the server for this component on the Web site for this book. This in-process, Automation server contains one COM class called `CTimeValue` that supports two interfaces: `ITimeValue` and `ITaxCalculation`. Perform the following steps to add this component to the COM+ application that you just created:

1. Right click on the `Components` folder beneath your COM+ application, as shown in Figure 11.24.
2. Select `New\Component` from the `Context` menu (the COM Component Install Wizard appears as shown in Figure 11.25).
3. Click `Next` (step 2 of the COM Component Install Wizard appears as shown in Figure 11.26).
4. Click the `Install New Components` button (step 3 of the COM Component Install Wizard appears as shown in Figure 11.27).
5. Click the `Add...` button (The Select Files to Install dialog appears).

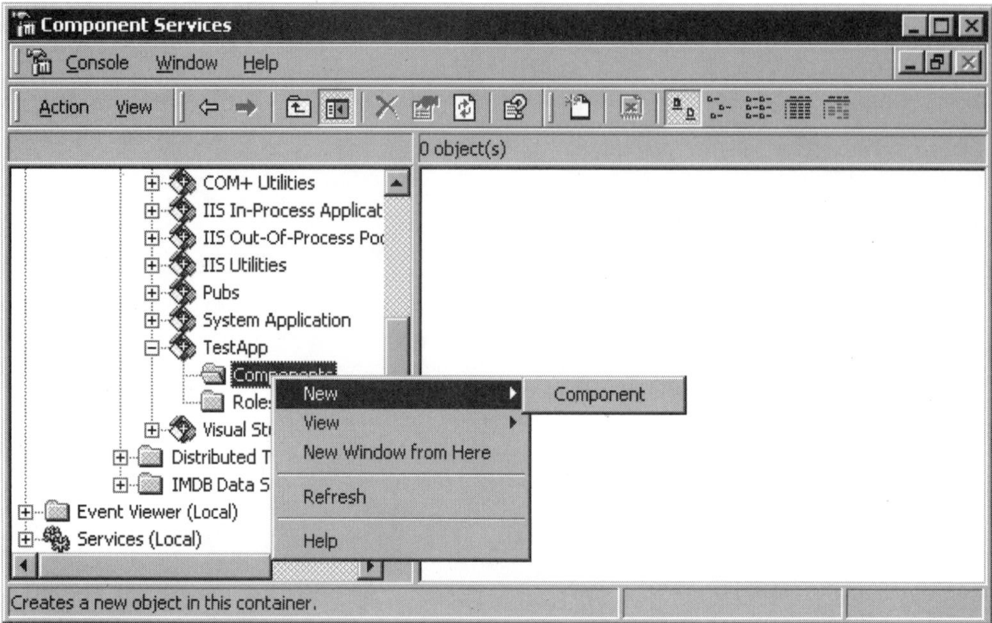

FIGURE 11.24 The Components Folder of a COM+ Application.

FIGURE 11.25 The Welcome Screen of the COM Component Install Wizard.

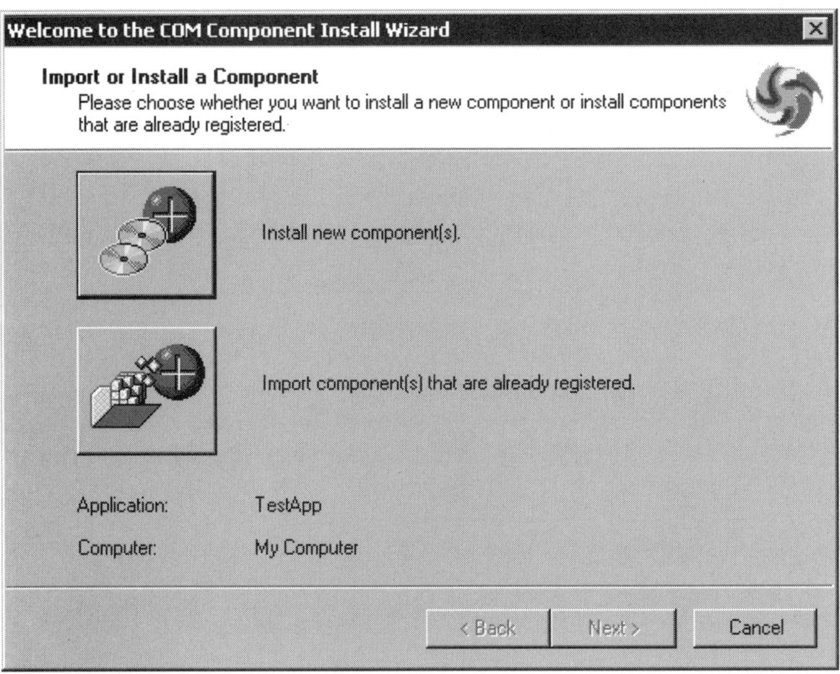

FIGURE 11.26 Install a New Component or Import One That Is Registered Already.

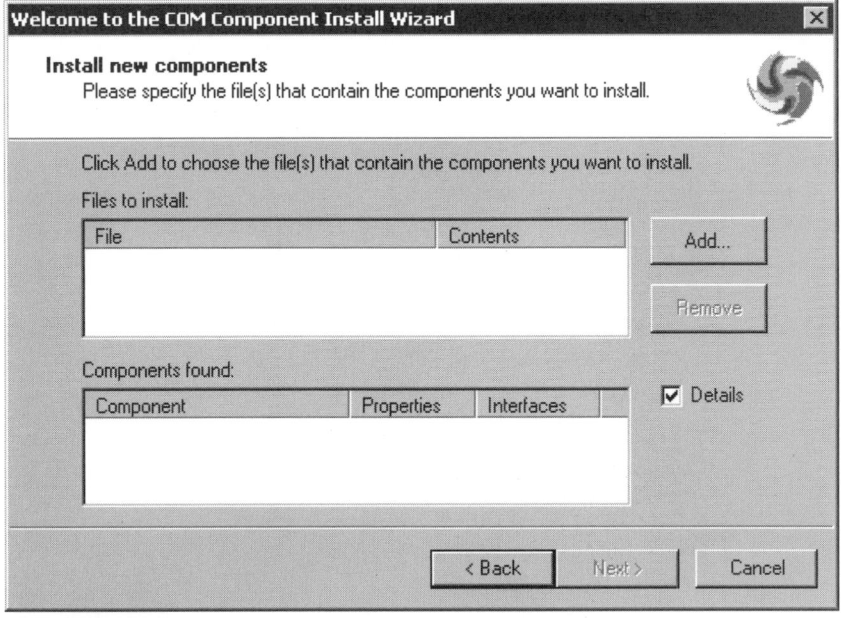

FIGURE 11.27 Select the Components You Wish to Install.

6. Navigate to where the DLL for the Financial Component resides on your machine.
7. Select the DLL and then click the `Open` button.
8. Click `Next` and then Click `Finished` on the Final dialog of the Wizard.

All of the classes that are implemented in the selected in-process server now appear in the components folder of your COM+ application as shown in Figure 11.28.

There is another, faster way you can add a new component to a COM+ application. You can use the Windows NT explorer to navigate to the directory where an in-process server resides. Then simply drag-and-drop the DLL into the Components subfolder of your COM+ application. Whichever method you choose to add a component to your COM+ application, once you have added components, you can view the class-level COM+ attributes by performing the following steps:

1. Right-click on a class in the `Components` tab.
2. Select `Properties` from the `Context` menu (the COM+ component properties dialog appears as shown in Figure 11.29).

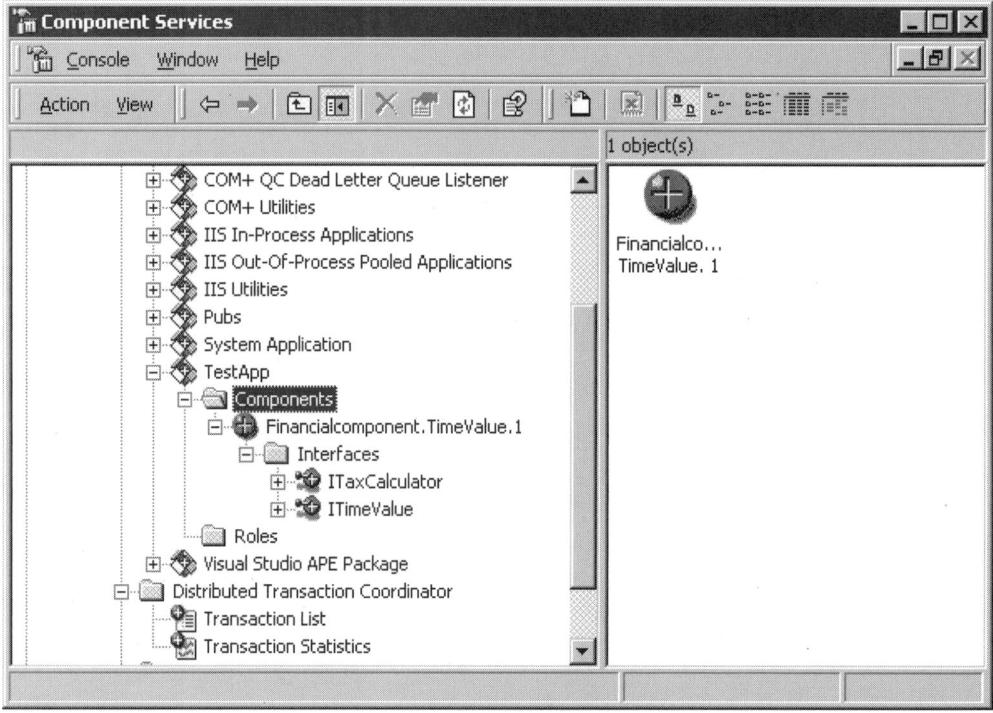

FIGURE 11.28 A Component in a COM+ Application.

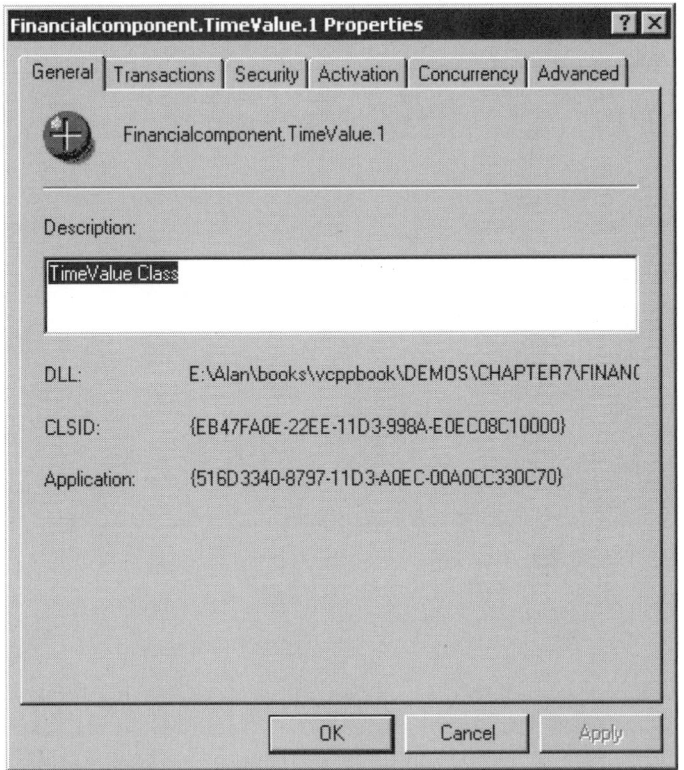

FIGURE 11.29 The COM+ Component Properties Dialog.

Once again, you can click on each tab if you wish, but I cover all the items on the tabs in the next chapter when I discuss the COM+ services one-by-one.

RUNNING A COM+ COMPONENT

Before going any further, it's probably a good idea to run your financial component now that it is configured. The client for the financial component is a Visual Basic Application you can find on the Web site for this book. Double-click on the executable in this directory to run the client application. The financial client application is shown in Figure 11.30.

It should take a second or two for the application to startup. This is because the application is now running out-of-process. If you bring up the task manager, you should see two instances of the `dllhost.exe` process running. One of these instances is the surrogate process that your component is running within (one instance of this process always stays up, that's why you see two). Now go to the Component Services Explorer. If you click

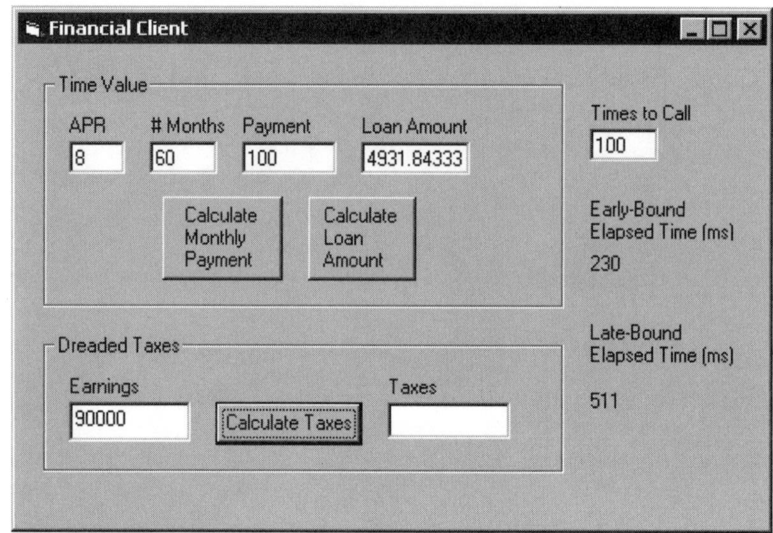

FIGURE 11.30 The Financial Client Application.

on the `Components` folder beneath your COM+ application, you should see the little ball icon that represents the `CTimeValue` class spinning. Whenever an instance of a configured class is running, its icon in the Components folder spins. If you click on the toolbar button on the far right on the Component Services Explorer, you see a display that shows the number of objects and the number of objects activated, the number of pooled objects, the number in call, and the time of the last call as shown in Figure 11.31.

This display only updates if the Component Supports events and statistics attribute for the Component is set to On. If you shut-down the client, you'll notice the number of objects and the number of objects activated goes almost immediately to zero, but if you check the task manager you see the two `dllhost` processes are still running. How long these processes run is determined by the setting you have for the Server Process Shutdown attribute. If you refer back to Table 11.1, you can see there are two possible settings for this attribute: Leave running when idle, or Shutdown after a specified number of minutes. The default is that the server process shuts down after it has been idle for three minutes. You can change this setting by going to the COM+ application Properties dialog (which is shown in Figure 11.23) and clicking the `Advanced` tab shown in Figure 11.32.

You often need to shutdown the process immediately. This happens most often when you are developing a server application that uses COM+. Each time you compile your application, you won't be able to overwrite your component server DLL while the server process is running. To shut-

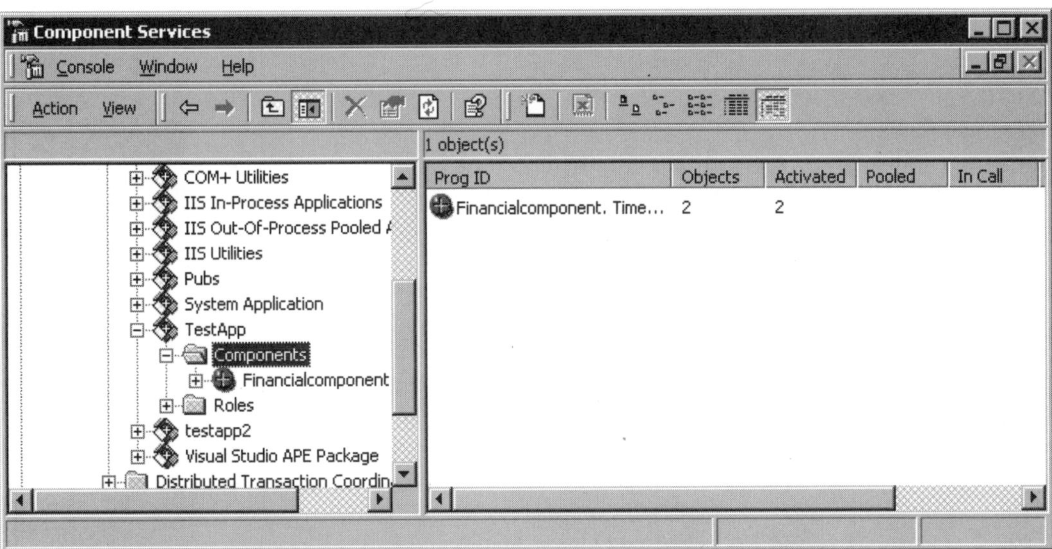

FIGURE 11.31 Viewing the Events and Statistics for a COM+ Component.

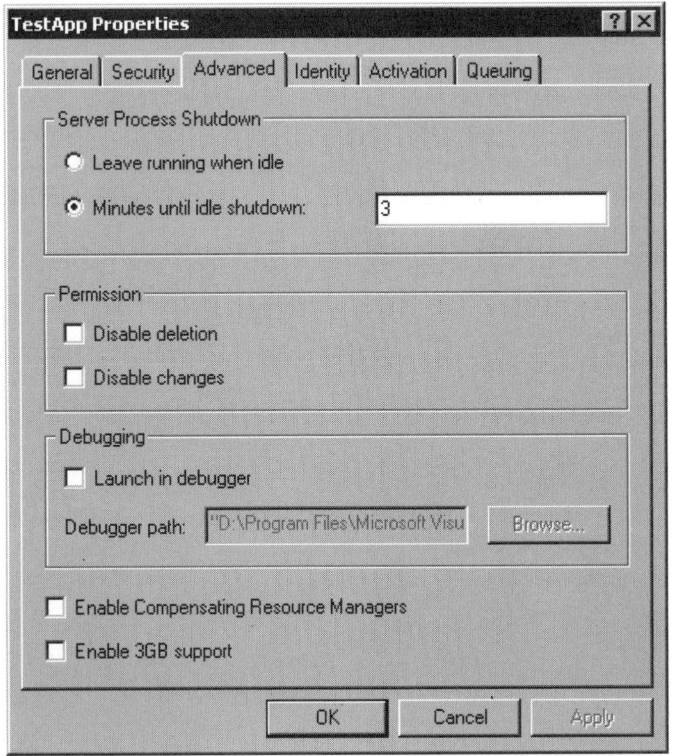

FIGURE 11.32 The Advanced Tab of the Application Properties Dialog.

down the COM+ application at any time, right-click on the COM+ application in the Component Services Explorer and select Shutdown from the context menu.

Summary

In this chapter, I defined COM+ and gave an introduction to the COM+ architecture. You learned that COM+ is a set of system services that provides COM objects with distributed transactions, fine-grained security, enhanced scalability through JIT activation and pooling of objects and database connections, thread synchronization, store and forward method invocation, and load balancing. COM+ implements these features through Attribute-Based Programming, Contexts, and Interception. Each COM+ component has a set of attributes associated with it. You can configure the settings for each of these attributes using the Component Services Explorer. When an instance of the component is created, the COM+ runtime reads these attributes and provides the specified services in an almost transparent way to your objects. To do this, the COM+ runtime provides an environment called a Context for each COM+ object. Through a process called interception, the COM+ runtime can execute its logic both before and after method calls on the object and in this way implements these value-added services.

I concluded the chapter by creating a COM+ server application and demonstrated how to add components to the application and configure application-level attributes. In the next chapter, I explore each of the COM+ services further and explain how to configure the components in your COM+ application to use these services.

TWELVE

An Introduction to the COM+ Services

With an understanding of the COM+ architecture under your belt, you are now ready to explore in greater depth each of the services that COM+ offers. COM+ provides fine-grained security, distributed transactions, enhanced scalability through object and connection pooling, thread synchronization, store and forward method invocation, and load balancing.

There are three steps you must perform to use these services in your COM components:

1. Create a COM+ application.
2. Add your COM components to the COM+ application.
3. Configure the components to use the COM+ services.

Steps 1 and 2 were covered in the previous chapter. Step 3 is the subject of this chapter. But which services should you use in a particular component? And what settings should you select for each of the attributes associated with a particular service? In this chapter, I go through the COM+ services one-by-one and explain how to configure them to implement your desired functionality.

Fine-Grained Security

In Chapter 10 you learned about DCOM and how to configure security settings using a tool called `dcomcnfg`. `Dcomcnfg` is simple to use because it lets you configure your security settings declaratively (without writing code). The main problem with `dcomcnfg` is that it only lets you configure security settings for an entire server. All the COM classes in that server share the same security settings. This is not sufficient for servers that contain COM classes or interfaces that have very different security requirements. For instance, imagine that you had a COM class with two interfaces. One of these interfaces lets users submit Field Service (heating repair, air conditioning repair, and so on) work orders to an accounting system for billing. The other interface lets users view work orders. Only certain users (supervisors, billing clerks) should be allowed to submit work orders for billing, but anyone should be allowed to view work order information. To provide a solution for this scenario, you need to configure your security settings on a per-interface basis. Unfortunately, `dcomcnfg` does not provide this capability. In the past, the only way to implement fine-grained security in DCOM components was to use the COM security API. But this API is difficult to use and you cannot use it from 4GLs such as Visual Basic.

With COM+, you can control access to a server on a per-class, per-interface, or even a per-method basis. The best part is that COM+ performs this using attribute-based programming so you don't have to write any code. There are still some situations where using attribute-based programming alone is not sufficient. As an example, imagine you are developing software for a bank. At this fictional bank, a bank teller is allowed to make withdrawals from a customer's account as long as the transaction involves less than $1,000.00, but the approval of a bank manager is required for a withdrawal where the amount is greater than $1,000.00. You have to write code to enforce this kind of access control even if you are using COM+. You cannot implement this type of access control using attribute settings alone. Fortunately, COM+ provides a simple solution that lets you implement this kind of programmatic security logic easily and without having to resort to the DCOM security API. Whether you use COM+'s fine-grained security declaratively or programmatically, to understand COM+'s security features, you must first understand *roles*.

Roles

COM+ implements a new security model that utilizes the concept of a *role*. A role is a group of users of a COM+ application that have the same security profile (they are allowed to perform the same operations and disallowed from performing the same operations). In most cases, the roles you define are the same as the real-life roles of the users who will use your application. For instance, a COM+ application that is designed for a bank will most likely have a Teller role, a Manager role, and a Loan Office role. Each of these types of users share a security profile: they are allowed to do the same kinds of things and are disallowed from doing the same kinds of things. As a COM+ programmer, you define the roles that your application requires. The System Administrator responsible for your application decides which users will belong to each role after your application is deployed.

Once you have defined the roles for your application, you (or an administrator) can add users and groups to those roles (you'll see how to do this shortly). You can then use these roles two ways: using the Component Services Explorer, you can declaratively specify that only users in a particular role are allowed to use a particular component, interface, or method. You can also programmatically query your call context to see what role the current caller belongs to and throw an error if the user is trying to do something he is not allowed to do.

CREATE ROLES

You can add roles to your COM+ Application immediately after you create it. The financial component that you built in Chapter 7 has two interfaces: `ITimeValue` and `ITaxCalculation`.

For this discussion, you can use the Financial component that you built in Chapter 7 and the TestApp COM+ Application you built in Chapter 11.

Let's say that only Loan Officers should be allowed to use the methods in `ITimeValue` and only Tax Preparers should be allowed to use the methods in `ITaxCalculation`. To create these two roles, perform the following steps in the COM+ Component Services Explorer:

1. Right-click on the `Roles` Folder in your TestApp COM+ Application as shown in Figure 12.1.
2. Select `New\Role` from the `Context` menu (the New Role dialog is displayed as shown in Figure 12.2).
3. Enter the `LoanOfficer` for the new role.
4. Click `OK`.
5. Repeat steps 1–4 and select `TaxPreparer` for the `Role` name.

You now need to do two things to use COM+ security declaratively: (1) Add Users to the role, and (2) Specify which entities in the COM+ application: Components, Interfaces, and Methods, that users in the role are allowed to access.

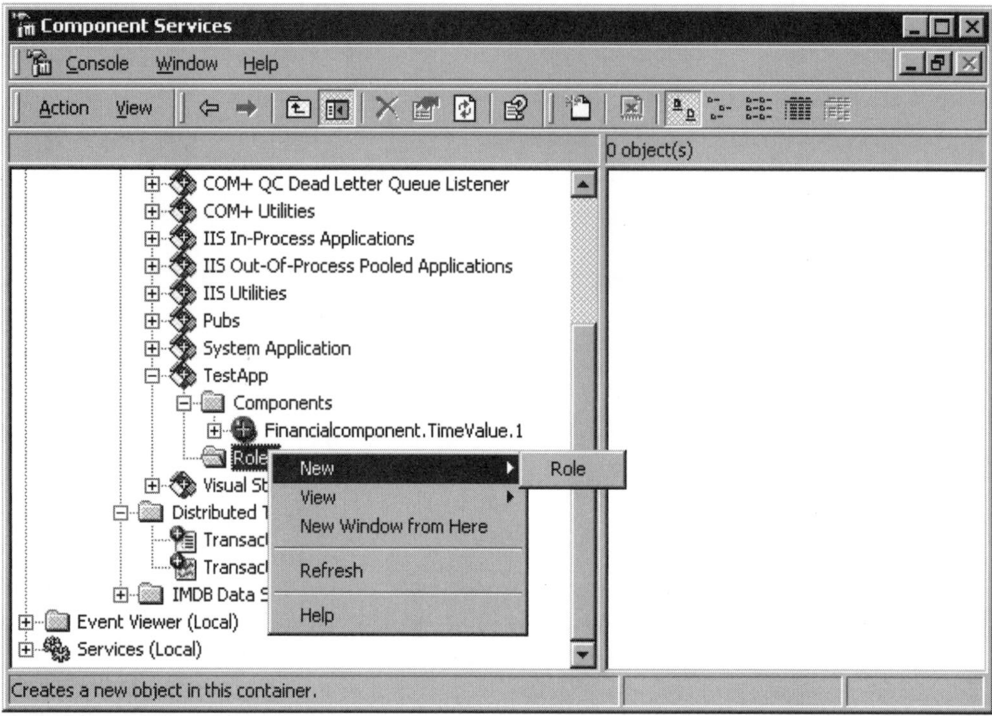

FIGURE 12.1 Create a New Role.

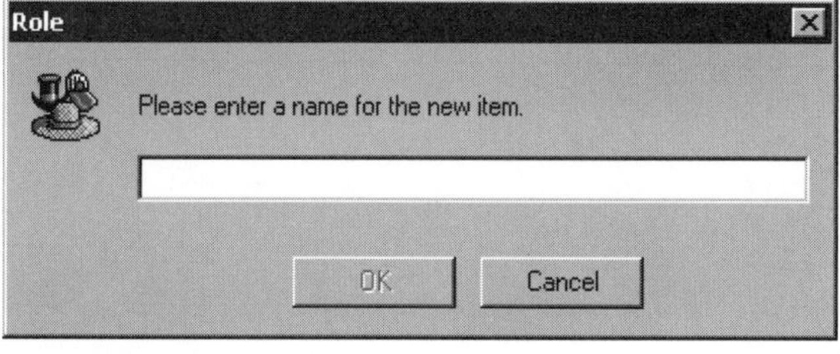

FIGURE 12.2 The New Role Dialog.

ADD USERS TO A ROLE

Perform the following steps to add new users to a role:

1. Right-click on the `Users` folder beneath the `LoanOfficer` role in the `Roles` folder as shown in Figure 12.3.

2. Select `New\Users` from the `Context` menu that appears (the next window that you see depends on whether you are using the Active Directory Service).
3. Select your user name in the list of Users and Click the Add button.
4. Click `OK`.
5. Repeat steps 1 thru 3 using the `TaxPreparer` role.

Remember that by adding a user to a role, you are saying this user is allowed to use all the classes, interfaces, and methods that you will allow this role to access.

SPECIFY THE ENTITIES EACH ROLE IS ALLOWED TO ACCESS

You need to specify the classes, interfaces, and methods that each role is allowed to access. But before you do this, you have to tell COM+ that you want it to enforce Access Control. By default, COM+'s enforcement of Access Control is turned off. To get COM+ to enforce Access Control, perform the following steps in the Component Services Explorer:

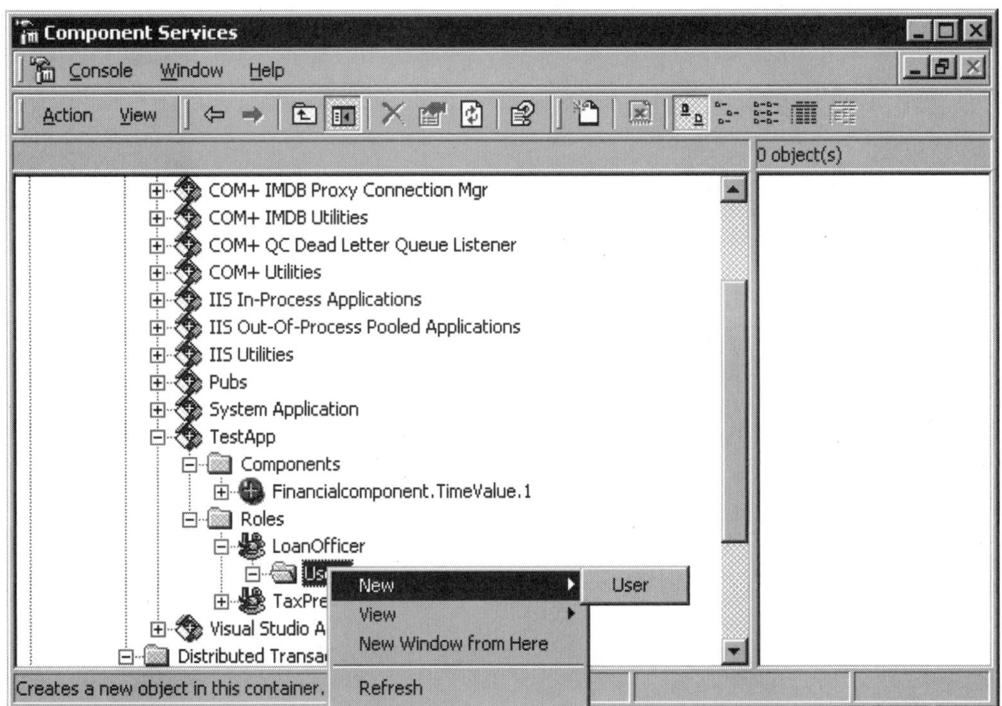

FIGURE 12.3 Add a User to a Role.

1. Right-click on your COM+ Application (`TestApp`) as shown in Figure 12.4.
2. Select `Properties...` from the `Context` menu (the component properties dialogs appear).
3. Click on the `Security` tab of the component properties dialog (you should see the dialog shown in Figure 12.5).
4. Set the check box that says `Enforce Access checks for this Application`.
5. Click `OK`.

Changes to COM+ security settings do not take effect until the server process is restarted. Make sure the server process has been shutdown by right-clicking on the COM+ Application in the Component Services Explorer and then selecting `Shut down` from the `Context` menu. Now try running the client for the financial component again.

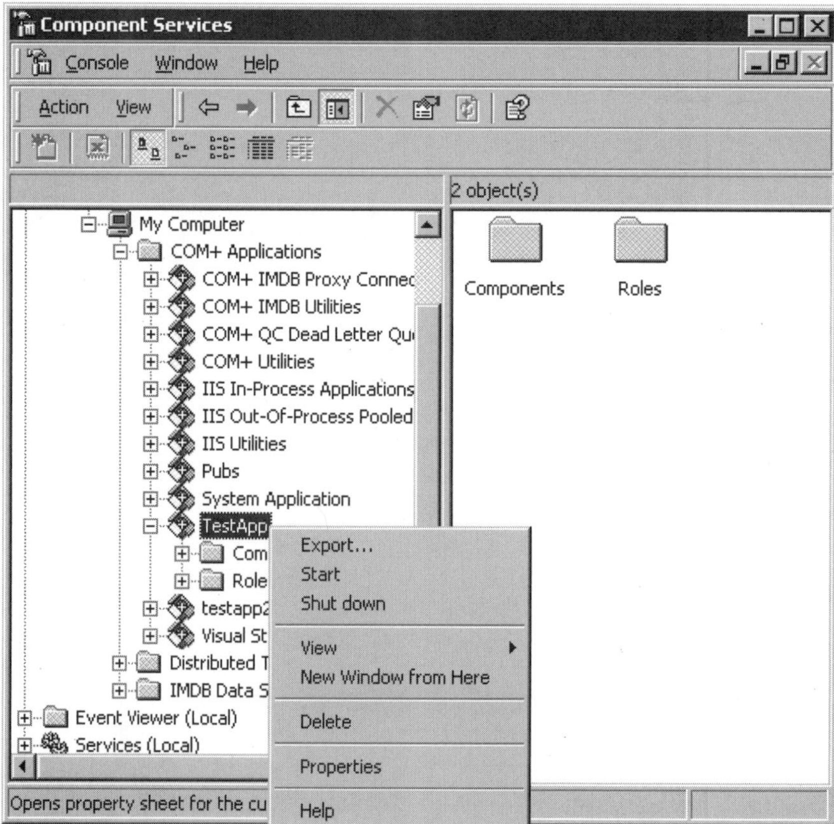

FIGURE 12.4 Bring Up the Application Properties Dialog.

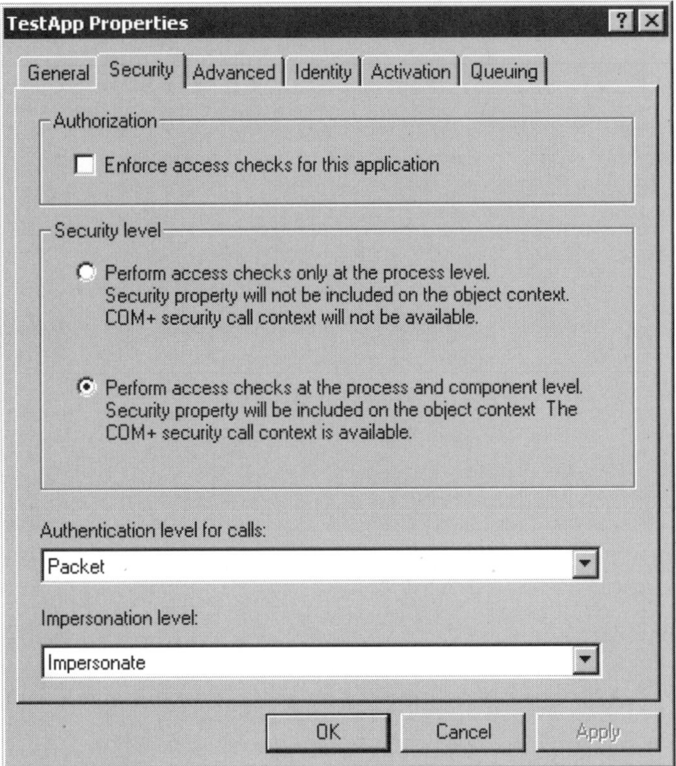

FIGURE 12.5 The Security Tab of the Application Properties Dialog.

Any time you change the security settings for a COM+ application, you should always shut down the server process before you test to see the effects of the change. The new changes will not take effect until a new process is created.

You should see a permission denied error as shown in Figure 12.6.

Understand that COM+ is not actually showing the message box shown in Figure 12.6. COM+ returns the standard, COM, permission denied error. The financial client is catching the error in an error handler and displaying the error description in a message box.

To get this permission denied error to go away, you first need to specify which role(s) are allowed to use the `ITimeValue` interface. As long as the calling user is in one of the roles that are allowed to use the interface, your call will succeed. Perform the following steps to specify that the `LoanOfficer` role is allowed to use the `ITimeValue` interface:

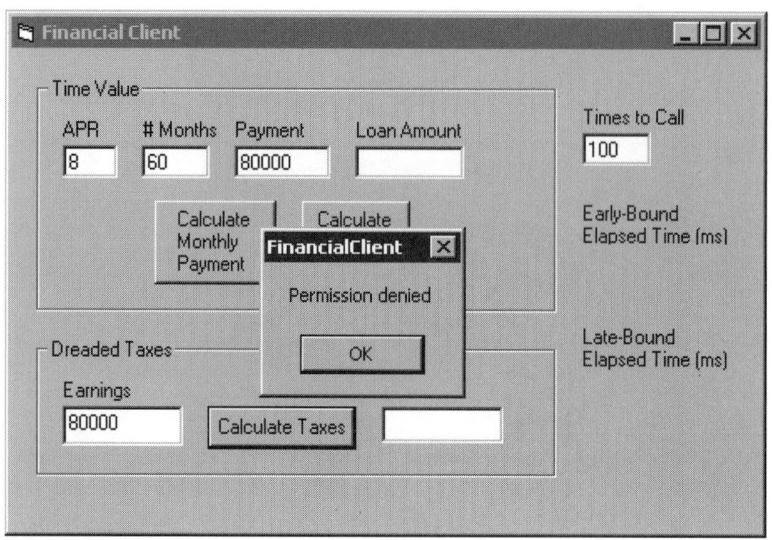

FIGURE 12.6 COM+ Denying Permission to Use a Component.

1. Right-click on the `ITimeValue` interface beneath the `Interfaces` subfolder as shown in Figure 12.7.
2. Select `Properties...` from the `Context` menu (the interface Properties dialog appears as shown in Figure 12.8).
3. Click the `Security` tab of the interface properties dialog.
4. Set the Checkbox next to the `LoanOfficer` role.
5. Click `OK`.

Make sure you shut down the server process before you try to run the financial client again. When you do run the financial client, you should be able to use the `Calculate Monthly Payment` and `Calculate Loan Amount` buttons at the top of the screen, as long as the current user has been added to the `LoanOfficer` role. These buttons use the `ITimeValue` interface. Now try using the tax calculation functionality. You should once again receive the permission denied error. The tax calculation functionality in the financial client uses the `ITaxCalculation` interface and no roles have been allowed to use the `ITaxCalculation` interface as yet.

Congratulations. You have just successfully implemented fine-grained security without writing a single-line of code. If nothing that I have said before has convinced you of the elegance and simplicity of COM+ and the beauty of attribute-based programming, hopefully this demonstration has. You were able to add new functionality to an existing component without writing a single line of code. I leave it as an exercise for you to add yourself

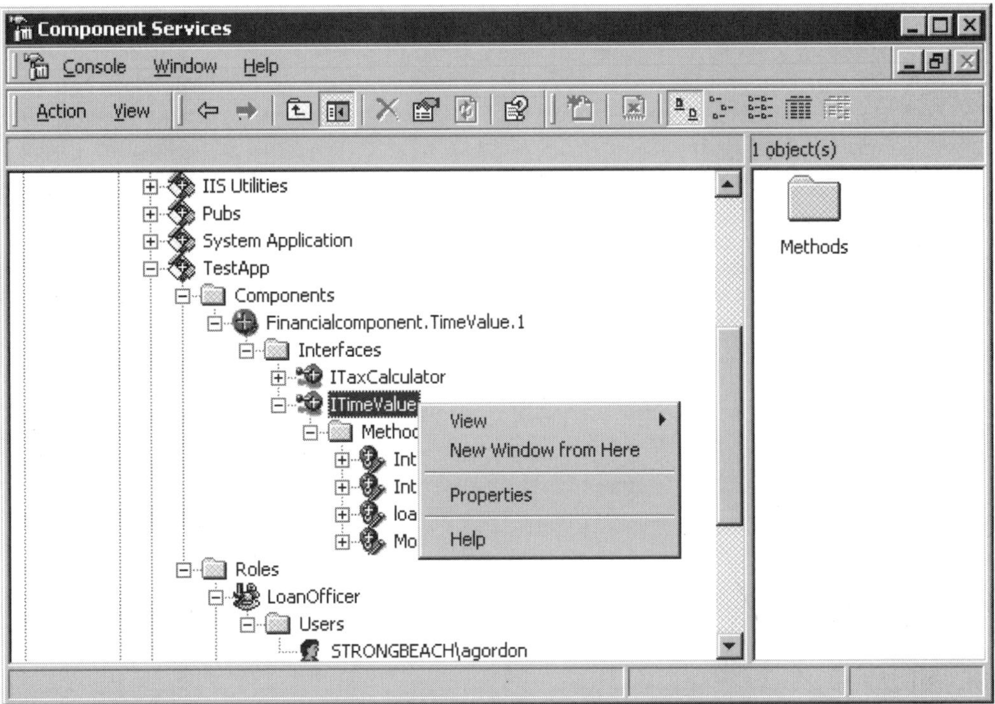

FIGURE 12.7 Configure Security for the ITimeValue Interface.

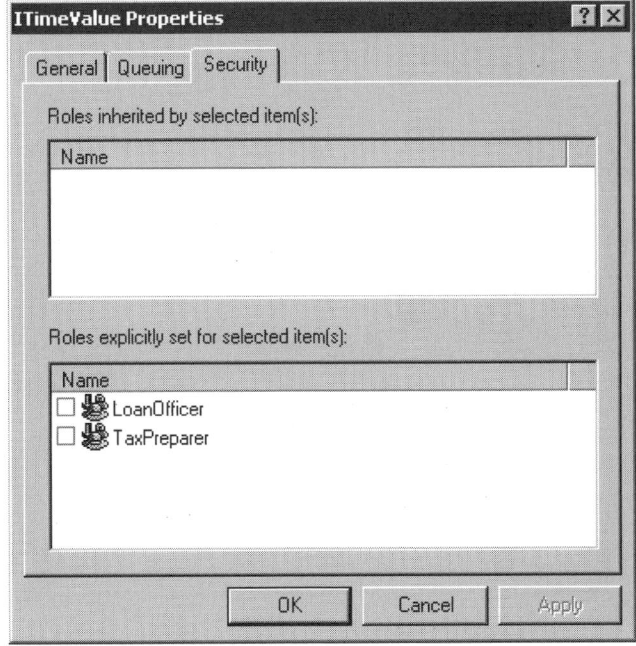

FIGURE 12.8 COM+ Interface Properties Dialog.

to the `TaxPreparer` role and then configure the `ITaxCalculation` interface to support the `TaxPreparer` role. After you have done this, you should be able to use the tax calculation functions in the Financial client.

In this scenario, you specified access permissions on a per-interface basis. You can also specify access permissions on a per-method basis. Perform the following steps in the Component Services Explorer to specify access permissions for a particular method:

1. Right-click on a method beneath the `Methods` folder as shown in Figure 12.9.
2. Select `Properties...` from the `Context` menu (the method properties dialog appears as shown in Figure 12.10).
3. Click the `Security` tab of the method properties dialog (shown in Figure 12.10).
4. Set the `CheckBox` for the role you wish to add to this method.
5. Click `OK`.

In this way you can specify different allowed roles individually for each method in an interface.

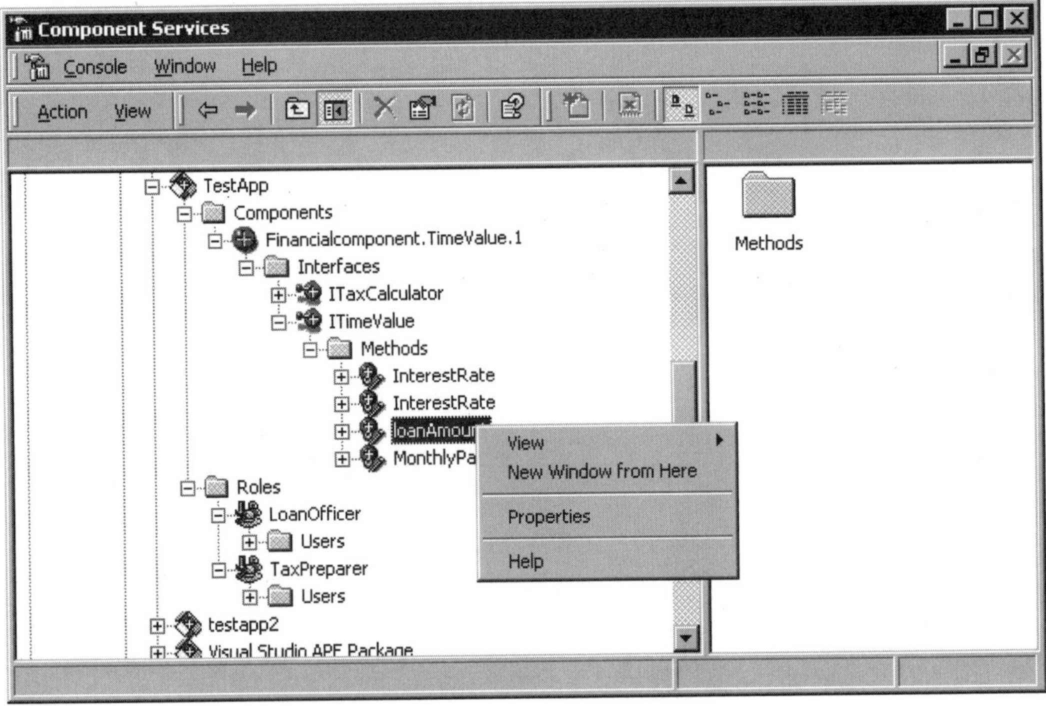

FIGURE 12.9 Configure Security for the LoanAmount Method.

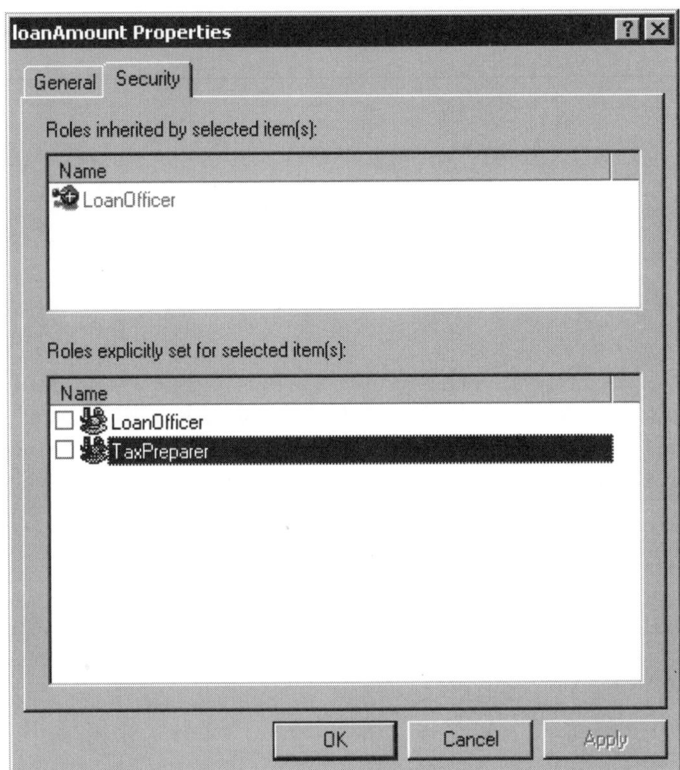

FIGURE 12.10

COM+ Method Properties Dialog.

Use COM+ Security Programmatically

There are certain situations where you need to use COM+ security programmatically. Imagine that a bank was using your financial component, and at that bank only managers are allowed to process loans involving amounts over $100,000. Declarative security won't work in this scenario because whether a user is allowed to use a method is a function of the parameters they pass to the method. You have to determine if a method call is allowed at runtime. To add support for this business rule, you first need to add a Manager role to your COM+ Application.

Hopefully by now you should have no problems adding a Manager role to your COM+ application and adding yourself to this role.

After you add the Manager role, you can enforce your security constraint using the IsCallerInRole method of the ISecurityCallContext interface on the call context.

Remember from Chapter 11 that the Call Context contains context-related information that is specific to a particular method call.

With the IsCallerInRole method, you can determine if the calling user is in the Manager role and if they are not, you can check to see that the LoanAmount they passed to you is less than $100,000. Listing 12.1 shows an updated version of the MonthlyPayment method in the CTimeValue class that uses COM+ programmatic security.

LISTING 12.1 *USING COM+ PROGRAMMATIC SECURITY*

```
STDMETHODIMP CTimeValue::MonthlyPayment(short numMonths, double
loanAmount, double *monthlyPayment)
{
   HRESULT hRes, hRetval;
   double monthlyRate, tempVal;
   LPOLESTR errDescription;
   BOOL bIsInRole;
   ISecurityCallContext *pCallContext;
   bstr_t strManagerRole("Manager");
   hRes=CoGetCallContext(IID_ISecurityCallContext,(void **)&pCallContext);
   if (SUCCEEDED(hRes))
   {
      pCallContext->IsCallerInRole(strManagerRole,&bIsInRole);
      if (loanAmount > 100000.0 && !bIsInRole)
      {
         *monthlyPayment=0;
         errDescription=L"The caller is not a manager";
         hRetval=E_CALLERNOTMANAGER;
      }
      else
      {

         monthlyRate=mInterestRate/1200;  // Convert A.P.R. to decimal,
                                                          monthly rate
         tempVal=pow((1+monthlyRate),(double)numMonths);
         *monthlyPayment=loanAmount*monthlyRate*tempVal/(tempVal-1);
```

```
            hRetval=S_OK;
        }
    }
    else
    {
        *monthlyPayment=0;
        errDescription=L"This component must be configured";
        hRetval=E_MUSTBECONFIGURED;
    }
    if (0!=pCallContext)
        pCallContext->Release();
    if (hRetval!=S_OK)
        return Error(errDescription,IID_ITimeValue,hRetval);
    else
        return S_OK;
}
```

I have highlighted the two key lines of code in this function. Notice that you call `CoGetCallContext` to retrieve the `ISecurityCallContext` interface on the call context and then you call `IsCallerInRole` on the interface pointer to test if the user is in the Manager role. If the loan amount is over $100,000 and the user is not in the manager role, then you throw an error. You also throw an error if the component is not configured. To test these changes, you need to add the Manager role to your COM+ application.

After you add the Manager role and make the changes shown above to the financial component, run the application before you add yourself to the Manager role. You should get an error as soon as you try to calculate the monthly payment for a loan greater than $100,000. If you add yourself to the Manager role, you can calculate the monthly payment on any loan. The COM+ security service made it simple to implement programmatic security.

In most cases, you should try to use declarative security; only use programmatic security in situations where declarative security won't work. The example I showed you—where the access permissions for a method are dependent on the values of the parameters that are passed in to the method—is a classic example where declarative security will not work. Declarative security is best because it is easy to use and more flexible. You can change the security behavior of a method without having to alter your source code. With declarative security, it is easy for end-users to change their security configuration. Also, keep in mind that in many situations where it seems that only programmatic security will work, you can still use declarative security if you are willing and able to change your interfaces. For instance, in the scenario that I just sketched out, you could create two methods to calculate loan payments: `MonthlyPayment` and `MonthlyPaymentJumbo`. `MonthlyPayment` always rejects loans over $100,000; `MonthlyPaymentJumbo` accepts any amount. You can then use declarative security to allow only Managers to call `MonthlyPaymentJumbo`.

Transactions

One of the key features of COM+ is its support for transactions. But before I can talk about COM+ support for transactions, I need to talk about transactions in general. The word transaction is used in so many different contexts (I'm not talking about COM+ contexts now) that most people have an intuitive sense of what it means. In the field of computer science, here's a precise definition of what a transaction is.

What is a Transaction?

A transaction is a series of operations that have the following properties:

- Atomicity
- Consistency
- Isolation
- Durability

These properties make an easy to remember acronym (ACID). You can understand what these four properties mean by considering what happens when you go to the bank and decide to transfer $500.00 from your savings account to your checking account. There are actually two operations that take place in completing this operation: (1) $500.00 is withdrawn from your savings account, and (2) $500.00 is deposited into your checking account. If both operations succeed, both the bank and you are happy. If both operations fail, neither you nor the bank is necessarily happy, but you can both live with this outcome as long as you can try the operation again later. Now imagine what would happen if the bank's computer failed in the middle of this account transfer operation. First consider the case where the bank's computer failed right after $500.00 was withdrawn from your savings account but before it was deposited into your checking account. You would have lost $500.00. This is not an acceptable outcome. Now consider what would happen if the bank's computer crashed after $500.00 was credited to your checking account, but before the monies were withdrawn from your savings. You would be happy but this is not acceptable to the bank. Both operations must succeed or they must both fail. This is what *Atomicity* means. *Consistency*, in this example, means the amount deposited into your checking account should be the same as the amount withdrawn from your savings account. Consistency is enforced by application logic with the help of a DBMS and/or a Transaction Processing (TP) Monitor.

A TP Monitor is a piece of software that can, among other things, coordinate a distributed transaction involving multiple resources. As you will learn shortly, COM+ contains most of the functionality of a TP Monitor.

Isolation means that a separate transaction that is executing concurrently with your account transfer should not see an invalid intermediate state such as where the $500.00 has been withdrawn from savings, but has not yet been deposited into checking. Isolation is usually implemented using locking. The *Durable* property of a transaction means that after the transaction is committed, the updates made by the transaction should never be lost. A system crash, network failure, or even someone inadvertently pulling the power cord, should not cause updates to be lost. Most databases (and other types of transactional resources) implement durability by first writing all intended changes to a journal file in durable storage. Once the journal file is written the database has a permanent record of the changes that need to be made to the system. The database can still apply the changes at a later time, even if there is a catastrophic failure while the resource was being updated.

Most Database Management Systems (DBMS) have built-in support for the Begin, Commit, and Rollback transaction-handling primitives. The basic steps of using these transaction primitives are shown in the following psuedo-code:

```
try
{
   Transaction.Begin
   Withdraw $500.00 from savings account
   deposit $500.00 dollars into checking account
   Transaction.Commit
}
catch (Exception)
{
// if anything goes wrong, rollback the entire operation
   Transaction.Rollback
}
```

The Begin operation starts a transaction. When all the operations in the transaction are complete, you can call the `Commit` function to commit the transaction. If the transaction fails at any time, you can call the `Rollback` function, which undoes everything since the call to `Begin`. You can make several updates to the database, but none of these updates are visible to anyone outside the transaction until the `Commit` function is called. The `Commit` function applys all the updates in an atomic step. Moreover, once the `Commit` function succeeds, you are guaranteed that the operation will succeed even if someone pulls a power cord. The code just shown also emphasizes the time-saving aspect of transactions. Without transactions you, the developer, would have to write code to undo a partially complete set of operations if one of the operations fails. With transactions, you push the work of undoing the effects of a partial failure onto the database. If anything goes wrong, you simply rollback the transaction.

Distributed Transactions

Using the transaction management functions that are built into your DBMS will work okay as long as all of the information is stored in a single database. Unfortunately, most enterprises don't store all their important information in a single database. In many cases, the information is spread among many databases. Take an online retailer as an example. A database of customer account information might be stored in an Oracle database at the corporate office. But many e-commerce businesses do not fill their orders themselves; they simply run the Web site and advertise. One or more partners actually fill the orders. In this situation, when the online retailer receives an order, it must be able to send the order information to its partners. The mechanism used to send this information could be to write directly to the partner's SQL Server database, or they might send a message to their partner using a message queuing product like Microsoft Message Queue (MSMQ). In either case, you need the placing of the order to be filled and the debiting of the customer's account to be done in an ACID way. The problem in this case is that you have multiple, distributed *resource managers* involved in the transaction.

A resource manager is a term from the field of transaction processing. It is a system that can provide ACID operations on the objects it implements. The canonical resource manager is an RDBMS such as Microsoft SQL Server. But MSMQ is also a resource manager and now, thanks to the COM+ Compensating Resource Manager (CRM) service, you can easily create your own custom resource managers.

Either all of the servers must commit their part of the transaction or, if any of the resource managers are unable to commit their part of the transaction, all of them must rollback.

2-Phase Commit Protocol

The key to implementing distributed transactions is the 2-phase commit protocol. In this protocol, the activity of the resource managers must be controlled by a separate piece of software that is sometimes called a transaction manager or a transaction coordinator. The steps in this protocol are shown below.

- An application invokes the commit method in the transaction coordinator.
- The transaction coordinator contacts each resource manager involved in the transaction and tells it to prepare to commit the transaction (this is the beginning of phase 1).
- To respond in the affirmative to the prepare phase, a resource manager must put itself into a state where it can guarantee to the transaction coordinator that it will commit the transaction if told to do so, or rollback the transaction if told to do so. Most resource managers will write a journal file (or the equivalent) with its intended changes to durable storage. If the resource manager is unable to prepare the transaction, it replys to the transaction coordinator with a negative response.
- The transaction coordinator collects all of the responses from the resource managers.
- In phase 2, the transaction coordinator informs each resource manager of the outcome of the transaction. If any of the resource managers responded in the negative, then the transaction coordinator sends a rollback command to all of the resource managers involved in the transaction. If they all responded in the affirmative, then the resource managers are instructed to go ahead and commit the transaction. Once the resource managers are told to commit, the transaction cannot fail after that. By responding in the affirmative to phase 1, each resource manager was guaranteeing that the transaction would not fail if it were told to commit later.

The 2-phase commit protocol is actually ubiquitous. If you are married, or have attended a wedding, you have seen the 2-phase commit protocol in action. In a wedding ceremony, the clergyman performing the ceremony is the transaction coordinator and the two resource managers are the bride and groom. In the prepare phase, the clergyman asks each resource manager to prepare to commit the transaction: he asks each person if they take the other to be their lawfully wedded spouse. Assuming each responds in the affirmative, he then turns to the crowd (who, in some sense, are a third resource manager) and asks if anyone objects to the marriage. If either the bride or the groom gets cold feet, or someone in the crowd objects, the clergyman can rollback the transaction, which in this case means to cancel the wedding. Assuming both the bride and groom say yes to the marriage and everyone in the crowd stays silent, the ceremony moves to the commit phase where the happy couple exchange rings, the clergyman pronounces them man and wife, and the couple kisses to signify that the transaction (marriage) has been committed.

If you don't like my marriage analogy and you prefer to look at pictures, Figures 12.11 and 12.12 show the 2-phase commit protocol as a pair of sequence diagrams. Figure 12.11 shows the sequence diagram where the

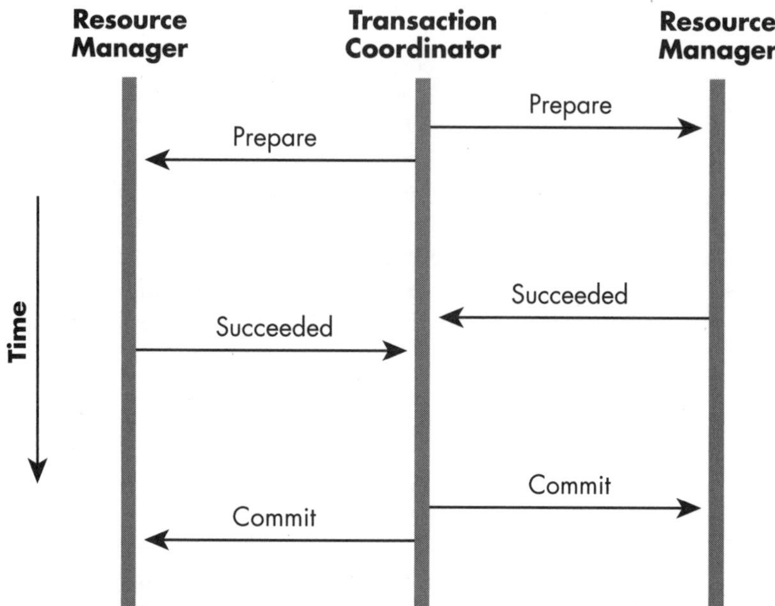

FIGURE 12.11 The 2-Phase Commit Protocol When the Transaction Commits.

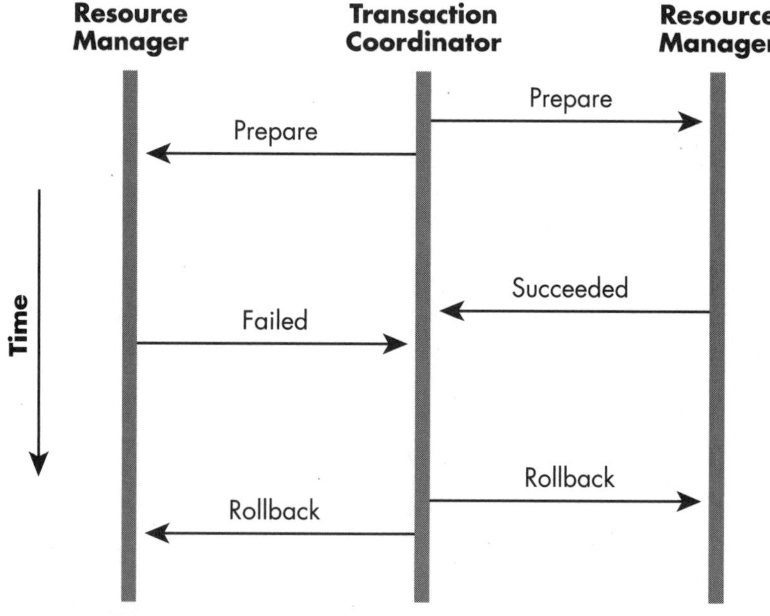

FIGURE 12.12 The 2-Phase Commit Protocol When the Transaction Is Rolled Back.

transaction succeeds (commits). Figure 12.12 shows the 2-phase commit protocol when one of the resource managers is unable to commit for some reason.

Transactions and COM+

Using COM+, you can add support for distributed transactions to your COM components with the barest minimum of code. The process is simple.

1. Configure your object to run within COM+.
2. Set the Transaction Attribute of the Object to Requires a Transaction, Requires a New Transaction, or Supports Transaction.
3. Call `SetComplete` on the object context when you are ready to commit a transaction.
4. Call `SetAbort` on the object context to indicate when a transaction must be rolled back.

Table 12.1 summarizes the meaning of all the possible values that may be set for the transaction attribute of an COM+ object.

TABLE 12.1 Transaction Attributes

Transaction Attribute	Description
Requires a Transaction	This object must run within a transaction. COM+ only starts a new transaction for this object if some other object running in the same context has not already started a transaction.
Requires a New Transaction	This object must run within a transaction. COM+ starts a new transaction as soon as the object is created.
Supports Transactions	This object should only run within a transaction if its creator has already created one. If its creator has not started a transaction this object runs without a transaction.
Does Not Support Transactions	This object does not require a transaction and COM+ will not run this object within a transaction (the default).
Disabled	This object ignores completely the value of the transaction attribute when determining context placement. This setting makes your configured component behave like an unconfigured one.

You can configure the transaction attribute on a per-class basis in the Component Services Explorer by performing the following steps:

1. Right-click on a component in the `Components` folder of your application.
2. Select `Properties...` from the `Context` Menu (the Component Properties dialog appears as shown in Figure 12.13).

3. Click the `Transactions` tab (shown in Figure 12.13).
4. Select one of the transaction settings.
5. Click `OK`.

That's all there is to it. You never have to code the typical `Begin`, `Commit`, `Rollback` logic again. When you start using an object that is configured to use transactions, COM+ starts a transaction. Remember COM+ can do this because it uses Interception. The COM+ runtime receives client requests before the actual object does and it can perform actions on behalf of the object.

START A TRANSACTION

After you have configured a COM+ component (class) to use transactions, the COM+ runtime reads the transaction attribute when it creates an object. It then contacts COM+'s transaction coordinator, which is called the Distributed Transaction Coordinator or (DTC). It asks the DTC to start a transaction for the object. The DTC starts a transaction for the object and returns the GUID for the transaction (the DTC assigns a GUID to each transaction). The GUID for

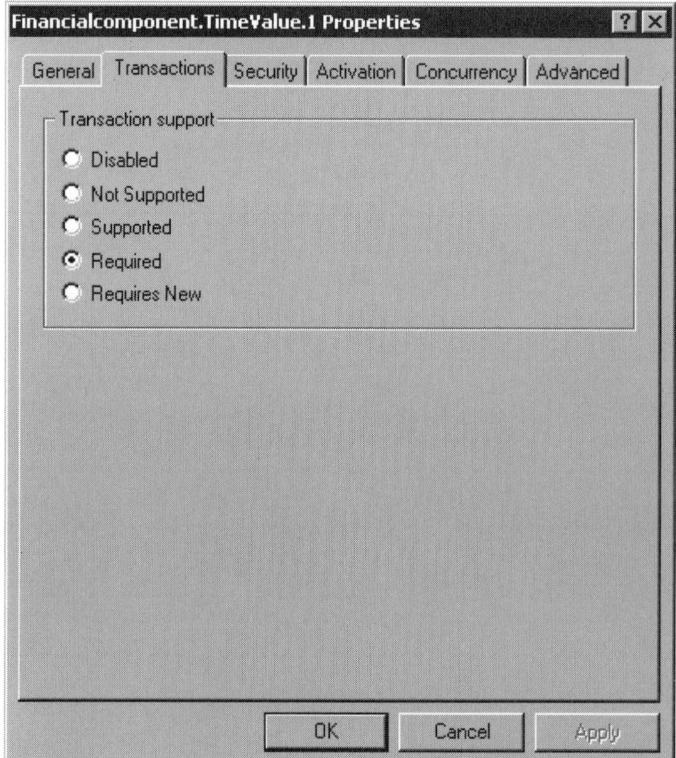

FIGURE 12.13

The Transaction Tab of the Components Properties Dialog.

the transaction is carried with the object in its context. You can determine if your object currently is running within a transaction and determine the GUID of its transaction by calling `CoGetObjectContext` and requesting the interface `IObjectContextInfo`. You can then use the `IsInTransaction` and `GetTransactionId` methods of `IObjectContextInfo` to determine if the object is in a transaction and retrieve the GUID of the transaction. The following code shows how this is done:

```
GUID aGUID;
BOOL bIsInTransaction;
IObjectContextInfo *pContextInfo;
hRes=CoGetObjectContext(IID_IObjectContextInfo,(void **)&pContextInfo);
if (SUCCEEDED(hRes))
{
   bIsInTransaction=pContextInfo->IsInTransaction();
   if (bIsInTransaction)
      pContextInfo->GetTransactionId(&aGUID);
   pContextInfo->Release();
}
```

The object that actually causes a new transaction to be created is called the root object of the transaction. The root object is important because the COM+ runtime won't attempt to commit the transaction until the root object is deactivated. Other objects can enlist in the transaction after the transaction has been created and these other objects can vote as to whether the transaction can commit. But, the root object (actually the deactivation of the root object) determines *when* the transaction commits.

When a COM+ object that has enlisted in a transaction makes a connection to a COM+ Resource Manager (in most cases this is a COM+ aware relational database), the Resource Manager also enlists in the transaction. The resource manager contacts the DTC and lets the DTC know that it is now a participant in the transaction. If the object connects to multiple resource managers, for instance, an Oracle database containing customer information, and a Microsoft SQL Server database containing order fulfillment information, each of these resource managers enlist in the transaction.

Most of the major database vendor's products are COM+ aware (or will be by the time COM+ is released). All versions of Microsoft SQL Server after 6.5 are COM+ aware, as are Oracle 7.3 and 8.0, Sybase SQL Server, IBM DB2, Informix, and CA Ingress. Other products, such as Microsoft Message Queue (MSMQ), are also COM+ Resource Managers.

As you perform operations on one or more resource managers, they buffer the operations maintaining a journal of your actions. When you have completed all of the work and are happy with the current state of the transaction, all you have to do is call SetComplete on the Object Context. If at any time you receive an error you simply call SetAbort. Listing 12.2 contains example code showing how this is done.

LISTING 12.2 *USING COM+ TRANSACTION WITH IOBJECTCONTEXT*

```
HRESULT hRes;
   IObjectContext *pObjectContext;
hRes=CoGetObjectContext(IID_IObjectContext,(void**)&pObjectContext);

   try
   {
   // Perform work here;

      pObjectContext->SetComplete();
   }
   catch(exception err)
   {
      pObjectContext->SetAbort();
   }
   pObjectContext->Release();
```

When you call SetComplete, you are voting to commit the transaction. Once the root object of the transaction indicates that it is ready to commit (by calling SetComplete), the DTC goes to work and using the 2-phase commit protocol it commits the transaction on all of the resource managers involved in the transaction. If any of the resource managers is unable to commit the transaction, the DTC rolls the entire transaction back.

TRANSACTIONS INVOLVING MULTIPLE OBJECTS

The case just described is where you have one COM+ object executing a transaction against 2 or more resource managers. In many cases, a transaction involves multiple COM+ objects. A good example is for an online book retailer where you might have an Order COM+ object that is used as a transaction root. This Order object may create and use a Customer COM+ object and a Book COM+ object in its processing of an order as shown in Figure 12.14.

When a configured COM+ instantiates another configured COM+ object, the new object can do one of three things with its creator's transaction: (1) it can share its creator's transaction, (2) it can create its own transaction, (3) it can not run within a transaction at all. How the new object behaves depends on the setting for the transaction attribute on both the creating and created objects. Table 12.2 looks at the example of an Order

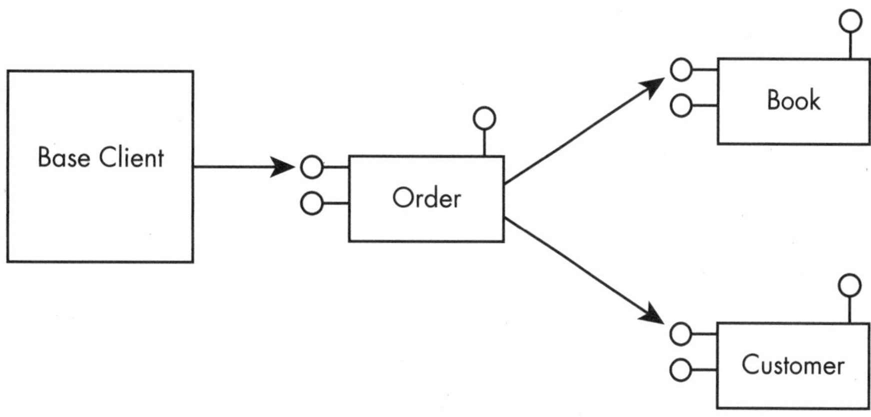

FIGURE 12.14 Multiple Objects in a COM+ Transaction.

object instantiating a Customer object and shows the transaction state for each possible transaction setting on each object (I left the disabled setting out of the table).

TABLE 12.2 Transaction Attributes

Order Transaction Attribute	Customer Transaction Attribute	The Order Object will run in a transaction	The Customer Object will run in a transaction	The Customer and Order Objects will share the same transaction
Requires a New Transaction	Requires a New Transaction	Yes	Yes	No
Requires a New Transaction	Requires a Transaction	Yes	Yes	Yes
Requires a New Transaction	Supports Transactions	Yes	Yes	Yes
Requires a New Transaction	Does not Support Transactions	Yes	No	N/A
Requires a Transaction	Requires a New Transaction	Yes	Yes	No
Requires a Transaction	Requires a Transaction	Yes	Yes	Yes
Requires a Transaction	Supports Transactions	Yes	Yes	Yes

Order Transaction Attribute	**Customer Transaction Attribute**	**The Order Object will run in a transaction**	**The Customer Object will run in a transaction**	**The Customer and Order Objects will share the same transaction**
Requires a Transaction	Does Not Support Transactions	Yes	No	N/A
Supports Transactions	Requires a New Transaction	Only if the object that activated the Order has a transaction.	Yes	No
Supports Transactions	Requires a Transaction	Only if the object that activated the Order has a transaction.	Yes	If the Order object has a transaction, the Customer will share it. If not, the Customer will have its own transaction.
Supports Transactions	Supports Transactions	Only if the object that activated the Order has a transaction.	Only if the object that activated the Order has a transaction.	If the Order object has a transaction, the Customer will share it. If not, the Customer will have its own transaction.
Supports Transactions	Does Not Support Transactions	Only if the object that activated the Order has a transaction.	No	N/A
Does Not Support Transactions	Requires a New Transaction	No	Yes	N/A
Does Not Support Transactions	Requires a Transaction	No	Yes	N/A
Does Not Support Transactions	Supports Transactions	No	No	N/A
Does Not Support Transactions	Does Not Support Transactions	No	No	N/A

If the Order object and the Customer object each have their own transaction, then they are each on their own as it regards committing their transaction. The operations performed by the Order object can commit while the Customer's transaction can abort. In some cases, this may be what you want, in most cases, this is *not* what you want. In most cases, you want the Order object and the Customer object to share the same transaction. If the Order object and the Customer object share the same transaction, then the outcome of the transaction depends on how each of the objects *vote* on whether the transaction should commit. An object can vote to commit a transaction by calling the `SetComplete` method on the `IObjectContext` interface of its object context. An object can vote to abort (rollback) a transaction by calling `SetAbort` on the `IObjectContext` interface of its object context. If both objects vote to commit the transaction, the transaction commits; if *either* object votes to rollback the transaction, then the transaction is rolled back. It's just like a wedding. If the bride says *no* when asked if she takes the groom to be her husband, it really doesn't matter if the groom had already said *yes*; the entire ceremony is aborted. This last point is an important one because it has another implication: once the groom gives his consent to the wedding, the outcome of the ceremony is still in doubt until the bride gives her consent. The same is true for COM+ objects. Once an object calls `SetComplete`, it doesn't know if the transaction will commit or not. The object is only giving its acceptance to the commitment of the transaction. This has an important implication for the management of the state of a transactional object. A transactional COM+ object should not assume that the state it has when it calls `SetComplete` will be valid after the transaction is committed. For instance, if the Customer object debits a customer's account in a database, it should not maintain state that contains the customer's new account balance; it should refresh itself with the new balance from the database after the transaction is committed. Even if the Customer object was pleased with its updates, the Book object could still rollback the transaction (perhaps because the book is no longer in print), and if it did, the Customer object is now in an invalid state. To prevent problems like this from happening, COM+ deactivates all the objects involved in a transaction when the transaction commits. This forces you to reinitialize your objects after each transaction. Deactivating objects like this also helps scalability, but the main reason it is done is to ensure the correctness of a transaction.

Deactivating an object means different things depending on whether object pooling is turned on (I talk about object pooling shortly). If object pooling is not turned on, then the deactivated object is actually destroyed. If object pooling is turned on, the deactivated object is returned to the object pool where another client can use it later.

MANAGING STATE IN COM+ OBJECTS

There is a big problem with this deactivate-on-transaction-commit approach. The definition of an object (in the computer science sense) is that it is an entity that has behavior and *state*. If the state of a transactional COM+ object is lost as soon as you commit a transaction, it makes it difficult to maintain the association between behavior and state that is the essence of an object. The real question is: how do you keep track of the state of your transactional COM+ objects?

You have a number of choices as to maintaining object state: You can make your object stateless, you can cache your object's state in the shared property manager, or you can persist the object's state into a database or some other durable storage.

Stateless Objects • Stateless objects are objects that do not maintain any member variables. This means that all of the information the object requires to execute a method must be stored somewhere (usually on the client), then passed into each method, or retrieved from a database or some other persistent storage. Some people have the misconception that to use COM+ (or MTS), your COM objects *must* be stateless. This is not true. Using COM+ requires you to think carefully about how you manage state in your objects. Building stateless objects is only one way to use COM+.

The Shared Property Manager • Another way to manage state in a COM+ object is to store the object's state in the Shared Property Manager, which is affectionately called the SPAM. The SPAM is an in-memory cache that is maintained within the COM+ surrogate process. It is essentially an indexed collection. The SPAM is good for maintaining process-wide, transient data (that's a fancy name for global variables). Because the SPAM runs in the surrogate process, all data in the SPAM is lost when the surrogate process shuts down. By default, that is three minutes after there has been no activity. You can alter this setting in the Component Services Explorer.

You can place data of any type in the SPAM and index it via a string key. When you wish to fetch the data later, you ask for it by its key. Listing 12.3 shows how to maintain a global counter in the SPAM. Each time this code is run it increments the counter. For clarity and brevity, I've omitted error checking from this code.

LISTING 12.3 *USING THE SPAM*

```
1. STDMETHODIMP CTestObject::TestSpam(long *counter)
2. {
3.     LONG lIsolationMode = LockMethod;
4.     LONG lReleaseMode = Process;
5.     _variant_t vtNextNumber;
6.     HRESULT hRes;
7.     ISharedPropertyGroupManager* pPropGrpMgr;
8.     ISharedPropertyGroup* pPropGrp;
9.     ISharedProperty* pPropNextNumber;
10.    VARIANT_BOOL bExists;
11.
12.    hRes=CoCreateInstance(CLSID_SharedPropertyGroupManager,NULL,
13.          CLSCTX_ALL,IID_ISharedPropertyGroupManager,
         (void**)&pPropGrpMgr);
14.
15.    hRes=pPropGrpMgr->CreatePropertyGroup(L"SharedCounters",
16.       &lIsolationMode, &lReleaseMode, &bExists,&pPropGrp);
17.    pPropGrpMgr->Release();
18.
19.    pPropGrp->CreateProperty(L"NextNumber",&bExists,&pPropNextNumber);
20.    pPropGrp->Release();
21.
22.    vtNextNumber.vt=VT_I4;
23.    hRes = pPropNextNumber->get_Value(&vtNextNumber);
24.    *counter=vtNextNumber.lVal++;  // Increment the counter
25.    hRes = pPropNextNumber->put_Value(vtNextNumber);
26.    pPropNextNumber->Release();
27.    return S_OK;
28.}
```

In this code, you call the CoCreateInstance method to obtain the ISharedPropertyGroupManager interface on a SharedProperty-Manager object on lines 12 and 13. Next, create a property group called SharedCounters using the CreatePropertyGroup method of ISharedPropertyGroupManager as shown on lines 15 and 16. This method opens the property group if it already exists, or it creates the property group if it does not. A property group is just a collection of properties. Next, you can attempt to create a property called NextNumber using the CreateProperty member function of the property group as shown on line 19. Once again, this method returns an existing property if it exists already or creates a property with the name if it does not. Finally, on lines 22–26 you get the value associated with the property (if the property is being created for the first time, its initial value is zero). You then increment the value and store the new value back into the property. The helpful thing about using the SPAM to maintain data like this is that it is global to the server not the client. This means that all clients see the same value for this property. Remember that once the server process shuts down, all data in the SPAM is lost.

Storing State in Persistent Storage • Your final choice for dealing with state in COM+ objects is to store the object state in persistent storage: a file or a database. When your object is deactivated, you can write its state to persistent storage and later, when an object is activated again, it can read its state back from the database. The `IObjectControl` interface comes in handy when implementing this functionality. If a COM+ object implements the `IObjectControl` interface, COM+ calls the `Deactivate` method on `IObjectControl` when it deactivates the object and it calls the `Activate` method on `IObjectControl` when it activates the object. You can put logic in the `Deactivate` method to write state to a database or file and then read the data back in from the database or file when the `Activate` method is called. I talk more about `IObjectControl` and you will see how to implement it when I discuss object pooling.

Stateful, Transactional Objects: Don't Do It! • You can create stateful, transactional objects in COM+ if you really want to. As long as you never indicate to COM+ that the object is done with its work (basically, that means you don't call `SetComplete` or `SetAbort`), an object is not deactivated until the base client deactivates the object by releasing its reference. Of course, an object designed this way does not commit any of its transactions until the client releases the object. This fact alone makes it impractical in most situations to design your objects this way. But there are other problems, too: shared resources used by the object (database connections and memory) are also not reclaimed until the client releases its references to the object, ruining scalability. In short, trying to create stateful, transactional COM+ objects is a bad idea.

DEACTIVATE-ON-RETURN BIT AND THE TRANSACTION-VOTE BIT

So far, I have simplified my discussion of how a transaction is controlled and committed so you would understand the basics. Now that you have a better understanding of the relationship between a transaction and the lifetime of an object, I can tell you that the situation is actually slightly more complicated (for good reasons) than what you have seen to this point. To understand how a transaction is controlled in COM+, you must understand the role of the deactivate-on-return and transaction-vote bits in the object context.

Each object's context contains two bits: a transaction-vote bit that indicates if the object is happy with the transaction as it currently exists (if it would vote to commit the transaction right now), and a deactivate-on-return bit that indicates if the object has completed its work and can be deactivated (remember COM+ must deactivate an object when it commits a transaction). The transaction-vote bit is also sometimes called the Happy bit and the deactivate-on-return bit is sometimes called the Done bit.

Under MTS (which COM+ replaces), the transaction-vote and deactivate-on-return bits were always called the Happy and Done bits, respectively. Under COM+, the terminology has officially changed. Transaction-vote and deactivate-on-return are the new, more accurate names for these bits. Throughout the rest of this chapter, I stick with the official terminology and use transaction-vote and deactivate-on-return for these bit names.

A COM+ object can change its transaction-vote bit any time until it is deactivated. Once an object is deactivated, the state of its transaction-vote bit at that time becomes its vote as to whether its transaction should succeed or fail. If the transaction-vote bit is set, when an object is deactivated, the object is voting to commit the transaction; if the transaction-vote bit is cleared, the object is voting to abort the transaction. Continuing with the marriage analogy, setting its transaction-vote bit is a COM+ object's way of saying I do. Clearing its transaction-vote bit is a COM+ object's way of saying I don't.

Under COM+, an object can be deactivated in two ways: (1) the client can release its reference to the object (call Release on an interface), or (2) an object can set its deactivate-on-return bit. If a COM+ sets its deactivate-on-return bit inside a method, the COM+ runtime deactivates the object when the method returns. Because the COM+ runtime won't actually attempt to commit a transaction until the object that created the transaction (the root object) is deactivated, setting the deactivate-on-return bit also has the effect of telling the COM+ runtime it can commit the transaction anytime it is ready.

Now that you understand these bits you can understand exactly what happens when a COM+ object calls `SetComplete` on the `IObjectContext` interface of its object context inside of a method. `SetComplete` sets both the transaction-vote and deactivate-on-return bits to true. This has the effect of telling COM+ that you are happy with the transaction and it can go ahead and commit it any time it is ready. Calling `SetAbort` on the `IObjectContext` interface of the object context clears the transaction-vote bit and sets the deactivate-on-return bit. This causes the object to be deactivated with its transaction-vote bit cleared and causes the transaction to abort.

So far, you have only looked at transactions that last for a single method. In these cases, the method calls `SetComplete` or `SetAbort` before it returns. What happens if you want to create a transaction that spans multiple method calls on an Object? Let's say you're designing an Order object. The use case for the object is as follows: the user first fills in the Master information for the order (customer name, delivery address, credit card information, and so on). Next, the user fills in the line items for the order and finally submits the order. The `Submit` method performs some required validity checks on the order and then submits the order for processing. If you cannot submit the order for any reason, all information associated with the order should be removed from the database. A sequence diagram for this use case is as shown in Figure 12.15.

In this use case, you don't want the transaction to commit until the client calls the `Submit` method. So the sequence of events for a transaction is as follows:

1. The User creates an Order object, which starts a transaction.
2. They then call `AddLineItem` one or more times within the same transaction.
3. The user calls `Submit` to submit the order and commit the transaction.

Obviously, you don't want to call `SetComplete` in `SetMasterInfo` because that commits the transaction. You also don't want to call `SetComplete` in `AddLineItem` because that also commits the transaction.

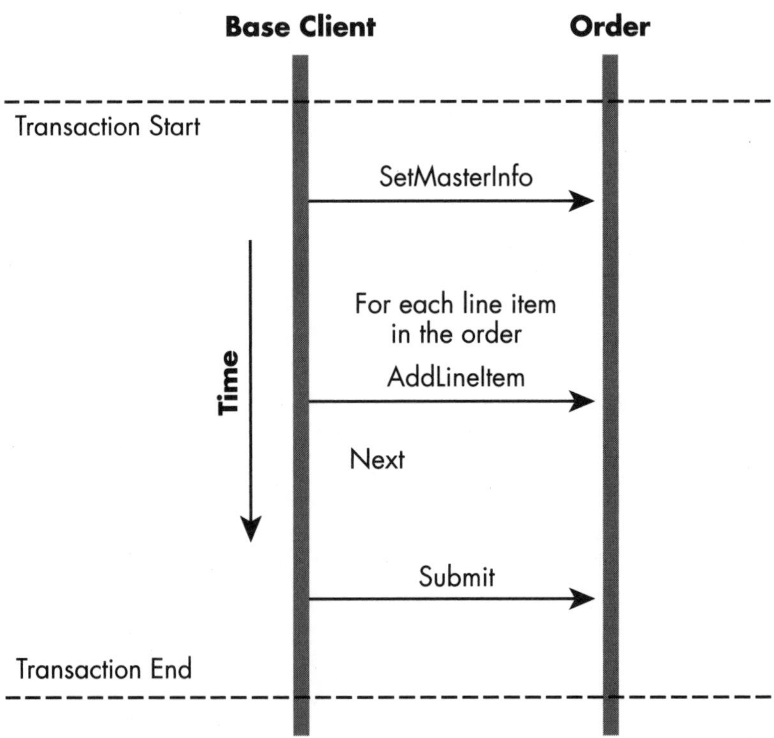

FIGURE 12.15 A Sequence Diagram for Placing an Order.

You only want to call SetComplete in the Submit method. Moreover, if the Order object is deactivated before the Submit method is called, you want the transaction to automatically abort. You can implement this functionality using the DisableCommit method on the IObjectContext interface of the object context. DisableCommit clears both the transaction-vote bit and the deactivate-on-return bit. The COM+ runtime does not attempt to deactivate the object and if the base client releases its last reference to the object (which causes the object to be deactivated), the fact that the transaction-vote bit is false causes the transaction to be aborted. In the scenario sketched out in Figure 12.15, you should call DisableCommit in SetMasterInfo and AddLineItem and then call SetComplete in the Submit method.

If you create a table showing all the possible states of the deactivate-on-return and transaction-vote bits as shown in Table 12.3, you will see that we have explored the first three of the four possible states.

TABLE 12.3 Possible States for the Deactive-On-Return and Transaction-Vote Bits in the Object Context

Deactivate-on-return Bit	Transaction-Vote Bit	IObjectContext Method	Object Deactivated on Method Return	OK to Commit Transaction
On	Off	SetAbort	Yes	No
On	On	SetComplete	Yes	Yes
Off	Off	DisableCommit	No	No
Off	On	EnableCommit	No	Yes

What about the last state? This is where the deactivate-on-return bit is cleared, so the object is not deactivated when the current method returns, but the transaction-vote bit is set, so the transaction is committed if the object is deactivated by the base client releasing its reference. You can put the deactivate-on-return and transaction-vote bits in this state by calling EnableCommit on the IObjectContext interface. An object should call EnableCommit if it is *not* yet done with all the work it would *like* to do, but if the object is deactivated, its transaction should be committed anyway. EnableCommit is the default action if a method in a COM+ object returns from a method without calling any methods on IObjectContext.

With Microsoft Transaction Server on NT 4.0, the only way you could manipulate the transaction-vote and deactivate-on-return bits was through the IObjectContext interface. Under COM+, the object context supports a number of interfaces including IContextState, which allows you to manipulate the transaction-vote and deactivate-on-return bits explicitly. IContextState contains the four methods shown in Table 12.4.

TABLE 12.4 The Methods in the IContextState Interface

Method Name	Description
SetDeactivateOnReturn	Sets the deactivate-on-return bit to true or false
GetDeactivateOnReturn	Gets the Done bit
SetMyTransactionVote	Sets the transaction-vote bit to true or false
GetMyTransactionVote	Gets the transaction-vote bit

Using `IContextState`, you can write the following code to either commit or abort a single-method transaction.

LISTING 12.4 *USING A COM+ TRANSACTION WITH ICONTEXTSTATE*

```
HRESULT hRes;
IContextState *pContextState;
hRes= CoGetObjectContext(IID_IContextState,(void **)&pContextState);

try
{
// Perform work here;

   pContextState->SetMyTransactionVote(TxCommit);
}
catch(exception err)
{
   pContextState->SetMyTransactionVote(TxAbort);
}
ContextState->SetDeactivateOnReturn(VARIANT_TRUE);
pContextState->Release();
```

If you have a transaction that spans multiple methods, you can call `SetMyTransactionVote` in each method and call `SetDeactivateOnReturn` with a `VARIANT_FALSE` parameter to prevent the object from deactivating. Then, in the method where you commit the transaction, you can call `SetDeactivateOnReturn` and pass in `VARIANT_TRUE`.

Using the `IContextState` interface is equivalent to using `IObjectContext`. I'm not sure which is the preferred way to manipulate a transaction. An article by Don Box in the September 1999 edition of *MSJ* stated that the use of `IObjectContext` is deprecated under Windows 2000, but almost all of the COM+ examples on Microsoft's Web site use `IObjectContext`. I use `IContextState` in the COM+ example you build in the next chapter.

I should make a couple of points before leaving the subject of transactions. First, a transaction is doomed once one of the objects involved in the transaction returns from a method with its deactivate-on-return bit set to true and its transaction-vote bit set to false (an object can do this explicitly using `IContextState` or by calling `SetAbort` on `IObjectContext`). You might as well set up your error handling so the error is immediately returned to the calling object (if there is one) so it can also abort. It's like the groom saying no when asked if he takes the bride to be his wife. Once he says no, you might as well call off the wedding immediately; there's no point in asking the bride if she takes him to be her husband. There's an example of how to setup your error handling in Chapter 13 when you build a complete COM+ example.

Second, you can change the default behavior that COM+ has in regard to transaction management. You can do this on a method-by-method basis by setting the Auto-Done bit to true. Perform the following steps in the Component Services Explorer to set the Auto-Done bit to true for a method:

1. Right-click on the method beneath the `Methods` folder under the `Components` folder in your COM+ Application (see Figure 12.16).

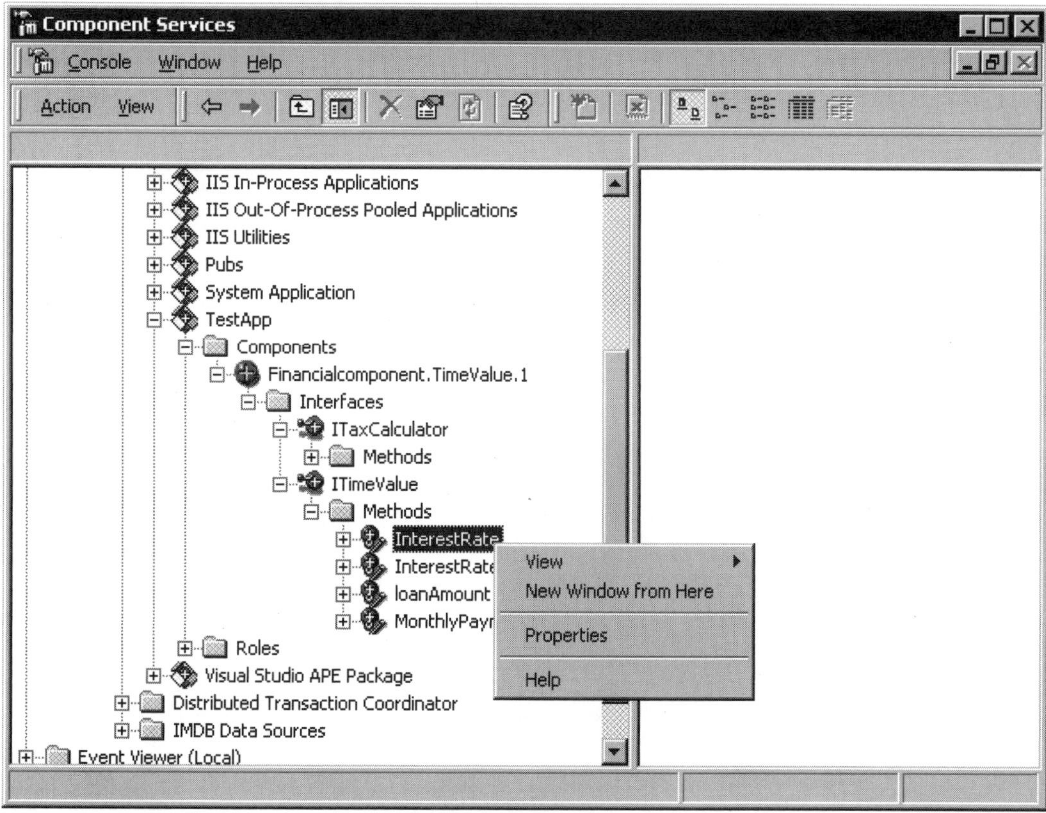

FIGURE 12.16 Setting the Attributes for a Method.

2. The Method Properties dialog appears as shown in Figure 12.17.
3. Set the `Automatically deactivate this object when the method returns` check box.
4. Click `OK`.

After you set the auto-done bit, then the `Deactivate-on-return` bit is set to true as soon as you enter the method. The state of the transaction vote bit is set based on the return value from the function. If you return `S_OK` from the method, the transaction vote bit is set; this is the same as if you had called `SetComplete`. If the method returns unsuccessfully, for example, it returns an HRESULT indicating an error, then the transaction vote bit is cleared. This is the same as calling `SetAbort`. The user can override the automatic setting of the `Deactivate on return` bit by explicitly calling methods on the `IContextState` interface.

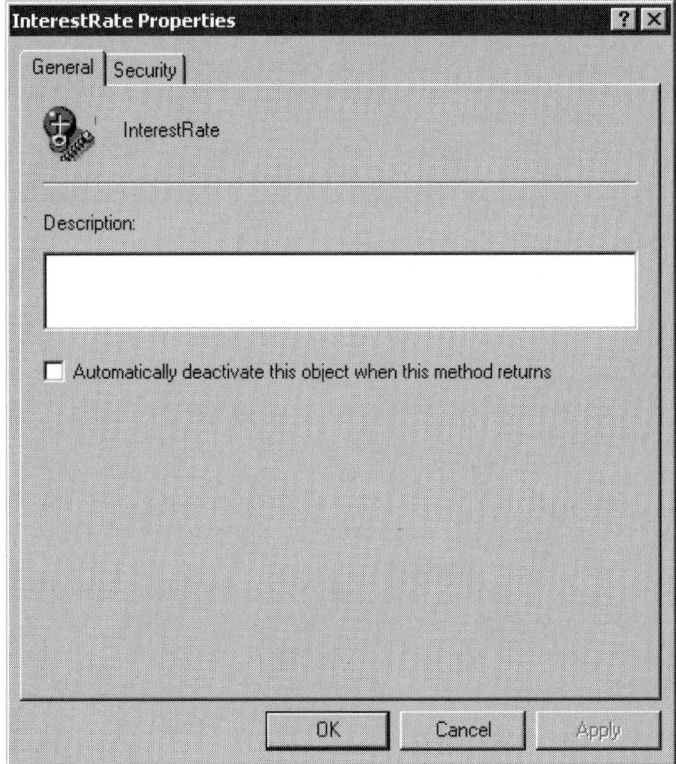

FIGURE 12.17 The Method Properties Dialog.

Scalability

COM+ also provides you with a number of services you can use to improve the scalability of your COM objects. In this context, scalability means how your application handles an increased workload.

Imagine if you installed a COM+ component on a server machine and suddenly a thousand people decided they wanted to simultaneously use your server. Each of those clients resides on a separate machine and each of those client applications (as most applications tend to do) creates a COM+ object and then holds on to an interface pointer on that object for the life of the user's session. The problem is that each object uses some quantum of server resources: each object uses some memory and may have its own thread; if your COM+ object does talk to a database, it will also have a database connection. An application designed this way does not scale well. The server machine would likely crash under the load before you reach a thousand users. So how can COM+ improve the scalability of this application?

To understand how COM+ works, imagine you are the manager of a successful rental car company. You know that in a typical year you will have 10,000 customers. Would you run out and buy 10,000 cars to rent to each of these customers? Of course not. Each customer's car would be gathering dust on your lot when that customer was not renting it from you.

You could probably service all of your customers with a pool of 200 cars. When someone arrives and wants to rent a car, you give them the first available car of their requested type. They can use this car for the length of their stay. When they're done, they bring the car back, you clean it up, and then it goes back into your pool to wait for the next customer who wants a car of that type. Maintaining a pool of some scarce resource allows you to service a given number of users of that resource with the smallest possible number of that resource. With COM+, you can achieve the same optimum sharing of a scarce resource using a combination of Just In Time (JIT) Activation and Object Pooling.

JIT Activation

People often write COM client applications so that they instantiate all the objects they need when they are started and then hold on to those objects for the life of the application. Most of the clients that you have built in this book work this way. In many situations, it makes sense to do this because the cost of instantiating a COM object can be high. At a minimum, a registry lookup is required. If the server is out-of-process, then a server process must be started. And if the server is a remote server, then activating an object requires a network round-trip. While it is simpler and seems more efficient from the client's perspective to hold onto object references for the length of a user's session, from the server's perspective this ruins scalability.

A thousand clients may be holding onto their object references but it's likely that only a small number of those clients are actually executing a method on one of those objects at any given moment. Meanwhile, each of those thousand objects is using some quantum of server resources. Without COM+, the solution to this problem would be to place the burden on developers of client applications to be smarter in the way they create and use objects. You can require that they instantiate a COM object only when they need one to execute a transaction and then release it as soon as the transaction is committed or rolled back. This places a great deal of additional work on client developers.

The whole idea of COM+ is to take enterprise-class functionality that would be difficult for most developers to implement in code and make it simple to use. So it is with the functionality I just described. Rather than require the client to manage the efficient allocation and deallocation of objects, COM+ implements this functionality for you. It's called Just In Time (JIT) Activation and is controlled using attributes like all the other services of COM+. Using JIT Activation, when the client first creates an object, the COM+ runtime creates the standard proxy and stub with an RPC channel between the object and its client as shown in Figure 12.18.

When the object sets its `Deactivate-on-return` bit, the COM+ runtime deactivates the object. The object is either destroyed or returned to the object pool (depending on the setting of the object pooling attribute). However, the client still holds the proxy for the object, the RPC Channel is in place, and the stub still exists as shown in Figure 12.19. So as far as the client is concerned, the server-side object is still there. When the client calls a method on the object again, the COM+ interceptor, which sits between the RPC channel and the stub, instantiates another instance of the object (or fetchs an instance from the object pool) and attaches it to the stub and the method can execute as normal.

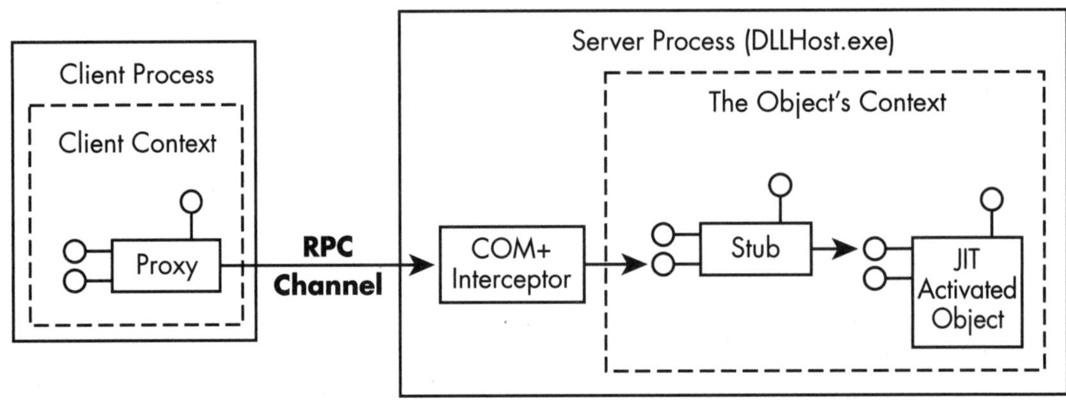

FIGURE 12.18 An Object That Supports JIT Activation in Its Activated State.

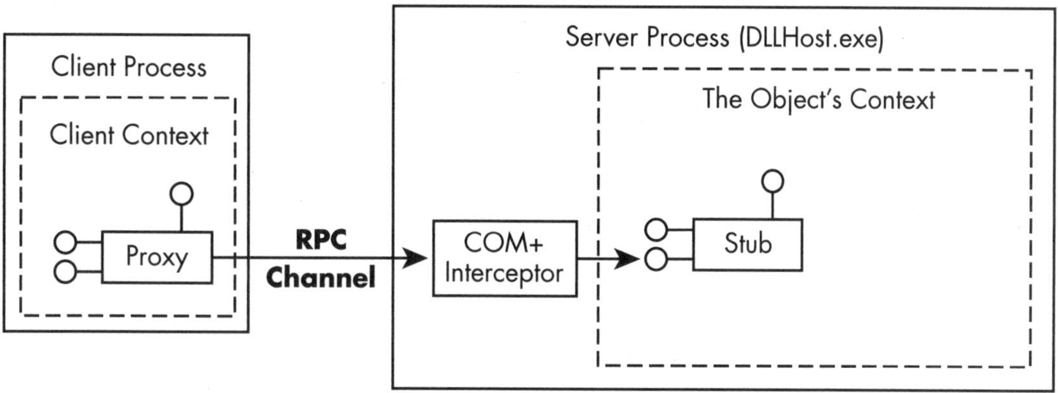

FIGURE 12.19 An Object That Supports JIT Activation in Its Deactivated State.

All transactional COM+ objects must use JIT Activation; this is to enforce transactional correctness. You can turn on JIT activation on a per-class basis using the Component Services Explorer. Perform the following steps to enable JIT activation for a COM+ component:

1. Right-click on the component in the `Components` folder of your Application.
2. Select `Properties...` from the `Context` Menu (the Component Properties dialog appears as shown in Figure 12.20).
3. Click the `Activation` tab.
4. Set the `Enable Just In Time Activation` checkbox.
5. Click OK.

You can see the dependency between transactions and JIT activation if you first go to a COM+ object in the Component Services Explorer and make it non-transactional by selecting *transactions not supported* for the transaction attribute and then turning off JIT activation. If you then go back to the Transaction tab and try to make it transactional again while JIT activation is still turned off, you see the warning message shown in Figure 12.21 as the system turns JIT activation back on. JIT activation serves two purposes. It not only enforces the correctness of your transactions, it also enhances the scalability of your application by minimizing the number of objects that need to be activated at any given time to service a given number of clients.

Object Pooling

An application that uses JIT activation activates and deactivates a large number of objects. Depending on how the object is implemented, it may be

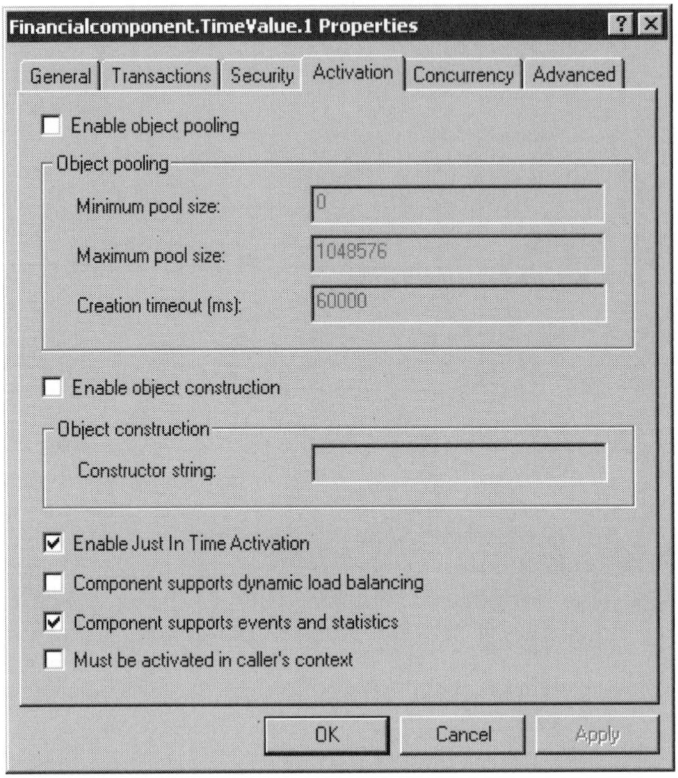

FIGURE 12.20 The Activation Tab of the Components Properties Dialog.

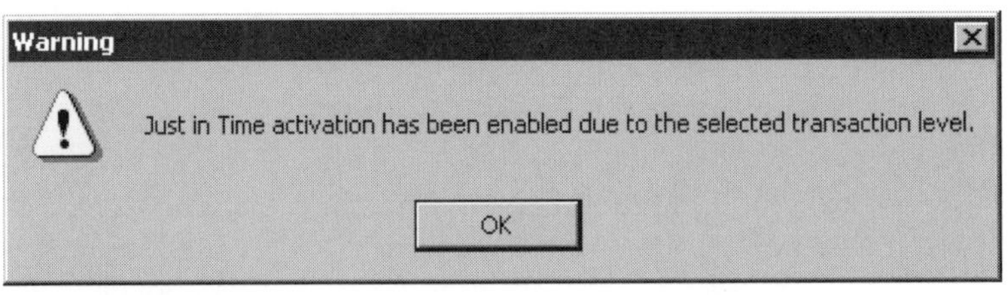

FIGURE 12.21 Trying to Make an Object That Does Not Support JIT Activation Transactional.

expensive in terms of time to create a new instance of an object whenever you start a new transaction. To alleviate this problem, COM+ supports object pooling. With object pooling, the COM+ pool manager maintains a pool of objects. When a client attempts to activate an object of that type, the COM+ runtime returns an instance from the pool if one is available, instead of creating a new instance from scratch. The client can use the object for as long as it likes. When the client releases its last reference to the object, or the object returns from a method with its deactivate-on-return bit set, the object is deactivated. If object pooling is turned on, instead of being destroyed, the deactivated object is returned to the object pool as shown in Figure 12.22.

You configure a COM+ class to support object pooling the same way you configure all COM+ services: using the Component Services Explorer. Perform the following steps to *view* the object pooling-related COM+ attributes:

1. Right-click on the component in the `Components` folder of your Application.
2. Select `Properties...` from the `Context` Menu (the Component Properties dialog appears as shown in Figure 12.20).
3. Click the `Activation` tab (shown in Figure 12.20).
4. Set the `Enable object pooling` checkbox.
5. Click `OK`.

Notice I say *view* the pooling-related attributes because most of the COM components that you have created up to now will *not* be poolable. You can tell if an object is poolable if the Enable Object Pooling checkbox

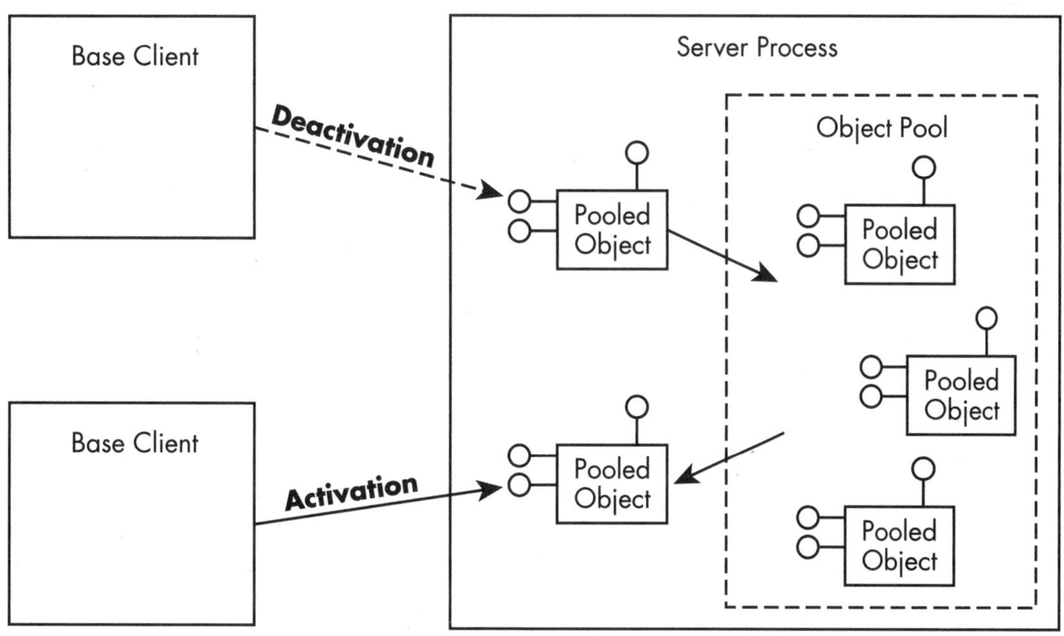

FIGURE 12.22 Object Pooling.

on the Activation tab of the class-level properties is enabled. A COM+ component must meet the following requirements before it can be poolable.

- It must reside in the Thread Neutral or Free-Threaded Apartment of a process.
- It must be stateless.
- It must not have thread-affinity.
- It must be aggregateable.

Assuming that a COM+ component is poolable, you can configure a minimum number of objects that should be instantiated immediately when the process for the COM+ application starts. You can also specify a maximum number of objects allowed in the pool and a creation timeout. As activation requests are received, the COM+ runtime services them from the initial (minimum) number of objects. If all the objects in this initial pool are being used and additional activation requests arrive, the COM+ runtime creates additional objects to service those requests until the specified maximum number of objects is reached. After that, additional activation requests are queued and they wait the specified creation timeout period for an object to become available before failing. The total number of objects, both activated and pooled (deactivated), is never allowed to exceed the specified maximum.

IObjectControl

There is a problem with object pooling as you understand it so far and it relates to state again. When a client receives an object from the pool, that object has the same state that it had when the last client that used it returned it to the object pool. In most cases, the object should be reinitialized when it is handed to a new client. Moreover, when a client is done with an object and returns it to the pool, you may want to run a termination routine. This termination routine might close a database connection or free some other shared resource the object is using. There is no point in the object holding on to some shared resource while it is sitting idling in the object pool.

If a poolable object wishes to be notified when it is being activated (fetched from the pool) or deactivated (returned to the pool), it should implement the `IObjectControl` interface. The `IObjectControl` interface also allows the object to specify programmatically if it is poolable. Table 12.5 lists the name and the description of the methods in `IObjectControl`.

TABLE 12.5 The Methods in the IObjectControl Interface

Method Name	Description
Activate	Called when an object is activated.
Deactivate	Called when an object is deactivated.
CanBePooled	Allows an object to let COM+ know whether it can be pooled.

COM+ objects that use object pooling *should* implement `IObjectControl`. If an object implements `IObjectControl`, when the object is deactivated (either released by its client or as a result of JIT activation) the COM+ runtime calls the `Deactivate` method on `IObjectControl`. After that it calls the `CanBePooled` method. If `CanBePooled` returns `TRUE`, the object is placed under the control of the pool manager. If the object is later activated on behalf of another (or the same) client, the COM+ runtime calls the Activate method on the object before the object is reactivated.

If a transactional object holds on to a managed resource like a database connection while it is pooled, it must indicate when the resource cannot be used by returning `FALSE` from `CanBePooled`; when `CanBePooled` returns False, it causes the transaction to abort. Also, if a pooled object holds on to a managed resource (like a database connection) while it is pooled, it should turn off the resource manager's auto-enlistment and manually enlist any resources it holds in transactions. The details of doing this are resource-manager dependent and beyond the scope of this book. Suffice to say, you should think long and hard before you decide to have a pooled object hold on to a managed resource like a database connection while it is deactivated in the object pool. The bold code shown in Listing 12.5 illustrates how to implement `IObjectControl` in a COM class that has been implemented with ATL.

LISTING 12.5 *IMPLEMENTING IOBJECTCONTROL*

```
class ATL_NO_VTABLE CBook :
    public CComObjectRootEx<CComMultiThreadModel>,
    public CComCoClass<CBook, &CLSID_Book>,
    public IDispatchImpl<IBook, &IID_IBook, &LIBID_PUBSBOSERVERLib>,
    public IObjectControl
{
public:
    CBook()
    { }

BEGIN_COM_MAP(CBook)
    COM_INTERFACE_ENTRY(IBook)
    COM_INTERFACE_ENTRY2(IDispatch, IBook)
    COM_INTERFACE_ENTRY(IObjectControl)
END_COM_MAP()
public:
// IBook methods go here …

// IObjectPool
    STDMETHOD_(BOOL, CanBePooled) ()
```

```
    {
        return TRUE;
    }
    STDMETHOD(Activate) ()
    {
    // Initialization logic goes here
        return S_OK;
    }
    STDMETHOD_(void, Deactivate)()
    {
    // Termination logic goes here
    }
};
```

Database Connection Pooling

COM+ also increases the scalability of COM objects by helping them effectively share server-side resources like database connections. A good portion of the COM+ components that you write will make a connection to a database. You can manage this connection within your object in one of two ways: (1) you can open a connection to the database when the object is activated and then close the connection when the object is deactivated, or (2) you can open a connection to the database in each method and close the connection before the method returns.

The first approach creates the same scalability problem that you have when a client tries to hold on to a COM object for the lifetime of a user's session: If you have a thousand users currently trying to use your server, then they will have a thousand database connections open. But it is likely that at any given moment only a small fraction of those connections will be used. Meanwhile your database server has to maintain a thousand connections. If enough connections are open, the server slows down to a point where performance becomes unacceptable. Moreover, maintaining a large number of connections can be expensive from a financial standpoint. Many database servers are licensed on a per-connection basis.

The second approach minimizes the number of connections that are used at any time and, thus, improves scalability, but it has an adverse effect on performance. For most RDBMS servers, making the initial connection to the database is a slow operation.

The natural solution to this problem is to maintain a pool of database connections. When a COM+ object wishes to make a connection to a database, it first checks the pool of available database connections. If a suitable connection to the desired database server is already available, the COM+ object can simply grab the connection from the pool and start working.

A suitable connection is one that has the same connection string (i.e., the same server, user name, password, and other connection properties).

If no suitable connections are found in the connection pool, then the object can make a new connection to the database. When the COM object is done with the connection, instead of closing the connection, it simply returns it to the pool where it is available for another object that might need a similar connection.

Now, if you are a true glutton for punishment you could implement this logic yourself, but you don't have to. Once again COM+ makes this functionality available to you without requiring you to write a line of code. As long as you write your COM+ business objects so they access databases using either Open DataBase Connectivity (ODBC) or OLEDB, then your objects automatically use the connection pooling provided by these data access technologies.

ODBC and OLEDB: Universal Data Access APIs

ODBC and OLEDB are universal data-access APIs. ODBC (which is much older) is implemented as a C language API; OLEDB is implemented as a set of COM interfaces that abstract the functionality of a DataBase Management System (DBMS).The idea is that you write your applications to the ODBC API or use the OLEDB interfaces.Then, to make your application work with any DBMS, you simply get an ODBC driver or an OLEDB provider for the DBMS.An ODBC driver and an OLEDB provider do the same thing: they map calls on the standard interface (ODBC or OLEDB) to calls on the native API of the DBMS.The only difference is the way they are implemented.An ODBC driver is a DLL that implements a specified set of functions.An OLEDB provider is an in-process COM server.

With ODBC, a piece of software called the Driver Manager sits between your application and each ODBC driver as shown in Figure 12.23.

With OLEDB there is no equivalent to the ODBC Driver Manager.Your application talks directly to the OLEDB provider, which talks to your database as shown in Figure 12.24.

The OLEDB Architecture is actually far more complex then that shown in Figure 12.24. I discuss this technology in greater detail in the next chapter. The architecture shown in Figure 12.24 is of sufficient detail for the discussion at hand.

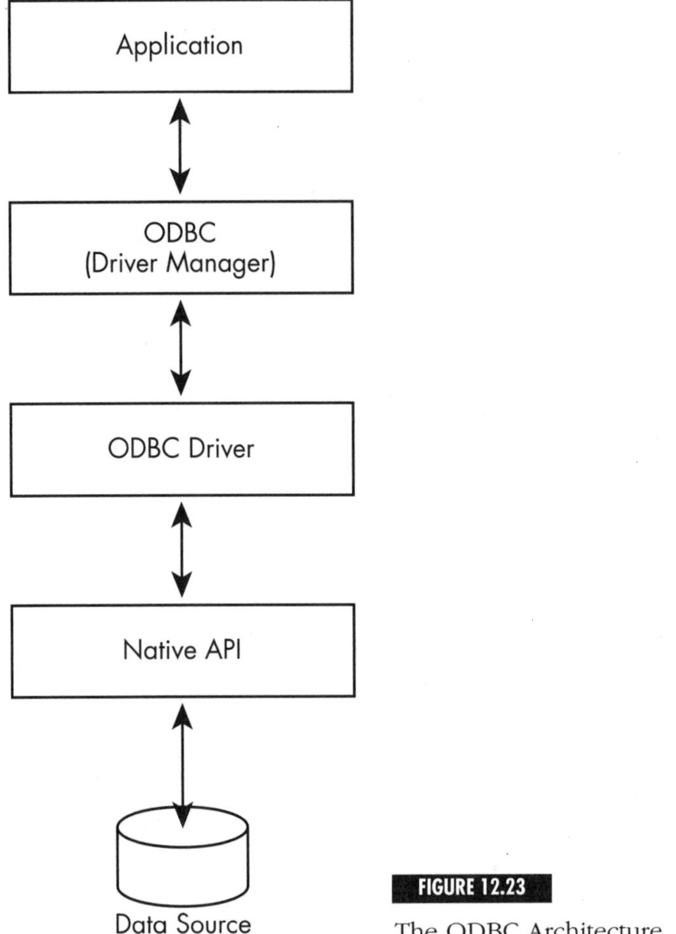

FIGURE 12.23

The ODBC Architecture.

Resource Dispensers • COM+ can implement connection pooling using either ODBC or OLEDB because the ODBC Driver Manager and most OLEDB providers are *Resource Dispensers*.

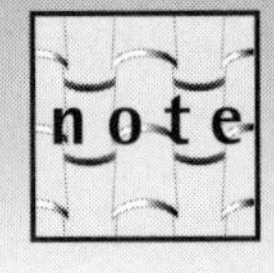

Check the documentation for your OLEDB provider to see if it implements connection pooling.

In the language of transaction processing, a resource dispenser is a piece of software that works with a transaction manager to manage a pool of some non-durable, shared resource. In this case, the *non-durable*, shared

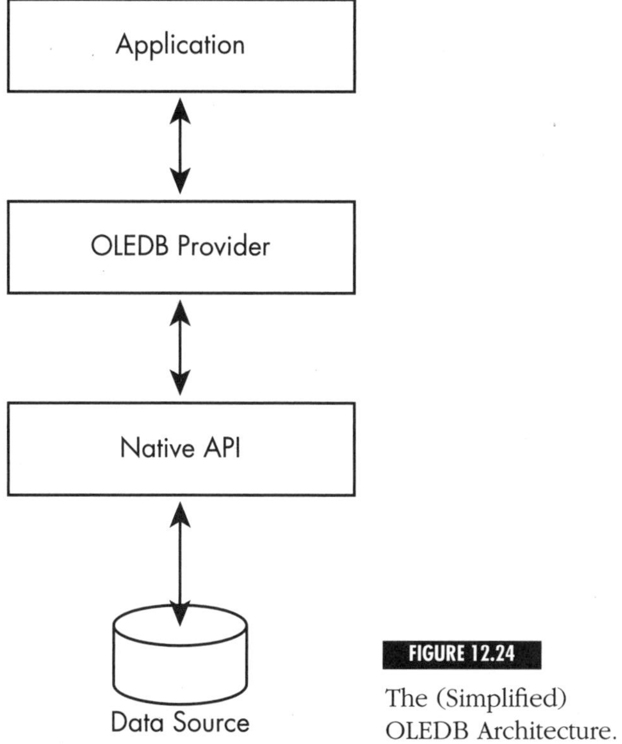

FIGURE 12.24

The (Simplified) OLEDB Architecture.

resource is a database connection; it could also be a socket connection or a file. Microsoft publishes an API you can use to create your own resource dispensers.

A Resource Manager, which you learned about earlier, manages *durable* state and can participate with a transaction manager and other resource managers in implementing the 2-phase commit protocol.

When you make a connection to a database server using OLEDB or ODBC, the ODBC Driver Manager (in the case of ODBC) and some OLEDB providers, first check their database connection pool to see if a connection to the requested database server already exists with the same connection string. The connection string includes the user ID and password and sometimes other parameters. If an unused connection exists in the pool that has a matching connection string, the Driver Manager or Provider returns the already open connection. The object can now use the connection as it sees fit. When the object is done with the application, it closes the connection.

Instead of destroying the connection, the resource dispenser returns the connection to the pool where it can be reused again.

To get the most out of connection pooling (or any other pooled resource that is managed by a resource dispenser), you need to follow two simple programming tenets: (1) acquire the resource as late as possible, and (2) release the resource as soon as possible. Remember the whole idea of resource pooling is that you have a resource that is in short supply; you don't want to hold on to the resource if you are not using it. So, the methods in your COM+ objects should create a connection only in a method that actually executes operations on the database. The method should close the connection before it returns. If you've done database programming before, you know that without connection pooling, using an approach like this can have poor performance. Creating a connection on a remote database is usually an expensive operation in terms of time. But with connection pooling, this is not a problem.

You do not configure database connection pooling in the Component Services Explorer. Database connection pooling is not specific to COM+. Any application using ODBC can take advantage of connection pooling. Perform the following steps to examine the ODBC connection pooling parameters in effect on your machine:

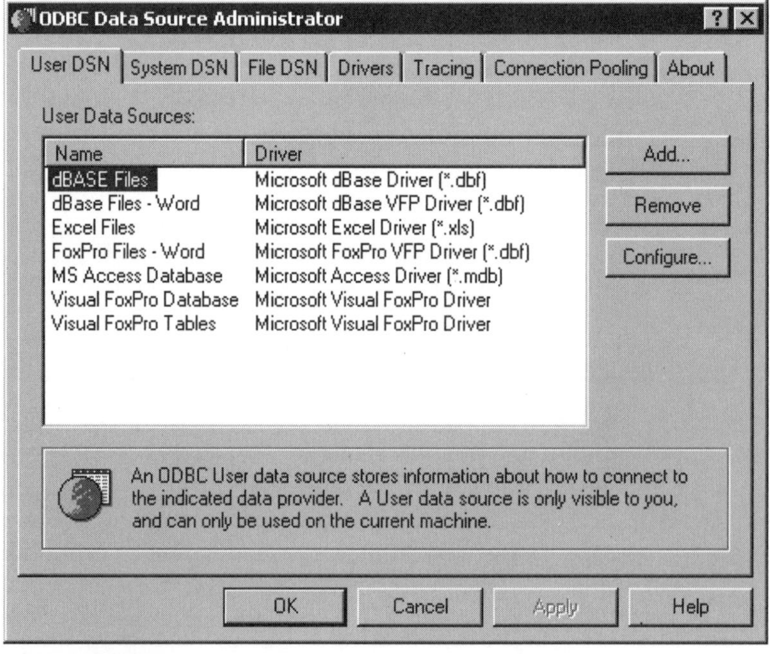

FIGURE 12.25 The ODBC Data Source Administrator.

1. Click the `Start` button.
2. Select `Programs\Administrative Tools\Data Sources` (the ODBC Data Source Administrator appears as shown in Figure 12.25).
3. Click the `Connection Pooling` tab (you should see the window shown in Figure 12.26).
4. Double-click the SQL Server entry in the ODBC Drivers list (the Set Connection Pooling Attributes dialog appears as shown in Figure 12.27).

Notice that in Figure 12.27 you can configure whether the driver pools the connections and how long an open connection remains in the pool.

If you are using OLEDB, you have to check the documentation for your OLEDB provider to see if it supports connection pooling and how to configure connection pooling for the provider.

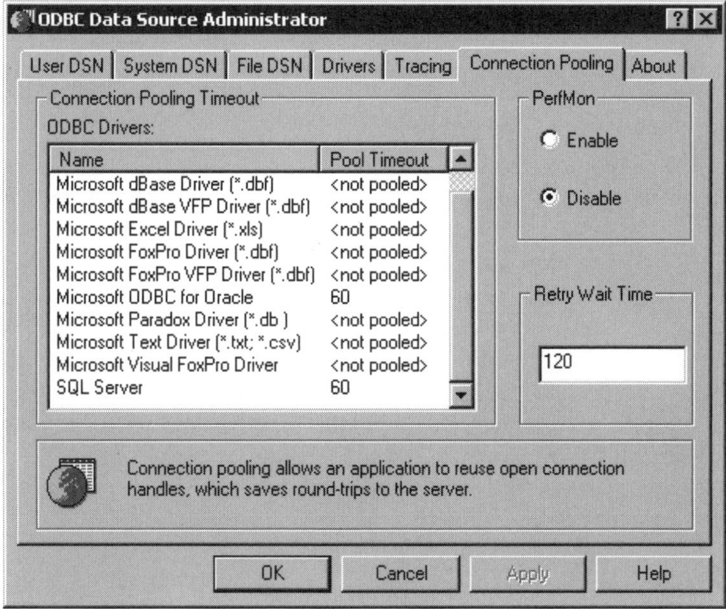

FIGURE 12.26 The Connection Pooling Tab of the ODBC Data Source Administrator.

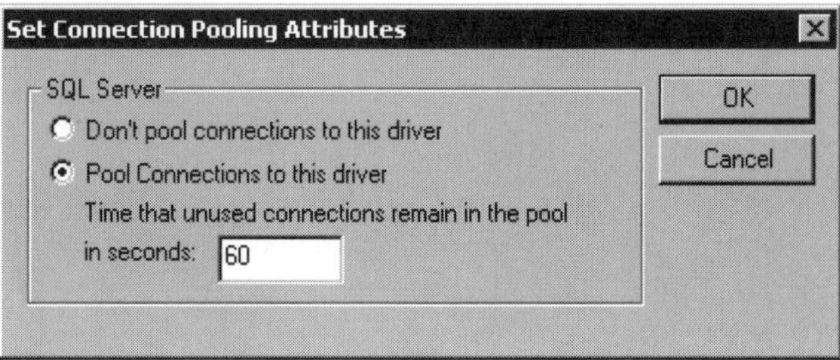

FIGURE 12.27 The Connection Pooling Attributes Dialog.

Synchronization

Both single and multi-threaded clients may use COM+ objects. You want your objects to be usable by both types of clients but you don't want to require developers of COM+ objects to have to write complicated thread synchronization code for all of their objects. COM used Apartments to provide thread-safety for objects that were not coded to be thread-safe. If your object is thread-safe, you can specify that the object should run in the Multi-Threaded Apartment (MTA). In this case, multiple threads may access the object simultaneously. MTA objects have the best performance when used in a multi-threaded environment, but the developer of this object has to implement code to make the object thread-safe. If an object is not thread-safe, you can specify that it should only run in the Single-Threaded Apartment (STA). An STA is intimately tied to one thread and only that thread is allowed to directly call a method on a COM object in an STA.

Unfortunately, STAs are not a good thread-safety solution for COM+ objects. The main problem is that STA objects also have thread-affinity. To maximize concurrency and performance, the surrogate process that COM+ uses is multi-threaded. You would like this process to have the liberty to choose which thread it uses to best service a particular method call. This runs counter to the whole concept of COM apartments. Apartments place strict limits on *which* thread is allowed to call a COM object directly. If the COM+ runtime tried to call into the object using a thread that is not the one thread associated with the object's STA, then intra-process marshaling must be used to send the method call to the thread in the object's STA. This thread switch is almost as slow as cross-process marshaling.

In addition, STA objects are unsuitable for use in an object pool. If it is not clear why this is so, imagine that you did try to implement object pooling with STA objects. Let's say you have a pool of five STA threads (Threads 1-5) that are to be used to create and manage a pool of STA COM objects. Thread 1 creates object A, executes some methods on the object, and then instead of deactivating the object when it is done with it, it places the object in the object pool. It's work done, thread 1 goes back to the thread pool. Now imagine that another activation request is received for a different type of object, and thread 1 is used to service this request. While thread 1 is busy servicing this request, an activation request for an object of the same type as object A is received. Because object A resides in the pool, it's natural that this object should be used instead of creating a new object (that's what object pooling is all about). But you have a problem. Because object A is an STA object, it can only be used by thread 1, which is busy servicing another request. So, even though there are four other threads available, any of which could service the request, you have to wait until thread 1 is free before you can use object A again.

As I mentioned in Chapter 9, the solution to all of these problems is the new COM+ Thread-Neutral Apartment (TNA). A thread in any apartment in a process can access an object that lives in the TNA. This allows the COM+ runtime to have the highest performance and concurrency that it possibly can and it also allows the COM+ runtime to implement object pooling. The problem here is that if you allow any thread to call into an object anytime it wants, you are faced with the very problem that apartments were designed to solve: How do you make your COM+ objects thread-safe without writing a lot of complex code?

Once again, COM+ and Attribute-Based Programming is the answer. COM+ provides activity-based synchronization support. You can specify that you want the system to provide thread synchronization support for your COM+ objects using the synchronization attribute.

Providing thread-safety for COM+ objects is more complex than just keeping a per-object lock and allowing only one thread to execute an object's methods. A COM+ object may call the methods of another COM+ object that resides in a different process, maybe even on a different machine. You would not want to get into a situation where one object is adding items to an order as another item is canceling the order. Using COM+'s synchronization support, you can synchronize the processing of multiple objects so no unwanted concurrency occurs even if the objects reside on different machines. To implement this functionality, COM+ introduces the concept of an *activity*.

Activities

An activity is defined as a set of objects performing work on behalf of a single client, within which concurrent calls from multiple threads are not allowed. Think of an activity as a logical thread that can span processes and machines. COM+ makes sure that two physical threads are not running at the same time within this logical thread of activity. This is actually a much stronger way of saying that more than one thread is not allowed to call into an object at the same time. You can specify that an object should support synchronization using the Component Services Explorer. There are five possible settings for the synchronization attribute: Table 12.6 gives the name and a description of each of these settings.

TABLE 12.6 Possible Settings for the Synchronization Attribute

Synchronization Setting	Description
Not Supported	The Object does not run within an activity.
Supported	The object runs within an activity if its creator runs within an activity.
Required	The object runs within its creators activity if the creator had one. It creates its own activity if its creator does not have one.
Requires New	The object always creates its own activity.
Disabled	This object ignores completely the value of the synchronization attribute when determining context placement. This setting makes your configured component behave like an unconfigured one.

Perform the following steps in the Component Services Explorer to set the Synchronization attribute for a COM+ component:

1. Right-click on the component in the `Components` folder beneath the Application.
2. Select `Properties` from the `Context` menu (the Component properties dialog appears).
3. Click the `Concurrency` tab (see Figure 12.28).
4. Set the radio button for the attribute that you would like to set.
5. Click `OK`.

It's likely that most of the options you see in this Window are disabled. There are a couple of important dependencies regarding synchronization that effect which settings are available.

- All STA components must reside in an activity whether or not they are transactional. An STA component, therefore, is only allowed to have either the Required or Requires New settings.
- All transactional COM+ components must reside within an activity so they also may only choose between the Required and Requires New settings.
- An object that supports JIT Activation whether it's transactional or not is allowed only the Required and Requires New settings.

An object that is running with COM+ synchronization support has an Activity ID in its Context just like an object that is running within a transaction has a Transaction ID in its Context. You can retrieve the Activity ID for an object by calling the `GetActivityId` method on the `IObjectContextInfo` interface of your object context. Let's see how activities work by looking at a single, synchronized object (in this case, let's consider an object whose synchronization attribute is Required and its creator is not currently running within an activity).

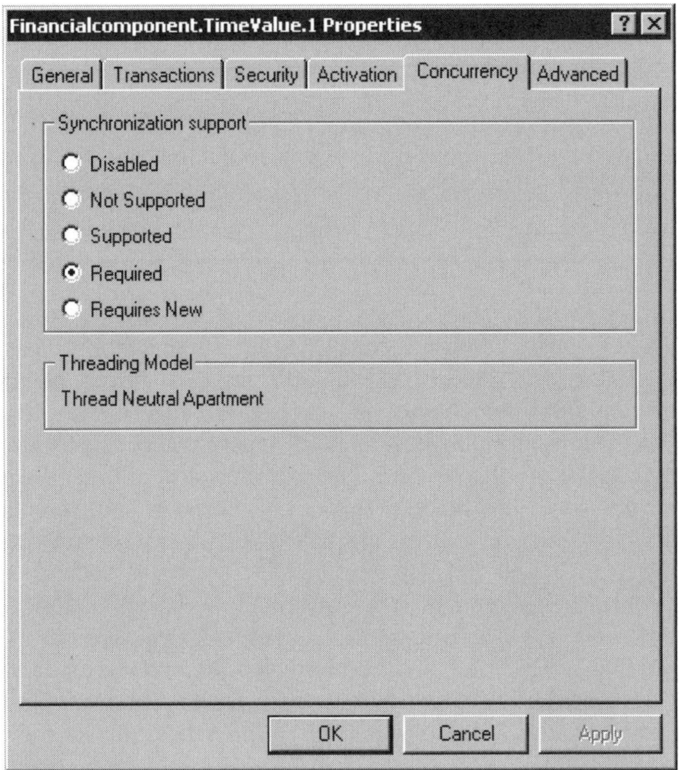

FIGURE 12.28 Configuring Synchronization for a COM+ Component.

When the object is first created, a new activity is created. Each activity contains a process-wide synchronization lock. Whenever a thread calls a method on the object, it acquires this lock. The lock is not released until the thread returns from the method. If a second thread tries to call into the method, it also attempts to lock the synchronization lock for the object's activity. This second thread cannot obtain this lock and enter the method until the first thread returns. Now let's consider what happens if, while within a method, a thread attempts to activate a second COM+ object.

Whether the activity flows to this second object depends on the synchronization setting that this second object has. Table 12.7 gives the activity status for an object when created from an object that is currently running within an activity.

TABLE 12.7 Activity Status of an Object Whose Creator Is within an Activity

Synchronization Setting	Activity Status
Not Supported	Does not run within an activity.
Supported	Runs within its creator's activity.
Required	Runs within its creator's activity.
Requires New	Runs within its own activity.

If you understood how transactions are created and propagated from object to object, then understanding how activities propagate from object to object isn't a big step for you. Let's say this second object has a synchronization attribute of Required. It shares the activity and, hence, the process-wide synchronization lock with its creating object. For a thread to make a method call on this second object, it must obtain this process-wide synchronization lock. If a method in the first object is still executing, it cannot do this. So a method call on the first object and a method call on the second object are never running simultaneously. If this second object has a synchronization setting of Not Supported or Requires New, it does not run within the same activity as its creating object so a method call on this second object may run concurrently with a method call on the first object.

Let's think about what happens if the first object activates an object that resides on a separate machine. The synchronization attribute still flows from the first object to the newly activated second object. If the second object is marked with a synchronization attribute of Supported or Required, then this second object shares the same activity as its creator. Because these objects are in different processes (on different machines), they cannot share the same physical thread. Not to worry, the COM+ runtime on the second machine creates a process-wide lock on the other machine.

There still is another problem, however. Consider what happens if the first object makes a method call to the second object and this second object makes a call back to the first object. The first object is blocked waiting for its method call on the second object to return (remember, method calls in COM and COM+ are synchronous by default). So the second object also blocks when it makes its call back to the first object. This is the classic case of deadlock. COM+ handles this situation using the concept of *Causality* (actually DCOM does the work here). Causality is a logical name for a set of nested function calls. A causality ID (which is a GUID) is sent along with every method call made via DCOM. When the second object calls back to the first object, it uses the same causality ID that the first object used to initiate the sequence of method calls. The first object checks the causality ID and sees that it is the same as the causality ID that it is waiting on. The first object realizes that a deadlock will be caused if it does not allow the call through, so it allows the method call to continue.

Queued Components

Think for a moment about your telephone. If you ignore answering machines and voice mail for a moment, when you call someone on the telephone, they must be available to answer the phone or no communication can take place. This is an example of synchronous communication. Both the sender and the receiver must be ready to receive the communication and their lifetimes must overlap. But waiting until someone is in his or her office and ready to receive a phone call is inconvenient. In many cases, it's not important that you talk to the person at that exact moment, you just need to get a message to them that they can listen to whenever they are ready. That's why voice mail was invented. With most telephones used in a business setting, if the person is not available to receive the phone call, you are automatically given the person's voice mail. You leave your message and the person will receive your message at a later time. This is an example of asynchronous communication. E-mail is another example of asynchronous communication. When you send an e-mail to someone you wouldn't expect your e-mail to be rejected just because the person you are sending the e-mail to is not available to receive it at that exact moment. You expect the message to be sent to the e-mail server on that person's domain where it patiently sits until the person is ready to read it. The COM+ Queued Components (QC) Service allows you to implement the equivalent of Voice Mail for your COM+ components. When using COM+ objects without the Queued Components Service, the client and object communicate over an RPC channel using a marshaling proxy and stub as shown in Figure 12.29.

The client has a proxy in its address space that turns a method call on a COM interface into an RPC message that is sent to a stub on the server machine. The stub receives and interprets the message and sends return values and output parameters back to the proxy. If someone accidentally killed

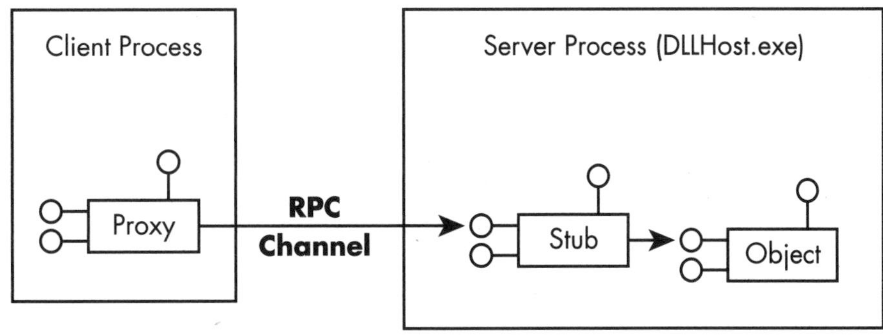

FIGURE 12.29 A COM/COM+ Client and Server Component without the Queued Components Service.

the server process or if for any other reason the server was not available at the time you made the method call, everything would fail. With Queued Components, the situation changes completely as in Figure 12.30 illustrates.

As shown in Figure 12.30, once you configure a COM+ class to use the QC Service (you'll see how to do this shortly), the COM+ runtime creates a set of queues using Microsoft Message Queue (MSMQ) between the client and server. When an object of a QC class is instantiated, the COM+ runtime creates a QC Recorder on the object's client. When you make a method call on this queued component, the QC recorder on the client transparently turns the set of method calls that you make into a single MSMQ message. When the object is deactivated, the QC service sends this message to the queue that the COM+ runtime had setup when you configured the component to support Queued Components.

On the server side, a component called the QC Listener Helper checks the queues looking for messages as shown in Figure 12.30. When the QC Listener Helper sees a message waiting in the queue for a component, it extracts the message from the queue and forwards it to a system-provided component called the QC Player. The QC Player then plays the method calls back to the component. Because the system is using MSMQ as its transport mechanism, you receive all the robustness and availability benefits that MSMQ provides. MSMQ caches the messages in its persistent store. If the server that the component is running on is down at the time the message is sent, this is not a problem. The next time the server comes up the QC Listener Helper reads the Queue, sees there is a message, and forwards the message to the QC Player that plays the method calls back to the queued object. As I said, it's conceptually similar to Voice Mail. In many ways, Queued Components is just a simplified way of using MSMQ.

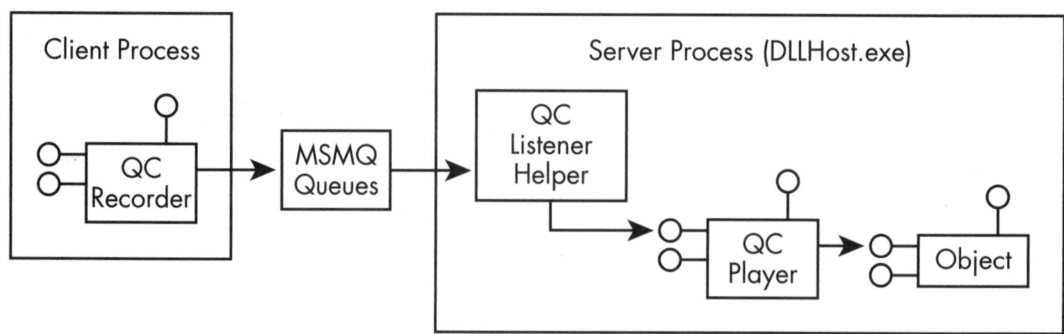

FIGURE 12.30 A COM+ Client and Server Component Using the Queued Components Service.

Design Restrictions on Queued Components

You have to be careful how you design your components if they are to function successfully as Queued Components. To run as a Queued Component, a COM component must obey the following rules:

- The interfaces the component implements cannot contain output parameters.
- The component cannot return application-specific HRESULTS.
- The methods implemented by the component cannot depend on additional information or interaction from the client after the initial method call.

NO OUTPUT PARAMETERS

Queued Components cannot implement interfaces that contain output parameters. These are parameters defined with the IDL attributes `[out]`, `[in,out]`, or `[out,retval]`. So the `ISpellChecker` interface, which was defined as shown below, could not be implemented as a Queued Component because the parameter `isCorrect` on the `CheckSpelling` method is an output parameter:

```
interface ISpellChecker : IUnknown
{
    HRESULT CheckSpelling([in,string] char *word,[out,retval] BOOL *isCorrect);
    HRESULT UseCustomDictionary([in,string] char *filename);
}
```

Queued Components cannot implement output parameters because the client will most likely not be around to receive the return values. When the client invokes a method on a Queued Component, it has no idea when that method will be executed. It is quite possible that the client itself will have terminated long before the queued component ever executes the method call. In fact, all of the rules previously stated basically arise from a single rule you must keep in mind when writing Queued Components: Never assume that the lifetime of the client and server will overlap.

NO APPLICATION-SPECIFIC HRESULTS

If you understand the basic rule about no overlapping lifetimes, then it should be clear why a queued component couldn't return an application-specific HRESULT. Who will be there to receive the HRESULT? When a client calls a queued component, the COM+ runtime returns an HRESULT that tells whether the message was successfully queued. After that, the client has no idea when the server actually executes the method.

NO DEPENDENCIES ON ADDITIONAL INFORMATION

Once you call a method on a Queued Component, the method that is called cannot depend on receiving additional information from the client. So the Stock Server component that you built in Chapter 8 definitely won't work as a Queued Component. This component cached an interface pointer that was implemented by the client, and the server invoked a method on this cached interface pointer whenever a stock price changed by more than a certain delta. This component would not work as a Queued Component because by the time the component runs, there may not be a client available for the server to call back on. When you get right down to it, the real client of the Queued Component is the QC Player that plays back method calls sent via MSMQ from the QC recorder on the client. The QC player knows nothing about the stock server's callback interfaces.

WHAT IF YOU MUST RECEIVE A RETURN VALUE?

What if you want to use the Queued Component Service, but your client application must be able to receive a return value from its queued components? A client application can receive a response from a queued component using a *response object*. A response object must be configured as a queued component itself. The client must instantiate this response object specifying the client machine as the destination server for the object. The client then passes the response object as one of the input parameters to the queued component (you must modify your queued interfaces so they accept this additional parameter). The queued component can then call methods on the response object when it wants to send its return values back to the client. The queued component actually sends its return values back to the response object not to the client application. That's why you must specify the client machine as the destination server for the response object. You want the response to return to the client machine. The client application does not have to be running when the queued component calls the response object. Typically, a response object writes to a database, sends an e-mail, or writes to a log file. The Queued Component example that you'll build in Chapter 14 won't use a response object, but the Web site for this book contains an enhanced version of this example that does use a response object.

Queued Components and Transactions

One of the best features of COM+ Queued Components is that they work with COM+ transactions. The underlying transport mechanism for Queued Components, MSMQ, is a COM+ Resource Manager just like SQL Server or Oracle (see the sidebar entitled the Role of MSMQ in COM+). If you send a message to an MSMQ queue within a transaction, MSMQ buffers the message until the outcome of the transaction is known. If the transaction commits, the message will be sent to the queue; if the transaction aborts, the message is not sent to the destination queue. Queued components can piggy back on this mechanism to allow you to make transactional method calls. The QC recorder takes on the same transaction attribute as its client. If the client is currently running within a transaction, the QC recorder enlists in the transaction. When the QC recorder is deactivated, it sends its message to MSMQ within the context of this transaction. If the transaction is aborted, the message is not sent to the queue, so it's as if the queued method calls never happened. Queued components also use transactions on the server side. The QC Listener Helper is a transactional component. It dequeues the message and sends it to the QC player within the context of a transaction. If the method call fails, the QC Recorder aborts the transaction and the message is returned to the queue so it can be tried again.

Configuring a Queued Component

As always, you configure Queued Components using the Component Services Explorer. To use the COM+ Queued Component service, first make your COM+ Application Queued. This causes COM+ to create the necessary message queues for your application. To make your COM+ application queued, perform the following steps:

1. Right-click on the COM+ application in the Component Services Explorer.
2. Select `Properties` from the `Context` Menu (the Application Properties dialog appears as shown in Figure 12.31).
3. Click the `Queuing` tab (shown in Figure 12.31).
4. Set the `Queued` and `Listen` checkboxes (the Listen checkbox enables when you set the Queued checkbox).
5. Click `OK`.

These steps cause COM+ to generate the message queues needed for your application. You can view these queues by going to the Computer Management Explorer, which is a Snap-In for the Microsoft Management Console just like the Component Services Explorer. To view the main queue for the application, perform the following steps in Windows 2000:

1. Click the `Start` menu.
2. Select `Programs\Administrative Tools\Computer Management` (the Computer Management Explorer appears as shown in Figure 12.32).
3. Open the `Services and Applications` item in the Tree on the left side of the Windows.
4. Open the `Message Queuing` item in the tree.
5. Open the `Public Queues` folder.

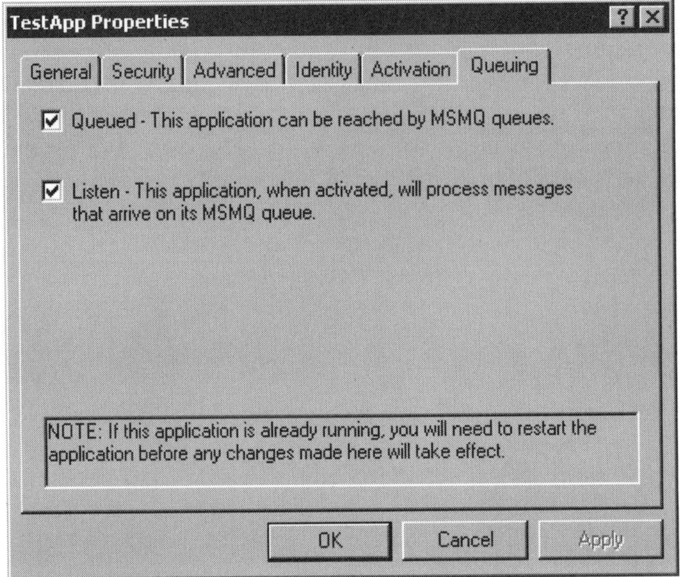

FIGURE 12.31 Configuring a COM+ Application to Support Queuing.

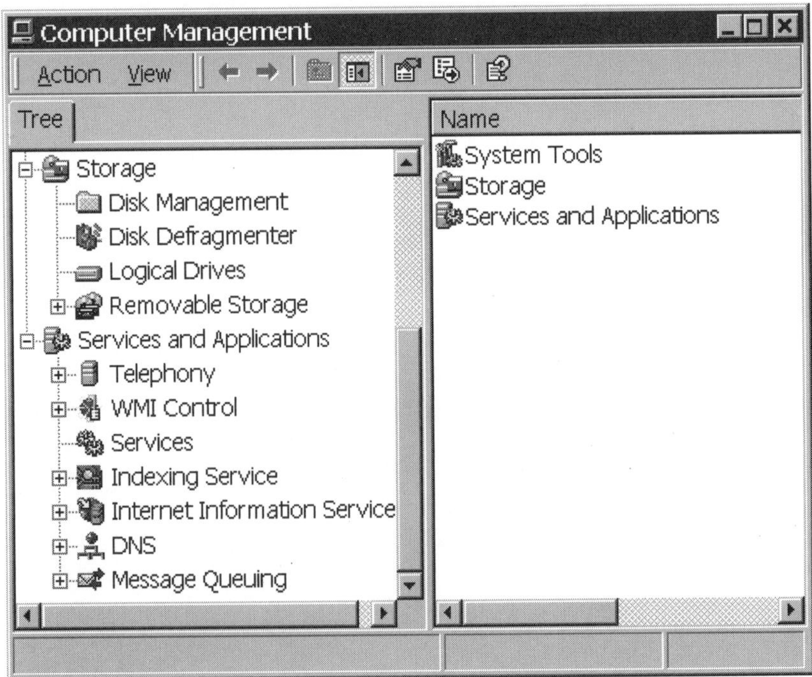

FIGURE 12.32 The Computer Management Explorer.

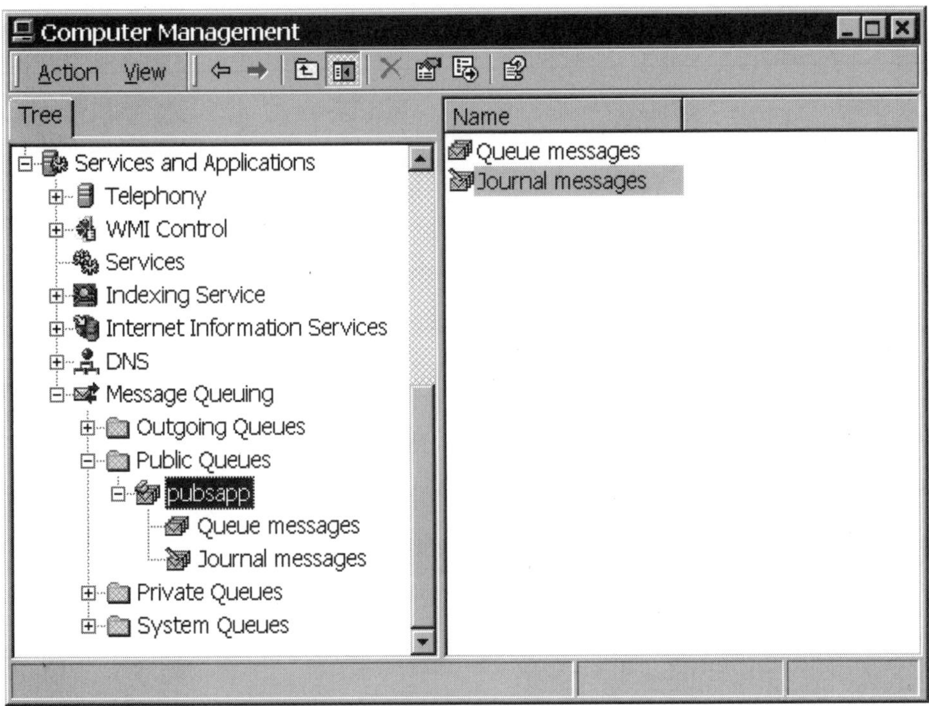

FIGURE 12.33 The Main Queue for a COM+ Application.

You should see a queue beneath there that has the same name as your COM+ application as shown in Figure 12.33.

The queue shown in Figure 12.33 is the queue for a COM+ Application called pubsapp. If the calls that you make to a queued interface in the pubsapp COM+ application succeed the first time, this is the only queue that is used. COM+ also creates additional queues that are used if the Queued Component Service tries and fails to deliver a message to a queued component. I talk about these other queues shortly when I discuss poison messages.

After you make a COM+ application queued, you must specify which interfaces within the COM+ Application should be queued. Perform the following steps to make an interface queued:

1. Right-click on an interface in the Component Services Explorer as shown in Figure 12.34.
2. Select `Properties` from the `Context` menu (the interface properties dialog appears as shown in Figure 12.35).
3. Click the `Queuing` tab (shown in Figure 12.35).
4. Set the `Queued` checkbox.
5. Click `OK`.

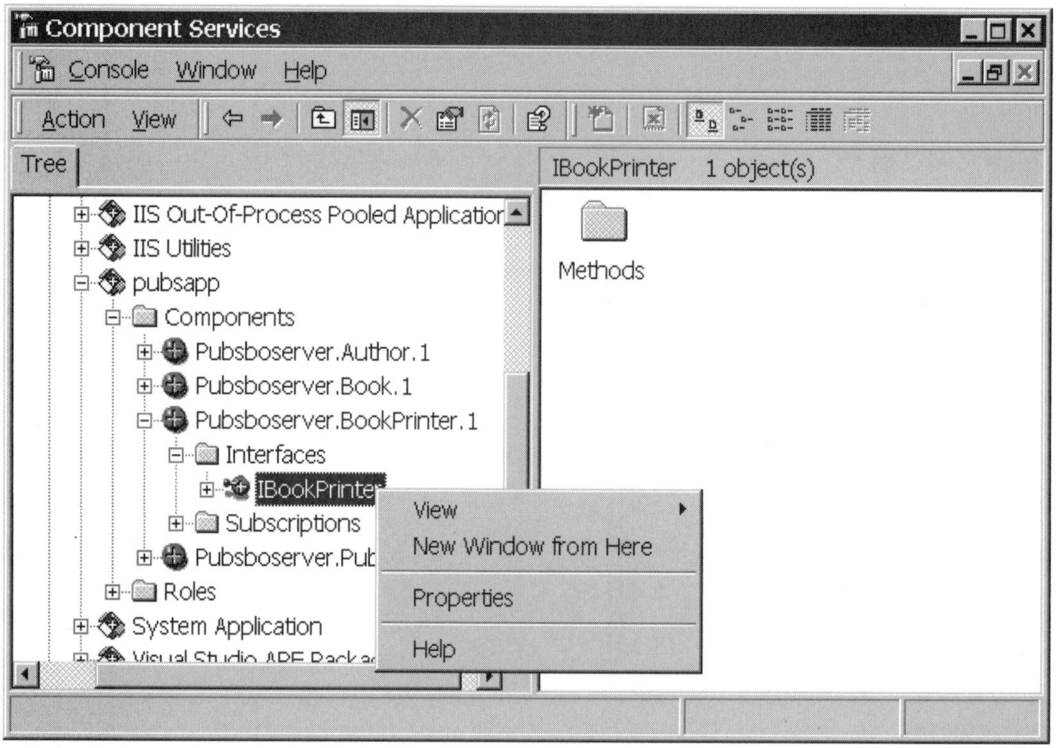

FIGURE 12.34 The First Step to Making an Interface Queued.

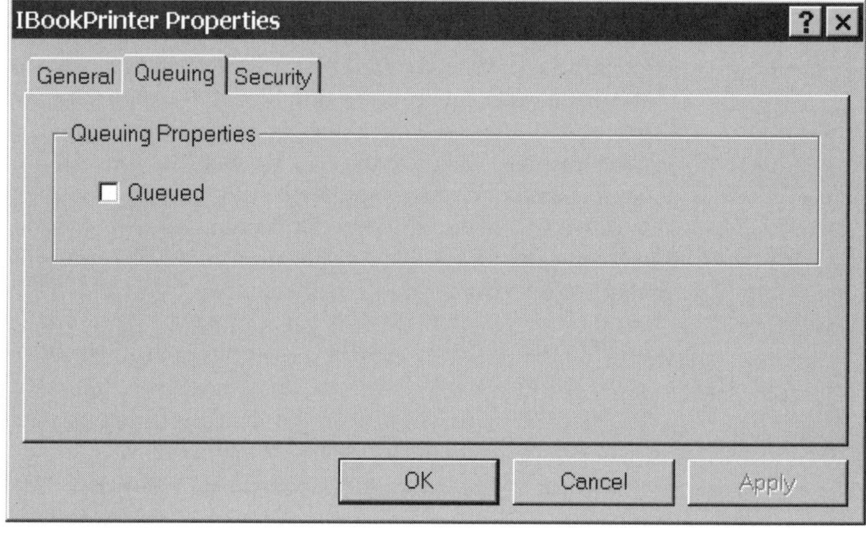

FIGURE 12.35 Enabling Queuing for an Interface in the Application.

If the Queued checkbox is disabled, that means the interface cannot be queued. Most likely this is because the interface violates one of the design rules for queued components.

Using Queued Components

Once you have configured your components to be queued, there are a few things that you have to do to use them via the queued component service. First, you must instantiate your component using the Queued Moniker.

In the introduction to this book, I mentioned that it was my intention to concentrate on the 90% of COM that application developers most often use. I agonized over whether to include Monikers. Eventually, time constraints made the decision for me and I could not create an entire chapter on Monikers. Since Monikers are used in Queued Components, I decided to cover them (albeit briefly) in this chapter. If you already understand Monikers, you can skip ahead to the section entitled *The Queue Moniker*; if not, go ahead and read this section on Monikers. It is not critical that you understand all the information in this section (especially on your first read through). If you find yourself getting lost, by all means skip ahead.

What Is a Moniker?

So far, you have only created COM objects using the `CoCreateInstance(Ex)` functions. In some scenarios, these functions are not sufficient. For instance, what if you want to store the state of object persistently in a file and then reconstitute the object from the information in that file. What if you just want to assign a textual name to an object that is being persisted to a database or file so you can reconstitute it later using this name. Or what if you want to do something even more complex than that. Perhaps you have a COM object located at an Internet URL and when the user attempts to instantiate the object, you would like to download the object's server to the local machine, register it, and then instantiate the object in the normal manner (this is how ActiveX controls are used over the Internet). The solution to all of these problems is *Monikers*.

A `Moniker` is a COM component that implements the `IMoniker` interface. Think of a `Moniker` as an object that lets you locate and activate other objects. The business logic associated with locating and activating an object is unique to each particular type of `Moniker`. There are a number of standard `Monikers` that are provided for you by COM and you can also create your own.

You call the `BindToObject` method on the `IMoniker` interface to create a COM object from a `Moniker`; this is called binding the `Moniker`. For instance, the File `Moniker` (one of the standard `Monikers` provided by the COM) lets you create an object from the contents of a file. To use the File Moniker, you first call the `CreateFileMoniker` API function to create a File Moniker. `CreateFileMoniker` is defined as follows:

```
HRESULT CreateFileMoniker(
    LPCOLESTR pPathName, // [Input] The path of a file
    IMoniker  **ppMoniker // [Output] The IMoniker interface pointer.
    )
```

Next, you call the `BindToObject` method to bind the contents of the file to an object. The logic within the File Moniker first finds the CLSID of the COM class associated with the file contents. The File Moniker creates an instance of this class and passes the contents of the file to the object. The File Moniker has a pre-defined search strategy it uses to find the CLSID of the COM class associated with the file contents. It first searches the contents of the file for a CLSID. If it doesn't find the CLSID in the file, it looks in the registry for the server object associated with the file extension (for instance, a `.doc` is associated with the Microsoft Word Document object).

The `CreateFileMoniker` function uses the `GetClassFile` API function to find the CLSID of its associated COM class. See the documentation for `GetClassFile` for an in-depth discussion of how this search strategy works.

The File Moniker instantiates an instance of the COM class that it finds. It will `QueryInterface` the object for the `IPersistFile` interface and then pass the contents of the file to the `Load` method of `IPersistFile`. The COM class associated with the file contents must implement the `IPersistFile` interface to work with the File Moniker. The code shown in Listing 12.6 creates a File Moniker using a .doc file and then binds the Moniker to an instance of its associated COM class: the Microsoft Word Document.

LISTING 12.6 *USING THE FILE MONIKER*

```
void CMonikertestclientDlg::OnTestfilemonikerButton()
{
    HRESULT hRes;
    IBindCtx *pBindCtx;
    IMoniker *pMoniker;
    IDispatch *pDispatch;
    _Application WordApp;
    _Document WordDoc;

    hRes=CreateFileMoniker(L"c:\\alan\\filemonikertest.doc",&pMoniker);
    if (FAILED(hRes))
    {
        _com_error err(hRes);
```

```
14.         AfxMessageBox(err.ErrorMessage());
15.     }
16.     hRes=CreateBindCtx(0,&pBindCtx);
17.     hRes=pMoniker->BindToObject(pBindCtx,NULL,IID_IDispatch,
            (void **)&pDispatch);
18.     pBindCtx->Release();
19.     pMoniker->Release();
20.     if (FAILED(hRes))
21.     {
22.         _com_error err(hRes);
23.         AfxMessageBox(err.ErrorMessage());
24.     }
25.     WordDoc.AttachDispatch(pDispatch);
26.     WordApp.AttachDispatch(WordDoc.GetApplication());
27.     WordApp.SetVisible(VARIANT_TRUE);   // Microsoft Word Will Appear
28. }
```

On line 10 of Listing 12.6, you create a File Moniker using the `CreateFileMoniker` function. To bind any Moniker to an object, you need a Bind Context, an object that stores information about a particular Moniker's binding operation. On line 16, you call the `CreateBindCtx` API function to create a Bind Context. On line 17, you call the `BindToObject` function on the File Moniker and request the `IDispatch` interface. This returns the default interface on the Microsoft Word Document Object. In this code, you used the MFC COleDispatchDriver to make it simple to work with the Automation interfaces exposed by Microsoft Word. You created two `COleDispatchDriver`-derived classes (`_Document` and `_Application`) using the MFC ClassWizard and the Microsoft Word type library. On line 25, you attach the `IDispatch` pointer you received from the File Moniker to a `_Document` object, then on line 26 you call `GetApplication` on the `Document` object and attach the return value to an `_Application` object. Finally, on line 27, you make Microsoft Word Visible. Notice how the File Moniker hides all the file handling logic involved with opening a Word Document. All of this logic is encapsulated within the File Moniker.

There are several other system-provided Monikers available including the URL Moniker (used to download and activate ActiveX controls given a URL), the Class and New Monikers (used to instantiate new objects given a CLSID), the Item Moniker (that can be used to create an object from a specified portion of a file), and the Composite Moniker (used to combine two or more Monikers). Remember, you can also create your own custom Monikers. I don't want to go into each one of these Moniker types, but I encourage you to read more about them (and other Moniker types) in the MSDN library (`msdn.Microsoft.com/library` or on CD-ROM).

I talk about the New Moniker and the Class Moniker after I discuss the `MkParseDisplayName` function.

Most Monikers have a Create function. The COM API contains a `CreateFileMoniker` function and a `CreateClassMoniker` function. However, the easiest and most flexible way to create a Moniker is using the `MkParseDisplayName` function. `MkParseDisplayName` is defined as shown here:

```
HRESULT MkParseDisplayName(IBindCtx *pbc,
        LPCOLESTR strDisplayName,
        ULONG *pEaten,IMoniker **pMoniker);
```

The `MkParseDisplayName` function creates a Moniker using a user-friendly string called a *Display Name*. The general format of a Display Name is as follows:

```
MonikerType:MonikerSpecificInformation
```

The display name for a File Moniker is constructed as follows:

```
File:Path
```

You can omit the File: prefix if you like. Two (equivalent) Display Names for a File Moniker are shown here:

```
File:c:\alan\filemonikertest.doc
c:\alan\filemonikertest.doc
```

The Display Name for a class Moniker is defined as follows:

```
Clsid:{CLSID}
```

An example Display Name for the class Moniker is shown below. You can omit the curly braces if you want:

```
Clsid:{ CF166FD0-958C-11D3-A0F5-00A0CC330C70}
```

You can construct a display name for the New Moniker using either the CLSID or the ProgID of a COM class. Two (equivalent) example Display Names for the New Moniker are shown here:

```
new:pubsboserver.book
new:{CF166FD0-958C-11D3-A0F5-00A0CC330C70}
```

You could have created and bound a File Moniker using the following call to `MkParseDisplayName` instead of using the `CreateFileMoniker` function:

```
    HRESULT hRes;
    IBindCtx *pBindCtx;
    IMoniker *pMoniker;
    IDispatch *pDispatch;
    ULONG lEaten;

    hRes=CreateBindCtx(0,&pBindCtx);
    hRes=MkParseDisplayName(pBindCtx,L"c:\\alan\\filemonikertest.doc",
         &lEaten,&pMoniker);
    hRes=pMoniker->BindToObject(pBindCtx,NULL,IID_IDispatch,
         (void **)&pDispatch);
```

Microsoft has even provided an API function called CoGetObject that encapsulates the preceding logic. CoGetObject is defined as follows:

```
HRESULT CoGetObject(LPCWSTR strDisplayName,BIND_OPTS *pBindOpts,
                                REFIID riid,void **ppv);
```

CoGetObject creates a BindContext, calls MkParseDisplay, and then calls BindToObject on the Moniker to create a COM object. Listing 12.7 shows how you would use CoGetObject to implement the same logic shown in Listing 12.6.

LISTING 12.7 *USING COGETOBJECT WITH THE FILE MONIKER*

```
void CMonikertestclientDlg::OnCoGetObjectButton()
{
    HRESULT hRes;
    IDispatch *pDispatch;
    _Application WordApp;
    _Document WordDoc;

    hRes=CoGetObject(L"c:\\alan\\filemonikertest.doc",NULL,
               IID_IDispatch,(void **)&pDispatch);
    if (FAILED(hRes))
    {
        _com_error err(hRes);
        AfxMessageBox(err.ErrorMessage());
    }
    WordDoc.AttachDispatch(pDispatch);
    WordApp.AttachDispatch(WordDoc.GetApplication());
    WordApp.SetVisible(VARIANT_TRUE);
}
```

Notice how much simpler this code is.

You can also use the CoGetObject together with the Class or New Monikers as an alternative to CoCreateInstance(Ex). You can create a new instance of an object using the Class Moniker as shown in Listing 12.8.

LISTING 12.8 *USING COGETOBJECT WITH THE CLASS MONIKER*

```
void CMonikertestclientDlg::OnClassMonikerButton()
{
   HRESULT hRes;
   IClassFactory *pFactory;
   IDispatch *pDispatch;

   hRes=CoGetObject(L"clsid:{CF166FD0-958C-11D3-A0F5-00A0CC330C70}",
                    NULL,IID_IClassFactory,(void **)&pFactory);
   if (SUCCEEDED(hRes))
   {
      hRes=pFactory->CreateInstance(NULL,IID_IDispatch,
           (void**)&pDispatch);
      pFactory->Release();
      // Use pDispatch here…

      pDispatch->Release();
   }
   else
   {
      _com_error err(hRes);
      AfxMessageBox(err.ErrorMessage());
   }
}
```

The Class Moniker only lets you bind to the Class Object for a COM class. So in Listing 12.8, you request the IClassFactory interface on the class object and then call CreateInstance on the IClassFactory interface pointer to create the desired COM object.

The New Moniker lets you bind directly to one of the interfaces that a COM class supports. The following code shows how to instantiate a COM object using CoGetObject and the New Moniker.

LISTING 12.9 *USING COGETOBJECT WITH THE NEW MONIKER*

```
void CMonikertestclientDlg::OnNewMonikerButton()
{
   HRESULT hRes;
   IDispatch *pDispatch;
```

```
    hRes=CoGetObject(L"new:pubsboserver.book",
                    NULL,IID_IDispatch,(void **)&pDispatch);
    if (SUCCEEDED(hRes))
    {
        // Use pDispatch here...

        pDispatch->Release();
    }
    else
    {
        _com_error err(hRes);
        AfxMessageBox(err.ErrorMessage());
    }
}
```

The `GetObject` function in Visual Basic is the equivalent of `CoGetObject`. Listing 12.10 shows how to use the New Moniker via `GetObject`. The code shown in Listing 12.10 is the Visual Basic equivalent of Listing 12.9.

LISTING 12.10 *USING VB, GETOBJECT WITH THE NEW MONIKER*

```
Private Sub Command1_Click()
    On Error GoTo errHandler
    Dim Book As Object
    Set object = GetObject("new:pubsboserver.book")
    ' Use the object here...

    Exit Sub
errHandler:
    Call MsgBox(Err.Description)
End Sub
```

You're probably wondering how `MkParseDisplayName` (and `CoGetObject`) works. It's actually quite simple. When `MkParse-DisplayName` receives a Display Name, like new:`pubsboserver.book`, it looks beneath the `HKEY_CLASSES_ROOT\` key in the registry for a key with the same name as the string to the left of the colon in the Display Name (*new* in this case). The CLSID for the Moniker associated with the Display Name is stored beneath a registry key with this name. Figure 12.36 shows the Registry key and the CLSID for the New Moniker. `MkParseDisplayName` then instantiates the COM class identified by this CLSID and requests the `IMoniker` interface. Then it creates a bind context and uses the bind context to pass the information on the right side of the colon to the `BindToObject` function of the Moniker. This is the additional information the Moniker needs to do its

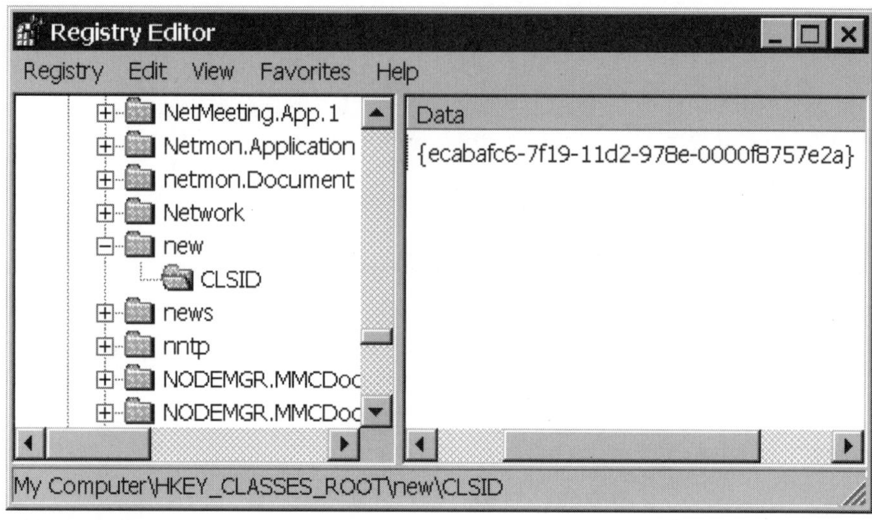

FIGURE 12.36 The Registry Key and CLSID for the New Moniker.

work. You can create your own Monikers that use the registry and the `MkParseDisplayName` function.

The Queue Moniker

Now that you understand a bit about Monikers in general, let's bring this discussion back to Queued Components and the Queue Moniker. To use the Queued Component Service, a client must instantiate the queued component using the Queue Moniker. If the client does not use the Queue Moniker (it uses `CoCreateInstance`, for example), the queued component is not queued (the method call is synchronous). This is actually good news; it means you can use queued components with or without the queuing service, depending on your needs at the time.

Although I have not seen the implementation of the Queue Moniker, it's not too difficult to imagine how it works. Instead of activating the queued object directly, the Queued Moniker must activate the QC Recorder and pass it the type library information for the requested object. The QC Recorder also has to know where to send its message when the QC Recorder is deactivated. The message the QC Recorder creates must also contain enough information for the QC player to instantiate the queued component on the server, so the Queue Moniker must also pass this information to the QC recorder. Figure 12.37 shows the Registry key and the CLSID for the Queue Moniker.

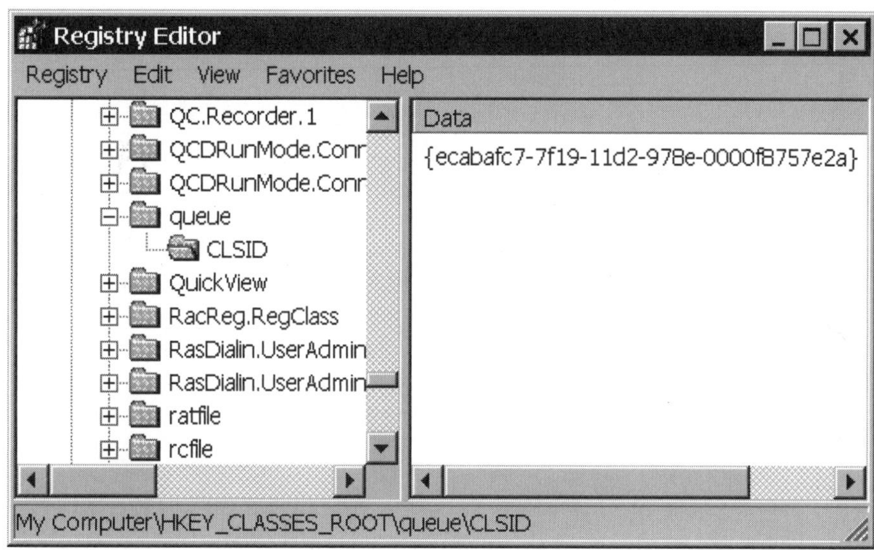

FIGURE 12.37 The Registry Key and CLSID for the Queue Moniker.

The display name for the Queue Moniker has the following form:

```
Queue:[options]/New:CLSID
```

Notice there are actually two Monikers being used here: the Queue Moniker and the New Moniker. The Queue Moniker expects to receive the CLSID of the queued component from the new Moniker to its right. The following examples show how to use the Queue Moniker and the `CoGetObject` function to instantiate a queued component whose progID is `pubsboserver.bookprinter`:

```
CoGetObject(L"queue:/new:pubsboserver.bookprinter,
        NULL,IID_IDispatch,(void **)&pDispatch);
CoGetObject(L"queue:Priority=5,ComputerName=agordon1/" \
   Lnew:pubsboserver.bookprinter ",NULL,
   IID_IDispatch,(void **)&pDispatch);
```

From Visual Basic you can use the Queue Moniker as follows:

```
Set objPrinter = GetObject("queue:/new:pubsboserver.BookPrinter")
```

The Queue Moniker accepts a number of options that affect how it works; Table 12.8 gives the name and description of *some* of the parameters that can be passed to the Queue Moniker. See the MSDN library for the rest.

TABLE 12.8 Parameters for the Queue Moniker

Parameter	Description
ComputerName	The computer that the Queued Component service should send the message to. If this parameter is not specified, the ComputerName associated with the configured application is used.
QueueName	The name of the MSMQ queue that the Queued Component service should send the message to. If this parameter is not specified, the QueueName associated with the configured application is used.
PathName	The complete path of the MSMQ queue that the QC Recorder should use. This string is of the form ComputerName\QueueName.
AuthLevel	Should MSMQ authenticate messages using digital signatures? MQMSG_AUTH_LEVEL_NONE MQMSG_AUTH_LEVEL_ALWAYS
Delivery	Are MSMQ messages recoverable? MQMSG_DELIVERY_EXPRESS (not recoverable) MQMSG_DELIVERY_RECOVERABLE
Priority	A message priority level: MQ_MIN_PRIORITY (0) MQ_MAX_PRIORITY (7) MQ_DEFAULT_PRIORITY (3) Any number between 0 and 7
PrivLevel	A privacy level, used to encrypt messages: MQMSG_PRIV_LEVEL_NONE MQMSG_PRIV_LEVEL_BODY MQMSG_PRIV_LEVEL_BODY_BASE MQMSG_PRIV_LEVEL_BODY_ENHANCED

Poison Messages

Once the QC Listener Helper receives a message on the server machine, it dequeues the message within the context of a transaction and then passes the message to the QC Player, which attempts to play the message back to the queued component. If one of the method calls fails or the transaction aborts for any other reason, the QC Listener Helper aborts its transaction, which returns the message to the queue. Since the message is now back on the queue, the QC Listener eventually tries to deliver the message again. If the queued component failed repeatedly, this could go on forever using up computing resources. This is called a *poison message*. MSMQ was designed to support high-availability and must strike a balance between handling poison messages and ensuring the system tries more than once to deliver a message to a queued component.

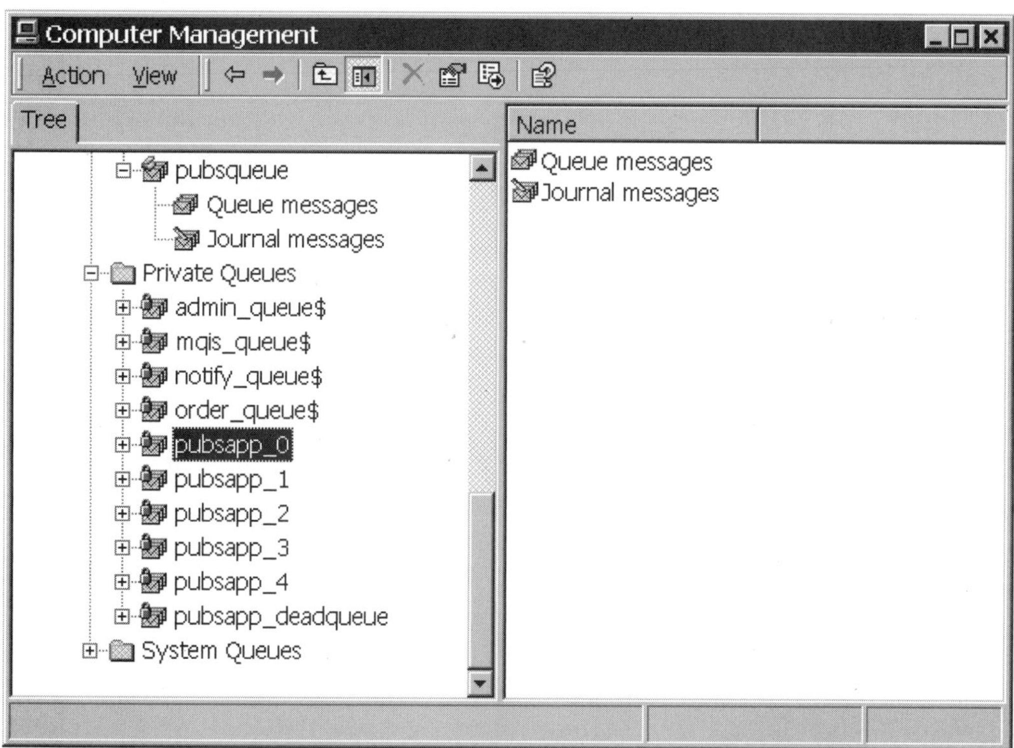

FIGURE 12.38 The Retry Queues for a Queued COM+ Application.

The solution to this problem in the COM+ Queued Component Service is a series of six, private, retry queues. The COM+ runtime generates these queues automatically when you configure a COM+ application to support queuing. The retry queues for a COM+ Application are named as follows: there are five queues with the name `COM+ApplicationName_N` (where N = 0 to 4), and one queue with the name `COM+ApplicationName_deadqueue`. Figure 12.38 shows the private queues for a COM+ Application called pubsapp.

These retry queues are used as follows (this algorithm is subject to change by Microsoft at any time):

- **COM+ApplicationName_0**: If the transaction fails repeatedly on the main, public queue, the message is moved here. Messages in this queue are retried once each minute. After three unsuccessful attempts, the message is moved to the queue called `COM+ApplicationName_1`.
- **COM+ApplicationName_1**: Messages on this queue are processed every two minutes. After three unsuccessful attempts, the message is moved to the queue called `COM+ApplicationName_2`.

- **COM+ApplicationName_2**: Messages on this queue are processed every four minutes. After three unsuccessful attempts, the message is moved to the queue called `COM+ApplicationName_3`.
- **COM+ApplicationName_3**: Messages on this queue are processed every eight minutes. After three unsuccessful attempts, the message is moved to the queue called `COM+ApplicationName_4`.
- **COM+ApplicationName_4**: Messages on this queue are processed every 16 minutes. After three unsuccessful attempts, the message is moved to the queue called `COM+ApplicationName_deadqueue`.
- **COM+ApplicationName_deadqueue**: The final resting place. Messages remain on this queue until they are manually moved or purged using the Computer Management Explorer.

If you want to be notified when a message is being sent to the dead queue, you can register an exception handling class for your queued component. The exception class is just a configured COM+ class that implements the `IPlaybackControl` interface. You associate an exception class with a queued component by performing these steps:

1. Right-click on a component in a COM+ application.
2. Select `Properties...` from the `Context` menu (the component properties dialog appears as shown in Figure 12.39).
3. Click the `Advanced` tab (shown in Figure 12.39).
4. Enter the ProgID for the exception class in the Queuing exception class field.
5. Click `OK`.

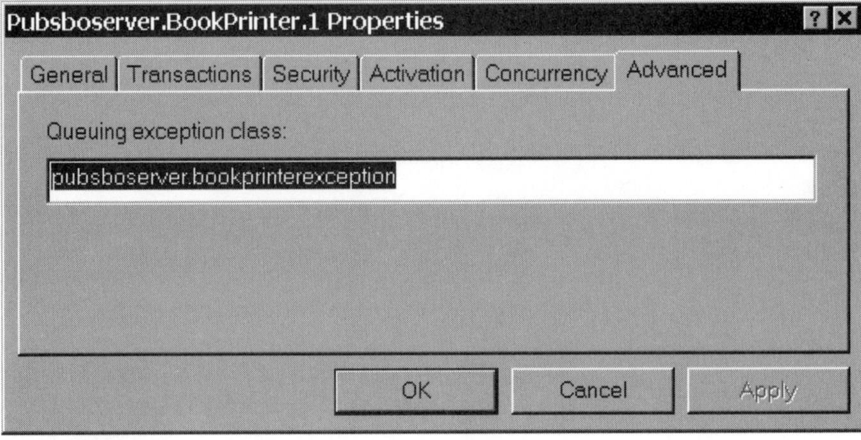

FIGURE 12.39 Configuring a Queuing Exception Class.

The QC Service calls this exception class right before it sends the message to the deadqueue. At a minimum, this exception class should implement the `IPlaybackControl` interface. `IPlaybackControl` has two methods: `FinalClientRetry` and `FinalServerRetry`. The QC Service calls `FinalClientRetry` if (after executing the algorithm described above) it is unable to send a Message to the message queues on the server. The method is called right before the message is placed on the client-side deadqueue. In your implementation of `FinalClientRetry`, you can send an e-mail message to an administrator or write a notification to a log file or database. The QC Service calls `FinalServerRetry` on the server if (after executing the algorithm described above) it is unable to playback the message to the queued component. Once again, in your implementation of this method you can send an e-mail message to an administrator or write a notification to a log file or database. You can also attempt to complete the transaction.

Notice that `FinalClientRetry` and `FinalServerRetry` do not have any arguments. Your Exception class may want to know the value of the arguments that were passed to the queued component. To receive the arguments, your Exception must implement the queued interface that is being used. For instance, in Chapter 14 you will create a queued interface called `IBookPrinter`. If the Exception class wishes to see the values of the arguments that were passed to the `PrintCopies` method of `IBookPrinter`, then it must implement the `IBookPrinter` interface. The QC service replays the `PrintCopies` method to the exception class after it calls `FinalServerRetry`. The Queued Component example that you build in Chapter 14 won't use an exception class, but the Web site contains an enhanced version of this example that does use an exception class.

The Role of MSMQ in COM+

Microsoft Message Queue (MSMQ), which was a part of the NT 4 Option Pack, lives on almost unchanged in Windows 2000. With Queued Components, I suspect that fewer people will use MSMQ in its raw form. Queued Components are the COM+ way to use MSMQ. As if to reinforce this, MSMQ is not administered in the Component Services Explorer. You administer MSMQ in the Computer Management Explorer as shown in Figure 12.33. Think of MSMQ as just a communication mechanism for COM+ Queued components. But you can use the Windows 2000 version of MSMQ in the same manner you used MSMQ on Windows NT 4. I explore MSMQ further when you build an example using queued components in Chapter 14.

Load Balancing

COM+ was designed to facilitate the development of enterprise-class, distributed applications. In many cases, these applications need to support a large enough number of users or a processing load large enough that you cannot deploy your business objects on a single-server machine. You could solve this problem by adding multiple business object servers, but how do you divide the processing load between these servers? You could use a static load-balancing scheme. Perhaps all the people in one department could use one business object server and all the people in a different department could use another one. Aside from being more difficult to administer, this approach has a tendency to make inefficient use of your available computing resources. It is quite possible that one department taxes its server to the max, while another department's server is sitting idle most of the time. You would make far better use of your available resources if you used a dynamic load-balancing scheme. To make the most efficient use of multiple servers, you would like an activation request from *any* client to be automatically serviced by the server that currently has the lightest load.

You could implement this logic if you had the time and expertise. First you'd have to create a broker object that all clients must go to first when they want to instantiate a COM object. All the server machines that share the processing load for your application have to register themselves with the broker. The broker is then responsible for finding the server machine with the lightest load and instantiating the requested COM object there. Thanks to COM+, you do not have to implement this logic yourself. It is provided by the COM+ runtime and it is called the Component Load Balancing Service (CLBS). Although Microsoft's plans could change at any time, it appears you can only use CLBS if you have a server running the AppCenter Server version of Windows 2000 which is *not* scheduled to ship when the other versions of Windows 2000 ship in the first quarter of 2000.

AppCenter Server is a version of Windows 2000 that will include deployment, management, and monitoring tools for Web applications running in server farms and will provide increased scalability and reliability for people who are deploying and managing high-volume, high-availability Web applications. The release version of AppCenter Server is not available as this book is going to press. However, CLBS was available in beta versions of Windows 2000 Advanced Server. The information and screen snapshots you see in this chapter are from Release Candidate 2 of Windows 2000 Advanced Server. Keep in mind that some of the information in this chapter may change by the time AppCenter Server is released, but the essence of the information should remain the same.

The architecture of CLBS is shown in Figure 12.40.

To use CLBS, you have to designate one machine on your network as the load-balancing server as shown in Figure 12.40. This machine is the bro-

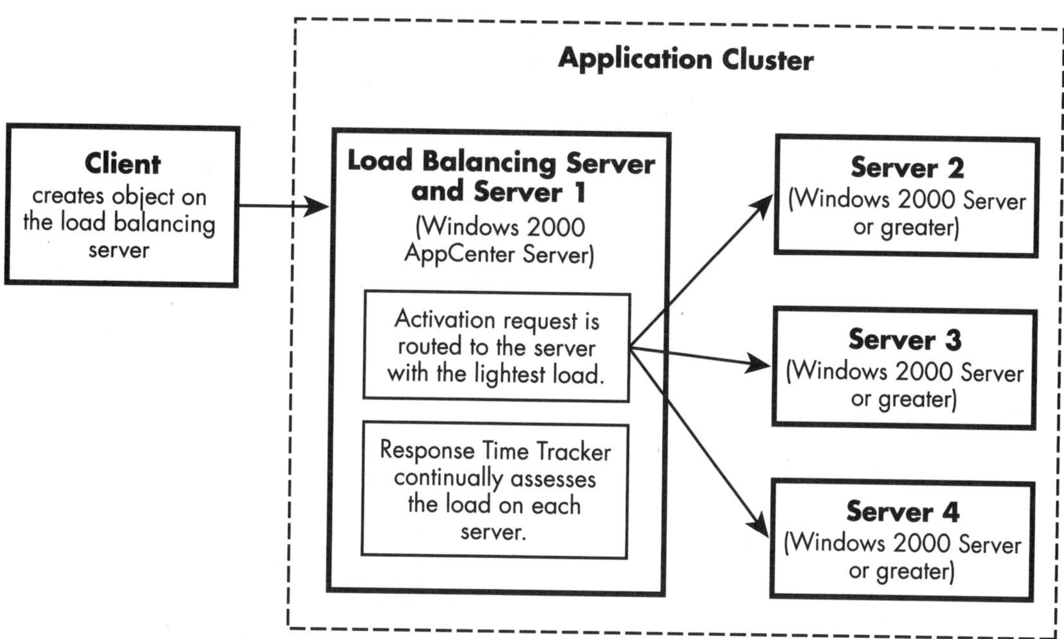

FIGURE 12.40 The Architecture of the Component Load-Balancing Service.

ker that routes an activation request to the server that has the lightest load. This is also the machine that must be running AppCenter Server. Next, you must create an application cluster. This is just the group of machines that together dynamically share the load for your application. The load-balancing server itself is automatically made a part of this cluster and you can add other machines to the cluster manually. To configure a machine to be a load-balancing server and define an application cluster, perform the following steps in the Component Services Explorer:

1. Right-click on a machine in the Component Services Explorer as shown in Figure 12.41.
2. Select `Properties` from the `Context` menu (the computer properties dialog appears as shown in Figure 12.42).

3. Click the `CLBS` tab (Figure 12.43).
4. Set the `Use this computer as the load balancing server` checkbox.
5. Click the `Add...` button and add other machines on your network to the Application Cluster.

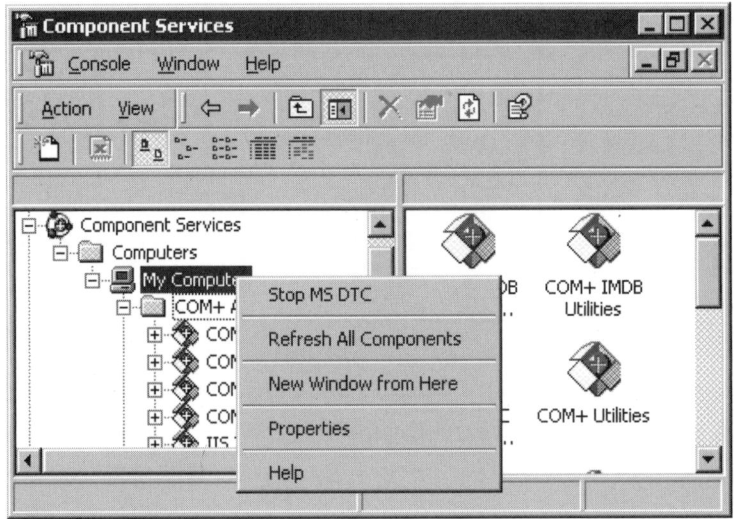

FIGURE 12.41 Viewing the Computer Properties.

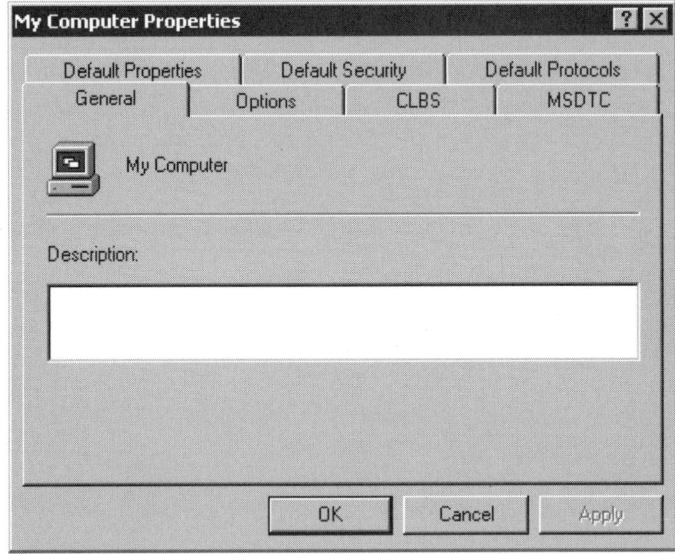

FIGURE 12.42 The Computer Properties Dialog.

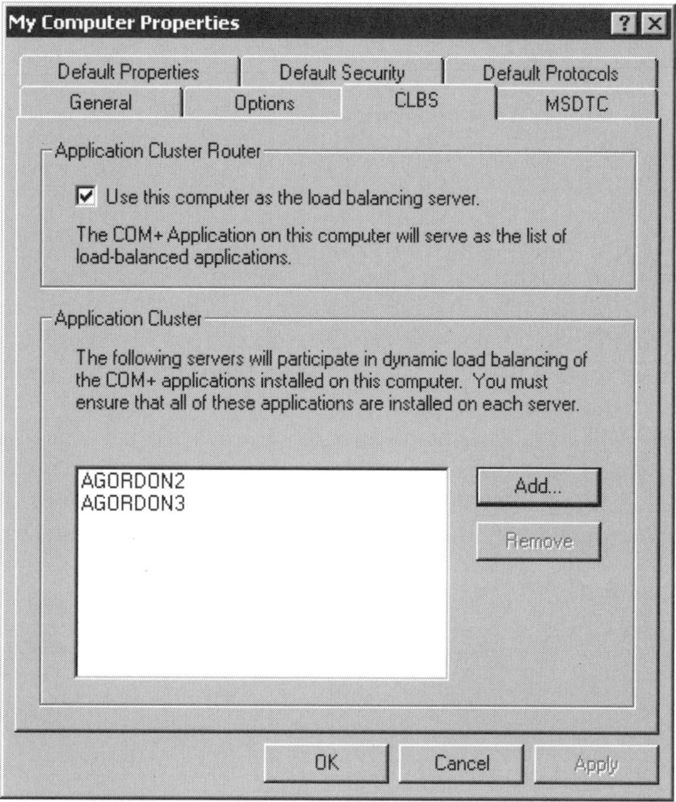

FIGURE 12.43 The CLBS Tab of the Computer Properties Dialog.

If you do not see the CLBS tab on the computer properties dialog, that means the machine you are using does not support CLBs.

Once you have configured a machine to be your load-balancing server, you must also specify which components (classes) are allowed to work with the CLBS. To do this, perform the following steps in the Component Services Explorer:

1. Right-click on a component in a COM+ application.
2. Select `Properties...` from the `Context` menu (the component properties dialog appears as shown in Figure 12.44).
3. Click the `Activation` tab (shown in Figure 12.44).

4. Set the `Component Supports Load Balancing` checkbox.
5. Click `OK`.

Any classes you configure to work with CLBS must be location independent. By that I mean they should not have any dependencies that require them to run on a particular machine. Beware of hard-code directory paths (which are always a bad idea) and registry settings. Also, all software that the load-balanced components are dependent on (third-party software) must be installed on all machines in your cluster and (this should be obvious) the load-balanced component must itself be installed on all machines in the cluster. A good test you should always run prior to using the CLBS is to verify that the component you are using can be instantiated normally on each machine in your cluster.

All instantiation requests made on a load balanced component must be made on the machine that you have configured to be the load-balancing server. So if the load-balancing server is called agordon1, you should make all activation requests on that machine. The object may actually be instanti-

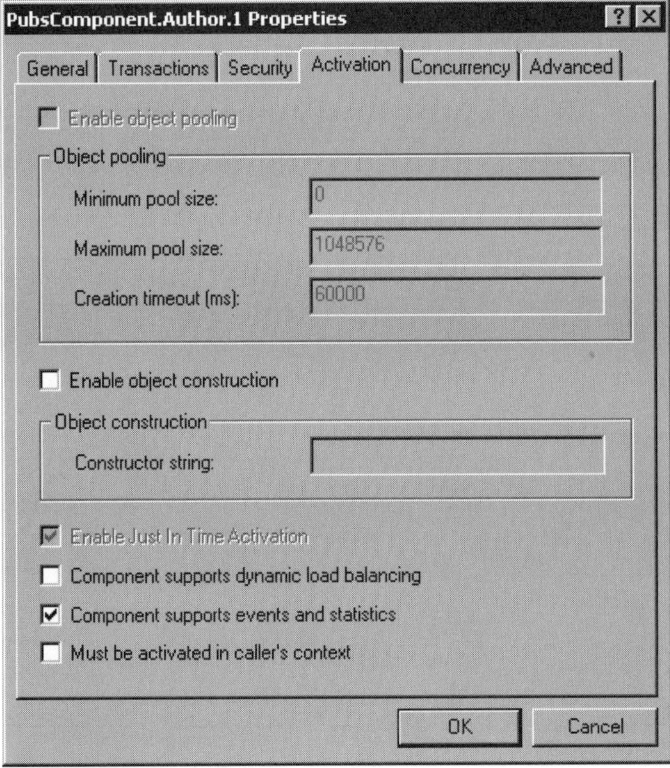

FIGURE 12.44 Configuring a Component to Support Load Balancing.

ated on any machine in the application cluster, however. The load-balancing server runs a response-time tracker service. This service pings each machine in the application cluster and times how long it takes to receive a response. This is the load-balancing server's way of gauging the load on each machine in the cluster. The exact details of this algorithm are still up in the air and eventually you will be able to plug in your own algorithm. The load-balancing server maintains statistics that tell it which machine in the cluster (including itself) currently has the lightest load. It instantiates the object on the machine with the lightest load and returns a reference to the client. All communication after this occurs directly between the client and the machine on which the object was instantiated. The load-balancing server is not used as a go-between after the initial activation. The load-balancing mechanism is only used once: when the client first activates the object. If your component uses Just In Time (JIT) Activation, your object will *never* be instantiated on one machine in the cluster, deactivated because of JIT activation, and then re-activated on a different machine.

One of the best things about the CLBS is that using it is primarily an administrative task. An administrator has to setup the application cluster and then make sure your component is installed on each machine in the cluster. Aside from making sure that your components are location-independent you, the developer, really don't have to do anything special to allow your components to work with the CLBS.

Compensating Resource Managers

A Compensating Resource Manager is any COM+ object that uses the Compensating Resource Manager (CRM) service provided by COM+. The COM+ CRM service is a set of tools provided by COM+ that make it simple to create your own resource managers. Unfortunately, the COM+ CRM service is another poorly named COM technology. Although you will often use *compensating transactions* to implement a CRM, this is not a requirement. A better name for this technology might have been the Resource Manager Framework, and a Compensating Resource Manager probably should just be called a Custom Resource Manager (you wouldn't even have to change the acronym).

See the sidebar "What is a Compensating Transaction"? on page 540 if you are not familiar with this term.

The COM+ CRM functionality lets you create your own resource managers with a minimum amount of effort. You're probably thinking why would you want to create your own resource manager? Using custom resource managers, you can make any operation part of a transaction. For example, on the application I am working on we send billing information via XML to third-party accounting systems. When we send an XML file to the third-party accounting, we update tables in our database to indicate the bill has been exported.

This application uses MTS not COM+, but the problem is still the same.

In this use-case, two operations are performed: (1) you write an XML file to disk, and (2) you update the database to indicate that the XML file has been sent. Obviously, the database update is a transactional operation; it's rolled back if the transaction is aborted. But what about the writing of the XML file? This is not a transactional operation. The Windows 2000 file system is not a resource manager, although it eventually may be. This causes several problems for you. Imagine that you wrote the XML file first and then attempted to perform your database updates, but the updates failed. Your transaction rollbacks the database operations, but the XML file is still sitting on your file system. You could try reversing the order of the operations—performing the database updates first and then writing the file. This is better because if the database updates fail, you won't even attempt to write the XML file, and if the generation or writing of the XML file fails, you can just rollback the database transaction. There is still a potential problem with this approach, however. What happens if you encounter a system failure after you perform both operations? COM+ rollbacks the transaction (restoring the database to its state prior to the transaction). But once the file is written you can't take it back. You really need a COM+ aware resource manager to write the file to disk. It then becomes the resource manager's responsibility to ensure that the file is only written if the transaction commits. The COM+ CRM service provides all the tools you need to quickly and (relatively) easily build a resource manager like this. The architecture of a Compensating Resource Manager is shown in Figure 12.45.

It's easy to understand this architecture if you remember how the 2-phase commit protocol works. Remember that to work with the 2-phase commit protocol, a resource manager must perform its operations in two phases: (1) It must place the resources that it controls in such a state that it can guarantee it can make the changes permanent if the transaction commits, or undo the changes if the transaction is rolled back, and (2) it must wait for the transaction coordinator to inform it of the outcome of the transaction.

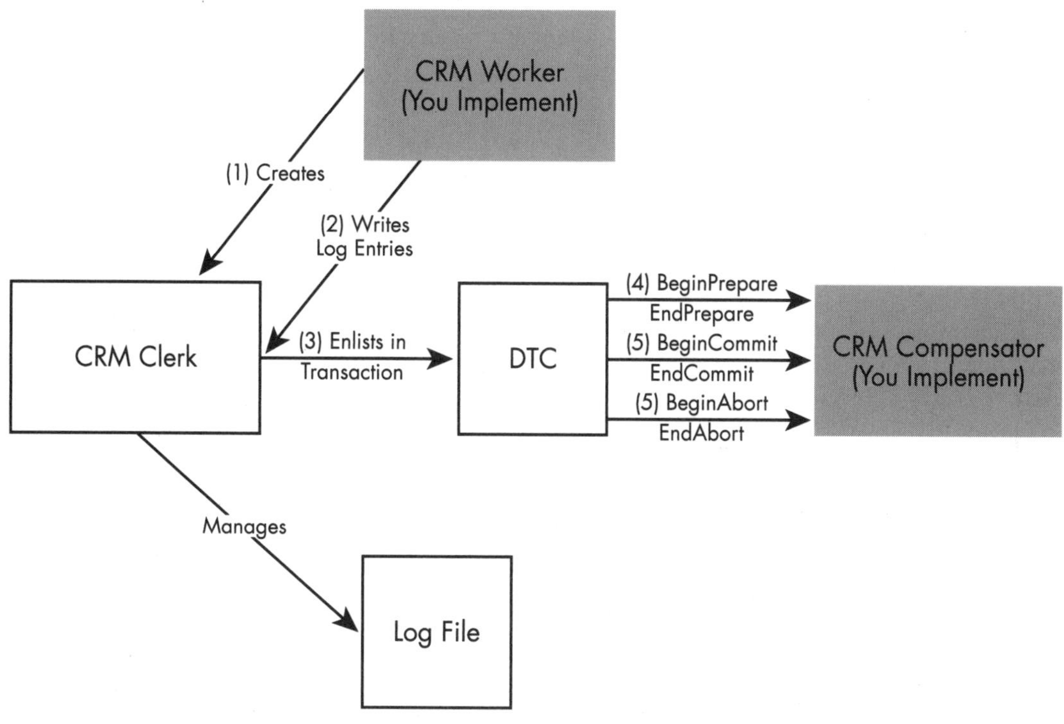

FIGURE 12.45 The CRM Architecture.

Most resource managers implement this logic using a durable log file. In phase 1, the resource manager writes to the durable log file a record of all the work it intends to perform and then performs whatever work is necessary to place itself in a state that guarantees the outcome of the transaction. After these steps are performed, the resource manager can respond in the affirmative to phase 1 (see the sidebar entitled, "What's a Durable Log File" on page 539). What happens in the second phase depends on the outcome of the transaction. If the transaction commits, the resource manager must read the log file records and make the updates on its resources permanent. If the transaction aborts, the resource manager must read the log file records and undo whatever changes it made.

What's a Durable Log File?

The log file used with a resource manager is called a *durable log file* because if the machines shut down abnormally (someone pulls the plug out of the wall, for example) on restart, the operating system (or transaction coordinator) reads the log file and checks to see if there are any transactions that did not complete in their entirety. If there are incomplete transactions, the operating system or transaction coordinator passes these log records to the resource manager so it can try again to complete the operation. This is called *recovery*. The CRM support provided by COM+ implements a durable log file and recovery. Unfortunately, it does not automatically attempt recovery on system restart. The DTC does not attempt recovery until the COM+ application that contains the CRM is started. If recovery must occur on system restart, you should build your own mechanism to start the CRM's COM+ Application.

What's a Compensating Transaction?

A Compensating Transaction is a transaction that reverses the affects of a previous transaction. For instance, if you buy an item using your credit card and then return the item, the merchant does not delete the original debit that was placed on your account. Instead the purchase price of the item is credited to your account, which cancels out the debit.

As Figure 12.45 shows, you must implement two COM components to create a CRM: a CRM Worker and a CRM Compensator. The CRM Worker contains the actual business logic that the CRM performs. So if your CRM writes XML files, your CRM Worker may likely contain a `WriteXML` method. The CRM Worker uses the services of the CRM Clerk component (provided by COM+) to register its CRM Compensator and to write records to a durable log file that the CRM Clerk maintains. When the DTC attempts to commit the transaction, it communicates with the CRM Compensator and call methods in the `ICRMCompensator` interface (that the CRM Compensator must implement) informing it of the outcome of the transaction. The DTC passes the log records written by the CRM Worker to the CRM Compensator so the CRM Compensator has all the information it needs to undo or make permanent the work depending on the outcome of the transaction.

When the CRM Worker is activated, it should create an instance of the CRM clerk. The CRM clerk implements the `ICrmLogControl` interface. The key methods in this interface are summarized in Table 12.9.

TABLE 12.9 The Methods in the ICrmLogControl Interface

Method Name	Description
RegisterCompensator	Registers the CRM compensator component that goes with this worker.
WriteLogRecord	Writes unstructured data to the log. You must call ForceLog before the records become durable.
WriteLogRecordVariants	Writes an array of variants to the log. You must call ForceLog before the records become durable.
ForceTransactionToAbort	Force the transaction to abort immediately.
ForceLog	Makes all log records that have been written durable so they can be retried if the machine shuts down abnormally.

The CRM Worker should call the RegisterCompensator method on ICRMLogControl and pass in the ProgID of its CRM Compensator as shown in Listing 12.11.

LISTING 12.11 *INITIALIZING A CRM WORKER COMPONENT*

```
HRESULT CCRMWorker::Activate()
{
   HRESULT hRes;
//  m_pCRMLogControl is a member variable declared as follows:
// ICrmLogControl *m_pCRMLogControl ;

   hRes = CoCreateInstance(CLSID_CRMClerk, NULL, CLSCTX_SERVER,
            IID_ICrmLogControl,(void **)&m_pCRMLogControl);

   hRes = m_pCRMLogControl-
>RegisterCompensator(L"Crmserver.MyCompensator",
            L"MyCompensator",CRMREGFLAG_ALLPHASES);

   return hRes;
}
```

You won't build a CRM example in this book, but I have implemented a file writer CRM you can download from this book's Web site, and the code that you see in Listings 12.11 and 12.12 is from my file writer CRM.

In its business logic, a CRM Worker should write its log file records and call ForceLog before it makes any system updates so that if the system crashed while it was making its updates, there would be enough information in the log to undo the changes. The CRM Worker should write enough information into the log so the CRM Compensator can undo or redo the operation. An example is shown in Listing 12.12. Some error checking is omitted from this code for clarity and brevity.

LISTING 12.12 *PERFORMING WORK IN THE CRM WORKER COMPONENT*

```
STDMETHODIMP CCRMWorker::WriteToFile(BSTR strText, BSTR strPath)
{
    HRESULT hRetval;
    _bstr_t strDescription;
    IObjectContext *pObjectContext;
    _bstr_t path(strPath);
```

```
7.      _bstr_t text(strText);
8.      ofstream outputFile;
9.      BLOB blob;
10.     hRetval=CoGetObjectContext(IID_IObjectContext,
            (void **)&pObjectContext);
11.
12.     blob.pBlobData = (unsigned char *) ((char*) path);
13.     blob.cbSize = path.length( ) * 2 ;
14.     hRetval = m_pCRMLogControl->WriteLogRecord (&blob, 1);
15.
16.     blob.pBlobData = (unsigned char *) ((char*) text);
17.     blob.cbSize = text.length( ) * 2 ;
18.     hRetval = m_pCRMLogControl->WriteLogRecord (&blob, 1);
19.
20.     m_pCRMLogControl->ForceLog();
21.
22.     outputFile.open(path);
23.     if (outputFile.is_open())
24.     {
25.         outputFile << text << endl;
26.         outputFile.close();
27.         pObjectContext->SetComplete();
28.         hRetval=S_OK;
29.     }
30.     else
31.     {
32.         pObjectContext->SetAbort();
33.         strDescription=L"Could not open file";
34.         hRetval=E_COULD_NOT_OPEN_FILE;
35.     }
36.
37.     if (SUCCEEDED(hRetval))
38.         return hRetval;
39.     else
40.         return Error((LPOLESTR)strDescription,IID_ICRMWorker,hRetval);
41. }
```

On lines 12–18 in Listing 12.12, you write the path of the file that is to be written and the contents of the file to the log. This is enough information to undo the operation (you can just delete the file) or redo the operation (you have the file path and contents so you can recreate the file if you have to). On line 20, you call `ForceLog` to make the log records durable. Then, on lines 22–29, you can attempt to write the disk file. If you successfully write the file, you call `SetComplete` on `IObjectContext`.

Let's explore the implementation of a CRM Compensator. A CRM Compensator must implement the `ICrmCompensator` interface. The methods in this interface are shown in Table 12.10. The DTC calls the methods in this interface as it is attempting to commit the transaction.

TABLE 12.10 The Methods in the ICrmCompensator Interface

Method Name	Description
SetLogControl	Delivers an ICRMLogControl pointer to the compensator so that it can write additional log records.
BeginPrepare	Notifies the compensator of the beginning of phase 1 of the transaction.
PrepareRecord	Called once for each log record that has been written.
EndPrepare	Notifies the compensator of the end of phase 1 of the transaction. The (logical) return value allows the compensator to vote on the outcome of the transaction.
BeginCommit	Notifies the compensator that the commit phase (phase 2) of the transaction is about to begin.
CommitRecord	Called once for each log record.
EndCommit	Notifies the compensator that the commit phase of the transaction is about to end.
BeginAbort	Notifies the compensator that the abort phase (phase 2) of the transaction is about to begin.
AbortRecord	Called once for each log record.
EndAbort	Notifies the compensator that the abort phase of the transaction is about to end.

The sequence of method calls depends on whether the transaction is being committed or aborted, or if recovery is in process. If the transaction is being committed, the sequence of method calls on the CRM Compensator is as follows:

(1) `SetLogControl`
(2) `BeginPrepare`
(3) `PrepareRecord` (called once for each log record written in the CRM Worker)
(4) `EndPrepare`
(5) `SetLogControl`
(6) `BeginCommit`
(7) `CommitRecord` (called once for each log record written in the CRM Worker)
(8) `EndCommit`.

If the client aborts the transaction, none of the prepare calls are made on the compensator. The sequence of method calls in this case is as follows:

(1) `SetLogControl`
(2) `BeginAbort`
(3) `AbortRecord` (called once for log record written in the CRM Worker)
(4) `EndAbort`

If the CRM Compensator is being called for recovery, you will see first a call to `SetLogControl` and then either a sequence of commit method calls (`BeginCommit`, `CommitRecord`, `EndCommit`) or abort method calls (`BeginAbort`, `AbortRecord`, `EndAbort`), depending on whether the recovered transaction was committed or aborted. You use these methods to implement the transactional logic of your CRM. In the `Prepare` method calls, you can verify that the system is in a state that allows the transaction to commit. In the `Commit` methods, you perform whatever processing is necessary to make your changes permanent. In the `Abort` methods, you should perform whatever processing is necessary to return the system to its state prior to the start of the transaction. For instance, my transactional file writer CRM deletes the file that was written by the CRM worker if the transaction aborts. If the transaction commits, it leaves the file alone.

You must keep some things in mind as you implement your CRM compensator. You cannot assume that the same instance of the CRM compensator that processes the set of method calls in the prepare phase will process the method calls in the commit phase. Each phase must be implemented so it is independent of the others. That's why `SetLogControl` is called at the beginning of each phase and the log records are passed to the CRM compensator in each phase. If a client attempts to commit a transaction and then someone pulls the power cord out of the wall or there is some other system failure in the commit phase, the `Prepare` method calls will not be repeated during recovery, the CRM compensator will only receive a set of `Abort` or `Commit` method calls.

Another point to keep in mind as you implement your CRM compensator is that the CRM architecture does not address *isolation*. Isolation (the "I" in ACID) means code that is running outside of the transaction should not see the results of the transaction until the transaction is complete. Usually isolation is implemented using locking. Your file writer CRM writes its file to disk in the CRM worker and then deletes it in the CRM Compensator, if the transaction aborts. But if some other piece of software tried to read the file after the CRM worker has performed its job but before the CRM compensator has had a chance to delete the file, the file could be read even when a transaction aborts. For the file writer, it is simple to fix this problem. Since you wrote the contents of the file to the durable log, you can delay writing the disk file until the transaction commits (the

`EndCommit` method). The CRM worker would just perform some validity checks (verify that the specified directory exists, for example) and then write the file path and contents to the durable log.

Another point to keep in mind is to make sure that the updates you make in the commit and abort phases are *idempotent*. An idempotent operation is one where the end result of the operation is the same even if the operation is performed several times. For instance, appending text to a file is *not* an idempotent operation. If you perform the operation several times, the text in the file is repeated several times. But opening and writing to a file in truncate mode so that its existing contents are discarded *is* an idempotent operation, because the file always contains the same contents regardless of how many times you perform the operation. The commit and abort phases in your CRM compensator must be idempotent because these operations may be performed many times.

After you have implemented your CRM Worker and Compensator, you must still perform some configuration to make them work properly. Your CRM worker and Compensator must be configured, so you must create a COM+ application and add both of these components to it. The COM+ documentation recommends that you configure your CRM Worker as shown in Table 12.11.

TABLE 12.11 Configuration Settings for a CRM Worker

Configuration Item	Setting
Transaction	Required
Synchronization	Yes
JIT	Yes
ThreadingModel	Apartment or Both

Your CRM compensator should be configured as shown in Table 12.12.

TABLE 12.12 Configuration Settings for a CRM Compensator

Configuration Item	Setting
Transaction	Disabled
Synchronization	Disabled
JIT	No
ThreadingModel	Apartment or Both

After you have configured both of the components, you must also enable CRM in the COM+ application. To do this, perform the following steps:

1. Right-click on the COM+ Application as shown in Figure 12.46.
2. Select `Properties...` from the `Context` menu (the Application properties dialog appears as shown in Figure 12.47).
3. Click the `Advanced` tab (shown in Figure 12.47).
4. Set the `Enable Compensating Resource Managers` checkbox.
5. Click `OK`.

If a COM+ server application has the Enable Compensating Resource Managers option selected, then the first time the COM+ application starts up it creates a CRM log file to be used by all CRMs in the server application process. The name of the log file is synthesized from the GUID that was assigned to the COM+ application when it was first created. You can find the log file in the `DtcLog` directory beneath your windows system directory. CRM log files have the extension crmlog.

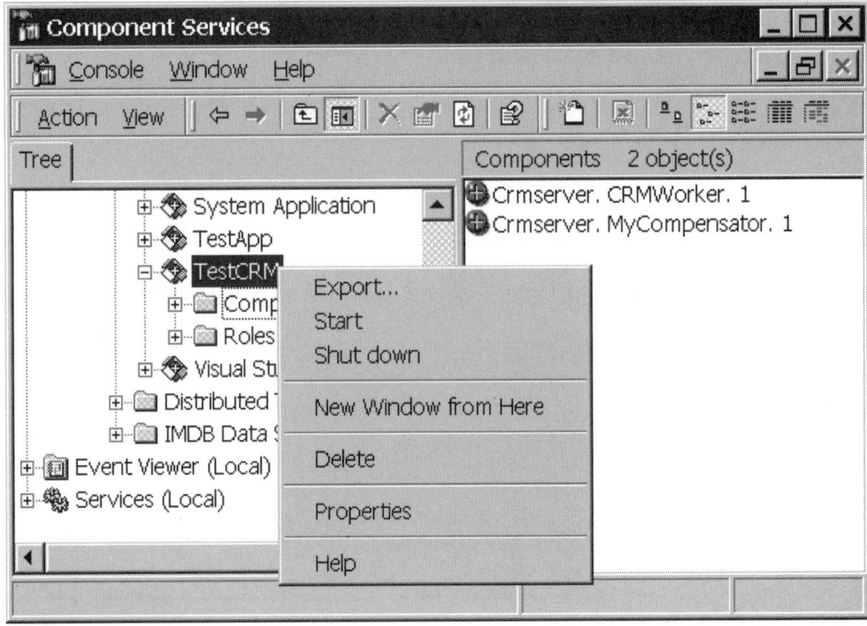

FIGURE 12.46 The First Step to Enabling CRM.

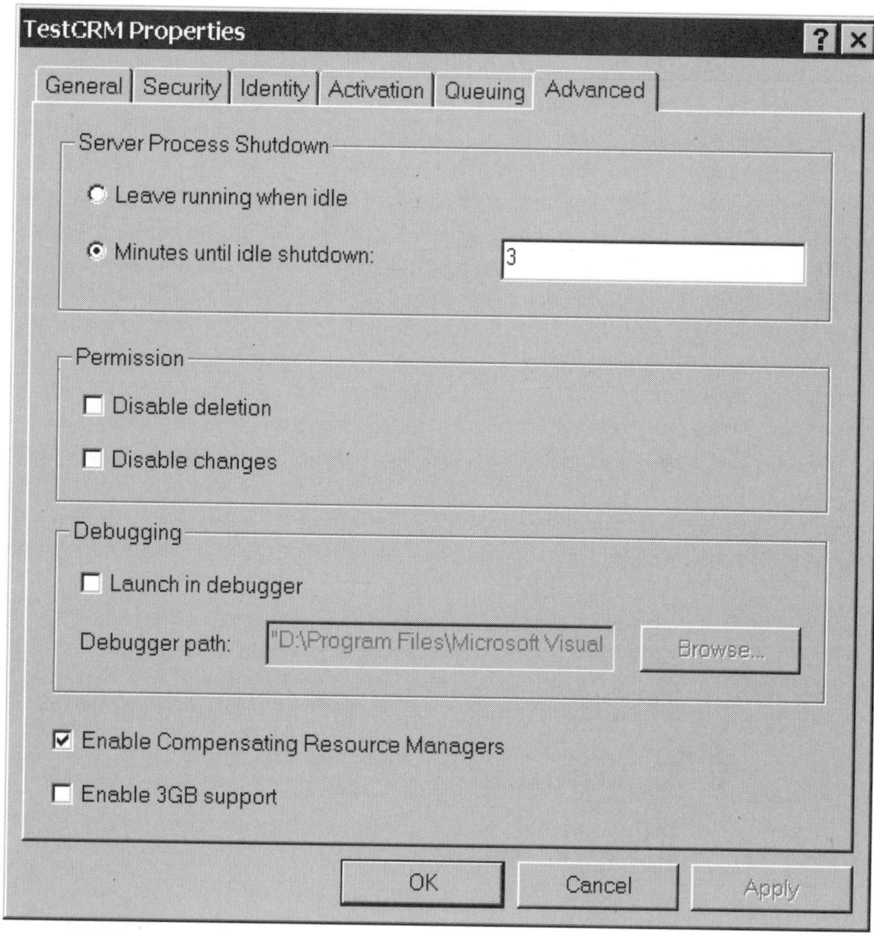

FIGURE 12.47 Enabling Compensating Resource Managers.

What Happened to the In-Memory Database?

In a nutshell, the In-Memory DataBase (IMDB) was removed from the release versions of COM+ and Windows 2000 because, as implemented, it would not meet the needs of most developers. It's likely that an improved version of this technology may find its way into later versions of COM+, but Microsoft has made no promises on this. Because it is not a part of the released version of COM+, I do not discuss it extensively, but since it will likely reappear sometime down the road, I thought it was at least worth a sidebar.

Anyone who has bought additional RAM for a PC knows about the amazing performance improvements you can gain from this upgrade. I recently upgraded my home PC from 128 to 256 MB of RAM and the improvement in performance was stunning. If you have a fixed amount of money to spend to improve the performance of a computer, that money is usually best spent on RAM rather than getting a faster processor. Why? Because additional memory means the operating system can keep more applications and data in main memory instead of paging it out to disk. Main memory access is typically two or three orders of magnitude faster than disk access. This same rule applies to databases. Accessing database tables from a disk file is two or three orders of magnitude slower than accessing the database table once it is cached in memory. A significant performance improvement can be realized in any database application, regardless of how it is implemented, by caching frequently-used, read-only information into in-memory data structures. Of course you have to write code to query and cache the data, and you may also have to write some sort of indexing mechanism to make it easy and fast to extract information from the cache. The In-Memory DataBase (IMDB) was designed to do this work for you. Using IMDB, you could specify tables (you could not do sub-queries within tables and this was part of the reason for the cancellation) that IMBD should load into shared memory when its server process is started. This data is then made available to business objects or client code through an OLEDB provider (you learn what OLEDB and an OLEDB Provider is in Chapter 13). You could not perform SQL queries on the cached data through this OLEDB provider. You were only allowed to either browse the tables or use indexes to sort and filter. This was another major limitation that eventually caused IMDB to be canceled. A transactional version of the Stored Property Manager (the TSPAM) was also removed from COM+ at the same time that IMDB was.

Summary

In this chapter, you received an introduction to the COM+ services. I discussed each of the COM+ services in detail and you learned how to configure your COM+ component to support these services. In the next chapter, I put all this knowledge to use and build a complete, 3-tiered, thin-client application using COM+ and Windows DNA 2000.

THIRTEEN

Building a 3-Tiered Application Using COM+ and Windows DNA 2000

In the last two chapters, you learned about the COM+ architecture and various services that COM+ provides to COM objects. But COM+ is just one piece of a complete architecture that Microsoft has assembled to enable you to build enterprise-class, distributed applications. In addition to COM and COM+, this architecture includes data-access and Web-enabling technologies. All these technologies work together in a synergistic way: COM is the glue that ties everything together and provides the communication infrastructure between the different tiers. COM+ provides the services you need to implement a secure, scalable, and transactional middle-tier. Universal Data Access and the Microsoft Data Access Components (MDAC) provide access to any data source in a uniform way. Internet Information Server (IIS) and Active Server Pages (ASP) make it easy to Web-enable your applications. This architecture is called the Windows Distributed interNet Applications Architecture (Windows DNA). Microsoft has updated this technology for Windows 2000 and it is now called the Windows DNA 2000. In this chapter you learn about Windows DNA and Windows DNA 2000. You also put everything you have learned in the previous two chapters to use as you build a 3-tiered, Web-enabled application using COM+ and other technologies in the Windows DNA. You will see how to build a COM+ server application step-by-step and then build a Web client and a native Windows client.

Hold on to your hat! This is biggest chapter of them all with lots of code and step-by-step instructions. Don't be alarmed. This chapter isn't long because it is complicated, it is long because you're doing a lot of work. You're going to be building three applications: a COM+ server application, a Visual Basic client, and an HTML client. Along the way you learn how to access a SQL Server database using Active Data Objects (ADO) and how to build a Web application using Active Server Pages (ASP). This chapter is the culmination of everything you have learned so far. So fire up Visual C++ and Visual Basic and let's get going.

What is the Windows DNA?

The best description I've ever heard of the Windows DNA is that it's a market-tecture, a combination of marketing and software architecture. The Windows DNA is not a product; there is nothing to buy. It's your style guide to using Microsoft technologies to implement enterprise-class, distributed applications. It is a set of ideas and white papers you can find on Microsoft's Web site (www.microsoft.com/dna) or in the MicroSoft Developer Network (MSDN) library (msdn.Microsoft.com/library or CD-ROM). In this chapter, I cut through the marketing hype and talk mostly about the architecture. The central ideas in the Windows DNA are that:

- Microsoft has all the technologies and tools you need to build enterprise-class, distributed applications.
- To use these technologies and tools to their best effect, you should partition your application into three logical layers: presentation, business, and data-access.
- There are Microsoft technologies and tools you can use to implement each layer.
- COM/COM+ is the glue that binds everything together.

Figure 13.1 shows all the tools and technologies in the Windows DNA.

Presentation Layer

Microsoft provides a rich set of technologies you can use to implement the presentation layer of your Windows DNA applications. Which technology you should use depends on your needs. In many cases, you may have both a Win32 native client and an HTML-based client. In the Windows DNA, Win32 executables, plain HTML, Dynamic HTML, client-side scripting (VB script and ECMA Script), and ActiveX Controls can be used to implement the presentation layer. Microsoft ships its Web browser, Internet Explorer

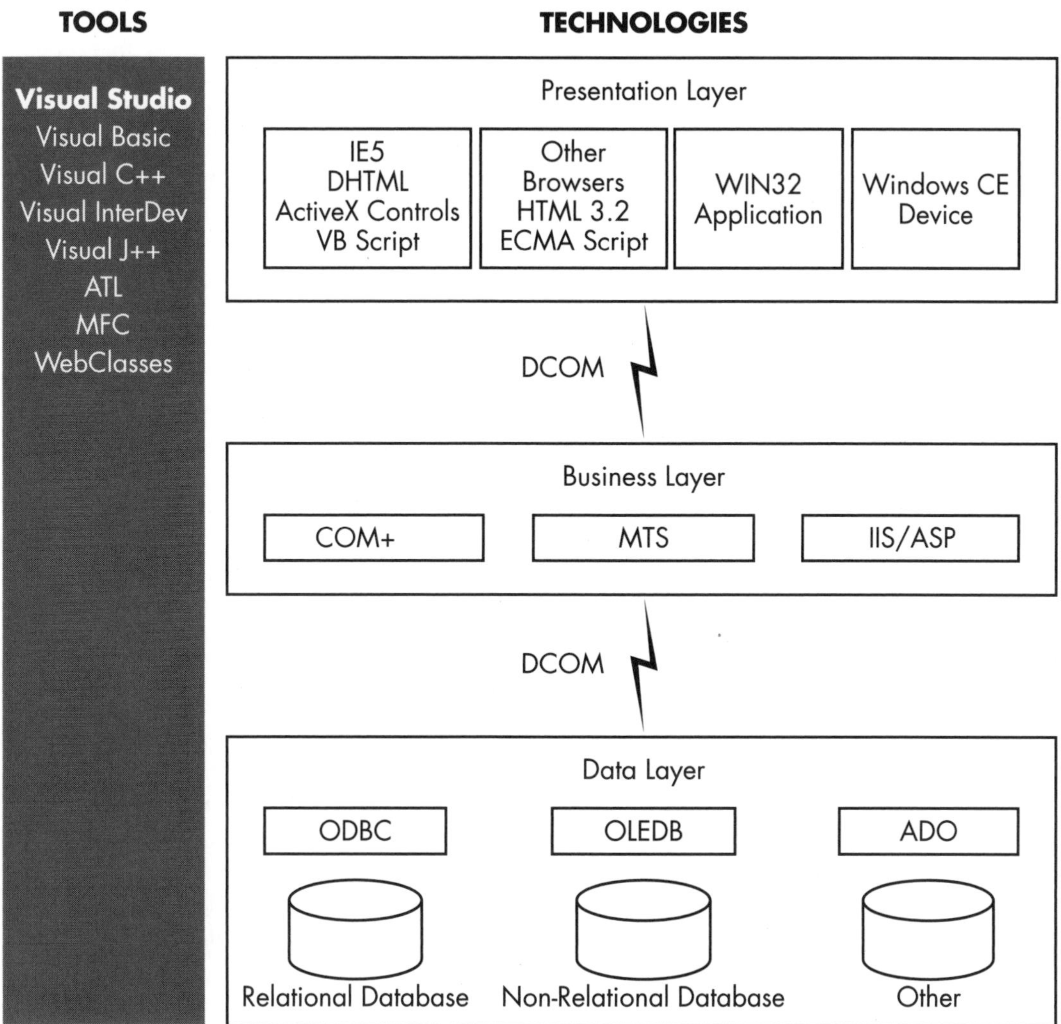

FIGURE 13.1 The Windows DNA.

5.0, with Windows 98 and Windows 2000. It provides support for plain HTML as well as Dynamic HTML (DHTML). It also provides support for ActiveX Controls and Java Applets.

If you use plain HTML, your users can use any browser on any platform as a client for your application. Unfortunately, it is difficult to create a rich user interface using plain HTML. With DHTML, you can write richer user interfaces using either VBSCRIPT or ECMA Script (Java Script). Using DHTML all the elements on the Web page are exposed as elements you can manipulate programmatically. You can change the content, structure, and look of a DHTML page using client-side script. You can also use client-side scripting to perform certain kinds of data validation as well as sorting and searching of data that has been fetched from the server without having to make another trip back to the server. Unfortunately, DHTML is implemented differently in Netscape and Internet Explorer. Unless you are careful and plan to do a lot of testing, you must specify a client browser (IE or Netscape Navigator) if you plan to use it.

Microsoft also provides versions of Visual C++ and Visual Basic you can use to build client applications for the Windows CE platform, thus, allowing you to create native Windows clients for the booming Personal Digital Assistant (PDA) market. Microsoft also ships a version of Internet Explorer for Windows CE so HTML-based presentation logic is also available to PDA clients.

Business Layer

On the business layer, the middle-tier is where Microsoft is doing its most important work, and is also the tier that COM+ addresses. The business layer is where you implement the business processing of your application. In the Windows DNA, you implement this business processing using *business objects* that you implement with COM+.

All of the technologies that Microsoft provides to implement the business layer can be summed up in one Word: COM+. As long as you implement your business objects as in-process COM servers, COM+ will provide you with fine-grained security, distributed transactions, thread synchronization, load balancing, asynchronous store and forward method invocation, and enhanced scalability through Just In Time (JIT) Activation and pooling of objects and database connections. In short, everything you need to build a high-performance, secure, scalable, transactional, business layer.

There is one thing missing from the middle-tier that I have not talked about yet—how to make it Web-enabled. This is where two of the most important pieces of technology in the Windows DNA come in: Internet Information Server (IIS) and Active Server Pages (ASP).

IIS AND ACTIVE SERVER PAGES

Internet Information Server (IIS) is Microsoft's Web server product. It can receive requests from any Web browser, including IE or Netscape Navigator, and it responds with HTML pages, images, and other information the HTML pages link to. But just downloading static HTML pages is not all that interesting (depending on what's in the images). To build Internet-capable applications, you must be able to generate HTML pages dynamically, using information retrieved from your data stores. For instance, if someone goes to Barnes and Noble's Web site to buy a book about COM+, they will likely use the book search tab and do a keyword search using COM+ as the keyword. This Web site has to dynamically generate an HTML page that contains a listing of all the COM+ books they currently sell.

Active Server Pages (ASP) let you write server-side scripts that are executed by IIS. Typically, your ASP scripts utilize the services of your business layer to dynamically generate HTML pages. Together IIS and ASP form the link between HTML-based clients and the business layer of a Windows DNA application.

ASP is not a stand-alone product; it is bundled with IIS. It is also included with Microsoft's lite version of IIS, Personal Web Server (PWS), that runs on Windows 2000 Professional, NT Workstation, and Windows 95/98.

ASP is, by far, the most successful Web technology Microsoft has ever produced. Thousands of large-scale commercial Web sites are successfully using this technology (barnesandnoble.com and ditech.com are just two examples).

You can tell if a Web site is using ASP by looking at the extension of the files being displayed in your Web browser. If you see the extension asp, the site is using Active Server Pages.

Using ASP is simple. An ASP page is just a text file, with the extension asp, that contains HTML and scripting code that is written with VB script or Java script. The scripting code is enclosed in the delimiters <% and %>. When IIS receives a request for an ASP page, it interprets the script between the delimiters before it sends back the response. The ASP script runs on the Web server machine. It can run in-process with the Web server or out-of-process. Figure 13.2 shows the ASP architecture.

The code between the <% and %> delimiters in an ASP file can instantiate and use COM+ objects, connect to a database, and generally do most things one expects from Visual Basic code. In many cases, this server-side script instantiates COM+ business objects and calls methods on these objects to retrieve and update information and implement business rules. The script can then take the information it receives from these business objects, format it as HTML and send it back to the Web browser.

The ASP runtime exposes an object model that the script can use as shown in Figure 13.3.

ASP scripts can retrieve the values the user entered into an HTML form using the Request object. They can write HTML into the Web server's response using the Response object. They can store information that can be

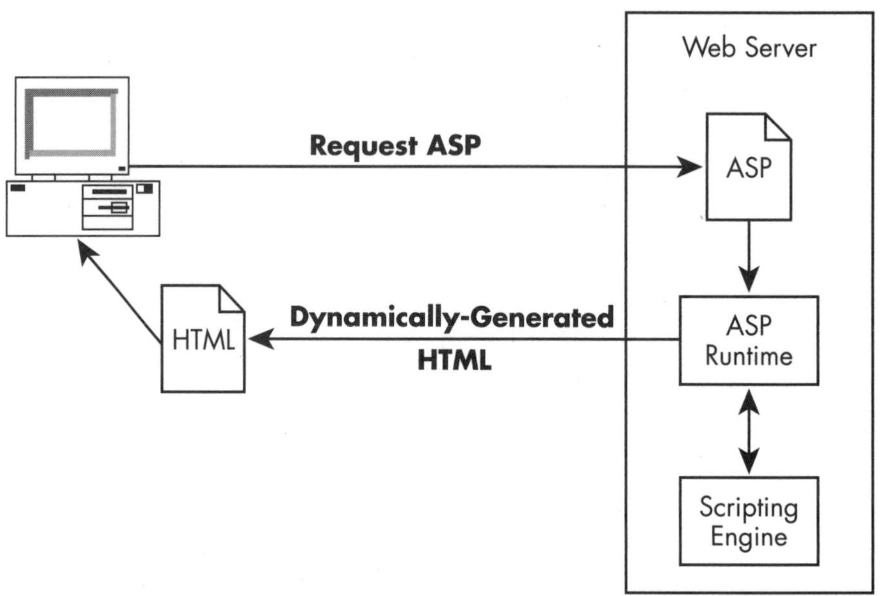

FIGURE 13.2 The Active Server Pages Architecture.

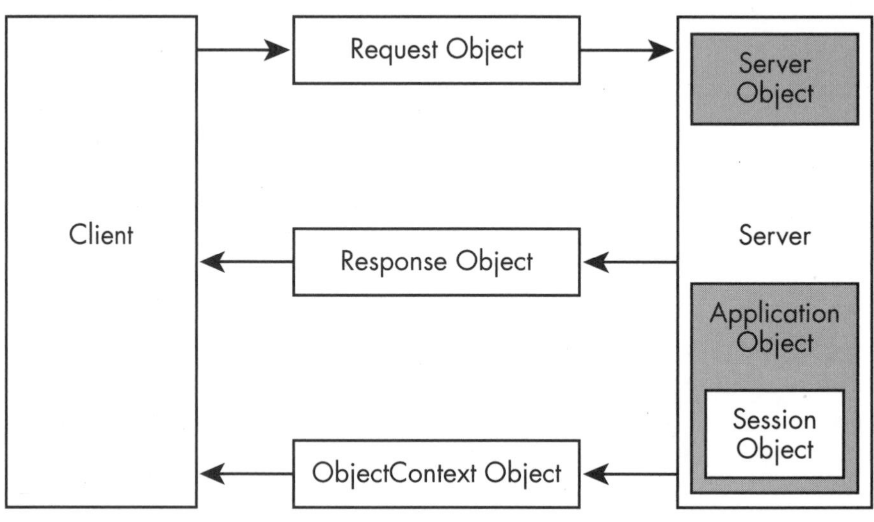

FIGURE 13.3 The Active Server Pages Object Model.

used across pages using the Session or Applications objects. And an Active Server Page can commit or rollback an MTS transaction using the `ObjectContext` object. In most cases, you encapsulate your transaction processing logic within COM+ business objects that you invoke from your

ASP pages, so there is no need to use the `ObjectContext` object. But there may be situations when you want your Active Server Page to start a transaction and you can use the `ObjectContext` for this.

ASP is cross-platform because, as long as you are careful to only generate platform-neutral HTML in your ASP files, any Web browser on any platform can be used as a client. In addition, while most people use IIS as their Web server when they are using Active Server Pages, you can buy implementations of Active Server Pages that run on other Web servers (such as Netscape Enterprise Server and Apache) from a company called ChiliSoft (www.chillisoft.com).

What I have given you here is a high-level introduction to Active Server Pages. You will learn more about ASP and use it later in this chapter. If you want an in-depth introduction to ASP, I highly recommend the following two books: *Beginning Active Server Pages 2.0* by Francis and colleagues and *Professional Active Server Pages 3.0* from Francis and colleagues. Wrox Press publishes both.

Data Layer

Enterprise-class, distributed applications must be able to access data from disparate data sources. The problem is that these different data sources have completely different APIs. SQL Server has a native API called Open Client. Oracle's DBMS has an API called the Oracle Call Interface (OCI). If you are accessing data from a non-relational database, such as an object-oriented database, there is still another API to write to. And if your data is stored in an operating system file, like an Excel spreadsheet or a comma-delimited text file, there is yet another API that you must use to access your data. This wide variety of data sources makes it difficult to write applications because developers have to learn multiple APIs. The solution to this problem in the Windows DNA is a set of technologies that together are called Universal Data Access.

UNIVERSAL DATA ACCESS

Universal Data Access (UDA) is Microsoft's name for a set of technologies that make it possible to access almost any piece of data in a uniform way. There are a number of technologies that together implement UDA and the key idea behind all these technologies is shown in Figure 13.4.

UDA implements a data-source independent layer. This layer can take the form of a C language API or a set of COM interfaces. You call the methods or functions in this layer in the exact same way whether you are working with SQL Server, Microsoft Access, or some other type of database. This data-source independent layer talks to a piece of software that maps method calls that you make in the data-source independent layer to the native API of the data source. This API mapping software is usually implemented as a DLL.

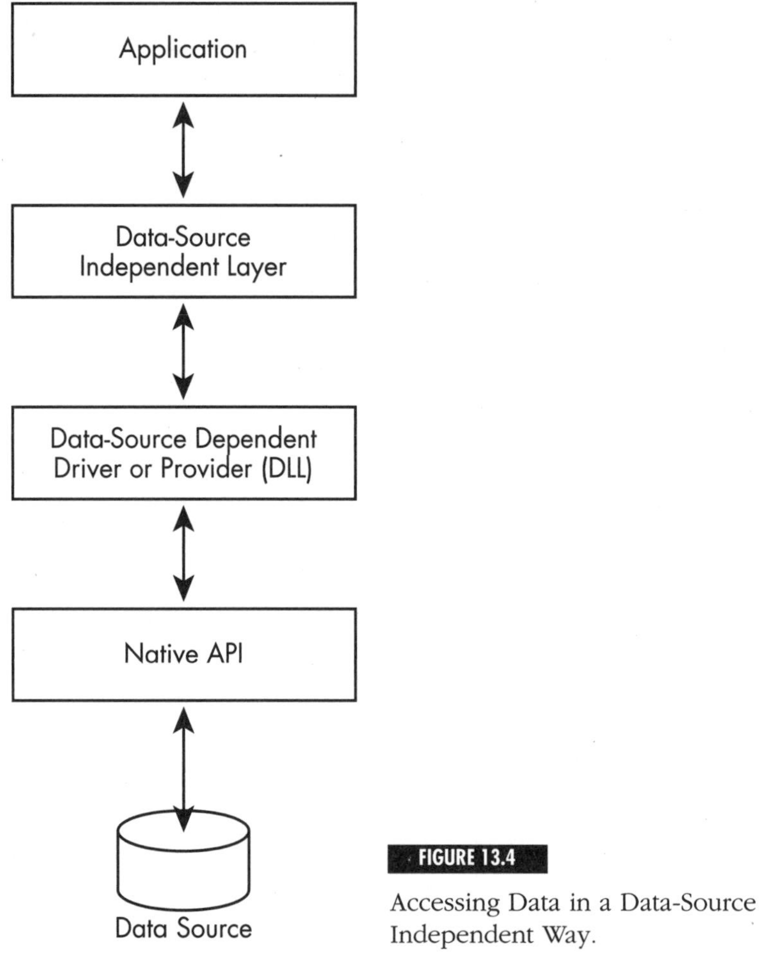

FIGURE 13.4

Accessing Data in a Data-Source Independent Way.

Microsoft has two data-source independent layers: Open DataBase Connectivity (ODBC) and OLEDB. OLEDB is implemented as a set of COM interfaces and ODBC is a C-language API. Both of these technologies are difficult to use and are not easily called from the 4GL development tools—Visual Basic, Delphi, PowerBuilder, and so on—that most database programmers prefer. To solve this problem, Microsoft created the Active Data Objects (ADO). ADO is a set of COM, automation classes that wrap OLEDB and make it much easier to use with 4GL development environments. You can also use ADO to access ODBC by using the OLEDB-to-ODBC provider.

MDAC

The Microsoft Data Access Components (MDAC) is a software distribution that implements Universal Data Access. The MDAC contains the latest

OLEDB system files and OLEDB providers. It also contains the latest ODBC system files and drivers and the latest version of ADO. The MDAC is included with all Microsoft development tools such as Visual Basic, Visual C++, and the Visual Studio suite. You can also download the latest version of the MDAC (new versions come out quite often) from www.microsoft.com/data.

ODBC

ODBC was Microsoft's first data-source independent layer. The first version of ODBC was released in 1992. The current version is 3.5. ODBC implements its data-source independent layer as a C language API. Although ODBC was designed primarily for client/server relational databases, it can be used with non-relational data sources from desktop, Indexed Sequential Access Method (ISAM) databases like Dbase, Microsft Excel files, to comma-delimited text files. Figure 13.5 shows schematically how ODBC works.

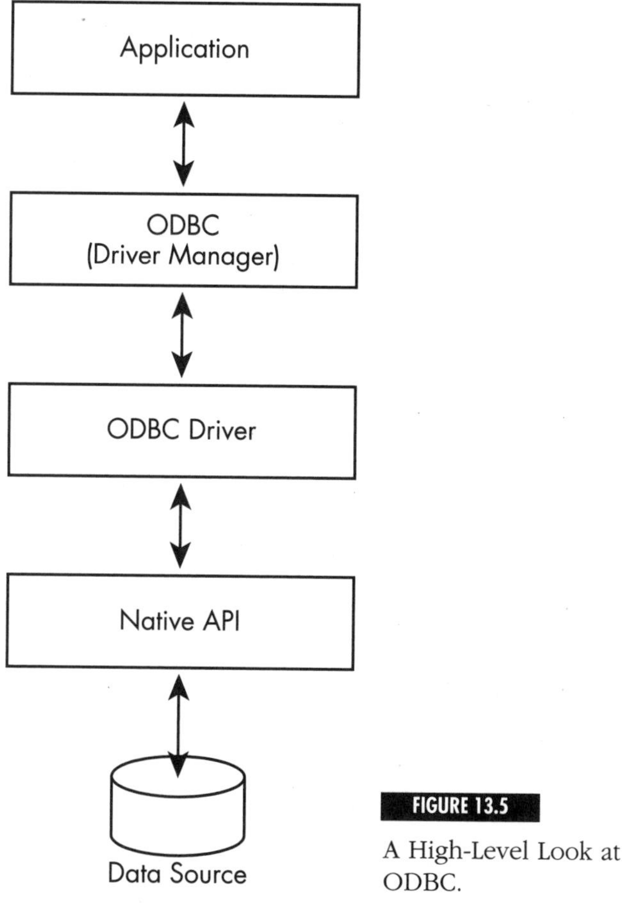

FIGURE 13.5

A High-Level Look at ODBC.

Microsoft did not create ODBC alone. Microsoft, Sybase, DEC, and Lotus all worked together to define the first version of ODBC.

The methods in the ODBC API are implemented in the ODBC driver manager, which is a system DLL (`odbc32.dll`) you can find in your Windows system directory. To use ODBC for a particular type of data source, you must have an ODBC driver for that data source. An ODBC driver is just a DLL. It translates ODBC method calls that it receives from the ODBC Driver Manager to calls on the Native API of the data source.

The MDAC ships with ODBC drivers for the most popular data sources on the PC platform, including SQL Server, Access, Oracle, Excel, and comma-delimited text. You can buy ODBC drivers for most other data-sources (Sybase SQL Server, IBM DB2, Informix, and so on) from a number of third parties. A company called Merant (previously known as InterSolv) is probably the most well known third-party developer of ODBC drivers. Its Web site can be found at www.merant.com.

DSN

Different databases require the client to provide different information to connect to the database. If the database is a desktop database, then the client must provide the path to the database file to connect to the database. For a client/server database, you must provide the network address of the server machine and possibly other information like the network protocol and other protocol-related information such as a TCP/IP socket port. ODBC hides all of this complexity behind an abstraction called a Data Source Name (DSN). A DSN maps all of the information required to connect to a data source to a logical name. To connect to a data source, you specify the DSN as the source that you wish to connect to.

Windows 2000 contains a GUI tool you can use to create ODBC DSNs called the ODBC Data Source Administrator. To start the ODBC Data Source Administrator on Windows 2000, perform the following steps:

1. Click the `Start` Menu.
2. Select `Programs\Administrative Tools\Data Sources` (ODBC). The ODBC Data Source Administrator appears as shown in Figure 13.6.

Using the ODBC Data Source Administrator you can create DSNs that are specific to a particular user, or you can create System DSNs that are available to all users on the machine. To see how you would go about creating a DSN for Microsoft Access (you won't actually create one), perform the following steps:

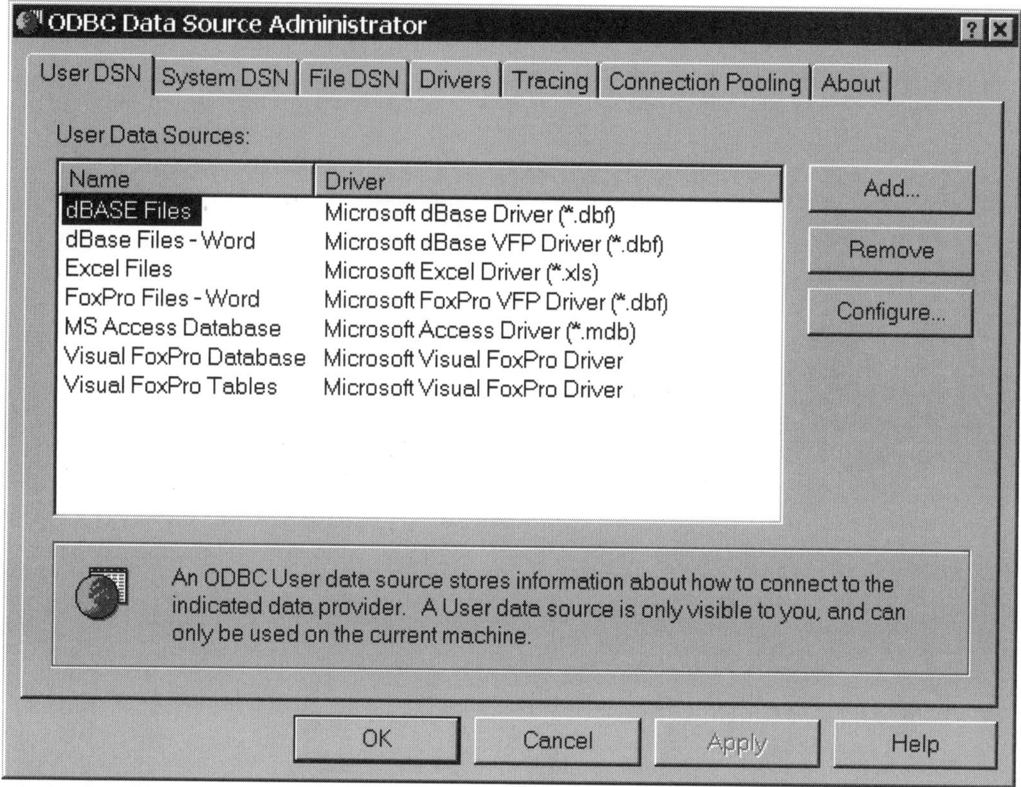

FIGURE 13.6 The ODBC Data Source Administrator.

1. Click the `Add...` button on the ODBC Data Source Administrator (the Create New Data Source dialog appears as shown in Figure 13.7).
2. Select `Microsoft Access Driver` from the list of drivers that appear (this is a list of the ODBC drivers currently installed on the system).
3. Click the `Finish` button (the ODBC Microsoft Access Setup dialog appears).

The ODBC Microsoft Access Setup dialog is implemented within the ODBC driver for Microsoft Access. This dialog is shown in Figure 13.8.

Notice in this dialog that you are allowed to select an .mdb file. Click cancel on the ODBC Microsoft Access Setup dialog, since you don't need to setup a DSN now. Perform the following steps to see how you would setup a DSN for Microsoft SQL Server:

1. Click the `Add...` button on the ODBC Data Source Administrator again.
2. On the Create New Data Source Window, select `SQL Server` from the list of installed ODBC drivers.

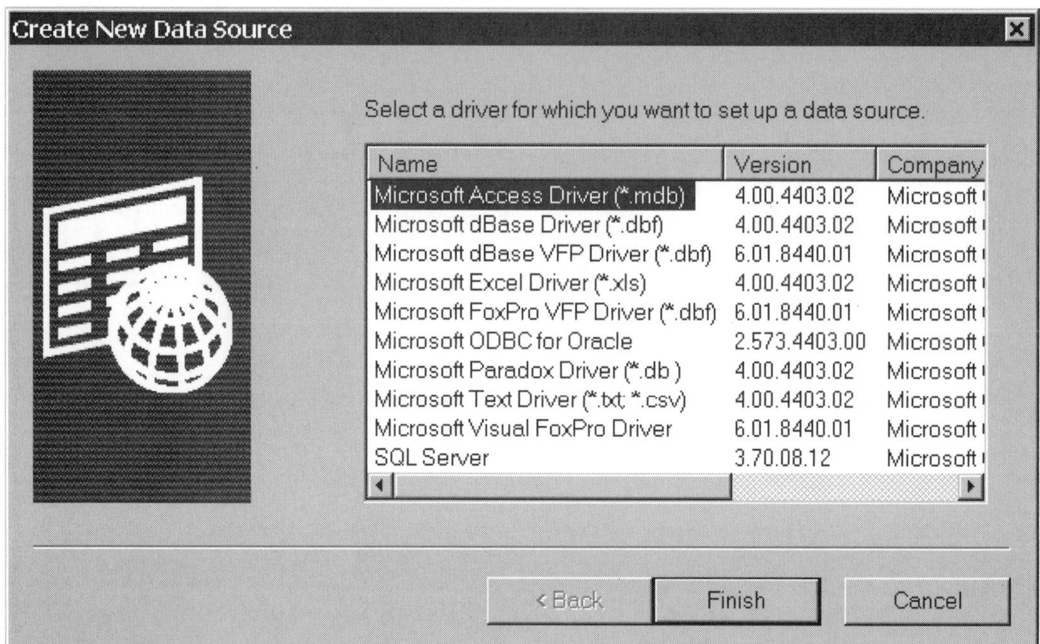

FIGURE 13.7 The Create New Data Source Dialog.

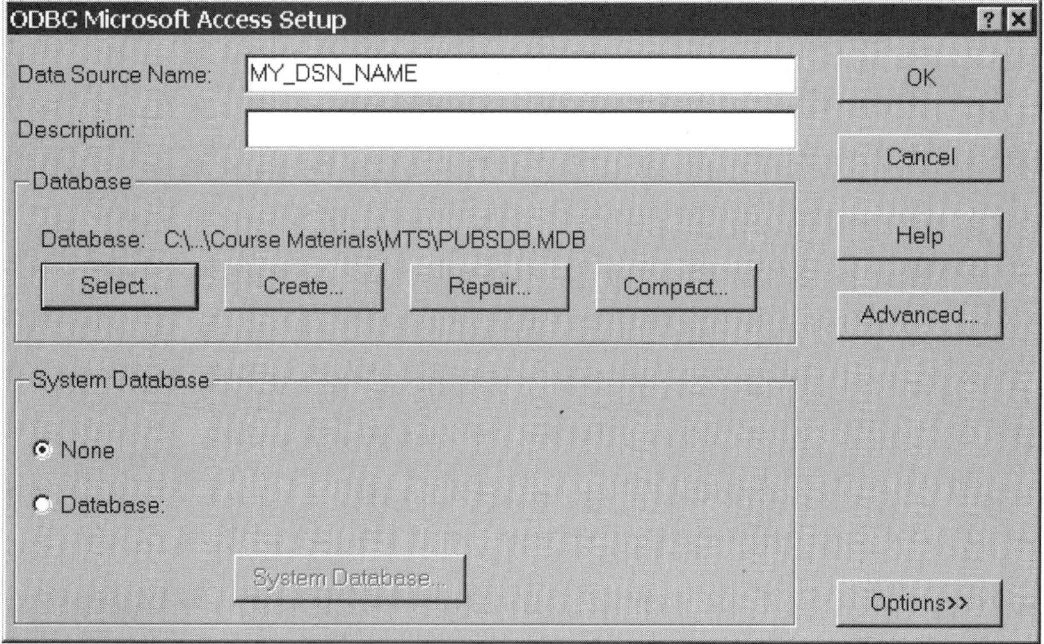

FIGURE 13.8 The DSN Setup Dialog for Microsoft Access.

3. Click the `Finish` button (the Create a New Data Source to SQL Server dialog appears as shown in Figure 13.9.

Figure 13.9 is the first step in a four-step wizard. In this wizard, you can select a remote machine (or the local one) where SQL server resides. You can select the authentication method to be used to log into the database as well as the default user name and password that someone connecting through this DSN will use. You can then use whatever mechanism your development environment provides to connect to the DSN. In Visual C++, use the ClassWizard to create a wrapper class that derives from an MFC class called `CRecordSet`. In Visual Basic, you can use Active Data Objects (ADO) or the Remote Data Objects (RDO). If you're a glutton for punishment, you can use the `SQLConnect` function in the raw ODBC API.

OLEDB

OLEDB is Microsoft's latest data access technology. OLEDB is a set of COM interfaces that provide access to a wide range of data sources in a uniform way. Although you can definitely see a relational flavor to OLEDB (it does have rows and fields, and the primary query language is SQL), it was designed from the beginning with other kinds of data sources in mind. Figure 13.10 shows the OLEDB Architecture.

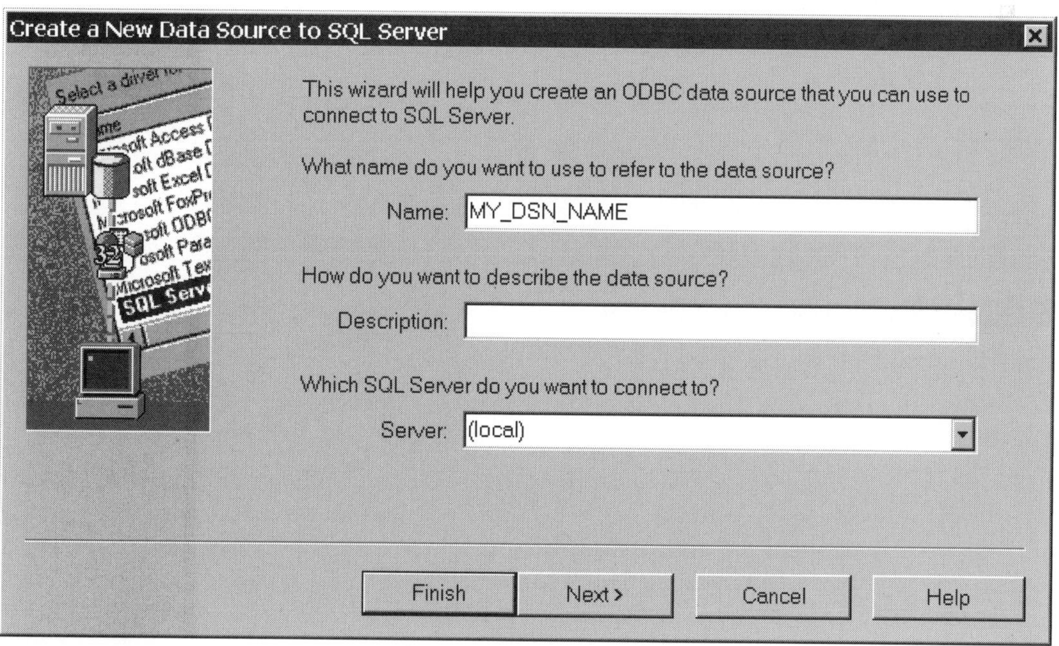

FIGURE 13.9 The DSN Setup Dialog for SQL Server.

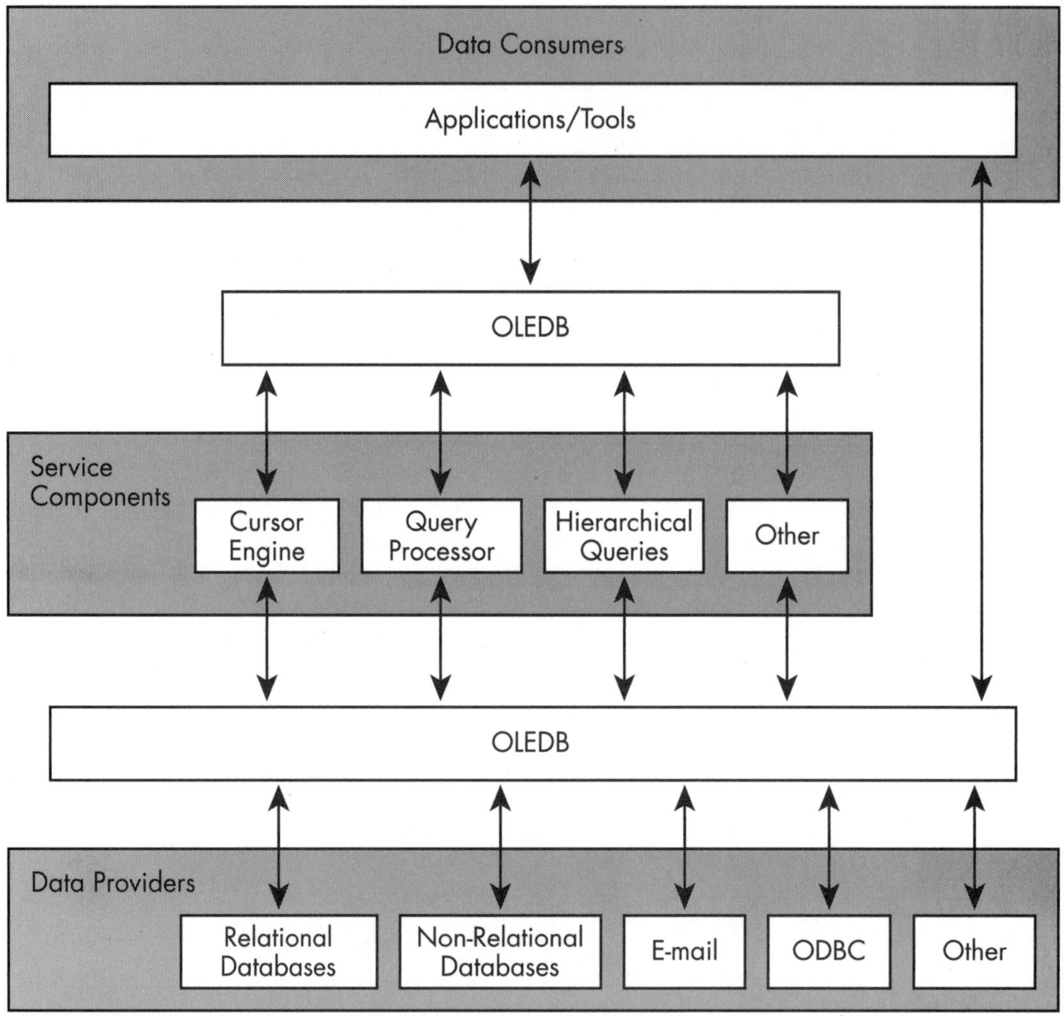

FIGURE 13.10 The OLEDB Architecture.

Although it seems similar to ODBC in concept, the OLEDB architecture represents a fundamental change. In addition to providing a data-source independent interface, OLEDB also partitions the functionality of a relational database into three types of components: data consumers, service components, and data providers. This partitioning makes OLEDB far easier to use with non-relational data sources.

DATA CONSUMERS

Data consumers are either development tools or applications that use the OLEDB interfaces to retrieve data from a data source. Notice that data consumers, as shown in Figure 13.10 can either use the service components or go directly to the OLEDB data providers. The OLEDB interfaces are rather complex and difficult (and in some cases impossible) to call from 4GLs. So, most applications tend not to use OLEDB directly. Instead they use the Active Data Objects (ADO), which I talk about shortly. Most data consumers that use the OLEDB interfaces directly are either system level software or development tools.

DATA PROVIDERS

Data providers allow basic tabular access to a data source. The job of a data provider is to represent the data in data source as rows and columns. If the data is already stored in that format, as it is in a relational database, then this job is simple. But it takes more work to implement the MAPI data provider that makes e-mail stored in Microsoft Exchange available through OLEDB.

In some cases, an OLEDB data provider is a separate piece of software (a DLL). These providers are similar to ODBC drivers.

Most of the companies that were making ODBC drivers, Merant for example, are also making OLEDB providers.

Microsoft hopes that people will begin creating data sources that use OLEDB as their native interface, thus obviating the need for a separate provider.

If you look closely at Figure 13.10, you'll see there is an OLEDB provider for ODBC. This provider allows you to access any ODBC data source through the OLEDB interfaces. Microsoft created this OLEDB provider because there were few native, OLEDB providers available when OLEDB first shipped. With the OLEDB provider for ODBC, people could begin to use the OLEDB interfaces immediately by using OLEDB to access their ODBC data sources. Now there are good, native OLEDB providers available for all the popular database products on the PC platform (Microsoft SQL Server, Oracle, Access, Excel, and Text). There is little need to use the OLEDB-ODBC provider with these data sources. Another good reason not to use the OLEDB-ODBC driver is that it is slow relative to native OLEDB providers. If you are using OLEDB with one of the less popular database products (on the PC platform) such as IBM DB2, Sybase SQL Server, or Informix, you may still need to use the OLEDB-ODBC provider.

SERVICE COMPONENTS

Service components provide additional data-access functionality above and beyond that provided by a simple data provider. A service component does not own data; it provides some value added processing on the data that is returned from a data provider. Examples include SQL queries or scrollable and updateable cursors. If the underlying data store is a relational database, there is no need for a separate service component. The OLEDB provider just has to map the OLEDB interfaces to the native API of the database. But if you are trying to access e-mail through OLEDB, you can use a data provider that is built on top of MAPI to provide tabular access to the data and then buy an OLEDB service component that provides SQL queries and database cursor functionality such as scrollable and updateable cursors.

CONNECTION STRINGS

One key difference between OLEDB and ODBC is that OLEDB does not require a DSN. To specify a particular data source, you simply pass a *Connection String* to one of the OLEDB connection methods. The connection string identifies the provider to be used and the actual database file or server that the user is trying to connect to. The following connection string connects to the Microsft SQL Server pubs database located on a machine called gordon1 using the login ID, sa:

```
"Provider=SQLOLEDB.1; User ID=sa;Initial Catalog=pubs;Data Source=GORDON1"
```

The provider string, `SQLOLEDB.1`, identifies the OLEDB provider to be used, which in this case is the native OLEDB provider for Microsoft SQL Server. The following connection string is used to connect to a Microsoft Access database:

```
Provider=Microsoft.Jet.OLEDB.4.0;Data Source=C:\Program
Files\Microsoft Visual Studio\VB98\Biblio.mdb
```

The following connection string uses the OLEDB-ODBC provider to connect to an ODBC DSN called PUBSDB:

```
Provider=MSDASQL.1;Data Source=PUBSDB
```

If you don't specify a provider explicitly, the OLEDB-ODBC provider is used by default. The documentation for your OLEDB provider should contain complete details on how to construct a connection string for that Provider. If you want to find out more about OLEDB, see the documentation online at www.microsoft.com/data.

ADO

The OLEDB interfaces are quite complex and difficult, and in some cases impossible to call from 4GLs. The Active Data Objects (ADO) are a set of automation objects that provide a higher-level interface to OLEDB. But ADO does more than just wrap OLEDB. It also implements a number of features that are important and useful for application developers that OLEDB does not provide, including a client-side cursor engine, disconnected record sets, and asynchronous queries.

Figure 13.11 shows the *key* portions of the ADO 2.5 object model. You can find complete documentation on ADO at www.microsoft.com/data.

Table 13.1 gives a description of each of these key objects.

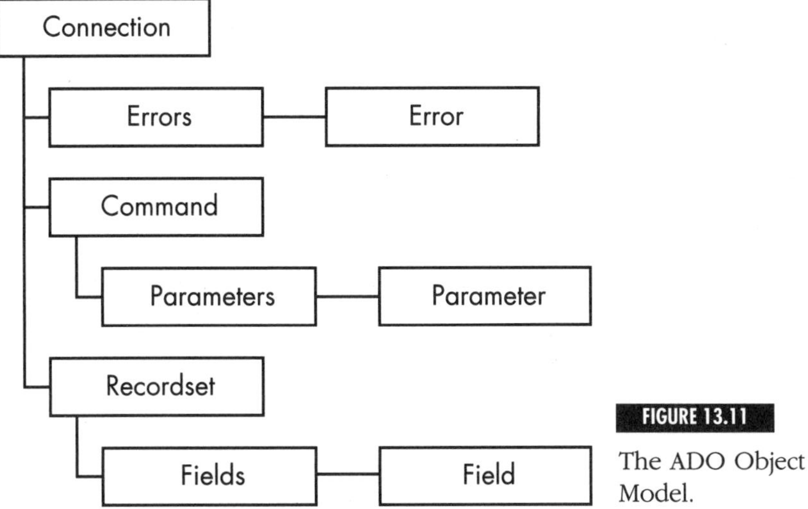

FIGURE 13.11

The ADO Object Model.

TABLE 13.1 ADO Objects

Object	Description
Connection	Represents an open connection to a data source.
Command	A definition of an operation that you intend to execute against a data source. You only need to use a Command when you are executing parameterized queries or calling a stored procedure.
Recordset	Represents the results of a query or an executed command.
Field	A column of data in a Recordset.
Parameter	A parameter or argument associated with a Command object. You only need to use Parameters when you are executing a parameterized query or calling a stored procedure.
Error	Contains details about data access errors.
Fields	A collection of Field objects.
Parameters	A collection of Parameter objects.
Errors	A collection of Error objects.

CLIENT-SIDE CURSOR ENGINE

The client-side cursor engine lets you send all the data in one batch from the database server to the client. It allows you to perform cursor operations and other kinds of operations including navigating through data, updates, and sorting and searching. Changes are made to a cursor that resides on the client and updates to this cursor can be sent to the server in one round-trip, thus reducing network traffic and improving performance.

DISCONNECTED RECORDSETS

Disconnected recordsets are recordsets that are created by running a query or executing a stored procedure and then disconnected from their source by setting their `ActiveConnection` property equal to NULL. Once an ADO recordset is disconnected from its data source, it becomes a powerful, self-describing collection. Disconnected recordsets can be passed easily between processes, stored in a file, and sorted and filtered. You can add data to the recordset, modify the data, or even delete data. When you are done with your modifications, you can set the `ActiveConnection` property of the recordset to an active database connection and apply your changes to the database using the `UpdateBatch` method of the RecordSet.

ADO recordsets also have custom marshaling support that makes them an efficient way to pass data between processes. Microsoft recommends that COM/COM+ business objects use ADO recordsets to pass data to and from the presentation layer.

ASYNCHRONOUS QUERIES

Asynchrounous queries let a client continue running immediately after it submits a query, even if the results of the query are not returned right away. ADO exposes a set of events (implemented with COM connection points) that are fired when the data is ready or if the query fails.

The Windows DNA 2000

Time does not stand still and neither does the Windows DNA. The computing world has changed dramatically in the less than two years the Windows DNA has existed. The major force driving these changes is electronic commerce (e-commerce). Many e-commerce (dot-com) businesses are virtual corporations. The dot-com company advertises and runs the Web site. The products are made, and in many cases, shipped and delivered by other companies. This requires a lot of communication and coordination between the companies involved. In addition, many e-commerce companies are selling build-to-order products. The computer I am writing these words on—a Micron Millenia Max—was custom-configured and purchased by yours truly just weeks ago on Micron's Web site. Delivering custom-made products at low cost and with short lead times requires a great deal of communication and coordination between the company making and selling the finished product and the dozens of companies that make sub-components used to build the product. In short, e-commerce requires that busineses be able to share information and communicate better with each other than they ever did in the past. Microsoft realized it was unrealistic to believe that all of these companies would adopt the Windows DNA; it, therefore, became critical for the Windows DNA to integrate better with other platforms like IBM mainframes, AS400, and UNIX.

In addition to this, the growing volume of business in e-commerce means that any application development technology that wants to play in this arena now must be able to handle heretofore unheard of transaction rates. Robust clustering and higher-performance and more scalable database and Web servers are required.

Microsoft's solution to all these problems is the Windows DNA 2000. The Windows DNA 2000 is an update that adds several new technologies to the Windows DNA architecture. These technologies include: Windows 2000, Host Integration Server 2000, Application Center 2000, BizTalk Server 2000, Commerce Server 2000, and Microsoft SQL Server 2000. Windows 2000 should be available by the time this book is available. The other products in this architecture are expected to ship by the middle of 2000. The objective of these tools is to make the Windows DNA more heterogeneous and scalable.

Windows 2000

Windows 2000 provides a better platform for Windows DNA 2000 than Windows NT. The difference isn't just COM+. Windows 2000 is more scalable and secure than Windows NT and was designed to work with the Active Directory. It is also the first operating system to have integrated support for Extensible Markup Language (XML). Windows 2000 comes with a high-performance, validating XML parser that is compliant with the latest standards.

Host Integration Server 2000

Host Integration Server 2000 (formerly known as Babylon) provides a variety of tools that can be used to integrate your Windows DNA applications with software that runs on other platforms such as IBM mainframes, AS400, and UNIX. These tools can be divided into three categories: Network and Security Integration Services, Data Integration Services, and Application Integration Services.

NETWORK AND SECURITY INTEGRATION SERVICES

The Network and Security Integration Services include support for SNA and LAN protocols, support for password synchronization and single sign-on, and support for Active Directory on other platforms.

DATA INTEGRATION SERVICES

Host Integration Server 2000 will also include a variety of tools that make it easier to share data across platforms, including bi-directional data replication tools that work between Microsoft SQL Server, IBM DB2, and Oracle. It will also include a wider range of ODBC drivers and OLEDB providers than are currently available. Drivers and providers will be delivered for DB2, VSAM, AS400 file system, and Sybase, in addition to the popular ones on the PC platform that Microsoft always shipped. Host Integration Server 2000 will also include a facility that allows users of IBM DB2 to access Microsoft SQL Server as though it were a peer DB2 data source.

APPLICATION INTEGRATION SERVICES

The COM Transaction Integrator (COMTI) and the XML Transaction Integrator (XMLTI) highlight the Application Integration Services in Host Integration Server 2000. COMTI allows COM+ and MTS applications to access Mainframe applications built with the CICS or IMS transaction processing environments. With COMTI, Mainframe applications appear as COM+ or MTS components to a Windows application. XMLTI provides an XML interface to COMTI components; this allows XML-formatted documents and messages to initiate transactions. XMLTI will be particularily useful for business-to-business e-commerce, especially when used with BizTalk Server 2000 and BizTalk-compatible XML schemas.

Host Integration Server also includes a tool called the COMTI Component Builder that provides a graphical, drag-and-drop environment that developers can use to generate a COM+ component or an XML interface from existing business logic.

A bridge between the MSMQ and MQ Series message queuing products (MQ Series is available on a number of platforms) is also provided by Host Integration Server, as is a Software Developer's Kit (SDK) that lets developers extend Host Integration Server to work with any platform.

Application Center Server 2000

Application Center Server 2000 is the same product I talked about in Chapter 12 during the discussion of the Component Load Balancing Service (CLBS). Application Center Server 2000 is a version of Windows 2000 that includes deployment, management, and monitoring tools for Web applications running in server farms; it provides increased scalability and reliability for people who are deploying and managing high-volume, high-availability Web applications.

BizTalk Server 2000

XML is shaping up to be as important a technology to the Web as HTML. If you don't know about XML, see the sidebar in this chapter entitled "The Importance of XML." BizTalk server 2000 was designed to make it easy for companies to exchange information via XML. Biztalk server provides a standard gateway for sending and receiving XML documents over the Internet. Biztalk server and XML will be a powerful combination for implementing business process integration and business-to-business e-commerce. As part of its biztalk strategy, Microsoft has also created a Web site where companies can collaborate to define standardized XML schemas for various industry segments (www.biztalk.org).

Commerce Server 2000

Commerce Server 2000 is a software solution for creating e-commerce web sites; it is an improved version of Microsoft's successful Site Server product. Commerce Server 2000 now features tight integration with the other products in the Windows DNA 2000. The integration with Windows 2000 and SQL Server 2000 makes Commerce Server 2000 a higher-performance, more scalable, easier-to-manage, and more secure product. The integration with Biztalk Server and Host Integration Server makes it easier for businesses to integrate their e-commerce Web sites with other business systems such as Enterprise Resource Planning (ERP).

Microsoft SQL Server 2000

Finally, Microsoft will be rolling out a new version of SQL Server to complete Windows DNA 2000. SQL Server 2000 (formerly called Shiloh) will feature improved scalability and managability. It will also have improved data warehousing and Online Analytical Processing (OLAP) as well as XML integration and improved data access via the web.

The Importance of XML

Extensible Markup Language (XML) is developing in Internet time precisely because it is the perfect solution for the communication needs of e-commerce. XML is a markup language for describing information. XML, like HTML, is a sub-set of the Standard Generalized Markup Language (SGML). XML is similar to HTML, which is also a computer language for describing information. XML, like HTML, is a sub-set of the Standard Generalized Markup Language (SGML). XML is similar to HTML, which is also a computer language for describing information. But, HTML only allows you to specify how information will be displayed. For instance, the following HTML displays a table of information about books:

```
<HTML>
<HEAD>
<TITLE>Browse for a book by keyword</title>
</HEAD>
<BODY>
<TABLE BORDER="1">
   <TR>
      <TD><H4>Title</H4></TD>
      <TD><H4>Author Last</H4></TD>
      <TD><H4>Author First</H4></TD>
   </TR>
   <TR>
      <TD>The COM and COM+ Programming Primer</TD>
      <TD>Gordon</TD>
      <TD>Alan</TD>
   </TR>
   <TR>
      <TD>XML by Example</TD>
      <TD>McGrath</TD>
      <TD>Sean</TD>
   </TR>
</TABLE>
</BODY>
</HTML>
```

There is a lot of information in this file that defines how the information will look when it is displayed. But there is no meta-information carried with this HTML; nothing that tells what the data *means*. Let's look at the same information displayed as XML:

```
<BOOKS>
   <BOOK>
      <TITLE>
         The COM and COM+ Programming Primer
      </TITLE>
      <AUTHORLAST>
         Gordon
      </AUTHORLAST>
      <AUTHORFIRST>
         Alan
      </AUTHORFIRST>
   </BOOK>
   <BOOK>
      <TITLE>
         XML by Example
      </TITLE>
      <AUTHORLAST>
         McGrath
      </AUTHORLAST>
      <AUTHORFIRST>
         Sean
      </AUTHORFIRST>
   </BOOK>
</BOOKS>
```

The two files contain the same information and both can be displayed in IE5 (try it), but that's where the similarities end. The XML file contains a great deal of meta-information that describes the meaning of the information in the file, which makes this file ideal for use as a medium for information exchange.

You can generate this XML file on any platform, perhaps even from data stored in a database. This file can be sent over the Internet (perhaps via Biztalk server) and then parsed by another piece of software (that runs on a different platform) and imported into some other database. All the meta-information that describes the meaning of the data in the file travels with the file. How is it displayed? However you want. A companion language called Extensible Stylesheet Language (XSL) can be used to format the XML file for display in any format you choose. I could go on like this for pages and pages since XML is an exciting technology. But this is not a book about XML. If you would like to learn more about XML, I recommend these books: *XML: Extensible Markup Language* by Elliotte Rusty Harold and IDG Books, and *XML IE5 Programmers Reference* by Alex Homer and Wrox Press.

Creating Your First COM+ Application

Now that you understand all the technology pieces in the Windows DNA that are required to create an enterprise-class, distributed application with COM+, it's time to start building your application. The first thing you need to do is configure Visual C++ to work with COM+.

Configuring Visual C++ to Work With COM+

Visual C++ 6.0 does not include the necessary header files and libraries that you need to build applications for Windows 2000.

Microsoft has recently begun shipping what they call the Windows 2000 Readiness Kit that does include the Windows 2000 headers. Microsoft may also release an updated version of Visual Studio 6.0 (a stop gap until Visual Studio 2000 arrives) that makes it simple to build applications on Windows 2000 with Visual Studio 6. Check Microsoft's Web site and if they do release an updated version of Visual Studio 6, it is likely that some of the steps shown in this section will be unnecessary. Also, watch the Web site for this book. If there are updates made to Visual Studio after this book goes to print, I will post updated chapters there. Also, there will be a revised edition of this book when Visual Studio 2000 arrives. But don't wait until then to begin learning COM+. The latest intelligence indicates that Visual Studio 2000 will not ship until March of 2001. If you understand COM (and that's the real key), you can begin developing COM+ applications using Visual Studio 6.0 right now.

You will have to make a few changes to your Visual Studio configuration and to the projects that you build with Visual Sudio 6.0 before you can create applications for Windows 2000 and COM+. The steps are fairly simple and I show you how in this chapter.

Initially I debated about whether to do the example program for this chapter in Visual C++ or Visual Basic. The application that you can build in this chapter is a database application, and most database applications are being built with 4GLs such as Visual Basic. Relatively few people are building such applications with Visual C++. Even so, I eventually decided to stick with Visual C++ for the server part of my application (the business objects) and Visual Basic for the client for the following reasons:

1. There are several COM+ features (primarily object pooling) that you cannot use with Visual Basic 6.
2. You have used Visual C++ for most of your examples so far.
3. With Native COM Support and ADO, building an application with Visual C++ isn't much more difficult than building an application with Visual Basic.
4. Many projects I have had experience with use this configuration: Visual C++ for server-side development and Visual Basic for the client.

The Platform SDK

Before you can build applications with COM+, you need to obtain the Platform SDK. This Platform contains all the header files and libraries that you need to build applications for Windows 2000. After you install the Platform SDK, take note of the root directory of your platform SDK installation (the default for the September 1999 version is `c:\platform sdk\`). You need this directory for the next section where you configure Visual C++ to use the Platform SDK. The setup program does have an option to enable Visual Studio integration, but this did not work well for me. Fortunately, it's fairly easy to manually configure Visual C++ to use the Platform SDK directories.

Configuring Visual C++ to Use the Platform SDK

By default, Visual C++ 6.0 is configured to use the header files, libraries, and binaries in its own installation. You need to configure Visual C++ to use the header files, libraries, and binaries from the platform SDK if you want to work with COM+. To do this, start Visual C++ and open any project and perform the following steps:

1. Select `Options` from the `Tools` Menu (the Visual C++ options dialog should appear).
2. Click the `Directories` tab (the window should look like that shown in Figure 13.12).
3. Make sure that `Include Files` is selected in the `Show Directories for` combo box.
4. Click the `New` button, which is the left-most of the four icon buttons shown in Figure 13.12.
5. Add an entry for the Platform SDK include directory (for example, `c:\platform sdk\include`).
6. Add an entry for the ATL 3.0 include directory of the Platform SDK (for example, `c:\platform sdk\include\ATL30`).
7. Make sure these two directories are the first in the list (your window should look like that shown in Figure 13.12).
8. Select `Library` files in the `Show Directories for` combo box.
9. Add an entry for the Library directory of the Platform SDK.
10. Make sure this directory is the first in the list (your window should look as shown in Figure 13.13).
11. Select `Executable` files in the `Show Directories for` combo box.
12. Add an entry for the Bin directory of the Platform SDK.

13. Make sure this directory is the first in the list (your window should look like that shown in Figure 13.14).
14. Click OK.

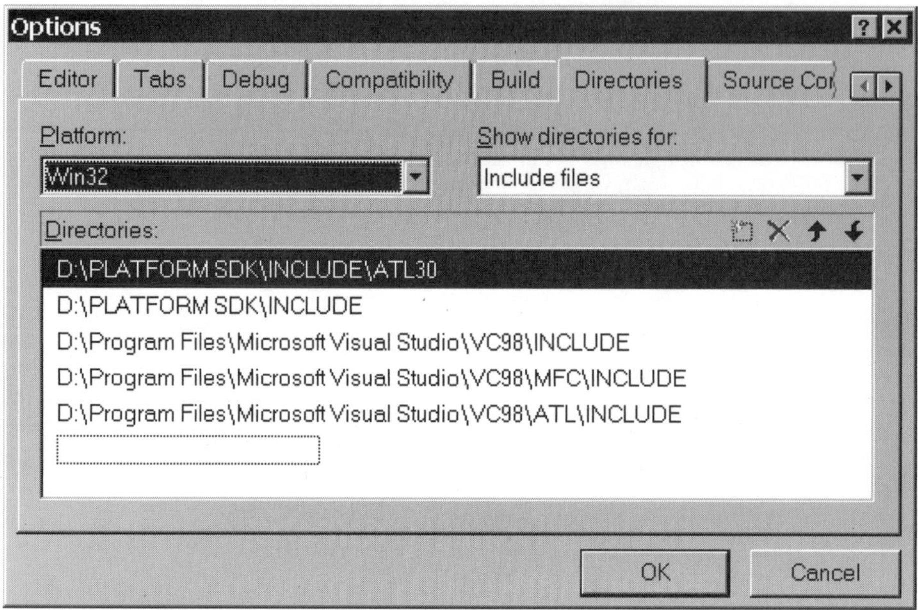

FIGURE 13.12 Include Directories in Visual C++ Options.

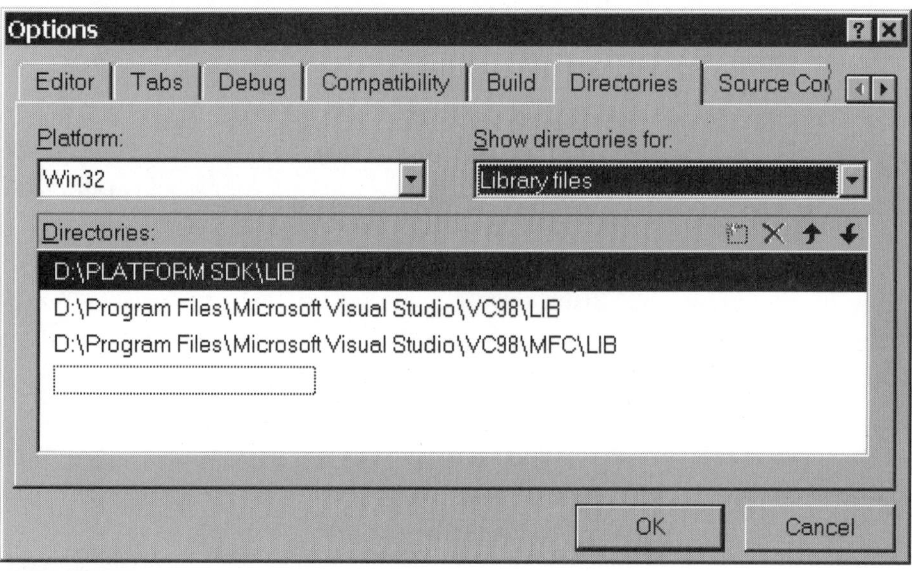

FIGURE 13.13 Library Directories in Visual C++ Options.

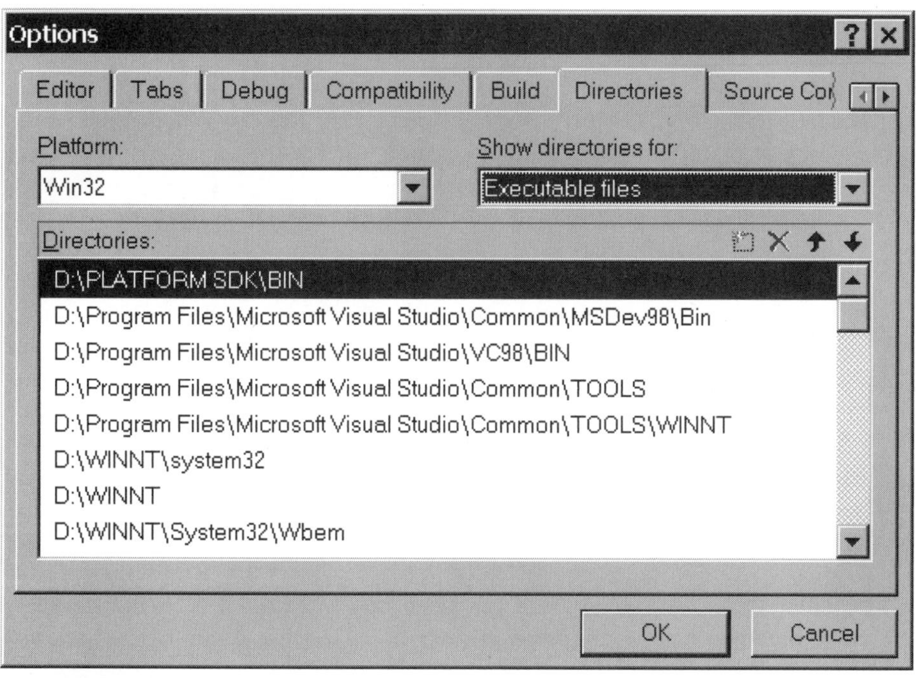

FIGURE 13.14 Executable Directories in Visual C++ Options.

The Publisher Example Program

The example program you can build in this chapter is a database application that uses the Pubs database that ships with Microsoft SQL Server 7.0 (it should ship with SQL Server 2000 as well). The Pubs database is a sample database that contains information that a book publisher might maintain, including titles, authors, publishers, and royalty information. The best part about using this database is that you won't have to create it. Once you install SQL Server 7.0, this database is automatically created for you. If you don't have SQL Server, one way to get it is to buy the book *Inside Microsoft SQL Server 7.0*; this book contains a 120-day evaluation copy of SQL Server 7.0. If you are going to build enterprise-class applications, you need to understand relational databases and this book does an excellent job of explaining one of the best database products on the market.

The application that we can build together in this chapter uses COM+ fine-grained security, transactions, and synchronization. This application has two client applications. The first application is a native Win32 application that you can build with Visual Basic. The second client application is an HTML-based client that uses Active Server Pages. This application shows off many of the elements of the Windows DNA, including COM+, ADO, OLEDB, IIS, ASP, and SQL Server.

From the native Win32 client application, the user can search for books via keyword. Once a book is found, users can view and (subject to security constraints) edit detailed information for the book, including the publisher, publication date, type, and so on. Users can also create new books with this application if they have permission. All employees are allowed to view information. But only Managers are allowed to edit or create new books. You can implement these security requirements using declarative, COM+ fine-grained security. The main window of the native application looks like that shown in Figure 13.15. When users double-click on a book in the main window, they see the dialog shown in Figure 13.16. On this window they may edit the information for the book and then update the book using the `Update` button, or they may create a new book using the `New` button. If they create a new book, the screen goes blank and users may enter all the information for their new book and then save it.

The HTML user interface for the application looks like that shown in Figure 13.17. Here I am using Internet Explorer on a Windows 2000 machine, but you can also use this user interface from a Netscape browser on other operating systems such as Sun Solaris (or other UNIX Variants)

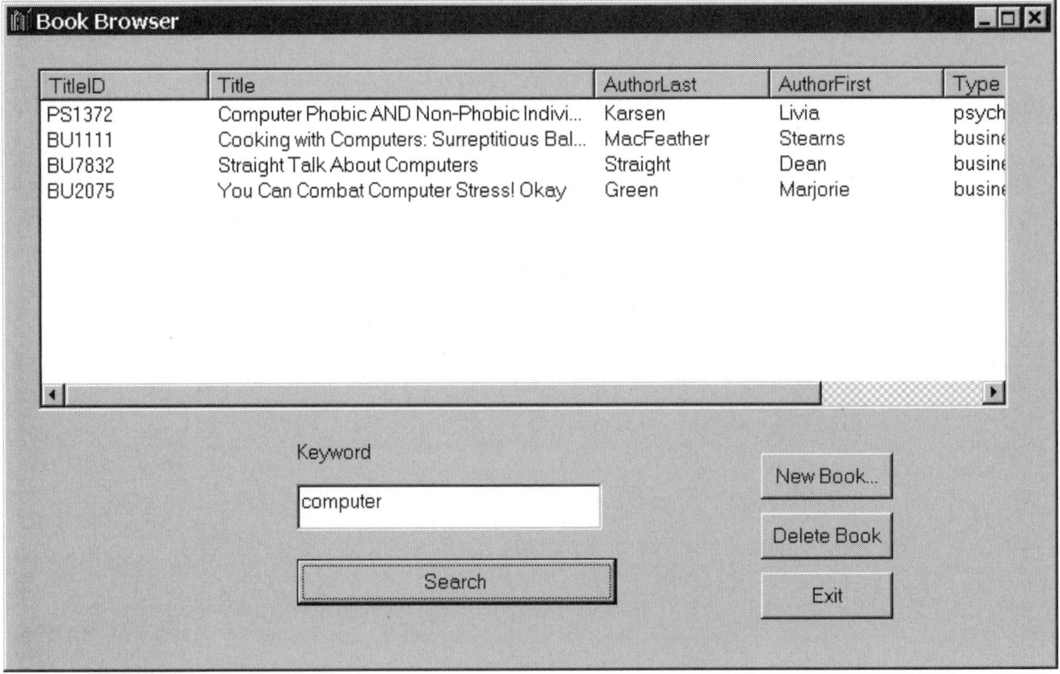

FIGURE 13.15 The Main Window of the Native Windows Client.

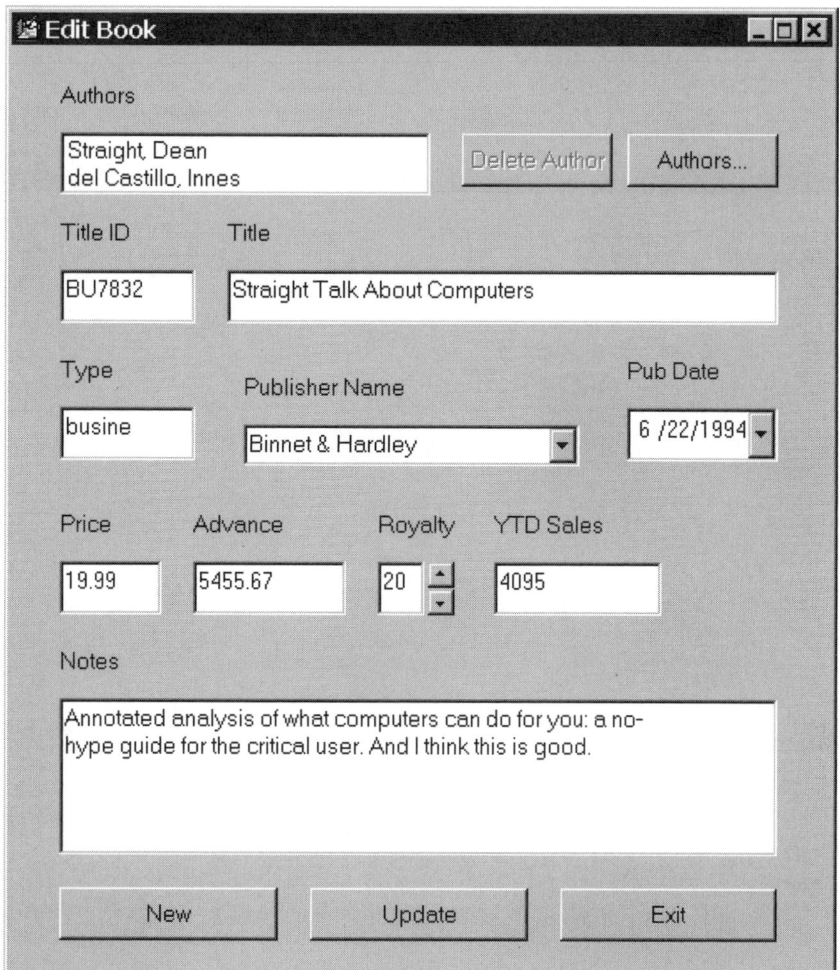

FIGURE 13.16 Editing Information for a Book in the Native Windows Client.

and, of course, Linux. From this user interface, users can retrieve a book by keyword. They can also update an existing book.

After users type in a keyword and click the `Submit` button, they see a list of the books whose titles contain the keyword as shown in Figure 13.18.

The user can then click on any of the hyperlinks in the table of books shown in Figure 13.18 and they will jump to a page where they can view and edit detailed information for the book as shown in Figure 13.19.

Users can modify the fields on the form in Figure 13.19 and click the `Submit` button to update the title in the database.

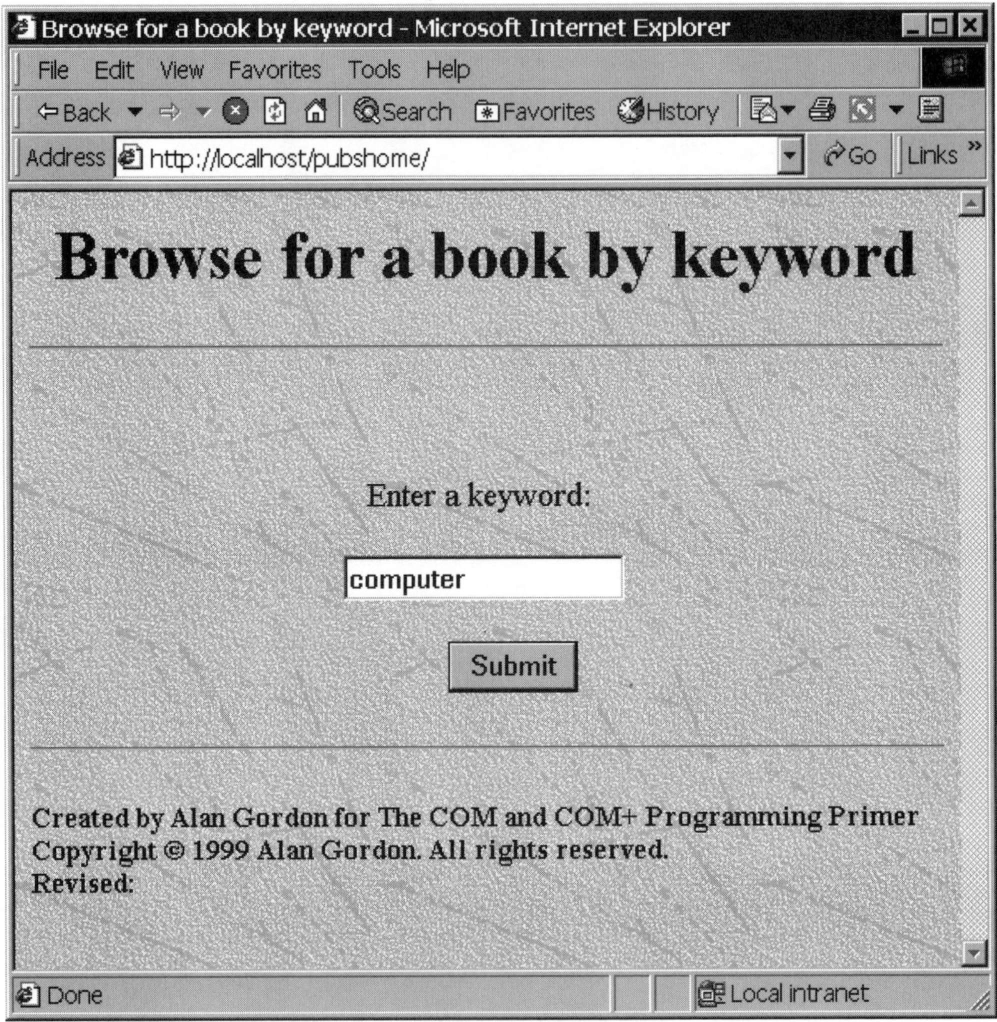

FIGURE 13.17 The Main Window of the HTML Client.

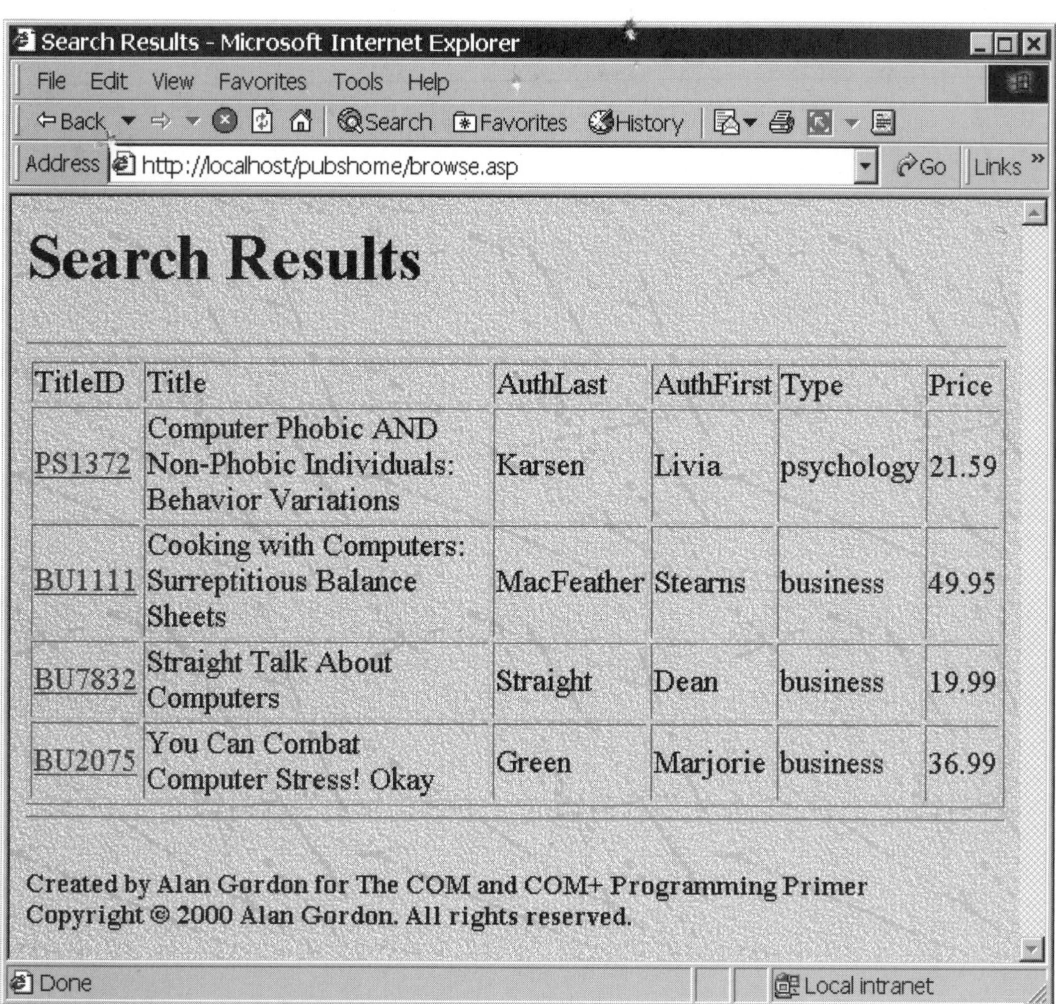

FIGURE 13.18 Browsing Titles in the HTML Client.

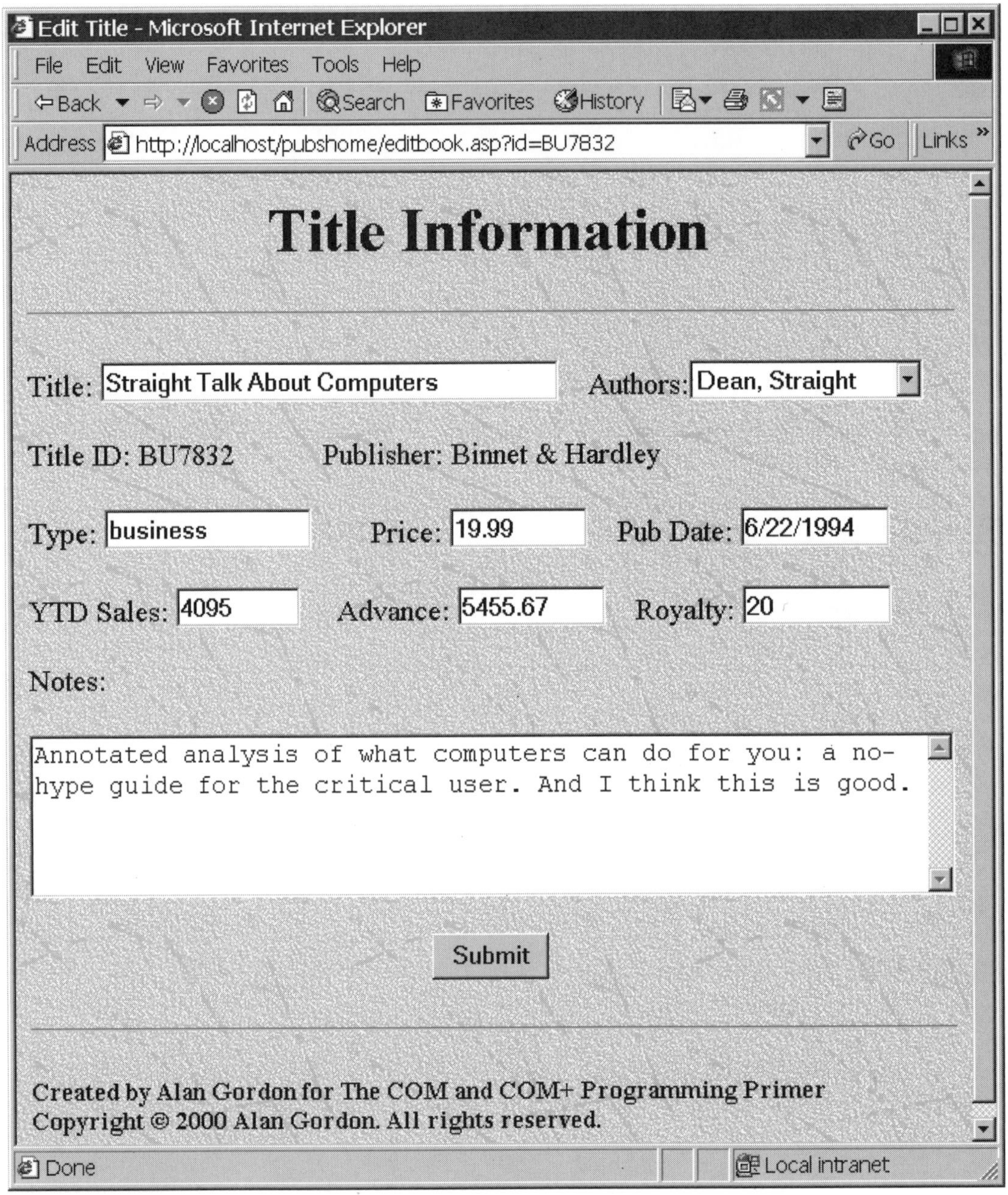

Edit Title - Microsoft Internet Explorer

File Edit View Favorites Tools Help

Back Search Favorites History

Address http://localhost/pubshome/editbook.asp?id=BU7832 Go Links

Title Information

Title: Straight Talk About Computers Authors: Dean, Straight

Title ID: BU7832 Publisher: Binnet & Hardley

Type: business Price: 19.99 Pub Date: 6/22/1994

YTD Sales: 4095 Advance: 5455.67 Royalty: 20

Notes:

Annotated analysis of what computers can do for you: a no-hype guide for the critical user. And I think this is good.

Submit

Created by Alan Gordon for The COM and COM+ Programming Primer
Copyright © 2000 Alan Gordon. All rights reserved.

Done Local intranet

FIGURE 13.19 Editing a Title in the HTML Client.

Building the Publisher Example Application

You can perform the following summarized steps to build your example application:

1. Create an ATL, DLL server project.
2. Add `Book`, `Author`, and `Publisher` classes to the project.
3. Modify the project to work with COM+ and ADO.
4. Add Methods to the `Book` class.
5. Add Methods to the `Author` class.
6. Add Methods to the `Publisher` class.
7. Add Support for the `IObjectConstruct` interface.
8. Implement the Methods in the `Book` class.
9. Implement the Methods in the `Author` class.
10. Implement the Methods in the `Publisher` class.
11. Compile your server.
12. Configure your components.
13. Implement the Visual Basic client.
14. Implement the ASP, HTML client.

Creating an ATL, DLL Server Project

To create an ATL, DLL-based server project, start Visual C++ 6.0 and then execute the following steps:

1. Select `New...` from the `File` menu (the New dialog appears).
2. Click the `Projects` tab.
3. Select ATL COM AppWizard from the presented list of project types.
4. Enter `pubsboserver` in the Project Name field.
5. Click the `OK` button (step 1 of the ATL, COM AppWizard appears).
6. Select `Dynamic Link Library` under Server Type.
7. Click `Finish`.

Visual C++ creates a project for an ATL, DLL-based server. You've done this so many times that there should be no need to discuss this further.

Adding Book, Author, and Publisher Classes to the Project Using the ATL Object Wizard

Your pubs business object server has three classes: `Book`, `Author`, and `Publisher`.

THE BOOK CLASS

The `Book` class lets you retrieve, update and create book-related information. Table 13.2 shows the names and descriptions of the methods supported by the lone interface in this class, `IBook`.

TABLE 13.2 Method for the Book Business Object

Object	Description
DeleteBook	Deletes the book with the specified titleID.
GetNewBookRecordSet	Creates an empty record set that contains all the fields that you need to specify for a new book. You fill the recordset and then send it back to the server for it to be saved to the database.
GetExistingBookRecordSet	Creates a record set that contains all the fields for one or more books. You can specify a search criterion (an SQL where clause) that is used to find the books.
RetrieveByID	Allows you to retrieve a recordset that contains book information by specifying the titleID for the book.
RetrieveByKeyword	Allows you to retrieve a recordset that contains book information by specifying a keyword in the title of the book. This method returns a record for all books that contain the keyword in its title.
UpdateBooks	Allows you to update an existing book in the database. You pass to this method a record set that you retrieve using either GetExistingBookRecordSet or GetNewBookRecordSet.

THE AUTHOR CLASS

The `Author` class lets you retrieve and modify author-related information. Table 13.3 gives the name and description of each of the methods supported by the `IAuthor` interface of the `Author` class.

TABLE 13.3 Methods for the Author Business Object

Object	Description
UpdateAuthorsForTitle	Allows the user to modify the list of Authors of a title.
GetNewTitleAuthorRecordSet	Creates an empty record set that contains all the fields that you need to create for a new title author recordset. You fill this recordset and then send it back to the server for it to be saved to the database
GetAuthors	Retrieves all the authors that have been entered into the system.
GetAuthorsForTitle	Retrieves all of the authors for the specified title.

THE PUBLISHER CLASS

The `Publisher` class lets you retrieve Publisher-related information from the database. Table 13.4 specifies the name and description for each of the methods supported by the `IPublisher` interface of the `Publisher` class.

TABLE 13.4 Methods for the Publisher Business Object

Object	Description
GetPublishers	Allows the user to associate a title with an Author. Basically they can specify that the author is one of the authors for that title.

Perform the following steps to add the `Book`, `Author`, and `Publisher` classes to your project.

1. Select `New ATL Object...` from the `Insert` menu (the ATL Object Wizard appears).
2. Make sure `Objects` is selected under `Category`, and `Select Simple Object` under `Objects` as shown in Figure 13.20.
3. Click `Next` (the ATL Object Wizard Properties dialog appears as shown in Figure 13.21).
4. Enter `Book` under `Short Name` (see Figure 13.21).
5. Click the `Attributes` tab (you should see the window shown in Figure 13.22).
6. Click `Free` under `Threading Model` and set the `Support ISupportErrorInfo` checkbox.
7. Click `OK`.
8. Repeat steps 1–7 and enter `Author` for the Short Name on step 4.
9. Repeat steps 1–7 and enter `Publisher` for the Short name on step 4.

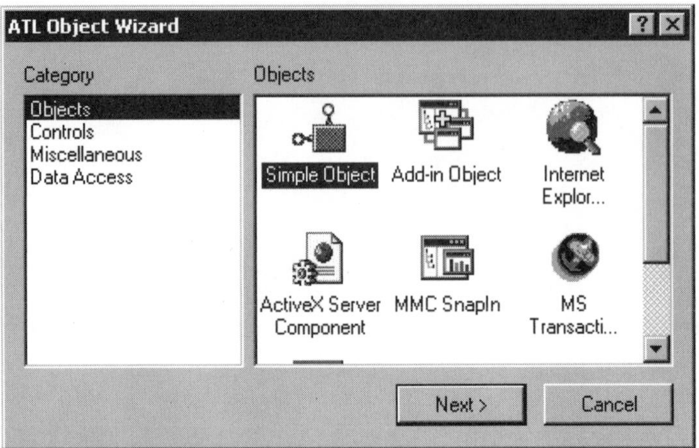

FIGURE 13.20 ATL Object Wizard.

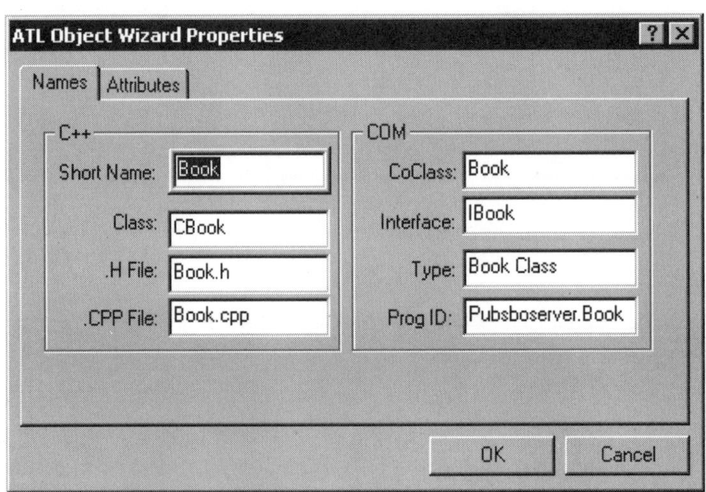

FIGURE 13.21 The Names Tab of the ATL Object Wizard Properties Dialog.

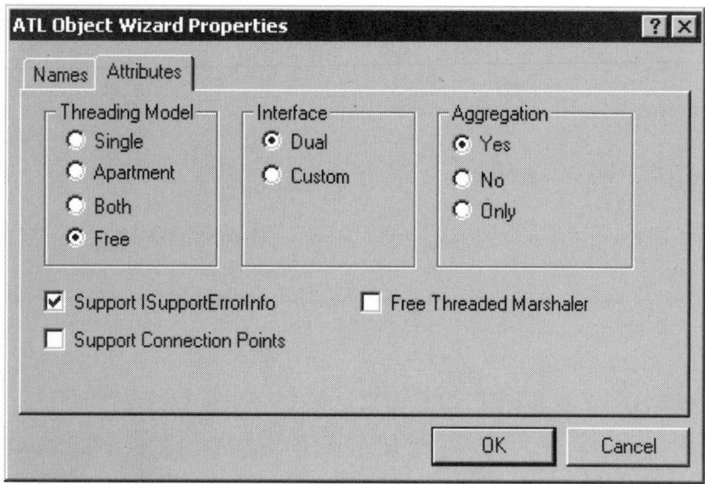

FIGURE 13.22 The Attributes Tab of the ATL Object Wizard Properties Dialog.

Modifying the Project to Work with COM+ and ADO

Now you need to modify your project so it works with COM+. As I mentioned earlier, it's quite possible that Microsoft will release an intermediate version of Visual Studio 6.0 that is designed to work with COM+, thus rendering these steps unnecessary. But for now, if you are using version 6.0 SP3 of Visual Studio, as I am, you need to make these modifications to your project if it is to work with COM+. Also, if you would like to use ADO with your Visual C++ project, you need to make additional modifications to your project.

The ADO modification are independent of COM+. You would need to make the modifications to support ADO if you wanted to use ADO in a Visual C++ project that was not using COM+.

MODIFYING YOUR PROJECT TO WORK WITH COM+

To make a Visual C++ 6.0 project work with COM+, you need to add an include file for `comsvcs.h`. This file contains the prototype for `CoGetObjectContext` and the declaration for a number of COM+-related interfaces such as `IContextState` and `IContextActivity`. To modify your project to support COM+, add the following include file to `stdafx.h`:

```
#include <comsvcs.h>
```

Click on the `FileView` tab in the Visual C++ Workspace and open the `Header files` folder beneath the main project folder to navigate to `stdafx.h`.

`Comsvcs.h` does not reside in the standard Visual C++ include directory. This file is included in the platform SDK. You must install the Platform SDK and configure Visual C++ to use the platform SDK as outlined in the section entitled "Configuring Visual C++ to work with COM+." If you do not do this, nothing else that I show you in this chapter will work.

MODIFYING YOUR PROJECT TO WORK WITH ADO

The easiest way to work with ADO in Visual C++ is to use native COM support to import the ADO type library and generate smart pointer wrapper classes for the objects in the ADO library: Recordset, Connection, Command, and so on. Add the following `#import` statement to the `stdafx.h` file in your project:

```
#import "msado15.dll" rename("EOF","adoEOF") no_namespace
```

Unfortunately, the file `msado15.dll` does not reside in one of the default directories that Visual C++ searches for include files and type libraries. `Msado15.dll` resides, by default, at the following location:

```
DRIVELETTER:\PROGRAM FILES\COMMON FILES\SYSTEM\ADO
```

To use `#import` without specifying the full path for the ADO type library, you must also add this directory to the list of extra include directories in Visual C++. Perform the following steps to add the ADO directory to Visual C++'s default search path:

1. Select `Options` from the `Tools` Menu (the Visual C++ options dialog should appear).
2. Click the `Directories` tab (the window should look like that shown in Figure 13.12).
3. Make sure that `Include Files` is selected in the `Show Directories for` combo box.
4. Click the `New` button.
5. Add an entry for the ADO System directory (your window should look like that shown in Figure 13.23).
6. Click `OK`.

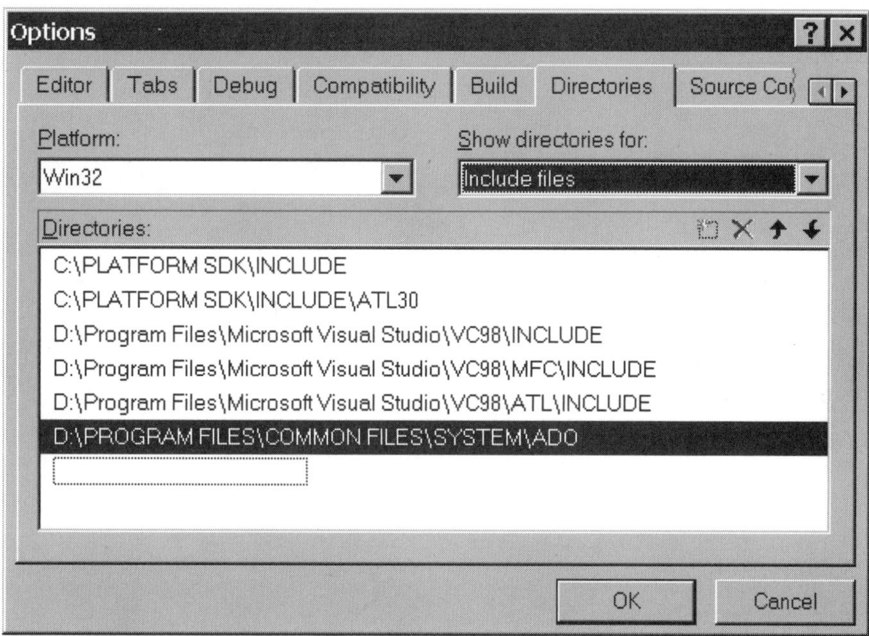

FIGURE 13.23 Adding the ADO System Directory to the Search List.

Using the `#import` statement imports all the needed enumerations and constants and it generates Smart Pointer classes for all the interfaces declared in the ADO type library. This allows the C++ code that you write to use the COM classes and interfaces declared in the type library. Notice that you used the `rename` attribute in the `#import` statement. This is required because the End Of File (EOF) property in the ADO recordset (which is a property you test to see if you have reached the last record in a recordset) conflicts with the EOF constant declared in the C++ standard library. Specifying the rename attribute on `#import` forces it to rename the EOF property to adoEOF. Keep this in mind when writing your code, because now, whenever you refer to the property documented as EOF in the ADO documentation, you need to reference it as adoEOF. The `no_namespace` attribute of `#import` forces the compiler to *not* put the generated classes and enumerations from the type library into a C++ namespace.

When you are done adding both COM+ and ADO support to your project, your `stdafx.h` file should look like that shown in Listing 13.1. The lines that I have added are shown in bold.

LISTING 13.1 *STDAFX.H*

```
if !defined(AFX_STDAFX_H__DA1DCC51_9588_11D3_A0F5_00A0CC330C70__INCLUDED_)
#define AFX_STDAFX_H__DA1DCC51_9588_11D3_A0F5_00A0CC330C70__INCLUDED_

#if _MSC_VER > 1000
#pragma once
#endif // _MSC_VER > 1000

#define STRICT
#ifndef _WIN32_WINNT
#define _WIN32_WINNT 0x0400
#endif
#define _ATL_APARTMENT_THREADED

#include <atlbase.h>
//You may derive a class from CComModule and use it if you want to override
//something, but do not change the name of _Module
extern CComModule _Module;
#include <atlcom.h>
#include <comsvcs.h>
#import "msado15.dll" rename("EOF","adoEOF") no_namespace

//{{AFX_INSERT_LOCATION}}
// Microsoft Visual C++ will insert additional declarations immediately
before the previous line.
#endif
```

Some (most) of the methods in your business objects either take ADO recordsets as inputs or return ADO recordsets to their clients, so you also need to import the ADO type library into your IDL file. You can do this using the `importlib` statement of IDL. This statement functions exactly like `#import` in C++; it imports all the classes, interfaces, and enumerations from the specified type library into the IDL file. This lets you use classes, interfaces, and other types from the ADO type library in the IDL definition of your interfaces. Add the bolded `importlib` statement shown here to the IDL file for your project. If you have followed my naming suggestions, this file should be called `pubsboserver.idl`. Make sure you add the `importlib` statement inside the library declaration for `PUBSBOSERVERLib` as shown here:

```
library PUBSBOSERVERLib
{
   importlib("stdole32.tlb");
   importlib("stdole2.tlb");
   importlib("msado15.dll");
```

```
    [
       uuid(CF166FD0-958C-11D3-A0F5-00A0CC330C70),
       helpstring("Book Class")
    ]
    coclass Book
    {
       [default] interface IBook;
    };
    [
       uuid(6EA2E880-9591-11D3-A0F5-00A0CC330C70),
       helpstring("Author Class")
    ]
    coclass Author
    {
       [default] interface IAuthor;
    };
    [
       uuid(3A5142B5-2705-4E1B-A819-4A29ABFFCB1F),
       helpstring("Publisher Class")
    ]
    coclass Publisher
    {
       [default] interface IPublisher;
    };
};
```

Unfortunately, I have found that just adding the `#importlib` statement to the library definition isn't enough to allow you to use ADO types in the argument lists or return types for your methods. You also need to move the definitions for the `IBook`, `IAuthor`, and `IPublisher` interfaces into the type library specification. Visual C++ initially creates the interfaces for your COM server outside of the type library specification as shown schematically below:

```
[...]
interface IDemo1 : IUnknown
{
}

[...]
interface IDemo2 : IUnknown
{
}

[...]
```

```
library DemoLib
{
   [...]
   class
   {
      interface IDemo1;
      interface IDemo2;
   }
}
```

To compile your application, you need to move the interface definitions inside the library specification so that your code looks similar to that shown below:

```
[...]
library DemoLib
{
   [...]
   interface IDemo1 : IUnknown
   {
   }

   [...]
   interface IDemo2 : IUnknown
   {
   }

   [...]
   class
   {
      interface IDemo1;
      interface IDemo2;
   }
}
```

Move the interface definitions into the library specification using the two listings shown above as a guide. When you have finished modifying the IDL file, it should look like that shown below. I have bolded the lines you should have moved. Remember, your IDL file contains different GUIDs than the one shown here:

```
import "oaidl.idl";
import "ocidl.idl";

[
   uuid(05EBEA10-957A-11D3-A0F5-00A0CC330C70),
   version(1.0),
   helpstring("pubsboserver 1.0 Type Library")
]
library PUBSBOSERVERLib
{
   importlib("stdole32.tlb");
   importlib("stdole2.tlb");
   importlib("msado15.dll");

   [
      object, uuid(73BDE500-9589-11D3-A0F5-00A0CC330C70),
      dual, helpstring("IBook Interface"), pointer_default(unique)
   ]
   interface IBook : IDispatch
   {
   };

   [
      object, uuid(6684B980-9591-11D3-A0F5-00A0CC330C70), dual,
      helpstring("IAuthor Interface"), pointer_default(unique)
   ]
   interface IAuthor : IDispatch
   {
   };

   [
      object, uuid(A456ACFC-1138-4F3F-B6B0-A93AA1DEF91C), dual,
      helpstring("IPublisher Interface"), pointer_default(unique)
   ]
   interface IPublisher : IDispatch
   {
   };

   [
      uuid(CF166FD0-958C-11D3-A0F5-00A0CC330C70),
      helpstring("Book Class")
   ]
   coclass Book
   {
```

```
        [default] interface IBook;
    };
    [
        uuid(6EA2E880-9591-11D3-A0F5-00A0CC330C70),
        helpstring("Author Class")
    ]
    coclass Author
    {
        [default] interface IAuthor;
    };
    [
        uuid(3A5142B5-2705-4E1B-A819-4A29ABFFCB1F),
        helpstring("Publisher Class")
    ]
    coclass Publisher
    {
        [default] interface IPublisher;
    };
};
```

Adding Methods to the Book Class

Perform the following steps to add the RetrieveByKeyword, RetrieveByID, GetNewBookRecordSet, GetExistingBookRecordSet, DeleteBook, and UpdateBooks and methods to the Book class:

1. Right-click on the IBook interface in the ClassView tab of the Visual C++ workspace (as shown in Figure 13.24).
2. Select Add Method... from the Context menu (the Add Method to Interface dialog appears as shown in Figure 13.25).
3. Enter RetrieveByKeyword in the Method Name field.
4. Enter [in] BSTR keyword, [out,retval] _Recordset** rs in the Parameters field.
5. Click OK.
6. Repeat steps 1–4, but enter RetrieveByID in the Method Name field and enter [in] BSTR id, [out,retval] _Recordset** rs in the Parameters field.
7. Repeat steps 1–4, but enter GetNewBookRecordSet in the Method Name field and enter [in] short numRecords,[out,retval] _Recordset **rs in the Parameters field.
8. Repeat steps 1–4, but enter GetExistingBookRecordSet in the Method Name field and enter [in] BSTR criterion,[out,retval] _Recordset** rs in the Parameters field.

9. Repeat steps 1–4, but enter `DeleteBook` in the `Method Name` field and enter `[in] BSTR id` in the `Parameters` field.
10. Repeat steps 1–4, but enter `UpdateBooks` in the `Method Name` field and enter `[in] _Recordset *rsBookInfo,[in] _Recordset *rsAuthorInfo` in the `Parameters` field.

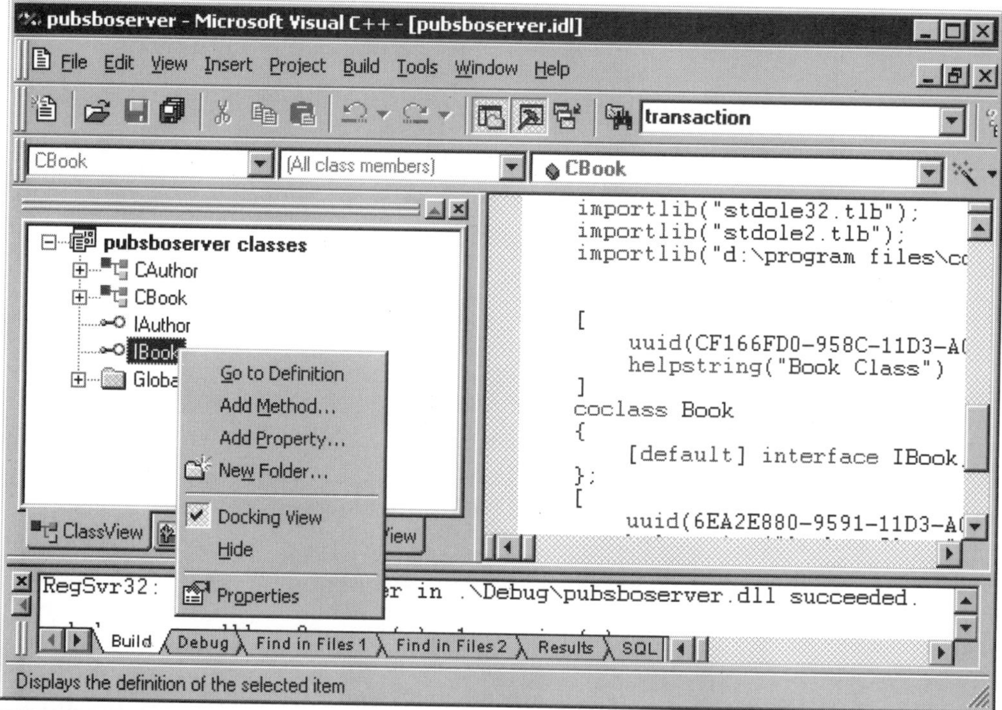

FIGURE 13.24 Adding Methods to the IBook Interface.

FIGURE 13.25 The Add Methods to Interface Dialog.

Visual C++ adds the methods to the IDL for the Book COM class and to the header file for the CBook implementation file. It also adds a skeleton implementation to the source file for the CBook implementation file.

Adding the Author Class Methods

Perform the following steps to add the UpdateAuthorsForTitle, GetAuthors, and GetAuthorsForTitles and GetNewTitle-AuthorRecordSet methods to the Author class.

1. Right-click on the IAuthor interface in the ClassView tab of the Visual C++ workspace.
2. Select Add Method... from the Context menu (the Add Method to Interface dialog appears as shown in Figure 13.25).
3. Enter UpdateAuthorsForTitle in the Method Name field.
4. Enter [in] _Recordset *rs in the Parameters field.
5. Click OK.
6. Repeat steps 1–4, but enter GetAuthors in the Method Name field and [out,retval] _Recordset** rs in the Parameters field.
7. Repeat steps 1–4, but enter GetAuthorsForTitle in the Method Name field and enter [in] BSTR titleID,[out,retval] _Recordset **rs in the Parameters field.
8. Repeat steps 1–4, but enter GetNewTitleAuthorRecordSet in the Method Name field and enter [in] short numRecords,[out,retval] _Recordset **rs in the Parameters field.

Adding the Publisher Class Method

Perform the following steps to add the GetPublishers method to the Publisher class:

1. Right-click on the IPublisher interface in the ClassView tab of the Visual C++ workspace.
2. Select Add Method... from the Context menu (the Add Method to Interface dialog appears as shown in Figure 13.25).
3. Enter GetPublishers in the Method Name field.
4. Enter [out,retval] _Recordset **rs in the Parameters field.
5. Click OK.

The next thing you need to do is to add the necessary code to make your classes work with the IObjectConstruct interface. Implementing this interface lets you configure an OLEDB connection string for each class using the Component Services Explorer.

Adding Support for the IObjectConstruct Interface

One weakness of COM is that it did not support constructors with parameter lists. In most object-oriented programming languages, you can define in each class a method that is called automatically whenever a new object of that type is created. This method is usually called a constructor. In most cases, you can specify that the constructor takes a user-defined set of parameters that you can use to initialize the state of an object. An example of this is the `Employee` class in Chapter 3.

```
#include<string>
using namespace std;
class Employee {
public:
    Employee(int id,const char *nm,float sal);
    virtual ~Employee();
    virtual float GetGrossPay() {
        return GetHoursWorked() * GetHourlyRate();
    }
    int GetHoursWorked() {
        return m_hoursWorked;
    }
    float GetHourlyRate() {
        return m_salary/40;
    }
// Omitted for clarity…
private:
    int m_id;
    string m_name;
    float m_salary;
    short m_hoursWorked;
    short m_numDependents;
};
```

The implementation of the `Employee` constructor is shown below:

```
Employee::Employee(int id,const char *nm,float sal)
{
    m_id=id;
    m_name=nm;
    m_salary=sal;
    m_numEmployees++;
    ::InitializeCriticalSection(&m_critSec);
}
```

With this constructor in the Employee class, you can write the following code to create an Employee object whose state is initialized to: ID=123, Name=Alan Gordon, Salary=250:

```
void main()
{
   Employee emp(123,"Alan Gordon",250.0);
   cout << emp.GetName() << endl;
}
```

With COM you cannot do this. The COM style of initializing an object is that you instantiate the object (using CoCreateInstance for instance) and then you explicitly call an initialization function on one of the object's interfaces. Or you can add an IEmployeeFactory interface to your class object (in addition to IClassFactory) and add a CreateEmployee method that takes the desired parameters. Unfortunately, neither of these solutions is exactly like the constructors in most programming languages because these methods aren't called automatically. You have to remember to call them yourself.

COM+ has a partial solution to the lack of constructors in COM. With COM+, you can define a construction string for each configured class. When the COM+ runtime instantiates a new instance of the class, it will QueryInterface the new instance for the IObjectConstruct interface and pass an object that contains the construction string to the Construct method of the IObjectConstruct interface.

To receive the construction string, a COM+ class must implement the IObjectConstruct interface and in its implementation of the IObjectConstruct::Construct method it should QueryInterface the object it receives for the IObjectConstructString interface. The object can then call the get_ConstructString method of this interface to receive a BSTR that contains the construction string.

The construction string can contain any information that you want. A good use for this string is to pass an OLEDB connection string to your COM+ components.

You can configure the string that will be passed to the component using the Component Services Explorer. To see how this works, right-click on a class in the Component Services Explorer, select Properties... from the Context menu to bring up the component properties dialog and click the Activation tab. You should see the window shown in Figure 13.26. You need to set the Enable object construction checkbox before you can enter a construction string.

To implement the IObjectConstruct interface in the Book, Author, and Publisher classes, add the code shown in bold in Listing 13.2 to the include file for each of these classes. Listing 13.2 contains the code for the Author class.

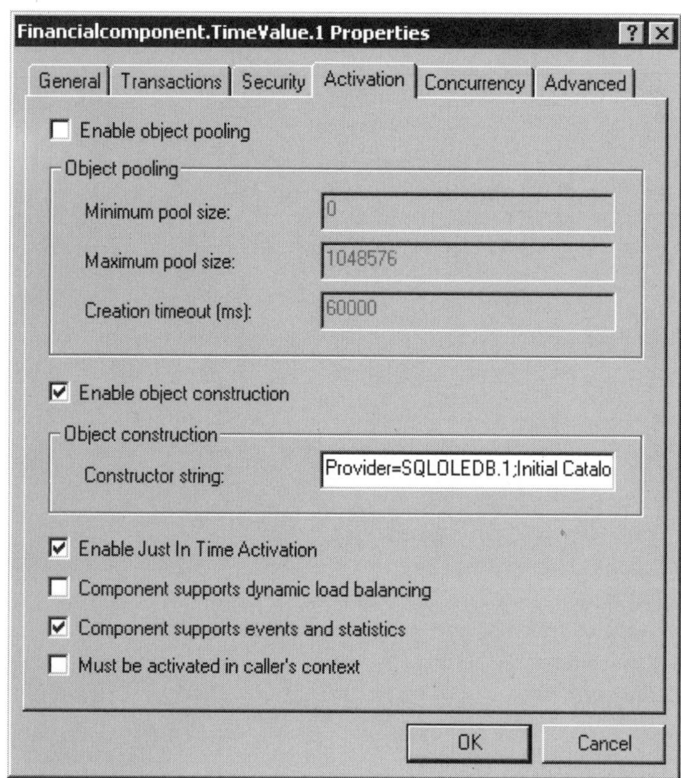

FIGURE 13.26 The Activation Tab of the Component Properties Dialog.

LISTING 13.2 *AUTHOR.H*

```
class ATL_NO_VTABLE CAuthor :
  public CComObjectRootEx<CComMultiThreadModel>,
  public CComCoClass<CAuthor, &CLSID_Author>,
  public ISupportErrorInfo,
  public IDispatchImpl<IAuthor, &IID_IAuthor, &LIBID_PUBSBOSERVERLib>,
  public IObjectConstruct
{
public:
  CAuthor()
  {
  }

DECLARE_REGISTRY_RESOURCEID(IDR_AUTHOR)

```

```
DECLARE_PROTECT_FINAL_CONSTRUCT()

BEGIN_COM_MAP(CAuthor)
   COM_INTERFACE_ENTRY(IAuthor)
   COM_INTERFACE_ENTRY(IDispatch)
   COM_INTERFACE_ENTRY(ISupportErrorInfo)
   COM_INTERFACE_ENTRY(IObjectConstruct)
END_COM_MAP()

// ISupportsErrorInfo
   STDMETHOD(InterfaceSupportsErrorInfo)(REFIID riid);

// IAuthor
public:
   STDMETHOD(UpdateAuthorsForTitle)(/*[in]*/ _Recordset *rs);
   STDMETHOD(GetNewTitleAuthorRecordSet)(/*[in]*/ short
numRecords,/*[out,retval]*/ _Recordset **rs);
   STDMETHOD(GetAuthorsForTitle)(/*[in]*/ BSTR titleID,/
  *[out,retval]*/ _Recordset **rs);
   STDMETHOD(GetAuthors)(/*[out,retval]*/ _Recordset** rs);
// IObjectConstruct
   STDMETHOD(Construct)(IDispatch * pCtorObj)
   {
      _bstr_t strDescription;
      HRESULT hRetval;
      IObjectConstructString *pStr;
      BSTR strConstruct;
      if (pCtorObj != NULL)
      {
         hRetval=pCtorObj->QueryInterface(
            IID_IObjectConstructString,(void **)&pStr);
         if (SUCCEEDED(hRetval))
         {
            hRetval=pStr->get_ConstructString(&strConstruct);
            if (SUCCEEDED(hRetval))
            {
               mConnectionString=strConstruct;
               SysFreeString(strConstruct);
            }
            pStr->Release();
         }
         else
         {
            _com_error err(hRetval);
            strDescription=err.Description();
```

```
57.                 ATLTRACE(err.ErrorMessage());
58.             }
59.         }
60.         else
61.         {
62.             hRetval=E_POINTER;
63.             strDescription=L"An invalid pointer was passed to Construct";
64.         }
65.         if (S_OK==hRetval)
66.             return hRetval;
67.         else
68.             return Error((LPOLESTR)strDescription,IID_IBook,hRetval);
69.     }
70. private:
71.     _bstr_t mConnectionString;
72. };
```

Notice on line 6 of Listing 13.2 that you have added `IObjectConstruct` to the inheritance list for your implementation class. You also added `IObjectConstruct` to the COM map for this class as shown on line 21. Next, you added a private member variable called `mConnectionString` to the class as shown on line 71. Now that you have done this, you can provide the implementation of the `Construct` function as shown on lines 34–69. This implementation first does a `QueryInterface` on the `IDispatch` interface that is passed in to the `Construct` method to get an `IObjectConstructString` interface pointer (see line 42). On line 45, you call the `get_ConstructString` method on `IObjectConstructString` to fetch the construction string into a BSTR. On line 48, you save the construction string into a local variable, `mConnectionString`. Now, whenever an Author object needs to get a connection string to create a new database connection, it can get it from `mConnectionString`. Remember that you need to add the code shown in Listing 13.2 to all the classes in your server: `Book`, `Author`, and `Publisher`.

Implementing the Book Class Methods

When writing code for COM+, or MTS for that matter, it is vital that you have a single exit point for your methods. In other words, you want to avoid this type of logic:

```
int my function(int param1)
{
    if (0 == param1)
        return 2;
    else
        return 1;
}
```

And instead, favor an implementation as follows:

```
int my function(int param1)
{
   int result;
   if (0 == param1)
      result = 2;
   else
      result = 1;
// cleanup code can go here
   return result;
}
```

Why? Because in the second implementation we can put any cleanup or exit code that the method requires at the end of the method. Regardless of which path is taken through the method, you always execute the line(s) at the end of the method.

When you are using COM+, there usually is a lot of cleanup that needs to be done in the methods of your business objects. In most of the business object methods you write, you will make a connection to a database at the start of the method and then close the connection when the method ends. This is the best approach when you are using database connection pooling. You want to acquire your database connection as late as possible and release it as soon as possible. In each method, you may also call `CoGetObjectContext` and/or `CoGetCallContext` to retrieve an interface on either the object context or the call context. You need to make sure that any interface pointers that your business objects acquires in its methods are released before the method returns. It's a good idea to put all of this cleanup logic together at the end of each method and structure the logic of the method so that the cleanup logic is always executed regardless of the path that a thread takes through the method. You will see how to do this in the next section.

RETRIEVEBYKEYWORD

The `RetrieveByKeyword` method allows the user to look up a book by specifying a keyword in the title. You can implement this method as shown in Listing 13.3.

LISTING 13.3 *THE CBOOK::RETRIEVEBYKEYWORD METHOD*

```
STDMETHODIMP CBook::RetrieveByKeyword(BSTR keyword, _Recordset **rs)
{
   _bstr_t strDescription;
   HRESULT hRetval;
   _ConnectionPtr pConn;
   _RecordsetPtr pRS;
   _CommandPtr pCmd;
   _ParameterPtr pParam;
   _variant_t blank(DISP_E_PARAMNOTFOUND, VT_ERROR);
   _bstr_t processedKeyword;
   IContextState *pContxState=NULL;

   if (0==mConnectionString.length())
   {
      hRetval=E_CONFIGURATION;
      strDescription=L"You must configure a connection string";
      goto exit_cleanup;
   }
   hRetval=CoGetObjectContext(IID_IContextState,(void **)&pContxState);
   if (SUCCEEDED(hRetval))
   {
      processedKeyword="%" + bstr_t(keyword) +"%";
      _bstr_t sql("SELECT titles.title_id, titles.title,"\
         " authors.au_lname, authors.au_fname,"\
         " titles.type, titles.price"\
         " FROM authors"\
         " INNER JOIN titleauthor ON authors.au_id=titleauthor.au_id"\
         " INNER JOIN titles ON titleauthor.title_id=titles.title_id"\
         " WHERE (titleauthor.au_ord = 1) AND (titles.title LIKE ?)"\
         " ORDER BY titles.title");

      try
      {
         pConn.CreateInstance( __uuidof(Connection));
         pConn->Open(mConnectionString,"","",-1);
         pCmd.CreateInstance( __uuidof(Command));
         pCmd->CommandType=adCmdText;
         pCmd->CommandText=sql;
         pCmd->ActiveConnection=pConn;
         pParam=pCmd->CreateParameter(_bstr_t(L""),adVarChar,
            adParamInput,80,processedKeyword);
         pCmd->Parameters->Append(pParam);
```

```
            pRS.CreateInstance( __uuidof(Recordset));
            pRS->CursorLocation=adUseClient;
            pRS->Open(pCmd.GetInterfacePtr(),blank,adOpenStatic,
               adLockBatchOptimistic,-1);
            pRS->AddRef();
            *rs=pRS;
            pRS->PutRefActiveConnection(NULL);
        }
        catch ( _com_error err)
        {
            strDescription=err.Description();
            hRetval=err.Error();
        }
    }
    else
    {
        _com_error err(hRetval);
        strDescription=L"Could not retrieve the object context. " \
                       L"Your component is probably not configured";
    }
// Exit and cleanup code
exit_cleanup:
    if (NULL != pContxState)
    {
        if (SUCCEEDED(hRetval))
            pContxState->SetMyTransactionVote(TxCommit);
        else
            pContxState->SetMyTransactionVote(TxAbort);

        pContxState->SetDeactivateOnReturn(VARIANT_TRUE);
        pContxState->Release();
    }
    if (NULL != pConn)
    {
        if (adStateOpen==pConn->GetState())
            pConn->Close();
        pConn=NULL;
    }
    if (SUCCEEDED(hRetval))
        return hRetval;
    else
        return Error((LPOLESTR)strDescription,IID_IBook,hRetval);
}
```

You'll study this method in-depth because the essence of this method is repeated in all the others. On lines 3-11, you have your variable declarations. You first declare a string that you will use to return an error description if something goes wrong. You also declare an HRESULT (`hRetval`) that will be your return value. Next, declare four ADO smart pointers: a Connection, a RecordSet, a Command, and a Parameter. Then you declare a blank variant to pass to methods that take optional parameters. Because C++ is a strongly typed language, you must pass a variable for every argument in the parameter list of a method (including the optional ones). You can pass a variant that has been setup to indicate that it should be ignored, for any optional parameters that you do not wish to use (the method uses the default value for the parameter). Next, declare a `_bstr_t` called `processedKeyword`. `ProcessKeyword` holds the keyword for your query after you append and prepend `%` symbols to the keyword so you can use it in an SQL Like statement. Your last local variable declaration is an `IContextState` interface pointer.

You start the actual processing of this method on line 13. On lines 13–18, check to see if the component has a zero length connection string (indicating the user has not configured an OLEDB connection string). You perform this check in the `RetrieveByKeyword` method because it is the entry point for both of the client applications. For production quality code, you would perform this check in *all* methods. On line 19, you obtain the `IContextState` interface on your object context. On line 20, we check to see if the call to `CoGetObjectContext` succeeded. If it didn't succeed, that most likely indicates the component has not been configured.

You next start the database processing of your method. You are going to use an SQL query with a `Like` clause in order to do our keyword match. You use the SQL `Like` clause to do wildcard searches. For instance, to find all people whose last name begins with G, you would use the following `Where` clause:

```
WHERE last_name like G%
```

The `Like` clause uses the `%` symbol as its wildcard symbol; `%` represents any number of characters. In your case, you want to find all the books that contain a certain word in their title; the `Where` clause for this query is as follows:

```
WHERE titles.title LIKE %keyword%
```

You don't want your users to have to put the % before and after their requested keyword, so you can append these as shown on line 22. On lines 23–30, define the SQL query that you will execute. I really don't want to go in-depth into the syntax of this query. Suffice to say that if you want to develop enterprise-class, distributed application with any technology—COM+, CORBA, or Java Beans—you need to learn SQL. In this query, I perform two joins to receive data from the titles, titleauthor, and authors tables. Notice that I use a parameterized query in this case (that's why the question mark appears in the `Where` clause). You could just as easily issue this query by building up the entire SQL string programmatically. I usually like to use parametrized queries (in some situations you have no choice but to construct the query string programmatically) because they are less error-prone and easier to port to different database products.

All COM methods are supposed to return an HRESULT. The COM style of error handling is that you should test this HRESULT after each method call. The smart pointers classes generated by the Visual C++ `#import` statement retrieve the HRESULT after each method call and throw C++ exceptions if there is an error. You can override this behavior if you want, but personally I prefer this style of error handling.

You can tell the `#import` statement not to generate smart pointer using the `raw_interfaces_only` attribute to `#import`.

To catch the exceptions from your ADO smart pointer classes, you must enclose your ADO method calls in a try block as shown on lines 32–55. If you do use C++ exception handling, then you should enable exception handling in the Visual C++ compiler. To do this, perform the following steps in the Visual C++ Workspace:

1. Select `Settings...` from the `Project` menu (the Project Settings dialog appears as shown in Figure 13.27).
2. Click the `C/C++` tab.
3. Make sure that `C++ Language` is selected for the Category.
4. Set the `Enable exception handling` checkbox.
5. Click `OK`.

On lines 34–49, use ADO to execute your database query. On lines 34 and 35, you create and open a database connection using the connection string in the `mConnectionString` member variable. If you are doing a parameterized query, you must construct an ADO Command object so you can specify values for the query parameters. On line 36, create an ADO Command object.

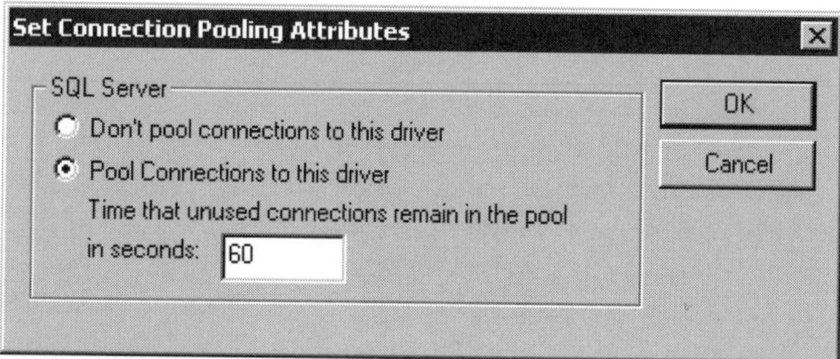

FIGURE 13.27 The C/C++ Tab of the Project Settings Dialog.

On line 37, you specify that the ADO Command object is used to execute an SQL query (you can also use Commands to execute stored procedures). And on line 38, you set the query text for the Command object equal to the SQL string that you defined on lines 23–30. On line 39, set the active connection of the Command object equal to the connection that you created and opened on lines 34 and 35. On lines 40 and 41, you create a parameter that you can use when you execute your query, and on line 42 you append the parameter to the Command. On lines 43, 44, and 45, you create an ADO recordset object, set the cursor location for the recordset to be on the client (the client of the database is your business object), and then you open the recordset by passing the underlying Interface pointer for the Command object to the Open method of the RecordSet. This causes the query to actually execute.

On line 47, we call the `AddRef` method on the record set. You must do this because you are using smart pointers. The destructor for the smart pointer instance, pRS, is called when the `RetrieveByKeyword` method returns and this destructor calls the `Release` method on its underlying Recordset pointer. Unfortunately, this is the same Recordset pointer that you want to return to your base client. But, if you increment the reference count before you return, then the RecordSet object is not destroyed. On line 48, you assign the output Recordset to the Recordset smart pointer, and then on line 49 you set the active connection on the recordset to NULL. This last step is important because it creates a disconnected recordset. I talked about ADO's ability to support disconnected recordsets earlier in this chapter. When you are passing ADO recordsets between processes, as you are here, they should be disconnected recordsets. On line 51, you start the catch part of your try statement where you handle any errors generated by the try block. In your case, the only exception you need to catch is the one that is fired by the smart pointers, `_com_error`. If you catch an exception, you call the `Error` method on `_com_error` to retrieve the HRESULT number from the `_com_error` object and then you call the `Description` method to get a textual description of the error.

On line 65–84, you perform the cleanup logic for this method. You use the same cleanup logic for all the methods so it is important to understand how it works. Remember that you must be careful how you write this code because you execute this cleanup logic each time you call the method. So it has to handle all possible failure modes. For instance, notice on line 65 that you check to see if the Context State is NULL before you try to set the Transaction Vote and DeactivateOnReturn bits. This is so you correctly handle the case where you weren't able to obtain the `pContextState` interface pointer from the `CoGetObjectContext` method. If you did receive a valid `IContextState` interface pointer, then on line 67 you check to see if the `RetrieveByKeyword` method was successful. If the method was successful, call the `SetMyTransactionVote` method on your `IContextState` interface pointer and pass `txCommit` for the parameter. If the method was unsuccessful, you pass `txAbort` to the `SetMyTransactionVote` method. The `RetrieveByKeyword` method only does queries, so there really is no need to use `txAbort` (there are no updates to rollback), you just need to end the transaction and you can do that with `txCommit`. I leave the logic this way for consistency with the methods that do require a rollback.

On line 72, you call the `SetDeactivateOnReturn` method on `IContextState` and pass in an argument of `VARIANT_TRUE`. This causes the object to be deactivated when the method returns. The DTC can commit the transaction anytime after this. The DTC waits until all the other participants in the transaction have voted on its outcome. You then release the `IContextState` interface pointer on line 73.

On lines 75–80, make sure you cleanup your database connection. On line 75, check to see if the connection is NULL; if it isn't, then check to see if the connection is open. If it is open, close it and then set the connection object to NULL.

On lines 81–84, you return an HRESULT back to your client. If the method executed successfully, you return the variable `hRetval`, which contains the value `S_OK`. If the method did *not* return successfully, call the ATL Error function to send rich error information to your client. You pass the error description, the IID for the `IBook` interface, and `hRetval`. The ATL Error function sets up a COM error that the client's programming environment can map to its native error handling mechanism.

The `RetrieveByKeyword` method uses a user-defined HRESULT, `E_CONFIGURATION`, so you must add a declaration for this HRESULT to the `Book.cpp`. Add a declaration for `E_CONFIGURATION` below the include files in the `Book.cpp` file as shown in bold below.

```
//  Book.cpp  :  Implementation of Cbook
#include  "stdafx.h"
#include  "Pubsboserver.h"
#include  "Book.h"
const E_CONFIGURATION=MAKE_HRESULT (SEVERITY_ERROR, FACILITY_ITF,
0x200+108);
```

RETRIEVEBYID

The RetrieveByID method is similar to RetrieveByKeyword. The main difference is that the RetrieveByKeyword method allows you to find a book by specifying its titleID (its primary key) instead of a keyword in its title. The implementation of the RetrieveByID method is shown in Listing 13.4.

LISTING 13.4 *THE CBOOK::RETRIEVEBYID*

```
STDMETHODIMP CBook::RetrieveByID(BSTR id, _Recordset **rs)
{
   HRESULT hRetval;
   _bstr_t strDescription;
   _variant_t blank(DISP_E_PARAMNOTFOUND, VT_ERROR);
   _bstr_t sql("SELECT titles.title_id, titles.title, titles.price,"\
      " titles.advance, titles.royalty, titles.ytd_sales, "\
      " titles.notes, titles.type,titles.pubdate, titles.pub_id,"\
      " publishers.pub_name, authors.au_id, authors.au_lname,"\
      " authors.au_fname"\
      " FROM titles "\
      " INNER JOIN publishers ON titles.pub_id=publishers.pub_id "\
      " INNER JOIN titleauthor ON titles.title_id=titleauthor.title_id"\
      " INNER JOIN authors ON titleauthor.au_id=authors.au_id"\
      " WHERE (titleauthor.au_ord = 1) AND (titles.title_id = ?)");
   _ConnectionPtr pConn;
   _RecordsetPtr pRS;
   _CommandPtr pCmd;
   _ParameterPtr pParam;
   IContextState *pContxState;

   hRetval=CoGetObjectContext(IID_IContextState,(void**)&pContxState);
   if (SUCCEEDED(hRetval))
   {
      try
      {
         pConn.CreateInstance( __uuidof(Connection));
         pConn->Open(mConnectionString, "", "",-1);
         pCmd.CreateInstance( __uuidof(Command));
         pCmd->CommandType=adCmdText;
         pCmd->CommandText=sql;
         pCmd->ActiveConnection=pConn;
         pParam=pCmd->CreateParameter(_bstr_t(L""),adVarChar,
            adParamInput,6,id);
         pCmd->Parameters->Append(pParam);
         pRS.CreateInstance( __uuidof(Recordset));
```

```
            pRS->CursorLocation=adUseClient;
            pRS->Open(pCmd.GetInterfacePtr(),blank,adOpenStatic,
                adLockBatchOptimistic,-1);
            pRS->AddRef();
            *rs=pRS;
            pRS->PutRefActiveConnection(NULL);
        }
        catch ( _com_error err)
        {
            strDescription=err.Description();
            hRetval=err.Error();
        }
    }
    else
    {
        _com_error err(hRetval);
        strDescription=L"Could not retrieve the object context. " \
                       L"Your component is probably not configured";
    }
// Exit and cleanup code
    if (NULL != pContxState)
    {
        if (SUCCEEDED(hRetval))
            pContxState->SetMyTransactionVote(TxCommit);
        else
            pContxState->SetMyTransactionVote(TxAbort);

        pContxState->SetDeactivateOnReturn(VARIANT_TRUE);
        pContxState->Release();
    }
    if (NULL != pConn)
    {
        if (adStateOpen==pConn->GetState())
            pConn->Close();
        pConn=NULL;
    }
    if (SUCCEEDED(hRetval))
        return hRetval;
    else
        return Error((LPOLESTR)strDescription,IID_IBook,hRetval);
}
```

Notice that this method is similar to `RetrieveByKeyword`. In fact, the only difference is that it performs a different query and I don't check for a zero length connection string.

GETNEWBOOKRECORDSET AND GETEXISTINGBOOKRECORDSET

The `GetNewBookRecordSet` and `GetExistingBookRecordSet` methods are needed to make it easy for the client to do updates. When the client wants to create a new book, it calls `GetNewBookRecordSet` and receives a disconnected ADO recordset that contains all the fields it needs to fill in to create a new book. The client can then fill in these fields and pass them to the `UpdateBooks` method on the Book object. Updating an existing book is similar. To update an existing book, the client calls `GetExistingBookRecordSet` to receive a Recordset that contains all the fields for an existing book. The client can then alter the fields and pass the modified Recordset to the UpdateBooks method to be saved.

GETNEWBOOKRECORDSET • The implementation of `GetNewBookRecordSet` is shown in Listing 13.5.

LISTING 13.5 *CBOOK::GETNEWBOOKRECORDSET*

```
STDMETHODIMP CBook::GetNewBookRecordSet(short numRecords, _Recordset **rs)
{
    _bstr_t strDescription;
    HRESULT hRetval;

    _ConnectionPtr pConn;
    _RecordsetPtr pRS;
    _CommandPtr pCmd;
    _ParameterPtr pParam;
    int i;
    _variant_t blank(DISP_E_PARAMNOTFOUND, VT_ERROR);
    IContextState *pContxState;

    hRetval=CoGetObjectContext(IID_IContextState,(void **)&pContxState);
    if (SUCCEEDED(hRetval))
    {
            bstr_t sql("SELECT titles.title_id, titles.title,"\
                " titles.price, titles.advance, titles.royalty,"\
                " titles.ytd_sales, titles.notes, titles.type,"\
                " titles.pubdate,titles.pub_id"\
                " FROM titles"\
                " WHERE (1 = 2)");
        try
        {
```

```
         pConn.CreateInstance( __uuidof(Connection));
         pConn->Open(mConnectionString,"","",-1);
         pRS.CreateInstance( __uuidof(Recordset));
         pRS->CursorLocation=adUseClient;
         pRS->Open(sql,pConn.GetInterfacePtr(),adOpenStatic,
            adLockBatchOptimistic,-1);
         pRS->AddRef();
         for (i=0;i<numRecords;i++)
            pRS->AddNew();
         pRS->MoveFirst();
         *rs=pRS;
         pRS->PutRefActiveConnection(NULL);
      }
      catch ( _com_error err)
      {
         strDescription=err.Description();
         hRetval=err.Error();
      }
   }
   else
   {
      _com_error err(hRetval);
      strDescription=L"Could not retrieve the object context. " \
                    L"Your component is probably not configured";
   }
// Exit and cleanup code
   if (NULL != pContxState)
   {
      if (SUCCEEDED(hRetval))
         pContxState->SetMyTransactionVote(TxCommit);
      else
         pContxState->SetMyTransactionVote(TxAbort);

      pContxState->SetDeactivateOnReturn(VARIANT_TRUE);
      pContxState->Release();
   }
   if (NULL != pConn)
   {
      if (adStateOpen==pConn->GetState())
         pConn->Close();
```

```
65.         pConn=NULL;
66.     }
67.     if (SUCCEEDED(hRetval))
68.         return hRetval;
69.     else
70.         return Error((LPOLESTR)strDescription,IID_IBook,hRetval);
71. }
```

The implementation has some important differences from the `RetrieveByKeyword` and `RetrieveByID` methods. First, the query is different. Notice on line 22 that the `Where` clause used in this query is the rather odd `WHERE 1=2` statement. This is a trick I have seen done a number of times to quickly generate a new, empty recordset for a database table. Next, on lines 32 and 33, you call the `AddNew` method on the ADO RecordSet to create the number of new records the user requested. On line 34, you move the current position on the RecordSet back to the first record; Then, set the output RecordSet value and disconnect the RecordSet. The rest of the logic is error handling and cleanup.

GETEXISTINGBOOKRECORDSET • The implementation of `GetExistingBookRecordSet` is shown in Listing 13.6.

LISTING 13.6 *CBOOK::GETEXISTINGBOOKRECORDSET*

```
STDMETHODIMP CBook::GetExistingBookRecordSet(BSTR criterion, _Recordset **rs)
{
    _bstr_t strDescription;
    HRESULT hRetval;

    _ConnectionPtr pConn;
    _RecordsetPtr pRS;
    _CommandPtr pCmd;
    _ParameterPtr pParam;

    _variant_t blank(DISP_E_PARAMNOTFOUND, VT_ERROR);
    IContextState *pContxState;

    hRetval=CoGetObjectContext(IID_IContextState,(void **)&pContxState);
    if (SUCCEEDED(hRetval))
    {
        bstr_t sql("SELECT titles.title_id, titles.title, titles.price,"\
            " titles.advance, titles.royalty, titles.ytd_sales,"\
            " titles.notes, titles.type, titles.pubdate, titles.pub_id"\
            " FROM titles WHERE ");
```

```
        sql=sql+criterion;

        try
        {
            pConn.CreateInstance( __uuidof(Connection));
            pConn->Open(mConnectionString,"","",-1);
            pRS.CreateInstance( __uuidof(Recordset));
            pRS->CursorLocation=adUseClient;
            pRS->Open(sql,pConn.GetInterfacePtr(),adOpenStatic,
                adLockBatchOptimistic,-1);
            pRS->AddRef();
            *rs=pRS;
            pRS->PutRefActiveConnection(NULL);
        }
        catch ( _com_error err)
        {
            strDescription=err.Description();
            hRetval=err.Error();
        }
    }
    else
    {
        _com_error err(hRetval);
        strDescription=L"Could not retrieve the object context. " \
                        L"Your component is probably not configured";
    }
// Exit and cleanup code
    if (NULL != pContxState)
    {
        if (SUCCEEDED(hRetval))
            pContxState->SetMyTransactionVote(TxCommit);
        else
            pContxState->SetMyTransactionVote(TxAbort);

        pContxState->SetDeactivateOnReturn(VARIANT_TRUE);
        pContxState->Release();
    }
    if (NULL != pConn)
    {
        if (adStateOpen==pConn->GetState())
            pConn->Close();
```

```
        pConn=NULL;
    }
    if (SUCCEEDED(hRetval))
        return hRetval;
    else
        return Error((LPOLESTR)strDescription,IID_IBook,hRetval);
}
```

The implementation of this method is similar to GetNewBook-RecordSet, the only difference is that the user is allowed to specify a Where clause that is used to fetch one or more existing books.

UPDATEBOOKS

The implementation of UpdateBooks is shown in Listing 13.7.

LISTING 13.7 *CBOOK::UPDATEBOOKS*

```
STDMETHODIMP CBook::UpdateBooks(_Recordset *rsBookInfo, _Recordset
    *rsAuthorInfo)
{
    HRESULT hRetval;
    _bstr_t strDescription;
    _ConnectionPtr pConn;
    _RecordsetPtr pRS;
    _variant_t blank(DISP_E_PARAMNOTFOUND, VT_ERROR);
    _bstr_t strMsg;
    CComPtr<IAuthor> authorPtr;
    BSTR strError;
    IErrorInfo* pei;
    IContextState *pContxState;

    hRetval=CoGetObjectContext(IID_IContextState,(void **)&pContxState);
    if (SUCCEEDED(hRetval))
    {
        if (NULL != rsBookInfo)
        {
            try
            {
                pRS=rsBookInfo;
                pConn.CreateInstance( __uuidof(Connection));
                pConn->Open(mConnectionString, "", "",-1);
                pRS->PutRefActiveConnection(pConn);
                pRS->UpdateBatch(adAffectAll);
                pRS->Filter=_variant_t((short)adFilterConflictingRecords);
```

```
                if (pRS->RecordCount > 0)
                {
                    strMsg="The following books could not be updated: ";
                    while (pRS->adoEOF != VARIANT_TRUE)
                    {
                        strMsg+=_bstr_t(
                            pRS->Fields->Item["title_id"]->Value)+" ";
                        pRS->MoveNext();
                    }
                    strDescription=strMsg;
                    hRetval=E_CONFLICTS_FOUND;
                }
            }
            catch ( _com_error err)
            {
                strDescription=err.Description();
                hRetval=err.Error();
            }
        }
        else
            hRetval=S_OK;

        if (NULL != rsAuthorInfo && S_OK == hRetval)
        {
            hRetval=authorPtr.CoCreateInstance(__uuidof(Author));
            if (SUCCEEDED(hRetval))
            {
                hRetval=authorPtr->UpdateAuthorsForTitle(rsAuthorInfo);
                if (FAILED(hRetval))
                {
                    if (SUCCEEDED(GetErrorInfo(0, &pei)))
                        if (pei)
                            if (SUCCEEDED(pei->GetDescription(&strError)))
                                    pei->Release();
                    strDescription=strError;
                }
            }
        }
    }
    else
    {
        _com_error err(hRetval);
        strDescription=L"Could not retrieve the object context. " \
                    L"Your component is probably not configured";
```

```
71.    }
72. // Exit and cleanup code
73.    if (NULL != pContxState)
74.    {
75.       if (SUCCEEDED(hRetval))
76.          pContxState->SetMyTransactionVote(TxCommit);
77.       else
78.          pContxState->SetMyTransactionVote(TxAbort);
79.
80.       pContxState->SetDeactivateOnReturn(VARIANT_TRUE);
81.       pContxState->Release();
82.    }
83.    if (NULL != pConn)
84.    {
85.       if (adStateOpen==pConn->GetState())
86.          pConn->Close();
87.       pConn=NULL;
88.    }
89.
90.    if (SUCCEEDED(hRetval))
91.       return hRetval;
92.    else
93.       return Error((LPOLESTR)strDescription,IID_IBook,hRetval);
94. }
```

Because the implementation of `UpdateBooks` is different from anything you have seen so far, I need to discuss this method. `UpdateBooks` takes two disconnected, ADO Recordsets as input. One Recordset, `rsBookInfo`, contains purely book-related information: the title ID, title, price, notes, and so on. The second Recordset, `rsAuthorInfo`, contains a list of authors for the book. The book object updates the book-related information and then creates an Author object and delegates the saving of the author information to the Author object. You don't have to implement this method this way. I just wanted to have an example showing a multi-object transaction. Both the Book and Author objects do their updates by creating a database connection, reconnecting their input Recordsets to the database through this connection, and then using the `UpdateBatch` method on the ADO recordset to propogate the required changes to the database.

In the `Updatebooks` method shown in Listing 13.7, you first have variable declarations on lines 3–12. There are two variable declarations on lines 9 and 11 that you haven't seen before. On line 9, you declare a COM interface pointer using the generic `CComPtr` smart pointer class that is a part of ATL.

`CComPtr` class is an ATL smart pointer class similar to the smart pointers that are generated by `#import`.

This `CComPtr` instance holds an interface pointer on the Author object. On line 11, you declare an `IErrorInfo` interface pointer. You need this pointer because the Author object returns errors using COM programming language-independent exceptions. Because you are not calling the Author object through a `#import`-generated smart pointer, you cannot use exceptions to catch this error. You must manually write the logic to extract this error information (see lines 55–62 in Listing 13.7). To do this, you need an `IErrorInfo` interface pointer.

On line 14, you do the usual call to `CoGetObjectContext` to retrieve the `IContextState` interface on the object context. The `UpdateBooks` method in the Book business object is implemented so you can pass a NULL recordset for the book information if you just want to update author information or vice versa. You can pass a NULL recordset for the author-related information if you just want to update book information. So on line 17, you check that the recordset that contains book information is not NULL. If it isn't NULL, you begin updating the book information.

You first enter a try block and then on line 21 you assign a Recordset smart pointer to the raw RecordSet pointer that contains book information. Next, on lines 22 and 23, you create and open a connection using the database connection string that was cached in the `IObjectConstruct::Construct` method. On line 24, you reconnect the recordset to the database by assigning your new connection to the `ActiveConnection` property of the RecordSet. Then, on line 25, you call the `UpdateBatch` method on the smart pointer. `UpdateBatch` tries to save all the records in the recordset to the database. If a record has been updated, it tries to update the record; if the record has been deleted, it attempts a delete; if a record has been added, it attempts to insert the record into the database. `UpdateBatch` is not going to work properly with all recordsets. Your recordset must have been created with the `adLockBatch` Optimistic lock setting as shown below for `UpdateBatch` to work:

```
pRS->Open(pCmd.GetInterfacePtr(),blank,adOpenStatic,
          adLockBatchOptimistic,-1);
```

Also, if your query was created from a complicated join, `UpdateBatch` may not be able to update the recordset. That's why your Book business object provides the `GetNewBookRecordSet` and `GetExistingBookRecordSet` methods. These methods return a recordset that is not the result of a join. The idea is that when you want to do an update or insert, you first get a recordset from one of these methods

(GetNewBookRecordSet for inserts and GetExistingBookRecordSet for updates) and then you modify data in the Recordset and pass the recordset to the UpdateBook method.

UpdateBatch won't stop if it has problems updating a particular record in the recordset. It just keeps going. To see if any records failed to update, you can filter the recordset using adFilterConflictingRecords. This filters the recordset so that it contains only records that failed to update.

You can clear the filter (display all records in the recordset) by applying the adFilterNone filter to the recordset.

On lines 26, you apply the adFilterConflictingRecords filter. Then you check to see if the recordset contains any records after the filter has been applied (this indicates that some records failed to update). If you find any failed records, you build up an error description string that contains the title_id of all the records that failed to update. Then on line 36, you assign this conflicted records string to your error description string and set the return HRESULT equal to a user-defined value, E_CONFLICTS_FOUND. Since you will also use this user-defined HRESULT in the Author class, you might as well put it in a separate include file so you can use it easily in both places. To create this include file, perform the following steps in the Visual C++ Workspace:

1. Select New... from the File menu (the New dialog appears).
2. Click the Files tab.
3. Select C/C++ Header File from the Files list.
4. Enter errorcodes in the File name: field.
5. Click OK.

Visual C++ adds a file called errorcodes.h to your project. Add the following code to this file:

```
#ifndef ERROR_CODES_H
#define ERROR_CODES_H
const E_CONFLICTS_FOUND=MAKE_HRESULT(SEVERITY_ERROR,FACILITY_ITF,
0x200+109);
#endif
```

Make sure you add the following include statements to the .cpp file for the Book class:

```
#include "errorcodes.h"
```

Remember, `stdafx.h` must always be the first include file, in every source file unless you change the pre-compiled header settings. So make sure you add `errorcodes.h` below `stdafx.h`.

The code for the `UpdateBooks` method (Listing 13.7) starts getting interesting again on line 49, that's where you check to see if you need to update author information for the book. Notice that you check to see if there is author information to update (`NULL != rsAuthorInfo`) and that the update of the book information was successful (`S_OK == hRetval`). If either of these conditions are FALSE, there is no point in even attempting to update the Author information. If both of these conditions are true, you begin the Author information update by creating a new author object on line 51. Use the `CoCreateInstance` function on `CComPtr` and pass in the CLSID for the `Author` class.

On line 50 you are seeing a big improvement that COM+ made over MTS. With MTS, if one object wanted to create a second object and have this second object share the same transaction, you had to call the `CreateInstance` method on the `IObjectContext` interface. With COM+, this is no longer necessary. You just create the object as you normally would and the COM+ runtime decides if the two objects can share the same transaction (or other attributes) based on their configuration settings.

If the call to `CoCreateInstance` succeeds, you call the `UpdateAuthorsForTitle` method on line 54 and pass in the Recordset of author information. The Author object returns rich error information if any of its methods abort a transaction for any reason. To retrieve the HRESULT and description of the error, you call `GetErrorInfo` on line 57 to fetch an `IErrorInfo` interface pointer, then on line 59 you retrieve the description that was stored for the error and finally, on line 61, you store the error description in the string that you pass back to your base client.

All transactional, COM+ objects should return an HRESULT indicating failure (or preferably return rich error information) whenever one of their methods aborts a transaction. Remember, once one object involved in a muti-object transaction votes to abort the transaction by returning from a method with its deactivate-on-return bit set to TRUE and its transaction vote bit set to FALSE, the transaction is doomed; there's no point in going any further.

On lines 73–93, you perform the usual cleanup and exit logic. This time, it is critical that you abort the transaction by passing `txAbort` to the `SetMyTransactionVote` method if anything went wrong. In the read-only methods, you can commit the transaction in all circumstances because there is no danger that you might save partial or incomplete information to the database if one of the operations fail. But when you are doing updates, you might save partial or incomplete information if you commit the transaction when one of the operations has failed.

DELETEBOOK

The last method in the Book class is the DeleteBook method. This method deletes the book with the specified ID. The implementation of this method is shown in Listing 13.8.

LISTING 13.8 *CBOOK::DELETEBOOK*

```
STDMETHODIMP CBook::DeleteBook(BSTR id)
{
   _bstr_t strDescription;
   HRESULT hRetval;
   _variant_t blank(DISP_E_PARAMNOTFOUND, VT_ERROR);
   _bstr_t sqlDeleteTitleAuthor("DELETE FROM titleauthor"\
      " WHERE title_id = ?");
   _bstr_t sqlDeleteTitle("DELETE FROM titles"\
      " WHERE titles.title_id = ?");
   _RecordsetPtr pRS;
   _CommandPtr pCmd;
   _ConnectionPtr pConn;
   _ParameterPtr pParam;
   IContextState *pContxState;
   hRetval=CoGetObjectContext(IID_IContextState,(void **)&pContxState);
   if (SUCCEEDED(hRetval))
   {
      try
      {
         pConn.CreateInstance( __uuidof(Connection));
         pConn->Open(mConnectionString,"","",-1);
         pCmd.CreateInstance( __uuidof(Command));
         pCmd->CommandType=adCmdText;
         pCmd->CommandText=sqlDeleteTitleAuthor;
         pCmd->ActiveConnection=pConn;
         pParam=pCmd->CreateParameter(_bstr_t(""),adVarChar,
            adParamInput,6,id);
         pCmd->Parameters->Append(pParam);
         pCmd->Execute(&blank,&blank,-1);
         pCmd->CommandText=sqlDeleteTitle;
         pCmd->Execute(&blank,&blank,-1);
```

```
32.             hRetval=S_OK;
33.         }
34.         catch ( _com_error err)
35.         {
36.             strDescription=err.Description();
37.             hRetval=err.Error();
38.         }
39.     }
40.     else
41.     {
42.         _com_error err(hRetval);
43.         strDescription=L"Could not retrieve the object context. " \
44.                        L"Your component is probably not configured";
45.     }
46. // Exit and cleanup code
47.     if (NULL != pContxState)
48.     {
49.         if (SUCCEEDED(hRetval))
50.             pContxState->SetMyTransactionVote(TxCommit);
51.         else
52.             pContxState->SetMyTransactionVote(TxAbort);
53.
54.         pContxState->SetDeactivateOnReturn(VARIANT_TRUE);
55.         pContxState->Release();
56.     }
57.     if (NULL != pConn)
58.     {
59.         if (adStateOpen==pConn->GetState())
60.             pConn->Close();
61.         pConn=NULL;
62.     }
63.     if (SUCCEEDED(hRetval))
64.         return hRetval;
65.     else
66.         return Error((LPOLESTR)strDescription,IID_IBook,hRetval);
67. }
```

Before you delete a book, you must first delete the records in the titleauthor table that link the book to its authors. On lines 6–9 of Listing 13.8, you declare two queries. You use the first query to delete the titleauthor records; you use the second query to delete the book from the title table. On lines 20–32, you execute both queries. The rest of the code is the usual exit and cleanup logic.

Implementing the Author Methods

The Author business object in your server has four methods that you must implement: `UpdateAuthorsForTitle`, `GetAuthors`, `GetAuthors-ForTitle`, and `GetNewTitleAuthorRecordSet`.

GETAUTHORS

The `GetAuthors` method returns a recordset that contains all the authors that have been defined in the database. The implementation of this method is shown in Listing 13.9. This method doesn't contain any logic that you haven't already seen. It executes a query that returns the ID, first name, and last name of all the authors in the database. In this case, because the query doesn't have any parameters, you don't need an ADO Command object; you simply pass the query string and an open connection to the `Open` method of an ADO `RecordSet` object. You then perform the usual cleanup and exit logic.

LISTING 13.9 *CAUTHOR::GETAUTHORS*

```
STDMETHODIMP CAuthor::GetAuthors(_Recordset **rs)
{
    HRESULT hRetval;
    _bstr_t strDescription;
    _variant_t blank(DISP_E_PARAMNOTFOUND, VT_ERROR);
    _bstr_t sql("SELECT au_id, au_fname, au_lname FROM AUTHORS");
    _RecordsetPtr pRS;
    _ConnectionPtr pConn;
    IContextState *pContxState;

    hRetval=CoGetObjectContext(IID_IContextState,(void **)&pContxState);
    if (SUCCEEDED(hRetval))
    {
        try
        {
            pConn.CreateInstance( __uuidof(Connection));
            pConn->Open(mConnectionString,"","",-1);
            pRS.CreateInstance( __uuidof(Recordset));
            pRS->CursorLocation=adUseClient;
            pRS->Open(sql,pConn.GetInterfacePtr(),adOpenStatic,
                adLockBatchOptimistic,-1);
            pRS->AddRef();
            *rs=pRS;
            pRS->PutRefActiveConnection(NULL);
        }
```

```
        catch ( _com_error err)
        {
            strDescription=err.Description();
            hRetval=err.Error();
        }
    }
    else
    {
        _com_error err(hRetval);
        strDescription=L"Could not retrieve the object context. " \
                        L"Your component is probably not configured";
    }
// Exit and cleanup code
    if (NULL != pContxState)
    {
        if (SUCCEEDED(hRetval))
            pContxState->SetMyTransactionVote(TxCommit);
        else
            pContxState->SetMyTransactionVote(TxAbort);
        pContxState->SetDeactivateOnReturn(VARIANT_TRUE);
        pContxState->Release();
    }
    if (NULL != pConn)
    {
        if (adStateOpen==pConn->GetState())
            pConn->Close();
        pConn=NULL;
    }
    if (SUCCEEDED(hRetval))
        return hRetval;
    else
        return Error((LPOLESTR)strDescription,IID_IAuthor,hRetval);
}
```

GETAUTHORSFORTITLE

The `GetAuthorsForTitle` method returns a recordset that contains the author information for all the authors for a specified title. The implementation of this method is shown in Listing 13.10. Like the `GetAuthors` method, this method does not contain any logic that you haven't seen before. On lines 6–12, you define your query. For this query, you do a join on the author and titleauthor tables to fetch the ID, last name, and first name of the authors of the specified book. You order the results by the titleauthor.au_ord field in ascending order. The au_ord field in titleauthor contains the order of the authors, i.e., the author with au_ord=1 for a book is the primary author of the book.

On lines 24–38, you execute the query using an ADO command object so you can specify the title ID query parameter. As always, you do an AddRef on the recordset and then disconnect the recordset by setting its ActiveConnection property to NULL before you return it. On lines 53–72, you perform the usual cleanup and exit logic.

LISTING 13.10 *GETAUTHORSFORTITLE*

```
1.  STDMETHODIMP CAuthor::GetAuthorsForTitle(BSTR titleID, _Recordset **rs)
2.  {
3.      HRESULT hRetval;
4.      _bstr_t strDescription;
5.      _variant_t blank(DISP_E_PARAMNOTFOUND, VT_ERROR);
6.      _bstr_t sql("SELECT authors.au_id, authors.au_lname,"\
7.          " authors.au_fname, authors.phone, authors.address,"\
8.          " authors.city, authors.state, titleauthor.au_ord,"\
9.          " titleauthor.royaltyper" \
10.         " FROM titleauthor "\
11.         " INNER JOIN authors ON titleauthor.au_id = authors.au_id"\
12.         " WHERE (titleauthor.title_id = ?) ORDER BY au_ord ASC");
13.     _RecordsetPtr pRS;
14.     _ConnectionPtr pConn;
15.     _CommandPtr pCmd;
16.     _ParameterPtr pParam;
17.     IContextState *pContxState;
18.
19.     hRetval=CoGetObjectContext(IID_IContextState,(void **)&pContxState);
20.     if (SUCCEEDED(hRetval))
21.     {
22.         try
23.         {
24.             pConn.CreateInstance( __uuidof(Connection));
25.             pConn->Open(mConnectionString,"","",-1);
26.             pRS.CreateInstance( __uuidof(Recordset));
27.             pRS->CursorLocation=adUseClient;
28.             pCmd.CreateInstance( __uuidof(Command));
29.             pCmd->CommandType=adCmdText;
30.             pCmd->CommandText=sql;
31.             pCmd->ActiveConnection=pConn;
32.             pParam=pCmd->CreateParameter(_bstr_t(L""),
                    adVarChar,adParamInput,6,titleID);
```

```
            pCmd->Parameters->Append(pParam);
            pRS->Open(pCmd.GetInterfacePtr(),blank,adOpenStatic,
                        adLockBatchOptimistic,-1);
            pRS->AddRef();
            *rs=pRS;
            pRS->PutRefActiveConnection(NULL);
        }
        catch ( _com_error err)
        {
            strDescription=err.Description();
            hRetval=err.Error();
        }
    }
    else
    {
        _com_error err(hRetval);
        strDescription=L"Could not retrieve the object context. " \
                    L"Your component is probably not configured";
    }
// Exit and cleanup code
    if (NULL != pContxState)
    {
        if (SUCCEEDED(hRetval))
            pContxState->SetMyTransactionVote(TxCommit);
        else
            pContxState->SetMyTransactionVote(TxAbort);

        pContxState->SetDeactivateOnReturn(VARIANT_TRUE);
        pContxState->Release();
    }
    if (NULL != pConn)
    {
        if (adStateOpen==pConn->GetState())
            pConn->Close();
        pConn=NULL;
    }
    if (SUCCEEDED(hRetval))
        return hRetval;
    else
        return Error((LPOLESTR)strDescription,IID_IAuthor,hRetval);
}
```

GETNEWTITLEAUTHORRECORDSET AND UPDATEAUTHORSFORTITLE

The GetNewTitleAuthorRecordSet and UpdateAuthorsForTitle methods work together to let you set the authors for a title. To set the authors for a title, you call the GetNewTitleAuthorRecordSet method and specify the number of authors the book is to have. Next, you fill the recordset that you get with the ID of the authors of the title and the title ID. Then you call the UpdateAuthorsForTitle method. UpdateAuthorsForTitle does not try to do a merge with the existing authors for the title. Instead, it deletes all the existing authors for the title and then saves the Authors that you passed in.

GetNewTitleAuthorRecordSet • The implementation of the GetNewTitleAuthorRecordSet is shown in Listing 13.11.

LISTING 13.11 *CAUTHOR::GETNEWTITLEAUTHORRECORDSET*

```
STDMETHODIMP CAuthor::GetNewTitleAuthorRecordSet(short numRecords,
            _Recordset **rs)
{
   _bstr_t strDescription;
   HRESULT hRetval;
   int i;
   _ConnectionPtr pConn;
   _RecordsetPtr pRS;
   _variant_t blank(DISP_E_PARAMNOTFOUND, VT_ERROR);
   IContextState *pContxState;

   hRetval=CoGetObjectContext(IID_IContextState,(void **)&pContxState);
   if (SUCCEEDED(hRetval))
   {
      _bstr_t sql("SELECT titleauthor.au_id, titleauthor.title_id,"\
         " titleauthor.au_ord, titleauthor.royaltyper"\
         " FROM titleauthor WHERE 1=2");
      try
      {
         pConn.CreateInstance( __uuidof(Connection));
         pConn->Open(mConnectionString,"","",-1);
         pRS.CreateInstance( __uuidof(Recordset));
         pRS->CursorLocation=adUseClient;
         pRS->Open(sql,pConn.GetInterfacePtr(),adOpenStatic,
            adLockBatchOptimistic,-1);
         pRS->AddRef();
         for (i=0;i<numRecords;i++)
            pRS->AddNew();
         pRS->MoveFirst();
```

```
            *rs=pRS;
            pRS->PutRefActiveConnection(NULL);
        }
        catch ( _com_error err)
        {
            strDescription=err.Description();
            hRetval=err.Error();
        }
    }
    else
    {
        _com_error err(hRetval);
        strDescription=L"Could not retrieve the object context. " \
                       L"Your component is probably not configured";
    }
// Exit and cleanup code
    if (NULL != pContxState)
    {
        if (SUCCEEDED(hRetval))
            pContxState->SetMyTransactionVote(TxCommit);
        else
            pContxState->SetMyTransactionVote(TxAbort);

        pContxState->SetDeactivateOnReturn(VARIANT_TRUE);
        pContxState->Release();
    }
    if (NULL != pConn)
    {
        if (adStateOpen==pConn->GetState())
            pConn->Close();
        pConn=NULL;
    }
    if (SUCCEEDED(hRetval))
        return hRetval;
    else
        return Error((LPOLESTR)strDescription,IID_IAuthor,hRetval);
}
```

The implementation of this method is almost identical to the `GetExistingBookRecordSet` method in the `Book` class, so I won't discuss it further.

UPDATEAUTHORSFORTITLE • The implementation of the `UpdateAuthorsForTitle` method is shown in Listing 13.12.

LISTING 13.12 *CAUTHOR::UPDATEAUTHORSFORTITLE*

```
STDMETHODIMP CAuthor::UpdateAuthorsForTitle(_Recordset *rs)
{
   _bstr_t strDescription;
   HRESULT hRetval;
   _ConnectionPtr pConn;
   _RecordsetPtr pRS;
   _CommandPtr pCmd;
   _bstr_t strTitleInClause;
   _bstr_t strMsg;
   _bstr_t sql("DELETE FROM titleauthor WHERE title_id IN ");
   _variant_t blank(DISP_E_PARAMNOTFOUND, VT_ERROR);
   IContextState *pContxState;
   short authorOrder;
   short intAuthorOrder=1;

   hRetval=CoGetObjectContext(IID_IContextState,(void **)&pContxState);
   if (SUCCEEDED(hRetval))
   {
      if (NULL != rs)
      {
         try
         {
            pRS=rs;
            pConn.CreateInstance( __uuidof(Connection));
            pConn->Open(mConnectionString, "", "",-1);
            pCmd.CreateInstance( __uuidof(Command));
            pCmd->CommandType=adCmdText;
            strTitleInClause=GetInClause(rs,"title_id");
            sql+=strTitleInClause;
            pCmd->CommandText=sql;
            pCmd->ActiveConnection=pConn;
            pCmd->Execute(&blank,&blank,-1);
            pRS->PutRefActiveConnection(pConn);
            pRS->MoveFirst();
            authorOrder=1;
            while (pRS->adoEOF != VARIANT_TRUE)
            {
               pRS->Fields->Item["au_ord"]->Value=
                  _variant_t(authorOrder);
               authorOrder++;
               pRS->MoveNext();
```

```
            }
            pRS->MoveFirst();
            hRetval=pRS->UpdateBatch(adAffectAll);
            pRS->Filter=_variant_t((short)adFilterConflictingRecords);
            if (pRS->RecordCount > 0)
            {
               strMsg="Could not update the following records: ";
               while (pRS->adoEOF != VARIANT_TRUE)
               {
                  strMsg+=_bstr_t("(") + _bstr_t(
                     pRS->Fields->Item["au_id"]->Value)
                     + "," + _bstr_t(
                     pRS->Fields->Item["title_id"]->Value)+") ";
                  pRS->MoveNext();
               }
               strDescription=strMsg;
               hRetval=E_CONFLICTS_FOUND;
            }
         }
         catch ( _com_error err)
         {
            strDescription=err.Description();
            hRetval=err.Error();
         }
      }
   }
   else
   {
      _com_error err(hRetval);
      strDescription=L"Could not retrieve the object context. " \
                  L"Your component is probably not configured";
   }
// Exit and cleanup code
   if (NULL != pContxState)
   {
      if (SUCCEEDED(hRetval))
         pContxState->SetMyTransactionVote(TxCommit);
      else
         pContxState->SetMyTransactionVote(TxAbort);

      pContxState->SetDeactivateOnReturn(VARIANT_TRUE);
      pContxState->Release();
   }
   if (NULL != pConn)
```

```
86.     {
87.         if (adStateOpen==pConn->GetState())
88.             pConn->Close();
89.         pConn=NULL;
90.     }
91.     if (SUCCEEDED(hRetval))
92.         return hRetval;
93.     else
94.         return Error((LPOLESTR)strDescription,IID_IAuthor,hRetval);
95. }
```

The implementation of the UpdateAuthorsForTitle method is similar to the UpdateBooks method in the Book class. The main difference is on lines 36–42 where you make sure the order has been set for the authors before you call UpdateBatch. Because you use the E_CONFLICTS_FOUND in the Author class, you must include errorcodes.h in the source file for the Author class. Add the following line to the CAuthor.cpp file:

```
#include "errorcodes.h"
```

Remember that stdafx.h must be the first include file.

UpdateAuthorsForTitle also depends on a private method in the Author implementation class called GetInClause that is used to construct a SQL IN clause. You can add this method to your business object project by performing the following steps:

1. Right-click on the CAuthor implementation class in the ClassView tab of the Visual C++ workspace (as shown in Figure 13.28).
2. Select Add Member Function... from the Context menu (the Add Method Function dialog appears as shown in Figure 13.29).
3. Enter _bstr_t in the Function Type field.
4. Enter GetInClause(_Recordset *rs,const char *fieldName) in the Function Declaration field.
5. Select Private under Access.
6. Click OK.

The implementation of this method is shown in Listing 13.13.

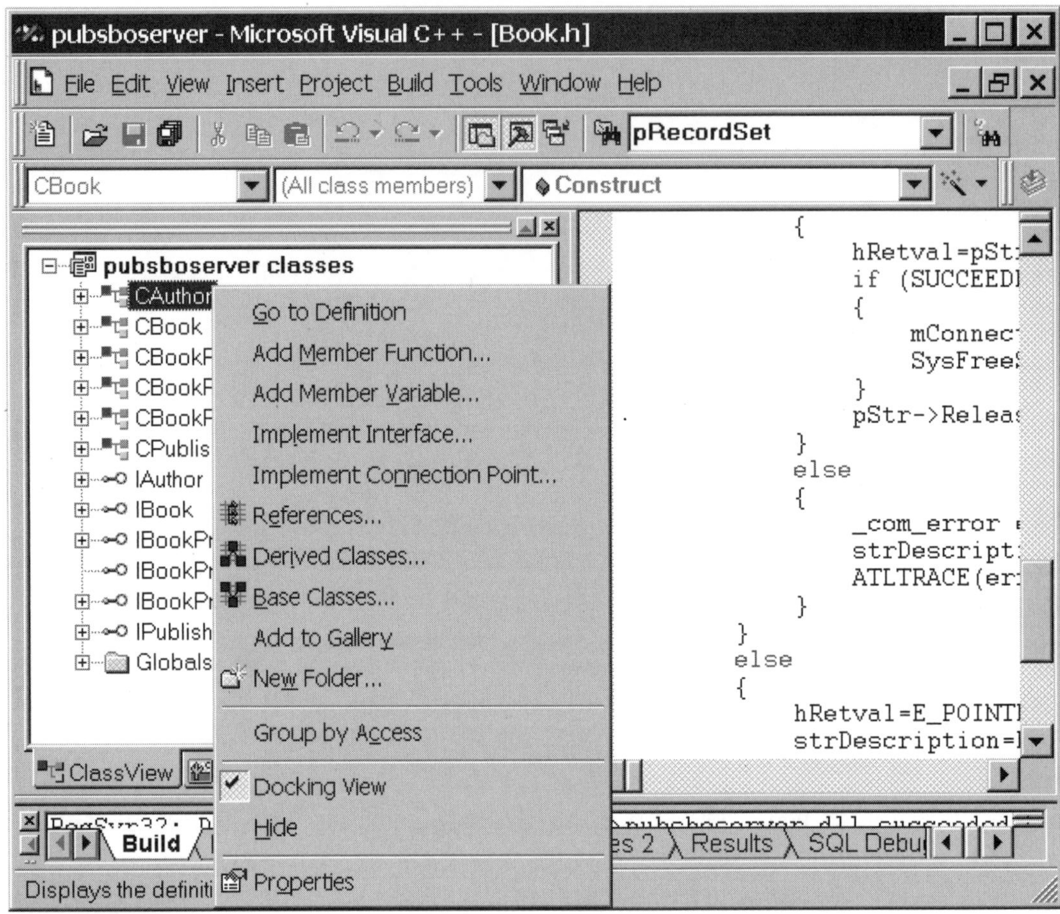

FIGURE 13.28 The First Step to Adding a Private Method.

Add Member Function

Function Type:
_bstr_t

Function Declaration:
GetInClause(_Recordset *rs,const char *fieldName)

Access
Public Protected Private

Static Virtual

OK
Cancel

FIGURE 13.29 The Add Member Function Dialog.

LISTING 13.13 *CAUTHOR::GETINCLAUSE*

```
_bstr_t CAuthor::GetInClause(_Recordset *rs, const char *fieldName)
{
   _RecordsetPtr pRS;
   _bstr_t strTitleID;
   _bstr_t strTitleInClause;
   if (NULL != rs)
   {
      pRS=rs;
      if (pRS->RecordCount > 0 )
      {
         pRS->MoveFirst();
         pRS=rs;
         strTitleInClause="(";
         strTitleID=_bstr_t("'")+
            _bstr_t(pRS->Fields->Item[fieldName]->Value)+"'";
         strTitleInClause+=strTitleID;
         pRS->MoveNext();
         while (pRS->adoEOF != VARIANT_TRUE)
         {
            strTitleID=_bstr_t("'")+
               _bstr_t(pRS->Fields->Item[fieldName]->Value)+"'";
            strTitleInClause+=_bstr_t(", ") + strTitleID;
            pRS->MoveNext();
         }
         strTitleInClause+=")";
         pRS->MoveFirst();
      }
   }
   return strTitleInClause;
}
```

Implementing the Publisher Methods

The Publisher business object has just one method, `GetPublishers`, that returns a RecordSet and contains all the Publishers that are currently defined in the database. For this example program, the Publisher information is read-only. The implementation of this method doesn't contain any logic you haven't seen already. In fact, the implementation of this method is almost identical to the `GetAuthors` method, except in this case you are querying for all of the Publishers instead of all of the Authors. The implementation of `GetPublishers` is shown in Listing 13.14.

LISTING 13.14 *CPUBLISHER::GETPUBLISHERS*

```
STDMETHODIMP CPublisher::GetPublishers(_Recordset **rs)
{
      HRESULT hRetval;
   _bstr_t strDescription;
   _bstr_t sql("SELECT * FROM PUBLISHERS");
   _RecordsetPtr pRS;
   _ConnectionPtr pConn;
   IContextState *pContxState;
   hRetval=CoGetObjectContext(IID_IContextState,(void **)&pContxState);
   if (SUCCEEDED(hRetval))
   {
      try
      {
         pConn.CreateInstance( __uuidof(Connection));
         pConn->Open(mConnectionString, "", "",-1);
         pRS.CreateInstance( __uuidof(Recordset));
         pRS->CursorLocation=adUseClient;
         pRS->Open(sql,pConn.GetInterfacePtr(),adOpenStatic,
            adLockBatchOptimistic,-1);
         pRS->AddRef();
         *rs=pRS;
         pRS->PutRefActiveConnection(NULL);
      }
      catch ( _com_error err)
      {
         strDescription=err.Description();
         hRetval=err.Error();
      }
   }
   else
   {
      _com_error err(hRetval);
      strDescription=L"Could not retrieve the object context. " \
                 L"Your component is probably not configured";
   }
// Exit and cleanup code
   if (NULL != pContxState)
   {
      if (SUCCEEDED(hRetval))
         pContxState->SetMyTransactionVote(TxCommit);
      else
         pContxState->SetMyTransactionVote(TxAbort);
```

```
        pContxState->SetDeactivateOnReturn(VARIANT_TRUE);
        pContxState->Release();
    }
    if (NULL != pConn)
    {
        if (adStateOpen==pConn->GetState())
            pConn->Close();
        pConn=NULL;
    }
    if (SUCCEEDED(hRetval))
        return hRetval;
    else
        return Error((LPOLESTR)strDescription,IID_IPublisher,hRetval);
}
```

Compiling Your Server

Now compile your project by pressing F7. Visual C++ registers your server once it is done compiling. You are now ready to configure your components.

Configuring Your Components

It's time to configure your components. The steps to do this are fairly simple.

1. Create a COM+ application
2. Add your in-process server to the COM+ application.
3. Set the transaction attribute for your classes.
4. Create Employee and Manager Roles.
5. Configure fine-grained security so that only Managers are allowed to call the methods that do updates.
6. Add a Construction String for each Component.

CREATING A COM+ APPLICATION

To create a new COM+ application, perform the following steps in the Component Services Explorer. I went through this process step-by-step in Chapter 11, so I won't repeat the figures here.

1. Right-click on the folder console `root\component\services\Computers\My Computer\COM+ application\` (see Figure 11.17).

2. Select New from the Context menu that appears (the COM+ application Install Wizard appears, see Figure 11.18).
3. Click Next (step 2 of the COM+ application Install Wizard appears, see Figure 11.19).
4. Click Create an empty application (step 3 of the COM+ application Install Wizard appears, see Figure 11.20).
5. Enter PubsApp for the application name and Accept the default activation type (Server Application).
6. Click Next (step 4 of the COM+ application Install Wizard appears, see Figure 11.21).
7. Accept the default Identity (Interactive User).
8. Click Next and then Click Finished on the final screen.

ADDING YOUR IN-PROCESS SERVER TO THE COM+ APPLICATION

Using the Windows NT Explorer, navigate to where you built your DLL and drag-and-drop the DLL into the components sub-folder beneath your new COM+ application. After you do this, you should see the Book, Author, and Publisher classes displayed in the components folder as shown in Figure 13.30. Now you are ready to set the transaction attribute for these classes.

SETTING THE TRANSACTION ATTRIBUTE FOR YOUR CLASSES

You can set the transaction attributes for your classes by performing the following steps in the Component Services Explorer:

1. Right-click on the Book Component in the Components folder of your COM+ application.
2. Select Properties from the Context Menu (the Component Properties dialog appears).
3. Click the Transaction tab (the dialog should look like that shown in Figure 12.13).
4. Select Required for the transaction setting.
5. Click OK.
6. Repeat steps 1–5 for the Author class.
7. Repeat steps 1–5 for the Publisher class.

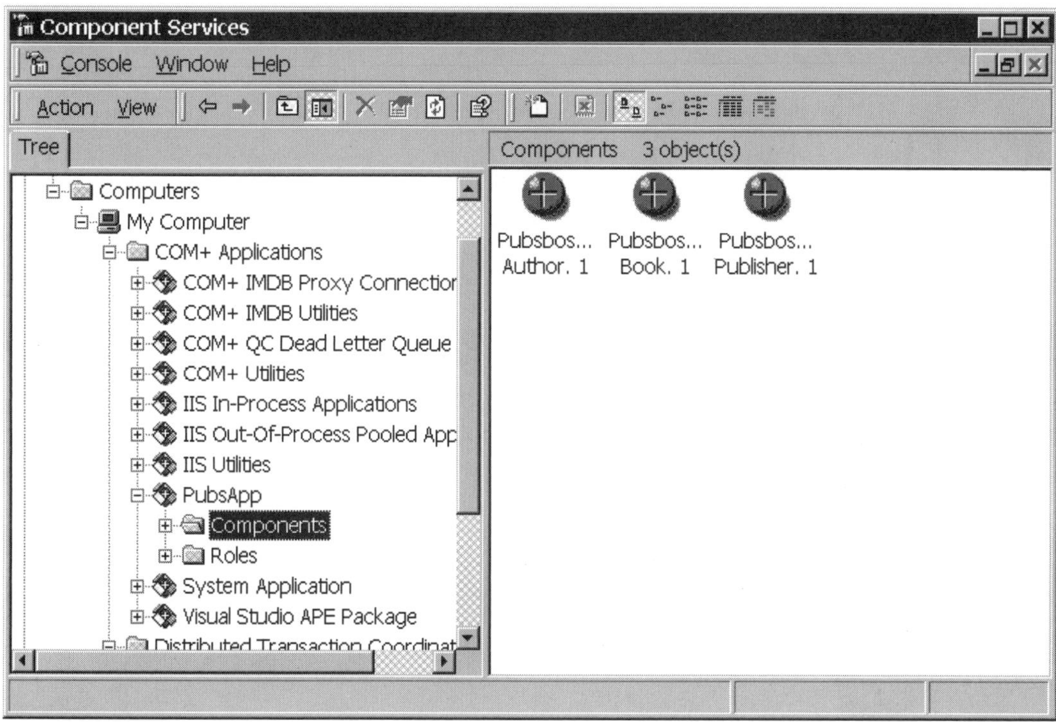

FIGURE 13.30 The Book, Author, and Publisher Components in Your COM+ Application.

I went through this process step-by-step in Chapter 12, so I won't repeat the figures here.

All of your classes have been configured to require a transaction. This setting means that if one object has a transaction and it creates another object, as the Book object does in the `UpdateBook` method, the second object shares its creator's transaction.

CREATING EMPLOYEE AND MANAGER ROLES

You can now create two Roles for your component. The first role, Employee, is the role for all users of your application. In other words, someone has to at least be in the Employee role if they are to use your component at all. The Manager role is for Employees who wish to make updates to the Publisher information. To either add a new book, or modify an existing one, a user must be in the Manager role. Perform the following steps to create the Employee and Manager roles. Once again, you went through these steps in detail in Chapter 12, so I won't repeat the figures.

1. Right-click on the `Roles` folder in your PubsApp COM+ application.
2. Select `New` from the `Context` menu and select `Role` from the pull right menu as shown in Figure 12.1 (the New Role dialog is displayed as shown in Figure 12.2).
3. Enter `Employee` for the name of the new role.
4. Click `OK`.
5. Repeat steps 1–4 and select Manager for the role name.

When you are done, you should see the Employee and Manager roles displayed in the `Roles` folder of your COM+ application as shown in Figure 13.31.

At this point, you might as well add your user account to both the Employee and Manager roles. Perform the following steps in the Component Services Explorer to do this:

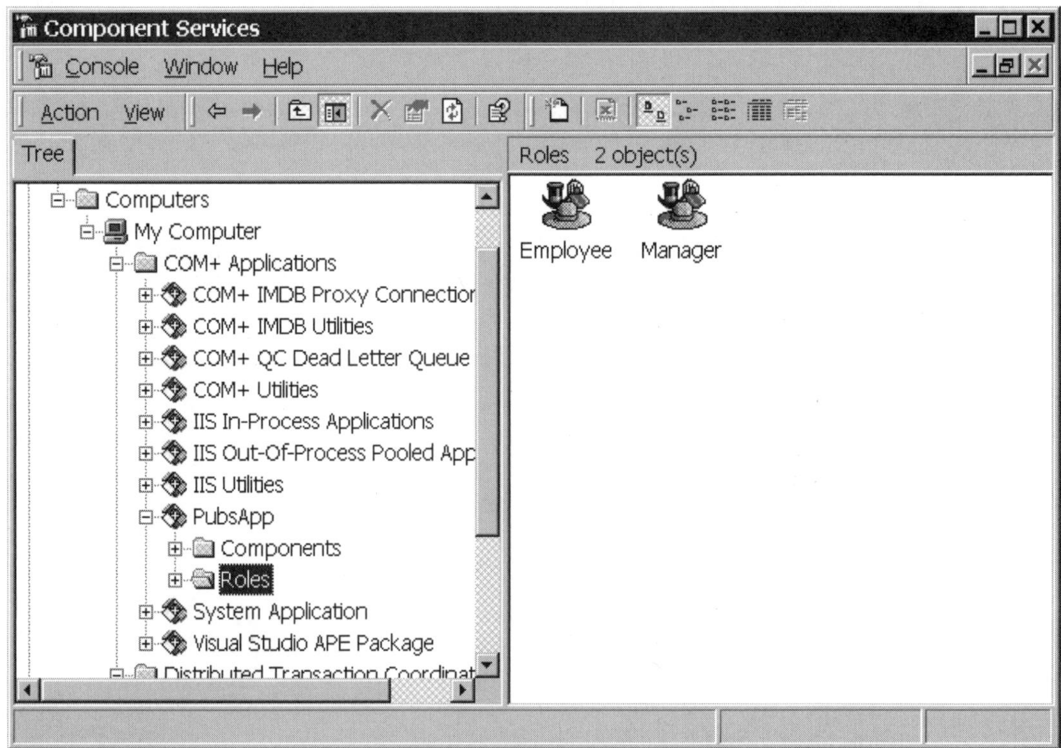

FIGURE 13.31 The Employee and Manager Roles Displayed in the Roles Folder.

1. Right-click on the `Users` Folder beneath the `Employee` Role as shown in Figure 13.32.
2. Select `New/User` from the `Context` menu (if you are using Active Directory, the Select Users and Groups dialog appears as shown in Figure 13.33).
3. Select yourself from the list of users and click the `Add` button.
4. Click `OK`.
5. Repeat steps 1–4 for the `Manager` role.

If you are not using the Active Directory, you will see the Standard NT Users and Groups dialog.

CONFIGURING FINE-GRAINED SECURITY

Now that you have created your roles, you can use these roles to implement fine-grained security in your application. To do this, you need to first

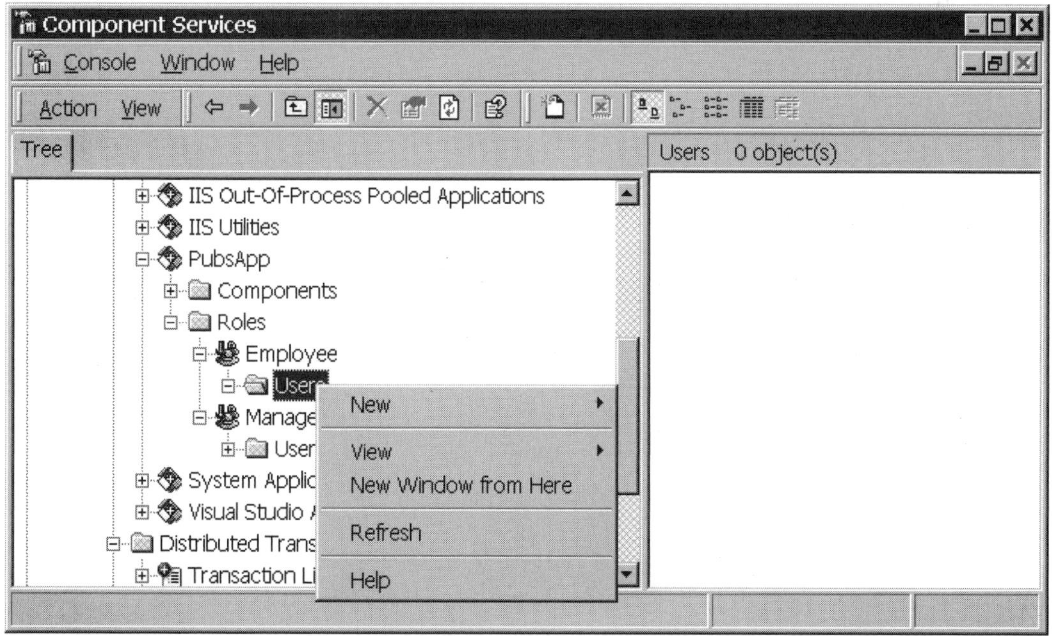

FIGURE 13.32 Adding a New User to the Employee and Manager Roles.

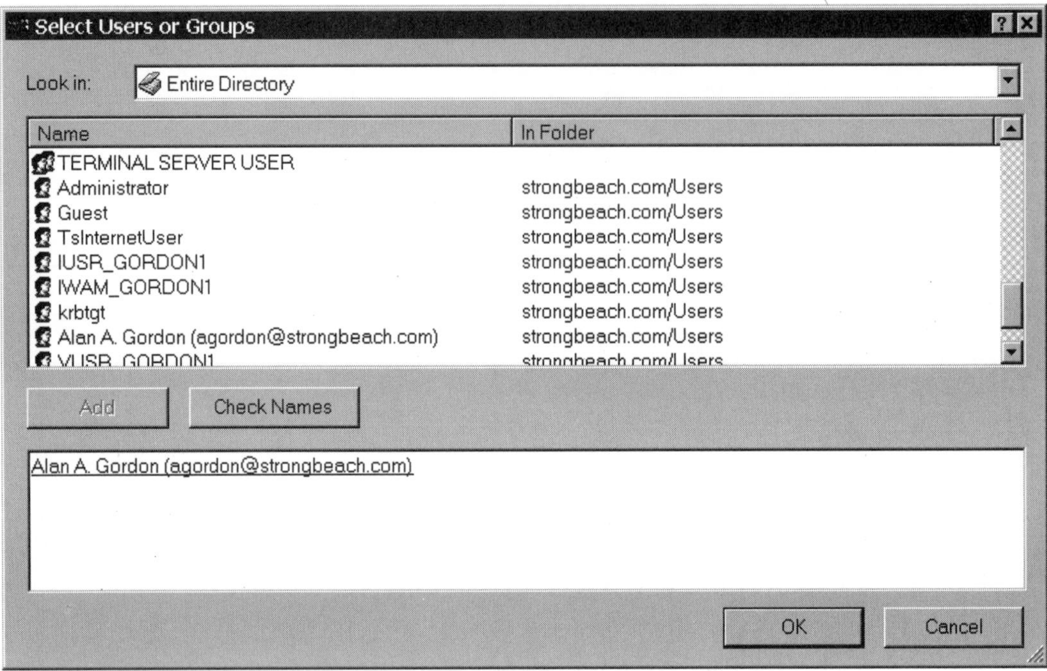

FIGURE 13.33 The Select Users and Groups Dialog.

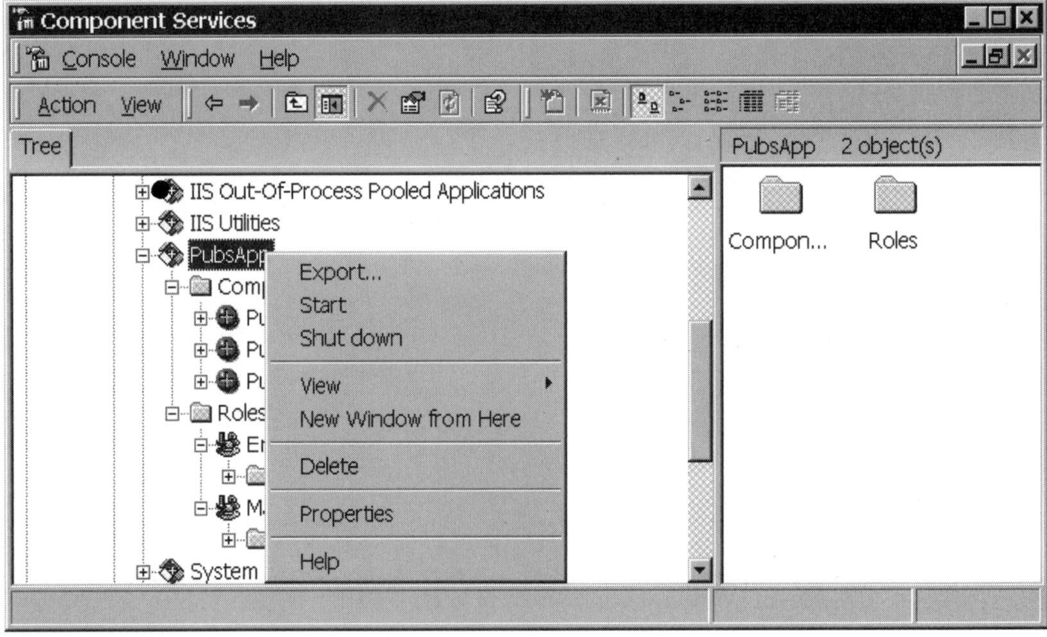

FIGURE 13.34 Right-click on the PubsApp COM+ Application.

enable COM+ access control, it is off by default. After you turn on COM+ access control, you need to configure which roles are allowed to call each method.

ENABLING COM+ ACCESS CONTROL • To turn on COM+ access control, perform the following steps in the Component Services Explorer:

1. Right-click on the `PubsApp` COM+ application as shown in Figure 13.34.
2. Select `Properties` from the `Context` menu.
3. Click the `Security` tab.
4. Set the `Enforce access checks for this application` checkbox as shown in Figure 13.35.
5. Click `OK`.

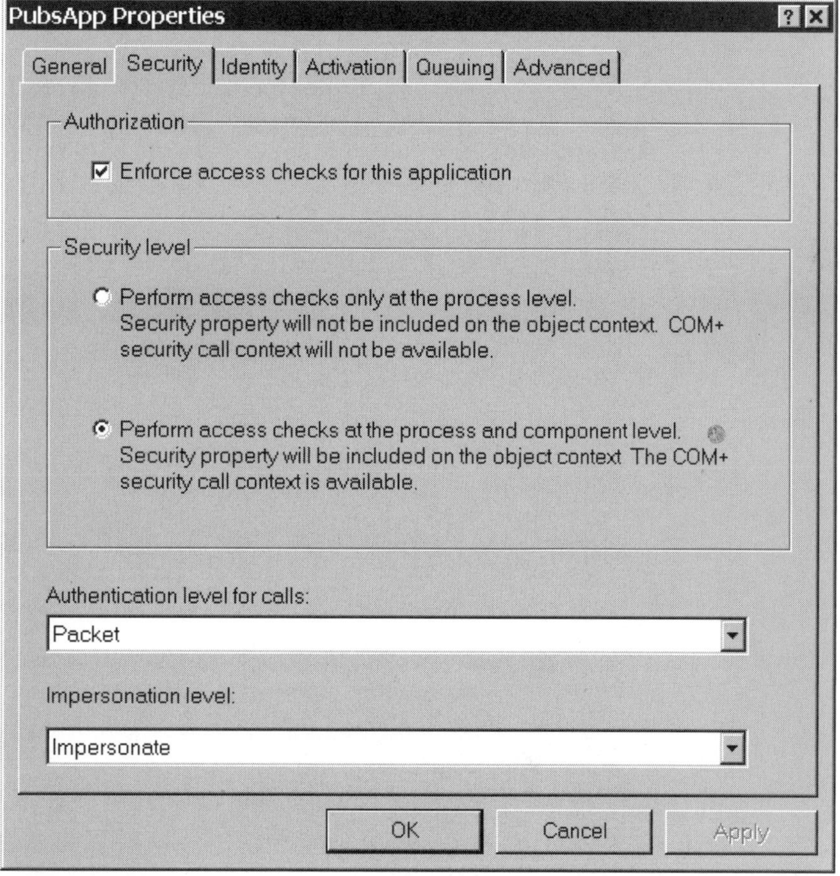

FIGURE 13.35 Enforcing Access Checks for the Application.

I noticed an interesting bug in the beta versions of Windows 2000 that I hope is fixed in the release version of the product. When you enable COM+ Access Control, COM+ does not return error information correctly. If my objects called the ATL Error function with a user-defined HRESULT, the error description would always be Automation Error. Once I turned off COM+ Access Control, the error description was returned correctly.

If you tried to use your components from a client application, right now they would not work. You would always get a permission-denied error. To get your components to work with COM+ security, you have to specify which roles are allowed to access each component, interface, or method. You can configure access control at whatever granularity you desire: component (class), interface, or per-method. In your case, your main security requirement is that only Managers should be allowed to edit existing books, create new books, or delete existing books. To enforce these constraints, you can configure security by allowing everyone (Employees and Managers) to access the following entities:

- All methods in the `Publisher` Class.
- The `GetExistingBookRecordSet`, `RetrieveByID`, and `RetrieveByKeyword` methods in the `Book` Class.
- The `GetAuthors` and `GetAuthorsForTitle` methods in the `Author` Class.

Only Managers are allowed to access methods that can update the database.

- The `GetNewBookRecordSet`, `DeleteBook`, and `UpdateBook` methods in the `Book` class.
- The `GetNewTitleAuthorRecordSet` and `UpdateAuthorsForTitle` methods in the `Author` class.

This means you can configure security for the `Publisher` class at the class level, but the `Book` and `Author` classes must be configured per-method.

Configuring the Publisher Class • To allow both the Employee and Manager roles to access all methods in the `Publisher` class, perform the following steps in the Component Services Explorer:

1. Right-click on the `Publisher` Class in the `Components` folder of your COM+ application as shown in Figure 13.36.
2. Select `Properties` from the `Context` menu (the Component properties dialog appears).
3. Click the `Security` tab (you should see the dialog shown in Figure 13.37).
4. Set the checkboxes next to the `Employee` and `Manager` roles.
5. Click `OK`.

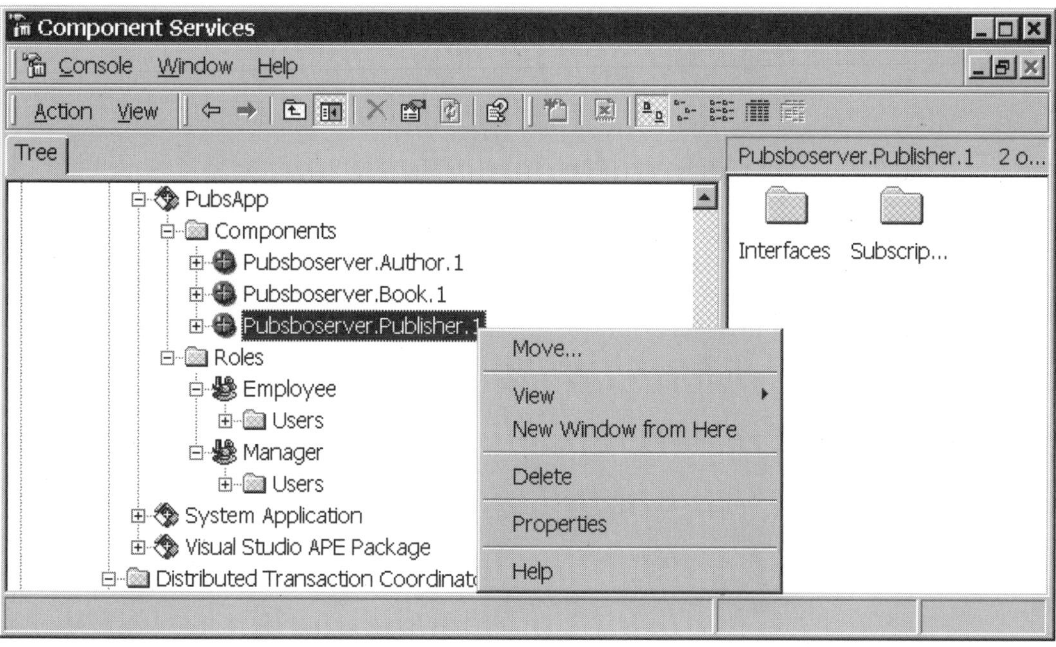

FIGURE 13.36 Right-Click on the Publisher Class.

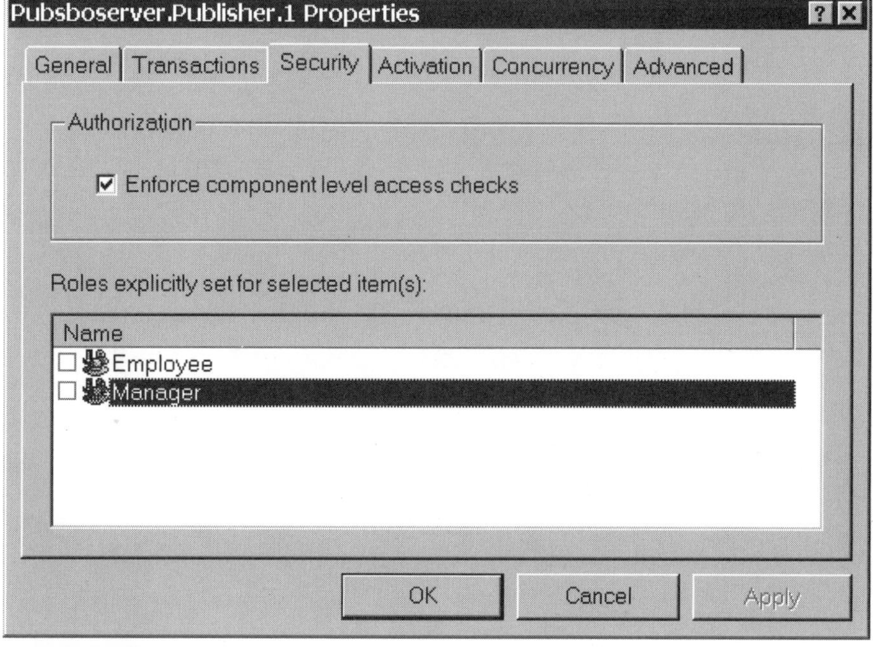

FIGURE 13.37 The Security Tab of the Component Properties Dialog.

Notice in step 3 that all of the roles that have been defined in the application appear in the Security tab of the properties dialog. All the defined roles in a COM+ application appear on the Security tab for each entity, class, interface, and method in the COM+ application.

CONFIGURING THE BOOK CLASS • For the `Book` class, you need to configure security for each method separately. You will configure some methods in the `Book` class to be accessible to both Employees and Managers and some to be accessible only to Managers. First, configure the methods that can be accessed by both Employee and Managers. Perform the following steps to do this:

1. Right-click on the `RetrieveByKeyword` method beneath the `IBook` interface as shown in Figure 13.38.
2. Select `Properties` from the `Context` menu.
3. Click on the `Security` tab (you should see a dialog similar to that shown in Figure 13.37).
4. Set the checkboxes next to both the Employee and Manager roles.
5. Click `OK`.
6. Repeat steps 1–5 for the `RetrieveByID` method.
7. Repeat steps 1–5 for the `GetExistingBookRecordSet` method.

Next, configure the methods that can only be accessed by members of the Manager Role.

1. Right-click on the `DeleteBook` method beneath the `IBook` interface.
2. Select `Properties` from the `Context` menu.
3. Click on the `Security` tab (you should see a dialog similar to that shown in Figure 13.37).
4. Set the checkbox next to the `Manager` role.
5. Click `OK`.
6. Repeat steps 1–5 for the `GetNewBookRecordSet` method.
7. Repeat steps 1–5 for the `UpdateBooks` method.

CONFIGURING THE AUTHOR CLASS • You also need to configure security separately for each method in the `Author` class. Configure the methods that are accessible by both Employees and Managers first. Perform the following steps to configure the methods that are accessible by members to both the Employee and Manager roles.

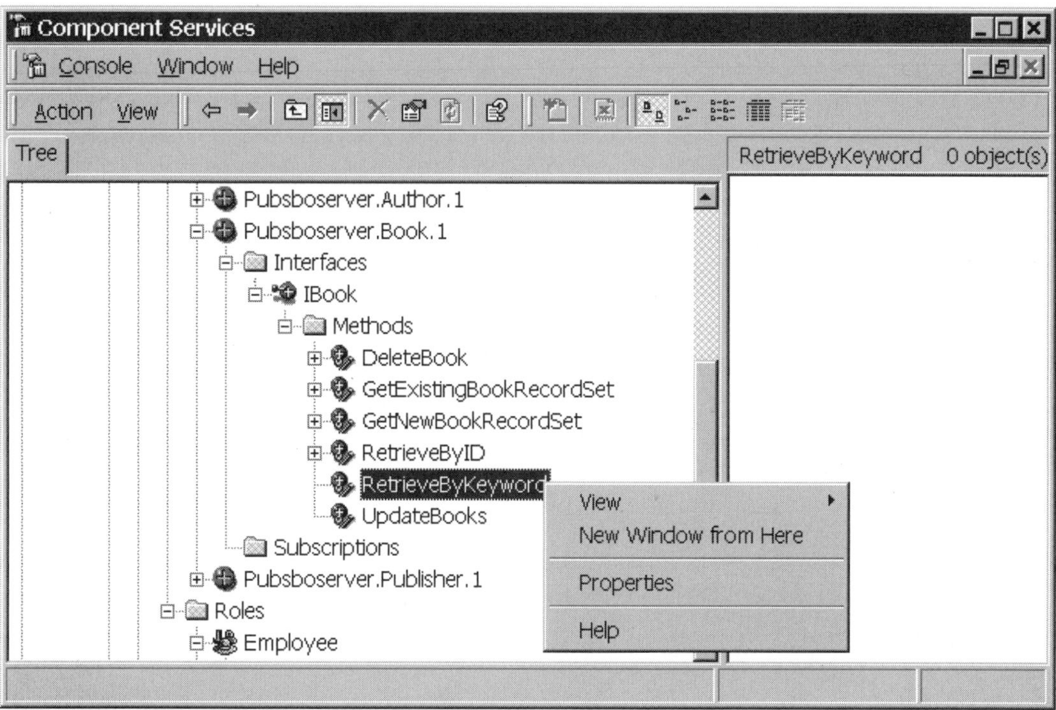

FIGURE 13.38 Right-click on a Method in a COM+ Application.

1. Right-click on the `GetAuthors` method beneath the `IAuthor` interface of the `Author` class.
2. Select the `Properties` item from the `Context` menu.
3. Click the `Security` tab.
4. Set the checkboxes next to both the `Employee` and `Manager` roles.
5. Click `OK`.
6. Repeat steps 1–5 for the `GetAuthorsForTitle` method.

Next, perform the following steps to configure the methods that are accessible only to Managers:

1. Right-click on the `GetNewTitleAuthorRecordSet` method beneath the `IAuthor` interface of the `Author` class.
2. Select `Properties` from the `Context` menu.
3. Click the `Security` tab.
4. Set the checkbox next to the `Manager` role.
5. Click `OK`.
6. Repeat steps 1–5 for the `UpdateAuthorsForTitle` method.

ADDING A CONSTRUCTION STRING FOR EACH COMPONENT

The Book, Author, and Publisher classes support the IObjectConstruct interface so you can configure a construction string for each class. The classes expect to receive their OLEDB Connection string in the construction string. To configure your connection string, perform the following steps in the Component Services Explorer:

1. Right-click on the Book class in the Components folder of your COM+ application.
2. Select Properties... from the Context menu to bring up the component properties dialog.
3. Click the Activation tab (you should see the window shown in Figure 13.26).
4. Set the Enable object construction checkbox.
5. Enter your connection string in the Constructor String field.
6. Click OK.
7. Repeat steps 1–6 for the Author class.
8. Repeat steps 1–6 for the Publisher class.

If you are using SQL Server, your connection string should be similar to the following string:

```
Provider=SQLOLEDB;User ID=sa;Initial Catalog=pubs;Data Source=GORDON1
```

The only thing you should need to change is the Data Source portion of the string, which should contain the name of the machine that your SQL Server is running on.

Although it should work, this connection string has not been tested with SQL Server 2000.

Your COM+ components are now ready for use. Let's build a client.

Implementing the Visual Basic Client Application

The first client to build is a native Windows application. You build this client with Visual Basic 6. To create a project, start Visual Basic 6 and perform the following steps:

1. Select `New Project` from the `File` menu (you may not need this step because Visual Basic starts up with the new Project dialog displayed).
2. Select `Standard Exe` from the `New Project` menu.
3. Click `OK`.
4. In the Visual Basic environment select `Properties` from the `Project` menu (the project properties dialog appears as shown in Figure 13.39).
5. On the `General` tab, change the project name to `BookClient`.
6. Click `OK`.
7. Click on the `Form1` form and change its name in the Property Window to `frmMain` as shown in Figure 13.40.

Now you can draw the main form for your application. Place the controls shown in Figure 13.15 on your form using Visual Basic. The grid that dominates this form is a ListView control. To use the ListView control in your Visual Basic project, perform the following steps:

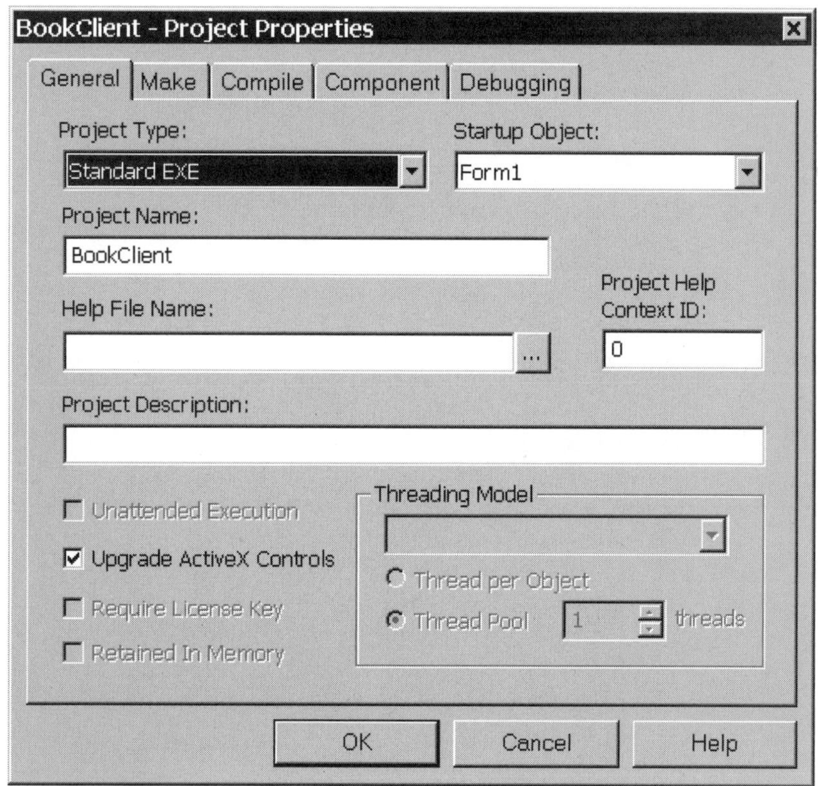

FIGURE 13.39 The Project Properties Dialog in Visual Basic.

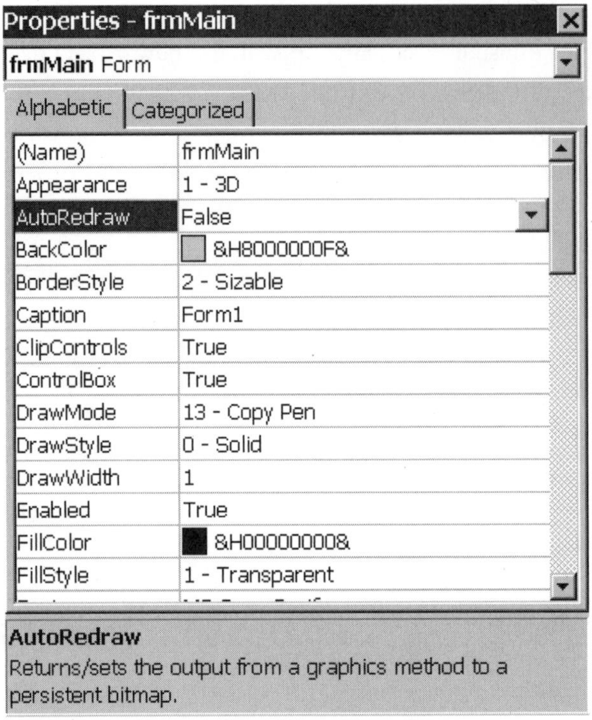

FIGURE 13.40

The Property Browser Displaying Your Form in Visual Basic.

1. Select `Components` from the `Project` menu.
2. Set the checkbox next to the Microsoft Windows Common Controls 6.0 entry.
3. Click `OK`.

After you perform these steps, you should see a number of new items in your tool palette. Select the one for the ListView. If you're not sure which one this is, just rest your mouse over each icon for one second until the tooltip appears. The tooltip for the ListView says ListView. Drag-and-drop an instance of this control on to your main Window form and perform the following steps to configure its properties:

1. Click on the `ListView` and change the Name Property of the ListView to `lvwBooks` in the VB property browser.
2. Right-click on `ListView` and select `Properties` from the `Context` menu (you should see the dialog shown in Figure 13.41).
3. Change the `View` property to `lvwReport`.
4. Change the `LabelEdit` property to `lvwManual`.

5. Set the `FullRowSelect` checkbox.
6. Click the `Column Headers` tab (your dialog should look like that shown in Figure 13.42).
7. Click the `Insert Column` button.
8. Enter `TitleID` for the `Text` Property.
9. Click the `Apply` button.
10. Repeat steps 7–9 but enter `Title` for the `Text` Property.
11. Repeat steps 7–9 but enter `AuthorLast` for the `Text` Property.
12. Repeat steps 7–9 but enter `AuthorFirst` for the `Text` Property.
13. Repeat steps 7–9 but enter `Type` for the `Text` Property.
14. Repeat steps 7–9 but enter `Price` for the `Text` Property.
15. Click `OK`.

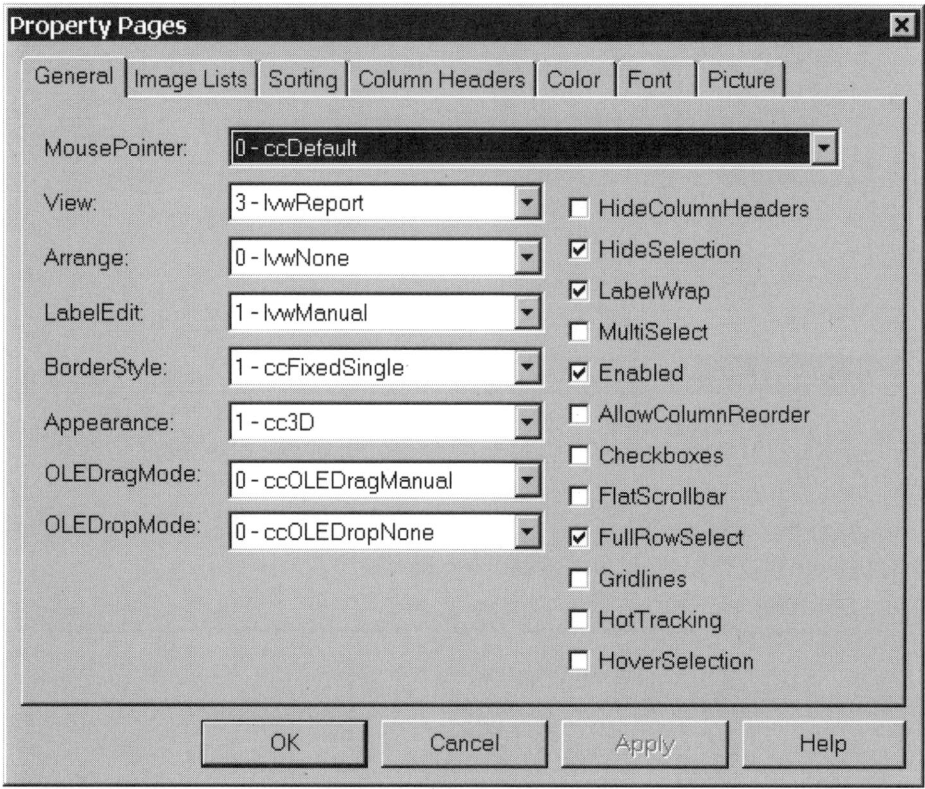

FIGURE 13.41 The Property Dialog for the ListView.

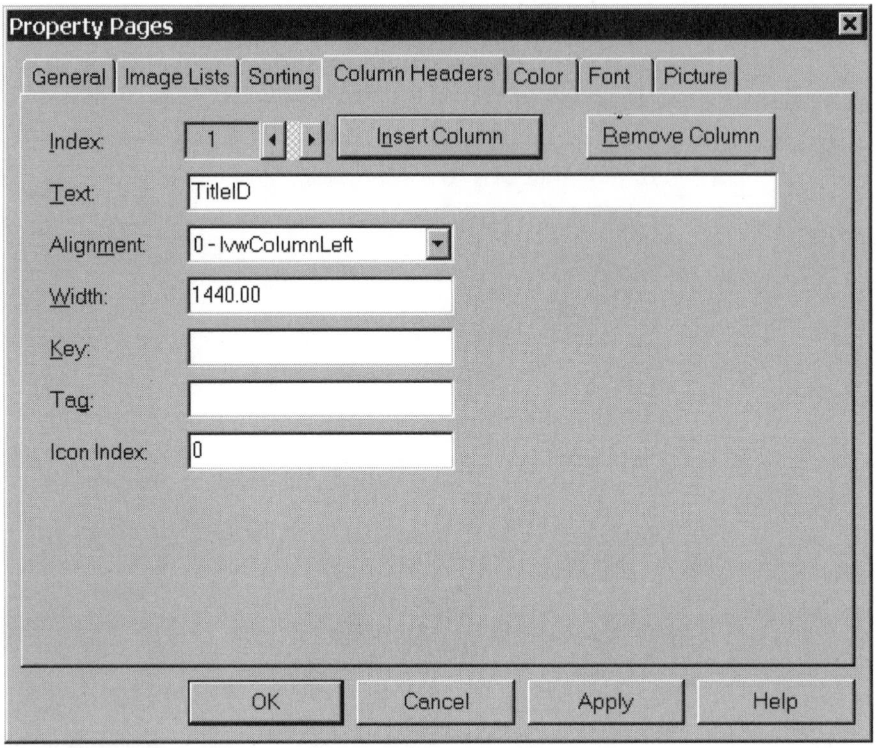

FIGURE 13.42 Setting Up The Column Headers for a ListView.

Add the other controls to the form, using Figure 13.15 as a guide. Name the other controls on the form as shown in Table 13.5.

TABLE 13.5 The Other Controls on the Main Window

Control Description	Control Name in VB Project
Keyword search text	txtSearch
Search button	cmdSearch.
New Book button	CmdNewBook
Delete button	CmdDeleteBook
Exit button	CmdExit

Before you can add code to your new project, you need to reference three COM type libraries. Referencing the type library for a component imports all the classes, interfaces, enumerations, and other entities in the type library into the project. It is similar to using the `#import` keyword in Visual C++. The three type libraries that you will reference are: (1) the ADO

RecordSet library, (2) the Microsoft Scripting Runtime Library, (3) the type library for your business object server. The ADO RecordSet is an abbreviated version of the full ADO library. This library was designed for clients that only need the RecordSet object from ADO, such as your client. Your client will need to use ADO recordsets, but it will not create any Connection or Command objects. You are importing the Microsoft Scripting Runtime library because it contains the definition for the Dictionary collection. The Dictionary is a much better collection class than the `Collection` class that is included with VB. Finally, you need to import the type library for your business object server. Because your server supports dual interfaces, you could actually use late binding and not have to do this last step. But it is so much easier and faster to use early binding. With early binding, you get intellisense, compile-time type checking, and syntax checking, and your code runs a little faster, too. To reference these three type libraries, perform the following steps in the Visual Basic environment:

1. Select `References` from the `Project` menu (the project references dialog appears).
2. Set the checkbox next to the entry labeled `Microsoft ActiveX Data Objects Recordset 2.5 Library`.
3. Set the checkbox next to the entry labeled `Microsoft Scripting Runtime`.
4. Set the checkbox next to the entry labeled `pubsboserver 1.0 type Library` (assuming that you named the library as you were instructed).
5. Click `OK`.

Now double-click on the form to bring up a code window and add the code shown in Listing 13.15 to the form.

LISTING 13.15 *THE CODE BEHIND YOUR MAIN FORM*

```
' frmMain.frm
Option Explicit
Private mServer As Book

Private Function GetServer() As Book
    On Error GoTo errHandler
    If mServer Is Nothing Then
        Set mServer = New Book
    End If
    Set GetServer = mServer
    Exit Function
errHandler:
    MsgBox (Err.Description)
```

```
End Function

Private Sub cmdDeleteBook_Click()
    On Error GoTo errHandler
    Set mServer = GetServer
    If Not lvwBooks.SelectedItem Is Nothing Then
        mServer.DeleteBook (lvwBooks.SelectedItem.Text)
        lvwBooks.ListItems.Remove lvwBooks.SelectedItem.Index
    Else
        MsgBox ("You must select an item first")
    End If
    Exit Sub
errHandler:
    MsgBox (Err.Description)
End Sub

Private Sub cmdExit_Click()
    On Error GoTo errHandler
    Call Unload(Me)
    Exit Sub
errHandler:
    MsgBox (Err.Description)
End Sub

Private Sub cmdNewBook_Click()
    On Error GoTo errHandler
    Dim frmEdit As frmEditBook
    Set frmEdit = New frmEditBook
    frmEdit.NewBookSelected = True
    Call frmEdit.Show(vbModeless, Me)
    Exit Sub
errHandler:
    MsgBox (Err.Description)
End Sub

Private Sub cmdSearch_Click()
    On Error GoTo errHandler
    Dim rs As ADOR.Recordset
    Dim lstItem As ListItem

    Set mServer = GetServer
    Set rs = mServer.RetrieveByKeyword(txtSearch.Text)
    lvwBooks.ListItems.Clear
    Do While Not rs.EOF
```

```
        Set lstItem = lvwBooks.ListItems.Add
        lstItem.Text = rs.Fields(0).Value
        lstItem.SubItems(1) = rs.Fields(1).Value
        lstItem.SubItems(2) = rs.Fields(2).Value
        lstItem.SubItems(3) = rs.Fields(3).Value
        lstItem.SubItems(4) = rs.Fields(4).Value
        lstItem.SubItems(5) = CheckNullCurrency(rs.Fields(5).Value)
        rs.MoveNext
    Loop
    Exit Sub
errHandler:
    MsgBox (Err.Description)
End Sub

Private Sub Form_Load()
    On Error GoTo errHandler
    Exit Sub
errHandler:
    MsgBox (Err.Description)
End Sub

Private Sub lvwBooks_DblClick()
    On Error GoTo errHandler
    Dim frmEdit As frmEditBook
    Dim lvwItem As ListItem
    Set lvwItem = lvwBooks.SelectedItem
    If Not lvwItem Is Nothing Then
        Set frmEdit = New frmEditBook
        frmEdit.TitleID = lvwItem.Text
        Call frmEdit.Show(vbModeless, Me)
    End If
    Exit Sub
errHandler:
    Call MsgBox(Err.Description)
End Sub
```

There is a lot of code and I really don't want to go through it all because it's just GUI code. I have bolded the code where you are using your COM+ business objects. If you compile now, you get an error because you need to add the `frmEditBook` form to your project. Add this form to your project by performing the following steps in Visual Basic:

1. Select `Add Form` from the `Project` menu.
2. Select `Form` on the `New` tab.

3. Click the Open button.
4. Change the Name property of the form in the VB property browser to frmEditBook.

Now draw the controls shown in Figure 13.16 on this new form. The control description, control type, and control name for each control are listed in Table 13.6.

If you don't want to create this form from scratch, you can copy it from the Web site and add it to your project by selecting Add Form from the Project menu and using the Existing tab. If you do copy it from the Web site, make sure you get both the frmEditBook.frm and frmEditBook.frx files.

TABLE 13.6 The Other Controls on the Main Window

Control Description	VB Control Type	Control Name in VB Project
Authors List	ListBox	lstAuthor
Delete Author	Command Button	cmdDeleteAuthor
Authors...	Command Button	CmdAuthors
Title ID	TextBox	txtTitleID
Title	TextBox	txtTitle
Type	TextBox	txtType
Publisher Name	ComboBox	CboPublishers
Price	TextBox	txtPrice
Advance	TextBox	txtAdvance
Royalty	TextBox	TxtRoyalty
Royalty spinner	UpDown (Spinner)	updRoyalty
YTD (Year To Date) Sales	TextBox	txtYTDSales
Notes	Multi-Line TextBox	txtNotes

You have used an UpDown (Spinner) control to let the user set the royalty for the book. To use the spinner control, you first need to reference the type library where it is contained. Perform the following steps in your Visual Basic project to do this:

1. Select Components from the Project menu.
2. Set the checkbox next to the Microsoft Windows Common Controls—2 6.0 entry.
3. Click OK.

Now you can draw a spinner control on the form. Next, the royalty text box and the spinner control need to be associated together so that when you click the up and down buttons on the spinner it changes the number in the royalty text box, but only in the range 0-100. To setup the spinner control, click on the control and set its properties in the VB property browser as shown in Table 13.7 (leave the defaults for all other properties). See Figure 13.43 for additional guidance.

TABLE 13.7 Property Values for the Royalty Spinner Control

Property Name	Property Value
BuddyControl	TxtRoyalty
BuddyProperty	Default
Max	100
Min	0

Now the notes text box needs to be configured so it behaves as a multi-line text box. Click on the text box and set its multi-line property to True. Also, the title field in the titles table in the Pubs database has a length of 6, the type field has a length of 12, and the Notes field has a length of 80. You may want to set the MaxLength property of each of these text

FIGURE 13.43 The Property Browser for the Royalty Spinner Control.

boxes to be the proper respective size. It's not a requirement that you do this, but if you don't you may see an error with the following text when you attempt to update or add a new book:

```
Multiple-step operation generated errors. Check each status value.
```

This indicates that you typed in text that is too long for one of these fields. Now double-click on the form to open an edit window and add the code shown in Listing 13.16 to this form.

LISTING 13.16 *THE CODE BEHIND THE BOOK EDIT FORM*

```
' frmEditBook.frm
Option Explicit
Private mTitleID As String
Private mAuthorCollection As Dictionary
Private mPublisherCollection As Dictionary
Private mRSPublisher As ADOR.Recordset
Private mRSBook As ADOR.Recordset
Private mRsAuthor As ADOR.Recordset
Private mBook As Book
Private mAuthor As Author
Private mNewBookSelected As Boolean
Private mStrNoPublisherSpecified As String

Public Property Let TitleID(ByVal intTitleID As String)
    On Error GoTo errHandler
    mTitleID = intTitleID
    Exit Property
errHandler:
    MsgBox (Err.Description)
End Property

Public Property Let NewBookSelected(ByVal bNewBook As Boolean)
    On Error GoTo errHandler
    mNewBookSelected = bNewBook
    Exit Property
errHandler:
    MsgBox (Err.Description)
End Property

Public Property Get NewBookSelected() As Boolean
    NewBookSelected = mNewBookSelected
End Property

Private Sub cmdAuthors_Click()
    On Error GoTo errHandler
```

```
    Dim frmDisplayAuthors As frmAuthor
    Set frmDisplayAuthors = New frmAuthor
    frmDisplayAuthors.TitleID = mTitleID
    Call frmDisplayAuthors.Show(vbModal)
    If frmDisplayAuthors.AddedTitleToAuthor Then
        If Not mAuthorCollection.Exists( _
                frmDisplayAuthors.SelectedAuthorID) Then
            lstAuthor.AddItem frmDisplayAuthors.SelectedAuthorFullName
            Call mAuthorCollection.Add( _
                frmDisplayAuthors.SelectedAuthorFullName, _
                frmDisplayAuthors.SelectedAuthorID)
        Else
           Call MsgBox("The selected author already exists for this title")
        End If
    End If
    Exit Sub

errHandler:
    MsgBox (Err.Description)
End Sub

Private Sub cmdDeleteAuthor_Click()
    On Error GoTo errHandler
    lstAuthor.RemoveItem (lstAuthor.ListIndex)
    Exit Sub
errHandler:
    MsgBox (Err.Description)
End Sub

Private Sub cmdExit_Click()
    On Error GoTo errHandler
    Call Unload(Me)
    Exit Sub
errHandler:
    MsgBox (Err.Description)
End Sub

Private Sub cmdNew_Click()
    On Error GoTo errHandler
    NewBookSelected = True
    Call SetupNewBook
    Exit Sub
errHandler:
    MsgBox (Err.Description)
End Sub

Private Sub SetupNewBook()
```

```
    On Error GoTo errHandler
    Set mRSBook = mBook.GetNewBookRecordSet(1)
    mAuthorCollection.RemoveAll
    Call PopulateForm(mRSBook)
    mRSBook.MoveFirst
    Exit Sub
errHandler:
    MsgBox (Err.Description)
End Sub

Private Sub SetupExistingBook()
    On Error GoTo errHandler
    Set mRSBook = mBook.GetExistingBookRecordSet( _
        "title_id='" & mTitleID & "'")
    If Not mRSBook.EOF Then
        Call PopulateForm(mRSBook)
    End If
    mRSBook.MoveFirst
    Exit Sub
errHandler:
    MsgBox (Err.Description)
End Sub

Private Sub cmdPrintCopies_Click()
    On Error GoTo errHandler
    Dim printerForm As frmPrintCopies
    Set printerForm = New frmPrintCopies
    If Not mRSBook Is Nothing Then
        printerForm.TitleID = txtTitleID.Text
        printerForm.TitleString = txtTitle.Text
        printerForm.Show (vbModal)
    Else
        Call MsgBox("You must have a valid book displayed displayed")
    End If
    Exit Sub
errHandler:
    MsgBox (Err.Description)
End Sub

Private Sub cmdUpdate_Click()
    On Error GoTo errHandler
    Dim rsAuthor As ADOR.Recordset
    Dim objBook As Book
    Dim objAuthor As Author
    Dim i As Integer
    Dim intAuthorCount As Integer
    Set objBook = New Book
```

```
    Set objAuthor = New Author
    Call SaveFormIntoRecordSet(mRSBook)

    intAuthorCount = lstAuthor.ListCount
    Set rsAuthor = _
        objAuthor.GetNewTitleAuthorRecordSet(intAuthorCount)
    For i = 0 To intAuthorCount - 1
        rsAuthor.Fields("au_id").Value = _
            GetAuthorID(lstAuthor.List(i))
        rsAuthor.Fields("title_id").Value = txtTitleID.Text
        rsAuthor.MoveNext
    Next
    rsAuthor.MoveFirst
    Call objBook.UpdateBooks(mRSBook, rsAuthor)
ex:
    mNewBookSelected = False
    Exit Sub
errHandler:
    Call MsgBox(CStr(Err.Number) & "   " & Err.Description)
    GoTo ex
End Sub

Private Sub SaveFormIntoRecordSet(ByRef rs As ADOR.Recordset)
    On Error GoTo errHandler
    rs.Fields("title").Value = txtTitle
    rs.Fields("type").Value = txtType
    rs.Fields("notes").Value = txtNotes.Text
    rs.Fields("pubdate").Value = dtpPubDate.Value
    rs.Fields("ytd_sales").Value = StrToLng(txtYTDSales.Text)
    rs.Fields("price").Value = StrToCur(txtPrice.Text)
    rs.Fields("Advance").Value = StrToCur(txtAdvance.Text)
    rs.Fields("Royalty").Value = StrToLng(txtRoyalty.Text)
    rs.Fields("title_id").Value = txtTitleID.Text
    rs.Fields("pub_id").Value = GetPublisherID(cboPublishers.Text)
    Exit Sub
errHandler:
    MsgBox (Err.Description)
End Sub

Private Sub Form_Load()
    On Error GoTo errHandler
    Dim strAuthorName As String
    Dim objPublisher As Publisher

    Set mAuthorCollection = New Dictionary
    Set mPublisherCollection = New Dictionary
```

```
    Set mBook = New Book
    Set mAuthor = New Author
    Set objPublisher = New Publisher

    Set mRSPublisher = objPublisher.GetPublishers
    If Not mRSPublisher.EOF Then
        Call PopulatePublishers(mRSPublisher)
    End If
    mRSPublisher.MoveFirst
    If Not NewBookSelected Then
        Call SetupExistingBook
    Else
        Call SetupNewBook
    End If

    Set objPublisher = Nothing

    Exit Sub
errHandler:
    MsgBox (Err.Description)
End Sub

Private Sub PopulateForm(ByVal rs As ADOR.Recordset)
    On Error GoTo errHandler
    Dim strPubID As String
    txtTitle.Text = NullToEmptyString(rs.Fields("title").Value)
    txtType.Text = NullToEmptyString(rs.Fields("type").Value)
    strPubID = NullToEmptyString(rs.Fields("pub_id").Value)
    mRSPublisher.Filter = adFilterNone

    If Len(strPubID) > 0 Then
        mRSPublisher.MoveFirst
        mRSPublisher.Filter = "pub_id = '" & strPubID & "'"
        If Not mRSPublisher.EOF Then
            cboPublishers.Text =
                        NullToEmptyString(mRSPublisher.Fields("pub_name"))
        Else
            cboPublishers.Text = mStrNoPublisherSpecified
        End If
    End If
    txtNotes = NullToEmptyString(rs.Fields("notes").Value)
    dtpPubDate.Value = NullToTodaysDate(rs.Fields("pubdate").Value)
    txtYTDSales.Text = NullToEmptyString(rs.Fields("ytd_sales").Value)
    txtPrice.Text = CheckNullCurrency(rs.Fields("price").Value)
    txtAdvance.Text = NullToEmptyString(rs.Fields("Advance").Value)
    txtRoyalty.Text = CheckNullCurrency(rs.Fields("Royalty"))
    txtTitleID.Text = NullToEmptyString(rs.Fields("title_id"))
```

```
    If Len(txtTitleID.Text) > 0 Then
        Set mRsAuthor = mAuthor.GetAuthorsForTitle(mTitleID)
        If Not mRsAuthor.EOF Then
            Call PopulateAuthors(mRsAuthor)
        End If
    Else
        lstAuthor.Clear
    End If
    Exit Sub
errHandler:
    Err.Raise Err.Number, Err.Source, Err.Description
End Sub

Private Sub PopulatePublishers(ByVal rs As ADOR.Recordset)
    On Error GoTo errHandler
    Dim strPublisherName As String
    Do While Not rs.EOF
        strPublisherName = rs("pub_name").Value
        cboPublishers.AddItem (strPublisherName)
        Call mPublisherCollection.Add(strPublisherName, rs("pub_id").Value)
        rs.MoveNext
    Loop
    mStrNoPublisherSpecified = "None"
    cboPublishers.AddItem (mStrNoPublisherSpecified)
    Exit Sub
errHandler:
    Err.Raise Err.Number, Err.Source, Err.Description
End Sub
Private Sub PopulateAuthors(ByVal rs As ADOR.Recordset)
    On Error GoTo errHandler
    Dim strAuthorName As String
    Do While Not rs.EOF
        strAuthorName = rs("au_lname").Value & ", " & rs("au_fname")
        Call lstAuthor.AddItem(strAuthorName)
        Call mAuthorCollection.Add(strAuthorName, rs("au_id").Value)
        rs.MoveNext
    Loop
    Exit Sub
errHandler:
    Err.Raise Err.Number, Err.Source, Err.Description
End Sub

Private Function GetAuthorID(ByVal strListText As String) As String
    Dim strRetval As String
    If mAuthorCollection.Exists(strListText) Then
        strRetval = mAuthorCollection.Item(strListText)
    End If
```

```
    GetAuthorID = strRetval
End Function

Private Function GetPublisherID(ByVal strListText As String) As String
    Dim strRetval As String
    If mPublisherCollection.Exists(strListText) Then
        strRetval = mPublisherCollection.Item(strListText)
    End If
    GetPublisherID = strRetval
End Function

Private Sub lstAuthor_Click()
    If lstAuthor.ListIndex <> -1 Then
        cmdDeleteAuthor.Enabled = True
    Else
        cmdDeleteAuthor.Enabled = False
    End If
End Sub
```

Once again, there is a lot of GUI code here that I really don't want to go through, and I have bolded the lines of code that I want to draw your attention to.

Now add another form to your project by performing the following steps in Visual Basic:

1. Select `Add Form...` from the `Project` menu.
2. Select `Form` on the `New` tab.
3. Click the `Open` button.
4. Change the name of the form in the VB property browser to `frmAuthor`.

This form is used to display a list of all the authors currently in the database so the user can select one to add to a book. Now draw the controls shown on Figure 13.44 on this new form.

The description, type, and name of each control is shown in Table 13.8.

TABLE 13.8 Controls for the Author Form

Control Description	VB Control Type	Control Name in VB Project
Authors List	ListBox	lstAuthors
Add to Title	Command Button	cmdAddToTitle
Exit	Command Button	cmdExit

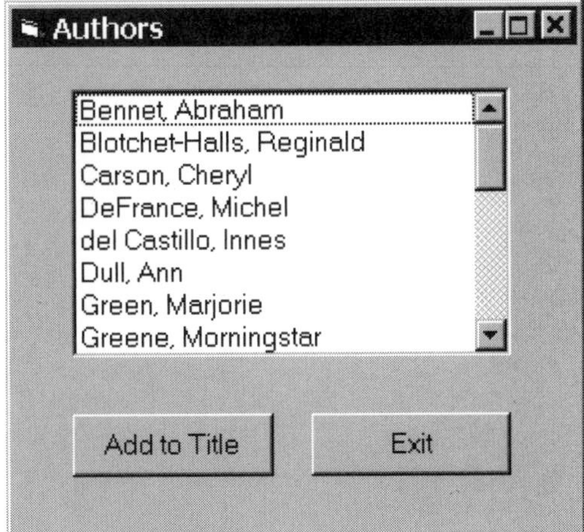

FIGURE 13.44

The Controls on the Author Form.

Now add the code shown in Listing 13.17 to this form.

LISTING 13.17 *THE CODE BEHIND THE AUTHOR FORM*

```
' frmAuthor.frm
Option Explicit
Private mSelectedAuthorID As String
Private mSelectedAuthorFullName As String
Private mAuthorCollection As Dictionary
Private mTitleID As String
Private mAddedTitleToAuthor As Boolean

Public Property Get SelectedAuthorID() As String
    SelectedAuthorID = mSelectedAuthorID
End Property

Public Property Get SelectedAuthorFullName() As String
    SelectedAuthorFullName = mSelectedAuthorFullName
End Property

Public Property Get AddedTitleToAuthor() As Boolean
    AddedTitleToAuthor = mAddedTitleToAuthor
End Property

Public Property Let TitleID(TitleID As String)
    mTitleID = TitleID
End Property

Private Sub cmdAddToTitle_Click()
    On Error GoTo errHandler
```

```
    Dim strSelectedAuthorName As String
    If lstAuthors.ListIndex <> -1 Then
        mSelectedAuthorFullName = lstAuthors.List(lstAuthors.ListIndex)
        mSelectedAuthorID =
mAuthorCollection.Item(mSelectedAuthorFullName)
    End If
    mAddedTitleToAuthor = True
    Call Unload(Me)
    Exit Sub
errHandler:
    Call MsgBox(Err.Description)
End Sub

Private Sub cmdExit_Click()
    On Error GoTo errHandler
    Call Unload(Me)
    Exit Sub
errHandler:
    MsgBox (Err.Description)
End Sub

Private Sub Form_Load()
    On Error GoTo errHandler
    Dim objAuthor As Author
    Dim rs As ADOR.Recordset
    Dim strAuthorName As String
    Set mAuthorCollection = New Dictionary
    Set objAuthor = New Author
    Set rs = objAuthor.GetAuthors
    Do While Not rs.EOF
        strAuthorName = rs("au_lname").Value & ", " & rs("au_fname")
        Call lstAuthors.AddItem(strAuthorName)
        Call mAuthorCollection.Add(strAuthorName, rs("au_id").Value)
        rs.MoveNext
    Loop
    Exit Sub
errHandler:
    Call MsgBox(Err.Description)
End Sub
```

Once again, the code here is fairly simple GUI code so I won't go through it, but the important lines are bolded. The last Visual Basic file is a module .bas file that contains some utilities for working with ADO Recordsets. To add this file to your project, perform the following steps:

1. Select `Add Module` from the `Project` menu (the Add Module dialog appears).
2. Click the `Open` button (this creates a new .bas file).

3. In the VB Property Browser, change the name of the file to RecordSetUtils.

   Now add the code shown in Listing 13.18 to this file.

LISTING 13.18 *ADO RECORDSET UTILITIES*

```
' RecordSetUtils.bas
Public Function CheckNullCurrency(ByVal curr As Variant) As Currency
    On Error GoTo errHandler
    Dim result As Currency
    If IsNull(curr) Then
        result = 0#
    Else
        result = curr
    End If
    CheckNullCurrency = result
    Exit Function
errHandler:
    Err.Raise Err.Number, Err.Source, Err.Description
End Function

Public Function NullToEmptyString(ByVal Var As Variant) As String
    On Error GoTo errHandler
    Dim strRetval As String
    If IsNull(Var) Or IsEmpty(Var) Then
        strRetval = vbNullString
    Else
        strRetval = Var
    End If
    NullToEmptyString = strRetval
    Exit Function
errHandler:
    Err.Raise Err.Number, Err.Source, Err.Description
End Function

Public Function NullToTodaysDate(ByVal Var As Variant) As String
    On Error GoTo errHandler
    Dim dtRetval As Date
    If Var = vbEmpty Then
        dtRetval = Now
    Else
        dtRetval = Var
    End If
    NullToTodaysDate = dtRetval
    Exit Function
errHandler:
    Err.Raise Err.Number, Err.Source, Err.Description
End Function
```

```
Public Function StrToLng(ByVal str As String) As Long
    On Error GoTo errHandler
    Dim lngRetval As Long
    If Len(str) = 0 Then
        lngRetval = 0
    Else
        lngRetval = CLng(str)
    End If
    Exit Function
errHandler:
    Err.Raise Err.Number, Err.Source, Err.Description
End Function
Public Function StrToCur(ByVal str As String) As Long
    On Error GoTo errHandler
    Dim curRetval As Currency
    If Len(str) = 0 Then
        curRetval = 0
    Else
        curRetval = CCur(str)
    End If
    Exit Function
errHandler:
    Err.Raise Err.Number, Err.Source, Err.Description
End Function
```

Now you can build your client executable. Select `Make book-client.exe` from the `File` menu. If you have trouble building your client, or you are an inexperienced Visual Basic programmer, you can download the client from the Web site.

You can run your Visual Basic client. You should be able to type in a keyword and push the search button. You should see a list of books that contain the keyword in their title. Double-click on a book to bring up the edit book dialog with the detailed information for the book. You can edit the information for the book, including adding and removing authors for the book, and then save the book. If you wish to add a new book, you can click the new book button. If you see a permission denied error, make sure you have added yourself to both the Employee and Manager roles. Try removing yourself from the Manager and try to do an update. You should definitely see a permission denied error. Now let's build your HTML client.

Implementing the ASP, HTML Client

Most enterprise-class applications need to support access via the Internet. HTML-based interfaces are becoming more important these days. Until recently, I was a believer in the strategy that you should have a native, client/server application for everyday power users; a Web interface should primarily be for occasional or remote users. The main reason I feel this way is that even with dyamic HTML, you still cannot provide as rich and intuitive an interface as you can with a native Windows app. Recently, I changed my mind in this area and I believe that for most new apps, you should try to create a Web-based interface that everyone can use. The main industry trend that has changed my opinion is the emergence of a new model for distributing business applications called the Application Service Provider Model.

The Application Service Provider Model is sometimes called the ASP Model, but I'm going to avoid using that acronym because I'm already using it for Active Server Pages.

In the Application Service Provider Model, businesses rent applications from Application Service Providers who will host and maintain the application. The easiest way to use applications in this model is to make them Web-based. The Application Service Provider Company can then host the application and its associated database on their servers and consumers can use the application over the Internet through their Web browsers paying either a per-use or a flat monthly rate. If this market does explode, as many people think it will, Web-based business applications may soon be the only kind of business applications that are built. Fortunately, the Windows DNA fits perfectly into this model. With COM+, ADO, and ASP, it is easy to build Web-based user interfaces.

To build your HTML/ASP client, perform the following summarized steps:

1. Create the HTML and ASP files.
2. Create a Virtual Directory in IIS.
3. Configure the Virtual Directory.
4. Create the HTML and ASP files.

I created the HTML and ASP files using Front Page 2000. You can use any HTML editor, Visual InterDev, or even notepad to create these files, or just copy them from the Web site. If you are following along, I recommend that you create a separate directory for these files; don't put them in the same directory as your Visual Basic or Visual C++ projects.

CREATING THE HTML AND ASP FILES

There is one pure HTML page in this Web application. This page lets the user specify a keyword to search for books. When displayed in Internet Explorer 5.0, it looks like that shown in Figure 13.45.

The HTML for this page is shown in Listing 13.19.

LISTING 13.19 *THE HTML FOR OUR MAIN PAGE, DEFAULT.HTM*

```
<html>
<head>
<meta http-equiv="Content-Type"
content="text/html; charset=iso-8859-1">
<meta name="GENERATOR" content="Microsoft FrontPage 4.0">
<title>Browse for a book by keyword</title>
</head>
<body background="ACEXPDTN.GIF">

<h1 align="center">Browse for a book by keyword</h1>
<hr>

<form action="browse.asp" method="post">
    <p> </p>
<P align="center">Enter a keyword: 
    </P>
<P align="center"> <input name="Keyword" >
```

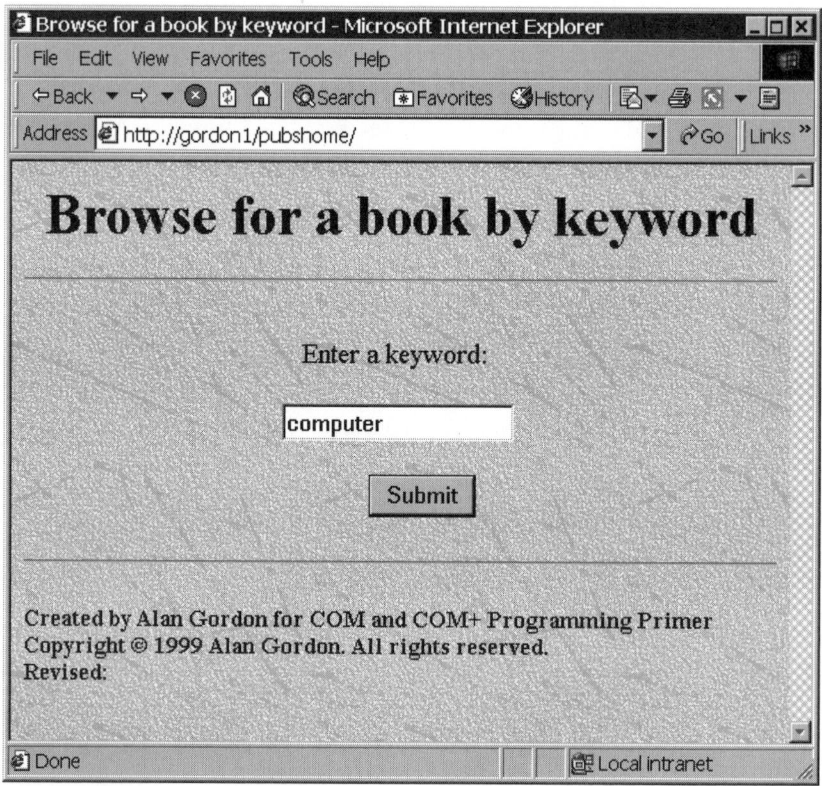

FIGURE 13.45 The Main Page for Your Application.

```
18.       </P>
19.       <p align="center">      
20.       <input type="submit" name="SubmitButton"
21.       value="Submit"></p>
22. </form>
23. <hr>
24. <h5>Created by Alan Gordon for The COM and COM+ Programming Primer<br>
25. Copyright © 1999 Alan Gordon. All rights reserved.<br>
26. </h5>
27. </body>
28. </html>
```

The HTML code shown here is fairly simply. The background image used on line 8 (`acexpdtn.gif`) is bundled with FrontPage 2000 and you can find it on the Web site. If you are following along, you need to copy it to the directory where you are creating your HTML and ASP files.

The only really interesting lines for this discussion are lines 13-22. On these lines, you define an HTML form. On line 13 you specify the action to be performed when the user presses the `Submit` button for the form. In this case, you are going to use the `http POST` method to invoke an Active Server page called `browse.asp`. Notice on line 17 the edit box that contains the keyword the user enters has been assigned the name Keyword. Save this HTML file under the filename, `default.htm`.

Listing 13.20 shows the code for the file `browse.asp` to be invoked when the user clicks the `Submit` button on the main page.

LISTING 13.20 *THE CODE FOR BROWSE.ASP YOUR APPLICATION*

```
<HTML>
<HEAD>
<META NAME="GENERATOR" Content="Microsoft FrontPage 4.0">
<META HTTP-EQUIV="Content-Type" content="text/html; charset=iso-8859-1">
<TITLE>Search Results</TITLE>
</HEAD>
<BODY background="ACEXPDTN.GIF">
<h1>Search Results </h1>
<hr>

<%
   set objBook=Server.CreateObject("pubsboserver.book")
   set rs=objBook.RetrieveByKeyword(Request.form("Keyword"))
   response.write("<TABLE BORDER=1>")
   strRow="<TR><TD>TitleID</TD><TD>Title</TD><TD>AuthLast</TD>" & _
      "<TD>AuthFirst</TD><TD>Type</TD><TD>Price</TD></TR>" & vbcrlf
   response.write(strRow)
   do while not rs.eof
      titleID=rs.fields("title_id")
```

```
20.         strRow="<TR><TD> <a href=" & chr(34) & "editbook.asp?id=" & _
21.             titleID & chr(34) & ">" & titleID & "</a></TD>" & _
22.             "<TD>" & rs.fields("title").value & "</TD>" & _
23.             "<TD>" & rs.fields("au_lname").value & "</TD>" & _
24.             "<TD>" & rs.fields("au_fname").value & "</TD>" & _
25.             "<TD>" & rs.fields("type").value & "</TD>" & _
26.             "<TD>" & rs.fields("price").value & "</TD></TR>" & vbcrlf
27.         response.write(strRow)
28.         rs.movenext
29.     loop
30.     Response.Write("</TABLE>")
31. %>
32.
33. <hr>
34. <h5>Created by Alan Gordon for The COM and COM+ Programming Primer<br>
35. Copyright © 2000 Alan Gordon. All rights reserved.<br>
36. </h5>
37. </BODY>
38. </HTML>
```

This file lets you browse information about the books that contain the specified keywod in their title. It displays the title ID, title, author last name, author first name, type, and price of each book in an HTML table. Figure 13.46 shows a typical response this file generates.

Remember that when a request is made on an asp document, the file is first sent to an interpreter on the Web server machine that executes all lines between the following markers: <% %>. The rest of the code in the asp file is treated like normal HTML. In this case, the bolded lines (12–30) lie between the script markers and contain the executable code for this asp file.

On line 12, you instantiate a Book object and assign it to the variable `objBook`. On line 13, you call the method `RetrieveByKeyword` and pass in the value in the Keyword control on the requesting form. The requesting form is the HTML file shown in Listing 13.19 and the Keyword control is the edit box users type their keyword into. The return value of the `RetrieveByKeyword` method is an ADO Recordset that is assigned to the variable `rs`. On lines 14–17, you create the header for the HTML table. On lines 18–29, you write out each row in the HTML table. The first column in each row contains a hyperlink that points to another Active Server Page called `editbook.asp`. This page contains detailed information about each title. Notice the syntax used on line 20 to call the editbook ASP file. You have the name of the asp file, a question mark, and then `id=` followed by the ID of the title. This is how you pass a parameter to an ASP file. If the user clicks this hyperlink, the `editbook.asp` file is invoked with an ID parameter equal to the ID of the title the user hyperlinked on. On lines 20 and 21, you write the symbol char(34) into the response HTML stream; this is how you write a quotation mark into the HTML stream that is sent back to the client.

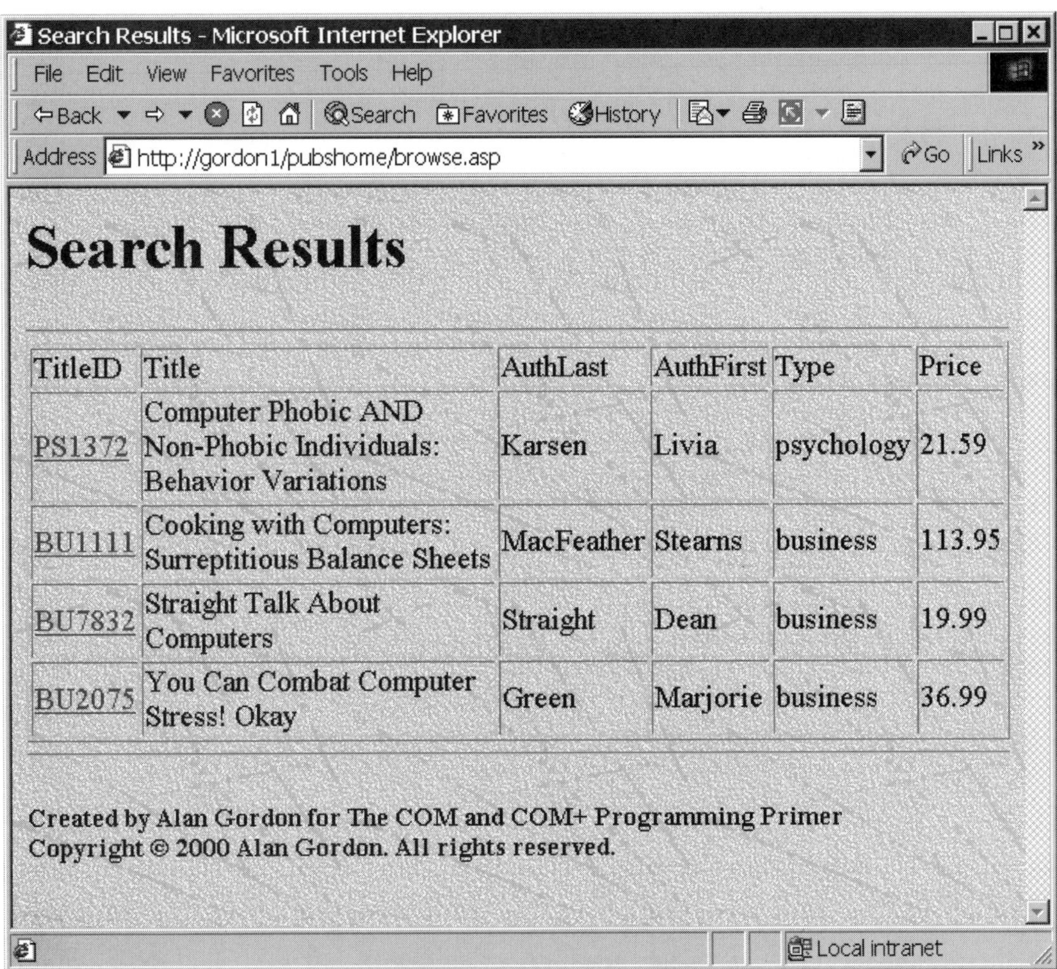

FIGURE 13.46 A Typical Response from the Browse.asp File.

Now let's look at the `editbook.asp` file, which is shown in Listing 13.21.

LISTING 13.21 *THE CODE FOR EDITBOOK.ASP*

```
<html>
<head>
<META NAME="GENERATOR" Content="Microsoft FrontPage 4.0">
<META HTTP-EQUIV="Content-Type" content="text/html; charset=iso-8859-1">
<title>Edit Title</title>
</head>
<body background="ACEXPDTN.GIF">
<h1 align="center">Title Information</h1>
```

```
<hr>
<form METHOD="POST" ACTION="updatebook.asp">
<%
    titleID=Request.querystring("id")
   set objBook=Server.CreateObject("pubsboserver.book")
   set rsBook=objBook.RetrieveByID(titleID)
   set objAuthor=Server.CreateObject("pubsboserver.author")
   set rsAuthors=objAuthor.GetAuthorsForTitle(titleID)

   strResp="<p>Title: <input type=text name=Title size=40 value='" & _
      rsBook.fields("title").value & "'>  " & vbcrlf
   strResp=strResp & _
      "Authors:<select size='1' name='AuthorList'>" & vbcrlf
   if rsAuthors.RecordCount > 0 then
      strResp=strResp & "<option selected value=" & _
         rsAuthors.fields("au_id").value & ">" & _
         rsAuthors.fields("au_fname").value & ", " & _
         rsAuthors.fields("au_lname").value & _
         "</option>" & vbcrlf
      rsAuthors.movenext
      do while not rsAuthors.EOF
         strResp=strResp & "<option value=" & _
            rsAuthors.fields("au_id").value & ">" & _
            rsAuthors.fields("au_fname").value & ", " & _
            rsAuthors.fields("au_lname").value & _
            "</option>" & vbcrlf
         rsAuthors.movenext
      loop
   end if
   strResp=strResp & "</select> </p>" & vbcrlf

   strResp=strResp & "<p> Title ID:" & rsBook.fields("title_id").value & _
         "       " & vbcrlf

   strResp=strResp & _
      "Publisher:" & rsBook.fields("pub_name").value & "</p>" & vbcrlf

   strResp=strResp & _
      "<input type=hidden name=TitleID value=" & titleID & ">" & vbcrlf

   strResp=strResp & _
      "<p>Type: <input type=text name=Type size=16 value='" & _
      rsBook.fields("type").value & "'>    " & _
      vbcrlf
```

```
    strResp=strResp & _
        "Price: <input type=text name=Price size=9 value='" & _
        rsBook.fields("price").value & "'>   " & vbcrlf

    strResp=strResp & _
        "Pub Date: <input type=text name=PubDate size=10 value='" & _
        rsBook.fields("pubdate").value & "'>  </p>" & _
        vbcrlf

        strResp=strResp & _
        "<p> YTD Sales: <input type=text name=YTDSales size=8 value='" & _
            rsBook.fields("ytd_sales").value & "'>  " & vbcrlf

    strResp=strResp & _
        " Advance: <input type=text name=Advance size=10 value='" & _
        rsBook.fields("advance").value & "'>   " & vbcrlf

        strResp=strResp & _
        "Royalty: <input type=text name=Royalty size=10 value='" & _
            rsBook.fields("royalty").value & "'>    </p>" & _
        vbcrlf

    strResp=strResp & "<p>Notes:    </p>" & _
        "<p><textarea rows=5 name=Notes cols=60>" & _
        rsBook.fields("notes").value & "</textarea></p>" & vbcrlf

    response.write(strResp)
%>
<p align="center"><input TYPE="submit" VALUE="Submit" style="text-
    align: Center"> </p>
</form>
<hr>
<h5>Created by Alan Gordon for The COM and COM+ Programming Primer<br>
```

```
Copyright © 2000 Alan Gordon. All rights reserved.<br>
</h5>
</body>
</html>
```

A typical response from this ASP file is shown in Figure 13.47.

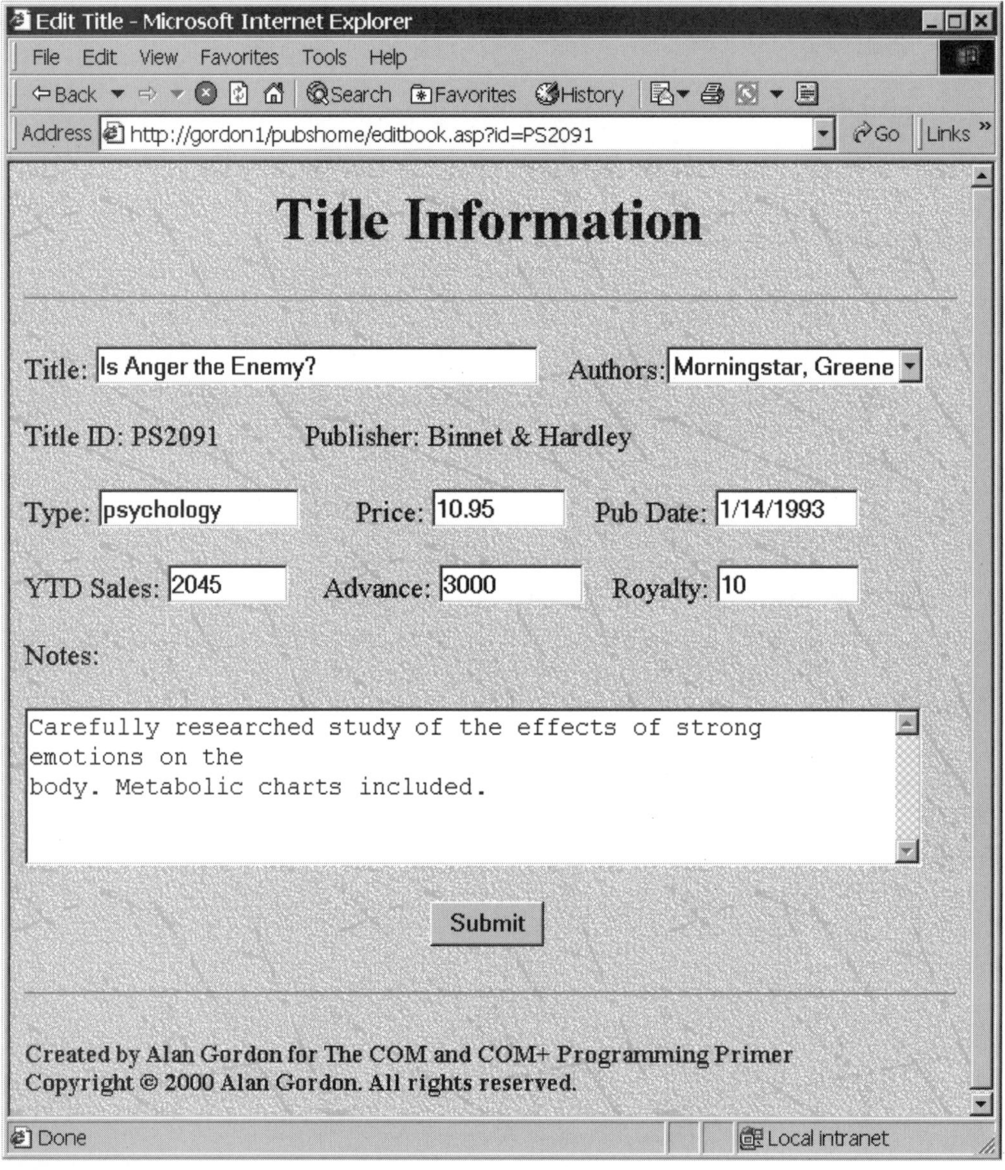

FIGURE 13.47 A Typical Response From the EditBook.asp File.

On line 10 is the Action statement for this form, which defines what happens when the user presses the `Submit` button. In this case, you invoke the `UpdateBook` asp file. Lines 11–81 (shown in bold) in this file contain the executable code that is interpreted by IIS on the server. Remember the Browse ASP file invokes the `EditBook` ASP file and passes the following parameter list:

```
Editbook.asp?id=<BookID>
```

On line 12, you retrieve the ID parameter that was passed to the ASP page and store it in a variable called titleID. Next, on lines 13 and 14, you instantiate a Book object and call the `RetrieveByID` method, passing in the titleID. The recordset that is returned from this method is stored in an ADO recordset called rsBook. On lines 15 and 16, you instantiate an Author object and call the `GetAuthorsForTitle` method passing in the titleID. The recordset that is returned from this method is stored in an ADO recordset called rsAuthor. On lines 18 and 19, you write the title, which is contained in the title field of the rsBook recordset, into an HTML text box in your response form. On lines 22–38 you populate an HTML drop-down list with the Authors for the book. On lines 40–80, you populate the other controls on the HTML form with data from the rsBook recordset. An important line of code is on lines 46 and 47 where the titleID for the book is stored in a hidden field in the form to make it easy for the `UpdateBook` ASP file to retrieve the titleID of the book that is to be updated. Finally on line 80, you write the response back to the client.

If you look at Figure 13.47, you'll see you can update all the fields except the titleID and Publisher. There's no reason why you couldn't update these fields also; I was just trying not to make this example more complicated than it already is. The update is performed in the `UpdateBook` ASP file, which is invoked when the user clicks the `Submit` button.

The `UpdateBook` ASP file is shown in Listing 13.22.

LISTING 13.22 *THE CODE FOR UPDATEBOOK.ASP*

```
<html>
<head>
<META NAME="GENERATOR" Content="Microsoft FrontPage 4.0">
<META HTTP-EQUIV="Content-Type" content="text/html; charset=iso-8859-1">
<title>Update Status</title>
</head>

<body background="ACEXPDTN.GIF">
<%
   on error resume next
   numErrors=0
```

```
set objBook=Server.CreateObject("pubsboserver.book")
titleID=Request.form("titleID")
set rsBook=objBook.GetExistingBookRecordSet("title_id='"&titleID&"'")

dtpub=cdate(request.form("PubDate"))
if err.number <> 0 then
   call ShowError("The publication date is not valid")
   err.number=0
end if

lngYTDSales=clng(request.form("YTDSales"))
if err.number <> 0 then
   call ShowError("The YTD sales is not a valid number")
   err.number=0
end if

sngRoyalty=csng(request.form("Royalty"))
if err.number <> 0 then
   call ShowError("The Royalty is not a valid number")
   err.number=0
end if
if sngRoyalty < 0 or sngRoyalty > 100 then
   call ShowError("The royalty must be > 0 and < 100")
   err.number=0
end if

curAdvance=ccur(request.form("Advance"))
if err.number <> 0 then
   call ShowError("Invalid entry for Advance")
   err.number=0
end if

curPrice=ccur(request.form("Price"))
if err.number <> 0 then
   call ShowError("Invalid entry for Price")
   err.number=0
end if

if numErrors=0 then
   rsBook.fields("title").value=request.form("Title")
   rsBook.fields("type").value=request.form("Type")
   rsBook.fields("pubdate").value=dtPub
   rsBook.fields("ytd_sales").value=lngYTDSales
   rsBook.fields("royalty").value=sngRoyalty
```

```
56.         rsBook.fields("advance").value=curAdvance
57.         rsBook.fields("price").value=curPrice
58.         rsBook.fields("Notes").value=request.form("Notes")
59.         call objBook.UpdateBooks(rsBook,nothing)
60.         if err.Number = 0 then
61.            response.write("<h1 align=center>Update Succeeded!!!</h1>")
62.         else
63.            ShowError("Business object error: " & err.description)
64.         end if
65.     end if
66.
67. sub ShowError(strDescription)
68.     if numErrors=0 then
69.         response.write("<h1 align=center>Update Failed!!!</h1><hr>")
70.     end if
71.     numErrors=numErrors+1
72.     response.write("<p>" & strDescription & "</p>" & vbcrlf)
73.     stop
74. end sub
75. %>
76. <hr>
77. <h5>Created by Alan Gordon for The COM and COM+ Programming Primer<br>
78. Copyright © 2000 Alan Gordon. All rights reserved.<br>
79. </h5>
80. </body>
81. </html>
```

The executable code is contained in lines 10-74. Because most of the fields in the form that invoke this page (see Figure 13.47) are free-form text, you need to do error handling in this function. So on line 10, you begin the VB Script portion of your active server page with an *on error resume next* statement. With other variants of VB, you have two choices of how to handle errors. You can tell VB to jump to an error handler when an error occurs. You do this with an on error goto <label> statement. Or you can tell VB if it encounters an error to just keep going, which you do with an *on error resume next statement*. If you choose the latter approach, then your VB keeps going when it encounters an error and you have to check the number property of the global *err* object for errors after each statement or group of statements. A non-zero value for err.number indicates that a failure occurred. With VB Script, your only error handling option is the *on error resume next* approach used here.

On line 11, you initialize a variable that contains the number of errors found so far. On lines 12–14, you instantiate a Book object, retrieve the titleID for the title that you'll be updating from the form (this is actually stored in a hidden field in the form), and call the `GetExistingBook-RecordSet` method on the Book business object to retrieve a recordset that contains the current information for the Book that you are updating.

On lines 16–20, you process the publication date in the form. You first call the cdate Visual Basic function to attempt to convert the information in the publication date field to a date. If the field contains a valid date, this function converts the text in the field to a date value, if not, it generates an error. So right after calling the `cdate` function, you check to see if `err.number` is non-zero. If it is non-zero, you call the `ShowError` subroutine with a descriptive string describing the problem. The `ShowError` function (shown on lines 67–74) builds up a well-formatted response when an error occurs).

You follow the similar pattern set by lines 16–20 on lines 22–48. You attempt to convert the data in the form field to the correct data type. If the conversion fails, call the `ShowError` function.

I don't consider the error checking that you're doing in this function business rules. This is just data validity checking. In fact, this sort of checking should ideally be done on the client. In a production application, I would probably use JavaScript (because it's more portable than VB script) to do this sort of data-validity checking on the client.

On lines 50–65, you update the recordset you received from the `GetExistingBookRecordSet` with the data from your form, and on line 59 you call the `UpdateBook` method in your Book business object to update the database. Notice on line 59 that you take advantage of the flexibility of this method and pass nothing for the Author information since you are not allowing the user to update Author information through the Web interface. On lines 60–65, you check the err.number value after the call to update books to see if your method call generated errors, and if it did, you call ShowError to display the error to your users.

CREATING A VIRTUAL DIRECTORY IN IIS

Now you are ready to setup your application so it can be used over an Internet or Intranet. To do this, you first need to setup a virtual directory for your ASP application. A virtual directory maps a directory name in a URL such as `http://myserver/mydirectory/` to a real directory on your hard drive. Hopefully, you followed my advice and created all your ASP and HTML files in a directory by themselves. You'll create a virtual directory using the Computer Management Explorer, which is a Snap-In for the Microsoft Management Console. The Computer Management Explorer is used for administering, among other things, Internet Information Server (IIS) and Microsoft Message Queue (MSMQ). You can invoke this application by performing the following steps:

1. Click the `Start` Menu.
2. Select `\Programs\Administrative Tools\Computer Management\`.

The Computer Management Explorer looks like that shown in Figure 13.48. To setup your virtual directory, perform the following steps:

1. Open the `Services and Applications` Tree.
2. Open the `Internet Information Services` Tree.
3. Right-click on `Default Web` site.
4. Select `New\Virtual Directory` from the Console (you should see step 1 of the Virtual Directory Creation Wizard as shown in Figure 13.49).

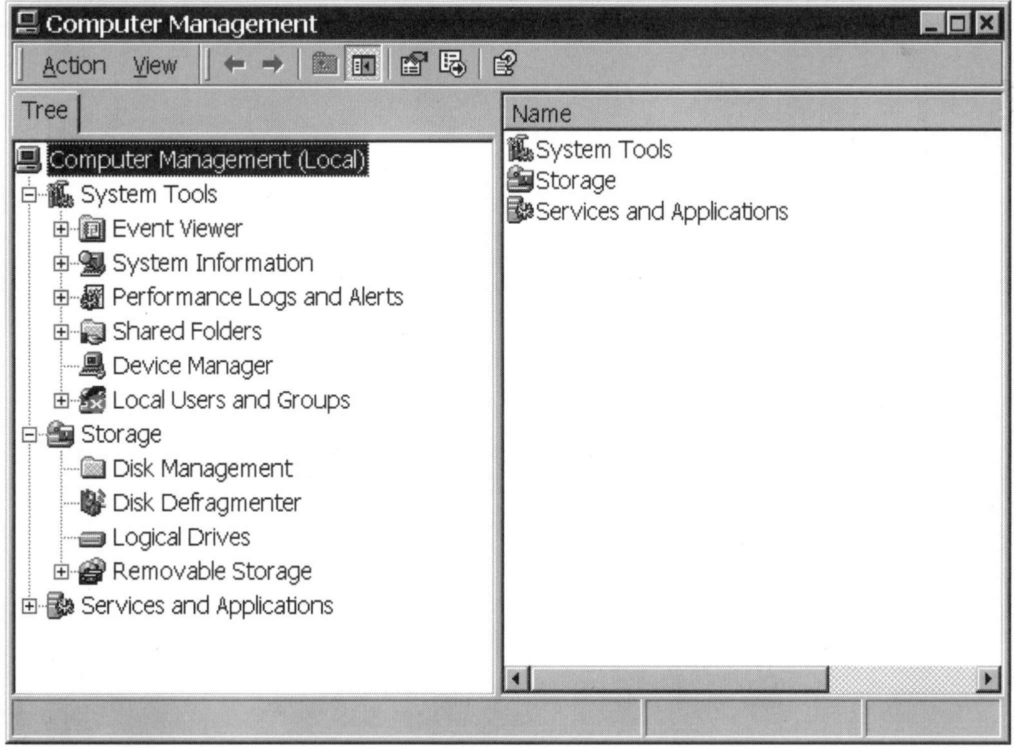

FIGURE 13.48 The Computer Management Explorer.

5. Click the `Next` button (you should see step 2 of the Virtual Directory Creation Wizard as shown in Figure 13.50).
6. Enter `PubsHome` in the alias field.
7. Click the `Next` button (you should see step 3 of the Virtual Directory Creation Wizard as shown in Figure 13.51).
8. Click the `Browse...` button and navigate to where the HTML files are stored on your hard drive.
9. Click the `Next` button (you should see step 4 of the Virtual Directory Creation Wizard as shown in Figure 13.52).
10. Accept the defaults shown in Figure 13.52 and click the `Next` button.
11. Click `Finish` on the last page of the Wizard.

It is important (and it should be obvious why) that the Run Scripts (Such as ASP) checkbox is checked in step 10. Now that you have created your virtual directory, you can try to access your application from Internet Explorer.

FIGURE 13.49 Step 1 of the Virtual Directory Creation Wizard.

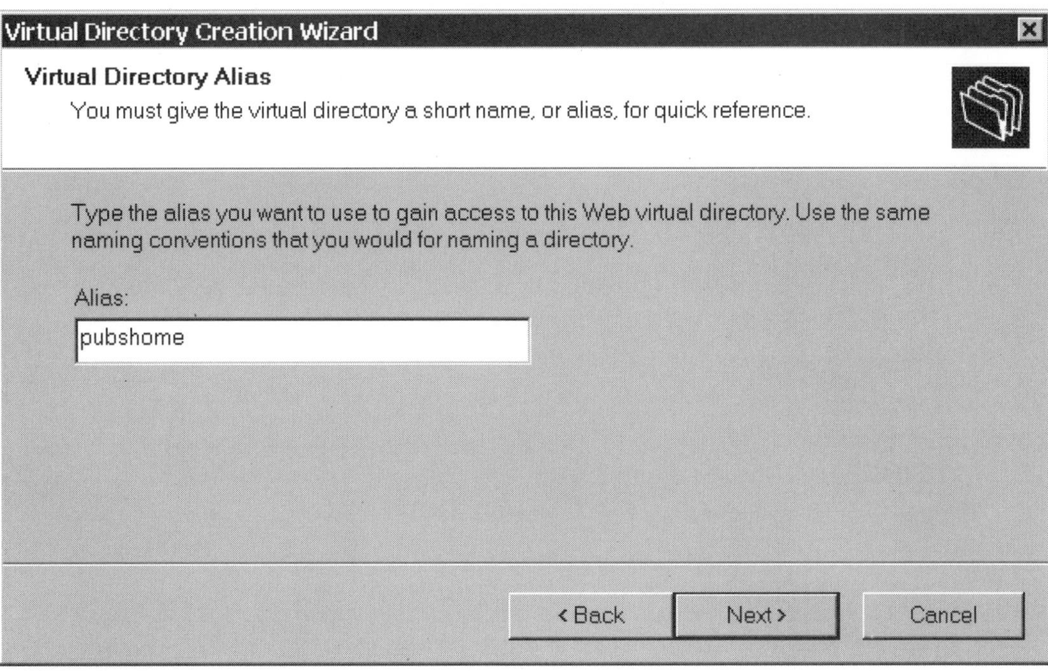

FIGURE 13.50 Step 2 of the Virtual Directory Creation Wizard.

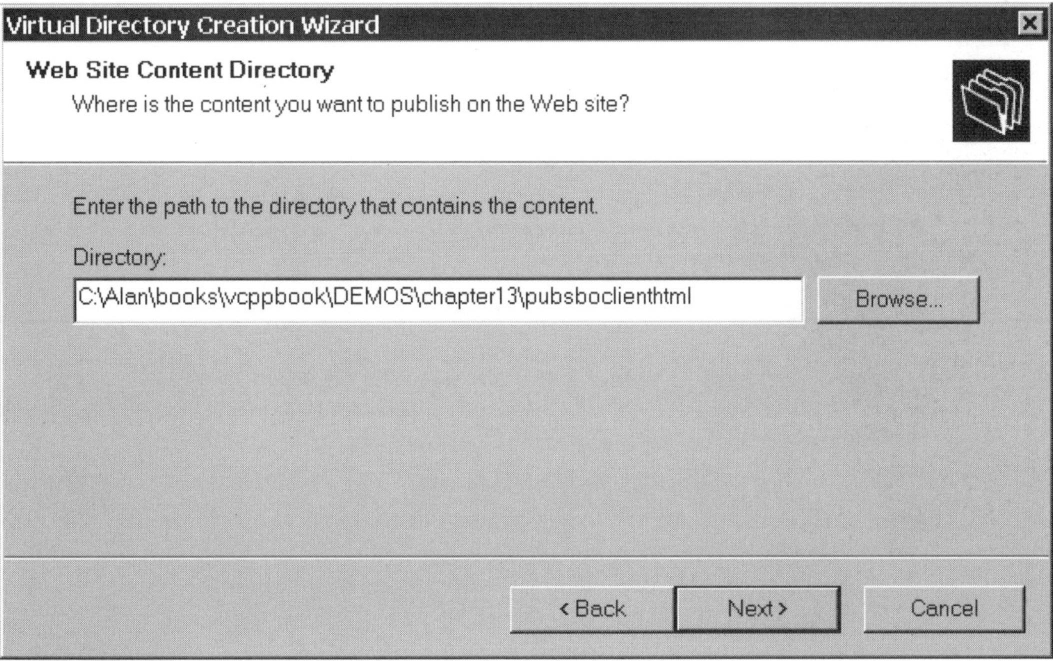

FIGURE 13.51 Step 3 of the Virtual Directory Creation Wizard.

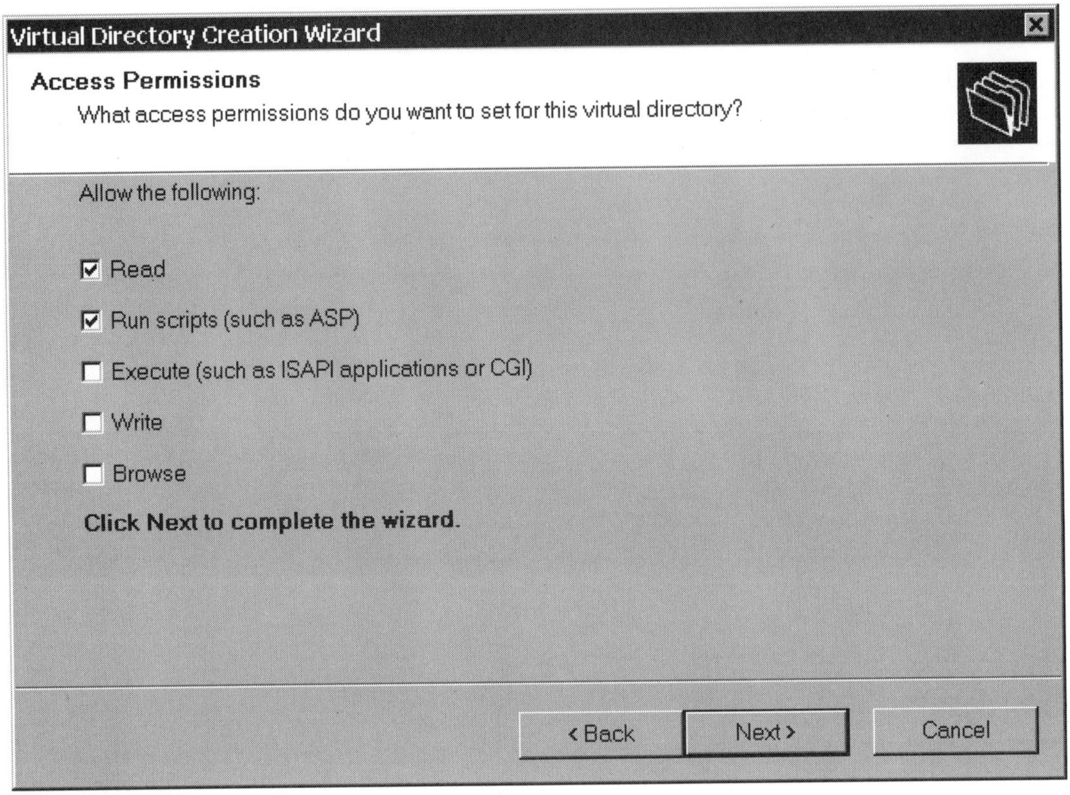

FIGURE 13.52 Step 4 of the Virtual Directory Creation Wizard.

For ASP files to be interpreted properly, you must run them through the Web server. Remember, it's the Web server that interprets the code between the <% %> symbols which generates the finished HTML. If you just double-click on the file in the NT File Explorer, you will not see the desired result.

Type the following URL into your Web browser:

```
http://localhost/pubshome/
```

You should be able to use either Internet Explorer or Netscape Navigator and see the main page of your application as shown in Figure 13.45. Now type in a keyword and click the `Submit` button. You should get a permission denied error when you try to instantiate your business object. To understand why you have this problem, think about the following question: Under whose security credentials is IIS running when it attempts to instantiate your business object?

You can see who IIS is running as by turning off COM+ access control and then writing the following code to see the username of the person instantiating the object:

```
ISecurityProperty *pSecProp;
SID *pSID;
TCHAR name[255], domain[255];
DWORD sizename=255, sizedomain=255;
SID_NAME_USE peUse;
CoGetObjectContext(IID_ISecurityProperty,(void **)&pSecProp);
pSecProp->GetDirectCallerSID((void**)&pSID);
LookupAccountSid(NULL,pSID,name,&sizename,domain,&sizedomain,&peUse);
ATLTRACE(name);  // You can see the user name in the debugger
pSecProp->Release();
```

If you run this code, you will see that the user name is `IUSR_<YOURMACHINENAME>`. In my case, my machine is called Gordon1 and the user name is `IUSR_GORDON1`. The description of this account in the Active Directory says that it is a "Built-in account for anonymous access to Internet Information Services." In other words, this is the account IIS uses if the user does not explicitly log in to the Web site. You can now go back to the Component Services Explorer and add the `IUSR_<YOURMACHINENAME>` username to the Employee and Manager roles. Make sure that you shut down your COM+ application by right-clicking on the application in the Component Services Explorer and selecting `Shut Down` from the `Context` menu before you test again. Your application should now work. But what if you don't want to allow anonymous access? You can disable anonymous access by performing the following steps in the Computer Management Explorer:

1. Right-click on the virtual directory name beneath the default Web site tree item.
2. Select `Properties` from the `Context` menu (the Virtual Directory Properties dialog appears as shown in Figure 13.53).
3. Click the `Directory Security` tab.
4. Click the `Edit...` button at the top of the screen (the Authentication Methods dialog should appear as shown in Figure 13.54).
5. Clear the `Anonymous Access` checkbox.
6. Click `OK` on the `Authentication Methods` dialog.
7. Click `OK` on the `Virtual Directory Properties` dialog.

If you want, you can go back and remove `IUSR_<YOURMACHINENAME>` from the Employee and Manager roles and the application will still work. You are now running the application as yourself.

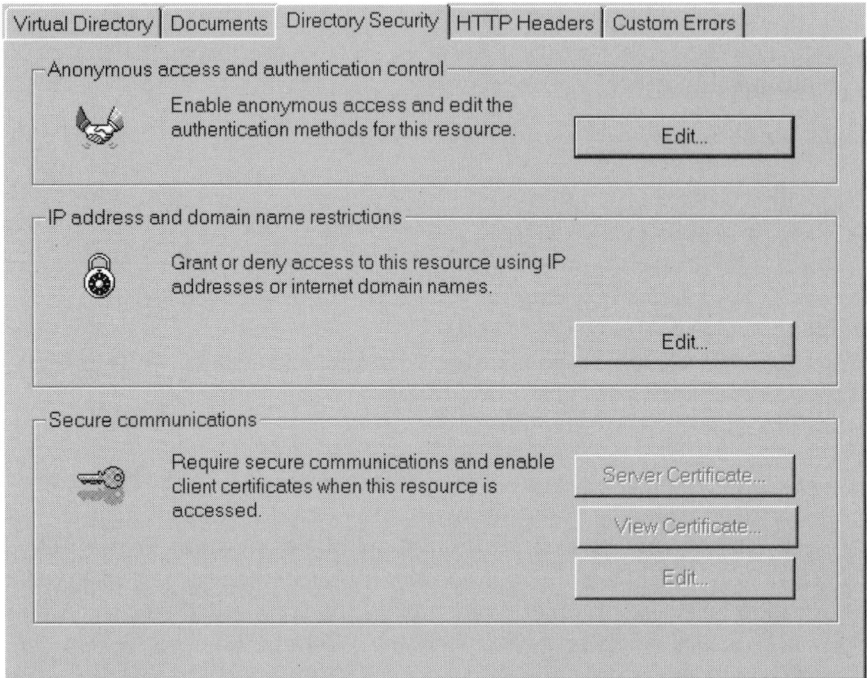

FIGURE 13.53 The Virtual Directory Properties Dialog.

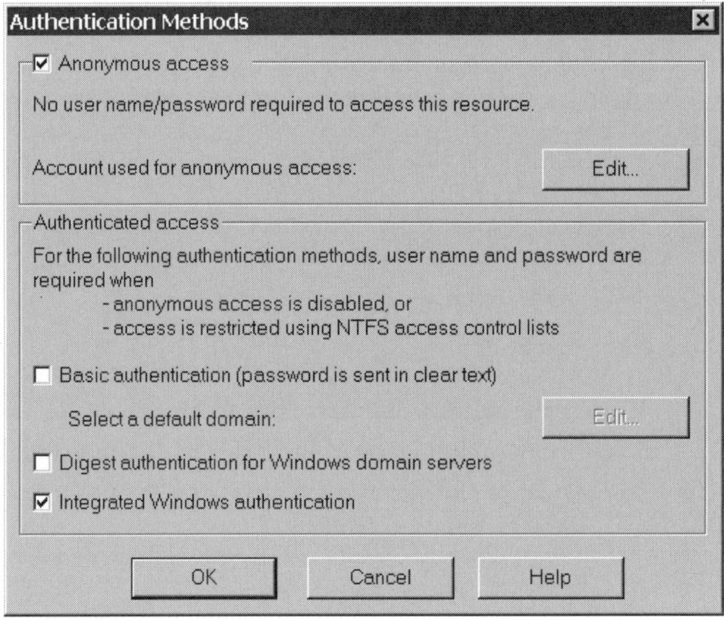

FIGURE 13.54 The Authentication Methods Dialog.

Object Pooling

You are now ready to configure object pooling for your COM+ application. Before doing this, let's first change the threading model for your component to use the neutral threading model.

You can use object pooling with free-threaded components also, but since the Thread Neutral Apartment (TNA) is now the recommended threading model for COM+ components, I decided it was worthwhile to show you how to create thread-neutral components with Visual C++.

One problem I found is that the COM+ runtime does not like it when you change the threading model of components that have already been configured.

Microsoft may fix this in the release version of Windows 2000.

Unfortunately, that means you have to remove the `Author`, `Book`, and `Publisher` classes from your COM+ application before you modify the threading model. You can then reinsert the classes back into the COM+ application. To remove the classes from your COM+ application, go to the `Component` folder in the left pane of the Component Services Explorer. Select all three components in the right pane. Right-click and select `Delete` from the `Context` menu. Changing the threading model for your components is also simple. Perform the following steps to do this:

1. Go to the `File` tab in the Visual C++ workspace as shown in Figure 13.55.
2. Open the Folder called `Resource Files`.
3. You should see a file with the name `Author.rgs` (there should be one each for `Author`, `Book`, and `Publisher`).
4. Double-click in the left pane to open the file.
5. In the right hand pane change the `Threading Model` to `Neutral`.

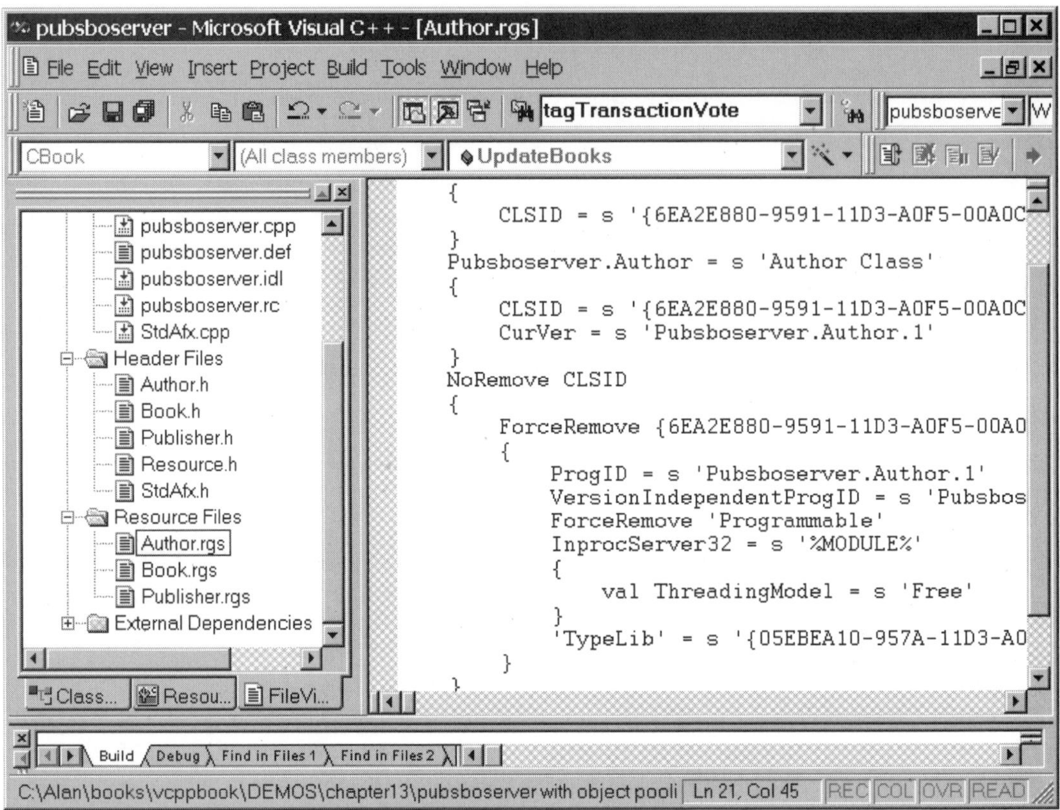

FIGURE 13.55 Changing the Threading Model.

You should have changed the following code in the `Author.rgs` file:

```
InprocServer32 = s '%MODULE%'
{
val ThreadingModel = s 'Free'
}
```

so that it reads as follows:

```
InprocServer32 = s '%MODULE%'
{
val ThreadingModel = s 'Neutral'
}
```

Vóila. Your objects are apartment neutral. Now you need to reconfigure your components. I won't go through the steps again to configure security and transactions and to setup the construction string. Refer to those sections in this chapter. To configure object pooling for each of your components (classes), perform the following steps in the Component Services Explorer:

1. Right-click on the Component in the `Components` folder.
2. Select `Properties` from the `Context` menu (the Component properties dialog appears).
3. Click the `Activation` Tab (see Figure 13.56).
4. Set the `Enable Object Pooling` checkbox.
5. Set the Minimum Pool Size to `4`.
6. Set the Maximum Pool Size to `100`.
7. Accept the default timeout period.
8. Click `OK`.

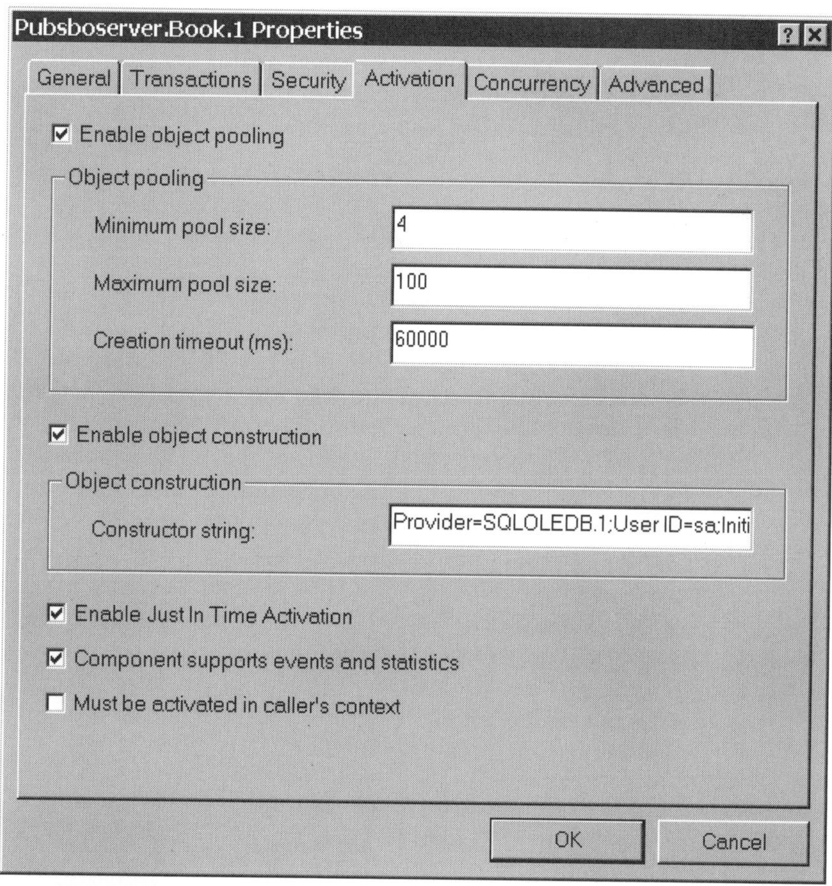

FIGURE 13.56 Configure Object Pooling.

The Minimum Pool Size specifies how many objects will be created immediately when the COM+ application starts. The COM+ runtime maintains at least the number of objects in the pool.

The current size of the Pool is the total number of both active (currently being used by a client) and inactive objects.

If the number of objects drops below the Minimum Pool Size, new objects are created to replenish the pool. If the number of *available* objects in the pool is above the minimum size, the extra objects are destroyed at the next cleanup cycle. If a client requests an object and there are no available objects in the pool, additional objects are created up to the Maximum Pool Size. After that, client requests are queued and they wait the specified timeout period for an object to become available before failing.

Now try running either client again. On my machine, I wasn't able to sense a significant difference. But using object pooling is definitely faster if you are doing lots of instantiations.

Deploying COM+ Applications

At this point you may be wondering how to deploy your COM+ application. There are two parts to this problem: (1) You must be able to easily and conveniently recreate the COM+ application including all of the components that it contains, the attribute settings (transaction, synchronization, and so on) for each component, and the security configuration including the roles and the assignment of those roles to the various entities (classes, interfaces, and methods) in the COM+ application, and (2) you must be able to easily and conveniently install onto a client the necessary registry entries and marshaling proxies so a remote client can access the components in the COM+ application. Fortunately, the Component Services Explorer provides you with all the tools you need to do both. Using the Component Services Explorer, you can generate an export file that contains all the information required to deploy a COM+ application easily and quickly. You can then take this file to another machine and use the Component Services Explorer on that machine to import the file.

You can also configure a remote machine using the Component Services Explorer. See the sidebar entitled "Configuring Remote Machines."

You can also bundle this export file into a setup program that performs all the steps required to setup your application (install client software, and create and populate a database). You can also create an Application Proxy, which contains the registry entries and marshaling proxies required to access the COM+ application from a remote client. Perform the following steps in the Component Services Explorer to create either a server export file or an Application Proxy:

1. Right-click on a COM+ application as shown in Figure 13.57.
2. Select `Export...` from the `Context` menu (the welcome screen of the Export Wizard appears).
3. Click `Next` (the Application Export Information dialog appears as shown in Figure 13.58).
4. On the Application Export Information dialog, select the path where you wish to export the file and whether you wish to export a server application (server export file) or an Application Proxy.
5. Click `Next` and then click `Finish` on the final screen.

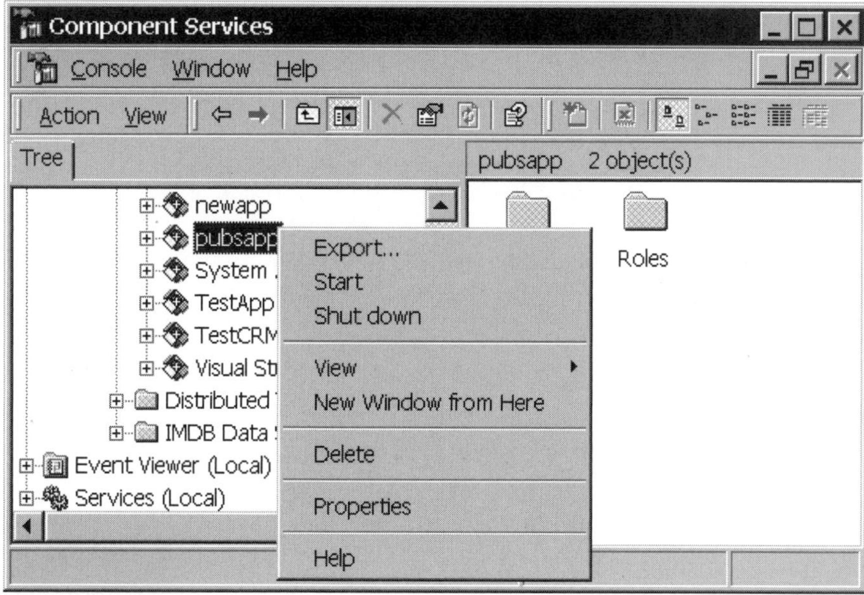

FIGURE 13.57 The First Step to Exporting a COM+ Application.

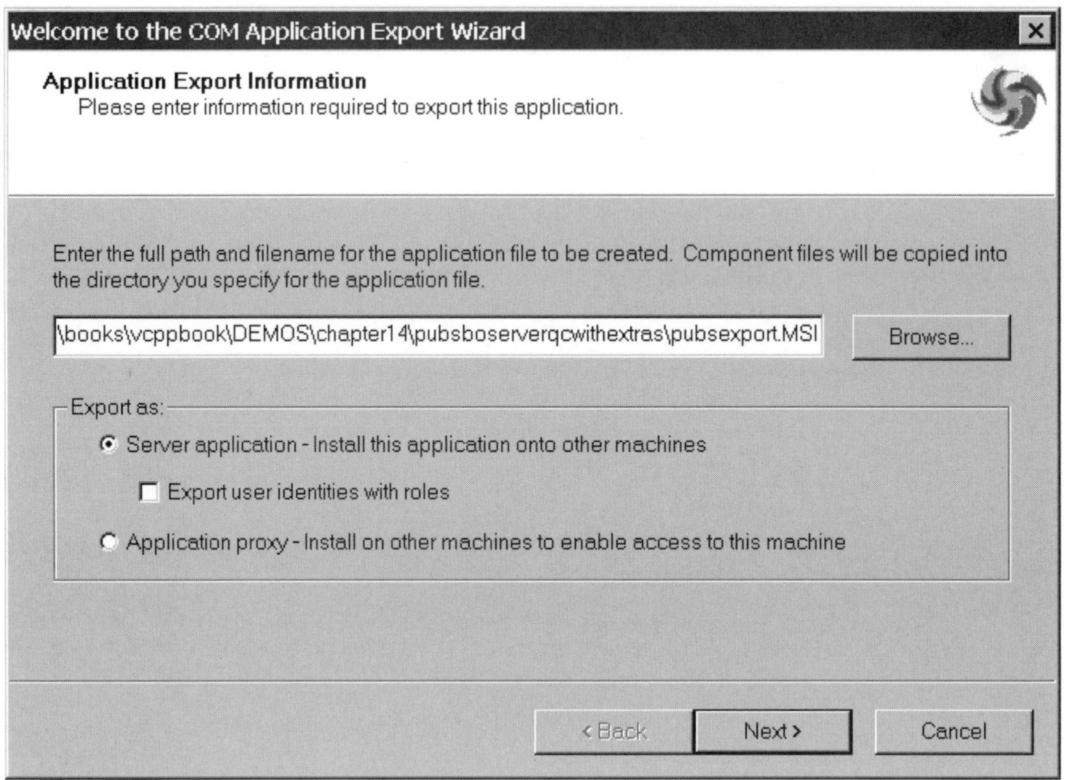

FIGURE 13.58 Step 2 of the Export Wizard.

The Component Services Explorer creates a file with the extension .msi. This file is a Windows Installer file and you can take it to another machine and double-click on it to install your COM+ application. That other machine must be running Windows 2000 for you to install a server export file, but you can install an Application Proxy on any machine that supports DCOM. You can also use the Component Services Explorer to import a server export file. Perform the following steps to do this:

1. Right-click on the `COM+ Applications` folder as shown in Figure 13.59.
2. Select `New\Application` from the `Context` menu (the welcome screen for the COM Application Wizard appears).
3. Click `Next` (the Install or Create a New Application dialog appears as shown in Figure 13.60).
4. Click the `Install pre-built Application(s)` button (a file selection dialog appears prompting you for the application file you wish to import).

5. Select the file to import and click `Open` (the Select Application Files dialog appears as shown in Figure 13.61).
6. Add additional files to import on the Select Application Files dialog.
7. Click `Next` (the Set Application Identity dialog appears as shown in Figure 13.62).
8. Select the Identity for the COM+ application.
9. Click `Next` (the Application Installation Options dialog appears as shown in Figure 13.63).
10. Specify an installation directory and whether you want to add the identities saved in the export file.
11. Click `Next` and then Click `Finish` on the final screen of the wizard.

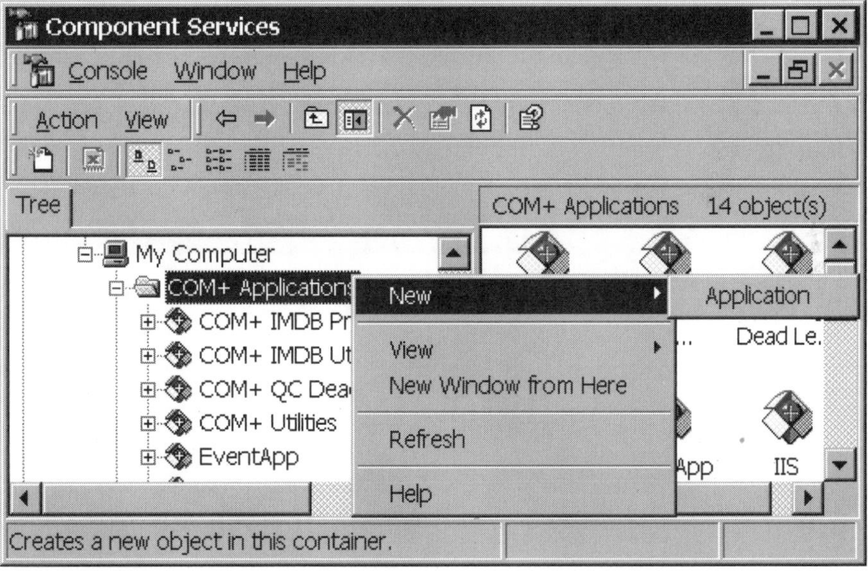

FIGURE 13.59 The First Step to Importing a COM+ Application.

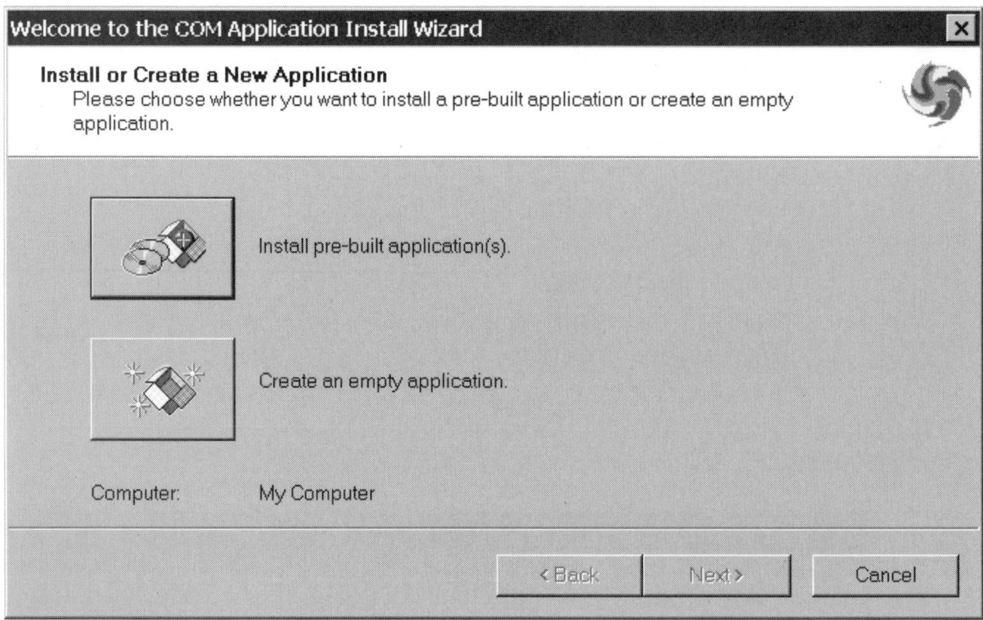

FIGURE 13.60 Step 1 of the Import Wizard.

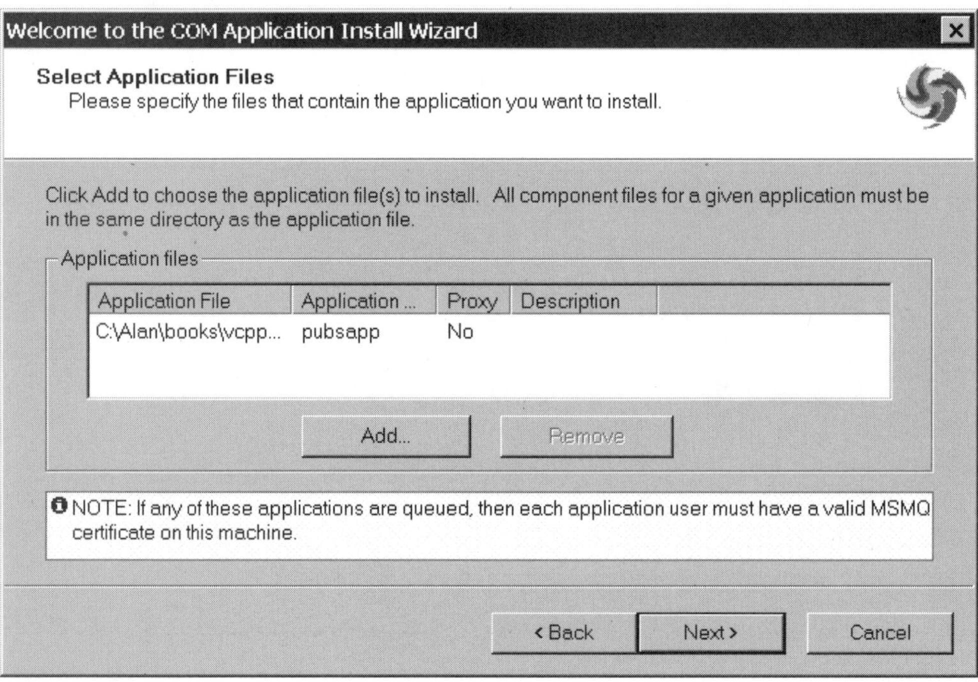

FIGURE 13.61 Step 2 of the Export Wizard.

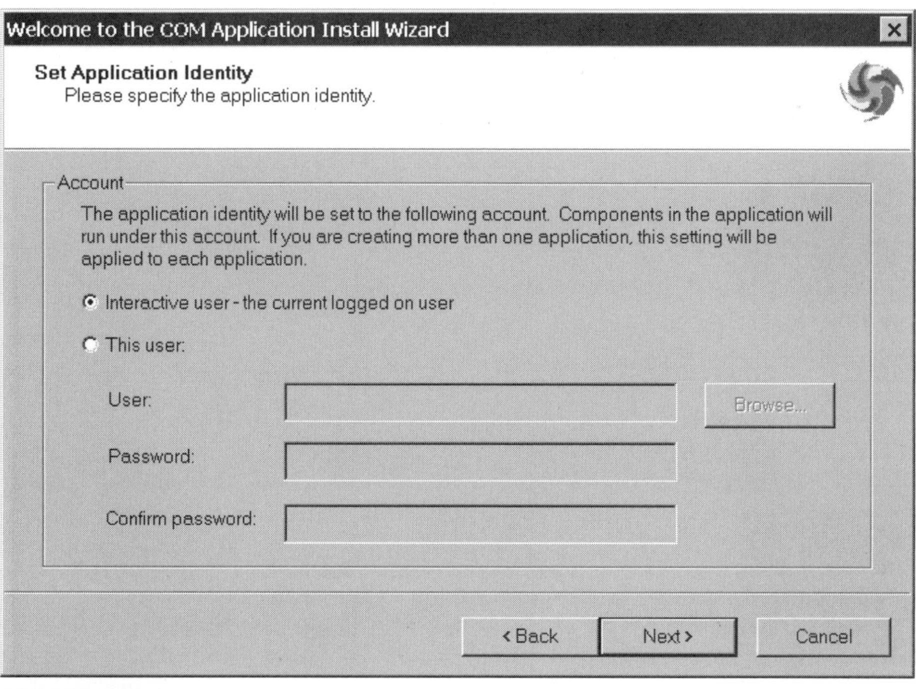

FIGURE 13.62 Step 3 of the Export Wizard.

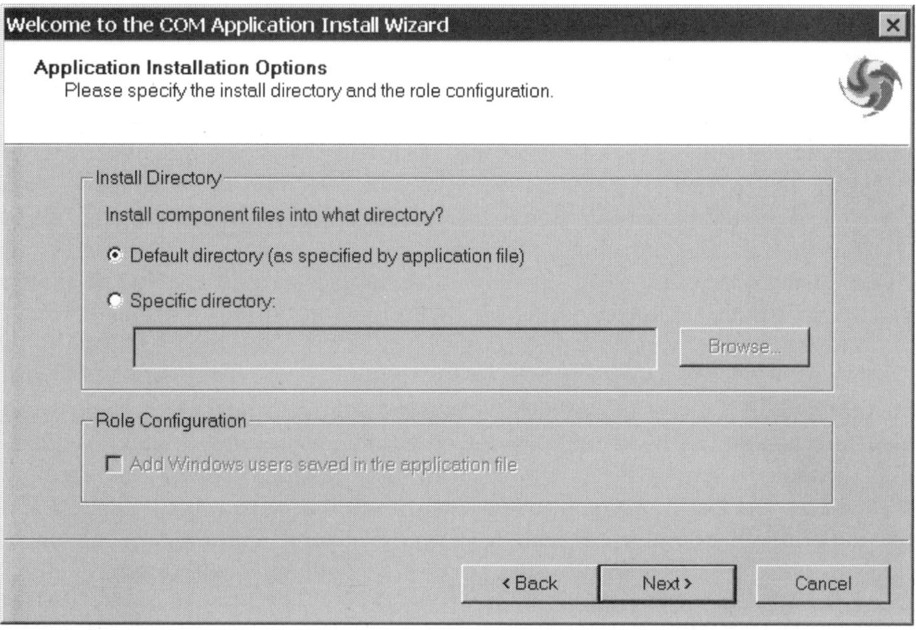

FIGURE 13.63 Step 4 of the Export Wizard.

Configuring Remote Machines

You can access remote machines using the Component Services Explorer.This is subject to security constraints, of course (you must be an administrator on the remote machine). To access a remote machine, perform the following steps in the Component Services Explorer:

1. Right-click on the folder labeled `Computers`.
2. Select `New\Computers` from the `Context` Menu (the Add Computer dialog appears).
3. Select the Remote Computer you wish to administer.
4. Click `OK`.

Differences Between COM+ and MTS

If you understand MTS already, learning COM+ won't be a major stretch for you. COM+ most does everything that MTS does, but COM+ has additional features and is easier to use. The main difference between COM+ and MTS is that COM+ is more tightly integrated with the operating system. That means the COM instantiation function, `CoCreateInstance(Ex)`, reads information from the COM+ catalog and knows how to establish the Context for an object. When you installed a component in an MTS package, MTS took over the registry entry of the component, inserting its own `LocalServer32` key beneath the CLSID of the component. That caused calls to `CoCreateInstance` to first go to MTS, which then created its surrogate process and loaded the component into that process. Problems occurred if you wanted two or more objects to participate in the same transaction. Because the `CoCreateInstance` function knew nothing about MTS Context, you had to call the `CreateInstance` function in the `IObjectContext` interface to create an object that could share the same transaction as its creator (whether it actually does or not depends on its transaction attribute settings). Under COM+, the `IObjectContext` interface still has the `CreateInstance` function so that code which was written for MTS still works under COM+, but you don't need `IObjectContext::CreateInstance` any more. Simply call `CoCreateInstance(Ex)` as you normally would and Context, Activity, Transaction, and other attributes flow between the created and creating objects. The `CoCreateInstance(Ex)` function now detects the Context and attributes of its caller and handles Context sharing and the propogation of attributes such as transactions from one object to another, automatically.

Another major difference between COM+ and MTS is in the area of fine-grained security. MTS only lets you configure security down to the interface level. With MTS, you could specify different security levels for each of the interfaces that a component supports, but you couldn't configure settings separately for the different methods in those interfaces. COM+ supports fine-grained security configuration at the method level.

Another difference is the factoring out of the Context information into multiple interfaces. Under MTS, an object interacted with its Context through the `IObjectContext` interface and the methods in that interface (`SetComplete`, `SetAbort`, `IsInRole`, and so on). There was also a method in the MTS library, called `GetObjectContext`, that you called to get the `IObjectContext` interface. Under COM+, the Object Context does a lot more things including thread synchronization and queueing so Microsoft created a new set of interfaces for the Object Context including `IContextState`, `IObjectContextActivity`, `ISecurityProperty`, `IGetContextProperties`, and `IObjectContextInfo`. There is also a new Windows API function called `CoGetObjectContext` you can use to request any of these interfaces on the object context.

MTS also did not provide support for thread synchronization as COM+ does. MTS relied on COM Apartments to provide the necessary protection against multiple threads. COM components that ran in MTS had to run in an STA (`ThreadingModel` registry value="`Apartment`"). COM+ provides thread synchronization through system-provided locking. Therefore, COM+ does not require objects to run in the STA. You can use free-threaded (MTA) objects under COM+, and COM+ actually prefers that you make your objects run in the Thread Neutral Apartment (`ThreadingModel` registry value="`Neutral`"). This last enhancement also allows COM+ to support object pooling, which MTS did not support.

As you can see, COM+ is a big improvement over MTS, but conceptually it is the same. In fact, if you do not have access to a Windows 2000 machine right now, one of the best ways you can prepare yourself to work with COM+ is to start learning MTS.

Debugging with COM+

Debugging configured COM+ components poses some additional challenges as compared to debugging COM components that have not been configured. The first problem is that configured COM+ components typically run in a separate process from their client (actually they run in the dllhost process provided by the COM+ runtime). Ideally, you would like to set break points in your business object code and have execution stop in the debugger at those points so you can trace the execution of the code from that point on. With Visual C++, you can do this three ways: (1) You can set the executable for your debug session to be the dllhost process and specify the GUID for your COM+ application as a parameter, (2) you can configure your COM+ application to start within the debugger, and (3) you can use the task manager to open the dllhost process in the debugger.

Setting the Executable for Debug Session in Visual C++

COM+ components must be packaged in an in-process server. In-process servers cannot run or be debugged by themselves. To debug an in-process server, you must specify a process for the server to run in. In the case of a component that is configured in a COM+ server application, the host process that you specify is the dllhost process. You have to pass the GUID of your COM+ application to the dllhost executable so it knows which COM+ application to work with.

Each COM+ application that you create has a GUID associated with it.

You can determine the GUID for a COM+ application by right-clicking on the COM+ application in the Component Services Explorer and selecting

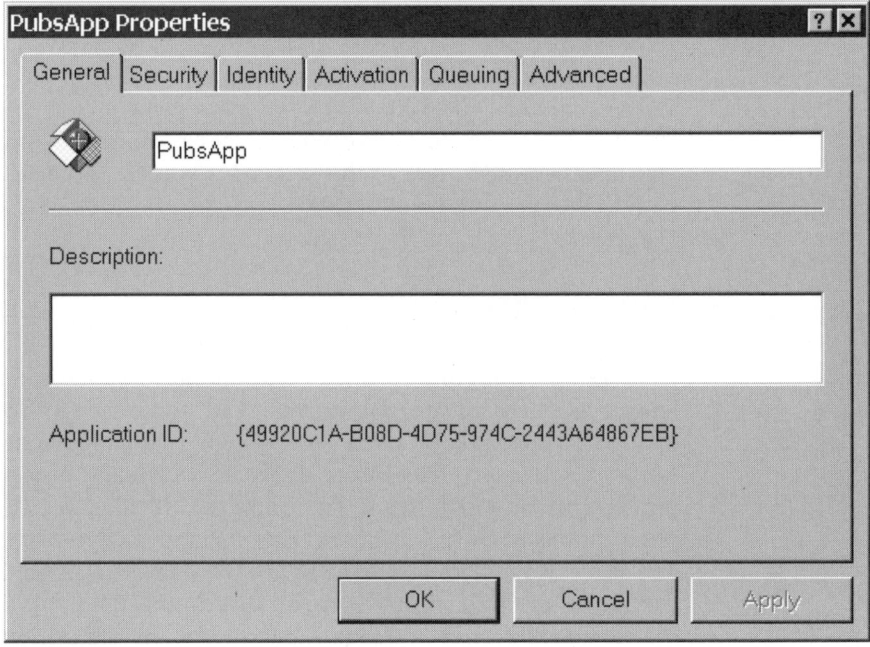

FIGURE 13.64 Viewing the GUID for a COM+ Application.

`Properties` from the `Context` menu. You should see the dialog shown in Figure 13.64. The GUID shown on this dialog is the GUID for your COM+ application.

To configure your Visual C++ project so you can debug a COM+ component, perform the following steps with the project open:

1. Select `Settings` from the `Project` menu (the Project settings dialog appears).
2. Click the Debug tab (your Window should look like that shown in Figure 13.65).
3. Enter the path to the dllhost executable in the `Executable for the debug session` field.
4. Enter `/ProcessID:{GUID for your COM+ application}` in the program arguments field (see Figure 13.65).
5. Click `OK`.

Set a breakpoint near the beginning of the `RetrieveByKeyword` method of the `Book` class.

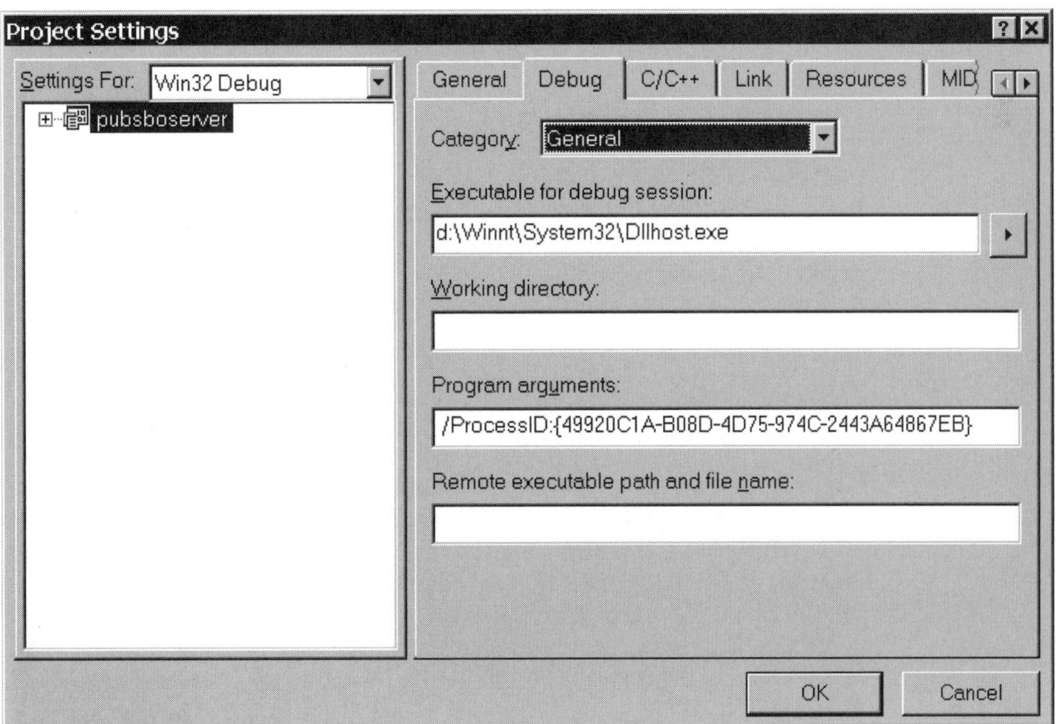

FIGURE 13.65 The Debug Tab of the Project Settings Dialog.

Press F5 (if you see a dialog warning you that dllhost does not contain debugging information, ignore it and click OK on the message box). Now start the Visual Basic client, type in a keyword and click the Search button. Execution should stop at your breakpoint in the Visual C++ debugger where you can put single-step through the code and set watches on variables.

Specifying That a COM+ Application Should Start within a Debugger

You can also specify, using the Component Services Explorer, that your COM+ application should start in the Visual C++ debugger. To do this, perform the following steps in the Component Services Explorer:

1. Right-click on the COM+ application.
2. Select `Properties` from the `Context` menu.
3. Click the `Advanced` tab (you should see the Window shown in Figure 13.66).
4. Set the Launch in debugger checkbox.
5. In the debugger path field, enter the path to the `msdev.exe` executable on your machine and pass `dllhost.exe /ProcessID:{YOUR_COM+ApplicationGUID}` as the parameter.
6. Click `OK`.

The Component Services Explorer actually tries to guess the correct path and GUID for you. On my machine it worked. Now start your Visual Basic client. Enter a keyword and click the `Search` button. Visual C++ starts; press F5 to continue running. Unfortunately, for me, Visual C++ was not finding the associated source code for my application. If it doesn't work for you either, you need to open the source files for your project and set breakpoints where you want.

Using the Task Manager to Open the Process in the Debugger

You can also specify that a process should run within a debugger using the task manager. To do this, start the task manager. An instance of the dllhost process is always running. You don't want to attach the debugger to this process; you want to attach your debugger to the process that is actually started when you make a component instantation request. The easiest way to do this is to make sure you shutdown your COM+ application by right-clicking on your application in the Component Services Explorer and selecting `shut-down` from the `Context` menu. Now look in the task manager and get the process ID of the dllhost process that is still running; this is the

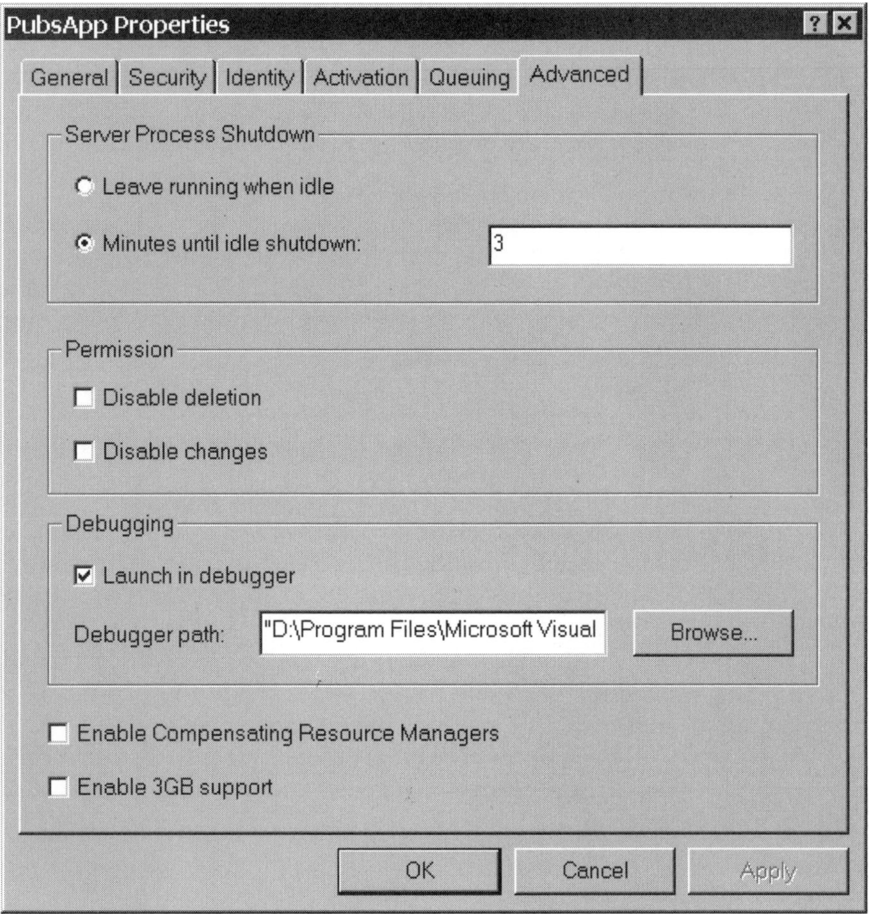

FIGURE 13.66 The Advanced Tab of the Project Settings Dialog.

one that stays up all the time. You don't want to attach to this process. Now start your Visual Basic application, type in a keyword, and then click the `Search` button. If you look back in the task manager you should now see two dllhost processes. The new one is the one you want to attach to. Right-click on this process and select `Debug` from the `Context` menu. Visual C++ starts and once again (at least on my machine) it won't find the associated source code for the executable, but that's okay. Open the `Book.cpp` source file, set a break point in the `RetrieveByKeyword` method and click `Search` in your client application. Once again execution should stop at the breakpoint.

■ Summary

In this chapter you have learned all about the Windows DNA and the Windows DNA 2000. The Windows DNA is an architectural style guide that shows you how to use Microsoft's technologies to build enterprise-class distributed applications. The key ideas in the Windows DNA are:

- Microsoft has all the technologies and tools that you need to build enterprise-class, distributed applications.
- To use these technologies and tools to their best effect, you should partition your application into three-logical layers: presentation, business, and data access.
- There are Microsoft technologies and tools you can use to implement each layer.
- COM/COM+ is the glue that binds everything together.

The Windows DNA 2000 is the latest version of the Windows DNA that includes tools to make the Windows DNA more scalable and interoperable with other platforms. It also includes integrated support for XML. These changes are designed primarily to make the Windows DNA more suitable for large-scale e-commerce.

In this chapter you also applied everything you learned about the Windows DNA and COM+ (most of the tools in the Windows DNA 2000 aren't available yet) and built a simple business application that has both a native Windows application client and an HTML-based client. In the next chapter, you will add a Queued Component to your application.

FOURTEEN

Queued Components

There is one important COM+ feature you did not use in Chapter 13 and that's Queued Components. I talked conceptually about Queued Components in Chapter 12. Queued Components implement a store and forward method call mechanism built on top of Microsoft Message Queue (MSMQ). When you use Queued Components, you are replacing the synchronous RPC-based communication layer used by COM with MSMQ messages. A client can make a method call to a Queued Component even if it currently does not have network connectivity to the server machine on which the Queued Component resides or the server machine is down. A message is buffered in an MSMQ and sent to the Queued Component the next time connectivity is established, or the server is up; this is great for wireless applications. Queued Components also fix one of the greatest weaknesses of COM/DCOM: its lack of support for asynchronous method calls. In this chapter, you can enhance the example program you built in the previous chapter so it will use a queued component to send an XML document to a fictional printer.

What are Queued Components?

When you configure an object to be queued, the COM+ runtime uses Microsoft Message Queue (MSMQ) as the communication mechanism between the client and server instead of RPC. As with all the COM+ services, using Queued Components requires almost no knowledge of the underlying mechanism used to implement the service. The COM+ queued component architecture abstracts away almost all the details associated with using MSMQ. A simplified view of the queued component architecture is shown in Figure 14.1

The COM+ runtime creates a set of MSMQs for a COM+ application when you first configure the COM+ application to support Queued Components. If a client elects to use the components through the queuing service (Queued Components can still be used synchronously), then the COM+ runtime instantiates a Queued Component (QC) Recorder on the client when the client requests a queued interface on the component. The QC Recorder supports the same methods as the component itself (the situation is not unlike the proxy that gets instantiated when you make a cross-apartment method call on a non-queued COM object). The client can then call whatever methods it desires on the Queued Component (the QC Recorder is actually receiving the method calls). The QC Recorder records these method calls. When the client deactivates the Queued Component, the QC Recorder turns the method calls that the client made into an MSMQ message and sends the message to a destination queue, which by default resides on the server on which the Queued Component was instantiated.

The client can explicitly specify the computer and the queue the message will be sent to using the `ComputerName` and `QueueName` parameters to the Queued Moniker.

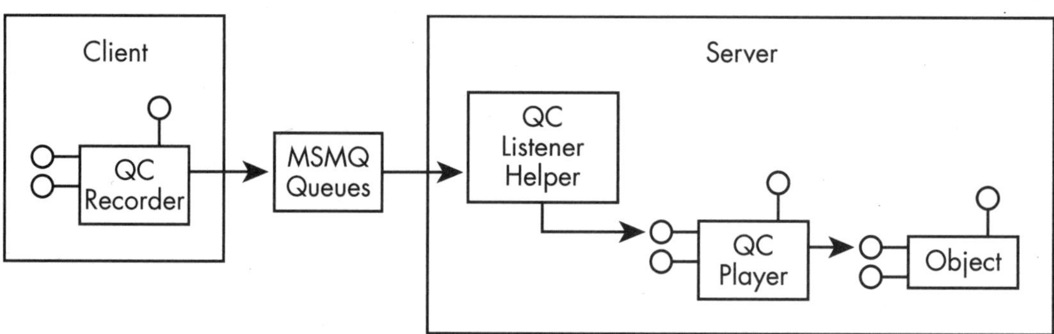

FIGURE 14.1 The Queued Component Architecture.

On the server, the QC Listener Helper checks the destination queue for messages. When it finds a message waiting, it instantiates a QC Player and passes the bundle of method calls to the QC Player, which plays the method calls back to the Queued Component. As I mentioned in Chapter 12, if you think of the queued components service as voice mail for COM+ objects, you've got the basic idea.

Why Do You Need Queued Components?

COM/DCOM has always been staunchly synchronous in its operation. The problem is a limitation of DCE RPC, on which COM/DCOM is built. As someone who has worked with COM/DCOM for a number of years, this has caused no end of frustration for me. There are two big problems with synchronous method calls: (1) the server has to be available (i.e., the machine must be up and the server must be ready to receive method calls) for the method invocation to be successful, and (2) the calling thread is blocked until the method returns. The first problem makes it difficult for us to build systems that operate in a disconnected environment such as an order-taking system that field service workers or salespeople can use on their PDA or laptop via a wireless network. The second problem is far more common and isn't a major issue until the method call takes more than a few seconds—then it becomes a big problem. When a synchronous method is called, the user's GUI is non-responsive while the synchronous method invocation is in progress. It has been my experience that most businesses have batch operations that aren't done very often (once a month, once a week) but when they are done, they take a significant amount of time. For example, in one application I helped develop, once a month the users of the application generated a publication that contained a listing of all the missions that would be run that month (sometimes there would be several hundred), and then all the missions for that month had to be transferred to a global mission repository. This operation could take several minutes.

As software developers, you have to implement these batch use-cases in your business applications. You don't want your user's machines to hang while they are performing one of these long operations. With COM/DCOM, you were left with two choices:

1. Simply run the operation synchronously (the application hangs while the operation is in progress) and cover your ears when the users complain about it.
2. Use multi-threading or some other solution to create a home-spun, asynchronous method invocation solution. You might think that most people would choose solution 2, but my experience has been that

most people choose 1. At my previous employer we used solution 1. At my current employer, we initially did 1 and then changed to a homespun solution built on MSMQ.

Although you can solve the disconnected operation and asynchronous method invocation problems with MSMQ alone, Microsoft realized that programming MSMQ is somewhat difficult. If you include production-level error handling, it takes on the order of 40 lines of code just to send a message. So Microsoft created the Queued Component Service, which is really just a tool that abstracts away all the difficulties of using MSMQ. Instead of having to worry about messages and queues, developers can still use method calls on objects. It is the job of the COM+ runtime to handle the complexity of MSMQ.

Microsoft Message Queue

To understand how Queued Components work, it helps to understand a little bit about MSMQ, so let's talk about this technology.

What Is Message Queuing

Message Queuing is really a lot like e-mail, but it is designed for sending data between applications not for sending messages between people. A message queue is just an ordered repository of messages that is accessible via the network through a message queue server as shown in Figure 14.2.

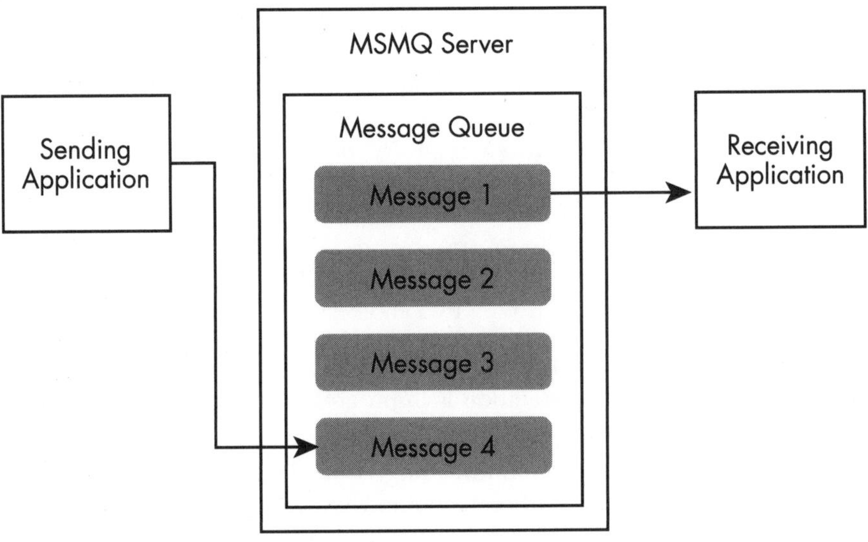

FIGURE 14.2 The MSMQ Architecture.

The sending application formats and sends messages to a message queue. These messages can be sent with different priorities (messages with higher priorities appear first in the queue and are received by the receiving application before lower priority messages).

The sending application, MSMQ server, and receiving application, shown in Figure 14.2, represent software services *not* machines. In other words, all of the boxes in the figure can reside on the same machine, on different machines, or two of the boxes can reside on the same machine. For instance, the message queue and the receiver application can reside on the same machine with the sending application on a different machine.

The message can contain whatever data the sending application wants: textual or binary. The message can contain a string that the receiving application must parse, or it can contain the persisted state of an object that implements the `IPersistStream` or `IPersistStorage` interface. A message can also contain a Visual Basic property bag (if you are using Visual Basic), or (and I love this one) an MSMQ message can contain a disconnected ADO Recordset. Of course, the receiver needs to have a priori knowledge of the format of the message content if it is to interpret it correctly.

An MSMQ message may be sent as part of a transaction, or not, to a message queuing server. The message queuing server stores the message in the destination queue. Once the message queue server has saved the message into a queue, the message is considered sent.

Depending on the network topology and the type of message queuing client that is being used, an MSMQ message may be sent to a queue other than the destination queue first. From there, the message is routed to the destination queue.

The sending client can continue to work immediately after the message is sent to a queue. Once the message gets to the destination queue, it sits there until the receiving application retrieves it from the queue (de-queues it). The receiving client can look at the message first before it de-queues the message (this is called peeking), but once the message is de-queued it is removed from the queue.

Being de-queued is not to be confused with disqualification.

De-queuing the message is done in a reliable fashion because the message queue server does not actually remove the message from the queue until it receives an acknowledgement from the receiving client that the message was received in its entirety. This protects against the situation where the receiver de-queues the message but then crashes while it is in the process of receiving the message. A receiving client can also opt to receive a notification (using connection point events) from the message queue server when there are messages in a queue. MSMQ has a set of COM automation classes you can use to interface with MSMQ and these classes have connection points that you can sink to receive these events.

The Web site contains a version of the example application that you built in Chapter 13 that uses MSMQ to send requests to print a book. This application uses a disconnected ADO Recordset as the message body. The Web site also has a client that uses connection point events to receive notifications when a message is waiting in the queue. You can then look (peek) at the information or process (de-queue) it.

The Advantages of Message Queuing

What does message queuing do for you? Using message queuing facilitates disconnected and asynchronous method invocation. It can also be used to implement load balancing and job scheduling, and makes it easier to integrate disparate systems together. To put it simply, if you are building distributed systems, there are things you can do rather simply *with* message queuing that are difficult to do *without* it.

DISCONNECTED OPERATION

In the disconnected operation scenario, there are two applications that are attempting to communicate with each other: either the network connecting the applications is unreliable, or you simply cannot guarantee that the lifetimes of the two applications will overlap. In other words, application A must be able to send a message to application B even if it does not have connectivity to application B or application B is not currently running at the time it wishes to send the message.

Disconnected operation is becoming more and more important as mobile computers and wireless networks gain popularity. Applications that are being built for use on mobile computers over wireless networks must be architected to compensate for the unreliability of the network and the fact that users of the application (who are mobile) will likely go in and out of network coverage. Message queuing handles this situation because it acts as a buffer between the two applications. If the application that is sending the message (Application A) is running on an MSMQ Independent Client (most MSMQ clients should be configured this way), you can send messages to a queue on a remote server. If the remote server is not available or you just drove out of wireless network coverage, the message is stored in a local queue. Your local message queue server (independent clients have one) forwards the message to the destination queue when you reestablish connectivity.

The latest version of Windows CE 3.0 contains a slightly abbreviated version of MSMQ.

ASYNCHRONOUS METHOD INVOCATION

Implementing asynchronous method invocation with MSMQ is simple: Instead of directly calling a method on a COM/DCOM object (which causes the client to block until the method call completes), a client can instead send a message to a queue. You then have to write a separate piece of code that reads from the queue and actually calls the method on the COM/DCOM object. Once the message is sent to the queue (which usually doesn't take long), the client can continue to run. The scheme just described is almost exactly how the Queued Component Service works.

LOAD BALANCING AND JOB SCHEDULING

Using MSMQ, you can implement a simple form of load balancing. Let's say you have one or more clients that need to execute some operation. This operation is computationally intensive so you have several server machines available to perform the task. You can setup a queue for this operation and when a client wants to perform this computationally intensive operation, it sends a message to the queue. You then have to write an application that reads from the queue and performs the operation. You can then put this application on each of your server machines. Each server as it becomes available checks the queue to see if it needs to perform the lengthy operation on behalf of a client. If it finds a message, it performs the operation. If all of your servers are busy and more messages arrive, they are simply buffered in the queue until a server becomes available and checks the queue again. This solution is scalable—you can handle more requests by adding more servers—and its fault-tolerant. If one of the servers goes down, the other servers continue to process messages.

Because COM+ has support for Component Load Balancing, you may be better off using COM+'s load balancing rather than implementing a scheme like this. I am just showing what you *can* do, not what you *should* do.

Because MSMQ messages can be assigned different priorities, you can also use MSMQ to implement job scheduling. Let's say an e-commerce Web site is using an `Order` business object that you implemented with COM+. There are two different operations that your business object needs to perform: (1) processing a new order from a customer, and (2) processing an order cancellation. Processing a new order is probably the highest priority operation (you want this to happen as quickly as possible); canceling an order is probably the lowest priority operation (you want new orders to be processed before cancellations). Whenever a client application wants to process an order, it sends this message with the highest priority. Whenever it sends a message to cancel an order, it sends the message with the lowest priority. If you have a farm of servers that read messages from the queue and then call your `Order` business object, the new order messages are always ahead of the cancellations in the queue so they are processed first.

Actually, in this scheme, cancellations are only processed when there are no orders. For this reason, you may not want to implement a scheme like this as is. A better solution might be to put the new orders and order cancellations on different queues and dedicate more servers to processing the new order queue.

Integrate Disparate Systems

MSMQ, with the help of some third-party products, makes it simple to integrate applications together that run on different platforms. Although MSMQ is a Windows-only product, a company called Level 8 Systems (www.level8.com) has an exclusive agreement with Microsoft to manufacture versions of MSMQ for other platforms. Their product, called Geneva, is available on Most UNIX platforms including Sun Solaris, IBM AIX, HPUX, and Linux. It is also available on mainframe platforms including IBM MVS, OS390 and 0S400, and Digital's VAX platform. In partnership with Level8, Microsoft is bundling a product called Message Queuing Connector with Windows 2000. This connector lets MSMQ applications on Windows platforms send and receive MSMQ messages to and from non-Windows, Geneva Message Queuing applications. With this solution, integrating disparate systems together is simple: from a Windows machine you send a message to a queue that resides on a UNIX or mainframe machine. A receiving application on the mainframe or UNIX machine can then read the queue, perform the requested operation and perhaps use a response queue to return a response to the Windows client.

Installing and Using MSMQ

To use Queued Components, MSMQ must be properly configured on your machine. Initially when I wrote this chapter, I was going to give complete details on setting up MSMQ, but eventually abandoned this idea for the following reasons:

- Setting up MSMQ on an enterprise network environment is a difficult task that requires a network administrator.
- All of this information is covered in the Help for MSMQ.
- I didn't want to be responsible for answering everyone's e-mail if they had problems setting up MSMQ using my instructions.

So please don't bombard me with e-mail if you have trouble getting MSMQ to work. I do my best to get you started and recommend places you can go to for more help.

What You Will Need

MSMQ 2.0 can operate in two environments: a domain environment or a workgroup environment. In the domain environment, a message queuing network is composed of one or more Windows 2000 sites. Each site must contain a domain controller (which must be running a Windows 2000 server) and each site must be using the Active Directory Service. In a workgroup environment, there is no domain controller and the Active Directory Service is not running. The capabilities of MSMQ are limited when it runs in a workgroup environment. To understand these limitations, you first have to understand the two different types of queues you can create in MSMQ: public queues and private queues. Public queues are published in Active Directory. Applications can locate these queues using the Active Directory service. Private queues are not published in Active Directory and are displayed only on the local computer that contains them. A client must know the full path name of a private queue to use it.

MSMQ 1.0 stored location information about its public queues in Microsoft SQL Server. That's why you had to install MS SQL Server 6.5 or greater before you could install MSMQ 1.0. MSMQ 2.0 in Windows 2000 no longer requires the installation of SQL Server.

In the domain environment, you can create both public and private queues. In the workgroup environment, you are limited to private queues. Because Queued Components require public queues, MSMQ must be operating in domain environment mode for queued components to work. I repeat this again because it has important implications: MSMQ must be operating in domain environment mode for Queued Components to work.

If you re-read the previous paragraph, the implications are clear: to setup MSMQ so that queued components work, you must have a machine that is running Windows 2000 Server that has been configured as a domain controller. Moreover, you must also have the Active Directory Service running on your network.

If you are following along at work or you have a network that has a Windows 2000 domain controller with Active Directory running already, there is nothing for you to do. As long as MSMQ is installed, Queued Components should work. I suspect that many people who buy this book may be using their home environment to run and/or build the example programs. In this environment, you might only have a single machine. If that's the case, then this machine must be running Windows 2000 Server, you must configure it to be a Domain Controller, and run the Active Directory Service. You may also have to fake Windows 2000 into believing that you are running on a network. The easiest way to do this is to get a network card and a hub to plug the card into. You can get a kit for about $100.00 that contains both from most places that sell computer hardware. If you have a home network, then you are good to go as far as hardware is concerned.

Once you have the hardware installed, your next step is to install Windows 2000 Server if it is not installed already. After you have installed Windows 2000 Server, you must configure your machine to be a domain controller and install Active Directory. With Release Candidate 2 of Windows 2000, it was fairly easy to do this. I suspect it to be the same or easier in the release version. After you have installed Windows 2000 Server, you can configure your server to be a domain controller and install Active Directory by performing the following steps:

1. Click the `Start` Menu and Select `Programs\Administrative Tools\Configure Your Server` (the Windows 2000 `Configure Your Server` Application appears as shown in Figure 14.3).
2. Click `Active Directory` on the left side of the Window.
3. The right side of the screen contains items you can click on to promote your server to a domain controller and install Active Directory. There is a wizard that guides you through the entire process. If the wizard tells you that you need to install the Domain Name Server (DNS), go ahead and install it.

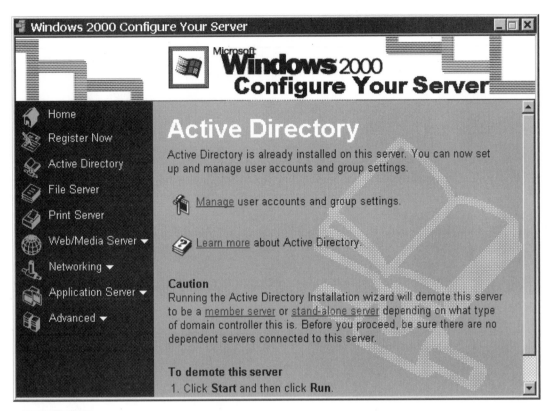

FIGURE 14.3 The Configure Your Server Application.

You may not need to bring up the Configure Your Server Application. After you install Windows 2000 Server, it always starts up immediately after you boot until you clear the checkbox that says: Show this screen at startup.

You also need to make sure that MSMQ is installed on your server. If it isn't, go to the `Add/Remove Programs tools` in the `Windows Control Panel` and use the `Add/Remove Windows Components` button to install MSMQ. See the Help for MSMQ for more details. The easiest way to test if MSMQ is installed properly is to attempt to create a public queue. To do this, perform the following steps:

1. Click the `Start` Menu and select `Programs\Administrative Tools\Computer Management` (the Computer Management Explorer appears as shown in Figure 14.4).

2. Open the `Services and Applications` item in the Tree on the left side of the Window.
3. Right-click on the `Public Queues` folder beneath `Message Queuing` and select `New\Public` Queue as shown in Figure 14.5.
4. The Queue Name dialog will appear as shown in Figure 14.6.
5. Enter `TestQueue` in the `Name` field.
6. Click `OK`.

If you were able to create a public queue, then MSMQ is probably setup okay for Queued Components to work. If you are unable to create a public queue, try creating a private queue. If you are able to create a private queue but not a public one, that means you are running in the workgroup environment. Uninstall MSMQ, make sure that you have a network card and a hub to plug it into, configure your machine to be a domain controller and install Active Directory (if this is not done already), and then reinstall MSMQ.

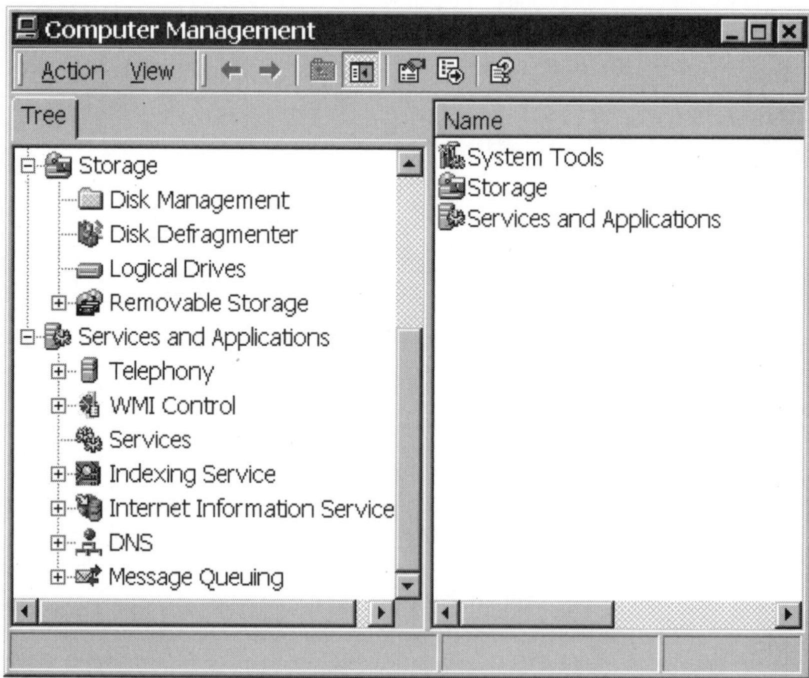

FIGURE 14.4 The Computer Management Explorer.

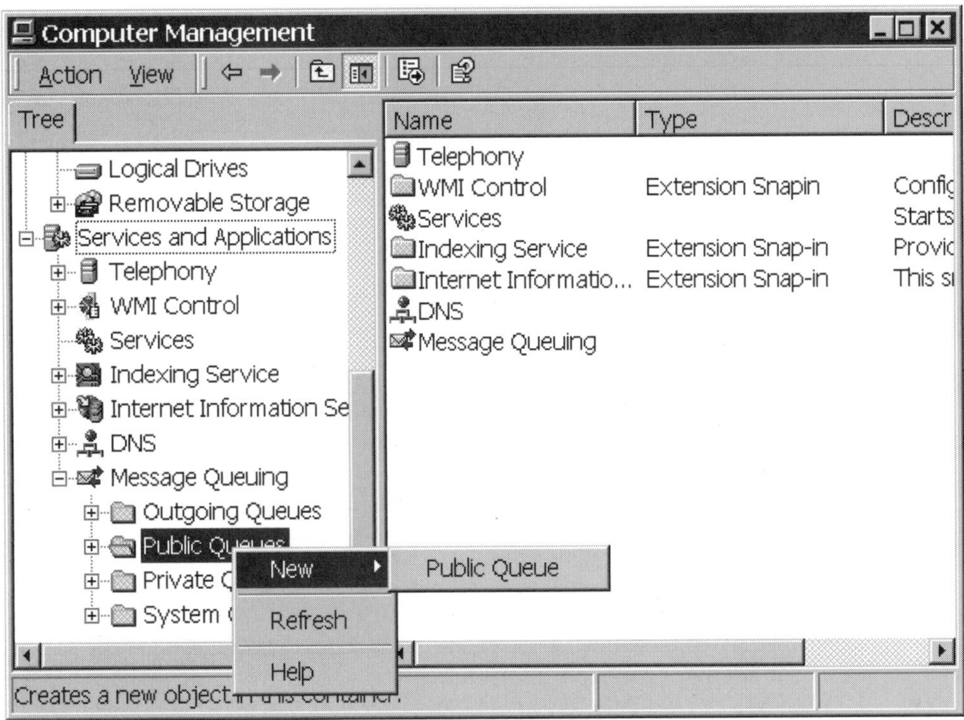

FIGURE 14.5 Creating a Public Queue.

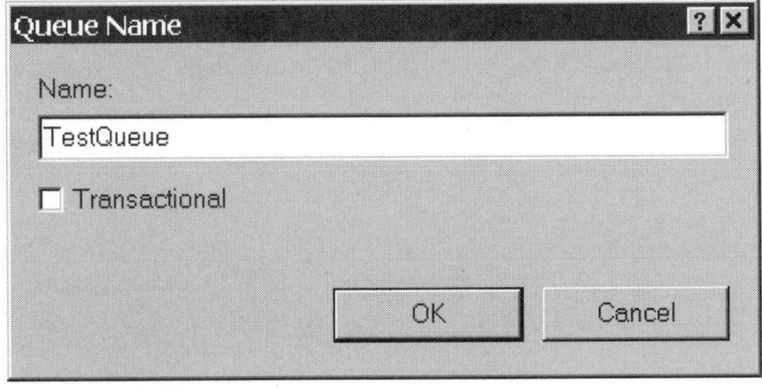

FIGURE 14.6 The Queue Name Dialog.

Places to Go for Help

If you have problems getting MSMQ installed and working, I can recommend the following sources for help: First try the MSMQ Help. To open this Help, perform the following steps:

1. Click the `Start` Menu and select `Help` (the Windows 2000 Help appears).
2. On the `Contents` tab, click the item that says `Application and Programming` Tools.
3. Click `Message Queuing`.

The Help contains a how-to section, concepts section, and troubleshooting section. If you don't find your answer there, try the documentation and the knowledgebase on the MSDN library which is available online at msdn.Microsoft.com/library or on the MSDN library CD if you have it.

As always with URLs in print, if you don't find the specified information at the URL, try a search at the domain level: www.microsoft.com, or try a search using your favorite search engine.

Search on the error message that you are receiving and check if there are any articles that address your problem. You can also try the following newsgroups: Microsoft.public.win2000.beta.msmq, Microsoft.public.win2000.beta.complus, and Microsoft.public.platformsdk.active.directory. You can also try any of the older NT Option Pack (MSMQ 1.0) newsgroups: Microsoft.public.msmq.*. I have found them to be useful on a few occasions.

Much like Web URLs, newsgroup names are subject to addition, deletion, and change. In particular, I expect that all of the win2000 newsgroups, like Microsoft.public.win2000.beta.complus, will lose the beta after Windows 2000 is released. Also, be careful with your e-mail address when using the newsgroups. Either disguise your e-mail address, get a hotmail account, or use a fake e-mail address. Spammers have software that plucks e-mail addresses from newsgroups and you may be bombarded with Spam if you start posting to newsgroups with your real e-mail address.

Another source of help is books. Because MSMQ was introduced in the NT Option Pack, there are lots of books already written about it. Windows 2000 contains a new version of MSMQ (2.0) that has some improvements over version 1.0 that was distributed with the NT Option Pack. But these improvements are mainly to integrate MSMQ with the Active Directory Service, so a lot of information in these books is still relevant. Also, I'm sure that new books covering the latest version of MSMQ will come out. The books that I have found most useful in learning about MSMQ are: *Programming Distributed Applications with COM and Microsoft Visual Basic 6.0* by Ted Pattison and Microsoft Press and *MTS MSMQ and VB with ASP* by Alex Homer, David Sussman, and Wrox Press. I suspect there will be new versions of both these books shortly.

Using Queued Components in Your Example Program

Now that you have gained an understanding of MSMQ and the environment that you need to setup to use the COM+ queued component service, it's time to use Queued Components in your example program. Since I talk so much about XML in Chapter 13, I decided to kill two birds with one stone and demonstrate how to use Queued Components and the Microsoft XML component.

The Microsoft XML Component is distributed with Internet Explorer 5.0 so you can also use it on Windows NT.

The use case is as follows: Imagine the publishing company that is using your software has decided to move to a Just In Time (JIT) production model. Rather than printing a large number of copies of a book when it is first released and hoping they can sell all the copies, the publishing company has instructed the printers that it sub-contracts with that it will be printing smaller batches of books more often. All the printers the publishing company uses are given the production version of manuscript as soon as they are complete. They must be prepared to print batches of the manuscript at any time. The use case is complicated by the fact that a print job that is sent at a later date may have a need-by date that is before a print job sent at an earlier date. So the printers need to do smart scheduling of their print jobs. To help the printers, the publishing company is providing them with new automation software. This software receives an XML file that contains the TitleID, Title, Number of Copies, a Need-by date, and special instructions for printing a book. An example XML file is shown here.

```
<PrintJobs>
  <PrintJob>
    <SentDateTime>12/8/1999 5:33:43 AM</SentDateTime>
    <TitleID>MC2222</TitleID>
    <Title>Silicon Valley Gastronomic Treats</Title>
    <NumCopies>963</NumCopies>
    <NeedBy>12/30/1999</NeedBy>
    <SpecialInstructions>here are special instructions
        that we should follow when printing copies of this
book</SpecialInstructions>
</PrintJob>
</PrintJobs>
```

You can define XML schemas or use Document Type Definitions (DTDs) to enforce the format you have defined for your XML document. See any of the XML books that I recommended in Chapter 13 for a discussion of XML schemas and DTDs.

The software parses the XML file (using the Microsoft XML component) and stores the information in a database. On any given day, scheduling software tells the printer which job they should do next to most efficiently meet their obligations. It also tells the printer if they have any jobs they won't be able to print by the need-by date.

So far there is nothing in this scenario that requires Queued Components. But let's imagine the printers are located at remote sites and the publisher does not want to depend on the printer's computers, or the network connecting them, being up when they wish to send an order to the printers. In other words, you want your software to support disconnected operation. Moreover, sending a print job may take a long time, in the future the publisher may want to send several print jobs at once.

Your XML document does support sending multiple print jobs in one document. You could have multiple `PrintJob` elements beneath the `PrintJobs` root element.

To make things interesting and so you can see the effect that queuing your component has, I'll also make the `BookPrinter` pause for five seconds when it is generating the XML file (you are pretending that the process takes much longer than it actually does).

You'll add a new COM+ class to the project that you built in Chapter 13. Your new `BookPrinter` class will have the methods shown in Table 14.1.

TABLE 14.1 Methods for the BookPrinter Business Object

Method	Description
PrintCopies	Called by a client to generate an XML document that contains instructions that a print shop would need to generate to print copies of a book on request.
AddPrintJob	A private (implementation only) method that is used in the generate of the XML.
AddPrintJobElement	A private (implementation only) method that is used in the generate of the XML.

Although the `BookPrinter` class has three methods, only one of these methods, `PrintCopies`, is a public method in the `IBookPrinter` COM interface. The other methods are private helper methods used by the implementation class in the generation of the XML. The steps to enhancing your example to support Queued Components are as follows:

1. Add the `BookPrinter` class to your project.
2. Import the MSXML type library.
3. Add the methods for the `BookPrinter` class.
4. Add the registry utility function.
5. Implement the Method in the `BookPrinter` class.
6. Configure the `BookPrinter` to be a Queued Component.
7. Modify the client.

Adding the BookPrinter Class to Your Project

To add the `BookPrinter` class to your Visual C++ project, perform the following steps in Visual C++ (I won't repeat the figures again):

1. Select `New ATL Object` from the `Insert` menu (the ATL Object Wizard appears).
2. Make sure `Objects` is selected under `Category`, and select `Simple Object` under `Objects`.
3. Click `Next` (the ATL Object Wizard Properties dialog appears).
4. Enter `BookPrinter` under `Short Name`.
5. Click the `Attributes` tab.
6. Click `Free` under `Threading Model` and set the `Support ISupportErrorInfo` checkbox.
7. Click `OK`.

Visual C++ adds a new, ATL implementation class to your project called `CBookPrinter`. This class has a COM interface called `IBookPrinter`. Before you add any methods to this class, you need to import the type library for the Microsoft XML component.

Importing the MSXML Type Library

The easiest way to use the Microsoft XML component is to use Visual C++ Native COM Support. To do this, you must first import the type library for the Microsoft XML component, which adds all the class, interface, and enumeration definitions from the type library to your project and generates a smart pointer class for each interface that the Microsoft XML component supports. To import the type library, add the following code to the `stdafx.h` file in your project:

```
#import "msxml.dll"
```

Notice that in this case you do not use the no_namespace directive on your #import statement. I tried using the no_namespace directive with this type library and when I did, the compiler generated a slew of errors. So the code that the #import statement generates is contained within a namespace called MSXML. That means you can either use the using namespace statement in your code like this:

```
using namespace MSXML;
```

or you must prefix the name of each interface that you use with MSXML. For example, the Microsoft XML component contains an interface called IXMLDOMDocument. If you don't use the using namespace statement, you can declare a smart pointer instance for this interface as follows:

```
MSXML::IXMLDOMDocumentPtr pDoc;
```

If you use the using namespace statement, then you can declare the smart pointer as follows:

```
IXMLDOMDocumentPtr pDoc;
```

Once you have imported the MSXML type library, you can add your three methods to the BookPrinter class.

Adding the Methods for the BookPrinter Class

The BookPrinter class has one method, PrintCopies, that is exposed through its COM interface and it has two private methods that implement the XML generation functionality. Perform the following steps in Visual C++ to add the public, PrintCopies method to the BookPrinter class:

1. Right-click on the IBookPrinter interface in the ClassView tab of the Visual C++ workspace.
2. Select Add Method... from the Context menu (the Add Method to Interface dialog appears).
3. Enter PrintCopies in the Method Name field.
4. Enter [in] BSTR titleID, [in] BSTR title, [in] short numCopies, [in] DATE needBy, [in] BSTR specialInstructions, [in] DATE sentWhen in the Parameters field.
5. Click OK.

Notice something important here: All the parameters for the PrintCopies method are inputs. When you configure this class to support queuing, you will configure queuing at the interface level (after you have enabled queuing at the COM+ application level). An interface cannot be queued if it has output parameters or a logical return value (a parameter declared using the IDL parameters [out,retval]). If an interface is to be queued, you must make the assumption that the lifetime of your Queued Components and their clients do not overlap. So, by the time the Queued Component actually processes a method call, the client may not be around to receive any output parameters or return values. If an interface is not queue-able (because it has output parameters or a logical return value), then the checkbox to enable queuing for that interface is disabled in the Component Services Explorer.

Now let's add the other two methods to the BookPrinter class: AddPrintJob and AddPrintJobElement. To add these methods to your project, perform the following steps in Visual C++:

1. Right-click on the CBookPrinter implementation class in the ClassView tab of the Visual C++ workspace.
2. Select Add Member Function... from the Context menu (the Add Member function dialog appears).
3. Enter void in the Function Type field.
4. Enter AddPrintJob(IXMLDOMDocumentPtr pDoc, IXMLDOMElementPtr pRootElement, BSTR titleID, BSTR title, long numCopies, DATE needBy,BSTR specialInstructions, DATE sentDate) in the Function Declaration field.
5. Select Private under Access.
6. Click OK.
7. Repeat steps 1–6 but on step 4 enter AddPrintJobElement (IXMLDOMDocumentPtr pDoc, IXMLDOMElementPtr pPrintJobRootElement, BSTR elementName, BSTR elementValue) in the Function Declaration field.

Visual C++ adds a prototype for both of these methods to the .h file for BookPrinter and adds an empty implementation for both of these methods to the source file for the BookPrinter. You will fill in the implementation shortly. In order to use the smart pointers generated from the Microsoft XML Parser (msxml.dll) you need to add a using namespace declaration to the header file for the BookPrinter class as shown here.

```
//  BookPrinter.h : Declaration of the  CbookPrinter
using namespace MSXML;
class ATL_NO_VTABLE CbookPrinter
public CcomObjectRootEx<CcomMultiThreadModel>,
```

```
public CcomCoClass<CbookPrinter, &CLSID_BookPrinter>,
public IsupportErrorInfo,
public IdispatchImpl<IbookPrinter, &IID_IbookPrinter, &LIBID_PUBSBOSERVERLib>
(
// The rest of the CbookPrinter class is omitted for clarity…
)
```

Next you need to create a utility function to read from the registry.

Adding The Registry Utility Function

Your BookPrinter class reads the path that it will write XML documents to from the registry. A construction string wasn't used in this case because I want to show you another way you can store application-specific configuration information. I'll create a utility function that can be used to make it simple to retrieve the XML output directory from the registry. To add this function, perform the following summarized steps:

1. Add header and source files to the project.
2. Add the function prototype and implementation to the header and source files.

ADDING HEADER AND SOURCE FILES TO THE PROJECT

To add a header file to your project, perform the following steps (you have done these steps many times, so I won't repeat the figures again):

1. Select New from the File menu (the New dialog appears).
2. Click the File tab.
3. Select C/C++ Header file from the list of file types.
4. Enter GetPathFromReg in the File Name field.
5. Click OK.
6. Repeat steps 1–5, but on step 3 select C/C++ Source file from the list of file types.

ADD THE FUNCTION PROTOTYPE AND IMPLEMENTATION

Add the following function prototype for a GetPathFromReg function to the GetPathFromReg.h file:

```
#ifndef GETPATHFROMREG_H
#define GETPATHFROMREG_H
_bstr_t GetPathFromReg(LPCTSTR lpszKeyName);
#endif // GETPATHFROMREG_H
```

Now add the following implementation for the `GetPathFromReg` function to the `GetPathFromReg.cpp` file (Listing 14.1).

LISTING 14.1 *THE GETPATHFROMREG FUNCTION*

```
1.  #include "stdafx.h"
2.  _bstr_t GetPathFromReg(LPCTSTR lpszKeyName)
3.  {
4.     CRegKey regXMLFileDir;
5.     LPTSTR lpszKeyValue;
6.     DWORD dwKeyCount;
7.     DWORD dwDisposition;
8.     LONG lRegReturn;
9.     _bstr_t bResult;
10.    dwKeyCount=64;
11.    lpszKeyValue=new TCHAR[dwKeyCount];
12.    lRegReturn=regXMLFileDir.Create(HKEY_LOCAL_MACHINE,
13.       _T("Software\\agordonbooks\\pubsboserver"),REG_NONE,
14.       REG_OPTION_NON_VOLATILE,KEY_ALL_ACCESS,NULL,&dwDisposition);
15.    lRegReturn=regXMLFileDir.QueryValue(lpszKeyValue,lpszKeyName,
16.       &dwKeyCount);
17.    if (ERROR_SUCCESS != lRegReturn) // indicates there is no value
18.    {
19.       regXMLFileDir.SetValue(_T("C:"),lpszKeyName);
20.       regXMLFileDir.QueryValue(lpszKeyValue,lpszKeyName,&dwKeyCount);
21.    }
22.    bResult=lpszKeyValue;
23.    delete [] lpszKeyValue;
24.    return bResult;
25. }
```

The code shown here isn't necessarily COM-related (the registry is used for more than just storing information about COM) but I'll go through it anyway. On line 4 of Listing 14.1, you declare an instance of the ATL class `CRegKey`. This class makes it fairly simple to manipulate the registry. On lines 5–11, you declare and initialize all the variables needed in our function. On line 12, you call the `Create` method on `CRegKey`, which opens the specified registry key if it already exists, or creates the key if it doesn't exist. In this case, you open or create the following key in the registry:

```
HKEY_LOCAL_MACHINE\Software\agordonbooks\pubsboserver\
```

Beneath this key you can store a string value called `OutputDir` that contains the directory your application writes its XML files to. You want the

GetPathFromReg function to be generic so the name of the string value is passed in as a parameter. On line 15, you call the QueryValue function to get the value at the requested string value beneath your specified key. If the string value has been created and contains a value, QueryValue returns ERROR_SUCCESS, so if the QueryValue function does not return ERROR_SUCCESSS, then on lines 19 and 20 you set the value (and hence the output path for the XML files) to C:\. Finally, on lines 22–24, you cleanup and assign the key value to a _bstr_t instance to return to your caller.

Implementing the Methods in the BookPrinter class

Now you can implement the methods in the BookPrinter class. First, you implement the PrintCopies method, which is a public method that is part of the IBookPrinter COM interface. The implementation of PrintCopies is shown in Listing 14.2.

LISTING 14.2 *PRINTCOPIES*

```
1.  STDMETHODIMP CBookPrinter::PrintCopies(BSTR titleID, BSTR title,
2.         short numCopies,DATE needBy, BSTR specialInstructions,
3.         DATE sentWhen)
4.  {
5.     HRESULT hRetval;
6.     _bstr_t bDescription;
7.     char strFileName[255];
8.     _bstr_t strFullPath;
9.     hRetval=S_OK;
10.    SYSTEMTIME dtSysDateTime;
11.    MSXML::IXMLDOMDocumentPtr pDoc;
12.    MSXML::IXMLDOMElementPtr pRootElement;
13.    IContextState *pContxState;
14.
15.    hRetval=CoGetObjectContext(IID_IContextState,(void **)&pContxState);
16.    if (SUCCEEDED(hRetval))
17.    {
18.       try
19.       {
20.          ::Sleep(5000);
21.          pDoc.CreateInstance( __uuidof(MSXML::DOMDocument));
22.          pRootElement=pDoc->createElement("PrintJobs");
23.          pDoc->documentElement=pRootElement;
24.          GetLocalTime(&dtSysDateTime);
25.          AddPrintJob(pDoc,pRootElement,titleID,title,numCopies,needBy,
```

```
26.                 specialInstructions,sentWhen);
27.             sprintf(strFileName,"printcopies%d%d%d_%d%d%d.xml",
28.                 dtSysDateTime.wMonth,dtSysDateTime.wDay,
29.                 dtSysDateTime.wYear,dtSysDateTime.wHour,
30.                 dtSysDateTime.wMinute,dtSysDateTime.wSecond);
31.             strFullPath=GetPathFromReg(_T("OutputDir")) +
32.                 _bstr_t("\\") + strFileName;
33.             pDoc->save(strFullPath);
34.         }
35.         catch ( _com_error err)
36.         {
37.             hRetval=err.Error();
38.             bDescription=err.Description();
39.         }
40.     }
41.     else
42.         bDescription=L"Could not retrieve the object context. " \
43.                     L"Your component is probably not configured";
44.
45.     if (NULL != pContxState)
46.     {
47.         if (SUCCEEDED(hRetval))
48.             pContxState->SetMyTransactionVote(TxCommit);
49.         else
50.             pContxState->SetMyTransactionVote(TxAbort);
51.             pContxState->SetDeactivateOnReturn(VARIANT_TRUE);
52.         pContxState->Release();
53.     }
54.     if (SUCCEEDED(hRetval))
55.         return S_OK;
56.     else
57.         return Error((LPOLESTR)bDescription,IID_IBook,hRetval);
58. }
```

On lines 5–13 of Listing 14.2 are your variable declarations. On line 15, you call `CoGetObjectContext` and request the `IContextState` interface. It may not be obvious why you need to do this since you are not using a database in this code. Remember, the queued components service is built on MSMQ, which is a COM+ resource manager and Queued Components can participate in transactions. If the client or component that is calling the

Queued Component is running within a transaction, the QC Recorder enlists in that transaction. When the QC Recorder is deactivated, it sends its method calls to MSMQ. Like any good resource manager, MSMQ buffers the messages pending the outcome of the transaction. If some other part of the transaction fails, perhaps because a related database update failed, the method calls are de-queued. You write this code so the `PrintCopies` method can participate in a transaction and vote on the outcome of that transaction.

If you successfully receive an `IContextState` interface pointer, you enter a try block on line 20. In this try block, you first sleep for five seconds. This is done to make this method seem longer than it actually is so you can see the effect that queuing has. Next, on line 21, you create an instance of the `DOMDocument` class from the Microsoft XML component. This class is the root class in the Microsoft XML component. On line 22, you call the `createElement` function in the `DOMDocument` object to create the root node of your XML document, which is called `PrintJobs`, and then you assign this element to the `documentElement` property of `DOMDocument` to actually make this element the root node of your document. Your XML document contains the date and time the XML document was sent. So, on line 24, you call the `GetLocalTime` function to retrieve the local, system time. You next call the `AddPrintJob` function passing in the `DOMDocument` object, the `rootElement` of your document, and all the information the function needs to generate the information in your XML file. This information includes the titleID, title, number of copies, need-by date, special instructions, and the date the document was sent. You want to save each XML file under a unique name, and on lines 27–30 you use the system time you generated earlier to construct a unique file name is a function of the time that the document was created. On lines 31 and 32, you construct the full path that you save the XML document to by adding the directory path that is stored at the following string value in the registry to your filename:

```
HKEY_LOCAL_MACHINE\Software\agordonbooks\pubsboserver\OutputDir
```

Finally, on line 33, you call the `Save` method on the `DOMDocument` object to save the generated XML to the path that you just constructed. After that you have the usual error handling code. In order to make this code work you have to add an include statement for the registry utility. Put this include statement near the top of the `BookPrinter` implementation (.cpp) file as shown here.

```
// BookPrinter.cpp : Implementation of CbookPrinter
#include "stdafx.h"
#include "Pubsboserver.h"
#include "BookPrinter.h"
#include "getpathfromreg.h"
```

Now let's implement the two private methods in your class that help generate the XML: AddPrintJob and AddPrintJobElement. AddPrintJob does just what its name suggests—it creates the root element of the XML document (PrintJobs) and add a PrintJob XML element below that. AddPrintJobElement is a helper function that AddPrintJob calls to add each leaf element of the XML document and fills in the data for that node.

A leaf element in an XML document is an element that has no children. So SentDate, Title, TitleID, and NumCopies are leaf elements in your XML document, but PrintJob is not.

The code in these two functions gives you a little taste of how to use the Microsoft XML component. The implementation of the AddPrintJob function is shown in Listing 14.3.

LISTING 14.3 *ADDPRINTJOB*

```
void CBookPrinter::AddPrintJob(IXMLDOMDocumentPtr pDoc,
               IXMLDOMElementPtr pRootElement,
               BSTR titleID,BSTR title,long numCopies,
               DATE needBy,BSTR specialInstructions,DATE sentDate)
{
  IXMLDOMElementPtr pElement;
  _bstr_t elementName;
  _bstr_t elementValue;
  _variant_t lngNumCopies(numCopies,VT_I4);
  _variant_t dtSentDateTime(sentDate,VT_DATE);
  _variant_t vNeedBy(needBy,VT_DATE);

  elementName="PrintJob";
  pElement=pDoc->createElement(elementName);
  pRootElement->appendChild(pElement);

  dtSentDateTime.ChangeType(VT_BSTR,NULL);
  elementName="SentDateTime";
  elementValue=dtSentDateTime;
  AddPrintJobElement(pDoc,pElement,elementName,elementValue);

  elementName="TitleID";
  elementValue=titleID;
  AddPrintJobElement(pDoc,pElement,elementName,elementValue);

```

```
26.     elementName="Title";
27.     elementValue=title;
28.     AddPrintJobElement(pDoc,pElement,elementName,elementValue);
29.
30.     lngNumCopies.ChangeType(VT_BSTR,NULL);
31.     elementName="NumCopies";
32.     elementValue=lngNumCopies;
33.     AddPrintJobElement(pDoc,pElement,elementName,elementValue);
34.
35.     vNeedBy.ChangeType(VT_BSTR,NULL);
36.     elementName="NeedBy";
37.     elementValue=vNeedBy;
38.     AddPrintJobElement(pDoc,pElement,elementName,elementValue);
39.
40.     elementName="SpecialInstructions";
41.     elementValue=specialInstructions;
42.     AddPrintJobElement(pDoc,pElement,elementName,elementValue);
43. }
```

On lines 6–11 of Listing 14.3 are the variable declarations. Notice on lines 9–11 that you declare a bunch of `_variant_t` convenience objects that you will use to process non-string data (`PrintCopies` is passed several dates and a long value). Using `_variant_t` means you can take advantage of the type-conversion functionality that is built into `_variant_t`. On lines 13–15, you create a new `PrintJob` element and it has a child of the root element. Next on lines 17–20 you write the `SentDateTime` element to the XML file. You first use the `ChangeType` function of `_variant_t` to convert the sent date-time to a string and then write it to the XML file using the `AddPrintJobElement` function. Next on lines 22–24 and 26–28, you write the TitleID and Title elements to the XML file. On lines 30–33, you write the `NumCopies` element to the XML file. On lines 35–38, you write the `NeedBy` element to the XMLfile, and finally on lines 40–42 you write the `SpecialInstruction` element to the XML file.

The implementation of the `AddPrintJobElement` method is shown in Listing 14.4.

LISTING 14.4 *ADDPRINTJOBELEMENT*

```
void CBookPrinter::AddPrintJobElement(IXMLDOMDocumentPtr pDoc,
                        IXMLDOMElementPtr pPrintJobRootElement,
                        BSTR elementName,BSTR elementValue)
{
   IXMLDOMElementPtr pChildElement;
   pChildElement=pDoc->createElement(elementName);
   pChildElement->text=elementValue;
   pPrintJobRootElement->appendChild(pChildElement);
}
```

The AddPrintJobElement method takes a DOMDocument smart pointer and a smart point for the PrintJob element as inputs. It creates a new child element using the createElement function of the DOMDocument object, sets the text property of the new element to the elementValue parameter that is passed in to the method, and then it appends the new child element as a child of the print job element. Now press F7 to compile your project again and then you need to reconfigure your new BookPrinter component.

Configuring the BookPrinter to be a Queued Component

You need to perform these three steps to configure the BookPrinter to be a Queued Component:

1. Add the BookPrinter to your COM+ application.
2. Make your COM+ application Queued.
3. Make the BookPrinter Component queue-able.

ADDING THE BOOKPRINTER COMPONENT TO YOUR COM+ APPLICATION

At least in the case of Release Candidate 2 (RC2), the Component Services Explorer does not sense the presence of new classes in a DLL. For the new class to appear in your COM+ application, you must drag-and-drop your DLL into your COM+ application again. After you drag-and-drop your DLL into your COM+ application again, you should see your new BookPrinter class displayed within the COM+ application as shown in Figure 14.7.

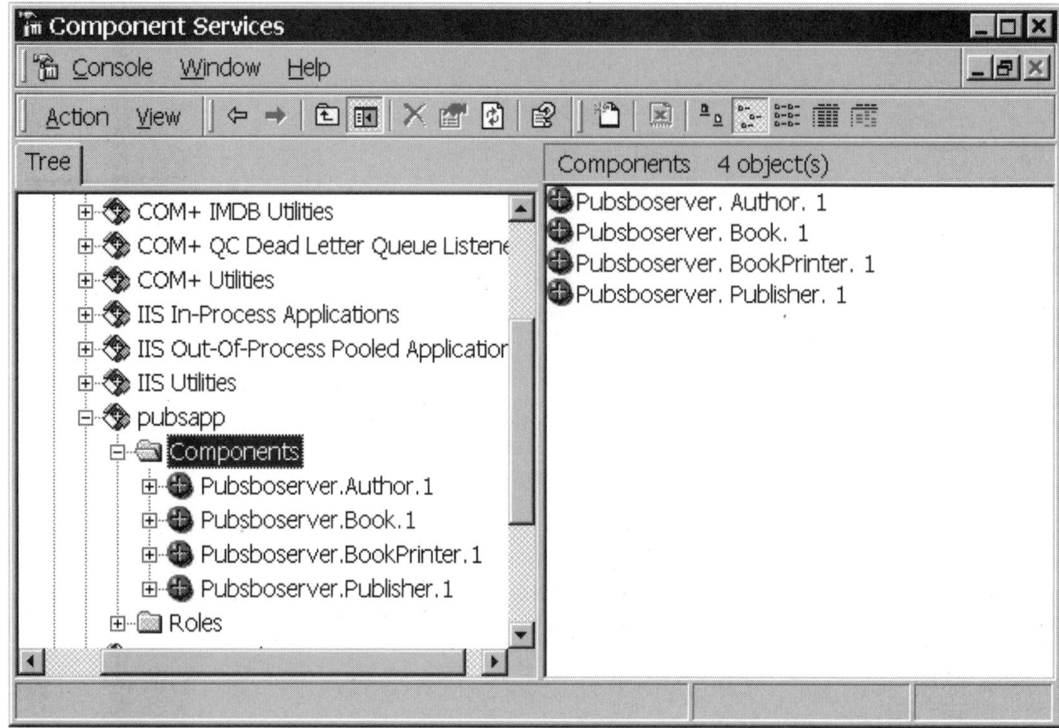

FIGURE 14.7 The BookPrinter Class Displayed within Your COM+ Application.

I noticed that whenever I dragged-and-dropped a DLL into a COM+ application that had previously been added to the COM+ application, the existing classes in the application would lose some of their attributes. I found that I had to reset the transaction, security and activation attributes. It was annoying and hopefully this problem will be fixed in the release version.

MAKING YOUR COM+ APPLICATION QUEUED

After you add the `BookPrinter` component to your COM+ application, you need to configure your COM+ application to support queuing. This causes the COM+ runtime to generate the MSMQ queues that your application needs to support the queued component service. To configure your COM+ application to support queuing, perform the following steps:

1. Right-click on your COM+ application as shown in Figure 14.8.
2. Select `Properties` from the `Context` menu (the COM+ applications properties dialog appears).

3. Click on the `Queuing` tab (your window should look like that shown in Figure 14.9.)
4. Set the `Queued` and `Listen` checkboxes.
5. Click `OK`.

Setting the Queued checkbox enables queuing. Setting the Listen checkbox enables the QC Listener Helper. Setting these checkboxes also causes COM+ to generate the message queues needed for your application. You can view these queues by going to the Computer Management Explorer for the Microsoft Management Console. To view your queues, perform the following steps in Windows 2000:

1. Click the `Start` menu.
2. Select `Programs\Administrative Tools\Computer Management`.
3. The Computer Management Explorer appears as shown back in Figure 14.4.
4. Open the `Services and Applications` item in the tree on the left side of the Windows.

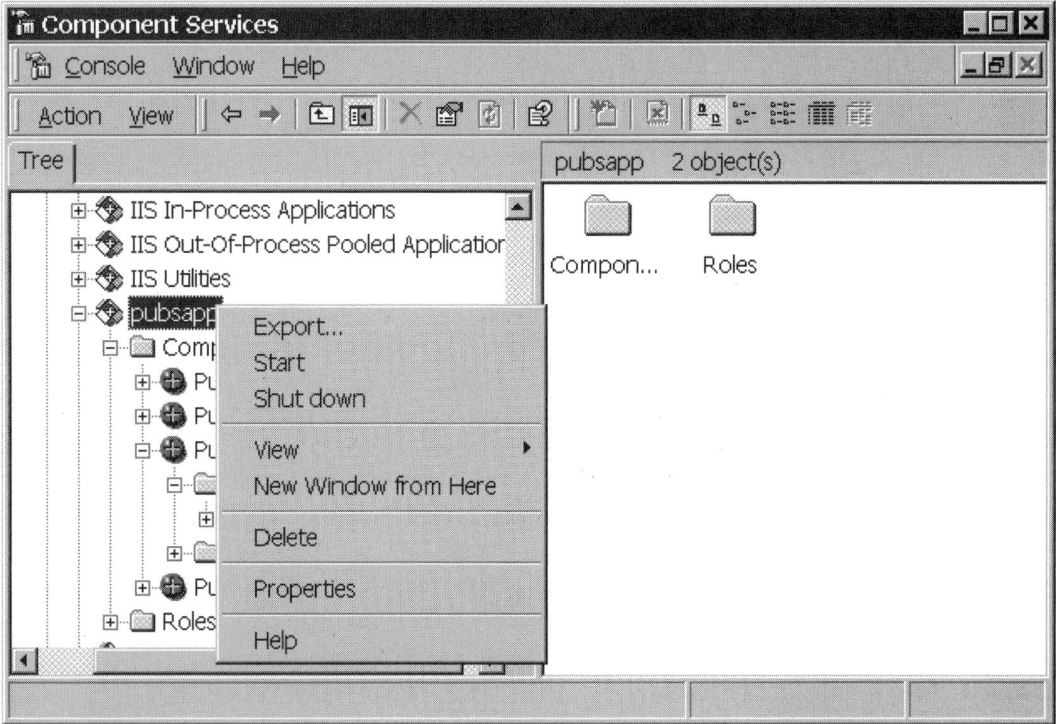

FIGURE 14.8 Right-click on Your COM+ Application.

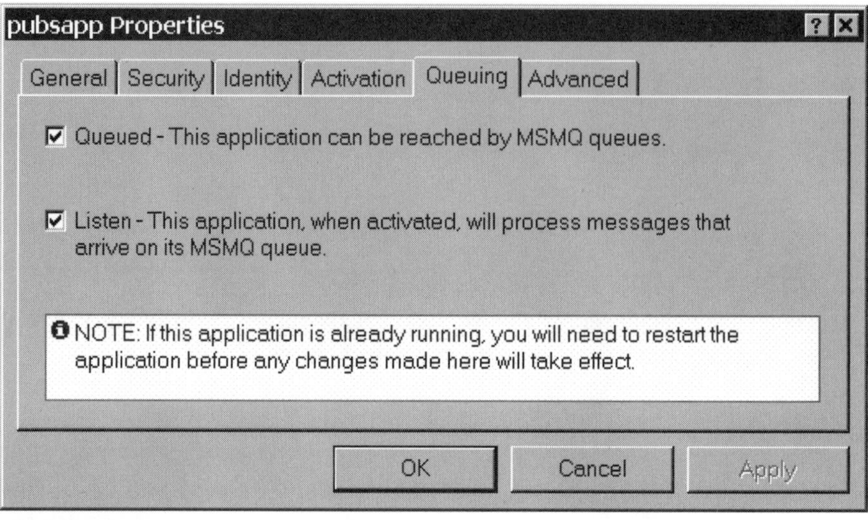

FIGURE 14.9 The Queuing Tab of Your COM+ Application.

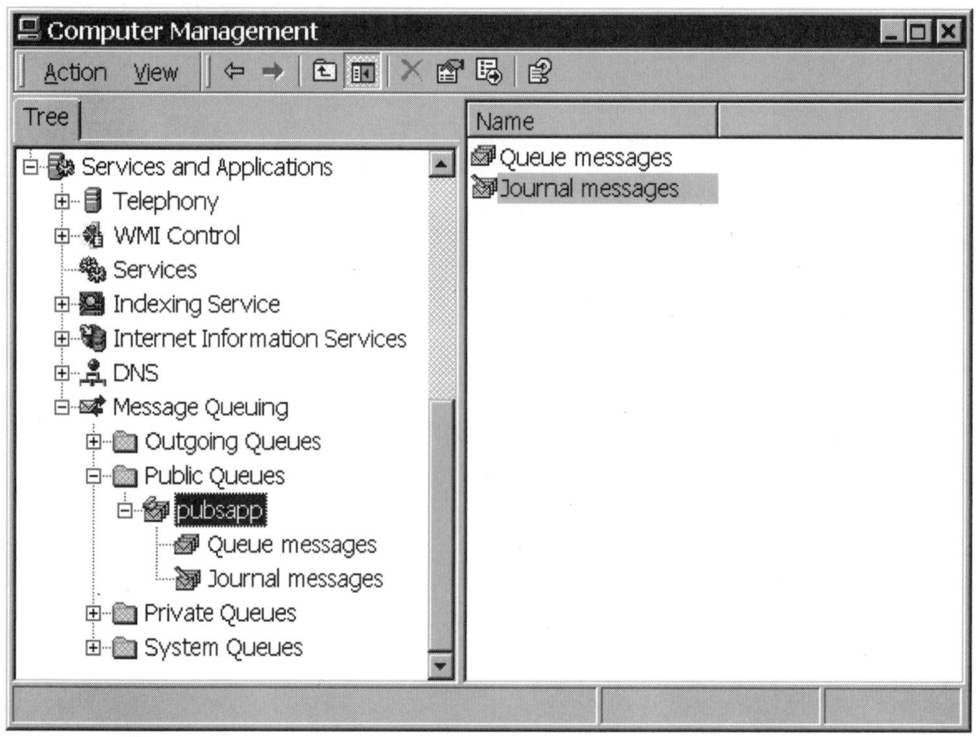

FIGURE 14.10 The Public Queue for Your COM+ Application.

5. Open the `Message Queuing` item in the tree.
6. Open the `Public Queues` folder.

You should see a public queue that has the same name as your COM+ application (as shown in Figure 14.10).

This is the message queue that's used by your COM+ application. Now open the private queues folder in the Computer Management Explorer. In the private queues you should see six queues that are related to your COM+ application as shown in Figure 14.11.

These private queues are used when a call to a Queued Component fails. See Chapter 12 for an explanation of how the private queues are used by the queued component service to retry failed methods.

MAKE THE BOOKPRINTER COMPONENT QUEUE-ABLE

Now you need to make the `IBookPrinter` interface in the `BookPrinter` component queue-able. To do this, perform the following steps in the Component Services Explorer:

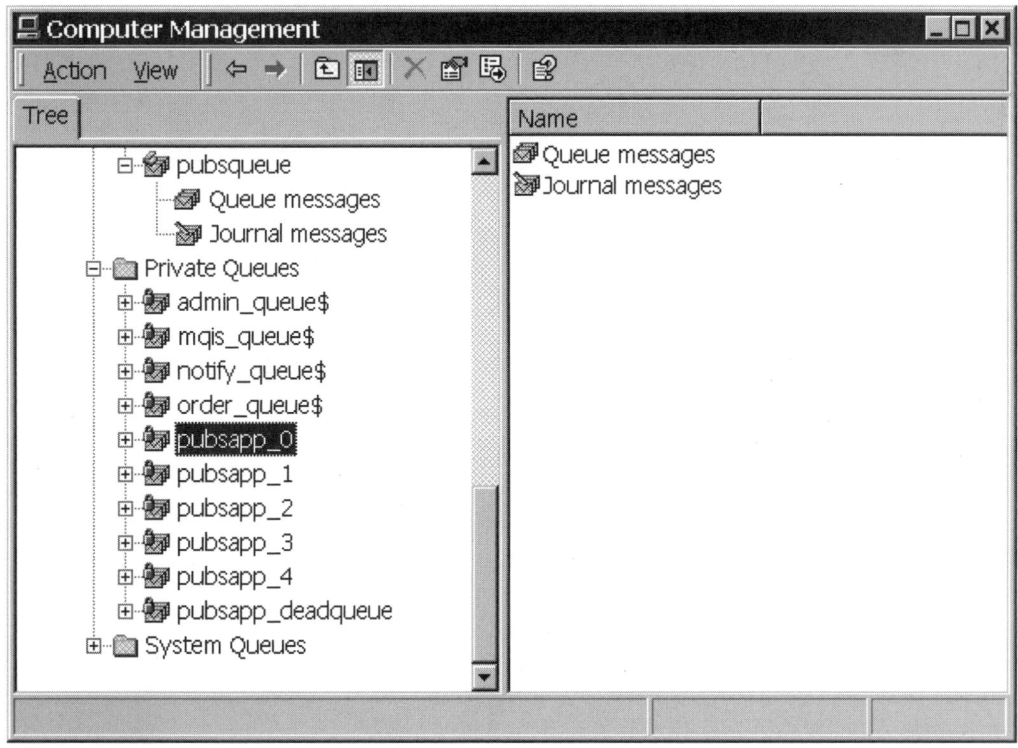

FIGURE 14.11 The Private Queues for Your COM+ Application.

1. Right-click on the IBookPrinter interface as shown in Figure 14.12.
2. Select Properties from the Context menu (the interface properties dialog appears).
3. Click the Queuing tab (your Window should look like that shown in Figure 14.13).
4. Set the Queued checkbox.
5. While you're here, you should probably configure security for this interface.
6. Click the Security tab and set the checkbox next to the Manager role. You have just allowed only managers to send orders for books to be printed.
7. Click OK.

Your BookPrinter class is now configured for queuing. Now let's modify your client to use your Queued Component.

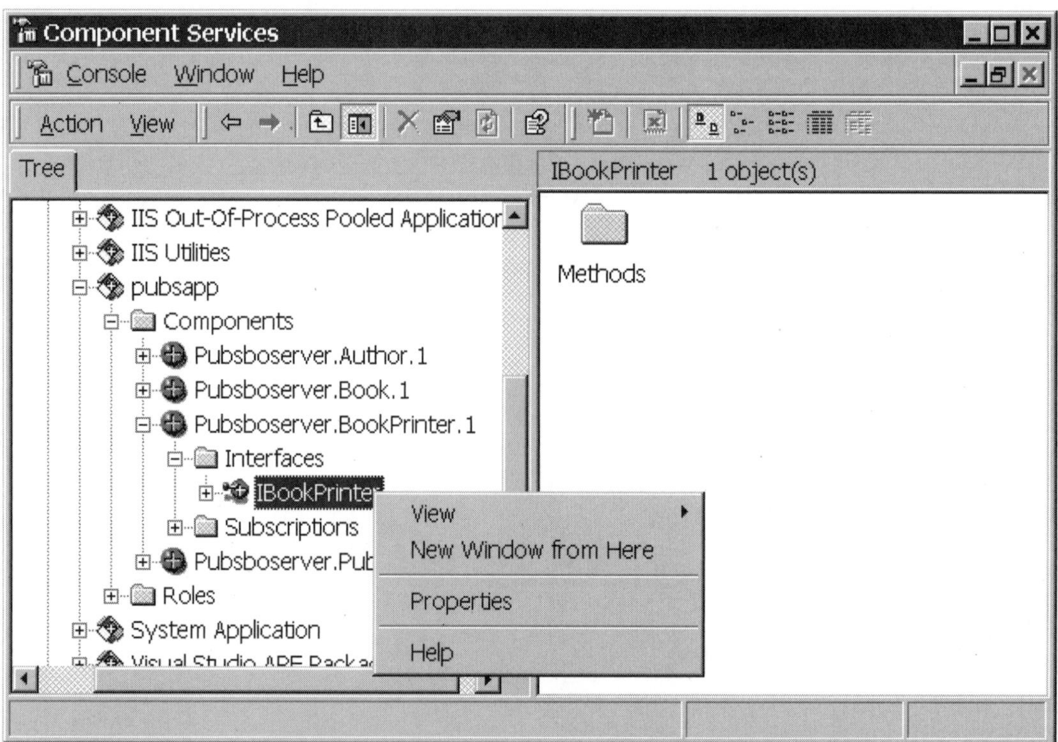

FIGURE 14.12 Right-click on the IBookPrinter Interface.

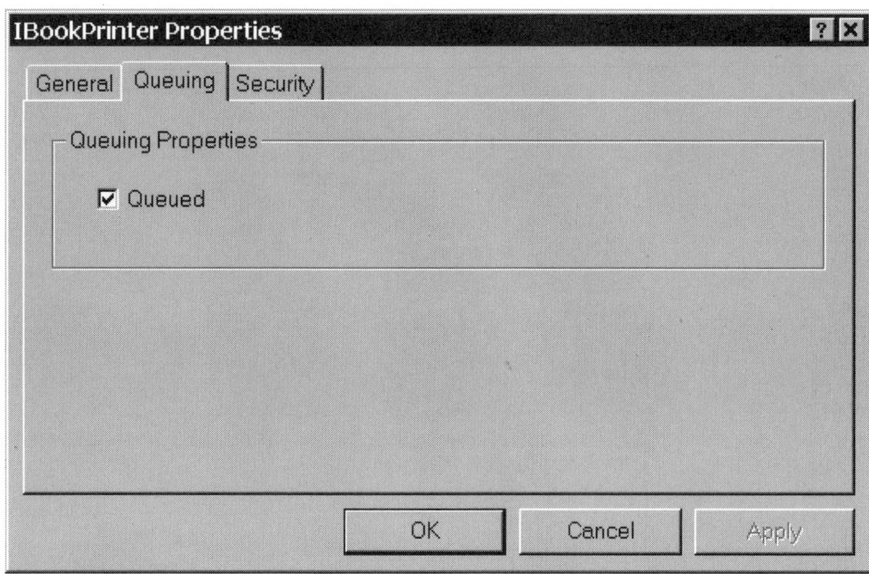

FIGURE 14.13 The Queuing Tab of the Interface Properties Dialog.

Modifying Your Client

First you need to create a Window that users can use to generate a print job XML document. The Window looks like that shown in Figure 14.14.

This Window has a check box the user can use to invoke the method call in either a queued or non-queued manner. To add this new Window to your Visual Basic client project, perform the following steps in Visual Basic:

1. Select `Add Form` from the `Project` menu (the Add Form dialog appears).
2. Select `Form` from the `New` tab of the Add Form dialog.
3. Click `Open`.

The new form is added to your project. It's called `form1` at this point. Make sure you click on the form and go to the Visual Basic property browser and change the name property of the form to `frmPrintCopies` as shown in Figure 14.15.

Now add controls to the form so it looks like Figure 14.14. The control description, control type, and control name for each control are listed in Table 14.2.

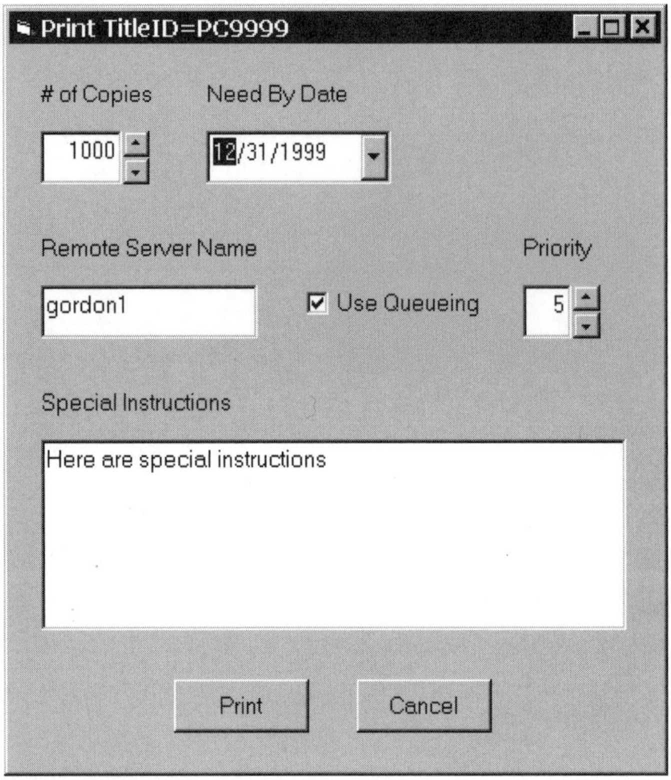

FIGURE 14.14 Your New PrintCopies Window.

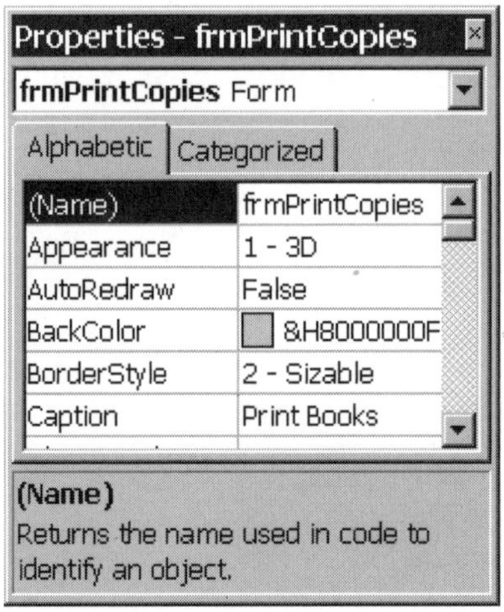

FIGURE 14.15 The VB Property Browser Showing the PrintCopies Form.

TABLE 14.2 Controls for the PrintCopies Form

Control Description	VB Control Type	Control Name in VB Project
# of Copies	TextBox	txtNumCopies
Need By Date	Date Time Picker	dtpNeedBy
Remote Server Name	TextBox	txtServerName
Use Queuing	CheckBox	chkQueueing
Priority	TextBox	txtPriority
Priority spinner	UpDown (Spinner)	updPriority
Special Instructions	Multi-Line TextBox	txtSpecialInstructions
Print	Command Button	cmdPrint
Cancel	Command Button	cmdCancel

The NeedBy date is a date time picker control. This control is found in the Microsoft Windows Common Controls-2 6.0 group of controls. These controls have already been added to your project because the UpDown control is in this group of controls. If you're not sure which control is the date time picker, rest your mouse over the tool palette. The date time picker has the tooltip `DTPicker`.

Now double-click on the print copies form to bring up a code window and add the following code in Listing 14.5 to the print copies form:

LISTING 14.5 *THE PRINT COPIES FORM*

```
Option Explicit
Private mTitleString As String
Private mTitleID As String
Public Property Let TitleString(ByVal strTitleString As String)
    mTitleString = strTitleString
End Property
Public Property Let TitleID(ByVal strTitleID As String)
    mTitleID = strTitleID
End Property

Private Sub chkQueueing_Click()
    On Error GoTo errHandler
    txtPriority.Enabled = chkQueueing.Value
    updPriority.Enabled = chkQueueing.Value
    Exit Sub
errHandler:
    MsgBox (Err.Description)
End Sub
```

```
19.
20. Private Sub cmdCancel_Click()
21.     On Error GoTo errHandler
22.     Call Unload(Me)
23.     Exit Sub
24. errHandler:
25.     MsgBox (Err.Description)
26. End Sub
27.
28. Private Sub cmdPrint_Click()
29.     On Error GoTo errHandler
30.     Dim objBookPrinter As BookPrinter
31.     Screen.MousePointer = vbHourglass
32.     If chkQueueing Then
33.         Set objBookPrinter = GetObject("queue:Priority=" & _
34.             CInt(txtPriority.Text) & ",ComputerName=" & _
35.             txtServerName.Text & "/new:pubsboserver.BookPrinter")
36.     Else
37.         Set objBookPrinter = CreateObject("pubsboserver.BookPrinter", _
38.             txtServerName.Text)
39.     End If
40.     Call objBookPrinter.PrintCopies(mTitleID, mTitleString, _
41.         CLng(txtNumCopies.Text), dtpNeedBy.Value, _
42.         txtSpecialInstructions.Text, Now)
43. ex:
44.     Screen.MousePointer = vbDefault
45.     Exit Sub
46. errHandler:
47.     MsgBox (CStr(Err.Number) & "   " & Err.Description)
48.     Resume ex
49. End Sub
50.
51. Private Sub Form_Load()
52.     On Error GoTo errHandler
53.     dtpNeedBy.Value = DateAdd("ww", 1, Date)
54.     Me.Caption = "Print TitleID=" & mTitleID
55.     Exit Sub
56. errHandler:
57.     MsgBox (Err.Description)
58. End Sub
```

I don't want to go through all of this GUI code line by line, but I've bolded the lines (32–42) that are really important. Notice on line 33 that if the user has checked the checkbox indicating that he wishes to use queuing, you instantiate your object using the Queue Moniker. I discussed the Queue Moniker in Chapter 12. You use the `Priority` and `ComputerName` parameters to the Queue Moniker to let the user specify a priority for the method call and to specify the server on which the method call executes. You can use either the domain name of the machine or an IP address for the `ComputerName` parameter. If the user has elected not to use queuing, then you instantiate the object normally using the `GetObject` function and the call proceeds in a synchronous manner.

Next you need to add a new button to your edit book window to let the user bring up the print copies window. This new button is shown in Figure 14.16.

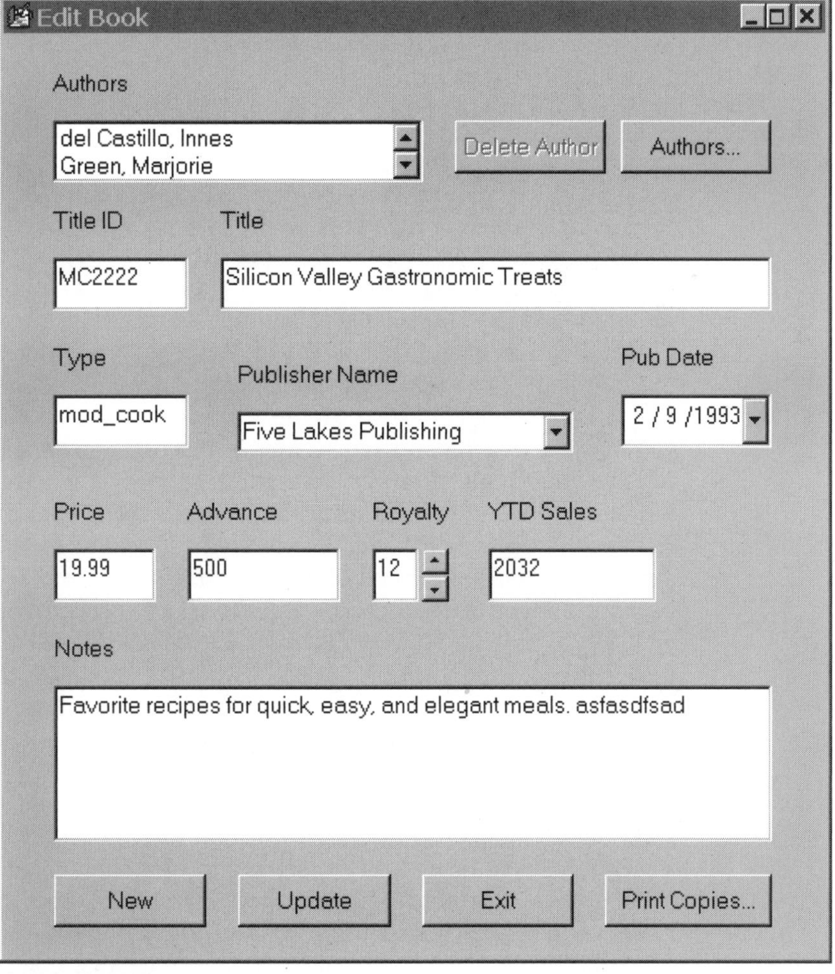

FIGURE 14.16 Print Copies Button on the Edit Book Form.

Add this button to the frmEditBook form in Visual Basic and then double-click on the button to bring up a code window and add the following code to the callback for the button:

```
Private Sub cmdPrintCopies_Click()
    On Error GoTo errHandler
    Dim printerForm As frmPrintCopies
    Set printerForm = New frmPrintCopies
    If Not mRSBook Is Nothing Then
        printerForm.TitleID = txtTitleID.Text
        printerForm.TitleString = txtTitle.Text
        printerForm.Show (vbModal)
    Else
        Call MsgBox("You must have a valid book displayed displayed")
    End If
    Exit Sub
errHandler:
    MsgBox (Err.Description)
End Sub
```

Now compile your client and test your application. You should be able to double-click on a book in the main window and bring up the edit window for the book. Now you can click the Print Copies button to bring up the Print Copies dialog. On this dialog enter a remote server name (if you are in a single-machine environment, enter the domain name of your machine [e.g., gordon1]) and then specify a priority for the method call or accept the default (5) and push the Print button. Notice that even though you have a five second pause in the PrintCopies method, the client hardly hangs at all. Now clear the queuing checkbox and then send a print job again. Notice that the client hangs until the method call is complete. Using a Queued Component without the Queued Moniker is useful for debugging. Remember that when you are using Queued Components, just because the initial method call from the client succeeds does not mean the method call will be successful. If the initial method call succeeds, that just means that the method call was successfully queued. The method call could still fail later when the QC Player plays the message in the queue to the Queued Component. When you run the method synchronously, you immediately see any errors that the method call generated.

In Chapter 12 I talked about exception classes and using a response Queued Component to return information to the client. I won't go step-by-step through the process of setting up an exception class for your Queued Component, or setting up a response object the server can use to return information to the client. But on the Web site for this book, I have included a version of the demo you built in this chapter that contains an exception class and a response object.

Asynchronous Method Invocation

I would be remiss if I left this chapter without at least a brief discussion of asynchronous method invocation. In Windows 2000 (I don't think this feature is considered a part of COM+; it actually is discussed in the COM portion of the Platform SDK documentation), it is possible to make an asynchronous method invocation without using Queued Components or MSMQ. I don't want to go into the details here because it is complicated. You can refer to an article in the Platform SDK entitled "Making an Asynchronous Call." Also check out the documentation for the `ICallFactory` interface. Making COM asynchronous calls is actually more complicated than using Queued Components and it isn't nearly as fault tolerant. In most cases, you are probably better off using Queued Components.

■ Summary

So there you have it. In the last two chapters, you built an example that uses most of the new services that COM+ provides. Your application has fine-grained security, transactions, it uses object and database connection pooling, system-provided thread synchronization, and now it also supports disconnected operation and asynchronous method invocation through the Queued Component Service. Pretty good considering you got all of this enterprise-enabling functionality without writing any code. In the last chapter of this book, you learn how to use the COM+ Event Service.

FIFTEEN

COM+ Events

COM+ Events is a service provided by the COM+ runtime that lets base clients or COM+ objects easily send notifications (events) to COM+ objects that wish to receive them. Objects or base clients that send events are called Publishers, and objects that receive events are called Subscribers. Because of this naming of its major participants, you may also hear COM+ Events referred to as Publish and Subscribe Events. COM+ Events solve many of the same problems as Connection Points that you learned about in Chapter 8. In fact, the example you can build in this chapter is a re-implementation of the stock monitor you built in chapter 8. You'll see that COM+ Events are better than Connection Points in a number of respects.

- With COM+ Events, the lifetimes of the Publisher and Subscriber do not have to overlap. A Subscriber can subscribe to events before a Publisher is started, and a Publisher can send events to a Subscriber that is not currently running.
- With COM+ Events, a Subscriber can easily filter the events that it receives. For instance in the Stock Monitor example you could elect to only receive price change events on Microsoft stock.
- Both Subscriptions (and filters) can be established and removed using the Component Services Explorer instead of using code.

This makes software built with COM+ Events more flexible than code that relies on Connection Points. All of these improvements create a loosely coupled relationship between the Subscriber that is receiving the events and the Publisher that is sending them. Because of this, COM+ Events are sometimes referred to as Loosely-Coupled Events. Whatever you choose to call them, COM+ Events simply add up to a better mechanism for sending events than Connection Points. In this chapter, you learn what COM+ Events are, what the COM+ Events architecture is and you'll build an example that illustrates everything you have learned.

Why Do You Need COM+ Events?

In Chapter 8 I discussed COM connection points. You learned that in certain situations the canonical client/server arrangement where a client uses the services of a COM object that passively waits for commands is not sufficient. Usually these are use-cases where some event that is of interest to the client may occur at random times (or at least is difficult to predict). That event could be a change in the price of a stock, a change in mortgage interest rates, or a change in the score of a football game.

One solution to these types of use-cases is to have the client poll the COM object, continually asking it if the event has occurred. Unless the event happens often, this approach wastes a lot of CPU cycles, and if the system is distributed, network bandwidth. A more efficient solution is to have the COM object notify the client whenever the event of interest occurs. The question now is: How can the client send these notifications back to the client?

COM connection points are a set of interfaces and a protocol for establishing bi-directional communication between a COM client and server. The best part about Connection Points is that they are generic. The COM interfaces used to implement connection points are a well-documented part of COM and most PC-based development tools make it simple to source and sink connection point events. In Visual Basic, you can add a handler for a connection point event with point-and-click ease. There are some problems with COM connection points, however. One problem is that it requires a total of five round trips just to establish a link between a COM client and server (see Chapter 8 for the details). In Chapter 8, you learned the solution to this problem: You can create your own custom (proprietary) callback interfaces. But custom callback interfaces don't work as well with most development tools. You have to do more manual coding to establish the link between your client and server.

Unfortunately, using custom callback interfaces won't fix another problem with connection points: tight-coupling between the client and server. When a client wishes to receive events from a COM object that fires them, the client must know ahead of time which mechanism it must use to establish a bi-directional link between itself and the COM object. In many cases, the mechanism is connection points, but the object also may use custom (proprietary) callback interfaces. In addition, both the client and the object that is firing the events must be running at all times during their interaction. Both sides must be running when the client establishes its link with the object, and both sides must be running when the object sends its events to the client. Moreover, the object must internally keep track of all the clients that it needs to send events to (the ATL implementation of connection points maintains a collection of outgoing interface pointers). As if this wasn't enough, there is also no (standardized) way to filter the events you receive from an object. Once a client registers itself to receive price change events, it receives all of them.

Before you start cursing Connection Points and everything for which they stand, know that Connection Points are the mechanism that ActiveX controls use to send events to their client (container). In this application, Connection Points work well. The object firing the events (the ActiveX control) runs in-process with its client so the five round trips to establish the bi-directional link is no problem. The lifetime of the ActiveX control and its container are usually the same, so there are no problems there. The simple truth of the matter is that ActiveX controls do have a tightly-coupled relationship with their containers, so the tightly-coupled nature of connection points is a good fit for that application. But in an enterprise-class distributed environment, the tightly coupled nature of connection points is a problem.

COM+ Events

The solution to all of these problems is a new COM+ technology called Loosely-Coupled Events (LCE), Publish and Subscriber Events, or simply COM+ Events. I've seen all three names used in various places, but the official name is COM+ Events.

COM+ Events work by decoupling the objects that wish to send Events (called Publishers) from the clients that wish to receive the events (called Subscribers).

Don't let my use of the word client confuse you here. The client does not have to be GUI code; it could be another COM+ object. When I refer to a client in this context I mean *any* piece of software that is using the services of a COM+ object.

Compare Figures 15.1 and 15.2.

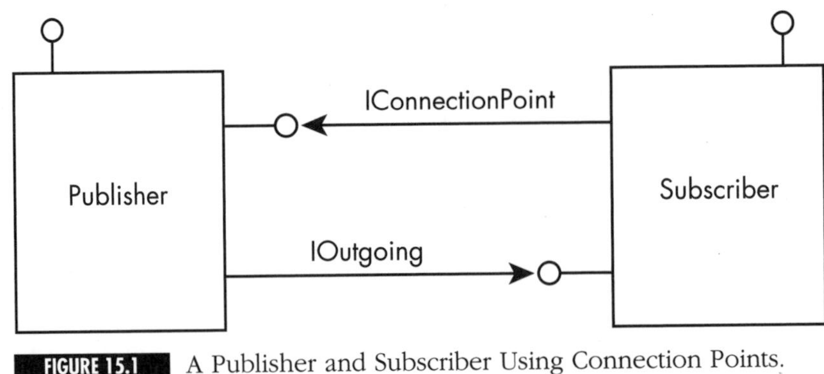

FIGURE 15.1 A Publisher and Subscriber Using Connection Points.

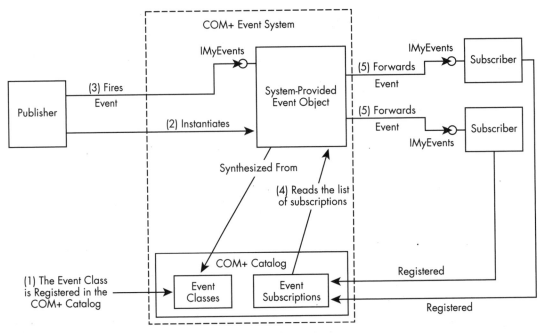

FIGURE 15.2 A Publisher and Subscriber Using COM+ Events.

Figure 15.1 shows the architecture of a Publisher and Subscriber when they are communicating using Connection Points. Notice that the Publisher and Subscriber are linked directly with each other. Now look at Figure 15.2, which shows a Publisher and Subscriber using COM+ Events. Notice that the Publisher and Subscriber do not hold direct references on each other. This is important in making the COM+ Event system more flexible and loosely coupled than Connection Points. As shown in Figure 15.2, there are five major elements in the COM+ Events architecture: an `Event` class, a system-provided `Event` object, the COM+ catalog and, of course, a Publisher and Subscriber. The steps to creating a Publisher and Subscriber using COM+ Events are as follows:

1. Create an Event class. To do this, perform these steps:
   - 1.1. Create a COM class that contains an empty implementation of one or more `Event` interfaces.
   - 1.2. Using the Component Services Explorer, configure the COM class to be an `Event` class.
2. Create a Publisher. To do this, perform the following steps:
   - 2.1. Instantiate an instance of the `Event` class.
   - 2.2. Fire an Event by calling a method on one of the interfaces in the `Event` class.
3. Create a Subscriber. To do this, perform the following steps:
   - 3.1. Create a COM class that implements one or more of the `Event` interfaces in the `Event` class. The implementation performs whatever actions you want to be done when an Event is received.
   - 3.2. Configure the COM class to be an event Subscriber.
   - 3.3. Add a Subscription to one or more of the Methods in the `Event` classes interfaces.

Creating an Event Class

Using COM+ Events begins with an `Event` class. The `Event` class is a COM class, which you create, that implements the interface(s) you will be using to send your events. Publishers call a method on one of the `Event` classes' interfaces to Fire an event. If a Subscriber wishes to receive those events, it must implement one or more of the interfaces defined by an `Event` class. The implementation you create for an `Event` class is typically empty. You really only need to create a type library and a self-registering DLL for your `Event` class. The easiest way to create a type library and a self-registering DLL is to use Visual Basic or the ATL Object Wizard in Visual C++ to create a COM class in an in-process server. You add your `Event` interfaces to this COM class, but you don't have to implement any of the methods in the event interfaces.

After you configure a COM+ class to be an `Event` Class, the COM+ runtime returns a system-provided event object whenever someone tries to create an instance of the `Event` class. This event object is synthesized from the type library that you provide. The event object forwards method calls to event Subscribers.

Configuring a COM class to be an `Event` class is simple. First you have to create a COM+ application in the normal way. Since I have shown how to do this several times in Chapters 11, 13, and 14, I won't repeat those steps again. Once you have created a COM+ application, the next step is to add a new COM class to the COM+ application and configure it to be an Event class. To do this, perform the following steps:

1. Right-click on the `Components` folder beneath the COM+ application as shown in Figure 15.3.
2. Select `New\Component` from the `Context` menu (the welcome screen for the Component Installation Wizard appears, see Figure 11.25 in Chapter 11).
3. Click the `Next` button (the Import or Install Component Screen appears as shown in Figure 15.4).
4. Click the `Install New Event Classes` button.
5. A file browsing dialog appears, navigate to where the DLL for your event class is located and either click `OK` or double-click on it. The Install New Event class dialog appears as shown in Figure 15.5.
6. Click `Next` and then Click `Finish` on the final screen.

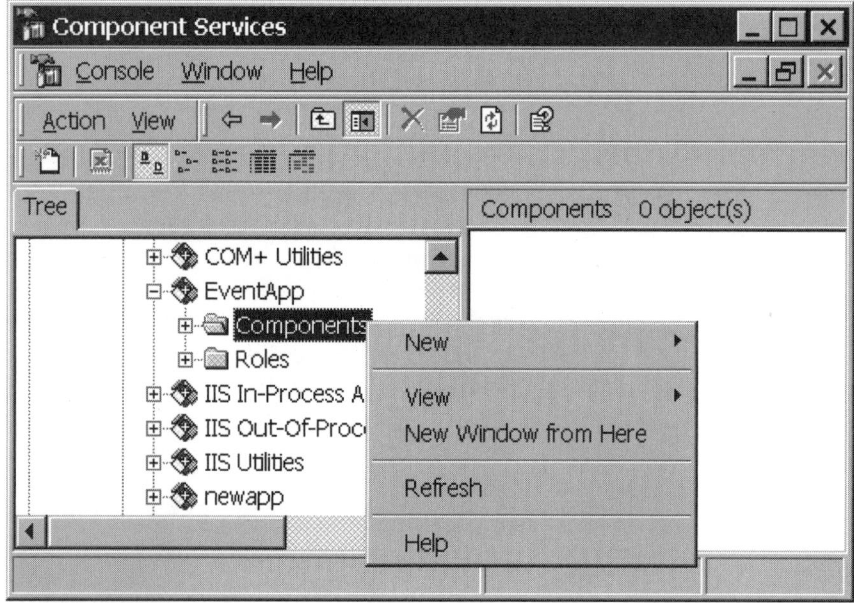

FIGURE 15.3 Adding a New Component to a COM+ Application.

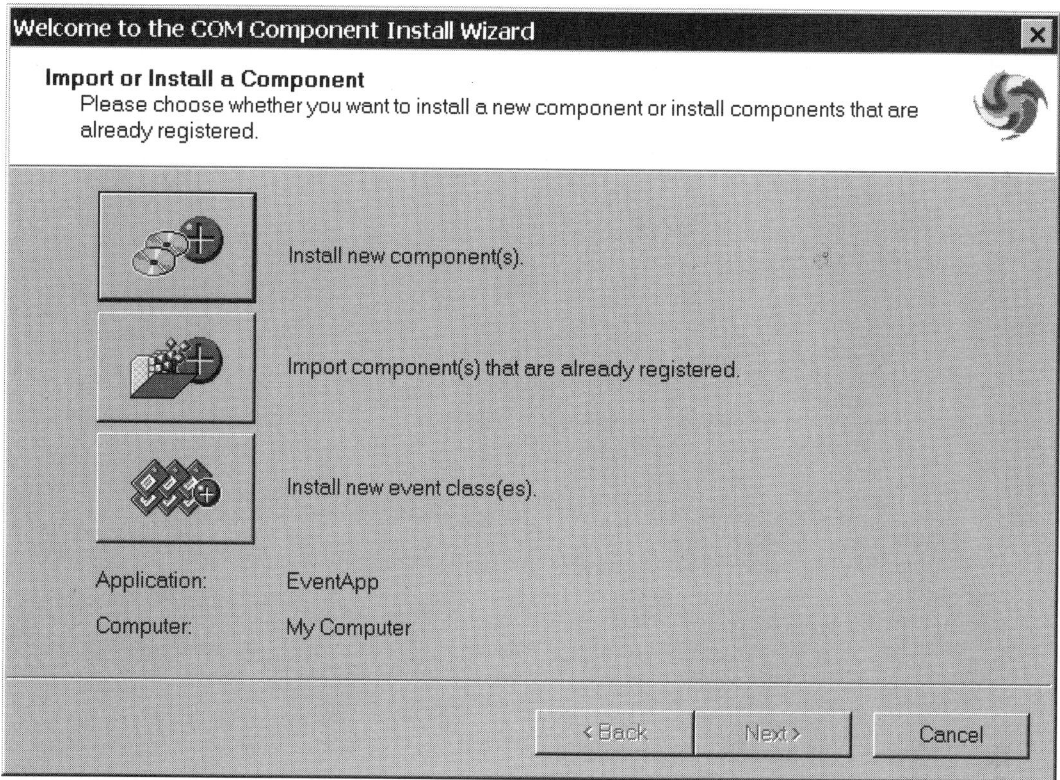

FIGURE 15.4 The Import or Install a New Component Dialog.

Now that your class is registered as an `Event` class, it appears in the Components folder of the COM+ application just like any COM class would. If you right-click on the class and select `Properties...` from the `Context` menu, you see the usual Component Properties dialog that you see for any configured COM+ component. All of the tabs look the same except for the `Advanced` tab, which is shown in Figure 15.6.

Notice that you can specify whether Events should be delivered in parallel to multiple Subscribers. If you set this checkbox, then the COM+ Event system uses multiple threads to deliver an event to more than one Subscriber. Setting this checkbox does not guarantee that the event is delivered at the same time to multiple Subscribers, but it instructs COM+ Events to permit this to happen. If this checkbox is cleared, then the event is delivered in serial fashion to multiple Subscribers.

On the `Advanced` tab, you can also specify whether in-process Subscribers are allowed. If the `Event` class and the Subscriber are both configured in COM+ library applications, the Subscriber runs in the same process

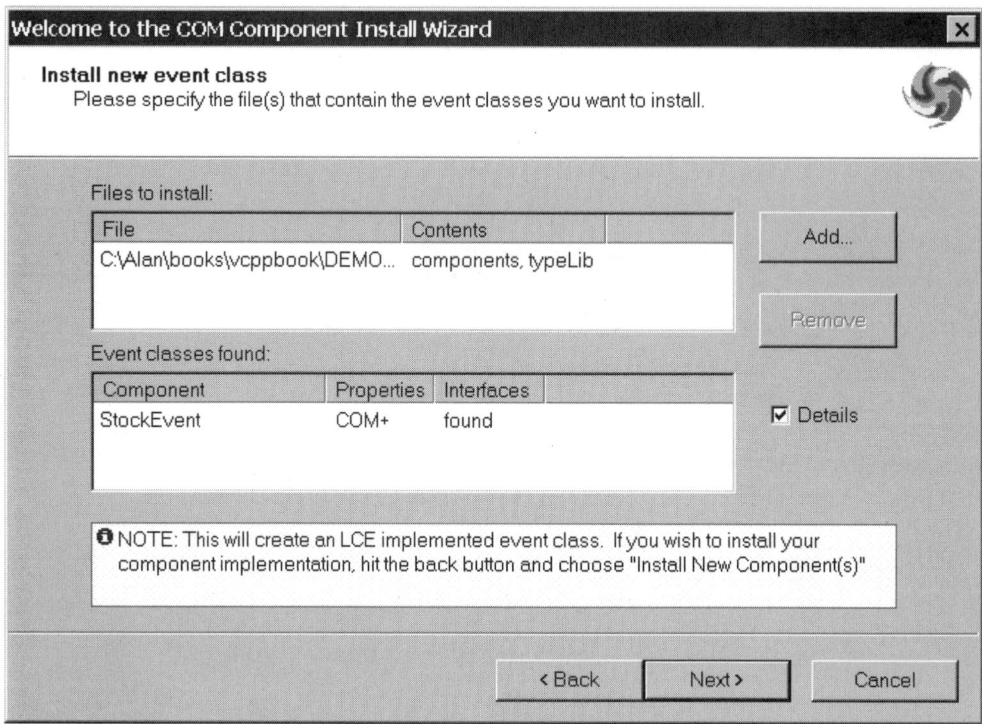

FIGURE 15.5 The Install New Event Class Dialog.

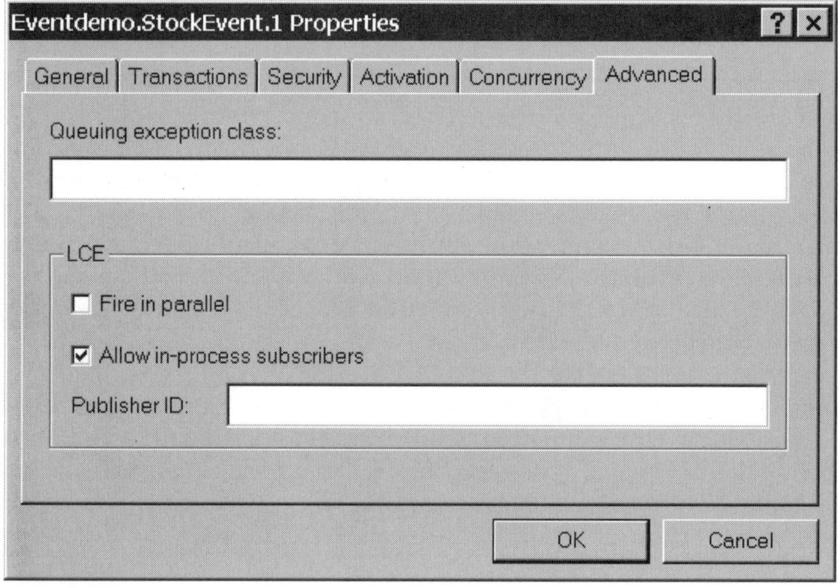

FIGURE 15.6 The Advanced Tab of the Component Properties Dialog for an Event Class.

as the Publisher. For security and/or robustness purposes, you may not want this to happen. If you clear the `allow in-process Subscribers` checkbox, then Subscribers are always created in a separate process even if they are configured in a COM+ library application.

You can also specify a Publisher ID for an `Event` class on the `Advanced` tab of the component properties dialog. The string that you enter here shows up in the Component Services Explorer when you add a Subscription for this `Event` class.

Creating Subscriptions

Now that you have created an `Event` class, you can immediately begin adding Subscriptions. You don't even need to create a Publisher yet. This is part of the beauty of COM+ Events: the lifetimes of Publishers and Subscribers are not linked. There are two types of Subscriptions you can create: Transient Subscriptions and Persistent Subscriptions.

TRANSIENT SUBSCRIPTIONS

Transient Subscriptions are tied to a particular `Subscriber` object (persistent Subscriptions are tied to all instances of a `Subscriber` class). Transient Subscriptions also do not survive a system shutdown. The next time you start the system the transient Subscription is gone. You cannot create transient Subscriptions using the Component Services Explorer. You must use the COM+ administrative interfaces (the `COMAdmin` component) to create or update a transient Subscription. To specify a Subscription as transient, you must add a new Subscription using the Administrative Interfaces and set the `SubscriberInterface` property of `IEventSubscription` (the interface that represents a Subscription) to the `IUnknown` interface of the transient `Subscriber` object. The COM+ Event system does not create a new instance of the `Subscriber` object when firing an event. It uses the `Subscriber` object whose `IUnknown` interface was set as the `SubscriberInterface` property of `IEventSubscription`. COM+ Events holds a reference on the `Subscriber` object until the Subscription is removed from the system. The main advantage of transient Subscriptions is that they are more efficient than persistent Subscriptions which instantiate and destroy an instance of the Subscriber class each time an event is sent.

PERSISTENT SUBSCRIPTIONS

Persistent Subscriptions are stored in the COM+ catalog and affect all instances of a `Subscriber` class. Persistent Subscriptions do survive a system shutdown. When a Publisher creates an instance of an `Event` class.

The system-provided event object that is synthesized from the `Event` class finds all the persistent Subscriptions in the COM+ catalog and creates a new instance of each Subscription class. The `Event` objects are released after the event is sent to each of these `Subscriber` objects. You can create Persistent Subscriptions using the Component Services Explorer. To create a persistent Subscription, perform the following steps:

1. Create a New COM+ class that implements an interface that is supported by an `Event` class.
2. Configure the `Subscription` class normally. You do not need to add the `Subscription` class to the same COM+ Application as the `Event` class.
3. Right-click on the `Subscriptions` folder beneath the `Subscriber` class as shown in Figure 15.7.
4. Select `New\Subscription` from the `Context` menu.
5. The welcome screen of the COM New Subscription Wizard appears as shown in Figure 15.8.
6. Click the `Next` button (the Select Subscription methods dialog appears as shown in Figure 15.9).
7. Select either a method or an interface that defines the event the Subscriber wishes to receive. If you select an interface, all methods in that interface are used.
8. Click the `Next` button. The Component Services Explorer finds all the `Event` classes that contain the specified interface as shown in Figure 15.10.
9. Select an `Event` class and click the `Next` button. The Subscription Options dialog appears as shown in Figure 15.11.
10. Enter a name for the Subscription and set the `Enable Subscription immediately` checkbox.
11. Click the `Next` button.
12. Click `Finish` on the final screen of the New Subscription Wizard.

Step 8 is very important. The New Subscription Wizard searches all the COM+ applications on the current machine for an `Event` class that implements this interface. Even if the `Event` class existed in a different COM+ application than the one the Subscriber resides in, the New Subscription Wizard still finds it. Also notice that the wizard lets you choose from several Event classes. That means you can have more than one `Event` class that implements the `IStockEvent` interface registered on your machine at once. When you create a Subscription, you have to choose which of these `Event` classes you want. Now that you have created a Subscription, you probably want to create a Publisher to generate events.

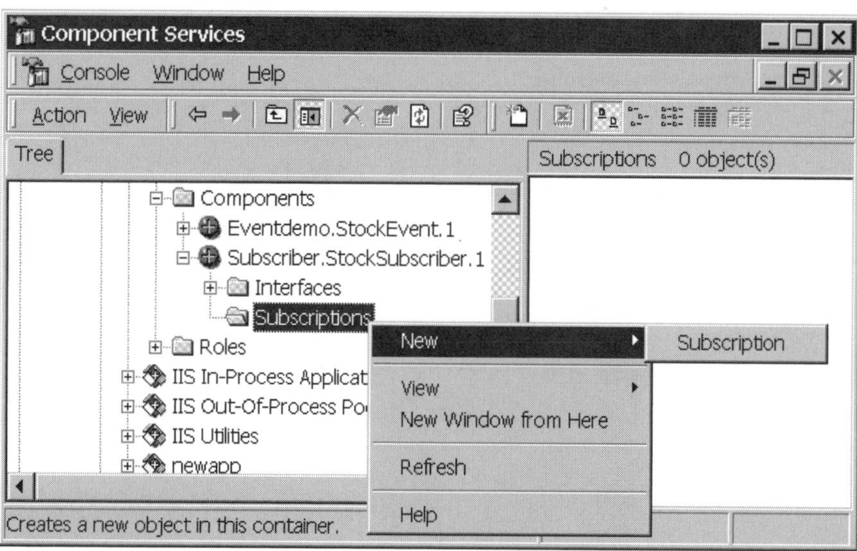

FIGURE 15.7 Adding a New Subscription.

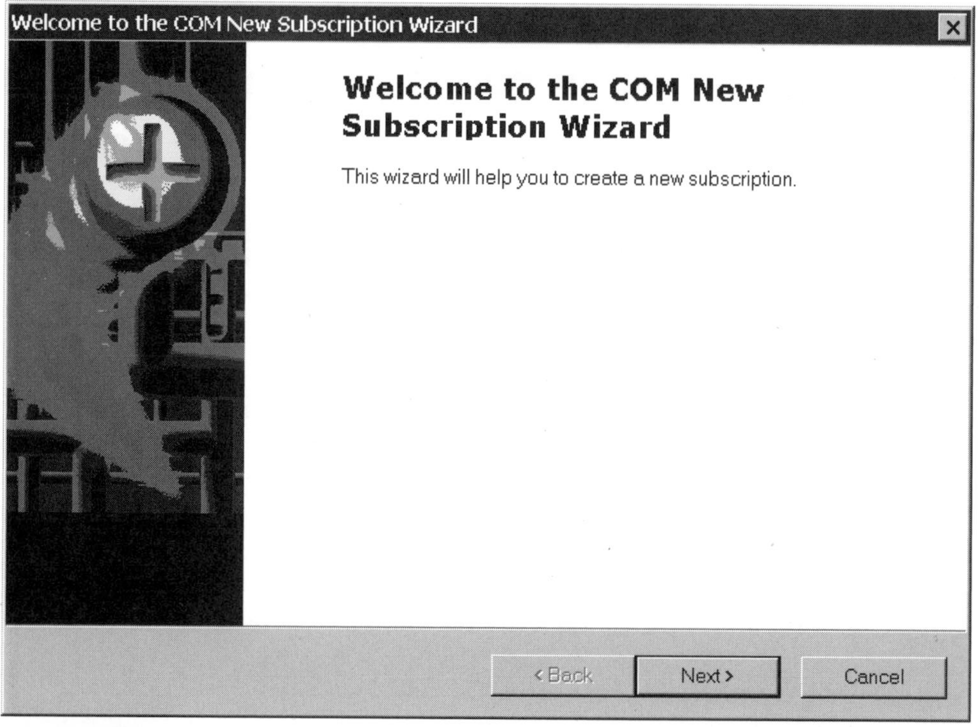

FIGURE 15.8 The Welcome Screen of the COM New Subscription Wizard.

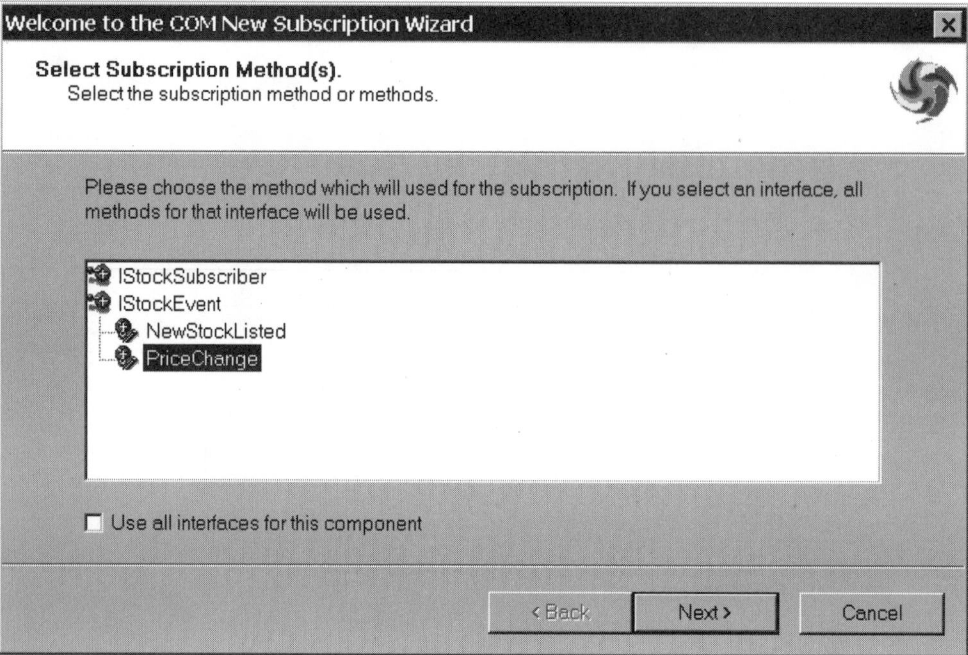

FIGURE 15.9 Selecting the Subscription Methods.

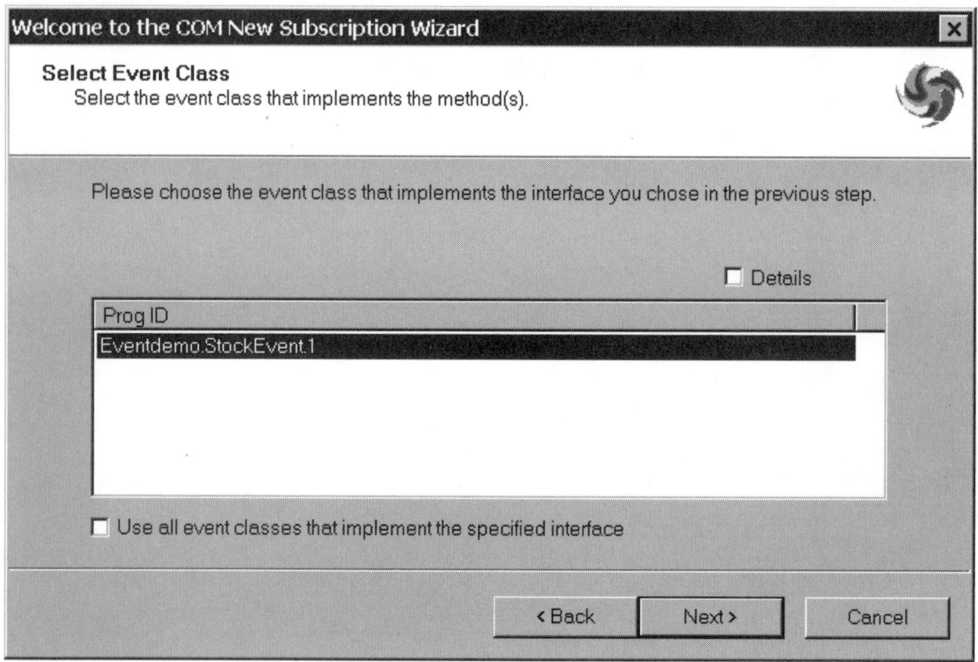

FIGURE 15.10 The Subscription Wizard Finds the Event Classes.

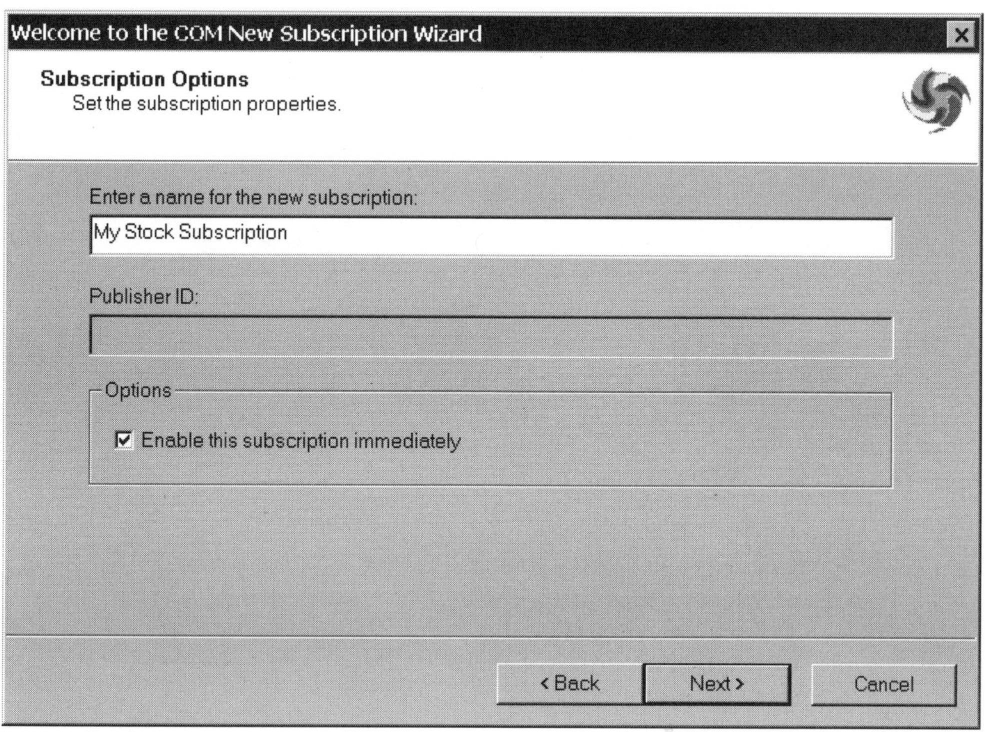

FIGURE 15.11 Subscription Options.

CREATING A PUBLISHER

Publishers are easy to create. All a Publisher has to do is create an instance of the Event class and then call a method on the Event class to fire an Event. The following code shows a Publisher creating an instance of an Event class, StockEvent, and then calling the PriceChange method on the IStockEvent interface to fire a PriceChange event:

```
void CPublishervcppDlg::OnFireEventButton()
{
   HRESULT hRes;
   CString strTicker;
   BSTR bTicker;
   IStockEvent *pEvent;
   UpdateData(TRUE);
   hRes=CoCreateInstance(__uuidof(StockEvent),NULL,CLSCTX_ALL,
      __uuidof(IStockEvent), (void **)&pEvent);
```

```
    if (FAILED(hRes))
    {
        _com_error err(hRes);
        AfxMessageBox(err.ErrorMessage());
    }
    m_stockList.GetText(m_stockList.GetCurSel(),strTicker);
    bTicker=strTicker.AllocSysString();
    hRes=pEvent->PriceChange(bTicker,m_newPrice,m_oldPrice);
    if (FAILED(hRes))
    {
        _com_error err(hRes);
        AfxMessageBox(err.ErrorMessage());
    }
    pEvent->Release();
    ::SysFreeString(bTicker);
}
```

Remember that when you call a method on an instance of an `Event` class (an event object), you are actually using a system-provided implementation that is synthesized from the `Event` class. The system-provided implementation of each `Event` method in the `Event` class can return one of the four values shown in Table 15.1.

TABLE 15.1 Return Codes for Event Methods

Return Code	Description
S_SUCCESS	The event was successfully delivered to all Subscribers.
EVENT_S_SOME_SUBSCRIBERS_FAILED	The error code is so descriptive it doesn't really need an explanation. It means the event could not be delivered to one or more Subscribers.
EVENT_E_ALL_SUBSCRIBERS_FAILED	The event could not be delivered to any Subscribers
EVENT_S_NOSUBSCRIBERS	The event was sent, but there are no Subscribers.

`EVENT_S_SOME_SUBSCRIBERS_FAILED` and `EVENT_S_NOSUBSCRIBERS` are warnings, not errors, so you won't catch these return values using the `FAILED` macro. The following logic catches these warnings.

```
hRes=pEvent->PriceChange(bTicker,m_newPrice,m_oldPrice);
if (SUCCEEDED(hRes))
{
    if (EVENT_S_SOME_SUBSCRIBERS_FAILED == hRes)
        AfxMessageBox("Some Subscribers Failed");
    else if (EVENT_S_NOSUBSCRIBERS  == hRes)
        AfxMessageBox("There were no Subscribers");
```

```
}
else
{
    _com_error err(hRes);
    AfxMessageBox(err.ErrorMessage());
}
```

You can create the event object normally using either the `CoCreateInstance(Ex)` function or using a Moniker. Typically if you use a Moniker, it's because you are using Queued Components with COM+ Events.

Using Queued Components with Events

You can use events with Queued Components in two ways: (1) you can use Queued Components between the Publisher and the `Event` class to fire events asynchronously, and (2) you can also deliver events asynchronously to Subscribers by using Queued Components between the `Event` class and the Subscribers. Both scenarios are shown in Figure 15.12.

Using Queued Components Between Publisher and Event Class

To use Queued Components between the Publisher and the `Event` class, you must instantiate the Event object using the Queued Moniker as shown below in C++:

```
hRes=CoGetObject (L"queue:/new:8796e0f6-552d-4e50-8146-eb69296065b6",
                  NULL, __uuidof(IStockEvent), (void**) &m_pEventObject);
```

or here in Visual Basic.

```
Set objEventClass = GetObject(
                    "queue:/new:8796e0f6-552d-4e50-8146-eb69296065b6")
```

To make this work, you also need to mark the COM+ application that contains the `Event` class as queued and you need to mark the `Event` interface(s) as queued also.

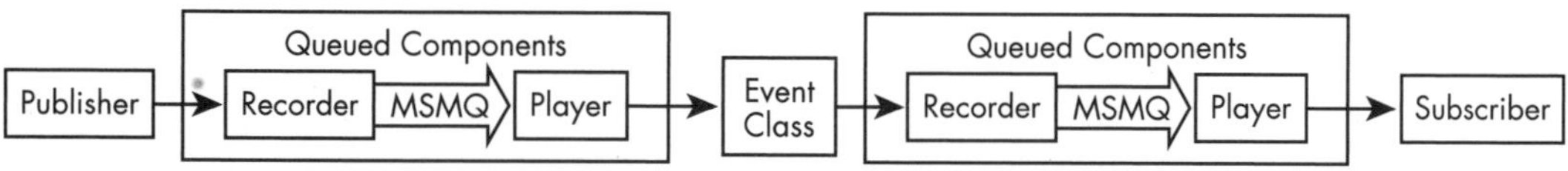

FIGURE 15.12 Two Ways to use Queued Components with Events.

Using Queued Components Between the Event Class and the Subscribers

To use Queued Components between the `Event` class and the Subscriber, you must set the queued attribute of the Subscription. You can do this by performing the following steps:

1. Right-click on the Subscription as shown in Figure 15.13.
2. Select `Properties` from the `Context` menu (the Subscription properties dialog appears as shown in Figure 15.14).
3. Click the `Options` tab.
4. Set the `Queued` checkbox.

The Subscriber also needs to reside in a COM+ application that is queued; I also had to mark the `Event` interface in the `Subscriber` class as queued to make this work. If the order of events is important to your application, you need to be mindful of an order-of-delivery problem when using Queued Components with COM+ Events. Remember from Chapter 14 that the COM+ Queued Components Service sends all the method calls made on a queued object to MSMQ in a single message. You are, therefore, guaran-

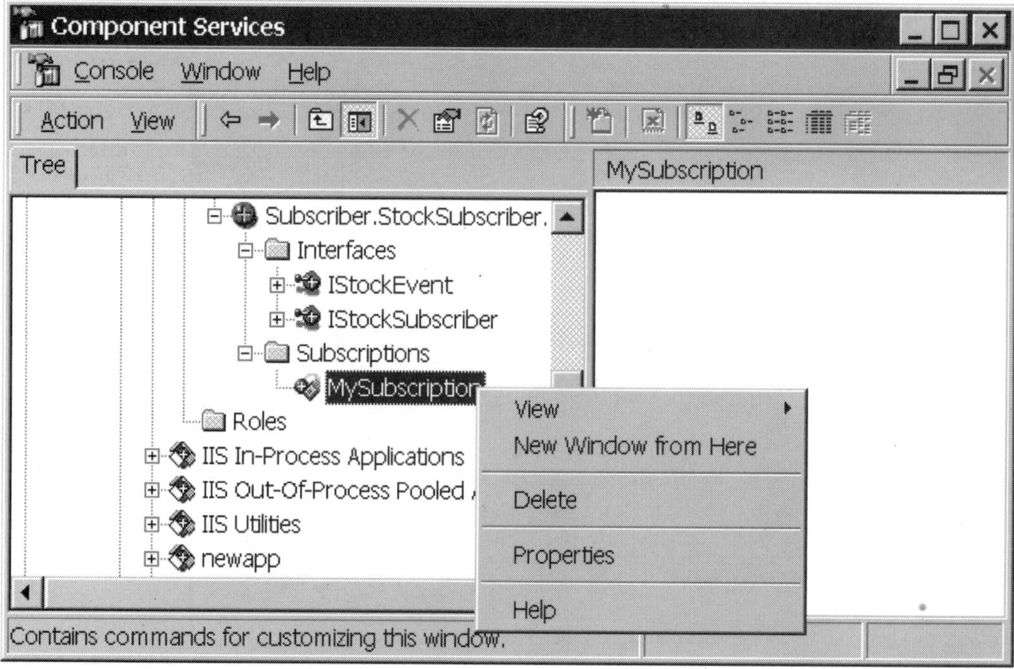

FIGURE 15.13 Displaying the Subscription Properties Dialog.

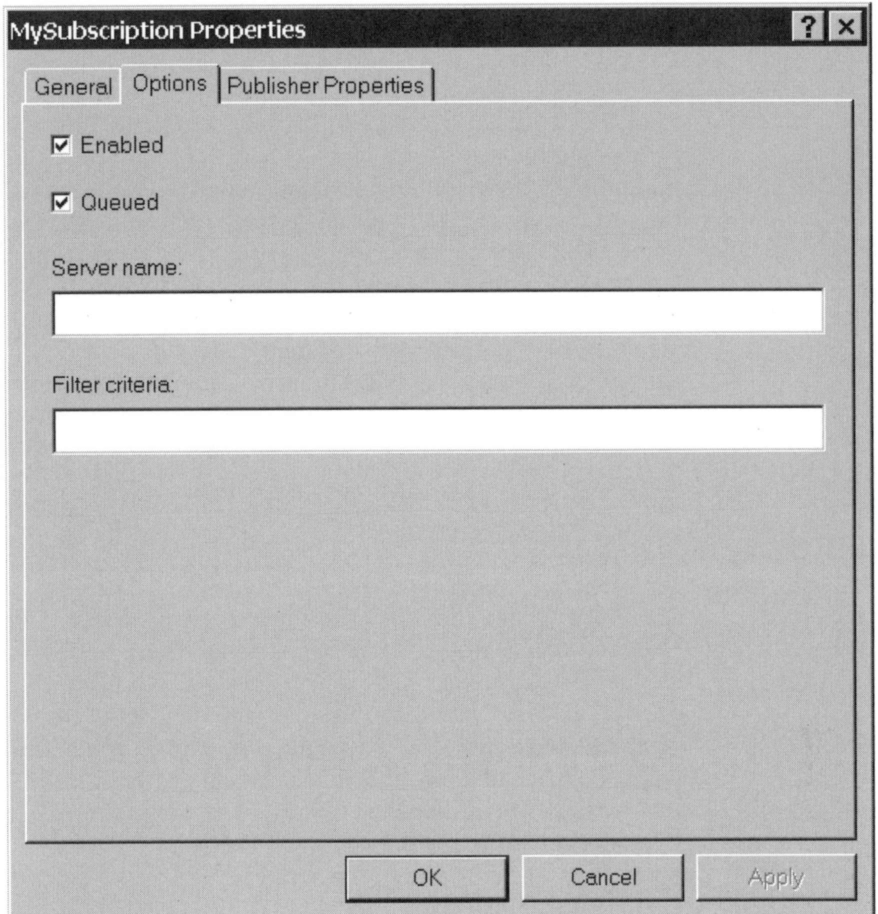

FIGURE 15.14 Option Tab of the Subscription Properties Dialog.

teed that all the method calls made on one instance of the `Event` class by the Publisher are played back to the Subscriber in the same order. However, if you use multiple instances of the `Event` class, then COM+ cannot guarantee the Subscriber receives events in the same order that the Publisher fired them. Whether this is a problem for you depends on your application. If the order that the events are received is important, you either need to make sure that all your events originate from a single instance of the `Event` class, or you need to avoid using Queued Components with events.

COM+ Events and Transactions

COM+ Events also works transparently with the COM+ transaction mechanism. You can cause events to be delivered in the context of a transaction by configuring the `Event` class to Support Transactions in the normal way using the Component Services Explorer. The Publisher's transaction propagates to the `Event` class and then to the Subscribers. Each Subscriber that receives the Event can then vote on the Transaction using either the `IContextState` or `IObjectContext` interfaces. In this way, a transactional Publisher can, for example, perform some operations on a resource manager (a database, for instance) and then fire an event. When the Subscriber receives the event, it can also perform some operations on a resource manager. If anything goes wrong with the Subscriber, it can rollback the transaction and the Publisher's operations are also undone.

Filtering Events

COM+ Events provides a standardized mechanism that Publishers can use to filter out events from certain Subscribers. There is also a mechanism that Subscribers can use to filter events they receive from a Publisher. You can do two types of filtering: Publisher filtering and Parameter filtering. The main difference between the two is the point at which the filtering is done. With Publisher filtering, the Publisher elects not to send events to certain Subscribers. With Parameter filtering, the Subscriber elects not to receive some of the events that are sent by a Publisher.

Publisher Filtering

Publisher filtering can be accomplished in two different ways. If the `Event` class is not queued, then a Publisher can query the event object for the `IEventControl` interface. The event object that is synthesized by the COM+ Event system from your `Event` class supports this interface. The `IEventControl` interface contains the methods shown in Table 15.2.

TABLE 15.2 Methods in the IEventControl Interface

Method	Description
SetPublisherFilter	Allows a Publisher to specify a filter class (I describe what this is shortly) at runtime.
AllowInprocActivation	Allows a Publisher to override in-proc activation setting at runtime.
GetSubscriptions	Returns a collection of Subscriptions.
SetDefaultQuery	Sets filter criteria.

Using SetDefaultQuery, you can filter out certain events. SetDefaultQuery is defined as follows:

```
HRESULT SetDefaultQuery(
  BSTR MethodName,
  BSTR Criteria,
  int *pErrorIndex
);
```

The first parameter to SetDefaultQuery contains the method name of the event that was fired (e.g., PriceChange). The second parameter contains the filter criteria. The syntax of the filter criteria is similar to an SQL Where clause; it may contain one or more Boolean expressions of the form:

```
[NOT] Property Operator Value
```

Valid operators are: ==, =, !=, <>, and ~=. The Value part of the expression can be one of the following: String, 'String', {GUID}, TRUE, FALSE, NULL. You can combine Boolean expressions with AND or OR and you can use nested parantheses to affect the order of evaluation of the expressions. The following are example filter criterion:

```
"EventClassID == {8796e0f6-552d-4e50-8146-eb69296065b6}"
"EventClassID == {8796e0f6-552d-4e50-8146-eb69296065b6} AND MethodName
= 'PriceChange'"
```

If the COM+ Event system encounters an error parsing the filter criterion, the third parameter to SetDefaultQuery, which is an output parameter, contains the location of the error as an offset from the beginning of the string.

Using the SetDefaultQuery method on IEventControl is not the recommended way to filter events from the Publisher side, however. This technique does not work for Event classes that are queued because SetDefaultQuery has an output parameter. The recommended way to filter events from the Publisher is to use a Publisher filter. A Publisher filter is a COM class that implements the IPublisherFilter interface. A Publisher filter sits between an Event object and its Subscribers as shown in Figure 15.15.

A Publisher filter should implement IMultiInterfacePublisherFilter if the Event class supports more than one interface.

You tell COM+ which Publisher filter to use for an Event class by setting the MultiInterfacePublisherFilterCLSID property on the Event class. You cannot do this using the Component Services Explorer;

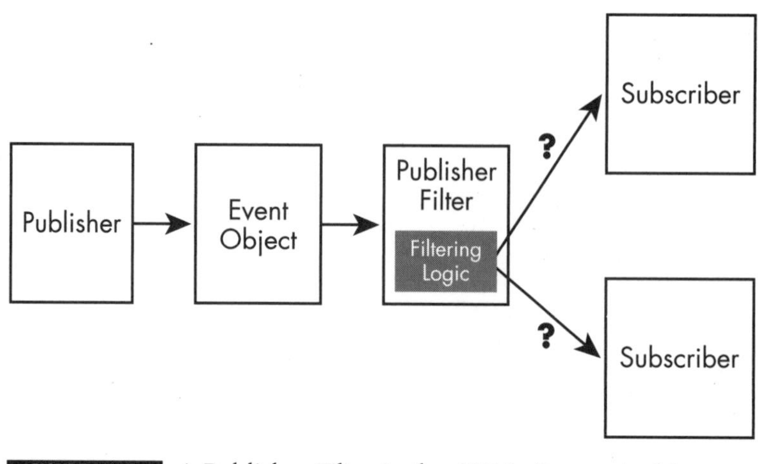

FIGURE 15.15 A Publisher Filter in the COM+ Events Architecture.

you must use the Administrative interfaces. The `IPublishFilter` interface has the two methods described in Table 15.3.

TABLE 15.3 Methods in the IPublisherFilter Interface

Method	Description
Initialize	Is called by the COM+ Event system when a Publisher creates an instance of an Event class. A Publisher filter can obtain a list of Subscribers from the second parameter to this method.
PrepareToFire	Called by the COM+ Event service to tell the Publisher filter to iterate through the list of Subscribers and determine which ones should receive the event.

The `PrepareToFire` method is declared as follows:

```
HRESULT PrepareToFire(
  BSTR MethodName,                    //Name of event method
  IFiringControl *pFiringControl      //Firing control
);
```

The first parameter contains the name of the event method that was fired. The second parameter contains an `IFiringControl` interface pointer. You call the `FireSubscription` method on `IFiringControl` for each Subscriber that you decide to forward the event to after executing your filtering logic. The list of Subscribers is passed to the Publisher filter in the `Initialize` method of `IPublisherFilter`.

If your filtering logic is not a function of the parameters that are passed to an Event method, the Publisher filter needs only to implement `IPublisherFilter` interface and then it can determine who to send the events to using business-specific logic. Perhaps you only send `PriceChange` to Subscribers who have paid their monthly Subscription fee, so the Publisher filter needs to query a database to see who has paid up. This is enough for some use cases, but for others you may want your Publisher filter to perform filtering based on the parameters that are passed to an Event method. Perhaps you are only interested in price changes on Emulex stock. If you want to do this, then your Publisher filter must also implement the Event interface in question. The COM+ Event Service will `QueryInterface` the Publisher filter for the Event interface after it calls `PrepareToFire`. If the Publisher filter supports the Event interface, the COM+ Event service calls the Event method on the Publisher filter passing in the parameters that were sent from the Publisher. For example, let's say you have an `Event` class called `StockEvent` with an interface called `IStockEvent`. If the Publisher calls the `PriceChange` method on this Event class with a stock ticker of MSFT and a new price of $110.00 and an old price of $100.00, the COM+ Event Service first calls the `PrepareToFire` method on `IPublisherFilter` passing in `PriceChange` for the `MethodName` parameter. If the logic that the Publisher filter uses to decide which Subscribers should receive the event is independent of the stock ticker and the new and old price, then the Publisher filter can execute its logic and call the Subscribers who should receive the event using the `FireSubscription` method on `IFiringControl`. If the `PublisherFilter`'s logic is dependent on the ticker and/or the new and old price, then the Publisher filter must also implement the `IStockEvent` interface. After calling the `PrepareToFire` method, the COM+ Event Service will `QueryInterface` for `IStockEvent` and call the `PriceChange` method on the `Publisher` filter passing in the stock ticker (MSFT in this case) and the old and new price ($100.00 and $110.00, respectively). The `Publisher` filter can then examine these parameters and decide if it wants to call each Subscriber.

Parameter Filtering

You can also easily do parameter filtering using the Component Services Explorer. If a Subscriber is only interested in price changes on Microsoft stock, for example, you can apply a filter criterion to the Subscriber that filters out price change events on other stocks. The steps to do this are shown here:

1. Right-click on the Subscription as shown in Figure 15.13.
2. Select `Properties` from the `Context` menu (the Subscription properties dialog appears as shown in Figure 15.16).
3. Click the `Options` tab.
4. Enter the filter criterion in the `Filter criteria:` edit box as shown in Figure 15.16.

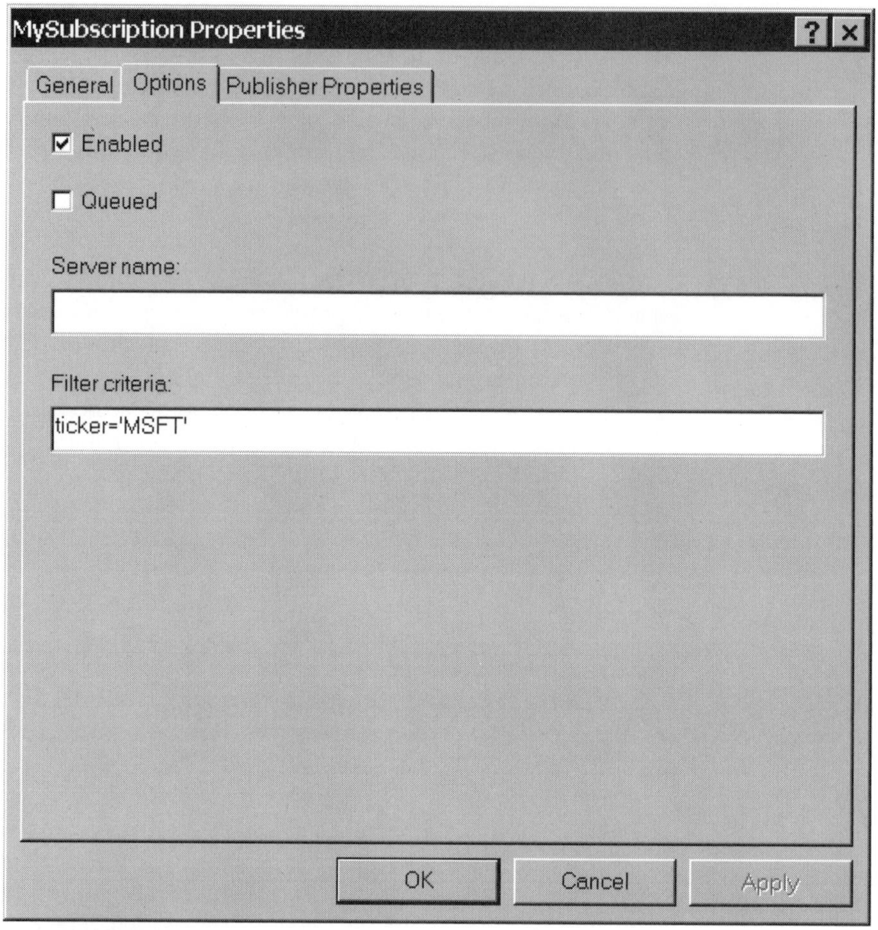

FIGURE 15.16 Parameter Filtering.

Figure 15.16 shows a simple filter criteria string. Like the filter criteria string that you used in the `SetDefaultQuery` method of `IEventControl`, the filter criterion that you specify to do parameter filtering recognizes standard relational operators, nested parentheses, and the logical keywords `AND`, `OR`, and `NOT`.

Using COM+ Events in a Distributed Environment

COM+ Events is not in itself a distributed technology. It would be helpful if COM+ allowed you to transparently store all your `Event` classes and Subscriptions on a central machine, but it doesn't. There is nothing stopping you from doing this yourself. Publishers would have to remember to instantiate the Event class on the central machine and Subscribers would receive their notifications from this central machine. You do pay the performance and bandwidth penalty of an extra network round trip to send the event from the Publisher to the central machine, but in most situations this is probably a minor price to pay.

Your COM+ Stock Monitoring Program

Let's build your example program for this chapter. Since you built a stock monitoring application in Chapter 8 using connection points, it makes sense to build a stock monitoring application for your COM+ Events example. Your application is a slightly more advanced version of the application you built in Chapter 8. It's composed of three parts: an Event class, an application that publishes events using the Event class, and an application that subscribes to the events. The Event class and the subscribing application are implemented using Visual C++ and the publishing application is written in Visual Basic. You use Visual C++ and the ATL object wizard to create your Event class, but you won't fill in the implementation of any of the methods. Remember, for the Event class you just need a type library and a self-registering DLL. The implementation of the Event class really doesn't matter.

Your Event class has a single interface called IStockEvent that is defined as follows:

```
interface IStockEvent : IDispatch
{
   [id(1), helpstring("method PriceChange")] HRESULT PriceChange(
            [in] BSTR ticker, [in] float newPrice,[in] float oldPrice);
   [id(2), helpstring("method NewStockListed")] HRESULT
            NewStockListed([in] BSTR ticker,[in] float price);
};
```

The PriceChange event is fired whenever the price of a stock changes. The parameters to this method are the name of the stock (ticker), the new price of the stock and the old price of the stock. The NewStockListed event is fired whenever a new stock is listed on your stock exchange. The parameters to this method are the name of the stock and the initial price of the stock.

Your publishing application looks like that shown in Figure 15.17.

This application will randomly generate price change events on 5 stocks: Northrop Grumman (NOC), Emulex (EMLX), Microsoft (MSFT), IBM, and COKE every 3 seconds. The application uses a random number generator to pick one of the stocks every 5 seconds and then apply a price change to the stock. Each stock has a different propensity to increase. Microsoft and

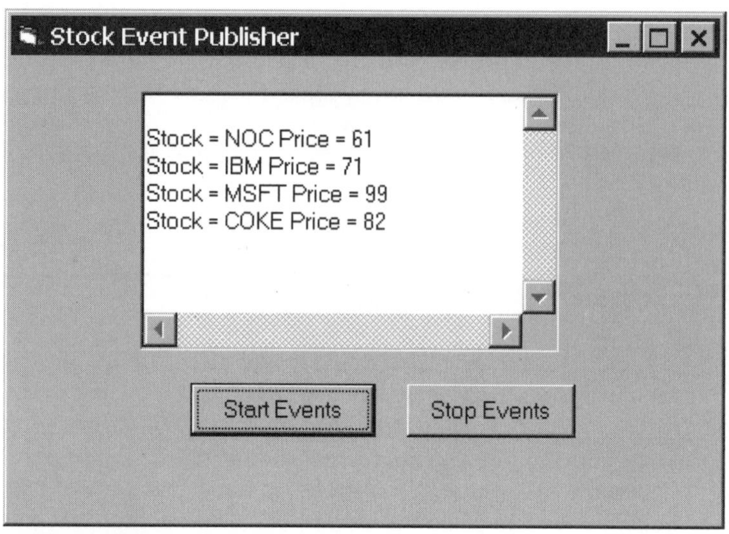

FIGURE 15.17 Your COM+ Events Publishing Application.

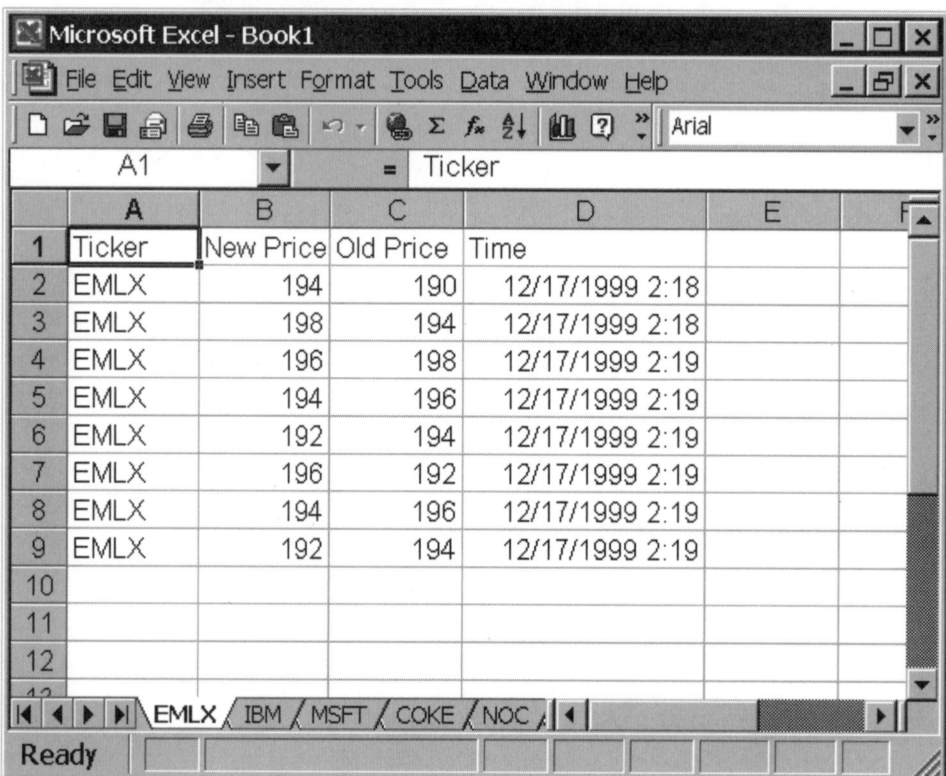

FIGURE 15.18 Your COM+ Events Subscriber Application.

Emulex—2 high flying tech stocks—have a high propensity to increase and Northrop Grumman—a defense company—has a lower propensity to increase.

The Subscriber is a component DLL that will be configured to run under COM+. This DLL will write information to an Excel workbook. Figure 15.18 shows events from the Subscriber components displayed in Microsoft Excel.

The example program uses Microsoft Excel 2000. You have to change the code slightly to use an earlier version of Excel.

The Subscriber component automatically updates Excel as events are received from the Publisher. I played around with several ways of using Excel. Eventually, I setup the Subscriber component so it writes to Excel if it is open. If Excel is not open, you won't see the events. Originally, I had Excel open automatically when the events started. The Subscriber even restarted Excel if it shut down, but eventually I found this annoying and I figured you would, too. The steps to implement your example application are as follows:

1. Create an ATL, DLL server project for your `Event` class.
2. Add the `Event` class to the Project using the ATL Object Wizard.
3. Add the `PriceChange` and `NewStockListed` methods to the `Event` class.
4. Configure the `Event` class.
5. Create the Publisher Application Project.
6. Implement the Publisher application.
7. Create the Subscriber Project.
8. Add the `Subscriber` class to the project using the ATL Object Wizard.
9. Import the Excel type library.
10. Implement the `Event` interface.
11. Build and configure the Subscriber component.
12. Test.

Creating the Event Class Project

Your first step in setting up a Publisher and Subscriber using COM+ Events is to create an `Event` class. The `Event` class must reside in an in-process (DLL-based) server. The easiest way to create an `Event` class in Visual C++ is to create an ATL, DLL server project and then add a COM class to it using the ATL Object Wizard.

Create an ATL, DLL Server Project

To create an ATL, DLL-based server project, start Visual C++ 6.0 and then execute the following steps:

1. Select `New...` from the `File` menu (the New dialog appears).
2. Click the `Projects` tab.
3. Select `ATL COM AppWizard` from the presented list of project types.
4. Enter `eventdemo` in the Project Name field.
5. Click the `OK` button (step 1 of the ATL, COM AppWizard appears).
6. Select `Dynamic Link Library` under Server Type.
7. Click `Finish`.

Visual C++ creates a new project for an ATL, DLL-based server.

Add the Event Class to Your Project

Perform the following steps to add an `Event` class called `StockEvent` to your project:

1. Select `New ATL Object` from the `Insert` menu (the ATL Object Wizard appears).
2. Make sure `Objects` is selected under `Category`, and select `Simple Object` under `Objects`.
3. Click `Next` (the ATL Object Wizard Properties dialog appears).
4. Enter `StockEvent` under `Short Name`.
5. Click `OK`.

We've been through these steps many times now, so I won't discuss the generated code any further.

Add the PriceChange and NewStockListed Methods to the Event Class

Perform the following steps to add the `PriceChange` and `NewStockListed` methods to the `StockEvent` class. Remember you don't need to provide an implementation for any of these methods:

1. Right-click on the `IStockEvent` interface in the `ClassView` tab of the Visual C++ workspace.
2. Select `Add Method...` from the `Context` menu (the Add Method to Interface dialog appears).
3. Enter `PriceChange` in the `Method Name` field.

4. Enter [in] BSTR ticker, [in] float newPrice, [in] float oldPrice in the Parameters field.
5. Click OK
6. Repeat steps 1–5 and enter NewStockListed in the Method Name field and enter [in] BSTR ticker, [in] float price in the Parameters field.

Now you are done with your Event class. Because this class is used as an Event class, you don't have to implement any of its methods. Compile your event project by pressing F7. Now you need to configure your Event class.

Configure the Event Class

To configure your Event class, the first thing to do is to create a new COM+ application. This was covered step-by-step in Chapters 12 and 13 so I won't repeat the figures, but I outline the steps below.

CREATE A COM+ APPLICATION

To create a new COM+ Application, perform the following steps in the Component Services Explorer:

1. Right-click on the folder console root\component\services \Computers\My Computer\COM+ Application\ (see Figure 11.17).
2. Select New from the Context menu that appears (the COM+ Application Install Wizard appears, see Figure 11.18)
3. Click Next (step 2 of the COM+ Application Install Wizard appears, see Figure 11.19).
4. Click Create an Empty Application (step 3 of the COM+ Application Install Wizard appears, see Figure 11.20).
5. Enter EventApp for the application name and accept the default activation type (Server Application).
6. Click Next (step 4 of the COM+ Application Install Wizard appears, see Figure 11.21).
7. Accept the default Identity (Interactive User).
8. Click Next and then Click Finished on the final screen.

After you create your COM+ application, you need to add your Event class. The steps to do this are new, so I cover them in more detail. Perform the following steps to add a new Event class:

1. Right-click on the Component folder beneath your COM+ application as shown in Figure 15.3.

2. Select `New\Component` from the `Context` menu that appears (the COM Component Install Wizard appears).
3. Click `Next` (step 2 of the COM Component Install Wizard appears, see Figure 15.4).
4. Click `Install new event Class(es)` (a file selection dialog appears).
5. Navigate to the file where the `eventdemo` component DLL is stored on your file system and double-click on it.
6. Click `Next`.
7. Click `Finish` on the last step of the COM Component Install Wizard.

The component appears in the component folder of the Component Services Explorer just like any configured COM+ component. Now you are ready to create your Publisher application. This application is created with Visual Basic.

Create Your Publisher Application

Start Visual Basic 6.0 and perform the following steps:

1. Select `New Project` from the `File` menu (you may not need this step because Visual Basic starts up with the new Project dialog displayed).
2. Select `Standard Exe` from the `New Project` menu.
3. Click `OK`.
4. In the Visual Basic environment, select `Properties` from the `Project` menu (the project properties dialog appears).
5. On the `General` tab, change the project name to `EventSender`.
6. Click `OK`.
7. Click on the `Form1` form and change its name in the Property Window to `frmMain`.

Now you can draw the main form for your application. Place the controls shown in Figure 15.17 on your form using Visual Basic. To keep it simple, I just used a multi-line text box for the control that displays the events. The controls are named as shown in Table 15.4.

TABLE 15.4 Controls on the Main Window of Your Publisher Application

Control Description	Control Type	Control Name in VB Project
List of Events	Text Box	txtEventList
Start Events button	CommandButton	cmdStartEvents
Stop Events button	CommandButton	cmdStopEvents
Timer Control (invisible)	Timer	tmStockEvents

The Timer Control is invisible at runtime. It appears at design time in the Visual Basic environment. You can set the period for the timer to three seconds by clicking on the timer control and entering 3000 for the interval property of the control (the interval is specified in milliseconds). Before you go any further, you need to add a reference to the type library for your Event class and to the type library for the Microsoft Scripting Runtime (for the Dictionary Collection class). Remember that Referencing a type library in Visual Basic is similar to using the `#import` keyword in Visual C++: it imports all the classes, interfaces, enumerations, and other entities in the type library into the project. To reference the type libraries, perform the following steps:

1. Select `References` from the `Project` menu (the project references dialog appears).
2. Set the checkbox next to the entry labeled `EventDemo 1.0 Type Library`.
3. Set the checkbox next to the entry labeled `Microsoft Scripting Runtime`.
4. Click `OK`.

Don't forget to set the `MultiLine Property` to `True` on the `txtEventList` textbox. Now add the following code to the main form for this application.

LISTING 15.1 *THE CODE BEHIND THE MAIN FORM OF YOUR PUBLISHER APPLICATION*

```
Option Explicit
Private objEventClass As EVENTDEMOLib.StockEvent
Private objStockList As Dictionary
Private objStockPropensityList As Dictionary

Private Sub cmdSendEvent_Click()
    Call objEventClass.PriceChange("MSFT", 45, 55)
End Sub

Private Sub cmdStartEvents_Click()
    tmStockEvents.Enabled = True
End Sub

Private Sub cmdStopEvents_Click()
    tmStockEvents.Enabled = False
End Sub

Private Sub Form_Load()
    On Error GoTo errHandler
```

```
    tmStockEvents.Enabled = False
    Set objEventClass = New EVENTDEMOLib.StockEvent
    Set objStockList = New Dictionary
    Set objStockPropensityList = New Dictionary
    Call LoadStockList
    Call Randomize
    Exit Sub
errHandler:
    Call MsgBox(Err.Description)
End Sub

Private Function PickAStock(ByRef sngNewStockPrice As Single, _
        ByRef sngOldStockPrice As Single) As String
    Dim intStockPropensity As Integer
    Dim intRandomPropensity As Integer
    Dim sngRandomNumber As Single
    Dim numStocks As Integer
    Dim index As Integer
    Dim strTicker As String
    numStocks = objStockList.Count
    sngRandomNumber = Rnd * 1000
    index = sngRandomNumber Mod numStocks
    strTicker = objStockList.Keys(index)
    sngOldStockPrice = objStockList.Item(strTicker)
    intStockPropensity = objStockPropensityList.Item(strTicker)
    intRandomPropensity = sngRandomNumber Mod 100
    If intRandomPropensity < intStockPropensity Then
        sngNewStockPrice = sngOldStockPrice + 4
    Else
        If sngOldStockPrice > 2 Then
            sngNewStockPrice = sngOldStockPrice - 2
        End If
    End If
    objStockList.Item(strTicker) = sngNewStockPrice
    PickAStock = strTicker
End Function

Private Sub LoadStockList()
    Call AddNewStock("MSFT", 95, 67)
    Call AddNewStock("NOC", 57, 45)
    Call AddNewStock("IBM", 67, 55)
    Call AddNewStock("COKE", 78, 44)
    Call AddNewStock("EMLX", 190, 34)
End Sub
```

```
64.
65. Private Function GetPrice(ByVal strTicker As String) As Single
66.     GetPrice = objStockList.Item(strTicker)
67. End Function
68.
69. Private Function GetPropensity(ByVal strTicker As String) As Integer
70.     GetPropensity = objStockPropensityList.Item(strTicker)
71. End Function
72.
73. Private Sub AddNewStock(ByVal strTicker As String, _
74.         ByVal price As Single, ByVal propensityToRise As Integer)
75.     On Error GoTo errHandler
76.     Call objStockList.Add(strTicker, price)
77.     Call objStockPropensityList.Add(strTicker, propensityToRise)
78.     Exit Sub
79. errHandler:
80.     Call MsgBox(Err.Description)
81. End Sub
82.
83. Private Sub tmStockEvents_Timer()
84.     On Error GoTo errHandler
85.     Dim strTicker As String
86.     Dim sngNewPrice As Single
87.     Dim sngOldPrice As Single
88.     strTicker = PickAStock(sngNewPrice, sngOldPrice)
89.     Call objEventClass.PriceChange(strTicker, sngNewPrice, sngOldPrice)
90.     txtEventList.Text = txtEventList.Text & vbCrLf & _
91.             "Stock = " & strTicker & " Price = " & sngNewPrice
92.     Exit Sub
93. errHandler:
94.     Call MsgBox(Err.Description)
95. End Sub
```

Most of this is GUI code and random number manipulation so I won't go into it in exhaustive depth. I did highlight in bold the two key lines. First, on line 21 in the `form_load` procedure, you create an instance of the Event class. And then on line 89 of the callback for the timer control, you call the `PriceChange` method on the event object to fire your event. Now compile the Publisher application by selecting `Make EventSender` from the `File` menu of Visual Basic. Now you are ready to create your Subscriber.

Create the Subscriber Project

You will create your Subscriber using Visual C++. Your Subscriber implements the `IStockEvent` interface of the Event class and performs some action in response to an event called on the interface. Once again, you use an ATL, DLL-based project. To create an ATL, DLL-based server project, start Visual C++ 6.0 and then execute the following steps:

1. Select New... from the File menu (the New dialog appears).
2. Click the Projects tab.
3. Select ATL COM AppWizard from the presented list of project types.
4. Enter Subscriber in the Project Name field.
5. Click the OK button (step 1 of the ATL, COM AppWizard appears).
6. Select Dynamic Link Library under Server Type.
7. Set the Support MFC Checkbox.
8. Click Finish.

Visual C++ creates a project for an ATL, DLL-based server.

Add the Subscriber Class to the Project Using the ATL Object Wizard

Perform the following steps to add an Event class called StockSubscriber to your project:

1. Select New ATL Object... from the Insert menu (the ATL Object Wizard appears).
2. Make sure Objects is selected under Category, and select Simple Object under Objects.
3. Click Next (the ATL Object Wizard Properties dialog appears).
4. Enter StockSubscriber under Short Name.
5. Click OK.

Import the Excel Type Library

Your Stock Subscriber will write information from the PriceChange events into Microsoft Excel. I figured this was a good opportunity to show you how to use the Automation interfaces exposed by a Microsoft Office Application to control an Office application from a Visual C++ program. The easiest way to do this is using the native COM support, and the first step to using native COM support is to import the type library for the server. There is a complication when using Microsoft Office applications: the Office type libraries tend to have dependencies. For instance, the type library for Excel 2000, Excel9.olb, depends on mso9.dll and vbe6ext.olb. Mso9.dll (and Excel9.olb) can be found (by default) at \Program Files\Microsoft Office\Office\. Vbe6ext.olb can be found at \Program Files\Common Files\Microsoft Shared\VBA\VBA6. To import the excel type library, you must import these type libraries. Add the following code to the `stdafx.h` file in your project:

```
#import <mso9.dll> no_namespace
#import <vbe6ext.olb> no_namespace
#import<excel9.olb>rename("DialogBox", DialogBoxXL")rename("RGB", RBGXL")
```

Notice that you also have to use the rename directive on `#import` to rename the DialogBox and RGB items in the Excel type library that clash with native Windows types. Remember to add the directories where `excel9.olb`, `vbe6ext.olb`, and `mso9.dll` reside to the search list for include files. Select `Options` from the `Tools` menu and click the Directories.

Implement the Event Interface

To receive events, the Subscriber must implement the event interface that the Publisher is calling to send its events (`ISTOCKEVENT` in your case). Before you actually implement the interface in a C++ class, you must modify the IDL for your Subscriber class to indicate that it implements the `ISTOCKEVENT` interface. Add the code shown in bold to the IDL file for your Subscriber class.

```
// The interface definitions were omitted for clarity…
library SUBSCRIBERLib
{
   importlib ("stdole32.tlb");
   importlib ("stdole2.tlb");
   importlib ("…\eventdemo\eventdemo.tlb");

   [
      uuid (C2FAD43F-7A97-4815-8FF5-51B52AD8F7E9),
      helpstring ("StockSubscriber Class")
   ]
   coclass StockSubscriber
   {
      [default] interface IStockSubscriber;
      interface IstockEvent
   };
};
```

This code uses a relative path to reference the `EventDemo` project. You may need to alter this path on your machine or you can set the search directories under `Tools\Options`.

Now you need to actually implement the `IStockEvent` interface in the `CStockSubscriber` class. The easiest way to do this is with the `Implement Interface` command in Visual C++. Perform the following steps to modify the `CStockSubscriber` class so that it implements `IStockEvents`.

1. Right-click on the Stock Subscriber implementation class (`CStockSubscriber`) as shown in Figure 15.19.
2. Select `Implement Interface...` from the `Context` menu (the Implement Interface dialog will appear as shown in Figure 15.20)
3. Click the `Add Typelib...` button (the Browse Type Libraries dialog will appear as shown in Figure 15.21).
4. Set the checkbox next to `eventdemo 1.0 Type Library`.
5. Click `OK` (the implementation Interface dialog will reappear with `IstockEvent` in the list of interfaces as shown in Figure 15.22).
6. Set the checkbox.

Visual C++ will add the code shown in bold (Listing 15.2) to the Stock Subscriber class.

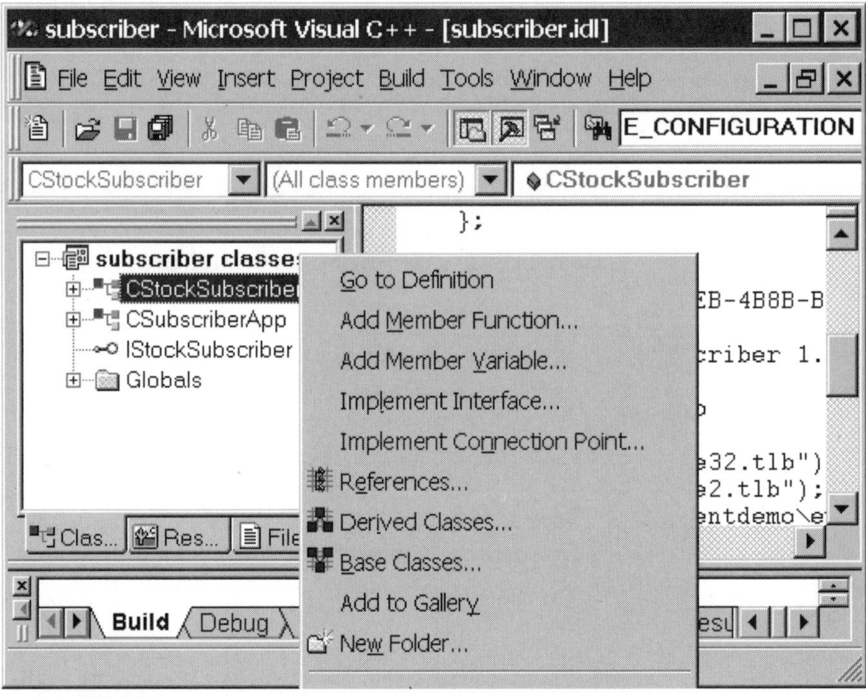

FIGURE 15.19 The First Step to Implement an Interface.

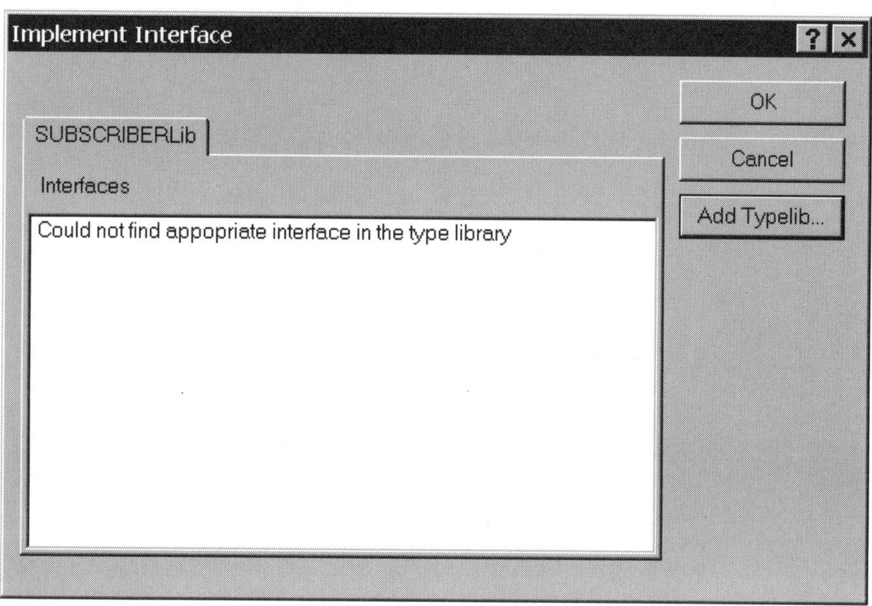

FIGURE 15.20 The Implementation Interface Dialog.

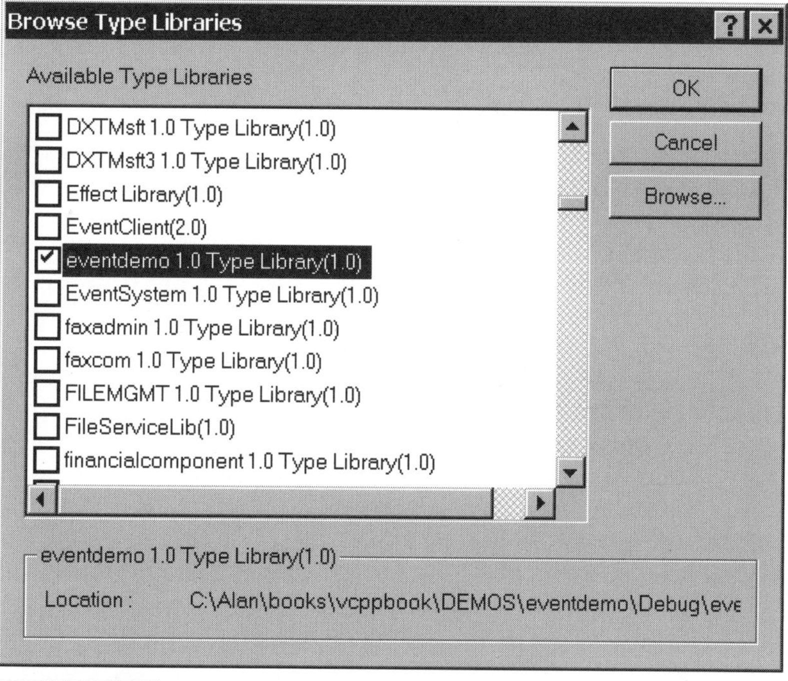

FIGURE 15.21 The Browse Type Library Dialog.

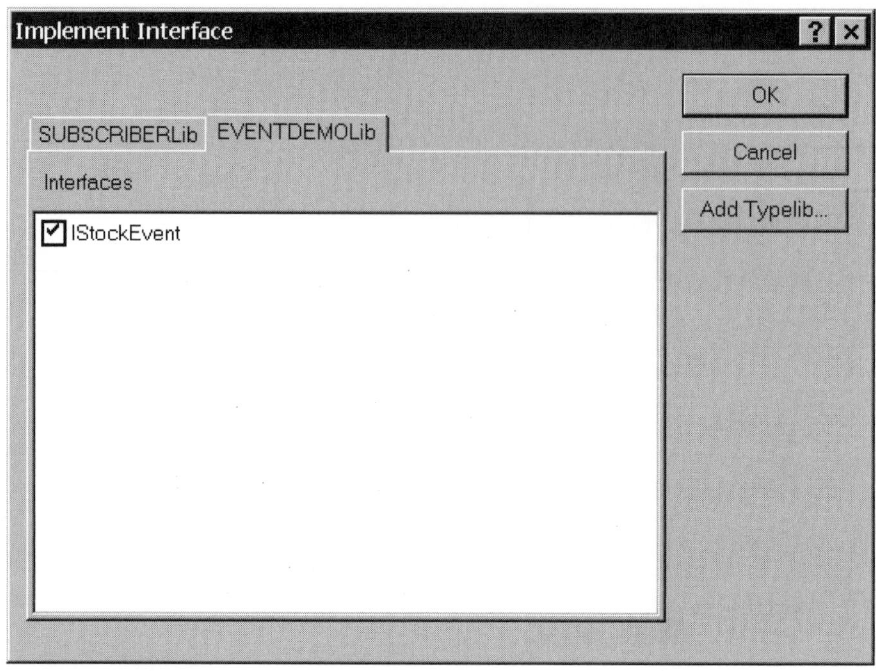

FIGURE 15.22 The Implementation Interface Dialog with IstockEvent.

LISTING 15.2 *CHANGES MADE BY THE IMPLEMENT INTERFACE COMMAND*

```
#import "C:\Alan\books\vcppbook\DEMOS\eventdemo\Debug\eventdemo.dll"\
   raw_interfaces_only, raw_native_types, no_namespace, named_guids
class ATL_NO_VTABLE CStockSubscriber :
   public CComObjectRootEx<CComSingleThreadModel>,
   public CComCoClass<CStockSubscriber, &CLSID_StockSubscriber>,
   public ISupportErrorInfo,
   public IDispatchImpl<IStockSubscriber, &IID_IStockSubscriber,
            &LIBID_SUBSCRIBERLib>,
   public IDispatchImpl<IStockEvent, &IID_IStockEvent,
            &LIBID_EVENTDEMOLib>
{
public:
   CStockSubscriber()
   { }

DECLARE_REGISTRY_RESOURCEID(IDR_STOCKSUBSCRIBER)
DECLARE_PROTECT_FINAL_CONSTRUCT()
```

```
BEGIN_COM_MAP(CStockSubscriber)
    COM_INTERFACE_ENTRY(IStockSubscriber)
//DEL  COM_INTERFACE_ENTRY(IDispatch)
    COM_INTERFACE_ENTRY(ISupportErrorInfo)
    COM_INTERFACE_ENTRY2(IDispatch, IStockSubscriber)
    COM_INTERFACE_ENTRY(IStockEvent)
END_COM_MAP()

// ISupportsErrorInfo
    STDMETHOD(InterfaceSupportsErrorInfo)(REFIID riid);

// IStockSubscriber
public:
// IStockEvent
    STDMETHOD(PriceChange)(BSTR ticker, FLOAT newPrice, FLOAT oldPrice)
    {
        return E_NOTIMPL;
    }
    STDMETHOD(NewStockListed)(BSTR ticker, FLOAT price)
    {
        return E_NOTIMPL;
    }
};
```

When you are implementing an interface that is declared in a type library, you do not need smart pointer; you just need the raw COM interfaces. So Visual C++ uses the `raw_interfaces_only` parameter on its generated `#import` statement to suppress the generation of smart pointers. Add the bolded code shown here to complete the implementation of the `CstockSubscriber` class.

LISTING 15.3 *IMPLEMENTING THE EVENT INTERFACE IN YOUR SUBSCRIBER*

```
using namespace Excel;
class ATL_NO_VTABLE CStockSubscriber :
    public CComObjectRootEx<CComSingleThreadModel>,
    public CComCoClass<CStockSubscriber, &CLSID_StockSubscriber>,
    public ISupportErrorInfo,
    public IDispatchImpl<IStockSubscriber, &IID_IStockSubscriber,
            &LIBID_SUBSCRIBERLib>,
    public IDispatchImpl<IStockEvent, &IID_IStockEvent,
            &LIBID_EVENTDEMOLib>
{
public:
    CStockSubscriber()
```

```
    { }

BEGIN_COM_MAP(CStockSubscriber)
    COM_INTERFACE_ENTRY(IStockSubscriber)
//DEL    COM_INTERFACE_ENTRY(IDispatch)
    COM_INTERFACE_ENTRY(ISupportErrorInfo)
    COM_INTERFACE_ENTRY2(IDispatch, IStockSubscriber)
    COM_INTERFACE_ENTRY(IStockEvent)
END_COM_MAP()

// ISupportsErrorInfo
    STDMETHOD(InterfaceSupportsErrorInfo)(REFIID riid);

// IStockSubscriber
public:
// IStockEvent
    STDMETHOD(PriceChange)(BSTR ticker, FLOAT newPrice, FLOAT oldPrice)
    {
        SYSTEMTIME dtSysDateTime;
        SheetsPtr pSheets;
        _bstr_t strTicker(ticker);
        _WorkbookPtr pBook;
        _WorksheetPtr pSheet;
        _variant_t dtCurrent;
        _variant_t var;
        _bstr_t strNumber;
        short i;
        if (ExcelIsRunning())
        {
            try
            {
                pExcel->put_Visible(LANG_USER_DEFAULT,VARIANT_TRUE);
                pBook=GetWorkBook();
                pSheets=pBook->Sheets;
                try
                {
                    pSheet=pSheets->Item[strTicker];
                    pSheet->Activate();
                }
                catch(_com_error )
                {
                    pSheet=pSheets->Add();
                    pSheet->Name = strTicker;
                    pSheet->Range[_bstr_t("A1")]->Value = "Ticker";
```

```
57.                pSheet->Range[_bstr_t("B1")]->Value = "New Price";
58.                pSheet->Range[_bstr_t("C1")]->Value = "Old Price";
59.                pSheet->Range[_bstr_t("D1")]->Value = "Time";
60.             }
61.             i=1;
62.             strNumber=i;
63.             var=pSheet->Range[_bstr_t("A")+strNumber]->Value;
64.             while (var.vt != VT_EMPTY)
65.             {
66.                i++;
67.                strNumber=i;
68.                var=pSheet->Range[_bstr_t("A")+strNumber]->Value;
69.             }
70.             GetLocalTime(&dtSysDateTime);
71.             dtCurrent.vt =VT_DATE;
72.             ::SystemTimeToVariantTime(&dtSysDateTime,
73.                &(dtCurrent.date));
74.             pSheet->Range[_bstr_t("A")+strNumber]->Value = ticker;
75.             pSheet->Range[_bstr_t("B")+strNumber]->Value = newPrice;
76.             pSheet->Range[_bstr_t("C")+strNumber]->Value = oldPrice;
77.             pSheet->Range[_bstr_t("D")+strNumber]->Value = dtCurrent;
78.             pSheet->Columns->AutoFit();
79.          }
80.          catch (_com_error err)
81.          {
82.             // Do nothing for now
83.          }
84.       }
85.       return S_OK;
86.    }
87.    STDMETHOD(NewStockListed)(BSTR ticker, FLOAT price)
88.    {
89.       return E_NOTIMPL;
90.    }
91. private:
92.    _WorkbookPtr GetWorkBook();
93.    BOOL ExcelIsRunning();
94.    _ApplicationPtr pExcel;
95. };
```

On line 1 of Listing 15.3 you use a `using` namespace statement so you don't have to prefix all the Excel types with the `Excel` namespace, On line 8, you add the `IStockEvent` interface to the list of interfaces that your

Subscriber class implements. IStockEvent is a dual interface, so you must use IDispatchIml with IStockEvent as a template parameter. Because CStockSubscriber now supports two IDispatch-derived interfaces, IStockSubscriber and IStockEvent, you must specify in the COM map which of these interfaces is the default IDispatch interface (the one that is returned when a client QueryInterfaces for IDispatch) using the COM_INTERFACE_ENTRY2 macro as shown on line 19. You must also add a COM_INTERFACE_ENTRY for IStockEvent as shown on line 20 and delete the original COM_INTERFACE_ENTRY for IDispatch on line 17. On lines 29–86, you have the handler for the PriceChange method. On line 40, you check if Excel is currently running. If it is running, enter a try block on line 44. In the try block, you first make sure that Excel is visible and then get a workbook. On line 46, you get the worksheets collection in the workbook. On line 49, you attempt to get the worksheet for the stock ticker associated with the event. If it exists, you activate the sheet on line 50. If the sheet does not exist, Excel throws an error. On lines 52–60, you catch this error and add a new worksheet for the stock, set the name of the stock to the stock ticker so you can find it next time, and fill in the column headers. On lines 61–69, you find the first empty row in the worksheet. Then on lines 70–77 we first get the local time and then write the stock ticker, new stock price, old stock price, and the time into the empty row of the worksheet. You then autofit the columns so they are displayed correctly. For simplicity, you have an empty implementation for the NewStockListed method. As an exercise, you could modify the Publisher to allow you to add new stocks and fire the NewStockListed event when a new stock is added. You could then modify the Subscriber to perform some action in the NewStockListed method. The implementation of the ExcelIsRunning and GetWorkBook methods used by the Subscriber in the PriceChange method are shown in Listing 15.4.

LISTING 15.4 *ADDITIONAL METHODS REQUIRED BY YOUR SUBSCRIBER*

```
BOOL CStockSubscriber::ExcelIsRunning()
{
    HRESULT hRes;
    hRes=pExcel.GetActiveObject("Excel.Application");
    if (S_OK==hRes)
        return TRUE;
    else
        return FALSE;
}

_WorkbookPtr CStockSubscriber::GetWorkBook()
{
    _variant_t blank(DISP_E_PARAMNOTFOUND, VT_ERROR);
```

```
    short i, intNumBooks;
    WorkbooksPtr pBooks;
    _WorkbookPtr pBook;
    SYSTEMTIME dtSysDateTime;
    char lpFileName[255];
    _bstr_t strFileName;
    _bstr_t strFullPath;

    pBooks=pExcel->Workbooks;
    intNumBooks=pBooks->Count;
    GetLocalTime(&dtSysDateTime);
    sprintf(lpFileName,"stock%d%d%d.xls", dtSysDateTime.wMonth,
       dtSysDateTime.wDay,dtSysDateTime.wYear);
    strFileName=lpFileName;
    strFullPath=GetPathFromReg(_T("OutputDir"))+_bstr_t("\\") +
       strFileName;

    for (i=1;i<=intNumBooks;i++)
    {
       pBook=pBooks->Item[_variant_t(i)];
       if (pBook->Name==strFileName)
          break;
    }
    if (NULL==pBook)
    {
       try {
          pBook=pBooks->Open(strFullPath);
       }
       catch ( _com_error )
       {
          pBook=pBooks->Add();
          pBook-
>SaveAs(strFullPath,blank,blank,blank,blank,blank,xlExclusive);
       }
    }
    return pBook;
}
```

GetWorkBook uses the GetPathFromReg function that you developed in Chapter 14. Perform the following steps to add this file to the Subscriber project:

1. Select New... from the File menu (the New dialog appears).
2. Click the File tab.

3. Select C/C++ Header file from the list of file types.
4. Enter GetPathFromReg in the File Name field.
5. Click OK.
6. Repeat steps 1–5 and on step 3 select C/C++ Source file from the list of file types.

Add the following function prototype for a GetPathFromReg function to the GetPathFromReg.h file:

```
#ifndef GETPATHFROMREG_H
#define GETPATHFROMREG_H
_bstr_t GetPathFromReg(LPCTSTR lpszKeyName);
#endif // GETPATHFROMREG_H
```

Add the following implementation for the GetPathFromReg function to the GetPathFromReg.cpp file:

LISTING 15.5 *THE GETPATHFROMREG FUNCTION*

```
#include "stdafx.h"
_bstr_t GetPathFromReg(LPCTSTR lpszKeyName)
{
   CRegKey registry;
   LPTSTR lpszKeyValue;
   DWORD dwKeyCount;
   DWORD dwDisposition;
   LONG lRegReturn;
   _bstr_t bResult;
   dwKeyCount=64;
   lpszKeyValue=new TCHAR[dwKeyCount];
   lRegReturn=registry.Create(HKEY_LOCAL_MACHINE,
      _T("Software\\agordonbooks\\pubsboserver"),
      REG_NONE,REG_OPTION_NON_VOLATILE,KEY_ALL_ACCESS,
      NULL,&dwDisposition);

   lRegReturn=registry.QueryValue(lpszKeyValue,lpszKeyName,
      &dwKeyCount);
   if (ERROR_SUCCESS != lRegReturn)
   {
      registry.SetValue(_T("C:"),lpszKeyName);
      _tcscpy(lpszKeyValue,_T("C:"));
   }
   bResult=lpszKeyValue;
   delete [] lpszKeyValue;
   return bResult;
}
```

or just copy these files from the demo that you built for Chapter 14. You also should add an include for `getpathfromreg.h` to the source file for the Stock Subscriber, `StockSubscriber.cpp`.

Configure the Subscriber Component

Now you are ready to configure your Subscriber component. You can either put the Subscriber in the same COM+ application as the `Event` class or in a different one. In most real-world situations, the Subscriber is probably in a different COM+ application than the `Event` class. In this case, for convenience, you can put it in the same COM+ application as its `Events` class. Perform the following steps to configure the Subscriber component this way: Drag-and-drop the Subscriber component DLL into the Components folder of the EventApp COM+ application (you should see both the Event class and the Subscriber class in the Components tab as shown in Figure 15.23).

Notice in Figure 15.23 there is a Subscriptions folder beneath your `Subscriber` class (as there is beneath every class). This folder is there so you can add Subscriptions to the class. Perform the following steps to add a Subscription to your class:

1. Right-click on the `Subscription` folder and select `New\Subscription` as shown in Figure 15.7.
2. The COM New Subscription Wizard appears as shown in Figure 15.8.

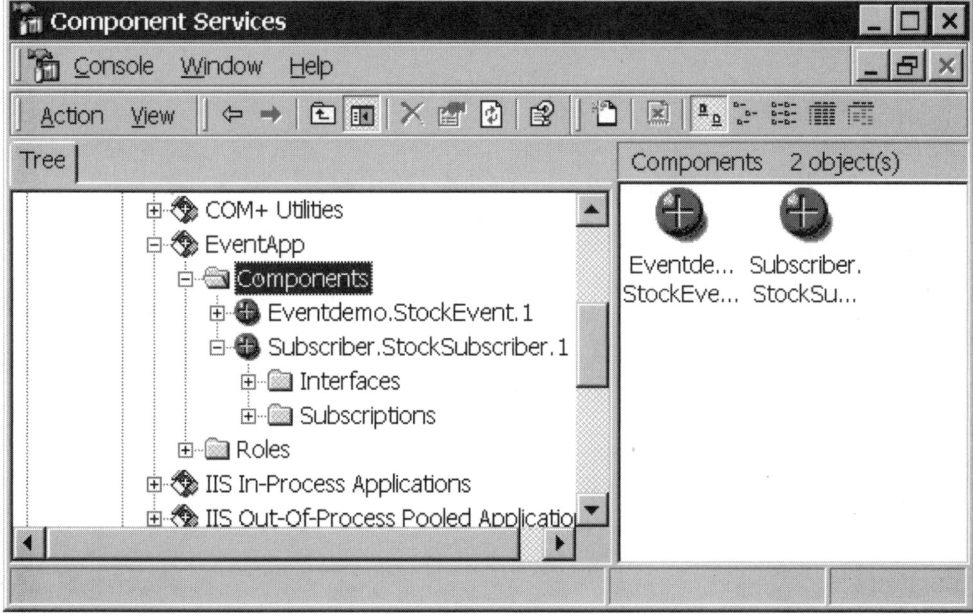

FIGURE 15.23 The Subscriber Component in Your COM+ Application.

3. Click `Next` (step 2 of the COM New Subscription Wizard appears as shown in Figure 15.9).
4. Select `PriceChange` under `IStockEvent` as shown in Figure 15.9.
5. Click Next (step 3 of the COM New Subscription Wizard appears as shown in Figure 15.10). Notice that the New Subscription Wizard is showing the Event class that you registered earlier.
6. Select the Event class and click `Next` (step 4 of the COM New Subscription Wizard appears as shown in Figure 15.11).
7. Enter `my stock Subscription` for the name of the new Subscription and set the `Enable this Subscription immediately` checkbox.
8. Click `Next` and then click `Finish` on the final screen.

Your new Subscription is now displayed in the Subscriptions folder of your COM+ application in the Component Services Explorer as shown in Figure 15.24.

Your example is now complete. Now you can test your Publisher and Subscriber. Start the Publisher VB application. Now start up Excel and then click the `Start Events` button on the Publisher. You should see stock price change events appearing on the screen. You should see the events appearing in Excel. A separate worksheet is created for each stock.

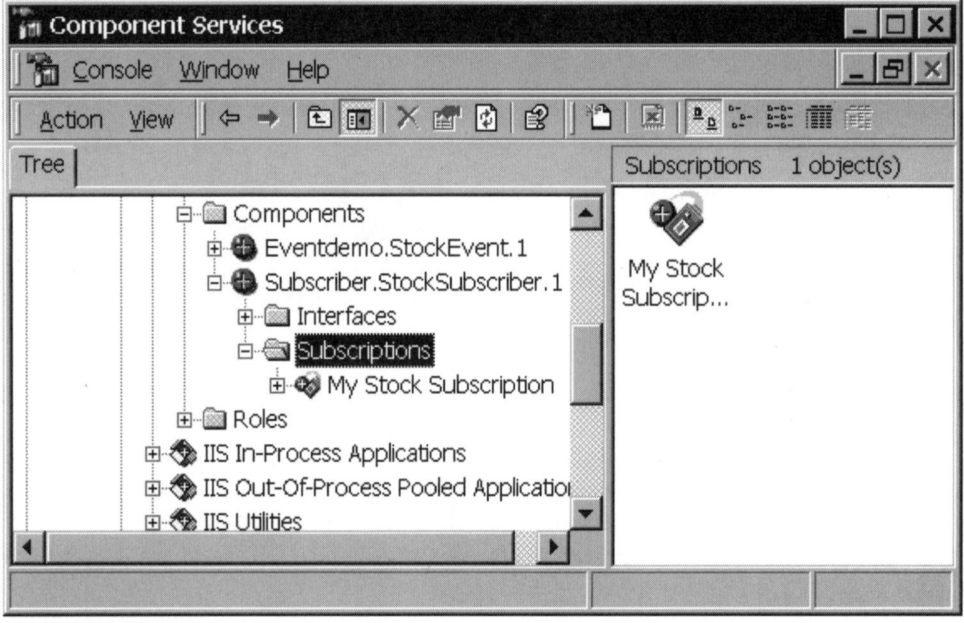

FIGURE 15.24 The Subscriber Component in Your COM+ Application.

I noticed an interesting quirk when I ran this example. If you start up the `Publisher` application and then immediately push the `Start Events` button and then start Excel, you do not see the events in Excel until you give focus back to the Publisher. The events appear in the Publisher window, you just don't see them in Excel.

Summary

In this chapter, you learned all about COM+ Events. COM+ Events is a service provided by the COM+ runtime that allows base clients or COM+ objects to easily send notifications (events) to COM+ objects that wish to receive them. Objects or base clients that send events are called `Publishers` and objects that receive events are called `Subscribers`. Using the COM+ Event Service is fairly simple. You first create a COM class and configure it to be an `Event` class using the Component Services Explorer. The `Event` class supports one or more interfaces that a Publisher can call methods on when it wants to send events. Next you must create a Publisher, which is just a piece of software that creates an instance of the `Event` class and calls methods on the event object to fire events. Finally, you must create a `Subscriber` class. The `Subscriber` class must implement one or more of the event interfaces that are supported by the `Event` class. Once you configure a class to be a subscriber to a particular event (an event is defined by a method in an `Event` class), the COM+ runtime takes care of notifying the `Subscriber` whenever a `Publisher` sends the event. COM+ events are far superior to connection points because the lifetimes of the Publisher and `Subscriber` do not have to overlap; the `Publisher` and `Subscriber` can filter the events that they send and receive; and Subscriptions can be created and removed using the Component Services Explorer instead of using code.

You have come a long way. You started by learning about all the confusing names in the COM namespace: ActiveX, OLE, COM, MTS, COM+, and the Windows DNA. Next you learned about object-orientation and why COM does not support implementation inheritance and places so much emphasis on interfaces. Then you learned some key COM concepts including: GUIDs, IDL, marshaling, and the `IUnknown` interface. Next you learned how to create a COM object from scratch. Then you received an introduction to the Active Template Library (ATL) and learned how to create a COM object more simply using ATL and the ATL Object Wizard in Visual C++.

Then you started diving deeper into COM. You learned how to create a server that ran in a different process from its client (an out-of-process server). You also learned about Automation, which uses the `IDispatch` interface to make COM accessible to simpler programming languages. Then you learned about Connection points, which allow COM objects to send events (callbacks, really) to their clients. You learned about threading and COM, and in the process (no pun intended) you learned about COM apartments. Then you started moving toward COM+. You first learned about DCOM, which provides the network communication and security infrastructure on which COM+ is built.

Finally, you learned about COM+. You learned that COM+ is a set of system services that facilitates the development of enterprise-class distributed applications. You first learned about the overall architecture of COM+ and the role of Context's, Interception and attribute-based programming in that architecture. You next learned about the various services that COM+ provides: fine-grained security, distributed transactions, queued components, concurrency control, publish and subscribe events, component load balancing, and enhanced scalability through Just In Time (JIT) Activation and pooling of objects and database connections. All of these tools make it much easier to build enterprise-class, distributed applications on the Windows platform than it ever was in the past. After learning about the COM+ architecture and services, you next built an example application using COM+ and the other technologies in the Windows DNA. You learned that the Windows Distributed InterNet Applications Architecture (Windows DNA) is your style guide to using Microsoft technologies to implement enterprise-class, distributed applications. You learned that COM+ is just one piece of this overall architecture. The architecture also includes data-access tools (such as ODBC, OLEDB, and ADO); it also includes tools to make it relatively simple to Web-enable your applications (IIS and ASP). The Windows DNA also includes technologies such as Microsoft SQL Server and Visual Studio. Windows DNA 2000 is an update to the Windows DNA that contains additional tools, such as XML and COMTI that enable e-commerce and allow Windows DNA applications to integrate better with other platforms. You finished off your study by learning about Queued Components and COM+ Events.

Hopefully, you are at the point where you are ready to begin tackling real-world problems with COM and COM+. There is still more for you to learn, though. Understanding COM and COM+ is just a start if you want to create enterprise-class distributed applications on the Windows platform. You also need to understand SQL, relational databases in general, ASP, ADO, and XML. This book has given you a start in these areas, but unless you have experience with these technologies already, you most likely need more study. I pointed you to additional references for further studies. The books I recommend are ones I have in my personal library and I have found useful.

Even though you need to understand other technologies to be a productive (and highly-paid) Windows DNA developer, understanding COM/COM+ is the key; it's the glue that ties everything together. With COM and now COM+ you can do with the selection of a few attributes what used to require man-months of labor. After using beta versions of Windows 2000 and COM+ for several months, I am excited about its upcoming release. I can't wait to see all the great applications that developers like you will write with this exciting new technology.

INDEX

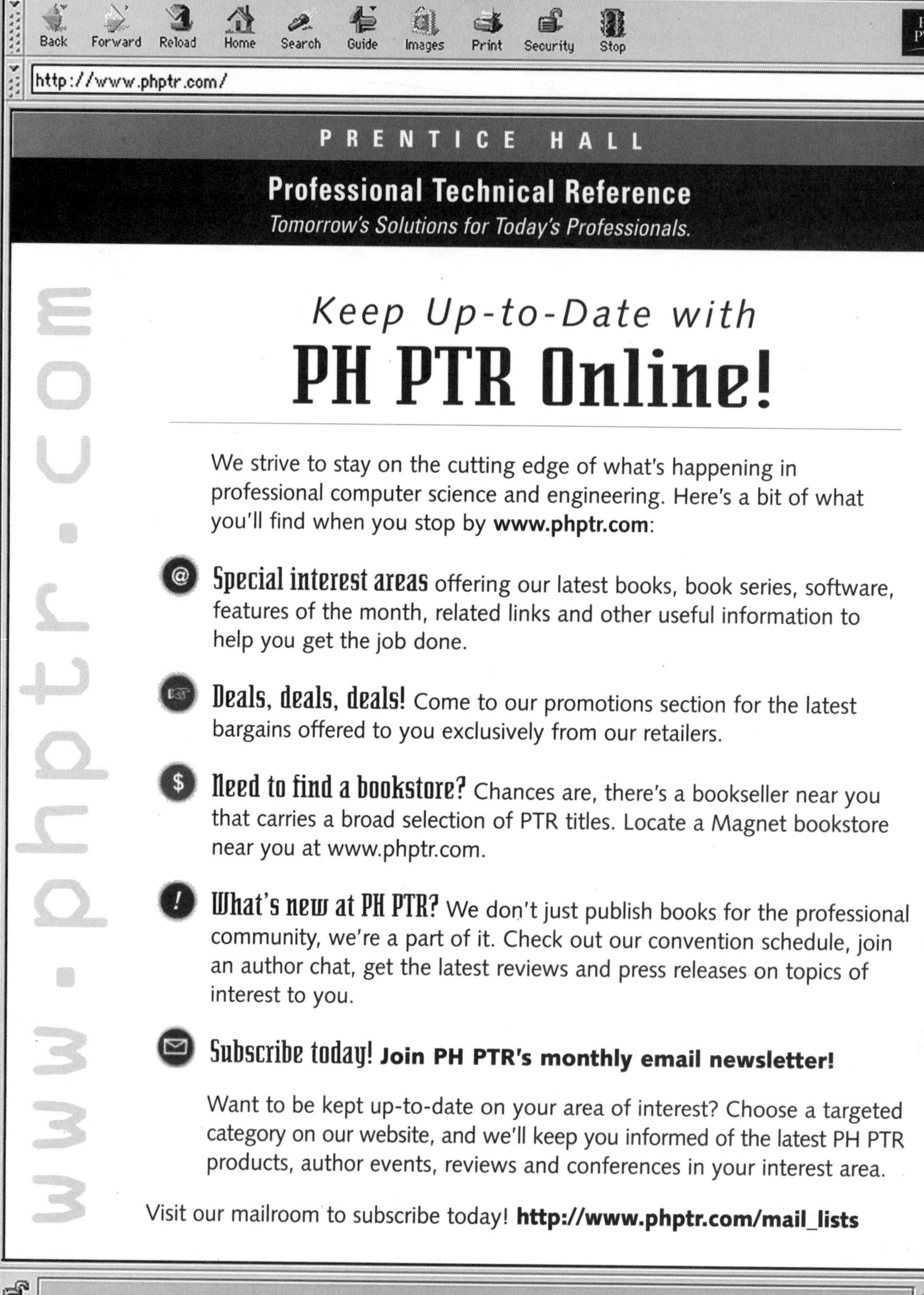

Prentice Hall: Professional Technical Reference
Back Forward Reload Home Search Guide Images Print Security Stop
PH PTR
http://www.phptr.com/
PRENTICE HALL
Professional Technical Reference
Tomorrow's Solutions for Today's Professionals.
www.phptr.com
Keep Up-to-Date with
PH PTR Online!
We strive to stay on the cutting edge of what's happening in professional computer science and engineering. Here's a bit of what you'll find when you stop by www.phptr.com:
Special interest areas offering our latest books, book series, software, features of the month, related links and other useful information to help you get the job done.
Deals, deals, deals! Come to our promotions section for the latest bargains offered to you exclusively from our retailers.
Need to find a bookstore? Chances are, there's a bookseller near you that carries a broad selection of PTR titles. Locate a Magnet bookstore near you at www.phptr.com.
What's new at PH PTR? We don't just publish books for the professional community, we're a part of it. Check out our convention schedule, join an author chat, get the latest reviews and press releases on topics of interest to you.
Subscribe today! Join PH PTR's monthly email newsletter!
Want to be kept up-to-date on your area of interest? Choose a targeted category on our website, and we'll keep you informed of the latest PH PTR products, author events, reviews and conferences in your interest area.
Visit our mailroom to subscribe today! http://www.phptr.com/mail_lists